Natural Disasters

· · · · · · · · · · · · · · · · · · · ·

NATURAL DISASTERS

· ·

FROM THE BLACK PLAGUE TO THE ERUPTION OF MT. PINATUBO

Lee Davis

Facts On File®

AN INFOBASE HOLDINGS COMPANY

NATURAL DISASTERS: FROM THE BLACK PLAGUE TO THE ERUPTION OF MT. PINATUBO

Facts On File, Inc.
460 Park Avenue South
New York, NY 10016

Library of Congress Cataloging-in-Publication Data

Davis, Lee.
Natural disasters : from the Black Plague to the eruption of
Mt. Pinatubo / Lee Davis.
p.   cm.
Includes bibliographical references and index.
ISBN 0-8160-2034-5
1. Natural disasters.   I. Title.
GB5014.D38   1991
904—dc20   91-38395

A British CIP catalogue record for this book is available from the British Library.

Facts On File books are available at special discounts when purchased in bulk quantities for businesses, associations, institutions, or sales promotions. Please contact our Special Sales Department in New York at 212/683-2244 or 800/322-8755.

Text design by Ron Monteleone
Jacket design by Soloway/Mitchell
Composition and manufacturing by the Maple-Vail Book Manufacturing Group
Printed in the United States of America

10 9 8 7 6 5 4 3 2

This book is printed on acid-free paper.

To Lisa,
who is the very antithesis
of disaster.

CONTENTS

· · · · ·

ACKNOWLEDGMENTS

· · · · ·

It is the custom, as if it were an awards ceremony, to thank everybody but your dog and your least favorite relative for help in the birthing of a book. That is not going to be the practice on this page. If I were to name all of the people over the passage of three years who, while I was writing about and therefore living through some of the world's worst times, kept me from getting depressed to the point of paralysis, I would compile a cast of—well—hundreds.

So, I won't, but will, instead, express my gratitude to the major players in this drama of disasters:

Particularly to Mary Lou Barber, who forfeited half a summer to help me endlessly and immeasurably in the accumulation of a small mountain range of reference material;

To Diane Johnston, who cut through a continent of red tape at the New York Public Library and made the portion of my life spent there infinitely more productive than it otherwise would have been;

To Jean Kaleda, Edana McCaffery Cichanowicz, Joanne Brooks, Patricia S. Tormey and the rest of the research staff at the Riverhead Free Library; to Shirley Van Derof, Phyllis Acard, Karen Hewlett, Susan LaVista, Jane Vail, Elva Stanley, Robert Allard, Jan Camarda and Nancy Foley of the Westhampton Free Library; to Selma Kelson and the research staff of the Patchogue-Medford Library; to the research staff of the library at the Southampton Campus of Long Island University; to the research staff of the print division of the Library of Congress;

To Elizabeth Hooks, of the American Red Cross photo library; to Reynaldo Reyes, of the United Nations photo library; to Pedro Soto, of the CARE photo library; to Michael Benson, Larry Crabil and particularly Bill McGruder of the National Transportation Safety Board; to Tim Cronen of the library of the Smithsonian Institution Air and Space Museum;

To Tom Deja for his picture research; to Fred Robertson for his patient photography of disintegrating copies of old newspapers;

To my agents, Elizabeth and Ed Knappman, for causing this to happen in the first place;

To my editors at Facts On File, during the long course of the birth of this book: Kate Kelly and Neal Maillet.

And to all of those unnamed friends and spiritual advisors who kept me sane for three years—my deepest and heartfelt thanks.

Lee Davis
Westhampton, N.Y.

INTRODUCTION

• • • • •

Sometimes it seems as if nature's way is some monumental system of checks and balances, designed to control the world's population. At other times it seems like some cruel cosmic joke. And at still others, it seems like pure happenstance, impure accident or random violence that proceeds mindlessly out of a universe without a pattern.

In fact, the very randomness and suddenness of some natural disasters are sometimes their most devastating qualities. Out of a freshly polished summer day in Pompeii, death in the form of white hot ashes both struck down and preserved a civilization, in one arrested moment of flight and surprise. In the Alps, families eating breakfast were instantly turned, by sudden avalanches, into recollections of a frozen fraction of time. Japanese fishermen, knitting nets and smoking, literally did not know what hit them when gigantic tsunamis, set in motion by undersea earthquakes hundreds of miles away, curled and broke 40 feet over their heads, smashing their villages to atoms in an instant.

All of this chaos is of course unsettling to scientists, and so, in an effort to make order out of disorder, they have tried to first identify and then track the patterns in natural disasters. To some extent, they have succeeded. Even the most cursory examination of the world's natural disasters indicates that human fatalities have steadily decreased, largely because humankind, through its scientists, has learned to pay attention to certain warning signs and signals.

Today, volcanologists have deduced that repeated earthquakes are an almost certain prelude to a volcanic eruption.

By comparing the relative heights of specific bodies of water over a fixed period of time, scientists are able to predict, with a fair amount of accuracy, the coming of a flood.

Meteorologists have now identified hurricane and tornado "seasons" and have developed sophisticated ways of tracking and gauging the storms within them.

With increased knowledge about sanitary conditions and the role of germs in the spreading of disease, and the discovery of vaccines and treatments, the unbridled spread of plague and epidemic has come under greater control.

And yet, there are always unpredictable variables.

Flash floods brought on by out of season rainfall can cause unpredictable catastrophes. Tornadoes and hurricanes often choose their own individual paths, confounding both computers and meteorologists. Dormant volcanoes have been known to come to life, inexplicably. These are the vagaries of nature that continue to confound both seers and scientists.

How else to explain city planners locating their creations on faults that will ultimately heave and split apart in some future earthquake? How to explain the inhabitants of the city of Catania, who rebuilt their city on the slopes of the volatile volcano Mount Etna? The statistics books bulge with fatalities that have come about this way, and yet, next year, in some place in the world, it will happen again, as regularly as the arrival of the seasons.

Throughout history, man has attributed natural disasters to a divine cause. For generations, perhaps eons, it was believed that the eruption of volcanoes was the cataclysmic expression of the dissatisfaction of the gods. To prevent such a monstrous eruption, the gods were offered a sacrifice of a goat, a virgin or a child. When the Black Death stalked Europe in the Middle Ages, it was thought to be a retribution exacted from Earth's sinners. Thus armies of flagellants whipped themselves publicly in atonement for the horror they felt they had brought upon mankind.

Other causes are complex and contemporary. Consider, for instance, poverty-ridden populations in countries like Bangladesh, who, through a multiplicity of economic factors, are forced to live in the direct path of monsoons and typhoons and are put at the mercy of floods caused by the rape of the ecology by uncaring governments—often of other, neighboring countries. Consider corrupt governments that absorb food, medical supplies, life-saving equipment, and the very seed grain that could, for future generations, alleviate the scourge of famine and starvation in Africa, Asia and the Middle East. Sometimes, mass inefficiency is the culprit. But, more pervasively, these natural disasters are exacerbated by simple, primal greed, and its immediate manifestation, corruption.

Nor should the most dramatic, appalling and contemporary example of human culpability in the face of a natural disaster be understated. By the 21st century, AIDS will become one of the most critical pandemics in the history of the world. And yet, whole governments have virtually ignored the disease, only recently making funds available for the treatment and research that could ultimately bring about a cure.

The United States government, until recently, has been grievously deficient in fighting AIDS. Compassion and intelligence seemed to absolutely desert the conservative administration of the 1980s, and the 1990s have not begun with an appreciable increase in either. As long as AIDS was perceived as a disease of homosexual men and drug addicts, the government refused to act. Indeed, some representatives postulated that AIDS was a form of divine punishment.

Now, with the AIDS epidemic spreading among the general population, governments are beginning to acknowledge the epidemic and its potential impact. But in the meantime, the disease continues to spread and will undoubtedly claim millions of lives and cause endless years of suffering, while governments scramble to undo years of foolish and destructive neglect.

Now, to the thinking that went into the criteria for inclusion in this compilation of natural disasters.

While it is absolutely and tragically true that any disaster that affects one human being is, for that human being and those around him or her, a horrible happening, any attempt at fairly representing all of these sorts of tragedies would be a hopeless and endless task for writer and reader alike.

Therefore, some attempt at constraint had to be made, and this, in turn, came about through a combination of scientific and subjective judgments. It would have been easy, perhaps, to be entirely scientific, and to include only natural disasters that were of a certain magnitude. But that would be inaccurate on a number of levels.

First of all, certain natural disasters affect more people than others. A volcanic eruption of enormous power occurring on a remote and sparsely inhabited island, for instance, will not kill as many people as a slightly lesser one near a populated city. In such a case I chose a lesser explosion that caused more human damage.

A plague that takes place before the development of modern medical science will have more human casualties than one that takes place after this development. Which to choose? I tried to balance casualties with contemporary medical discoveries.

The same considerations were made when casualty figures were measured before and after the development of modern meteorology, seismology and the entirely new science of volcanology. Obviously, those who are warned about approaching cyclones, tornadoes, typhoons and hurricanes will, in most cases, clear out, as will those who are warned of the possibility of earthquakes or volcanic explosions. And those who don't form a small enough minority to affect final statistics very little.

I picked no earthquake under 6.5 on the Richter scale, except when the human factor, the suffering caused to people, outweighed this. Major disasters that did not fit this criteria are included in the chronological listing at the beginning of each section. References covering these events appear in the bibliography.

Casualty figures for natural disasters seem to bear out Mark Twain's assertion that "There are three kinds of lies—lies, damned lies and statistics." No two sources for casualty counts seem to agree, and sometimes the differences are both wide and incredible. When there were huge discrepancies, the disparate figures were indicated in the text.

AVALANCHES AND LANDSLIDES

· · · · · · · · · · · · · · · · ·

THE WORST RECORDED AVALANCHES AND LANDSLIDES

* * * * *

CHRONOLOGY

* * * * * * * *

Marmolada, Switzerland
1920
  Kansu, China (see
    EARTHQUAKES)
1929
  July 22
    Northern Anatolia, Turkey
1934
  May 23–25
    Kwantung Province, China
1948
  September 18
    Assam, India
1951
  January 20
    * Vals, Switzerland
1954
  January 11
    * Blons, Austria
  October 22
    Berly, Haiti
1959
  October 29
    * Minatitlan, Mexico
1962
  January 10
    * Huascaran, Peru

1963
  March 8
    Tempayaeta, Southern Andes
  October 9
    * Belluno, Italy
  November 13–14
    * Grand Riviere du Nord, Haiti
1964
  July 18–19
    * Niigata, Japan
1966
  January 11–13
    * Rio de Janeiro, Brazil
  October 21
    * Aberfan, Wales
1967
  February 17–20
    * Rio de Janeiro, Brazil
1968
  October 1–4
    * Bihar, West Bengal and Assam,
     India
1969
  January 18–26
    * California
1971
  February 19

Lima, Peru
  March 19
    * Chungar, Peru
1972
  July 17
    * Japan
1973
  September 20
    Choloma, Honduras
1980
  May 18
    * Mt. St. Helens,
     Washington (see VOLCANIC
     ERUPTIONS)
  September 7
    * Darjeeling, India
1981
  May 18–20
    Sichuan Province, China
1983
  January 12–14
    China (Northwest)
  September 8
    Quito, Ecuador
1987
  September 27
    * Medellin, Colombia

• • • • •

AVALANCHES AND LANDSLIDES

• • • • •

Avalanches and landslides are usually secondary disasters, caused by such primary natural occurrences as heavy snowfalls, monsoon rains, volcanic eruptions or earthquakes.

To occur at all, an avalanche needs an insecure base. Snow that has accumulated upon a mountainside can be loosened by tremors, echoes or uneven melting of the snow base. Secure landmasses can be turned to mud by weeks of unrelieved rain. The underpinnings of cities can be rattled loose by repeated natural or man-made Earth tremors or by the superheating of subterranean depths under the soil brought on by volcanic activity.

Whatever the cause, an avalanche is sudden, unanticipated and violent. Mountains, lake and seaside waterfronts and entire population areas can be abruptly uprooted. Helped by accumulated force, speed and gravity itself, these avalanches generally grow in size and destructive power as they accumulate loose debris, rocks, soil, trees, water and anything that happens to be unlucky enough to find itself in their paths.

The most spectacular and lethal avalanches occur in regions of heavy snow and ice. In these places, as much as 1 million cubic yards of snow have been known to give way and thunder downslope at a time—an amount that would fill the beds of 10,000 10-yard dump trucks, which in turn is equivalent to a line of vehicles that would reach for approximately 200 miles.

Avalanches of snow can be triggered by the most delicate vibration, which is why some Alpine farmers muffle the bells on their livestock in winter. A falling stone, the movement of animals, thunder, the sonic boom of a jet, a man slicing across a slope on skis can become the genesis of an avalanche of snow and ice.

The results are sometimes instantaneous; sometimes, delayed. Several skiers may safely cross a slope before the cumulative effect of their passing sets off vibrations in the snow which catch the last members of the party in an avalanche. Or, a rupture may streak through compacted snow from a point of first impact to break the anchorage of nearby snow and start a second avalanche. Fractures can run through ice at speeds of 350 feet per second.

One final, lethal effect of dry snow avalanches should be noted: They travel quickly. On a 43-degree slope in the Swiss Alps, one of them was clocked at almost 300 mph. At these speeds, dry snow becomes airborne. Progressing downslope, its powdery clouds disturb the air in front of it, causing hurricane force winds, and these winds in turn whirl still more loose snow into frenetic suspension. Wind speeds within the vanguard of these avalanches have been recorded at nearly 400 feet per second, and the wind, like an unseen plow, can blast trees and buildings, toppling them even before the snow arrives. Death has struck skiers and mountain climbers and mountain residents untouched by the racing snow. When autopsied, their lungs have shown lesions of the sort produced by explosions.

Avalanches will occur wherever the conditions exist for them, and there is no avoidance except absence from them. Those who ski, who love to live amidst some of Earth's most beautiful and breathtaking scenery, or to travel to it, may well find this an unacceptable impossibility. For them, the experience is worth the risk.

The criteria for inclusion in this section are based upon size, fatalities, and/or unusualness. If the avalanche was a unique one, casualty figures were ignored. If not, large numbers of casualties—exceeding 1,000—became the yardstick.

• • • • • • • • • • • • • •

ALPS

218 B.C.

• • • • • • • • • • • • • • •

Impatience caused the deaths by avalanche of 18,000 of Hannibal's men, 2,000 of his horses, and several of his elephants as he ordered them across the Col de la Traversette pass of the Italian Alps following an early October snowstorm in 218 B.C.

Hannibal met his match in natural forces in the early days of October 218 B.C. when, commanding 38,000 soldiers, 8,000 horsemen and 37 elephants, he unwisely attempted to cross the Col de la Traversette pass in the Italian Alps. At least, according to incomplete records, that is the approximate location he had reached, in a heavy snowstorm and bone-numbing cold.

For two days, he and his expedition camped at the top of the pass. Finally, growing impatient, they resumed their march. A blanket of fresh snow covered the crusted snow of an earlier storm—a prime condition for an avalanche—and, as they began to descend, the animals' feet perforated the top layer of snow. That layer gave way and, in the words of the poet Silius Italicus, ". . . [Hannibal] pierce[d] the resistant ice with his lance. Detached snow drag[ged] the men into the abyss and snow falling rapidly from the high summits engulf[ed] the living squadrons."

Eighteen thousand men, 2,000 horses and several elephants perished in this historic and horrendous tragedy.

ALPS

TYROL

1915–1918

• • • • • • • • • • • • • • •

An estimated 40,000 to 80,000 men lost their lives during World War I in the Tyrolean Alps, not from enemy gunfire, but from avalanches caused by the sounds of war.

World War I was fought on many fronts, but one of the most dramatic—and disastrous—was in the Tyrol, where Italian and Austrian troops battled each other on forbidding terrain for four years.

During that time, there were appreciable casualties from gunfire. But by far the most lethal enemies of both armies were mountains and snow. Rattled by explosions and the noises of war, avalanche after avalanche cascaded down Alpine slopes, burying such villages as Marmolada, where, in one day, 235 men were lost, buried in their barracks.

The final death toll from avalanches was estimated to be between 40,000 and 80,000 men—an accumulation of lost life that eclipsed that of similar battles fought on more level terrain.

AUSTRIA

BLONS

January 11, 1954

• • • • • • • • • • • • • • •

The worst mass burial, by percentage, in history occurred when two avalanches roared into the small Austrian village of Blons on the same day—January 11, 1954. One hundred eleven of the 376 residents of the village were killed; 29 of its 90 homes were destroyed; 300 of the approximately 600 miners in the Leduc mine were buried alive.

The all-time record for mass burial by avalanche belongs to the twin slides that hit the small Alpine village of Blons, near Arlberg Pass in Austria at 9:36 in the morning and at 7:00 in the evening of January 11, 1954. Half of the miners in the nearby Leduc mine camp were killed; 111 of the 376 people who lived in the village perished outright; 29 of 90 homes were crushed.

This catastrophic loss of life came despite the villagers' constant preparation for the avalanches they had come to expect each winter. Every December, in fact, the village councilmen ordered the removal of the crucifix that stood close to a certain ravine so that it could survive the next months without damage. When villagers crossed a certain bridge over that same ravine, they automatically walked in widely spaced single file and stopped talking. If their voices or some other vibration began an avalanche, they reasoned that with wide distances between them, fewer would perish.

But there was no defense when these two slides—the largest and most powerful that have ever visited Blons—roared down the mountains. Of those who were buried, 33 extricated themselves, 31 were dug out alive by rescuers, and 47 were found dead. Eight survivors later died, and two residents were never found.

One woman perished from burns, even though she was buried in snow. She had been baking when the avalanche hit her house and coals from the oven seared her as she was swept downslope. A man who was trapped for 17 hours emerged alive when a search party reached him, but, according to wire service reports, he died of shock when they told him how long he had been under the snow. Others survived after being trapped under the snow for up to 62 hours.

BRAZIL
RIO DE JANEIRO

January 11–13, 1966; February 17–20, 1967

• • • • • • • • • • • • • • •

Inattention to maintaining the terrain of the hills above Rio de Janeiro, Brazil led to the enormous loss of life and property caused by the twin avalanches of January 11–13, 1966, and February 17–20, 1967. The slides, which followed a month of heavy rain in each case, killed 259, injured hundreds more and crippled the city's three power plants.

Prior to the punishing landslides of 1966 and 1967, not much attention was paid to the insecure terrain of the hills above Rio de Janeiro nor to the obvious fact that mountainsides deprived of the roots of vegetation are prone to erosion and resultant slides following heavy rains.

For generations, the poor of Rio had built their shanties in what was called the *favelados* district, chipped into the sides of the hills above the city. The shacks were ramshackle at best and clung precariously to the hillsides.

Torrential rains battered that part of Brazil in early January 1966, causing only inconvenience to the rest of the country. But near Rio, from the 11th through the 13th, mudslides began to rumble and then slide inexorably toward the city. Two hundred thirty-nine residents of the districts of Santa Teresa, Copacabana and Ipanema were killed and hundreds injured as their houses were either swept away or crushed by the walls of mud that caromed down the mountainside, burying or sweeping away everything in their paths.

The reaction of both residents and officials was either naive or philosophical. "Rains like this happen only once in a century," stated Governor Francisco Negrao de Lima of Rio. And so, the shacks were reconstructed, and still more foliage was stripped from the hills.

In February 1967, a little more than a year later, an 11-inch rainfall soaked the city of Rio de Janeiro. Once again, mudslides cascaded from the hills, toppling and smashing the primitively constructed homes, crushing and burying the *favelados* beneath them.

But this time, the wealthy and the white-collar workers who had been unaffected by the previous slides, felt the impact. Mudslides crept into Rio's three power plants, cutting the city's electrical supply to 40 percent, which in turn caused air conditioners to burn out and elevators to malfunction. A score of heart attacks felled businesspeople who were forced to climb countless stairs in skyscrapers, thus raising the total of persons killed because of the landslides to 259.

This time, Governor de Lima forbade more construction in and about the hills. He set up a geological "police force" to patrol the mountains, instituted new laws to prevent the destruction of vegetation and sent out military helicopters to see that his rules were enforced. In addition, concrete shorings were set into the slopes to prevent what geologists predicted could be a burial under mud of most of the city of Rio de Janeiro.

COLOMBIA
MEDELLIN

September 27, 1987

• • • • • • • • • • • • • • •

Mudslides caused by torrential downpours wiped out whole sections of the Villa Tina area of Medellin, Colombia on September 27, 1987. Five hundred residents disappeared and were presumed dead, the bodies of 183 were found, and 200 were injured. Only 117 residents of the district survived the catastrophe.

The Villa Tina area of Medellin, a city in the mountains 160 miles northwest of Bogota, Colombia is an achingly impoverished one, despite the affluence of the drug cartel based in the rest of the city. The entire population of approximately 1,000 lives from day to day, sometimes 10 to a dwelling, in improvised shacks.

On Sunday morning, September 27, 1987, tons of red soil, turned to thin mud by days of torrential rains, loosened from Sugar Loaf Mountain, and, picking up enormous boulders in their plummetting fall downslope, thundered into the Villa Tina section, just as a group of young children were receiving their first Communion.

An Associated Press reporter spoke to survivors. "We heard the noise that sounded like an explosion and soon afterward a huge mass of rocks and mud descended upon us," said Mary Mosquera, who lost three daughters in the avalanche. They were three of 43 children (seven died in church during the Communion ceremony) who would perish in a matter of minutes that Sunday morning. One hundred eighty-three people would be crushed under the roaring juggernaut of rocks and mud; nearly 500 would be missing and presumed dead; 200 would be injured. That would leave a mere 117 survivors to try to rescue their neighbors or families.

The destruction of the shanties in which they had lived was complete. Rescue workers, laboring for two days, were guided to many bodies by dogs howling at the spot where their owners were buried.

The mayor of Medellin, William Jaramillo Gomez, ordered that all victims, many of them unidentified, be buried immediately to prevent any outbreak of disease. At least 50 people were interred in a mass grave.

All of this was done while the soaking rains continued to fall, threatening new slides. Thousands of people took refuge in shelters more substantial than their homes as several small slides hurtled down the mountain the night after the avalanche.

HAITI
GRAND RIVIERE DU NORD
November 13–14, 1963

• • • • • • • • • • • • • • •

Mudslides brought about by long periods of tropical downpours killed 500 residents and tourists in Grand Riviere du Nord on November 13 and 14, 1963.

Five hundred persons were killed when landslides devastated Grand Riviere du Nord, Haiti's most prosperous area, on November 13 and 14, 1963.

The slides, brought about by days of relentless rain during and following a hurricane, covered villages with mud and rock, flattened dwellings and totally destroyed all of the crops in the region.

Scores were crushed in their homes; scores more drowned when rivers overflowed their banks after mudslides displaced their waters. A bus carrying 20 passengers was picked up and hurled from a highway, then buried beneath the landslide that had displaced it. All 20 passengers and the driver died.

Communications with Port-au-Prince and the outside world were down for days, thus hampering the arrival of adequate relief supplies.

INDIA
BIHAR, WEST BENGAL AND ASSAM
October 1–4, 1968

• • • • • • • • • • • • • • •

One thousand residents of Bihar, West Bengal and Assam were killed by a combination of landslides and floods and the pipeline linking Bihar and Assam was largely destroyed between October 1 and 4, 1968.

One thousand people were crushed or drowned when India's three northeastern states—Bihar, West Bengal and Assam—were inundated by floods and landslides between October 1 and 4, 1968.

The Tista River, just outside of Jalpaiguri, overflowed, submerging the town under 10 feet of water and thus accounting for many of the deaths. But equally vicious and lethal were the landslides, brought on by a combination

of floods and monsoon rains. These cascaded down from the Himalayas to the north and the Naga Hills to the east, crushing native homes and burying parts of the cities of Darjeeling and Jalpaiguri, which were left without electricity and drinking water for weeks.

The entire area, in fact, was cut off from the outside world and the 500-mile oil pipeline between Bihar and Assam was largely destroyed by the multiple mudslides which washed out the roadways and railbeds that connected this part of India with the rest of the subcontinent.

INDIA
DARJEELING
September 7, 1980

• • • • • • • • • • • • • • •

Thirty thousand residents of the Darjeeling area of India were cut off from the outside world and 250 were killed when avalanches, caused by monsoon rains, descended from the Himalayas on September 7, 1980.

Tons of earth and enormous boulders swept down the Himalayas in the tea-growing area of Darjeeling on September 7, 1980, killing 250 people and trapping 30,000.

Monsoon rains had ravaged this part of West Bengal for days before the landslides, which were brought on by the loosening of the earth from the pounding of the rains. Sheered off from the mountainsides, these huge walls of mud uprooted trees and rolled enormous boulders ahead of them as if they were snowballs. Entire villages were instantly crushed and obliterated.

The landslides, coupled with floods, increased the 1980 fatality total from monsoons to nearly 1,500.

ITALY
BELLUNO
October 9, 1963

• • • • • • • • • • • • • • •

An earthquake caused a landslide, which in turn caused a flood in the Piave River Valley of Italy on October 9, 1963. Over 4,000 residents of the area drowned.

At 11:15 P.M. on October 9, 1963, the Piave River Valley in northern Italy, which had been the scene of the Italian Army's stand against the Austrians after the Italians' defeat at Caporetto during World War I, and which was familiar to millions as the setting of Ernest Hemingway's novel *A Farewell to Arms*, faced a far worse natural disaster: The entire valley was flooded and the 873-foot high

Valmont dam was at first thought to have collapsed under the assault of a mountain landslide, caused by an earthquake. Over 4,000 people drowned in this multiple cataclysm.

The 72-foot thick dam, the world's highest, had not collapsed. The roar that survivors recalled hearing before an immense wall of water thundered into the valley was the cracking apart of the mountain on either side of the dam. Captain Fred R. Michelson, a United States Army helicopter pilot who flew out residents of the village of Casso above the dam (the village was threatened with destruction from residual landslides), described the scene: "There was a mile-long lake behind the dam, but it doesn't exist any more," he reported. "The entire tops of both mountains on either side slid into the lake and completely filled it."

The displaced water from the lake overflowed the dam, cracking it at the top and cascaded in an immense 1,500-foot waterfall at right angles to the Piave River Valley.

"You can see where the burst of water swirled down the [Piave] river on both sides for about 30 miles downstream and about 500 yards on either side of the river," continued Captain Michelson. "You can't find any buildings for about five miles. There aren't even any foundations. You can't find anything of the towns that once existed."

Longarone, a village directly in the water's path, disappeared entirely, along with 3,700 of its 4,700 residents. At Pirago, a few miles downstream, only a church bell tower, a chapel in a cemetery and one house remained standing. Nobody in the village lived.

"At first, there was a loud, distant roar, and then the window panes started trembling," was the way Alessandro Bellumcini, a resident of Longarone, who survived because he was watching a soccer match in a tavern in Fae, outside of his native village, put it. "I raced outside and saw flashes of light on the mountains in the direction of the Vaiont Valley. They were probably high-power electric wires snapping.

"All of us rushed toward the mountain and started running uphill. We had not covered more than 300 yards when we saw something like a whitish, rolling form engulfing the valley at fantastic speed. It was just visible in the light of the half moon. I saw the few homes of our little hamlet being wiped out in seconds. It was horrible."

Bodies were carried as far as 40 miles downstream; others were buried on the spot by the rubble of the landslide and other parts of the valley loosened and were carried along by the flood waters.

Huddled in an army blanket, Mario Faini, a survivor who had been asleep in his home on the fringes of the landslide and flood, recalled that he and his two sons ". . . felt what seemed like an earthquake. I got up and started

dressing. I heard a terrible wind blowing outside just like a tornado. Suddenly, the windows were smashed in and water poured into the house. We were thrown off our feet . . . ."

His son recalled that ". . . our pajamas were torn off our bodies, and after a few horrible moments . . . we found ourselves rushing out the back windows and up the mountain, shivering in the cold."

Mario Laveder, municipal secretary of Longarone, observed this sort of evacuation: "Some villagers rushed into the streets and tried to climb up the mountainside. A few of them succeeded. [Others] were engulfed by a wave of swirling waters and drowned. Others died under the debris of their homes."

American helicopters from Allied headquarters in Verona were successful in lifting out stranded survivors, among them, a pregnant woman who, assisted by the helicopter crew and a nurse, gave birth to a girl minutes after the copter had deposited her in a safe place.

Devastation was everywhere the next morning, augmented by a further, lethal danger. Authorities appealed to everyone in the area by radio not to drink water from the Piave or to allow their cattle to drink it. Five tons of potassium cyanide had washed from a riverside factory into the Piave, turning the waters poisonous.

Americans supplied 6,000-gallon tank trucks from Allied headquarters. The grim rescue work continued for weeks, but many of the villages that had been wiped from the face of the valley by this huge combination of earthquake, landslide and flood would never be rebuilt.

JAPAN
July 17, 1972

• • • • • • • • • • • • •

Torrential rains caused landslides that precipitated floods throughout Japan during the week of July 10, 1972. On Monday, the 17th, the destruction reached its climax. Three hundred seventy persons were killed; over $472 million in property damage was caused by the combination of landslides and flooding.

Three hundred seventy persons were drowned or crushed by landslides set off by floods, which were in turn brought on by a week of relentless rain throughout most of Japan in mid-July, 1972. Scores of major rivers and minor streams overflowed their banks, eroding them into rushing mudslides which embraced and then consumed whole villages and numerous farms.

It was, in fact, in the agricultural sections of Japan that calamity struck most clearly and widely. More than $472 million in both building and crop loss was caused by this combination of natural disasters.

JAPAN
NIIGATA

July 18–19, 1964

• • • • • • • • • • • • •

An earthquake combined with heavy rains caused landslides near Niigata, Japan on July 18 and 19, 1964. One hundred eight died; 223 were injured; 44,000 were rendered homeless.

Landslides that were caused by a combination of a minor earthquake and torrential rains in Niigata, Japan caved in river banks, destroyed 150 bridges and collapsed 50-year-old dikes during the two days of July 18 and 19, 1964. The five districts near Niigata and along the Sea of Japan were likewise devastated, swept clean of 295 dwellings, which were either buried under the landslides or carried away by the waters released by over 200 gaps that had been opened up in protecting dikes by the cascading mud.

Several villages were wiped out completely by landslides; in cities such as Ishikawa, Toyamma, Niigata, Tottori and Shimane, entire sections crumbled.

The final death count was 108. Two hundred twenty-three residents of the area were injured, and 44,000 were made homeless.

MEXICO
MINATITLAN

October 29, 1959

• • • • • • • • • • • • •

An earthquake, a tsunami and a series of landslides combined to kill 5,000 people in Mexico on October 29, 1959. The village of Minatitlan was obliterated, and 800 residents died in their beds.

A massive combination of natural forces conspired to kill 5,000 residents of Mexico on October 29, 1959. First, an earthquake that barely registered on the Richter scale brought on a giant tsunami that slammed into the Pacific Coast of Mexico, drowning thousands, sinking 10 small freighters and sending the passenger-freighter *Sinola* to the bottom of the Pacific with all on board.

That night, massive mudslides virtually buried the village of Minatitlan, crushing people in their beds. Eight hundred died within minutes when the landslide roared with comparatively little warning over virtually every building in the town.

Nearby, another 1,000 were killed when rocks and mud from the same surrounding hills cascaded murderously into their villages. The town of Zacoalpan in northern Colima state was obliterated by landslides and then flooded to the tops of the surviving buildings' roofs. A pilot flying over the area noted that only the church steeple protruded from the waters covering the town.

In the grim aftermath, swarms of snakes, scorpions and tarantulas, unearthed from their lairs when the landslides tore apart the hillsides, slithered and crawled into what was left of Minatitlan, killing another 200 residents before serum could be flown in from Mexico City.

PERU
CHUNGAR

March 19, 1971

• • • • • • • • • • • • •

Chungar, a mining camp 10,000 feet up in the Andes, was destroyed by an avalanche caused by an earthquake on March 19, 1971. Between 400 and 600 were killed; 50 were injured.

An avalanche rained tons of water, mud and rocks down upon the isolated mining camp of Chungar, high in the Andes of Peru, on the morning of March 19, 1971. Between 400 and 600 people were buried in seconds by the thundering slide.

The avalanche was touched off by an earthquake that struck at 8:30 A.M., crumbling a nearby mountaintop and toppling it into a lake. Water spilled over the banks of the lake and swept the nearby terrain, picking up soil, trees and immense boulders. The slide continued on, obliterating the main road to Chungar from Lima, wiping out bridges and demolishing living quarters.

The camp, 10,000 feet up in the Andes and an eight hour journey by foot from the nearest town, had been inhabited by about 1,000 people. But rescuers, after crossing a 12,000-foot mountain range on their trip in from Lima, Cerro de Pasco and Canta, found only a third of that population still alive. The others had been buried under tons of mud, rocks and the remains of their homes. Fifty injured people were flown out and taken to hospitals.

It was the worst disaster in Peru since an earthquake the previous May, which had struck an area 180 miles north of Lima, with a death toll estimated at 70,000. (See EARTHQUAKES.) As in this event, many of those killed in that quake had died when an avalanche of mud and rocks thundered down the slopes of Mount Huascaran, Peru's highest mountain, and buried two towns.

PERU
HUASCARAN

January 10, 1962

• • • • • • • • • • • • • •

A glacier at the summit of Mt. Huascaran in the Andes shattered and triggered an avalanche on January 10, 1962. Thirty-five hundred people died in the valley below.

At exactly 6:13 P.M. on January 10, 1962, 3 million tons of ice from Glacier 511, located 21,834 feet high at the top of Mount Huascaran cracked, loosened and began to slide towards the valley below. Within seven minutes, 3,500 people were dead.

Fattened by freak snows and warmed by unseasonal sunshine, the glacier simply came apart and, in seconds, started its highspeed, cataclysmic journey. A man in Yungay, looking upward at the instant that the glacier let loose, first thought it was a cloud turning golden in the sunset. "But I saw," he later reported, "that the cloud was flying downhill."

The ice sped into the gorge of the Callejon de Huailas with a roar "like that of ten thousand wild beasts," according to another man.

"I could feel the rumble in the walls of the belly," added still another.

This lethal barrage of ice first shaved down an uninhabited slope, then bounced in an insane ricochet back and forth from gorge to gorge, carving and collecting topsoil, boulders and flocks of sheep. Finally, it entered the village of Yanamachico and three others nearby, flattening them and killing all 800 residents. Sweeping the ruins of houses along with other debris, it continued on.

Now the avalanche flattened to 60 feet in thickness, slowing to 60 mph from hundreds of miles per hour moments before. Hills banked near a gorge diverted it from the town of Yungay, but the larger town of Ranrahirca, with a population of 2,700, still remained in its path.

Within an instant, the avalanche crashed into this town, toppling its church steeples and crushing houses as if they were cardboard. Ricardo Olivera, the chief engineer of the local power station, hearing the telltale roar growing closer, grabbed the hands of two young girls playing in a playground in an effort to get them to the church, a sturdily built shelter. But, as Olivera later described it, "The girls were torn from my hands—by the winds or by a wall of mud. Electric wires had fallen around me. Somehow, I came free. I regained my senses, and saw only a waste of mud and ice."

The girls, all of the buildings around him and the church itself had all been crushed, and every one of their inhabitants were dead. "I was impressed by a profound silence," Olivera went on. "Realizing that my wife, my children, my parents were all buried under the debris, I suddenly found myself sobbing."

According to *National Geographic* writer Bart McDowell, who came upon the scene shortly after the avalanche struck, the scene ". . . resembled an Old Testament visitation. White rock and pale mud stretched a mile across the green Andean valley. No ice was visible on the surface. Boulders were mortared together by a crusting mud of granite dust, and streaked by small, disoriented brooks of melt. Following a team of stretcher-bearers to recover the dead," McDowell sadly concluded, "we sank thigh-deep in mire."

The few surviving villagers were mute in their sorrow. According to McDowell, "As the priest intoned the Latin words [of absolution over the dead], some women wept, quietly, without sobbing. Their faces seemed numb beyond the curing salt of tears."

SWITZERLAND
ELM

September 11, 1881

• • • • • • • • • • • • • • • • •

The undermined peak of Plattenbergkopf mountain, hovering over Elm, Switzerland, collapsed upon the village on September 11, 1881. The village was destroyed; 150 villagers were killed; 200 were injured.

One hundred fifty people were killed when the peak of Plattenbergkopf mountain, undermined by years of slate mining, came loose and hurtled down on the village of Elm in the Sernf valley of Switzerland on Sunday afternoon, September 11, 1881.

Cracks had begun to appear in the mountain as early as 1876, and by 1881, one of them had opened to a width of five yards. The random and careless blasting away of parts of the peak and the random positioning of mine shafts had, by the middle of that year, produced cave-ins and minor rock slides which were enough to cause some alarm among the residents of the hamlet of Elm.

But all of this was merely a prelude to the rumbling that first began at 5:30 P.M. on September 11, 1881. At that moment, the roof of the largest slate quarry caved in with a roar. And then there was a pause, enough for the mountain residents to settle into a shortlived feeling of relief.

Seventeen minutes later, the top of the mountain came loose. Over 10 million cubic yards of rock broke loose and thundered downslope at hundreds of miles per hour, shoving boulders, livestock, houses and human beings before it. "Trees were snapped like matches," a survivor recalled, "and houses were lifted through the air like feathers and thrown like cards against the hillside."

The village inn, located above the village itself, was crowded with drinkers, gathered for the usual Sunday afternoon "social watch," of the daily discharge of random boulders from the mountaintop. Some, more sober than others, left after the first rumblings.

One of these was Meirad Rhyner, who, shortly after he quit the inn with a wheel of cheese under his arm, turned to see the entire building and its occupants disappear under tons of earth. Rhyner managed to escape the avalanche, but his family was not so lucky. Breathlessly reaching his home after the last of three separate slides, he found it intact. But the hurtling rocks loosed by the slide had killed every member of his fleeing family—his wife, daughter, son, daughter-in-law and two grandchildren. "The doors were open," he remembered later, "a fire burning in the kitchen, the table laid and coffee hot in the coffeepot, but no living soul was left."

Over half the village was flattened. Some residents escaped, like Kasper Zentner, the fastest runner in the village. He outpaced the slide for a while, then, when it threatened to engulf him, he saved himself by jumping over several stone walls and, with a broken leg, dropping into a deep gully while the slide passed over him.

Most others were far less lucky. One hundred fifty villagers lay dead, 200 more were seriously injured and the village was in ruins.

SWITZERLAND
GOLDAU VALLEY

September 2, 1806

• • • • • • • • • • • • • •

An avalanche caused by the sudden erosion of the top of Rossberg Peak in the Swiss Alps on September 2, 1806 set forest fires and inundated four villages in the Goldau Valley. Eight hundred were killed.

Eight hundred people in four villages were killed in a matter of minutes on September 2, 1806, when the entire top of Rossberg Peak in the Swiss Alps crumbled, then plummeted into the valley below.

A thick forest covered the slopes almost to the top of the peak, and this forest remained intact, sliding downward, in one destructive slab, at ferocious speed. Rock ground against rock, shooting geysers of steam in the air, finally erupting in flames as the friction increased. Horrified onlookers witnessed a flame-orange forest fire that rocketed downward at hundreds of miles an hour, filling up the entire valley and consuming everything in its path.

SWITZERLAND
LEUKERBAD

January 17, 1718

• • • • • • • • • • • • • •

Sixty-one people were killed and almost every building in the village of Leukerbad, Switzerland was smashed when cyclonic winds caused a snow avalanche on January 17, 1718.

The monster avalanche of January 17, 1718 was only one of a series that had plagued this popular tourist resort and hot springs for centuries. But it was by far the most devastating. Practically every building in the village was destroyed, and 61 people died—over half of Leukerbad's population.

It had snowed unrelievedly for two weeks before the avalanche, according to Stephen Matter, a local scribe. At the end of the two weeks, a large avalanche roared through the outskirts of the village, killing three young men. A search party, using sounding rods to detect bodies buried in snow, located the corpses and returned to the village that evening with them, thankful that Leukerbad had escaped a more destructive slide.

The party had hardly entered the village when a second, cataclysmic avalanche of tons and tons of powdered snow, preceded by cyclonic winds, thundered down the mountainside from the top of the 10,000-foot Balmhorn. The Church of St. Laurentius, where parishioners were gathered for evening vespers, was wrecked, killing all of those within. The three luxury baths were destroyed. Entire families were crushed and buried.

Even the stories of survivors were tempered by tragedy. One man, caught in his wine cellar as he was searching for a bottle of wine to accompany his evening meal, was trapped alive for eight days. Finally rescued, he died soon thereafter of malnutrition and frostbite.

SWITZERLAND
ST. GERVAIS

July 12, 1892

• • • • • • • • • • • • • •

One hundred forty people were killed in the giant avalanche caused by the calving of the Tete Rousse glacier on Mont Blanc on July 12, 1892.

Only 10 of 150 persons in the 19th century resort towns of St. Gervais and La Fayet survived the massive avalanche that occurred at 2:00 A.M. on July 12, 1892.

Mount Blanc, 14,318 feet tall, towered above these two resorts. St. Gervais was particularly crowded with tourists enjoying its luxurious hotel and sulfur springs baths. It was the middle of summer, and even to the seasoned mountaineers who lived in St. Gervais, thoughts of snow avalanches were distant, if not entirely absent.

But in the middle of that July night, the Tete Rousse glacier, suspended at the brink of a gorge above the Glacier de Bionnassay on the western side of Mount Blanc, broke off. Within an instant, it plummeted toward the two sleeping towns, sweeping rocks, trees, snow, debris and water along with it.

Not one person in the hotels was able to leave his or her bed. Every building—from the simplest lean-to to the stone edifices of the church and the hotel were crushed and mutilated. Only those on the very outskirts of the village survived.

SWITZERLAND
VALS

January 20, 1951

• • • • • • • • • • • • • • •

Two hundred forty people died, and over 45,000 were trapped on January 20, 1951, when a series of avalanches, caused by a combination of hurricane force winds and wet snow overlaying powder snow, thundered through the Swiss, Austrian and Italian Alps.

A horrendous series of avalanches—the worst since the 1916 series of slides that had buried hundreds of Italian and Austrian troops (see AVALANCHES, Alps, Tyrol, p. 6)—roared and raged through the Swiss, Austrian and Italian Alps on January 20, 1951. Before tranquillity returned to the mountainsides, more than 45,000 people were trapped for weeks, 240 were dead and dozens of villages were in ruins. Even the posh resorts of Davos, Zermatt, Arosa and St. Moritz did not escape the tragedy. Perhaps the hardest hit of all was the Swiss village of Vals, located 4,100 feet above sea level in the most picturesque region of the Swiss Alps. The village disappeared entirely, and 19 of its residents were crushed to death.

The conditions that caused the avalanche were classic. First, very little snow fell in December of 1950, disappointing hundreds of international skiers. Then, with the new year, extensive, powdery snow storms struck. Then rain. Then snow mixed with rain. And finally, rain entirely.

On January 20, the sides of Sustenhorn and Dammastock shuddered, and tons of wet snow overlaying the shifting and unstable mounds of powder snow broke loose at the higher elevations. Hurricane force winds ran ahead of the white wall of snow and rocks, helping to topple the trees that had been planted to slow just such an avalanche, and allowing the force of the slide to snap off or uproot every one of those that escaped the winds.

The St. Gotthard rail line between Switzerland and central Europe was rendered inoperable for a week, blocked by immense walls of snow, ice and rocks. Communication lines and towers were toppled, cutting off all contact with the outside world.

Dozens of bittersweet tales of survival surfaced, as survivors wandered into the few standing structures. Typical of these was the story of Johann Lutz, who buried his family in a common grave in Vals. When the first of the series of avalanches struck, Lutz climbed to the roof of his home to sweep the snow off the roof, lest it cave in. While he was there, four more avalanches roared down in quick succession. It was all he could do to hold on to the roof and not be swept into the valley with the rest of the debris. When he finally climbed down from the roof, he found that both his wife and two-year-old son had been crushed to death by the snow that had poured in through the windows and doors of his home.

UNITED STATES
CALIFORNIA

January 18–26, 1969

• • • • • • • • • • • • • • •

Ninety-five persons died and over $138 million in damage was caused in southern California by a series of mudslides, brought about by nine days of torrential rain, and a subtropical storm, from January 18 to 26, 1969.

For nine straight days, rain fell along the coast of California, fueled by a subtropical storm that slammed into the southern coast on January 18, 1969. By January 26, 10 inches of rain had eaten into the hillsides, particularly those insubstantial ones in the San Gabriel and Santa Monica mountains above Los Angeles.

Landslides began on the 22nd of January, as running yellow mud threatened the posh homes of movie stars and movie moguls on Rainbow Drive in Glendora and in Mandeville Canyon. The slides, some of them half mud and half water, oozed into estates, trapping some residents in their homes. Other houses tipped and fell, shoved by the mudslides into the valleys below.

On El Paso Drive, more and more homes were demolished, and more and more people perished as the force of the mudslides increased in size, speed and scope.

Santiago Creek rapidly filled with mud, rain water and floodwaters, and threatened Santa Ana. Five thousand volunteers arrived and for hours labored at creating dikes and levees to hold back the overflowing flood waters. Finally, Marine helicopters appeared, carrying wrecked cars in the slings beneath them. The combination of levees and junk cars formed a barrier that thwarted a potentially disastrous flood.

Movie sets in the Santa Monica mountains were swept away. Over 100 boats, large and small, were sunk at Ventura and Santa Barbara. The final total of dead came to 95, and over $138 million in damage was finally tallied when the rain and mudslides ceased. Federal relief funds of $3 million were immediately funneled into the devastated countryside, which was declared a disaster area by President Richard M. Nixon.

UNITED STATES
WASHINGTON
WELLINGTON

March 1, 1910

• • • • • • • • • • • • •

Snow loosened by rain broke loose from a mountain in the Cascade range of Washington on March 1, 1910, and buried the village of Wellington and a stranded train at its railroad station. Ninety-six died in one of the worst avalanches in U.S. history.

The worst single avalanche in United States history took place in the small mountain rail stop of Wellington, Washington, located partway up the Cascade range, at 1:20 A.M. on March 1, 1910.

A blizzard of enormous proportions had buffetted the area for nine days in February. The snow that fell at the alarming rate of a foot an hour—on one particularly ferocious day, 11 feet of snow accumulated—managed to close down the Great Northern Railroad completely.

Unfortunately, it also stranded a passenger train, loaded with over 100 travelers, which had stopped at the high outpost of Wellington. Plows brought in to free the train had become stuck in the mounting snow just outside of town. Several locomotives and a mail train, all equipped with special plows, were unable to break through the steadily increasing wall of heavy powdered snow surrounding this tiny rail stop.

Residents of the village surveyed the mountain range above them nervously. A huge forest fire had swept the slopes clean of the trees that could prevent or at least dissipate an avalanche. The conditions were ideal for a disaster.

Then, late on February 28, the snow stopped, and rain, accompanied by warm winds, began to fall. What had become a possibility rapidly turned into an inevitability, and shortly after 1 A.M., a slab of rain-heavy snow resting upon unstable powder broke loose from the side of the mountain. A 20-foot high, half-mile long, quarter-mile wide wall of snow roared down the slope, headed directly for the village of Wellington.

It missed the local hotel, but plunged, at enormous speed, directly toward the railroad depot. With the force of a thousand battering rams, it slammed into the locomotives, boxcars, engine house, water tower, mail train and passenger train, in which 100 unsuspecting people slept. Within seconds, it picked up the trains and buildings and plowed them into a 150-foot gorge.

Another minute, and it was all over. Trainmen who lived in the hotel rushed to the gorge with shovels and picks and, listening for muffled screams and groans for help from beneath the displaced mountain of snow, immediately started to dig for survivors.

Twenty-six people were rescued. Ninety-six died, buried in the pieces of the passenger train that had been crushed and transported into the gorge by the avalanche. The rescue work had to be abandoned within days; it took a late spring thaw to unearth all of the bodies and cars.

UNITED STATES
WASHINGTON

May 18, 1980

• • • • • • • • • • • • •

The volcanic explosion of Mt. St. Helens on May 18, 1980 triggered the largest recorded avalanche in history on the mountain's north slope. The velocity of the avalanche reached a record-making 250 mph.

The largest recorded avalanche in history thundered down the north slope of Mt. St. Helens on May 18, 1980, following the cataclysmic eruption of that mountain. (See VOLCANOS.) The landslide measured 2.8 cubic kilometers—enough to cover an area slightly larger than downtown Portland, Oregon to a depth that would bury the city's 40-story First National Bank Tower.

Its velocity reached an astonishing 250 mph, which is 125 mph faster than the wind speed in a maximum force hurricane.

According to George Plafker, a survey geologist who studied landslides in Alaska and South America, the Mt. St. Helens slide dwarfed even the cataclysmic 1963 Mount Huascaran avalanche in Peru (see p. 11).

WALES
ABERFAN

October 21, 1966

• • • • • • • • • • • • • •

The collapse of a slag heap outside of Aberfan, Wales on October 21, 1966 caused the worst landslide in Wales's history. One hundred forty-five persons—116 of them children—were killed.

"**B**uried alive by the National Coal Board," was the statement a score of ravaged and angry parents demanded be put on their children's death certificates in the wake of the worst landslide in the history of Wales. One hundred forty-five persons were killed in the collapse of an 800-foot high slag heap outside of the village of Aberfan on the morning of October 21, 1966. One hundred sixteen of those crushed by the landslide were children.

There was certainly culpability on the part of the owners of the colliery that had built this characteristic slag pile to such a mountainous height. But the primary cause was, according to geologist Robert Price, a "geological freak," an underground spring that had established itself beneath the slag pile after the pile had already grown to immense size.

Be that as it may, the combination of forces caused a cataclysm, which began, ironically enough, at the same moment that a maintenance man, sent by the mine operators, who had in turn been goaded by complaints from local residents, climbed around the peak of this man-made mountain, hoping to pronounce it safe.

A heavy ground fog clung to the land at dawn on October 21, but the slag heap inspector, David John Evans, remembered that ". . . it was like a summer's day on top."

Everything seemed normal to him at first. And then, suddenly, as he sat on it, the heap began to shift. "We could see the tip moving 300 yards away from us," he remembered, in disbelief even after it had happened. "Down it went, but we could not see the result because of the thick fog. . . . The movement was like thunder. We could hear the trees on the side of the tip being crushed. It was frightening."

Mr. Evans managed to scurry to safety in the mine office, which by now was a maelstrom of hysterical activity.

Two million tons of rock, coal and mud was catapulting down the hill, directly toward the Pantglas school, which had just begun its day. Almost every school-age child in the village was there, directly in the path of the avalanche.

One of these children was, however, late for school, and described the next few moments: "I could not see at first, because it was very foggy," he recalled. "When I could, it looked like water pouring down the hillside. It uprooted a great tree on its way. [My two friends] ran the other way. It just sucked them away and they ran right into it. It hit the school like a big wave, spattering all over the place and crushing the building. It was like a dream . . ."

According to another survivor, who by this time was, with miners and parents, running toward the school building, "I saw scores of houses, some with a slime-like river running through them. Running down the mountainside was a cataract, working itself through the tip which [had] collapsed."

The quarter-mile wide mass hit the school dead center, pitching it off its foundation and entering any open space, be it door, window or cracked shingling. The building folded like a paper box, crushing children and teachers within it.

Some managed to escape. One teacher, his leg broken, hobbled to a free, open window and handed surviving children out through it.

Hundreds of sobbing townspeople descended upon what was left of the school house and clawed at the wreckage, following the sounds of moaning survivors. One mining boss who directed a party to one of the collapsed rooms in the school related his findings: "We found four children underneath a lot of brickwork which had slipped down on top of them," he said. "One small boy was still alive. He was standing against the heater in the schoolroom and was crying because his leg had been caught in something. By his seat were three other children. They were dead."

The loss of any life is tragic; the loss of half of a village's children in a few horrible moments is almost beyond comprehension. A mass grave was dug for the children, marked by a hundred-foot cross upon which garlands, sent by miners from all over the world, would be hung, for months to come. Just before the grave was closed, mothers threw their dead children's stuffed animals into it as hardened police sergeants, sent to control the crowds, broke into unmuffled sobs.

EARTHQUAKES

· · · · · · · · · · · · · · · · · · ·

THE WORST RECORDED EARTHQUAKES

• • • • •

* Detailed in text

Africa
* (217 B.C.)

Algeria
  (1716)
* Al Asnam (1980)

Armenia (Soviet)
* (1988)

Asia Minor
  Cieilia (1268)

Caucasia
  Shemaka (1667)

Chile
* (1822)
* (1939)
* (1960)
* Valparaiso (1906)

China
* (1556—Largest death toll in
   history)
  Chihli (1290)
* Kansu (1920)
  Kansu (1927)
  Kansu (1932)
  Pekin (1731)
  Shansi (1038)
* Southwest (1988)
  Talifu (1925)
* Tangshan (1976)

Colombia
* (1875)

Ecuador
* (1949)
* Quito (1797)

Ecuador and Peru
  (1868)

Egypt
* Alexandria (365)
  Cairo (1754)

France and Italy
* French and Italian Rivieras (1887)

Greece
* Corinth (856)
* Sparta (464 B.C.)

Guatemala
* (1902)

* (1976)
  Santiago (1773)

India
  (893)
* Assam (1950)
  Calcutta (1737)
* Kangra (1905)
* Kashmir (1885)
  Quetta (1935)

Iran
  (1962)
* Northwest: Caspian Sea Area
   (1990)
  Qir Valley (1968)
  Qir Valley (1972)
* Tabas (1978)

Italy
  Avezzano (1915)
* Calabria (1783)
  Calabria (1797)
  Calabria and Naples
   (1805)
* Calabria (1857)
* Calabria (1905)
  Cantania (1693)
  Genoa (1819)
* Messina (1908)
  Naples (1456)
  Naples (1626)
  Naples (1693)
  Naples (1706)
* Southern (1980)

Jamaica
* Kingston (1907)
* Port Royal (1692)

Japan
  (1605)
* (1737)
  (1876)
  (1891)
* (1896)
  Tokyo (1703)
* Tokyo (1857)
* Tokyo and Yokohama
   (1923)
* Unsen (1793)
  Zenkoji (1847)

Martinique
  (1767)

Mexico
* (1973)
* Mexico City (1985)

Morocco
* Agadir (1960)

Nepal and India
* (1988)

Nicaragua
* Managua (1972)

Persia
  Gansana (1139)
  Northern Khorassan (1929)
  Tabriz (1040)
  Tabriz (1727)

Peru
  (1892)
* Yungay (1970)

Philippines
* Manila (1863)
* Mindanao (1976)

Portugal
  Lisbon (1531)
* Lisbon (1755)

Romania
* Bucharest (1977)

South and Central America
* (1868)

Syria
  (A.D. 19)
  (365)
  (742)
  Antioch (115)
  Antioch (526)

Turkey
  Deinar (1007)
* Erzincan, Sivas and Samsun
   (1939)
* Scio (1881)

United States
  Alaska (1964)
  California
   * Los Angeles (1971)
   * San Francisco (1906)
  Missouri
   * New Madrid (1811–1812)

South Carolina
• Charleston (1886)

Venezuela
• Caracas (1812)

Yugoslavia
• Skopje (1963)

CHRONOLOGY

• • • • • • • •

• Detailed in text

464 B.C.
• Sparta, Greece
217 B.C.
June
• Africa
A.D. 19
Syria
115
Antioch, Syria
365
Syria
July 21
• Alexandria, Egypt
526
May 26
Antioch, Syria
742
Syria
856
• Corinth, Greece
893
India
1007
Deinar, Turkey
1038
Shansi, China
1040
Tabriz, Persia
1139
Gansana, Persia
1268
Cieilia, Asia Minor
1290
September 27
Chihli, China
1456
December 5
Naples, Italy
1531
January 26
• Lisbon, Portugal
1556
February 2

• China (Largest death toll in history)
1605
January 31
Japan
1626
July 30
Naples, Italy
1667
May–June
Shemaka, Caucasia
1692
June 7
• Port Royal, Jamaica
1693
Naples, Italy
September
Cantania, Italy
1703
December 30
Tokyo, Japan
1706
November 3
Naples, Italy
1716
May–June
Algeria
1727
Tabriz, Persia
1731
November 30
Pekin, China
1737
• Japan
October 11
Calcutta, India
1755
November 1
• Lisbon, Portugal
1767
August
Martinique
1773
June 7
Santiago, Guatemala

1754
September
Cairo, Egypt
1783
February 5
• Calabria, Italy
1793
April 1
• Unsen, Japan
1797
February 4
• Quito, Ecuador
September
Calabria, Italy
1805
July 26
Calabria and Naples, Italy
1811
December 16–February 7, 1812
• New Madrid, Missouri
1812
March 12
• Caracas, Venezuela
1819
August–September
Genoa, Italy
1822
November 19
• Chile
1847
Zenkoji, Japan
1857
March 21
• Tokyo, Japan
December 16
• Calabria, Italy
1863
July 3
• Manila, Philippines
1868
August 13
• Ecuador and Peru
August 13–15
• South and Central America

1875
May 15
· Colombia
1876
June 15
Japan
1881
April 3
· Scio, Turkey
1885
June–July
· Kashmir, India
1886
August 31
· Charleston,
    South Carolina
1887
February 23
· France and Italy
1891
October 28
Japan
1892
Peru
1896
June 15
· Japan
1902
April 18
· Guatemala
1905
April 4
· Kangra, India
September 8
· Calabria, Italy
1906
August 16
· Valparaiso, Chile
April 18
· San Francisco,
    California
1907
January 14
· Kingston, Jamaica
1908
December 28
· Messina, Italy
1915
January 13

Avezzano, Italy
1920
December 16
· Kansu, China
1923
September 1–3
· Tokyo and Yokohama
1925
March 16
Talifu, China
1927
May 22
Kansu, China
1929
May 3
Northern Khorassan,
    Persia
1932
December 25
Kansu, China
1935
May 31
Quetta, India
1939
January 24
· Chile
December 27
· Erzincan, Sivas and Samsun,
    Turkey
1949
August 5
· Ecuador
1950
August 15
· Assam, India
1960
February 29
· Agadir, Morocco
May 21–30
· Chile
1962
September 16
Iran
1963
July 16
· Skopje, Yugoslavia
1964
March 27
Alaska

1968
August 31
Qir Valley, Iran
1970
May 31
· Yungay, Peru
1971
February 9
· Los Angeles, California
1972
April 10
Qir Valley, Iran
December 21
· Managua, Nicaragua
1973
September 29
· Mexico
1976
February 4
· Guatemala
July 28
· Tangshan, China
August 17
· Mindanao, Philippines
1977
March 4
· Bucharest, Romania
1978
September 16
· Tabas, Iran
1980
October 10
· Al Asnam, Algeria
November 23
· Italy (Southern)
1985
September 18–19
· Mexico City, Mexico
1988
August 21
· Nepal and India
November 6
· China (Southwest)
December 7
· Armenia (Soviet)
1990
June 21
· Iran (Northwest: Caspian Sea
    Area)

• • • • •

EARTHQUAKES

• • • • •

The rock-solid character of the Earth beneath our feet is only a comforting illusion, if a now fairly universally accepted theory termed plate tectonics is accurate. According to this postulation, the seemingly solid surface of the Earth is actually composed of a series of drifting plates.

According to the theory, which is a distillation of findings in geology, oceanography and geophysics, the lithosphere, or outer crust of the Earth, is divided into seven major plates and 12 minor ones. Each is about 60 miles thick, and each rests upon a less stable, softer layer called the asthenosphere. Imbedded in these plates and poking up irregularly above them are the continents, which are roughly 40 miles thick. Scientists theorize that the transfer of heat energy within the Earth causes the plates to drift.

In the course of this process, both continents and plates collide, and some slip over and under each other. Others drift apart. Along these boundaries, earthquake and volcanic activity occur.

There are two basic causes of earthquakes. One, the shallow earthquake influence, occurs when two plates slide past each other in a grinding, shearing manner along great transcurrent faults, such as the San Andreas Fault in California and the Alpine Fault in New Zealand. The other, deeper influence comes from subduction zones along the edges of the shifting plates, where the rims of these crustal masses dive steeply into the earth mantle and are reabsorbed at a depth of 400 miles.

The tremor of an earthquake results from vibrations set up when these masses collide or override each other, causing compressional or tensional stresses that eventually find their way to the surface.

Picture it this way: The skin of the Earth is like the surface of a sea, shifting with the tides. A solid object, once snagged in some subterranean place beneath this body of water, breaks free and shoots to the water's surface. Where the solid object emerges is exactly akin to the focus point of an earthquake. The water directly above the location of the erupting object is called the epicenter. The ripples cascading outward from this epicenter correspond precisely to the ripple effect of the shock waves of an earthquake.

The only improvement reality can make upon this analogy is this: Unlike the watery target of a pitched or erupting solid object, earthquakes usually have a multitude of epicenters occurring simultaneously along a fault line; thus, there is a certain irregularity and latitude in the shock waves and their effect.

An earthquake customarily begins with a slight tremor. Following this—sometimes with alarming rapidity—is a series of violent shocks, which can cause volcanic eruptions, rockfalls and explosions of the Earth's surface. Land areas can rise and fall during this time, triggering landslides and tsunamis, the giant Pacific Ocean waves that frequently and suddenly engulf land areas in Asia and the Pacific. (Elsewhere, these frightening walls of water are called seismic waves.) And finally, the third stage of an earthquake's life is marked by vibrations of gradually diminishing force.

When earthquakes take place in urban areas, the devastation is generally acute and cataclysmic. Flexible structures built upon bedrock weather earthquakes better than rigid structures built on loose soil, and the greatest tragedies have occurred in urban centers built in this latter way. In the last 4,000 years, over 13 million deaths have been caused by earthquakes and their aftereffects of fire, landslide, flood and flying debris.

The strength and destructive power of earthquakes are both measured by seismologists, who gather information, via a seismograph, of the velocity, depth and longevity of the quake. There are two types of body waves that pass through the earth: P, or primary waves, which are compressionary in nature and are fast travelers; and S, or secondary waves, which are transverse—which means that they cause the Earth to vibrate perpendicularly to the direction of their motion. S waves cannot pass through water; thus, tsunamis are caused by a third type of wave, called the L, or long wave, which churns around the earthquake's epicenter.

Interestingly enough, both P and S waves are affected by changes in the density and rigidity of the materials through which they pass, thus allowing scientists to theorize with great certainty regarding the precise boundaries between the three layers of the Earth—its core, mantle and crust. (Earthquakes originate in the mantle and crust; volcanic eruptions in the core.) Thus, the disappearance of S waves below depths of 1,800 miles indicates that at least the outer part of the Earth's core is liquid.

The intensity of earthquakes is measured in two ways: by the Richter scale and the Mercalli scale.

The Richter scale, devised in 1935 by the American seismologist Charles F. Richter, is a measurement of magnitude of the energy released by an earthquake at its point of origin. Since this is based upon measurements arbitrarily set at 62 miles from the epicenter, a combination of multiple seismographs and conversion tables too complex for other than a seismologist to unravel is used to arrive at a Richter number.

The scale is logarithmic—in other words, the energy release increases by powers of 10 in relation to the Richter magnitude numbers. Thus, the magnitude of an earthquake measuring 6 on the Richter scale has a force of 10 times that of one measuring 5.

There is no fixed lower or upper limit on this scale. Small earthquakes are measured at figures near 0, and some are actually given negative numbers. An earthquake of magnitude 1 can normally only be detected by a seismograph. One of magnitude 2 is the weakest disturbance that can be noticed by people. A magnitude 5 earthquake releases energy equivilant to that released by 1,000 tons of TNT.

Any earthquake with a Richter value of 6 or more is commonly considered to be a major disturbance, and a magnitude of 7 on the scale releases energy equivilant to 1 million tons of TNT. There have been earthquakes—the Alaskan earthquake of March 27, 1964 was one of them—that have hit 8.5 on the Richter scale.

The scale developed by the Italian seismologist Guiseppe Mercalli mixes in subjective factors. It measures the severity of an earthquake in terms of its effect upon the inhabitants of an area—the damage to buildings and people, or in the case of slight earthquakes, whether or not sleeping persons were awakened by it.

On the Mercalli scale, a quake can climb in intensity from Degree I to Degree XII. A Degree I earthquake is not felt except by a few people under especially sensitive or favorable conditions. A Degree II earthquake is felt by most people, and it causes delicately suspended objects to swing. A degree IV earthquake cracks walls and produces the sensation that a heavy vehicle has just struck the building.

A Degree IX earthquake is capable of shifting buildings off foundations and cracking them conspicuously. With a rating of XI, an earthquake leaves few if any masonry structures standing, pulverizes bridges and produces broad fissures in the ground. A Degree XII earthquake is one in which damage is total and waves are seen on ground surfaces.

All of the earthquakes in the following section registered at least 6.5 on the Richter scale and were classified as Degree IX or higher on the Mercalli scale.

• • • • • • • • • • • • • • •

AFRICA

June 217 B.C.

• • • • • • • • • • • • •

One hundred cities were affected and between 50,000 and 75,000 people were killed by a giant earthquake in North Africa in June 217 B.C.

According to Roman historians, a gigantic earthquake tore through all of North Africa early in June of 217 B.C., a moment in history best known for Hannibal's conquering of the Roman legions at Trasimeno Lake, which was a momentary stop in the Roman conquest of all of central and Southern Italy, and the continued building of the Via Appia from Capua to Tarentum.

The parts of the Appian Way that were in place by June, 217 B.C., however, must have been dislodged by this quake, which, according to the historians, ". . . tumbled lakes and streams from their beds . . ." in several Italian cities.

It destroyed 100 cities in North Africa and killed 50,000 to 75,000 people.

ALGERIA
AL ASNAM

October 10, 1980

• • • • • • • • • • • • •

Two earthquakes, rated at 7.5 and 6.5 on the Richter scale, swept through Al Asnam, Algeria on October 10, 1980. Six thousand died; 250,000 were rendered homeless and 80 percent of the city was destroyed.

Slightly after 12:30 P.M., while thousands of residents of the Algerian city of Al Asnam were at home celebrating the Muslim sabbath, a monstrous 7.5 earthquake raged through the city, followed closely by another 6.5 tremor that toppled most of the public buildings, including a hospital, a girls' high school and the central mosque.

"You could hear the screams of the injured and the dying," a French resident said, describing the impact of the first tremor, which lasted a full two minutes. "But it was mostly destroyed in the first 30 seconds," was the way the resident summed up the initial impact of this quake, which destroyed 80 percent of the city, killed 6,000 and left 250,000 homeless.

The shocks ripped through the countryside, forcing apart fissures in the sweeping plains and abrupt hills that surround Al Asnam and run down to the Mediterranean. In Al Attaf, two pink apartment buildings tilted crazily in opposite directions, a pair of leaning towers in imminent danger of collapse.

Rescue began immediately, but in a disorganized fashion. Reflecting the hysteria of the populace, officials initially released wildly inflated casualty figures, estimating between 17,000 and 25,000 dead. The highway leading from Algiers to Al Asnam quickly became snarled and choked with truck and automobile traffic. Guards at military checkpoints let only essential vehicles travel to the worst hit areas. Dozens of ambulances hurtled down the road, which buckled in places, while civilian cars moved over and waited patiently in line.

In some parts of the city center, hands and arms protruded from beneath heavy concrete slabs. Reports from the scene said that doctors and sometimes nurses ampu-

tated arms and legs without anesthesia to free trapped people.

As the night wore on, aftershocks panicked people as rescue workers toiled on by floodlights powered by portable generators. The Algerian government appealed to other countries for aid, and several moved swiftly—notably Switzerland, which sent in Alpine rescue teams, and France, which sent firemen and dogs trained to sniff out survivors. Soviet nurses arrived upon the scene, and planeloads of blood plasma, medical equipment, blankets and tents arrived from the Netherlands and West Germany. The United States sent $25,000 from its emergency fund.

In one bizarre footnote, rescue workers, digging through ruins two weeks after the quake hit, found six survivors who had been having a drink in a local cafe when the quake hit. They had managed to stay alive for 14 days, drinking lemonade.

ARMENIA (SOVIET)

December 7, 1988

• • • • • • • • • • • • •

An earthquake measuring 6.9 on the Richter scale struck Soviet Armenia on December 7, 1988, destroying two-thirds of Leninakan, Armenia's second largest city, and eliminating a score of villages and towns. Officially, 28,854 were killed, 12,000 were injured and 400,000 were made homeless. Unofficial reports stated there were 55,000 casualties.

The inefficiency of bureaucracy, the contrast between the Leonid Brezhnev and Mikhail Gorbachev years in the USSR, and the terrible capriciousness of natural disasters all collided in a catastrophic, 6.9 earthquake at 11:41 A.M. on December 7, 1988, in Soviet Armenia. Gorbachev, in New York City on a diplomatic mission to the United States, cut short his visit and rushed home when the news reached him.

It was the worst quake in the region in 80 years and one of the worst in Soviet history. "I have Chernobyl behind me," said Yevgen I. Chazov, the Soviet health minister, to the newspaper *Izvestia*, after surveying the region by air, "but I have never seen anything like this. The scope is just catastrophic."

Leninakan, the second largest city in Armenia, was two-thirds destroyed. Half of Korovakan, a city of 150,000, was toppled, and Spital, a town of 30,000, disappeared entirely, collapsed to its foundations by the quake. Tremors were felt as far west as Baku, the capital of the Soviet republic of Azerbaijan, and north to Tbilisi, the capital of Georgia.

A woman, in the wreckage of her home, surveys the extent of her belongings after the Armenian earthquake of December 7, 1988. Rudolph von Bernuth, CARE.

According to Dr. Robert Wallace of the U.S. Geological Survey's earthquake center in Menlo Park, California, the area is a "structural knot," made by the interactions of several rigid tectonic plates. A broad zone extending from the Mediterranean Sea to the Himalayan Mountains is a relic of Tethys, an ancient sea that once separated Eurasia from Africa and India. These continents converge over what once was a sea and press against each other. In turn, the pressure causes earthquakes, volcanic eruptions and the creation of nascent mountain ranges. In A.D. 893, a quake in the area was reported to have caused 20,000 deaths, and in 1667, in nearby Shemaka, another consumed 80,000 lives.

What was particularly horrendous about the 1988 Armenian earthquake was the extensive loss of life caused by the faulty construction of many of the houses in the area. Built cheaply and carelessly during the Brezhnev era, they

simply became unhinged and crumbled inward on their inhabitants. In Leninakan, the clock in the town square was eerily frozen at 11:42, one minute after the quake hit. All around it, slabs of concrete were piled in crazy confusion, twisted girders poked fingers at the sky where apartment buildings once stood, and hollow-eyed survivors wandered about, looking for familiar faces.

Trains were derailed, tracks were obliterated by landslides, cars were tossed off roads like toys and hundreds of fires were ignited by broken gas and electric lines.

"It was like a slow-motion movie," said Ruzanna Grigoryan, who was working at the stocking factory in Leninakan when the quake struck. "There was a concrete panel slowly falling down . . . I used every piece of concrete, every rod, and I was pulling myself out centimeter by centimeter," she continued. "Then I found out that I had been doing this for four hours."

"There was a loud humming noise, then steam burst out of the ground, buildings began to rock like boats and it

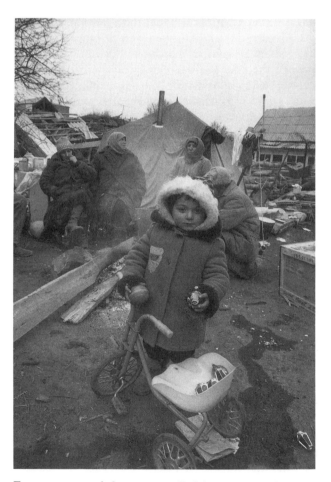

Emergency tent shelters are small defense against the winter cold of Soviet Armenia after the earthquake of December 7, 1988. Rudolph von Bernuth, CARE.

was as though the earth was boiling," said Leninakan resident Gevork Shakhnasaryan, as he described the first and strongest of three shocks.

Soviet television showed a distraught man standing in a pile of wood and concrete and pointing despairingly at a charred pile of rubble, which had once been his kitchen, and where his brother had been eating lunch when the quake struck. The body of his father had just been pulled from the wreckage. The brother had not been found. "No one could live there . . . The grief is horrible," said the man, in a choked and terrible voice.

Leninakan's Mayor, Emile Kirakosyan, lost his entire family of 15. "They're all gone," he wept on television, "I must just keep working."

Workers continued for days to dig through the wreckage. Four days after the quake, a crane operator, Anton Sukisikanyan, said on Soviet television, "We've brought out 23 people alive. I don't want to talk about how many bodies—but there were 280 people in this building."

One hundred twenty of Leninakan's apartment buildings disappeared entirely. What had been a nine-story structure close to the central square was reduced to a 40-foot mound of debris flecked with remnants of clothing, curtains and mattresses. Ironically, one of the buildings in Leninakan that collapsed into dust was the Seismic Institute of the Armenian Academy of Sciences.

In addition to the shoddy construction of prefabricated houses, the backward state of Soviet medicine affected local rescue efforts. However, Gorbachev's perestroika facilitated a quick response from the outside world, and an openness to international relief efforts that would have been impossible in earlier years. By December 10, a team of 160 French firefighters with 36 dogs was unloading two DC-8 airliners and a Hercules transport plane that contained tents, blankets, medical supplies and special equipment at Moscow airport.

And then, later that same day, heavy fog closed in on much of the USSR, and both supplies and help were further delayed. On December 11, a Soviet military transport plane crashed on its approach to Leninakan, killing nine crew members and 69 military personnel. A day later, a Yugoslav Air Force transport plane plummeted to earth near the congested airport in Yereven. Its crew of seven was killed.

Chaos now began to escalate, as *Pravda*, the Communist Party paper, blamed the unruliness on entrenched bureaucrats and the shoddy construction on the "period of stagnation" of the 18 years of power of Leonid Brezhnev. Still, 46 countries, in the greatest foreign aid effort since World War II, continued to work around the clock despite rain slickened roads, shortages of cranes, medical equip-

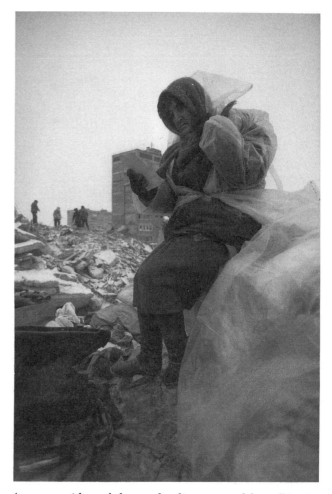

A woman without shelter reads a letter rescued from the ruins left by the Armenian earthquake of December 7, 1988. Rudolph von Bernuth, CARE.

ment, antibiotics and blood plasma, and two new problems: looting and an outbreak of ethnic tensions.

On December 12, Soviet television reported an attempted break-in at a savings bank in Spitak, a town leveled by the quake. An Army officer reported that soldiers had to restrain local crowds who wanted to kill the thief on the spot. "You can see that grief does not always unite people," chief Soviet spokesman Gennadi I. Gerasimov observed.

By the next day, trucks with loudspeakers were roaming the streets of Leninakan, advising the homeless to leave. But a virtual army of soot-covered survivors remained in the central city, hunting for relatives, belongings or, more insidiously, for mementos.

One hundred fifty people were arrested for looting, including one man in Kirovakan caught stealing jewelry and watches from corpses. Desperation drove some sur-

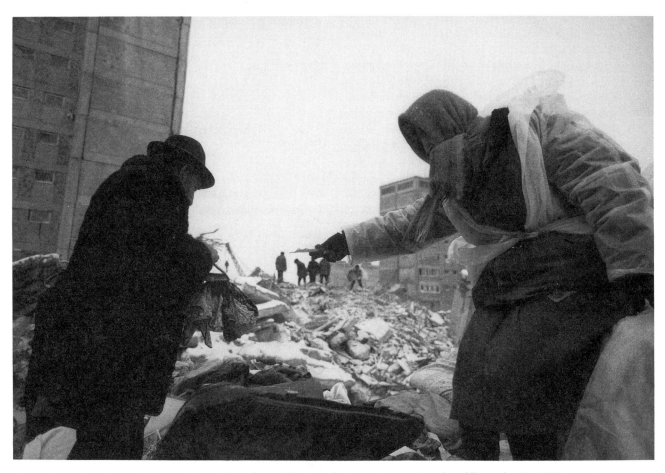

A couple searches through the wreckage of their home following the Armenian earthquake of December 7, 1988. Rudolph von Bernuth, CARE.

vivors to huddle in dangerously unstable ruins or to sleep around campfires in the rubble. Driven by despair, a 46-year-old man in a Leninakan hospital who had lost his entire family grabbed a knife and stabbed himself to death.

Gradually, the international rescue teams began to withdraw. Tent cities were erected for refugees, particularly in Spitak, once known for its sugar factory and elevator plant, and now reduced to nothing.

Thirty-five days later, in Leninakan, a miracle was reported. Six men, led by Aikaz Akopyan, a Soviet carpenter, were said to have been discovered in the basement of a wrecked building. They had, Akopyan told the world press, stayed alive on "pickles, canned fruit salad, jams, apples and smoked ham." Akopyan said he had kept up the spirits of the other younger men by singing and telling them stories.

But the rescue turned out to be a hoax. "It is understandable [that we all believed it]," reported Tass, the government news agency. "One wants so much to believe

in the miracle of six people being saved on the 35th day after the quake."

Hoaxes aside, there were lessons to be learned from the quake and its aftermath. Armenia and Azerbaijan, friendly for a few days after the quake, returned to armed conflict, as if nothing had happened. Staggering misery seemed to make no difference where ethnic rivalries were concerned.

The weaknesses of the old Soviet system and the strengths of the new were revealed as dramatically as the ribs of destroyed buildings. "These days of death and diplomacy have exposed backwardness and inflexibility in the Soviet system that are certain to provoke months of official recriminations," reported Bill Keller in the *New York Times*. "But they have also seen a society long secretive about domestic tragedies and ashamed of soliciting foreign help open itself to the world's pity—and defer to outside advice—as never before."

"It is a big transformation since Chernobyl," agreed Colonel Khludnev, the commander in the village of Stepanavan. "After Chernobyl, they allowed foreigners to participate in the investigation of why it happened, but that was it. This time, we are asking for concrete help."

In the rest of the world seismic experts applied lessons learned in Armenia in setting up a new network of highly sensitive seismic stations to monitor the Earth's tremors with greater accuracy. "A safer world awaits our resolve to act together," said Dr. Frank Press, president of the National Academy of Sciences.

Peter Wilson, a London fireman who was interviewed by the *Times* as he was packing up 11 days after the quake, concluded, "I wouldn't want to see anything like this again. It gives a very good impression, I suppose, of what the Second World War must have been like."

CHILE

November 19, 1822

• • • • • • • • • • • • • • •

An earthquake centered in Valparaiso, Chile on November 19, 1822 killed 10,000 people and raised the elevation of that city permanently.

The land around the central Chilean port city of Valparaiso, Chile was raised four feet by the earthquake that struck on November 19, 1822. The quake hit the Chilean coast, collapsing a number of towns and wiping out entire villages. Its focal point, however, was the city of Valparaiso, where 10,000 people died in massive building collapses, fires and open fissures.

According to observers, the quake raised the ocean bed so far that thousands of fish were stranded on dry land, where they died, sending a horrible stench through the city. Hundreds of boats, once used to gather in these fish, landed out of the water, where, left behind by their dead owners, they gradually deteriorated.

CHILE

January 24, 1939

• • • • • • • • • • • • • • •

A record 50,000 people were killed, 60,000 were injured and 700,000 were made homeless by the Chilean earthquake of January 24, 1939.

No earthquake in South American history claimed more lives than the earthquake of January 24, 1939. Striking at 11:35 P.M., it caught an unwary population asleep and unprepared. Over 50,000 people lost their lives, 60,000 were injured and 700,000 were rendered homeless by this

cataclysmic quake, which devastated five of Chile's oldest towns.

Concepcion lost 70 percent of its buildings, from the most historic churches to the lean-tos of some of its poorest inhabitants. Underground, hundreds of coal mine shafts collapsed, burying the miners working in them.

Coihueco, Coronal and Angol suffered similar devastation. But the worst force of the earthquake occurred in Chillan. Located 250 miles south of Santiago, Chillan was the city closest to the quake's epicenter. Of its hundreds of buildings, only three remained standing after the three minutes of tremors ceased.

Over 300 patrons of Chillan's National Theatre were crushed when the building collapsed on them. Bewildered survivors wandered the streets.

A night watchman working outside of the main power plant saw a score of live wires split, erupt in sparks and then snake toward the ground, obviously in the path of running refugees. The watchman ran into the power plant and turned off the power switch, thus saving hundreds from electrocution. A moment later, the building collapsed, crushing him to death.

Other individual tales of tragedy and heroism abounded, but the most chilling statistic from this particular disaster is a resounding one: Seventy percent—almost an entire generation—of the 50,000 dead were children.

CHILE

May 21–30, 1960

• • • • • • • • • • • • • • •

Multiple earthquakes occurring between May 21 and 30, 1960 killed 5,700 people, rendered 100,000 homeless and destroyed 20 percent of the country's industrial complex.

In a seven day trial by terror, a series of earthquakes very nearly destroyed the entire country of Chile during the period from May 21 to 30, 1960. Ninety thousand square miles of Andean countryside were ripped apart and reshaped by these multiple and, to the inhabitants, at least, seemingly unending series of major and minor quakes, volcanic eruptions and gigantic tsunamis. To some, it was as if the end of the world had arrived. Fifty-seven hundred people died; 100,000 were made homeless; 20 percent of the country's industrial complex was demolished. The cost of the wholesale destruction was estimated at $400 million.

There was some warning of the earthquake's approach; a series of minor tremors shook the ancient city of Concepcion, rebuilt with wider streets after the disaster of 1939 (see previous entry). But nobody could possibly have predicted the hammer blows of five earthquakes occurring within 48 hours. The first began shortly after 6 A.M. on the morning of May 21. And once more, the population of Concepcion ran into the streets to escape the slow-motion crumbling of ancient buildings, the tearing apart of the walls of their homes and the sickening heaving of the Earth as it opened up into fissures that swallowed homes, animals and people indiscriminately.

The city of Concepcion was almost entirely destroyed, as were Valdivia, Osormo and Puerto Montt. A 25-mile area of the Chilean countryside sank 1,000 feet.

Soon after the first quake had ravaged the country, the ocean waters began to fall alarmingly, a certain sign that a tsunami was in the making. It was. One of the largest and most terrifying tsunamis ever to roar into Chile, 24 feet high and traveling at a speed of 520 mph crashed over the coastline, flattening the fishing villages of Anoud, Lebu and Quelin and drowning everyone in its path. It flooded the entire coast from 500 yards inland to the former coastline. Withdrawing, folding back on itself, it then traveled in the other direction with equally withering force, breaking on the shore of Japan and killing 150 people there.

As the earthquakes continued, six dormant volcanoes sprang to life and three more were born. The erupting volcanoes spewed ash 23,000 feet into the air. The lava oozed into Lake Ranco, which burst its banks and created multiple landslides that drowned yet more people and livestock.

Thousands of homeless refugees were then subjected to a mixture of rain and sleet that fell on the ravaged countryside after the quakes finally subsided.

Millions of dollars in aid and supplies were flown into Chile from 35 countries. Eventually, this would allow Chile to rebuild, but not before 100,000 Chileans, some of them berserk and hungry enough to commit cannibalism and murder, rioted for crusts of bread and containers of milk.

A scene in the Waiakea area of Hilo, Hawaii following a tsunami caused by the Chilean earthquake of May 21, 1960. National Geophysical Data Center/U.S. Navy.

Men fought knife duels, and the police and the army fired into the hysterical mobs. It would be months before the doctors, nurses and relief workers flown into Chile from other countries could restore something even resembling their former living standards to hundreds of thousands in this country that had literally been torn asunder.

CHILE
VALPARAISO
August 16, 1906

• • • • • • • • • • • • • • •

A monster earthquake ripped apart Valparaiso, Chile on August 16, 1906. Fifteen hundred died, over 100,000 were made homeless and over $200 million in damage was caused by the quake.

The entire north-south axis of Chile was shaken by a major earthquake on August 16, 1906—a mere four months after the fabled San Francisco earthquake. (See p. 60.)

Far more were killed in Chile than in San Francisco, although the epicenters of both quakes occurred in the center of major cities. Perhaps because it was more populous, perhaps because its buildings were older and situated more closely together than those in San Francisco, or more probably because of the inequality and randomness of natural disasters, much of Valparaiso collapsed in upon itself. Fifteen hundred people were killed, over 100,000 were rendered homeless and over $200 million in damage was sustained by this city that had been damaged extensively by earthquakes many times before and would be many times again.

CHINA

February 2, 1556

• • • • • • • • • • • • • • •

Eight hundred twenty thousand people perished in an earthquake that took the largest toll of human life of any earthquake in all of recorded history, in China, on February 2, 1556.

As observers of natural phenomena, the Chinese are without equals in the ancient world. Besides noting astronomical events such as the appearance of new stars, comets and sunspots, they chronicled the statistics of every major earthquake since 1831 B.C. Their laborious and diligent recordkeeping thus left the world a virtually uninterrupted account of nearly 3,000 years of earthquakes.

So, although details are missing, and only a dispassionate list survives, it seems indisputable that the worst earthquake in terms of loss of life in all of recorded history took place on February 2, 1556, in an immense territory of Shenshi province in Central China, along the valley of the Wei-ho river, a tributary of the Hoang-ho.

A staggering total of 820,000 people perished in this cataclysm. And that is all that is known about it.

CHINA
KANSU
December 16, 1920

• • • • • • • • • • • • • • • •

One hundred eighty thousand people were killed outright by an 8.6-force earthquake in Kansu, China on December 16, 1920. Another 20,000 froze to death after their homes had been destroyed by the quake.

One of the most severe earthquakes of the 20th century—it registered 8.6 on the Richter scale—rolled through the remote province of Kansu, China on December 16, 1920. Villages, constructed mostly of flimsy material insulated with skins, were quickly destroyed by the huge quake. Ten ancient cities collapsed in ruins in a matter of moments. One hundred eighty thousand occupants were killed by the quake. Another 20,000 froze to death when their homes and the villages in which they had lived only a day before were wiped from the face of the Earth.

Adding to the destruction from the immediate rolling and opening of the Earth were landslides that were touched off by the quake. The area of Kansu is not only mountainous, but composed of caves in which there are deep deposits of loess, a fine and unstable sand. Set in motion by the quake, these loess deposits cascaded down the sides of mountains like falling water, loosening huge rocks and gigantic clods of turf.

In one case, a gigantic landslide actually saved a village and several thousand lives. Located at the junction of two valleys, Swen Family Gap suffered enough damage from the quake's first shock to kill one-tenth of its population and destroy roughly that percentage of its buildings. A giant landslide, set in motion by the same tremors roared down the mountainside, and would have buried the remainder of the population of the village if two bodies of earth hadn't collided just above the village and formed a natural dam that contained the rest of the landslide.

Other natural dams of timber and rockslide had to be demolished to prevent flooding. Ten thousand survivors of this monster quake set out to do just that within days of its occurence.

CHINA
SOUTHWEST

November 6, 1988

• • • • • • • • • • • • • •

In the thinly populated Southwest region of China, 938 people lost their lives on November 6, 1988. The quake measured 7.6 on the Richter scale.

An enormous earthquake that measured 7.6 on the Richter scale rumbled through Lancang and Menglian counties, a lightly populated area of China about 240 miles southwest of the Yunnan provincial capital of Kumming and slightly north of the Burmese border, at 9 P.M. on November 6, 1988. Oddly, for a quake of that magnitude, no reports of damage or injuries were reported in the city of Kumming, which contains 1.5 million inhabitants, even though there were aftershocks that registered a startling 7.2.

The scene was quite different in the two counties of Lancang and Menglian. There, the worst quake in China since the 7.8 monster that killed over 650,000 in Tangshan (see below) left only a handful of buildings standing and destroyed thousands more in the 14 surrounding counties.

A death toll of 938 was reported by the New China News Agency, a small enough figure, considering the magnitude of the quake, but the fact that the two counties were fairly sparsely settled—for China—might have accounted for this. Eighty-one thousand people live in Menglian County and 237,000 in Lancang. The region is one of dense jungle, and the poor roads into the area were rendered unusable. Neither communication with the quake area or accessibility for relief supplies was possible for weeks after the disaster.

CHINA
TANGSHAN

July 28, 1976

• • • • • • • • • • • • • •

Over 650,000 people were killed and more than 780,000 were injured in a monster earthquake that centered in the city of Tangshan, China on July 28, 1976.

The year of killer earthquakes was 1976. Twenty-three thousand were killed in Guatemala on February 4; the Friuli, Italy quake on May 6 caused over 900 deaths; a 7.1 shock on June 25 killed 6,000 people in Iran; an earthquake and tsunami killed over 4,000 in the Philippines on August 17; and over 4,000 lost their lives in a quake near Muradiye, Turkey on November 24.

But all of these pale alongside the staggering death toll of over 650,000 from an earthquake that virtually razed the industrial city of Tangshan, located some 95 miles east of Peking (now Beijing). The monster shock reverberated for nearly a hundred miles in all directions, collapsing mud walls and brick buildings and killing 100 people in Peking itself. Over 780,000 people were injured and hundreds of millions of dollars in damage was caused.

There were also political reverberations set off by the quake. The Chinese view that predates Communist doctrine maintains that natural disasters are a mandate from heaven, and earthquakes were considered a bad omen for governments as far back as the Sung dynasty. Local politicians credited their losses to the effects of this one.

COLOMBIA

May 15, 1875

• • • • • • • • • • • • • •

The brief earthquake that struck Colombia on May 15, 1875 claimed 16,000 lives.

More than 16,000 people were killed when a 45-second earthquake rumbled through the South American country of Colombia on May 15, 1875. Most of these fatalities occurred along the Venezuelan border, but the major cities of Colombia also suffered heavy casualties.

The city of San Cayetano sustained a large number of fatalities and severe damage to its business district. In Cucuta, a nearby volcano erupted simultaneously with the earthquake. Enormous fireballs were catapulted from the volcano into the city, some of them landing on churches and businesses, and burning them to the ground.

ECUADOR

August 5, 1949

• • • • • • • • • • • • • •

Over 6,000 died, 20,000 were injured and 100,000 were rendered homeless by the worst earthquake in the history of Ecuador on August 5, 1949.

There was no celebration of Ecuador's 140th birthday on August 10, 1949. Just five days before, the worst earthquake in Ecuadoran history decimated a 1,500-square-mile area of the central highland plateau, cut mountains in half and wiped out the entire city of Pelileo. Over 6,000 were killed, 20,000 were injured and 100,000 were made homeless. Fifty-three cities and towns were hit by the quake and damaged; some were decimated. The total dollar value of the destruction was placed at $66 million.

Fortunately, the earthquake sent out warning tremors shortly before it hit with full force at 2:10 P.M. As a result, thousands who might have been crushed by collapsing buildings had time to evacuate them. Not so fortunate were some who sought the shelter of churches. In the Ambato Cathedral, 70 children were crushed to death when the roof fell in.

Others were sucked into crevices that closed over them. One Indian woman held her baby over her head as she fell into a fissure. The woman was crushed to death; her baby, still held aloft in her arms, lived.

Numbed survivors of the vanished city of Pelileo (only 1,000 of the population of 3,500 escaped death) wandered about, unable to respond to the cries of their fellow citizens buried under the city's rubble. Enrique Mejia, a seven-year-old boy, lay buried beneath 12 feet of bricks for 117 hours, yelling for help. Red Cross workers finally dug him out, but it was too late. He died an hour later.

All that was left of Pelileo was a 20-foot-deep pit submerged under a river that had once meandered through the town.

Relief agencies arrived only hours after the quake stopped, but some rescuers from the United States and other South and Central American countries met with other disasters. A Shell Oil plane carrying 34 workers who were to help in the excavation of buried survivors of the city of Ambato crashed, killing all on board the plane. Relief crews climbing into remote towns on the upper reaches of the Andes were set upon and slaughtered by primitive tribes of Salasaca Indians.

ECUADOR
QUITO

February 4, 1797

• • • • • • • • • • • • • • •

Most of the population of Quito, Ecuador died in the earthquake of February 4, 1797. Forty thousand people were killed, and much of the city was destroyed in the first of two cataclysmic quakes to strike that area.

Two major earthquakes, one in 1797 and one in 1859, battered the Ecuadoran city of Quito, located on a 10,000-foot-high plateau in the Andes. Although the 1859 quake destroyed most of its historic monuments and buildings, including the Government Palace and the Archepiscopal Palace, the quake of February 4, 1797 took a far greater toll in human life, killing 40,000 people—most of the population.

Within a few seconds, this cataclysmic series of earth tremors buckled buildings, tore open the earth throughout the city and then radiated out into the countryside, activating Cotopaxi and Chimborazo, two immense volcanoes, which then showered lethal rainstorms of lava and stones upon Ambato, a town in the foothills.

ECUADOR AND PERU

August 13, 1868

• • • • • • • • • • • • • • •

An earthquake centered on the border between Ecuador and Peru killed 25,000 people in both countries on August 13, 1868.

Roaring and rolling along the border of Ecuador and Peru, a giant earthquake killed 25,000 people late in the afternoon of August 13, 1868. Very little is known except the statistics and this bizarre account by Lieutenant L. G. Billings, who was stationed at the time on the U.S. Navy ship *Wateree*, anchored in the harbor at Arica, a port that had been repeatedly beaten down and churned up by earthquakes:

> *The last rays of the sun were lighting up the Andes when we saw to our horror that the tombs in which the former inhabitants had buried their dead, in the slope of the mountain, had opened, and in concentric ranks, as in an amphitheater, the mummies of natives dead and forgotten for centuries appeared on the surface. They had been buried sitting up, facing the sea. The nitrate impregnated soil had preserved them astonishingly, and the violent shocks that had crumbled away the desert-dry earth now uncovered a horrifying city of the dead, buried long ago.*

EGYPT
ALEXANDRIA

July 21, A.D. 365

• • • • • • • • • • • • • • •

Fifty thousand people lost their lives in a giant quake that also toppled the Alexandria lighthouse—the fourth wonder of the ancient world—on July 21, 365.

On July 21, A.D. 365, the fourth wonder of the ancient world, the 600-foot-high lighthouse in Alexandria, Egypt, whose beacon lights reached 30 miles out to sea, was demolished in a huge earthquake that affected the greater part of the Roman Empire.

The gigantic tremors also toppled other, less monumental edifices and killed thousands. Enormous seismic waves formed in the waters surrounding Greece, Dalmatia, Sicily and Egypt, crashing onto their shore and pulverizing the ships and structures on them.

But the greatest destruction and loss of life occurred in Alexandria. In that city, 50,000 citizens drowned or were crushed by the quake, which left only the magnificently carved base of the lighthouse intact. It would remain in just that condition for another 500 years.

FRANCE AND ITALY
FRENCH AND ITALIAN RIVIERAS

February 23, 1887

• • • • • • • • • • • • • •

Two thousand people—almost all of them entertainers or workers—were killed when a huge earthquake struck the French and Italian Rivieras at the height of Mardi Gras, February 23, 1887.

All along the French and Italian Rivieras, Mardi Gras was drawing to an end. The climactic balls and parties roared on all night on Shrove Tuesday, February 22, 1887. When dawn broke on the morning of Ash Wednesday, February 23, revelers were still rollicking in the streets.

But at 6:02 A.M., a major earthquake tore apart the Riviera from Leghorn, Italy to Lyons, France. Two enormous shocks followed each other in quick succession, followed by several steadily diminishing ones. Huge sections of buildings cracked, wavered, and then tumbled, crushing thousands of costumed celebrants on the avenues and streets of Nice. The Jardin Public and the Place de la Liberte, relatively free from threatening buildings, were choked with terrified refugees.

Two thousand people perished in this earthquake, but ironically enough, they were mainly local residents. Not one of the well-heeled American, British, Russian or French tourists was even slightly injured by it. In fact, the *Illustrated London News* reported that the earthquake had ". . . caused a certain joy, because [it has] sent back to Paris some hundreds of people of leisure whose presence is desirable in the interests of luxury and elegance of life."

Meanwhile, back on the Cote d'Azur, life was considerably less elegant and more grim. On the Italian Riviera di Ponente, entire towns collapsed in tragic ruins. Following the first tremors, the entire population of Bajardo—1,500 persons—crowded into the local church. In the midst of their terrified prayers, another quake struck, bringing the heavy walls of the church down onto the townspeople, and killing 300 of them.

In Diano Marino, 250 dancers still celebrating in a ballroom were crushed to death when the building in which they were celebrating was split asunder. In Savona, the railroad was ripped apart. In Oneglia, a penitentiary was obliterated, and its prisoners moved to Genoa, where the Ducal Palace was scarred by huge, meandering cracks. When huge fissures opened in the earth in Cervo, 300 people were killed.

The shock waves were felt as far north as Switzerland, and seismographs as far away as Washington, D.C. leaped when shock waves from this horrendous quake, traveling at more than 500 mph, reached the east coast of the United States.

GREECE
CORINTH

A.D. 856

• • • • • • • • • • • • • •

A death toll of 45,000 was recorded in a cataclysmic earthquake that struck Corinth in A.D. 856.

The earliest accurate recording of an earthquake occurred in Corinth, Greece in A.D. 856. The city—which has been destroyed by earthquakes no less than nine times—was reduced to absolute rubble, as were several other Grecian cities. Statuary and temples alike collapsed; the countryside was reduced to torn, ruptured earth.

The death toll was terrible to consider: 45,000 residents of Corinth and the surrounding countryside were killed by what must have been a monstrous quake.

GREECE
SPARTA

464 B.C.

• • • • • • • • • • • • • •

Twenty thousand people died in a historically important earthquake that struck Sparta in 464 B.C.

The Peloponnesian War may have had its beginnings in a gigantic earthquake that tore apart a large section of Ancient Greece in 464 B.C., during the reign of Archidamus.

Sparta was unusually hard hit. In one account, a mere five houses remained standing in the entire state. Twenty thousand were killed and many more injured. "The flower of Spartan youth was overwhelmed . . ." was the way one overwrought chronicler of the time put it.

In the Spartan city of Ithome, which was horrendously ripped apart, the Helots, slaves to the Cacedemonians,

Refugees camp near Nice following the cataclysmic earthquake that devastated large sections of the French and Italian Rivieras on February 23, 1887. Illustrated London News.

were freed by the quake and rioted through that city's rubbled streets, murdering former masters who had survived the disaster. They eventually took control of the city.

Depleted by the earthquake, the Spartans called upon the Athenians for aid in putting down the uprising. When this alliance succeeded, the Spartans peremptorily dismissed the helpful Athenians, thus setting in motion resentments that would eventually grow into the Peloponnesian War.

GUATEMALA

April 18, 1902

• • • • • • • • • • • • • •

In a series of earthquakes that struck Guatemala on April 18, 1902, 12,200 people lost their lives.

The worst earthquake in 200 years of Guatemalan history devastated a large part of that country on the night of April 18, 1902. There were a score of earthquakes, actually, preceded by torrential rain, lightning and thunder.

Guatemala City was immediately flooded, as huge fissures opened in the streets, water mains burst and huts and cathedrals alike crumbled and fell, burying hundreds. Within an hour, 80,000 people were made homeless. Throughout the ravaged country, 12,200 were killed.

Fissures hundreds of feet deep opened in the countryside. In the town of Escuintla, 4,000 of the 10,000 inhabitants were killed as a shock lasting a full two minutes crisscrossed the village, ripping its center apart. Ocos, on the Pacific Ocean, was totally destroyed, first by fissures spouting lava, then by a giant tsunami which roared through the city. The banks of a nearby river were squeezed to-

35

Guatemala, February 4, 1976. View southward along a row of trees offset about 3.25 miles by strike-slip motion along the Motagua fault in Guatemala. The amount of offset is indicated by the distance between the row of trees on the right and the stake at which the man points. The stake is aligned with the row of trees in the background. U.S. Geological Survey.

gether, and the muddy bottom spit up a sailing vessel, intact. It had sunk in the river decades before.

The volcano Santa Ana, which had not erupted in so long it was thought to be extinct, suddenly leaped to fiery life, flinging lava and rocks into the nearby countryside and towns. San Marcus, San Pedro, San Juan Ostancalco, Champerico, Cuyoenango, Mazatenango and Tucana were all reduced to rubble.

GUATEMALA

February 4, 1976

• • • • • • • • • • • • • • •

Twenty-two thousand were killed, 70,000 were injured and over 1 million residents of Guatemala were made homeless on February 4, 1976, when a giant earthquake struck that country.

At two minutes after 3:00 A.M., on the morning of February 4, 1976, a huge earthquake rippled along the Mo-

tagua Fault, which is the boundary between the Caribbean and North American plates. The fault ruptured spectacularly and horrendously, opening up parallel fissures like bursting veins from Guatemala City eastward as far as the Gulf of Honduras and south to Puerto Barrios. An astounding 22,000 people lost their lives and another 70,000 were injured. Over 1 million people in a 3,400-square-mile area were made homeless.

The tragic loss of life and huge injury toll was undoubtedly caused by the timing of the quake. Families were sleeping at the time, and with no warning whatsoever, were buried beneath the exploding walls and falling roofs of their homes. In the towns of the Motagua River Valley and to the west of Guatemala City, most of the dwellings are constructed of adobe mud brick walls, which are notoriously unresistant to horizontal motion. Once the quake began, it was only a matter of seconds before the walls cracked and broke, allowing wood beams and tile roofs to thunder down upon the occupants.

In Guatemala City, which is built on an elevated plain deeply cut by ravines, there was no building code requir-

Guatemala, February 4, 1976. These railroad tracks were twisted and offset 1.07 miles by the Motagua fault, which runs perpendicular to the tracks. U.S. Geological Survey.

ing earthquake resistant design. This was despite the fact that 40 percent of the city had been destroyed by a 1917 earthquake, and Antigua, the city that had previously stood on the same site, had been totally destroyed by earthquakes in 1586, 1717, 1773 and 1874. Thus, when the quake hit, causing huge landslides and enormous, gaping fissures in the streets, damage was extreme. Thirty percent of the adobe dwellings were annihilated; some of the hospitals, the city's largest cathedral and its largest hotel were demolished, although its two steel, multi-story buildings remained unscathed.

In the countryside, there was extensive flooding when river banks closed in on each other, spilling the rivers through the countryside. Landslides buried villages, livestock and people, and dammed some rivers. In the resort settlements along Lake Atitlan, huge upthrusts in the sand, resembling giant boils, toppled and damaged hotels and holiday dwellings.

The immense devastation brought immediate aid in the form of medical supplies and food from the rest of the world within a few days.

INDIA
ASSAM

August 15, 1950

• • • • • • • • • • • • • •

The most severe quake ever recorded killed over 1,000 people in Assam, India on August 15, 1950.

More than 1,000 people perished in the most violent quake known to man, a quake so fierce that it sent needles skidding off seismographs. A reading of at least a 9 on the Richter scale was later assigned to it. The violence of this quake was so extreme it confused seismological extrapolations. American geologists thought it took place in Japan; Japanese geologists pinpointed it in America.

In the vicinity of Assam, India the situation was far less benign, though no less confusing. The catastrophic quake opened and closed the earth for five full days, sending geysers of steam and superheated liquid skyward and swallowing whole villages at a time. It wrecked dams, flooded fields and towns, and drove residents into the trees for safety— one woman was reported to have given birth in one of these trees.

The natives of this agricultural part of India likened the sound of the approaching quake to the stampede of elephants. British planters said it sounded like an express train entering a tunnel.

Its ruination exceeded that of the second most violent quake ever recorded, which also took place in this same province in 1897, and which claimed the lives of 1,542 people. Landslides spawned by the repeated tremors tumbled from the mountains, blocking off the tributaries that flowed into the Brahmaputra River. After the next quake struck, the blockages dissolved, sending huge waves of water into the fields.

In addition to the death toll of 1,000, 2,000 homes were destroyed. Damage estimates totalled $25 million.

INDIA
KANGRA

April 4, 1905

• • • • • • • • • • • • • •

An immense 8.7 earthquake killed 19,000 residents of Kangra, India on April 4, 1905.

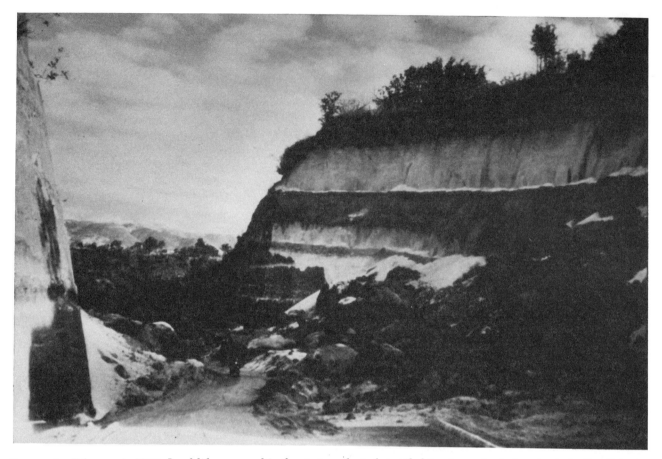

Guatemala, February 4, 1976. Landslides occurred in the steep roadcut of stratified pumice and ash deposits at the San Cristobal subdivision west of Guatemala City. U.S. Geological Survey.

At 6 A.M. on the morning of April 4, 1905, the sleeping city of Kangra, India was almost entirely destroyed by a monster earthquake that registered 8.7 on the Richter scale. Nineteen thousand inhabitants of the city were crushed to death, most of them in their beds.

The ancient and revered Bhowan Temple was filled with 2,000 chanting pilgrims when the earthquake struck. Every one of them, including the guru, was killed instantly when the temple collapsed on them. It has remained a communal tomb for the pilgrims to this day.

In the countryside, and for an area of approximately 1.6 million square miles, devastation was rampant. The neighboring towns of Dharmsala, Naggar, Sultenpur, Suket and Mandi were heavily damaged. Landslides, dammed rivers and flattened farms turned the landscape into one resembling that of a nation after a war. Entire tea plantations, lush and vital a day before, were now nothing but piles of blue slate, thatched roofs and ravaged crops.

INDIA
KASHMIR
June–July 1885

• • • • • • • • • • • • • • •

In a series of earthquakes that struck the Kashmir province of India in June and July 1885, 3,100 were killed and over 5,000 were injured.

In June and July of 1885, a relentless series of earthquakes opened huge fissures in the earth of India that swallowed entire herds of cattle.

On and on the earth rippled, and towns and villages throughout Kashmir province were either swallowed up or flattened. The death toll in the city of Serinagur and the surrounding countryside rose to 3,100 before the earth ceased to tremble on July 8. Over 5,000 hapless residents of this normally tranquil part of India were reported injured.

IRAN
NORTHWEST: CASPIAN SEA AREA

June 21, 1990

• • • • • • • • • • • • • • •

An earthquake that registered 7.3 on the Richter scale at Teheran University and 7.7 at the U.S. Geological Survey at Golden, Colorado ripped through northwestern Iran on June 21, 1990, killing an estimated 50,000, injuring 200,000 and rendering 500,000 homeless.

The worst earthquake to hit Iran in 12 years struck the historically quake-plagued northwestern part of that country at 12:30 A.M. on June 21, 1990. The epicenter was located in the Caspian Sea, but its destructive force cut a wide swath through Zanjan and Gilan Provinces, a region bordering the Caspian 100 to 200 miles northwest of Teheran. The massive tremor toppled mountains and buildings, and heavily damaged or destroyed over 100 towns and villages. Gilan's capital city of Rasht was particularly hard hit, and a dam south of it burst, flooding the countryside and causing even more casualties.

More than a dozen aftershocks—one of them measuring 6.5—terrorized the already hysterical survivors of the quake for four days after the initial impact, thus confirming the opinion of geologists that Iran and its surrounding region is an area prone to catastrophic quakes.

Ever since A.D. 700, when records of the area's earthquakes were begun, this part of Iran has undergone devastating earth tremors. Twelve earthquakes with a magnitude greater than 7 rumbled through the area from 1960 through 1990. (See following entry.) Iran lies in an earthquake belt extending from Turkey through the Caucasus Mountains and farther east into the Himalayas. This belt straddles the area in which the Arabian tectonic plate is grinding gradually northeastward, at a rate of an inch to five inches a year. As it works its way in this direction, it continually collides with the larger Eurasian plate, and energy, geologists at the National Earthquake Information Center in Golden, Colorado reason, is transferred from the collision to fault lines running from it. These fault lines run through Northwestern Iran.

Geological explanations aside, it was a night of continual, ascending terror for the 2.7 million residents of the area, most of whom were either in bed or watching World Cup soccer from Italy on television when the quake struck. "A rock as big as a building crushed my home," wailed a man in Rudbar, a mountainside village in Gilan province, when rescuers reached him. The rock, loosed from a mountain that collapsed onto the main road into this village and hampered the influx of rescue workers, killed four

of his six children and buried his wife for hours before help came.

"There is not a single house in this area that has been left standing," added Ali Mohammadi, a farmer from Rudbar, where 6,000 died and 90 percent of that city's buildings were destroyed. In the nearby towns of Abn-Dar and Bouin, all in Zanjan province, every building was flattened and every resident killed.

And it was much the same throughout the entire region of cities and villages located in the midst of inaccessible peaks, lush plains, vineyards and wheat fields. Particularly hard hit was the jewel-like city of Manjil, located in an abundant valley in the foothills of the Elborz Mountains. Rescuers, battling bad weather and blocked roads, descended by helicopter and found mile after mile of buildings that had been smashed flat, as if the boot of a giant had ground them into the soil.

"I saw how the earth was trembling, like nature kicking the cradle," said 71-year-old Baba Kamalyari to a reporter for the *New York Times*. He was standing outside of his crushed home in the nearby mountainside village of Hir. "I saw the mountain slide toward the village and said, 'Allah Akbar! I am ready to die!' But I lived, and all the younger ones were taken from me." His wife, his children, his brother and his brother's family were all crushed by a rock as big as a three-story house.

"The earth was whistling," a veteran of Iran's war with Iraq told a Reuters reporter. "It reminded me of the sound of an incoming mortar bomb."

In the city of Rasht, frantic young men clawed at the rubble with bare hands, digging through smashed concrete buildings in a search for survivors. Victims were extricated by hand, then taken out on stretchers and flown by helicopter to hospitals in Teheran, while the dead were hurriedly buried in mass graves. The haste of the operation and the efforts to bury the dead before disease spread made an accurate casualty count impossible.

Within days, international aid began to arrive, sparking a furious debate in the Iranian Parliament. Hardliners wanted no interference from the West, and, in some places, Western doctors and relief workers were turned away. In other places, like Rasht, French rescue workers used trained dogs to search for victims and aided in the search for survivors while cranes lifted concrete slabs and bulldozers cleared roads for ambulances and other rescue vehicles. Tons of supplies were funneled to Iran from the outside world through the Red Crescent.

In Rudbar, more than 50 hours after the quake struck, workers uncovered a woman who emerged with a dead child in her arms. She joined thousands of wailing refugees who were housed in tent cities. Others continued to wander from place to place, searching for missing family members.

On Sunday, June 24, three days after the original earthquake hit, a 6.5 aftershock roared through the area, burying some victims who were near rescue. Claude Sins, a French fireman who had come to Iran as a relief worker, told the *Times* that he was preparing to dig through to a woman who was only a few feet below the surface. She had been desperately pounding on a doorframe in answer to his knocks when the aftershock hit, and nearly buried him, too. "[The aftershock came,] I knocked again, and there was no answer this time," he said. The woman was later discovered, dead, by other workers.

In Hir, rescue workers broke through the rubble of a home into what once was a bedroom and found a woman wrapped in bedsheets and a blanket. She was still breathing, and workers dashed to her aid, pulled her from the wreckage and laid her gently on the ground. Moments later, she died.

All through the area, the stench of death filled the air, as, day by day, mass graves overflowed with victims, and confusion among the rescuers began to grow. "The scope of the damage is so massive that much may be going undone because of simple confusion and a lack of coordination," said a Western diplomat. The general consensus was that the official report from the Islamic Republic News Agency of at least 50,000 dead, more than 200,000 injured and 500,000 homeless was modest, by far.

There was even a discrepancy in the seismograph readings. Teheran University recorded 7.3 on the Richter scale; the United States Geological Survey at Golden, Colorado recorded 7.7. Either way, it was a major earthquake in a region that has been periodically ripped asunder by this natural disaster for 1,300 recorded years.

IRAN
TABAS

September 16, 1978

• • • • • • • • • • • • • • •

Twenty-five thousand people died in a sudden earthquake centered in the city of Tabas, in eastern Iran, on September 16, 1978. Fifteen thousand of the 17,000 residents of Tabas were killed in the quake.

The city of Tabas, an agricultural center in eastern Iran, was almost completely demolished by a huge earthquake whose epicenter was located directly in the thickly settled city on September 16, 1978. Twenty-five thousand perished in this 7.7-force quake, 15,000 of them in the city of Tabas itself, whose total population was only 17,000.

It could be said that because the quake struck in a relatively unpopulated section of Iran many lives were saved. But to the populace of this city on the edge of the central Iranian desert, 400 miles southeast of Tehran and close to Iran's border with Afghanistan, it was a devastating loss.

As in the case of the lesser, though still major quake of 10 years before, there was no warning. Thousands were crushed to death when the mud walls of their dwellings caved in on them. Others were swallowed alive when their fields opened up beneath them.

Although the greatest and most dramatic devastation occurred in Tabas and the surrounding countryside, the quake was strong enough to be felt throughout two-thirds of the area of Iran. More than 40 villages within a radius of 60 miles of the epicenter were completely leveled, and buildings in Tehran, 400 miles from Tabas, swayed.

ITALY
CALABRIA

February 5, 1783

• • • • • • • • • • • • • • •

One hundred eighty-one towns were destroyed and 60,000 residents of the Calabria region of Italy were killed during two months of earthquakes that began on February 5, 1783. During this period 949 separate earthquakes hit the region.

For two long, terrible months, beginning on February 5, 1783, a continuous series of earthquakes shook the entire western portion of Southern Italy. Nearly 60,000 people perished in the 949 recorded shocks that occurred during the period, most from the quakes, but 10,000 from epidemics that resulted from the rupturing of waterlines; massive injuries; the crowding of survivors into small, unsanitary shelters; and exposure to the elements.

The epicenter of the quake was the earthquake-prone region of Calabria, located in the instep of the boot of Italy, and bordering on the Gulf of Taranto and the Ionian Sea. Thirty thousand people died in this region during the first, most serious and disastrous quake, which was particularly terrifying to its inhabitants because of the immensely powerful thermal springs that were unleashed by the rupturing of the earth. Some of the fissures were described by eyewitnesses and scientists as 150 feet wide and 225 feet deep—enormous by any standards. Like the quake itself, these cracks in the earth opened without warning, swallowing hundreds of humans and animals that were almost instantaneously regurgitated on geysers of boiling lava. Those few who survived this terrible ordeal were so badly burned they spent the remainder of their lives hopelessly crippled.

In total, 181 towns in Calabria were leveled. Landslides occurred everywhere, but were most acutely felt by residents along the seacoast, who were set upon by landslides on one side and giant 20-foot tsunamis on the other. Sixteen hundred coast dwellers perished from one or the other of these two murderous side effects of the earthquakes.

ITALY
CALABRIA

December 16, 1857

• • • • • • • • • • • • • •

Over 10,000 people perished in the earthquake of December 16, 1857, in the Calabria region of Italy. The quake was the last in a series that rippled through the region for 74 years and killed 110,000 people.

According to the Italian historian Lacaita, 110,000 inhabitants of the region of Calabria lost their lives during the period between 1783 (see previous entry) and 1857. The 74-year period contained the most violent earthquakes to ever hit this often shaken region.

The final earthquake of this series struck on December 16, 1857, splitting the peninsula open from the Adriatic to the Mediterranean. Entire villages were either flattened, engulfed in landslides or swallowed up by gigantic earth fissures. Over 10,000 perished in this quake alone, the last of a series, but by no means the last earthquake to devastate Southern Italy.

Distressed refugees huddle in a public square in the town of Martirano, in the Calabria region of Italy, after the September 8, 1905 earthquake which killed 5,000 and destroyed over 25 villages. Illustrated London News.

ITALY
CALABRIA

September 8, 1905

• • • • • • • • • • • • • •

Twenty-five villages were demolished and 5,000 people lost their lives when an earthquake once again tore through the Calabria region of Italy on September 8, 1905.

The quake that struck in the middle of the night of September 8, 1905 throughout Southern Italy killed 5,000 people, most of them in their sleep. Over 25 villages were obliterated by the quake, including Conidoni, San Constantino, Sanfeo, Bratico, Zammaro, Tripapni and Piscopio. Martirano alone lost 2,000 of its populace to the series of 18-second shocks that traversed the countryside and rocked pantry shelves as far north as Naples and Florence.

On the island of St. Romboli, the volcano that gives the island its name was stimulated to erupt by the quake, strewing the night air with flaming rocks and lava and killing several dozen residents of the sparsely populated island.

Twenty thousand were made homeless by the series of shocks that forced the survivors of collapsed dwellings into the streets. Mobs of terrified refugees ran insanely through city streets, where they smashed storefronts, wrecked cafes and generally added to the unbridled turmoil brought about by the natural disaster.

A supremely ironic drama unfolded in the local jail in the town of Monte Leone. Terrified prisoners staged a riot in which several inmates and guards were killed. Free of their cells, scores of rampaging prisoners perished when a secondary quake loosened the already periously pitched walls of the prison, sending them crashing in on the newly liberated prisoners and burying them under the debris.

ITALY
MESSINA

December 28, 1908

• • • • • • • • • • • • • •

Depending upon the source of statistics, either 160,000 or 250,000 people were killed in the cataclysmic quake that demolished the city of Messina and 25 surrounding towns on December 28, 1908.

One of the most vicious quakes in all of recorded history began under the waters of the Straits of Messina at 5:25 A.M. on December 28, 1908. The official death toll was set at 160,000, but Professor Antonio Rioco of the Mount Etna Observatory reported 250,000 dead.

This unimaginable loss of life was matched by the fact that the entire Sicilian city of Messina was wiped out. Only one structure, an iron reinforced home built by an eccentric merchant, remained. Cities and towns within a 120-mile radius of the quake's epicenter were destroyed. Among them Reggio de Calabria (in which 25,000 of the city's 34,000 people were killed), Caltanissetta, Patti, Augusta, Mineo, Naro, Marianopoli, Terranova, Paterno, Vittoria, Chiaramonto, Noto, Floridia, Cannitella, Lazzaro, Scylla, San Giovanni, Seminaria, Riposta, Bagbara, Cosenza, Casano, Palmi, Catania and Castroreale.

The quake struck with the fury of an apocalypse, combining earth tremors, a 50-foot-high, 500-mph tsunami, hurricane force winds and driving, relentless rain—and all of this occurring in that deep darkness that precedes the dawn. Small wonder that so many of the few survivors went hopelessly insane. It was more than the most stable of minds could imagine, much less endure.

The preliminary shocks roused people from their beds at precisely 5:25 A.M. The second, rending one lasted roughly 10 seconds, and roused still more. And then, the shocks hit like an artillery barrage, each one lasting from 35 to 45 seconds, and each bringing down a series of buildings, a cathedral, a hotel, an entire city block.

The great Norman Cathedral of Annunziata dei Catalani which had sheltered ancient art treasures for centuries collapsed, burying the treasures under tons of granite. The architectural wonders of the Munizone and Victor Emmanuele Theatres crumbled to dust. Plush and thickly populated tourist hotels, the Victoria, Metropole, Trinacria and the France wavered and then toppled, crushing their occupants inside. The Duomo, another storehouse of centuries of priceless art, imploded, leaving only the colossal figure of Christ, in mosaic in the dome of the apse at the east end standing. In the words of survivor Alexander Hood:

. . . with serene countenance and hand uplifted in the act of blessing as for five hundred years or more it has remained, gazing benignly on [while] the monster monoliths of granite with gilded capitals, which were the columns of Neptune's Temple at Faro, lie half or wholly covered by the painted woodwork and debris of the roof, among which are fragments of marble tombs and inlaid altars, golden figures of angels and sculptured saints . . . with the mosaic and frescoes, with the arches and cornices which had made the Duomo so rich a treasure house of art.

Convents that had sheltered centuries of other art crumbled and destroyed their contents; the Castle Durante collapsed, burying its prehistoric artifact collection.

But that was only a small part of the tragic story. Homes buried families; complexes buried citizens. The Santelia army barracks collapsed, killing almost all of the soldiers sleeping there and creating tragedy. With the chief of police dead in his home and most civilian authorities also killed, 750 prisoners liberated by the quake from the Cappuccini prison were left free to roam the streets, creating a residual menace as they looted and murdered at will.

When the tremors finally quieted, 65,000 had survived out of the previous population of 147,000. The rest had been killed, some outright, some by the fires set by broken gas mains, some by the flooding caused by the splitting apart of the city's reservoirs; others along the port were drowned by the force of the tsunami.

Captain Owen of the Welsh steamer *Afonwen* described conditions in the port:

. . . It was a cyclone from all points of the compass. The wind howled and the waves battered and swept the decks. Amazing and terrifying things were happening all around us. Great holes opened in the sea itself and seemed to reach down twenty to thirty feet . . . the water at first appeared to grow livid and then became white with foam. . . .

Sailors from these ships rescued many and eventually restored order after the unbridled chaos that followed the quake. At the Trinacria Hotel, some survivors found themselves trapped in parts of rooms left after the rest of the structure had fallen away. Precariously perched, up to 10 stories above the street, some of them were rescued by the aforementioned Captain Owen and his first mate, Read.

One family, huddled on a balcony of the remains of the hotel called to the two sailors. Read and Smith, another sailor, climbed up a small ladder to a lower balcony and shouted to the trapped children to lower a string with a rock attached. Grabbing the rock, the two sailors attached an eighth-inch manila rope to it and told the terrified youngsters to secure it to the balcony railing. While the balcony still swayed from aftershocks, Smith shinnyed up the rope and, with Read at his side, lowered 10 children and several adults to safety.

Meanwhile, at ground level, chaos turned to madness. Looters hacked fingers from corpses to retrieve jewelry. Famished crowds fought each other to death over food in semi-collapsed warehouses.

Finally, at dawn, Russian battleships, informed of the tragedy, steamed into the straits of Messina from Agoata. Six hundred Russian sailors went ashore, organizing rescue parties and restoring some semblance of law and order. They rounded up looters, executed some of them on the spot and ultimately set up an open air hospital that treated over 1,000 wounded survivors during its first hour of operation.

By afternoon, the British Navy arrived, erecting soup kitchens and aiding the Russians in maintaining order.

The American Navy did not acquit itself nearly so well. Stung by its rejection the previous year by the British governor of the earthquake-struck island of Jamaica (see p. 44), the American fleet in the Red Sea refused to respond to distress calls unless they came personally from King Victor Emmanuel. However, within weeks, the civilian American government, apparently rethinking the situation, dispatched millions of dollars in supplies to the city that had been virtually wiped from the face of the Earth by the forces of the Earth.

ITALY
SOUTHERN

November 23, 1980

· · · · · · · · · · · · · · ·

A seven-part earthquake, measuring 6.8 on the Richter scale, devastated parts of southern Italy on November 23, 1980, killing over 3,000, injuring 3,000 and rendering 200,000 homeless.

The earthquake that roared through the south of Italy early on the evening of November 23, 1980, killing over 3,000, injuring 3,000 more and leaving 200,000 homeless, was the strongest to hit that quake-prone part of the world in 65 years. Measuring 6.8 on the Richter scale, the quake's epicenter was located at Eboli, a town near the Bay of Salerno and 30 miles southeast of Naples.

The first of seven shocks hit at 7:34 P.M., just as residents of some cities were sitting down to their Sunday meal, and just as others were beginning the ceremony of the Mass.

The parish priest at Balvano, the Reverend Salvatore Pagliuca, his vestments ripped and covered with dust from his efforts to free victims from his collapsed church, told a reporter, "There were at least 300 people at the Mass tonight, including many children. The front wall collapsed as people were trying to get out."

Thousands of people in Naples spilled hysterically out of their homes and into the streets, as their evening meals accumulated dust and debris from rocking walls and collapsing ceilings. Most roamed the streets, afraid to return to their homes.

In Potema, 90 miles east of Naples and near Balvano, virtually all of that city's 50,000 residents fled to the hills nearby, to spend the night either in their cars or in the open.

There and elsewhere, fires began to ignite from stoves left burning when apartment and home dwellers abruptly left their kitchens. Water mains were severed, hampering fire fighting efforts, but leaving firemen free to aid in the rescue work, which began as soon as the nation's doctors, who had scheduled a strike for the next day, decided to cancel their work stoppage.

As far away as Rome, the Leonardo da Vinci airport closed for 40 minutes when air traffic controllers fled their swaying 195-foot-high control tower.

At the Poggioreale prison in Naples, prisoners rioted as their cell walls began to crumble around them and fissures yawned in the prison yard. Afraid of an escape, guards hurled gas grenades and fired submachine guns into the air.

A heavy fog rolled in over Naples, making it slow going for teams with bulldozers, tents and medical supplies. Trains were halted south of Naples, and traffic was blocked on highways.

When rescuers finally reached isolated towns, they found heartrending desolation. Tiny Pescaopagano, the closest town to the center of the quake, was virtually razed. New tremors rumbled through the area, collapsing half demolished buildings and creating panic among the survivors.

But it was neither the aftershocks nor the terrain that ultimately hampered rescuers. It was the poverty of the people. The area of the Appenine Mountains along the spine of the Italian Peninsula is one of the poorest in Europe. There was virtually no modern heavy equipment, such as bulldozers, tractors or cranes, in the afflicted areas.

This, plus a bearuacracy that sent well equipped rescue teams into the larger towns like Potenza and Avellino and ignored the more inaccessible, smaller places in the mountains undoubtedly contributed to an increase in both suffering and casualties.

Still, by any standards, the rescue effort was massive. Not counting volunteers, 9,000 men joined in the search for bodies and survivors. Thirty army helicopters flew mercy missions, and regular airlifts were established to ferry in food and transport survivors out to hospitals. Six hundred army tents were brought in, five field hospitals and 28 field kitchens were erected in various sites.

And finally, belatedly, these rescuers climbed their way to remote villages, bereft of food, water, money or young men—most of their able bodied young men had long since left, to work in northern Italy, Germany, Switzerland and Scandinavia. Conza Della Compagna, formerly a town of 2,000 on a mountaintop, was transformed into a shapeless heap of stones, collapsed roofs, beams and debris. Firemen, their faces masked to avoid the pervasive stench of death, dug for bodies with bulldozers. Coffins were placed singly or in neat stacks in front of wrecked homesites.

Some of those who survived were housed in prefabricated barracks once used by construction workers at a nearby dam site. Others were put into tents. Some went to relatives in other towns. The small children, some of them with aged faces that reflected the holocaust they had experienced, were housed in a hotel in a nearby village, to await—perhaps fruitlessly—the return of their parents.

JAMAICA
KINGSTON

January 14, 1907

• • • • • • • • • • • • • •

The major earthquake that struck Kingston, Jamaica on January 14, 1907 destroyed most of the city and killed over 1,400 of its residents.

Over 1,400 inhabitants of Kingston, Jamaica were killed by a grueling earthquake that ripped that city apart on the afternoon of January 14, 1907. Not since the 1692 earthquake in nearby Port Royal (see next entry) had such devastation struck the island of Jamaica in such a concentrated space and time.

According to reports, the earth actually thrust upward for 36 seconds, toppling buildings, snapping water and electric lines, opening huge longitudinal cracks in roads, sidewalks and buildings, and setting off a tsunami which slammed, with gigantic force, into the dwellings and inhabitants rimming Anotta Bay. Within moments, hundreds of houses, with their inhabitants inside, were swept out to sea.

The Kingston powerhouse was one of the first buildings to be destroyed, but not before live wires split and broke, spewing sparks, electrocuting scores of people and setting a huge number of fires. With no available water, since all of the city's water mains were broken, the fires raged out

of control, destroying, along with the quake, more than 25 square blocks of dwellings and businesses. A cigar factory collapsed, killing all 125 workers trapped inside of it.

With no useable treatment facilities available on land, the wounded were taken to vessels in the harbor, which were quickly turned into hospital ships. On the *Arno*, a doctor, said to have gone crazy halfway through the quake, performed 79 amputations—not all of them, according to observers, necessary.

JAMAICA
PORT ROYAL

June 7, 1692

• • • • • • • • • • • • • •

One-third of the population of Port Royal, Jamaica—1,600 persons—was killed when the worst western hemisphere earthquake recorded to that time ravaged the island on June 7, 1692.

When, at 11:40 A.M., the most powerful earthquake to yet rock the western hemisphere made matchsticks out of the roaring port of Port Royal, Jamaica, it was regarded by many pastors as the just desserts of sin. A kind of combination Sodom and Gomorrah to some, a jolly good time to others, Port Royal consisted of 2,000 dwellings, some of which were fleshpots, some ship refitting centers, some homes to its natives. Within two minutes, 1,600 people— one-third of the population—would lie dead, the victims of a cataclysm that struck some distance north of the port and literally moved mountains—two of them—a mile to the south.

The first of three shocks was a major one, dislodging crockery, upsetting furniture and cracking walls. The second, longer and more violent (it lasted a full minute, which is an eternity during an earthquake) started the real damage, crumbling the wavering walls, sending them crashing down upon occupants of disappearing buildings, opening up huge crevices in the earth that would run the entire length of streets and consume vehicles, animals and human beings.

Simultaneously with the last two shocks, a tsunami was formed, which, combined with landslides, caused the entire northern portion of Port Royal to slide into the sea, drowning every inhabitant in that section of the city.

For some others, the tsunami was a lifesaver. The frigate *Swan*, resting on its side for repairs, was caught up in the tsunami as it roared inland. Skimming along over the submerged part of the city at what must have seemed unimaginable speed, it dragged its lifelines, which were grabbed by survivors thrashing about in the turbulent waters. Yanked along by the wildly racing frigate, they were able to emerge from the shallow water, shaken but safe, when the ship finally beached on the roof of a partially submerged building.

Others were far less lucky. Many were crushed by the closing of fissures into which they had slipped, only their heads protruding from the ground, and these heads, according to Reverend Emmanuel Heath, a surviving minister, turned into food for roving dogs.

One venerable city resident, merchant Lewis Galdy, had better luck when he fell into a fissure. Trapped under water and sand, he concluded that his time had come, only to feel, a moment later, a geyser erupting beneath him, which forced the fissure open again, and popped him, like a human cork, into the air. Mr. Galdy lived on to be one of the island's leading repositories of first-person anecdotes about the great earthquake of 1692.

This sort of selective salvation contributed to the legend that this particular earthquake had been the product of divine intervention.

JAPAN
1737

• • • • • • • • • • • • • • • •

An enormous earthquake struck Japan sometime in 1737 and launched what is believed to be the largest tsunami in recorded history.

Information is decidedly sketchy, but if that information is even remotely correct, possibly the greatest tsunami of all time was set in destructive motion by an earthquake that rocked Japan sometime in 1737. According to records that border on rumor, this tsunami reached a height of 210 feet as it curled away from, then rushed ashore from Yezo Island to Kamchatka. Thousands were killed by the earthquake; thousands more perished from the tsunami, which completely wiped out the coastal city of Kamaishi.

JAPAN
June 15, 1896

• • • • • • • • • • • • • • • •

Tsunamis set in motion by an earthquake in the Tuscarora Deep, off the coast of Japan, drowned nearly 28,000 people on June 15, 1896.

Sometime during the late morning of June 15, 1896, a subsea crater seismologists call the Tuscarora Deep col-lapsed. The shock waves hit the shore of the Sanriku District of Japan, where an ancient ceremony known as the "Boy's Festival" was at its height. Traditionally conducted at this time every year along Japan's northeast coast, it attracted thousands of people.

Although the shock seemed mild, many of the celebrants retreated to the hills, away from the coast, in case the quake spawned a tsunami. Rain fell, but no wave appeared, and by sunset, when the skies had cleared, so had the memories of the multitudes that had evacuated the beaches. They resumed their places on the sand for the conclusion of the ceremonies.

And then it happened. Not one, but a series of tsunamis, each traveling at 500 mph, varying in height from 30 to 110 feet, slammed into 100 miles of shore with a horrendous roar. They broke over the beach and then continued to blunder inland for almost 100 miles.

Nearly 28,000 people were consumed by these raging waters, which pounded and then pulverized scores of seaside towns. Kamaishi disappeared; when the waters receded, only 143 of its 4,223 buildings were left standing, and a mere 1,857 of its 6,557 people escaped drowning.

The story was the same in other nearby villages. In the obliterated village of Toni, only 97 of the village's 1,200 people escaped drowning. In the Kissen District, 6,000 were drowned or crushed. At Yamada, 1,200 survivors remained of a village that had once housed 4,000. Every person in the hamlet of Hongo died except for a group of old residents who were wiling away the time playing a game of tiles in a hilltop temple.

Some people were swept out to sea and then back again. Others were transported from one shore to islands offshore, and survived. But they were few, and many of these wandered listlessly among the mounds of rotting, dismembered corpses piled high in villages and along the beaches. Some villages would never be rebuilt; others would be years in reconstruction.

JAPAN
TOKYO
March 21, 1857

• • • • • • • • • • • • • • • •

Fires caused by an earthquake on March 21, 1857 swelled the total fatalities in Tokyo, Japan to 107,000.

An incredible 107,000 people died fiery deaths in the horrifying aftermath of an earthquake that rocked the city of Tokyo on March 21, 1857. Thousands perished in the first shocks that devastated large sections of the city, collapsing thousands of structures that had not been built to with-

Pools of standing water and a shattered landscape remain after a giant tsunami inundated the coast of Japan in 1896. A staggering 28,000 were drowned. Frank Leslie's Illustrated Newspaper.

stand earthquakes—nor would they be rebuilt to withstand them, either.

But the greatest and grimmest toll came from fires, fanned by 60-mph cyclonic winds that swept, uncontrolled, through the city. With its water mains split apart, the firefighters of Tokyo could only look on helplessly as huge sections of the city were eaten up by towering flames which spread with all the rapidity and power of a tsunami.

JAPAN
TOKYO AND YOKOHAMA

September 1–3, 1923

· · · · · · · · · · · · · · ·

The massive earthquake of September 1, 1923, combined with two days of heavy winds, which in turn fanned out of control fires, killed 143,000 residents of Tokyo and Yokohama, injured 200,000 and rendered 500,000 homeless.

There was horror enough for a hundred earthquakes in the great Kwanto Earthquake of September 1, 1923. Preceded by a rainless typhoon and followed by a tornado, this underwater quake that consumed Tokyo and Yokohama and its inhabitants in a fiery fury claimed a staggering 143,000 lives, injured another 200,000 and made a half-million people homeless.

The first tremors hit at noon, just as the charcoal burners were being lit for the midday meal—a circumstance that would add to the holocaust of flames that would rage unchecked through both cities for two full days.

Tokyo had already begun modern construction in 1923. Chief among these structures was the Imperial Hotel, designed by Frank Lloyd Wright, who had learned from the great San Francisco quake (see p. 60) and had specified that not only the hotel but the ornamental pool at its entrance be constructed of steel frames that would expand and contract, be sunk into bedrock, and be equipped with diagonal supports to protect the structure from an earthquake's lateral movements. His design was sound; the Imperial Hotel was one of the few structures to survive the quake, and its ornamental pool became the only source of water for the hardpressed fire fighters.

Fanned by high winds, the flames sent fiery fingers 20 and 30 feet into the air. Nothing beneath them, buildings or people, survived. On the Tokyo waterfront, thousands leaped into the water to escape the flames. Clinging to the sides of boats and to floating pieces of docks ripped apart by the earthquake, they at least felt safe from the fires. But their safety was abruptly shattered when the gigantic Standard Oil Building and its oil reserves suddenly exploded with an ear-shattering roar, flinging 100,000 tons of oil into Yokohama Bay, where it immediately caught fire around the swimming survivors, immolating thousands of them.

Yokohama suffered the same fate. Within hours, there were no identifiable landmarks. The city was one vast plain of fire that roared on unchecked, since there were neither water supplies nor firemen to fight the flames.

In Yokohama harbor, the liner *The Empress of Australia* was preparing to set sail. The wharf collapsed around those seeing their friends off on the festive trip, but most of these well-wishers managed to scramble to safety. The ship, tossed about sickeningly by swells in the harbor, was rendered inoperable when its propeller tangled with the anchor chain of another nearby ship. It was fortunate that it could not set sail; over 2,000 frantic swimmers, escaping the fires ashore, were pulled to safety aboard the *Empress*.

Others near the Yokohama waterfront were less lucky. In one public park, hundreds slid gratefully into pools, hoping to shield themselves from the flames. But they soon found that they were only partially protected. Flying, flaming debris began to ignite their hair. Only by slapping wet mud on each other were some of them able to extinguish the flames. In nearby Yokohama Park, 24,000 people were surrounded by flames. When the fire closed in on them, some dove into the park's lagoon, which had already been vaporized by flaming bits of buildings, and those in the water were literally boiled to death.

In the surrounding countryside, more chaos accumulated. The earth actually capsized upon itself in some places. A 750-year-old bridge near the village of Chigasaki was first buried under tons of mud, then flipped, intact, to the surface.

The ground turned to liquid and swallowed huge trees, so that only their tops were visible. Potatoes were pulled from the ground and flung about like baseballs.

Landslides roared through the countryside. An entire forest detached itself from the upper slopes of Mount Tanzawa and slid at 60 mph down the slopes, consuming a village and a railway and flinging the entire mass into Sa-

gami Bay, which turned the color of blood for miles around the site.

A passenger train that had stopped at the station at Nebukawa with 200 passengers aboard was hit broadside by another landslide that plowed the train and the entire village into Sagami Bay, killing everyone on the train and in its path.

At 4:00 P.M., when it seemed that no horror could exceed the present devastation, a new one occurred. A tornado appeared over the Sumida River, slamming into and crushing boats filled with wounded survivors of the fire. It then scooped up fireballs and flung them across the river and into a huge military clothing depot that had become a sanctuary for 40,000 survivors of the fire. In moments, this haven was turned into an inferno, burning to death all but a dozen of the 40,000 who were gathered there.

Hirohito, a regent at the time, shrugged off the traditional blame that would normally befall an emperor for a holocaust of these dimensions. (According to legend and religious lore, something of this vastness could only be caused by the sun goddess's displeasure with the reigning monarch.) Instead, he placed blame on Koreans and socialists who, according to his official dispatch, ". . . had offended the spirits before the earthquake and were taking advantage of the disaster by setting fires and pillaging shops."

Four thousand Koreans were publicly beheaded by the Emperor's Black Dragon Society, adding still more casualties to the tragic event.

JAPAN
UNSEN

April 1, 1793

• • • • • • • • • • • • •

The island of Unsen and its 53,000 inhabitants disappeared beneath Japan's Satsuma Sea during the earthquake of April 1, 1793.

Although the size and effect of disasters sometimes become distorted with time, there seems no doubt that the statistics recorded by the series of earthquakes and volcanic eruptions that played back and forth across Japan between 1780 and 1800 remain staggering, almost beyond belief.

The worst disaster took place on April 1, 1793, when the island of Unsen and all of its 53,000 inhabitants were swallowed up by the Earth, as an earthquake split the island apart while simultaneously igniting its volcano, which in turn blew asunder.

The fallout from this cataclysm formed dozens of small, new islands in the Satsuma Sea. Some said that the Asama volcano unleashed a lava stream 425 miles long and catapulted a steady arc of stone blocks, one of which was reported to be 42 feet in diameter, into the sky.

MEXICO
September 29, 1973

• • • • • • • • • • • • • •

Seven hundred residents of southeastern Mexico were killed and tens of thousands were made homeless by the earthquake of September 29, 1973.

Striking at 3:51 A.M. on the morning of September 29, 1973, a 6.5-force earthquake ripped apart 300 miles of southeastern Mexico, centering somewhere near the cities of Ciudad Serdan, Tehuacan and Orizaba. Seven hundred people, most of them asleep in their beds, were killed by the sudden quake. Twenty-one other villages, towns or cities in the provinces of Puebla and Veracruz, located in the Sierra Madre mountain range, were severely damaged by the tremors, leaving tens of thousands homeless.

Centuries-old churches were swallowed up by the huge fissures that opened in these villages. Particularly wide and deep crevices extended outward from Pico de Orizaba, the extinct volcano that rests in the midst of these provinces.

MEXICO
MEXICO CITY
September 18–19, 1985

• • • • • • • • • • • • • •

Two stupendous earthquakes, the first registering 8.1, the second registering 7.5 on the Richter scale, tore through Mexico City on two successive days, September 18 and 19, 1985, killing 5,526, injuring 40,000 and leaving 31,000 citizens of that city homeless.

The epicenters of the two monster earthquakes that roared through Mexico City on September 18 and 19, 1985 were located on a front along which the Pacific Ocean floor drives under the Mexican coast. Pushing under the land at this point, the sea floor is dragged down to form the Middle America Trench, which parallels the coast off shore. According to officials analyzing it afterward, the relentless pressure along these two colliding plates ". . . has caused scores of earthquakes . . . much like firecrackers on a string. It was," according to one seismologist, "just a matter of time before the next one struck."

That next time fell on the morning of September 18th, while many citizens were either at work, at school, or watching television, which at first flickered, then, as live announcers expressed disbelief and finally panic, went blank. Hundreds of buildings in Mexico City collapsed immediately. Others continued to crumble during the day as their weakened structures slowly gave way.

Many residents felt as if the buildings in which they found themselves were swinging back and forth, then heaving up and down. Furniture shot across rooms, windows shattered, refrigerators toppled, books and pictures went flying, doors and shutters flapped crazily on their hinges. For some, it was as if they were at sea in a terrible storm.

Others said they heard walls cracking with a powerful, horrifying force of a gun shot.

The 12-story Hotel Principiado collapsed, burying its 140 guests. Only 39 survived. Witnesses told of school-children standing on street corners sobbing for their parents as the city rumbled beneath their feet and its customary smog was slowly replaced by clouds of dust and smoke rising from the rubble. On the Avenida Juarez, rescue workers, troops and citizens used any available tool to dig out survivors.

In the city's suburbs, similar tragedies occurred. In Guzman, in Jalisco state, the cathedral collapsed during morning Mass, killing at least 26 people.

Then, at 7:37 the next night, just as rescue work had begun to reach an organized state, the second quake struck, collapsing buildings, sometimes on top of rescue crews. The Hotel del Carlo resembled a dissembling accordian as it cracked and then collapsed upon itself.

There were multiple, individual scenes of suffering. Arturo Lara Rivas wandered through streets looking for his family. As he picked his way past broken windows and fallen bricks, he occasionally whispered words of comfort to his canary, which he carried in its dented cage.

Mrs. Maria de los Angeles Lara Rivera talked expressively to reporters. "Oh, I was scared," she said to anyone who would listen. "It swayed and swayed and then people shouted, 'Run, run, the building will fall.' But oh, God, we didn't know where to run." As she spoke to newsmen, the Valentin Zamora Orozco public school collapsed behind her in a noisy geyser of green brick and broken glass.

Jose Costello, resting on a bench in a government shelter, his fedora still powdered with dust, said he had clung to a bedroom wall "like a drunk." His sister hung onto a doorknob and a chair. "When the thunder came," he said to reporters, "we scrambled out with only the clothes on our backs and our white dove, Linda."

Temporary morgues were set up at government offices in the 18 districts of the capital, and when they over-

Between 800 and 900 people were believed to have died in the collapse of the Nuevo Leon building during the 1985 Mexico City earthquake. U.N. photo/Jean Claude Constant.

flowed, bodies were brought to the city baseball stadium, where they were laid end to end on the playing field. Workers and pedestrians in the street donned blue surgical masks or held scarves or handkerchiefs to their faces as a defense against the rising odor of death.

As the rescue attempts began to reorganize themselves, it became apparent that the quake had limited itself to a small geographical area of the city. But, tragically, that particular area was also the most thickly populated one. The six square miles of absolute destruction were centered along Avenida Juarez, the Plaza de la Republica and the neighborhoods off the southern part of the Avenida Insurgentes. The giant Nueva Leon apartment building in Tiateloico had once housed 200 families. It had disappeared. The nearby General Hospital collapsed, burying 600 patients and staff members.

Specially trained dogs and relief experts from France, Switzerland, West Germany and the United States flew into Mexico City and immediately went to work seeking signs of life under tons of wreckage. When the dogs barked,

indicating the possible presence of a body, rescue workers rushed to the site to begin digging.

In one International incident, on Sunday morning, September 22, two days after the last quake, Mexican soldiers told French rescuers they were moving too slowly. The Mexicans proposed, none too politely, that they were about to tear holes in a main wall with heavy cranes. The French answered that it would collapse their tunnel and kill two survivors who were in it. The argument rapidly escalated into a shouting match, and the French, their pride injured, walked away, only to be entreated by the survivors' relatives to resume their work. A truce was arranged, and the Mexican soldiers dug elsewhere.

Another incident involved an infant who had been born just before the first quake. A premature child, she had been placed in an incubator. Just as the door on the incubator was shut, the hospital floors above it tumbled down, burying child and incubator under tons of steel and concrete.

Fifty-five hours later, rescuers reached the site. A steel beam had wedged itself above the incubator, protecting it

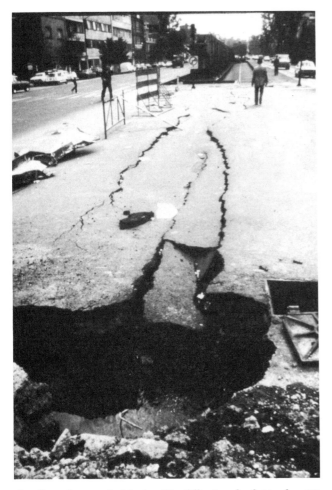

A collapsed street in Mexico City following the September 19, 1985 earthquake. National Geophysical Data Center/Munchener Ruck, Munich Re.

from the cascading concrete, and the baby was alive and unharmed, safe within the environment of its only slightly dented incubator.

MOROCCO
AGADIR

February 29, 1960

• • • • • • • • • • • • • • •

An earthquake and tsunami devastated the port city of Agadir, Morocco on February 29, 1960, destroying 70 percent of its buildings and killing 12,000 of its residents.

At 11:45 P.M. on February 29, 1960, the third day of the Muslim observance of Ramadan, one of the most destructive earthquakes of modern times swept through the international resort city of Agadir, in French Morocco. A few

seconds later, after the earth ceased to tremble, and the giant tsunami had receded, 70 percent of this once shining city would lie in ruins, and 12,000 residents would lie crushed to death beneath the remains of the formerly grandly designed buildings.

Some earthquakes strike without warning; others announce their imminence. In this case, a slight tremor ran throughout the city on February 28, 24 hours before the major jolt. It was a warning, heeded by most, misinterpreted by others as a loud knock at the door, or the backfiring of a car.

Two major shock waves passed through the city the next night. The first, at 10:50, was severe enough to cause some consternation. It was the third tremor that sealed the fate of thousands. It struck with the force of a cosmic fist, which instantaneously clawed the earth apart a full four feet, and then, within six seconds, slammed it back together again. Luxury hotels packed with American and European tourists, apartment buildings, office buildings, markets, the Casbah that had stood in squalor for centuries on the side of a hill all toppled, then disintegrated.

Simultaneously, water mains burst, sending up geysers of water that might have been used to extinguish the hundreds of fires that ignited. They would never be put out, since every fire station was destroyed, and most firemen were dead. Sewers exploded, releasing tens of thousands of marauding rats.

The Mediterranean, its floor buckled, gathered itself into a tsunami that rose, broke and rushed inland for 300 yards, drowning everything in its path.

In the harbor, boats bobbed like toy vessels, slamming into each other. Steam rose in gusts as underwater crevices opened and closed. A pilot flying above the city later commented that "it looked like a giant foot had stepped on the city and squashed it flat."

There was no possibility of rescue and relief operations from within the city. By dawn, French army personnel and sailors from the American Sixth Fleet anchored nearby descended upon the city, shooting rats that were already spreading plague among the survivors and taking part in a gigantic, often touchingly successful digging out of survivors who cried out from beneath the mountains of wreckage.

One rescue had a storybook quality about it. Mrs. Margaret Sue Martin, the wife of a U.S. Navy lieutenant, would lie pinned in the wreckage of the Saada Hotel for 40 hours. A French lieutenant, digging close to her, buoyed her spirits by noting her beauty. "How do you know that when all you can see is my feet?" Mrs. Martin is reported to have asked the lieutenant.

With classic French gallantry, he answered, "To have your courage, you *must* be beautiful."

It would take hours of painstaking digging to release her finally, long after a doctor examining her legs had predicted that she would be dead within an hour.

But she survived, remembering, for the press, that ". . . at the top of the hole I felt the sunlight on my face. People were crowding around. They were all cheering. They seemed to be crying. I think I was crying, too, with sheer happiness. . . ."

NEPAL AND INDIA
August 21, 1988

• • • • • • • • • • • • • • •

Northern India and the adjoining districts of Nepal were raked by a 6.5 earthquake on August 21, 1988. Impassable terrain made rescue and the tallying of casualty figures difficult, if not impossible. Between 1,000 and 1,500 people were thought to be killed, tens of thousands injured, and hundreds of thousands rendered homeless.

A 6.5 earthquake whose epicenter was located east of Darbhanga in northern India wreaked its greatest havoc across the border in neighboring Nepal. The worst quake in 54 years in either India's Bihar state or Nepal, it claimed over 700 deaths in Nepal and between 300 and 800 in India. Tens of thousands were injured and hundreds of thousands were made homeless in both countries.

Precise fatality figures were difficult to determine because of the area in which the quake hit.

The causes of the large loss of life were multiple. The third straight year of monsoon rains, which flooded India's Darbhanga district and washed away the summer rice crop also weakened buildings in cities and villages and accounted for the instantaneous collapse of thousands of structures in the city of Darbhanga. This, plus the fact that the first tremors were felt shortly before dawn, when most families were indoors, accounted in part for the immense casualty figures in this fairly unpopulated part of the world.

"It was a rumbling sound that seemed evil, demonic," was the way Ishrar Jha, an automobile mechanic living in the Indian city of Patna described the coming of the quake. He and others said that tens of thousands of people rushed into the streets and fields of this sprawling city when the first tremors occurred. "It was like the end of the Earth," remarked Beshan Jha, a farmer who brought his badly hurt wife and young son to the Darbhanga Medical College Hospital, which was so overcrowded that mattresses had to be spread on its floors to accommodate the overflow.

In Nepal, one of the world's least developed countries whose population is strung along the foothills of the Hi-malayas, the death toll was higher, and the damage more severe. Three days after the quake, 700 bodies had been dug from the rubble of villages in the quake zone. Thousands more were injured and far more were believed to be buried under the numerous landslides the earthquake had spawned. Unlike India, which has a widespread irrigation system based on ground water, Nepal is primarily dependent upon rain-fed irrigation for its farms, and these irrigation ditches added to the instability of the hillsides near many of the villages.

Nearly 18,000 buildings were either destroyed or severely damaged, and tens of millions of dollars in property loss was estimated. Over $1 million in funds was immediately funneled into the stricken country from the United States, the European community, Australia and Britain. The United States flew in 650,000 square feet of heavy duty plastic sheeting to be used to roof temporary shelters, since most families were afraid to reenter their former homes. "This heavy rain may be the next one, and it will all fall in," commented one farmer in Nepal, as his family huddled under a makeshift tent that was being pelted by yet another fierce rainstorm.

NICARAGUA
MANAGUA
December 21, 1972

• • • • • • • • • • • • • • •

Seventy-five percent of Managua, Nicaragua was destroyed on December 21–22, 1972 by earthquakes that killed 7,000 and made 200,000 homeless.

The first of a series of quakes struck the capital city of Managua, Nicaragua at 11:10 P.M. on December 21, 1972. Ten minutes later, a stronger shock hit, producing consternation but nothing more. At 1:30 A.M. on December 22, the third, heaviest, most terrifying tremors rumbled through the city, hitting 6.25 on the Richter scale and triggering an entire series of aftershocks that would tumble buildings as if they were children's blocks.

Managua had been destroyed twice before by earthquakes and fires, once in 1885, and again in 1931. This time, the city would again be leveled and turned into a roaring inferno that would kill 7,000 of its people and render 200,000 homeless. Seventy-five percent of its buildings would be destroyed, another 15 percent to 20 percent would be left uninhabitable. Its population of 325,000 was diminished to 118,000.

The first tremors on December 22 took their toll. Collapsing buildings were accompanied by explosions, the rending apart of the earth into huge fissures, the release of sulphurous fumes, and multiple fires which could not be put out because of the mass rupture of the city's water mains.

Survivors fled in panic, clogging the roads out of the city in the eerie predawn darkness. "Hundreds of mutilated bodies were strewn along the streets, some still wrapped in bedsheets, some missing heads, hands or feet," said one witness who was fleeing the city.

All communication with the outside world was cut off when transmitting towers toppled. One man, however, known only as "Enrique," managed to transmit news of the catastrophe over his ham radio. For hours, he was the only link between Managua and the rest of humanity. "People run through the streets like zombies, with terror," he said at one point. "Big buildings are cracked. There is blood on people's faces, legs, arms as they leave their houses. We have never seen a catastrophe like this."

Fires burned through the night. From the air, downtown Managua looked as if it had been under incendiary attack. At dawn, the commander of the Army Corps of Engineers, Lieutenant Colonel Jose Alagret, led his men into the city to control rampant looting and to aid in rescue attempts. He was appalled. "This is a city that was but is no more," he said, simply but eloquently.

The only solution would be to destroy what was precariously standing and begin again. Some survivors remained in the city, picking through the smoking ruins. In an attempt to clear the city of survivors before the decaying bodies beneath the rubble created an epidemic, the Nicaraguan government cut off food supplies, but distributed bottled water and drinks free.

An American demolition team stood by, ready to blow up the heavily damaged United States Embassy, among other buildings. The fire department declared part of the city a "contaminated area" and proceeded to level it, covering it with lime to serve as a mass grave for the unknown number of people who had died and were buried beneath the ruins.

Looting continued, then grew, as troops abandoned any attempt to contain it. Hundreds of people raided a market center and its warehouses, carrying away everything transportable, including washing machines and clothing.

Outside of the city, 2,000 people were buried in a mass grave. Other bodies were burned where they were found in the city.

The United States sent $3 million in aid, and transport planes began to arrive with food and supplies from all over the world.

There was almost no damage a mere few miles from Managua, thus giving credence to the repeated warnings of geologists, who had stated over and over that the city was built upon a fault and that, had it stood even 25 miles

from its present location, this and the previous two tragedies might never have occurred.

The lesson would not, however, be learned. The city would be rebuilt on the same fault and suffer more destructive earthquakes.

PERU
YUNGAY
May 31, 1970
• • • • • • • • • • • • • • •
Only 2,500 of the 20,000 residents of Yungay, Peru survived the 7.75 earthquake that devastated much of that country on May 31, 1970. A total of 70,000 were killed, 50,000 were injured and 200,000 were rendered homeless.

An awesome total of 70,000 people died in the cataclysmic 7.75-force earthquake that struck Peru at 3:24 P.M. on May 31, 1970. Fifty thousand people were injured, and 200,000 were made homeless. Government figures released immediately after the quake listed a mere 200 dead "to prevent panic" as they later explained it. But just 24 hours later, that figure had increased 150 times, and reports of horrendous devastation began to filter through to the outside world.

There were reasons for the inaccuracy of casualty figures. First, a combination of fog and cold would hamper rescue efforts for days. Also, much of the area affected was in the high Andes and therefore difficult to reach. And although the epicenter was located in the Pacific Ocean 210 miles northwest of Lima, much of the damage was outside the capital city. In fact, the quake was felt as far south as the village of Nazca, about 300 miles south of Lima, as far north as the southern part of Ecuador and as far east as the Amazon jungle city of Iquitos, where some damage was reported.

The immediate damage visible to observers who flew over Peru were scores of raging rivers that had not been there before. Landslides and burst dams turned formerly habitable valleys into river basins in a matter of minutes.

The city of Chimbote, a naturally protected harbor and the object of intense investment in the two years prior to the earthquake was located a mere 12 miles away from the quake's epicenter and suffered extreme and dramatic damage. Three-fourths of its flimsy housing was totally destroyed; over 200 people lost their lives. Nearby, the 10,000-feet-high resort city of Huaras—in which 6,000 people were killed in an avalanche in 1941—was totally leveled. Iquitos, with a population of 100,000, located in the middle of an area that produces gold, oil, iron, rubber, quinine and palm oil, was devastated.

Stone houses decimated in the Yungay, Peru earthquake of May 31, 1970. CARE.

But it was in the city of Yungay, located in the valley of Huaylas, that the most dramatic disaster took place. Only 2,500 of its 20,000 inhabitants survived the quake. Roaring flood waters, gigantic fissures in the ground that swallowed buildings and human beings alike, avalanches of rocks, ice and snow all conspired to virtually wipe out the city. The final blow was a wall of icy water that roared into the city from lakes high in the Andes. Dams had burst and lake shores had folded upwards, spilling these lakes beyond their banks and into the nearest valleys. The terrified survivors—all 2,500 of them—scrambled upward to a hillside cemetery, where they clung to the sides of the Andes and waited for help from the circling aircraft and helicopters that soon began to arrive from the United States and neighboring countries.

From the beginning, however, these paratroops and helicopter units were hampered by the seasonal fog that rolls in off the cold waters of the Pacific and becomes trapped on the eastern slopes of the Andes by the warm moist air from the Amazon. Pilots reported fog rising to 18,000 feet over parts of the affected region, and this made the dropping of supplies by parachute impossible. Thus the misery of the 200,000 made homeless by the quake intensified as the cold deepened and food and water began to run out.

Three days after the quake, the fog lifted, and supplies and rescue teams began to parachute in, meeting those on the ground who were frantically opening blocked roads in order to get medical supplies to the injured.

More and more died as too little effort and too few supplies finally determined the ending to the story. In Huaraz,

These two photographs show a city street in Huaraz, Peru before and after the earthquake of May 31, 1970. This adobe construction is typical of much of the housing that underwent complete collapse in the Andean townships. National Geophysical Data Center.

A young boy surveys the devastation left by the earthquake in Yungay, Peru on May 31, 1970. CARE.

a month later, there were still too few tents to protect homeless survivors from the cold. Two hundred thousand people in the area were without any kind of shelter, and many were forced to subsist on contaminated water and very little food.

According to one observer, the bulldozers that were seen in a few towns clearing away mountains of adobe rubble looked as if they were tidying up a cemetery rather than rebuilding a community.

Most cynically, this tragedy ultimately turned into a political parade ground. Lieutenant General Juan Velasco Alvarado, mindful of the fact that Peru's treasury was nearly empty, hoped that relief moneys would go towards replenishing it, and the magnitude of the disaster would unite the people of Peru behind, as his government put it, ". . . the programs of their revolutionary government."

Internationally, foreign governments went to extraordinary lengths to obtain maximum publicity for their donations to Peru. Premier Fidel Castro of Cuba personally donated a pint of blood for transfusion into an injured Peruvian child. Mrs. Richard Nixon toured Huaraz and other devastated towns as a compassionate representative of the United States government.

Both gestures were dutifully recorded by an army of television crews and newspaper reporters.

In Huaraz, ragged survivors were heard to grumble that the immaculately uniformed Peruvian generals who accompanied Mrs. Nixon had until then never set foot in the quake zone.

PHILIPPINES
MANILA

July 3, 1863

• • • • • • • • • • • • • • • •

One thousand people were killed and Manila was almost destroyed by a huge earthquake that struck that city on July 3, 1863.

Manila was nearly leveled by an enormous earthquake that struck at 7:30 P.M. on July 3, 1863. Only a few of the historic and magnificently carved churches and government buildings were left standing, but severely damaged. One thousand people were crushed to death, buried under tons of stone and rafters that trapped worshippers at vespers and shoppers in the main market.

Two shocks, each of a minute's duration, toppled the Binondo Cathedral and the huge Church of St. Domingo. Three Dominican convents collapsed, burying scores of nuns and friars, most of whom did not survive. At the Binondo Cathedral, seven priests remained unscathed by huddling underneath a gothic arch, which held; hundreds of others, worshipping beneath its dome, were crushed when the dome fell.

The nearby Pampasinga River overflowed its banks, causing huge mudslides that carried away warehouses, buildings and $2 million worth of tobacco, the mainstay of Manila's economy. The nearby volcanos of Taal, Albay and Arayat were nudged into borderline activity, but fortunately soon quieted.

The cataclysm of the earthquake was missed by Manila's governor, who was, at the moment of its arrival, riding with his son in the hills. His residence collapsed in his absence, narrowly missing his wife and his daughter, who, hours later, greeted the returning riders with plates laden with their dinners. The governor complained. His food, he said, was unpardonably cold.

PHILIPPINES
MINDANAO

August 17, 1976

• • • • • • • • • • • • • •

A huge earthquake struck the island of Mindanao in the Philippines on August 17, 1976, killing 5,000, and making 150,000 homeless.

Five thousand people were killed, 3,000 were reported missing and 150,000 were rendered homeless when a huge, 7.8 earthquake struck the Philippines at dawn on August 17, 1976. Mindanao, the largest island in the southern

Philippines was hardest hit, sustaining huge damage and enormous loss of life and property. The epicenter of the quake was located in the Celebes Sea, about 500 miles south of Manila and 100 miles east of Zamboanga City.

This epicenter, in the Moro Gulf, is about 250 miles west of the Philippine trench, where the Pacific Ocean floor is currently sliding into the Earth's interior, under the Philippine Islands. This overbiting of moving plates is scientifically explainable and almost predictable. But to the human beings caught in the quake, there was very little explanation and far less comfort in facts.

The fierce nature of the quake, which also spawned an 18-foot tsunami, plus the ramshackle nature of the dwellings of the fishermen and others who lived along the shoreline were no match for these twin forces of nature. Entire villages were wiped from the face of the earth, either swallowed up by the giant fissures the quake produced, or drowned by the giant wave that reached in and gathered up entire settlements and dragged them into the Pacific Ocean.

Hardest hit were the towns of Malabang in Lanao Province, where more than 300 were reported killed; Pagadian City, with 180 dead; and Margosatubig and Zamboanga City, where more than 200 were killed.

In Malabang, two squads consisting of 16 men of the 33rd Infantry Battalion were swept out to sea with all their equipment. The headquarters of the 41st Infantry Battalion in Curuan Zamboanga was likewise washed away.

Ralph Consing, a newsman from Colabato, said the tremor continued ". . . for what seemed an interminable time, the road cracked, fires broke out here and there and the flames cast a ghastly glow on the crumbling city."

"For a time people panicked," said a young teacher from Harvardian College, which, along with the bigger Notre Dame University, suffered extensive damage. "There was shouting. Soldiers began shooting in the air and common folk, recalling superstition, beat on drums and gongs to frighten away evil spirits."

Days later, hundreds were still without shelter. The 21st Infantry Battalion, which had a camp in Sangali, took in the homeless temporarily, doling out food rations and inoculations against cholera.

Syd Wigen of the International Tsunami Information Center, which assists nations in organizing local warning and evacuation procedures, voiced his frustration and that of his fellow scientists as they helped in the cleanup:

Five thousand people died. You can talk about statistics and they don't mean a hoot, but it's different when you know the people. Every day I'd meet someone I knew who had lost relatives or friends, and I'd go cry my eyes out. It gave me an awareness of the human situation, an awareness that reading never would.

But what really gets me, is that most of those deaths were needless—the people just didn't know how to react. They don't know that when they feel an earthquake they should take to the hills as fast as possible. They're fishermen, living on the beach or in huts just above the water, totally exposed to the waves. Today, they've rebuilt their homes, all in the same areas. Those places got whacked fifty years ago, too. Looks like the next time will be just as bad. But it doesn't have to be that way.

PORTUGAL
LISBON
November 1, 1755

• • • • • • • • • • • • • • •

Fifty thousand people died in the Great Lisbon earthquake—actually a series of over 500 shocks—on November 1, 1755. The entire city was destroyed, and along with it, priceless works of art and much of the momentum of the Age of Enlightenment.

The Great Lisbon earthquake of 1755—the most severe in modern times—was cataclysmic on a number of levels. First, it destroyed the entire city. What was not leveled by the tremors was consumed in fire, so that where once a proud city stood, only a smoldering, stench-ridden wasteland remained. On a deeper level, the human toll was staggering. The official estimate of loss of life was set at 50,000; other, equally reliable estimates ran as high as 100,000.

The range of the quake was awesome: Its destruction was felt over an area of 1.5 million square miles, and in North Africa, specifically in Fez and Mequinez, in Morocco, 10,000 died from the quake's ripple effects.

Finally, on a more profound level, the loss of enormous libraries and irreplaceable works of art—all of Lisbon's museums and libraries, both public and private, burned to the ground. The past was forever destroyed in the minds of some of the most influential thinkers of the Great Enlightenment. There was nothing left but the present, and it was at best uncertain. The Inquisition was still thriving in Lisbon, creating the same tremor as this natural disaster. But its opposite, the unbridled optimism of the Enlightenment, died that day in Lisbon. Reality rushed in with the first shock waves the morning of All Saint's Day, Saturday, November 1, 1755, and the world would never be the same for it.

The first tremors rumbled through the city at 9:30 A.M., while thousands crowded Lisbon's many cathedrals. Walls swayed, chandeliers gyrated wildly. Sacramental objects,

A contemporary engraving captures the horror of the great Lisbon earthquake of November 1, 1755. New York Public Library.

including the candles that would soon kindle the wildfires that would sweep through Lisbon, tumbled from altars and pulpits. In the harbor, a sea captain watched transfixed as, with a slow, almost stately grandeur, the stone structures of Lisbon, erected on terraced hillsides overlooking the River Tagus began to rock back and forth—"like a wheat field in a breeze," he would later recall.

It would be 40 minutes before the second of some 500 shocks and aftershocks (A Spanish nobleman would one day ask a Lisbon dignitary, "Will your earth never be quiet?") would strike the city, killing 50,000 in two minutes, opening a huge fissure 15 feet wide in the middle of the city and collapsing 18,000 buildings.

After the first shock, hundreds were buried under masonry and marble as churches—Santa Catarina and the Church of Sao Paulo among them—fell. The square before the Basilica de Santa Maria, Lisbon's ancient cathedral, became jammed with screaming, praying refugees. When the second, larger shock hit, the basilica and surrounding buildings collapsed inward with a horrendous roar onto the square, burying all of the refugees beneath them.

Hundreds of other refugees sought safety on a new marble quay recently built on the banks of the River Tagus. After the initial shock, the water in the Tagus receded, exposing the bottom all the way out to a sandbar at the river's mouth; none of the refugees noticed what seismologists would regard as a sure sign that a seismic wave would

soon appear. It did—measuring from 50 to 70 feet in height, and it washed horribly over the quay, carrying off every single person on it. Two more seismic waves followed and consumed people and boats in the bay in deadly whirlpools.

And then the fires began. Whipped by fierce northeast winds, flames ignited by altar candles toppling onto tapestries and timbers collapsing onto kitchen hearths became one uncontrollable inferno. The city burned for three days and nights, and when the flames finally died, the destruction was complete. Even the structures that had managed to survive the quake were consumed by fire.

Piled high upon the human loss was the loss of history. Lisbon's two convents burned to the ground, a new Opera House was leveled and the royal palace was destroyed. The palace of the Marques de Lourical, containing over 200 paintings by Rubens, Coreggio and Titian was obliterated. Also included in its priceless library were 18,000 books, among them a history written, in his own hand, by Charles V; maps and charts of the world made over centuries by Portugese seamen; and an especially valuable niche of Incunabula, those first-person views of the world published before 1500. Illuminated medieval manuscripts that had been stored within the Dominican convent were all consumed by the raging flames.

The tremors spread outside Lisbon and were so powerful that they were felt through all of Europe and North Africa. In addition to the calamity in Morocco, 500 soldiers died when a barracks collapsed in Luxembourg. As far north as Scandinavia, rivers and lakes overflowed their banks. In the English county of Derbyshire, nearly 1,000 miles from the quake's center, plaster fell off walls and a fissure opened in the ground.

In Lisbon, revenge for real or fancied responsibility for the disasters of the earthquake came swiftly. Gallows were erected by Dom Joseph, the young king, and hundreds of prisoners who had escaped when the walls of the prison collapsed, were rounded up and publicly hanged. Some confessed, before their deaths, to looting and setting some of the fires in the city.

Armies of priests in the black hoods of the Inquisition roamed the city looking for heretics to burn, rounding up and forcing some Protestant ministers to be baptized in penance over their sinful instigation of this natural calamity.

But fortunately for the 200,000 survivors, the level thinking of the secretary of state, the Marquis de Pombal, finally prevailed. Asked by the king for his rehabilitation plan, the Marquis uttered words that would echo for centuries: "Sire, we must bury the dead and feed the living."

That was what was done; tons of food were trucked in from the provinces, and the city would, for the next 15 years, be slowly rebuilt, this time with new streets that were 40 feet in width, bordered by wide pavements.

But the impact on the Age of Reason was lasting. Voltaire would immortalize the earthquake by letting Candide and Doctor Pangloss arrive in Lisbon in the midst of it. Jean-Jacques Rousseau would regard it as a vindication of his theory of natural man. If more people had lived outdoors, he wrote, more would have survived.

But for the other thinkers of the Enlightenment, it was a cold shower, a shocking, chastening immersion in pragmatism.

ROMANIA
BUCHAREST

March 4, 1977

• • • • • • • • • • • • • • • •

Fifteen thousand died, 10,500 were injured and tens of thousands were made homeless in Romania's worst earthquake, which was centered in Bucharest on March 4, 1977 and measured 7.5 on the Richter scale.

The worst earthquake in the history of Romania struck its capital city, Bucharest, on March 4, 1977. Although the greatest damage was done to the city itself, the effects of the 7.5 quake were felt throughout the Romanian coun-

tryside. Fifteen thousand people were killed, 10,500 were injured and tens of thousands were left homeless.

Seventy miles south of Bucharest, the Danube River port of Zimnicea lay in almost total ruin. Dumitru Sandu, its mayor, who had taken office only minutes before the quake hit, was faced with a horrendous disaster. "The earth swayed round and round . . . ." he said afterwards. "Eighty percent of my town vanished. We had no electricity, no gas, no water. Everywhere, I saw people crying. Some had to be pulled from the rubble; we didn't know if worse tremors would follow, so we took to the streets, where we lit fires and shared blankets to keep warm. Nobody slept that night for fear of aftershocks."

Thirty miles to the north of Bucharest, tremors crippled factories in the oil-rich Ploiesti. And in the capital itself, dozens of brick and cement buildings crumbled, burying hundreds. Some of the buildings were sliced in half and, poised in the early spring sky that followed the quake, resembled nothing so much as giant doll houses, their contents tumbling to the streets behind them.

Rescue work continued for weeks. The air hung heavy with plaster dust and chlorine, which was sprayed on the debris to avert epidemic. Some survivors were trapped under the wreckage for as many as eight days.

SOUTH AND CENTRAL AMERICA

August 13–15, 1868

• • • • • • • • • • • • • • • •

Multiple earthquakes ripped through South and Central America from August 13–15, 1868. Over 25,000 were killed, and 30,000 were made homeless.

Over 25,000 people died in a series of earthquakes that shook much of South and Central America for three days, August 13 through 15, 1868. Thirty thousand more were made homeless, and the damage totaled $300 million.

Damage was most severe and casualties most numerous in cities and villages, since population was dense, buildings were built in close proximity to each other, and—in the villages particularly—building materials were largely timber and mud. The cities of Arica, Arequipa, Iquique, Tacna and Chencha were wiped away totally.

Huge seismic waves slammed into coasts, engulfing villages and cities, and drowning thousands. Entire fishing fleets were demolished.

Suffering from depressed economies, the countries affected by the quake appealed for international relief. Most of this came from England, in the 1860s a thriving mercantile nation.

TURKEY
ERZINCAN, SIVAS AND SAMSUN

December 27, 1939

• • • • • • • • • • • • • •

Over 50,000 were killed in the seven shocks of an earthquake that struck the Erzincan, Sivas and Samsun provinces of Turkey on December 27, 1939. Hundreds of thousands were injured.

More than 50,000 inhabitants of the provinces of Erzincan, Sivas and Samsun, Turkey perished in the most violent earthquake ever to hit that country, at 2 A.M. on December 27, 1939. Hundreds of thousands were injured or made homeless, and even the homeless continued to die after the tremors stopped, as a huge blizzard tore into the countryside directly on the heels of the earthquake.

The worst hit city was Erzincan, which was totally leveled. But it was the severity of the winter weather that accounted for a large number of the deaths from the quake. As a primitive kind of insulation against the cold that often reaches 30 degrees below zero, citizens pile mounds of dirt and rock on their rooftops. When the first shock waves hit, the weight of these piles instantly collapsed roofs, caving in ceilings and walls on top of the sleeping inhabitants.

All in all, seven major shocks rocked the city, turning it into a tumultuous cemetery. Every building except the prison fell. All of its doctors and nurses were killed. Most of its government officials were buried under the rubble.

In an unusual act of heroism, dozens of prisoners, some of them convicted murderers, helped dig out over 1,000 buried victims of the quake. Finishing this task, they built shelters, provided warm clothing, often from their own backs, built fires against the raging blizzard and fought off hundreds of wild dogs that were roaming the city, feeding on the dead and the injured.

Although seismologists insisted that there was no interrelationship, a series of earthquakes traveled the globe for the next three weeks, while multiple aftershocks rumbled through Erzincan and part of the rest of Turkey. Minor quakes hit Los Angeles, Bolsena (on the outskirts of Rome), Nicaragua, El Salvador and Honduras. In South Africa's Rand, no less than 25 tremors struck during this period.

TURKEY
SCIO

April 3, 1881

• • • • • • • • • • • • • • •

Seven thousand died and 20,000 were injured in an earthquake that struck Scio, in the Aegean Sea off Greece on April 3, 1881.

The tiny island of Scio, located in the Grecian Archipelago in the Aegean Sea, but controlled, in the 19th century by Turkey, suffered three damaging tremors on April 3, 1881. Of a population of 80,000, 7,000 persons were reported killed and 20,000 were injured.

Scio is dotted with tiny villages, composed of earthquake-prone stone structures bereft of the support of either beams or adequate mortar. Thus, when the first of the three shocks hit, many of these structures immediately collapsed, crushing their inhabitants before they were able to escape.

Forty-four villages were virtually obliterated; 10 in Kempos, a district in the south, were absolutely leveled. In Kalimasia, the district's largest village, only 330 of 1,000 residents survived, and half of these were seriously injured.

Many of the fatalities were caused by the peculiar behavior of the residents. Panicked to the verge of insanity by the multiple quakes, many ran as fast as they could for the seashore, ignoring the cries of the injured, some of whom were only buried under light layers of debris. Hundreds of friends and family members were thus crushed to death by the hordes of refugees running helter-skelter over the wreckage.

UNITED STATES
CALIFORNIA
LOS ANGELES

February 9, 1971

• • • • • • • • • • • • • •

Fifty-nine were killed and several hundred injured in a 6.6 earthquake that struck Los Angeles on February 9, 1971.

At a few seconds after 6 A.M., on February 9, 1971, a 6.6 earthquake rattled Los Angeles and its surrounding environs. In most buildings in Los Angeles proper, this meant only minor inconvenience and a loss of sleep. To 59 people who died in this quake and the several hundred who were injured, it proved the adage that there is no such thing as a mild disaster.

The cause of the quake was determined to be a sudden earth movement along a minor fault in the San Fernando

The Call Building, the heart of San Francisco's communication network, burns out of control during the San Francisco earthquake of April 18, 1906. New York Public Library.

Valley, north of Los Angeles. This "minor movement" along a "minor fault" resulted in a quake that released more energy than the Hiroshima atom bomb and caused $1 billion in damage.

At the Sylmar Veterans Hospital, walls that had been built before earthquake-proof construction was legislated simply collapsed inward, killing 45 patients. There was a supposedly earthquake-proof hospital nearby, but it too was damaged, and two of its patients died when a power failure shut down their respirators.

Near the hospital, a freeway overpass collapsed, crushing a car and its occupants, and homes near the overpass were damaged, killing several more people. Nine more died from heart attacks. More than a thousand landslides touched off by the quake caused no injuries.

A great potential tragedy was averted by seconds. The old dam of the Lower Van Norman Reservoir, only par-

tially filled at the time, suffered immense damage. Experts later affirmed that a few more seconds of tremors would have brought down the entire dam, releasing a huge wall of water that would have swamped hundreds of houses built in the shadow of the dam. Tens of thousands of lives would have been lost.

UNITED STATES
CALIFORNIA
SAN FRANCISCO
April 18, 1906

• • • • • • • • • • • • • •

Close to 700 people perished, and most of San Francisco was destroyed in the great earthquake and fire of April 18, 1906.

No earthquake in the history of the world has been better recorded than the famous San Francisco quake and fire of April 18, 1906, in which an estimated 700 people died, 500 city blocks were obliterated and nearly $500 million of damage was done to what was once—and would be again—one of the most fabulous cities in the United States. On that day, and for two days afterward, San Francisco was practically burned to the ground.

The quake, which measured an awesome 8.3 on the Richter scale (later downgraded to a 7.8), struck at 5:13 A.M. The epicenter was a few centimeters from the Golden Gate Bridge and was created by a section of rock snapping along the San Andreas Fault, an inevitable (and, seismologists say, repeatable) circumstance caused by the inexorable movement of land masses on either side of this fault. Today, Los Angeles is grinding northward at a rate of two centimeters a year, which means that in 30 million years, it will be a suburb of San Francisco.

But back to 1906. The quake came in two shocks: one 40 seconds in duration, the other 75. The fire—set off by not only the quake but the bumbling efforts of troops trying to stop it by dynamite—lasted for three days.

The quake itself was, by all accounts, apocolyptic, tumbling huge buildings in seconds, caving in walls, splitting water and gas mains and igniting thousands of fires instantaneously. Cavernous cracks in the earth opened—and swallowed people and vehicles and then snapped shut, crushing them.

The product of several economic booms, the city had been built haphazardly in many sections, including the mansions of Nob Hill, the huge commercial establishments and hotels of Market Street, the subterranean catacombs of Chinatown, and the honkytonk structures of the Barbary Coast.

Spectacular damage to a freeway overpass that was under construction at the time of the February 9, 1971 earthquake in the San Fernando Valley. National Geophysical Data Center/J. R. Evans.

It was here, on the Coast, that some of the most dramatic destruction from the earthquake took place. Sitting on sandy landfill, this area was a prime target for the first tremors. Almost instantaneously, block after block of shoddily constructed, thin wood-frame dwellings resting on the shifting sands of the landfill splintered into unrecognizable ruins, burying the occupants within them. On the Barbary Coast, hundreds of shanties collapsed upon themselves. The wholesale district was an enormous 15-foot-high pudding of bricks, beams, dying produce and men and dead horses.

The rooming houses at Ninth and Brannon streets were leveled. Writer William Bronson described the crazily perched buildings along the roller-coaster landscape of buckled Dore Street as ". . . a row of tottering drunks."

Nearby, the $6 million, seemingly indestructible city hall, located at McAllister and Larkin Streets, crumbled into a mess of stone and cast iron. Its steel-framed dome resembled a cracked egg, its columns splayed into the surrounding streets, resting atop the unlucky pedestrians they had crushed in their precipitous fall.

In the Mission District, the Valencia Hotel simply slid into the street, then folded up like an accordian, the topmost of its four floors ending up where the first had been. All 80 of its occupants were crushed within the ruins.

The spires of churches—St. Patrick's, St. James's, St. Bridget's, St. Dominick's—buckled and became lethal spears falling at those fleeing in the streets beneath them. These streets filled with hysterical people soon after the first tremor hit. A survivor, Sam Wolfe described them vividly:

The street seemed to move like waves of water. On my way down Market Street the whole side of a building fell out and come [sic] so near me that I was covered and blinded by the dust. Then I saw the first dead come by. They were piled up in an automobile like carcasses in a butcher's wagon, all over blood, with crushed skulls, and broken limbs, and bloody faces. A man cried out to me,

61

Damage caused by the earthquake of February 9, 1971 in the San Fernando Valley, California. The photograph shows freeway compression of about 69 cm that occurred south of the interchanges of Routes 5/210 near San Fernando. National Geophysical Data Center.

"Look out for that live wire!" I had just time to sidestep certain death.

The ornate and grand hotels that had once given San Francisco part of its patrician identity went down like dominos. The Denver, the Cosmopolitan, the Brunswick, the Palace, the St. Francis were total losses; the Fairmont was heavily damaged.

World celebrities and millionaires were sleeping in some of these hotels when the quake struck, and their adventures added another layer of experience to the bizarre happenings of that April morning. Enrico Caruso, who had opened in *Carmen* at the San Francisco Opera House the night before, was in residence at the Palace Hotel. Ironically, he had heard the previous day that Vesuvius had erupted over his native Naples. Wiping his brow, he pro-

claimed, "Maybe it was God's will that, after all, I should come this far."

Caruso emerged from the quake shaken but uninjured, and one story has it that, although terrified that his voice would be ruined forever by the dust and the disturbance, he reared back and sang, loudly and clearly, thus bringing comfort to other survivors nearby.

Whether or not this or Caruso's supposed later meeting with an inebriated John Barrymore actually happened is highly questionable, but the lore and factual of this earthquake are so interwoven by now that perhaps it makes little difference.

Barrymore, the great actor and great consumer of spirits was, at the time, appearing in *The Dictator*, a play by Richard Harding Davis, at the Columbia Theatre on Powell Street. Barrymore had little interest in the play. He apparently had great interest in the fiancee of another man, and he was pursuing this interest in his suite at the St. Francis Hotel when the quake struck. Attired in the evening dress of the night before, he emerged from his suite unscathed (the story neglects to note the whereabouts or condition of the lady involved).

Failing to find the St. Francis bar open, he worked his way over the rubble to the street, where he found a sobbing Enrico Caruso atop a broken down peddler's cart. Caruso was clutching a picture of Theodore Roosevelt to his bosom—all he had rescued from his huge wardrobe bursting with possessions.

The dapper Barrymore, in his tails and diamond shirt studs, surveyed Caruso with an appraising eye. "Hello, old boy," he is supposed to have said. "Rather dumpy about the whole thing, eh?"

Caruso looked at his sartorial colleague for a moment, then reportedly smiled, his depression disintegrating in the absurdity of the moment. "Mr. Barrymore," Caruso said, "You know, you're the only man in San Francisco—the only man in the world who would dress for an earthquake!"

This was the legend. The very real conflagration roared on for three days, fed not only by the overturned coal burners and ruptured gas mains of the city, but by foolhardiness brought on by criminal corruption.

Dennis T. Sullivan, the farsighted and inventive chief of the San Francisco fire department had evolved a logical plan of dynamiting to control a fire of this magnitude. But he was killed in the quake's first moments.

The mayor of San Francisco was a corrupt embezzler (he was later removed from office and jailed) named Eugene Schmitz, who was in turn elevated to office by a grafter named Abe Ruef. Both of these scoundrels had so looted the city treasury that no funds had been appropriated for Sullivan's safety measures. Moreover, Schmitz had no idea of how to run a city, much less save it from a fiery demise.

That task fell to a self-appointed military dictator named Brigadier General Frederick Funston, who, without consulting civil authorities, declared martial law and ordered troops from the nearby Presidio garrison mobilized. The troops descended upon San Francisco with fixed bayonets at 7 A.M., with orders to shoot any looters on sight.

Undoubtedly, they were needed to stem the tide of wholesale mayhem that immediately followed the quake. Homeless toughs from the Barbary Coast broke into bars, consumed the stock, and thus fortified, rampaged through the city, looting stores, breaking down the doors of banks and rifling their safes.

At the height of this chaos, a ragtag mob tried to loot the United States Mint building. They were fortunately met by a phalanx of policemen, armed clerks, vigilantes and troops who turned them back in an exchange that left 34 of the mob dead and the Mint's $39 million in gold, silver and currency intact.

While Mayor Schmitz did what only the president of the United States had a right to do—authorize General Funston's unconstitutional action after the fact—troops, often joined by vigilante groups, stalked looters, set up instant firing squads and makeshift gallows. Lawbreakers—and some who did not break the law—were executed on the spot. Told of these executions, Mayor Schmitz gave them his full endorsement. So, while legitimate arrests were made, the swiftness and indescriminateness of the punishment grew. In one instance, three men were dragged from a basement of a building on Stockton Street where they were rummaging through belongings. They were lined up against a nearby wall and shot to death.

Even more disturbing were the soldiers' attempts to stop the fire. Laying down dynamite charges without design, they managed to set more fires than they put out. Most of the time, they used too much powder and instead of creating a backfire, leveled whole blocks, sending flaming mattresses into the air in one instance, thus setting fire to the whole of Chinatown.

This "unmasking," as one writer of the period put it, of Chinatown unearthed more than opium caverns. Thousands of rats—a large number of them infected with bubonic plague carried across the Pacific from the Orient—swarmed out of their lairs, driven streetward by the red hot coals descending into the catacombs of Chinatown. They fanned out throughout the city, and within a year, more than 150 cases of bubonic plague would be reported by victims of rat bites.

Half the city went up in flames. The next day, the survivors boarded crowded ferries to Oakland or climbed to higher ground to escape the flames. All of the water mains in the city had burst, and on Telegraph Hill, the Italian community improvised successfully, clearing their wine cellars of 1,000 gallons of wine in order to put out the flames. According to one observer, ". . . barrel heads were smashed in, and the bucket brigade turned from water to wine. Sacks were dipped in the wine and used for beating out the fire. Beds were stripped of their blankets, and these were soaked in the wine and hung over the exposed portions of the cottages, and men on the roofs drenched the shingles and sides of the house with wine."

All night and into the next day, explosions rocked the city and the fire burned on. Gougers began to charge $1 for a loaf of bread. Drivers extracted as much as $1,000 to transport a load of family belongings 10 or 12 blocks. A glass of water went for 50 cents.

In retaliation, troops broke open standing warehouses and distributed food to the starving. More than 75,000 residents of the burning city took ferries to Oakland and went from there to Berkeley, Alameda and Benicia.

Finally, on the third day after the quake, the fire was halted at Van Ness Avenue, where troops and firemen were able to create successful backfires.

The devastation was horrible to behold. Five hundred million dollars of damage in 1906 translates into hundreds of billions of dollars today. Funds that might have begun the restoration were burned up in the banks that housed them. The small, privately owned Bank of Italy, headed by Amadeo Giannini, managed to salvage $80,000 of its deposits and to lend this to all who wished to rebuild. This one altruistic stroke marked the beginning of the Bank of America.

The city would rise like a stately phoenix. But to those who were there that day, it would be all they would need to know about hell. An old man who had heeded the pleas of another man crushed beneath a collapsed building and committed a mercy killing turned himself in to an exhausted police sergeant. The overworked policeman looked at him for a moment and then said: "Go home, old man. All of San Francisco is dying this day and it no longer matters how."

UNITED STATES
MISSOURI
NEW MADRID

December 16, 1811–February 7, 1812

• • • • • • • • • • • • • • • •

A series of earthquakes that began in the tiny town of New Madrid, Missouri on December 16, 1811 with a pre-Richter scale estimated force of between 7 and 7.5, eventually affected 50,000 square miles of the United States and parts of Canada. New Madrid was destroyed and six known deaths occurred. It was the greatest recorded natural disaster in the United States to that date.

At 2 A.M. on the morning of December 16, 1811, the worst natural calamity to hit the United States to that date struck the small town of New Madrid (population 800), on the Mississippi River in what was then the Louisiana Territory. In a place that on the surface seemed an unlikely location for an earthquake to strike, a force estimated between 7 and 7.5 pounded the countryside for a full minute.

Trees were torn apart, chimneys buckled and fell, furniture overturned, and the terrified populace fled outdoors into the night.

It turned out to be just the beginning. At dawn, a stronger tremor ran through the settlement, and this time,

as one eyewitness wrote, " . . the whole land trembled like the flesh of a beef just killed." In nearby Kentucky, naturalist John James Audubon wrote that ". . . the ground weaved like a field of corn before the breeze."

Long fissures split the earth, swallowing homes and stores, and sulfurous fumes, escaping from these upheavals, sent an odor of brimstone through the settlement.

The normally placid Mississippi went wild. During the repeated series of quakes, pressures deep underground exploded through the riverbed from bank to bank; this in turn sent a wall of water upstream, thus allowing a steamboat captain accurately to observe that, for a moment at least, the Mississippi actually reversed its flow.

As the tremors continued for an unconscionable two months, land masses began to rise, fall and shift. The tremors radiated south, north and east. Chimneys fell in Tennessee, Georgia, South Carolina and Virginia. Church bells began to ring in Charleston, South Carolina, pendulum clocks stopped in Washington, D.C., and windows rattled in New York City. Lesser effects were felt as far away as Boston and Canada. All in all, nearly 50,000 square miles of land area were affected by this endless string of quakes.

But the greatest damage was caused nearest the epicenter, which was located directly under the village of New Madrid. A nearby stretch of land measuring approximately 25 square miles was raised 20 feet and earned the name of Tiptonville Dome.

In northwest Tennessee, a region of swampy area fed by creeks sank, while an adjacent area was thrust upward, cutting off the creeks' outlet. The water accumulated itself into what is now known as Reelfoot Lake—a highly descriptive title for a body of water formed by an earthquake.

In some locations, the shocks and upheavals created new channels of the Mississippi, and by the middle of January, what was left of New Madrid was largely under water.

Fortunately, no more than 3,000 people lived around the settlement at the time, and this undoubtedly kept down the loss of life. Only half a dozen residents are confirmed to have been killed. Still, as many as 100 deaths may have gone unrecorded, mostly of travelers trapped on the Mississippi. To this day, farming in the region suffers from the sandy soil spewed out of the earth in those terrifying months.

New Madrid became newer still. The survivors rebuilt it on the banks of the Mississippi redefined by the quake. Today, the 3,000 descendants of these survivors seem to consider the possibility of a future earthquake. A popular T-shirt sold in the local novelty store reads: VISIT NEW MADRID (WHILE IT'S STILL THERE).

A contemporary newspaper lithograph depicts the fate of some of the citizens of Charleston, South Carolina during the earthquake of August 31, 1886. Most of the 100 who died were killed as they ran through the streets shouting that the end of the world had arrived. In the inset: refugees huddling on Battery Place, Charleston. Frank Leslie's Illustrated Weekly.

UNITED STATES
SOUTH CAROLINA
CHARLESTON

August 31, 1886

• • • • • • • • • • • • •

Ancillary shocks from the Charleston, South Carolina earthquake of August 31, 1886 were felt over 2 million square miles. One hundred were killed.

According to contemporary accounts, most of the 100 persons who died in the Great Charleston Earthquake of 1886—one of the most widely felt earthquakes in United States history—were killed while running hysterically through the streets. Some of them shouting that the end of the world had arrived. Secondary shocks sent buildings toppling on them; fissures spouting sulfuric fumes swallowed them.

The damage to historic buildings in Charleston itself was extensive, surpassing the 1687 quake, which had likewise been regarded by the citizenry as the Day of Judgment.

What was particularly unique about this quake, however, was its extensive ancillary effect. The shock was felt over 2 million square miles—as far north as New York and Chicago, as far south as Mobile, Alabama and as far west as Omaha, Nebraska.

Gas flames flickered, walls cracked and office workers were knocked from their chairs in New York City. In Richmond, Virginia, prisoners in a federal penitentiary rioted, prompting officials to call in troops to surround the prison walls to prevent an escape. In Cincinnati, Ohio, panicked office workers leaped from second story windows when buildings began to sway.

One of the most curious stories surviving from this quake deals with a Professor Capen, a New York City weather forecaster who had eerily predicted the date and time of the quake. Despite turmoil in the offices around him, he failed to notice any of the effects of the cataclysm he had predicted, and had to be told about it after the fact.

VENEZUELA
CARACAS

March 12, 1812

• • • • • • • • • • • • •

Twenty thousand people died in an earthquake that destroyed nine-tenths of the city of Caracas, Venezuela on March 12, 1812.

The course of history was changed for Venezuela on Holy Thursday, March 12, 1812, when the worst quake in that country's history destroyed nine-tenths of Caracas and laid waste to the countryside surrounding it. The viciousness of the quake, the enormity of its destruction—20,000 people perished in Caracas and its environs—and its timing on a holy day when the cathedrals were filled with worshippers, convinced multitudes of people that God was displeased with their efforts to overthrow Spanish rule and its leader Simon Bolivar. Wholesale defections took place in the armies of Miranda, the revolutionary leader, who had managed, to make large inroads into Spanish landholdings and military installations. Terrified peasants deserted the cause, and efforts to establish the United States of Colombia were crushed in one terrible day. Buoyed by this unexpected turn of events, the Royalists returned to power, claiming divine intervention.

The magnitude of the quake and the resulting terror must have seemed like an omen. Striking after dark, its epicenter erupted in the northern part of the city of Caracas, a hilly promontory thickly populated with both people and churches. The first tremors toppled the churches of Alta Gracia and Trinity, both built of stone. The splendor of Alta Gracia was made particularly impressive by the presence of 15-foot-thick pillars supporting its massive, 150-foot height. Not one worshiper emerged alive from either church.

In the streets, chaos abounded. Gigantic fissures swallowed people, livestock, vehicles—even entire houses. In one horrible moment, the entire complex of San Carlos barracks was consumed, along with every soldier sleeping within it.

All of this had taken a mere minute, but the rest of the night and days afterwards would be spent extricating the 2,000 survivors trapped in the wreckage of what once was a city. Ten thousand were killed in Caracas alone. In the surrounding villages of San Felipe, La Guaya, Merida, Antimano, La Vega, Baruta and Mayquetia, 5,000 more perished.

The Caracas authorities, fearful of an epidemic of plague resulting from unburied bodies and rats attracted to the carnage, ordered gigantic funeral pyres of hundreds of bodies apiece to be erected throughout the ravaged city. Their flames could be seen for miles throughout the night.

What the authorities had not planned for was famine and dysentery spread by a polluted water supply caused by the rupturing of fresh water conduits. Another 5,000 would die as a result, lending further credence to the exhortations of priests that this was God's revenge for straying from the cruel, inhuman, vicious but nevertheless devout Spanish rulers.

YUGOSLAVIA
SKOPJE

July 16, 1963

• • • • • • • • • • • • •

Two thousand people died, 3,000 were injured and 170,000 were made homeless by a monster 9-point earthquake that leveled Skopje, Yugoslavia on July 16, 1963.

A cataclysmic 9-point earthquake destroyed the city of Skopje, Yugoslavia when it struck at 5:15 A.M. on the morning of July 16, 1963. Two thousand were killed outright; more were buried under the rubble and never found. Three thousand were injured and more than 170,000 were made homeless.

A tourist transfer point at a road and rail junction 125 miles north of Salonika, Greece and 110 miles west of the Bulgarian capital of Sofia, the city lies on a direct fault line with the Italian and French Rivieras, which had experienced tremors just days before the devastating quake hit Skopje.

"I thought it was a hydrogen bomb," a Skopje man said. "There was a terrible roar. I woke up, looked out the window and saw the Hotel Macedonia swaying from side to side."

The Macedonia, a popular hotel, was full, its 180 beds occupied by tourists. It collapsed into a 20-foot-high rubble heap of stone and steel, killing all but a few of its guests and staff.

The Macedonia had company in destruction. Nearby, the Skopje Hotel disintegrated. The main post office collapsed, leaving only one wall remaining upright. The center of the railroad terminal fell in on hundreds of travelers waiting to catch the early morning train for Belgrade.

The Kaarpus, a five-story office building, suddenly shrank to three stories as the earth swallowed up its bottom two floors. An ancient mosque on the left bank of the Vardar River was completely shattered.

From the moment the tremors ceased, a haze of brick and mortar dust hung like a curtain over the city. From the air, it seemed as if a giant foot had stamped it out. The scene up close was appalling. Silent groups of homeless men and women dug wordlessly through the ruins, trying to save whatever they could.

There was nothing left of the city. Its two movie houses, library, museums, the Yugoslav National and Investment Bank, many schools, the City Council, radio station, and 85 percent of its dwellings were simply no more.

Ironically, the Emperor Duahan Bridge, originally built in A.D. 520, in the reign of Justinian and now a main thoroughfare which connected the old city of Skopje on the left bank of the Vardar River with the newer part on the right bank, remained unscathed.

Thirteen survivors of the railway station underwent a similar, miraculous escape. The 13, trapped in a tunnel beneath the wreckage of the railway station, were detected by a French supersensitive listening device that heard them through 26 feet of rubble. They had spent more than 72 hours under the tangle of steel and stone.

The rebuilders of Skopje consulted seismologists before undertaking the task of reconstruction of their demolished city. Fearful of a typhus epidemic, they were eager to begin construction.

But one epidemic almost certain to strike any disaster site did not roar through Skopje. Hundreds of stores lay with their display windows shattered. Goods were there for the taking. But there was no looting, none whatsoever, despite the citizens' desperation and homelessness.

FAMINES AND DROUGHTS

• • • • • • • • • • • • • • • • •

THE WORST RECORDED FAMINES AND DROUGHTS

· · · · ·

* Detailed in text

China
    (1333)
    (1810–11)
    (1846)
    (1849)
   * (1876–78)
    (1920)
    (1928)
   * (1939)
   * (1942–43)
Denmark
    (1087)
Egypt
   * (Earliest recorded famine) (3500 B.C.)
   * (1708)
   * (A.D. 1064)
   * (1199)
    Fustat (A.D. 968)
England
    (A.D. 680)
    (695–700)
    (822)
   * (1069)
    (1235)
    (1563)
   * (1976)

Ethiopia and the Sudan
   * (1983–1988)
France
    (987–1059)
Greece
    (1942)
Holland
   * (1944–45)
India
    (1669)
    (1745)
   * (1769)
    (1782)
   * (1790)
    (1812)
   * (1833)
    (1837)
   * (1866)
   * (1876–1877)
   * (1898)
   * (1943)
   * (1972)
    Hyderabad (1677)
Ireland
    (1316)
    (1816)
   * (1845–1850)
Italy
    (A.D. 450)

Jamaica
   * (1788)
Nigeria
   * (1968)
Roman Empire
    (A.D. 79–88)
Russia/USSR
    (1650)
    (1906)
    (1914)
   * (1921–1923)
    (1932)
   * (1975)
Scotland
    (A.D. 856)
    (936)
    (1047)
Sudan (see ETHIOPIA AND THE SUDAN)
United States
    Midwest
   * (1909–1914)
   * (1934–1941)
    Virginia
   * Jamestown (1607)
Yemen
    (1970)

CHRONOLOGY
· · · · · · · · ·

(There are no specific dates for famines. Thus, only the year of the famine's origin is noted.)

* Detailed in text

3500 B.C.
   * Egypt (Earliest recorded famine)
1708 B.C.
   * Egypt

A.D. 79–88
   Roman Empire
450
   Italy
680
   England
695–700
   England
822

England
856
   Scotland
936
   Scotland
968
   Fustat, Egypt
987–1059
   France

1047
Scotland
1064
• Egypt
1069
• England
1087
Denmark
1199
• Egypt
1235
England
1316
Ireland
1333
China
1563
England
1607
• Jamestown, Virginia
1650
Russia
1669
India
1677
Hyderabad, India
1745
India
1769
• India
1782
India

1788
• Jamaica
1790
• India
1810–1811
China
1812
India
1816
Ireland
1833
• India
1837
India
1845–1850
• Ireland
1846
China
1849
China
1866
• India
1876
• China (1876–1878)
• India (1876–1877)
1898
• India
1906
Russia
1909–1914
• Midwestern United States
1914

Russia
1920
China
1921–1923
• USSR
1928
China
1932
USSR
1934–1941
• Midwestern United States
1939
• China
1942
• China (1942–1943)
Greece
1943
• India
1944–1945
• Holland
1968
• Nigeria
1970
Yemen
1972
• India
1975
• USSR
1976
• England
1983–1988
• Ethiopia and the Sudan

FAMINES AND DROUGHTS

• • • • •

Most natural disasters are mercifully brief. An earthquake usually lasts under a minute. A tornado careens through a midwestern town in something under five minutes. Cyclones and hurricanes lay waste to cities in hours. Even the duration of floods can usually be measured in days.

But not so famine and drought. These are long-lasting disasters that can go on for decades, and their effects continue for generations. There is a Fourth World, some social scientists assert, and it consists of the half billion people on this Earth today who live their lives under conditions of famine.

The reasons for drought and famine are likewise more complex than those for all other natural disasters. Along with nature and the changing state of the earth, there are distinctly human, economic, cultural and political causes for both drought and famine. And although drought is the most common cause of famine, it is by no means the only one. In fact, famine can be brought about by just the opposite phenomenon—flood. Other natural causes abound: heavy rains; unseasonably cold, hot or dry weather; typhoons; pest infestation; and plant disease.

All of these are reasonably beyond the control of human beings, although much has been invented and put to use to counteract pests and disease.

Similarly, drought, which occurs naturally when evaporation and transpiration (the movement of water in the soil through plants into the air) exceed precipitation for a considerable period, is also affected by human behavior.

There are four basic kinds of drought: permanent drought, which occurs in the driest climates, where nothing could possibly grow without constant irrigation; seasonal drought, which occurs in climates that have well defined dry and rainy seasons; unpredictable drought, which occurs as a result of a sudden reduction in rainfall; and invisible drought, which is a borderline situation in which high temperatures induce abnormal evaporation and transpiration, so that even regular rainshowers fail to irrigate crops, and they die.

All of these are typical conditions in nature. Yet human beings often choose to live on and farm land that hasn't a prayer of supporting them. Or, human beings take good land in a benign climate and turn it into worthless dust by misfarming it.

The natural causes of famine that frequently elude human correction sometimes occur outside of the region that is affected. Drought, for instance, may occur in the headwaters of a major river used for irrigation, thus causing famine in an irrigated region hundreds of miles downstream—possibly across a national border.

And so, the famines of Egypt and the Middle East, regions whose environments are naturally hostile to intense sedentary agriculture. Because of this, sources of irrigation often occur miles away across national boundaries.

Asia is another example. It has land that is resistant to predictable planting. Alternately drought- and flood-prone, this land has traditionally been incapable of supporting its population; thus the reputation—unfortunately not well documented—of China as the most drought- and famine-prone country in the world, with India closely behind. Each has farmland that is irrigated from rivers with their headwaters in the other's country, and their needs—often conflicting—have caused some of their most terrible droughts and famines.

Also entering into the famine picture of both of these countries are political and cultural factors. And these make natural causes pale by comparison.

Consider the severe food shortages of Roman times, in which citizens purportedly flung themselves into the Tiber rather than starve. The shortages were caused by Roman emperors who hoarded valuable grain.

Or consider another common human cause of famine: warfare. One way of conquering a country is to starve it to death, and the blockade of food supplies was widely employed in Europe between 1500 and 1700. In 1812, the "scorched earth" policy of the Russians not only deprived Napoleon's armies of needed food, but inflicted the same deprivation on the Russian people. During World War II, the German policy of starvation in occupied Holland was a particularly infamous use of famine as a weapon of war. And in the late 1970s, the genocidal policies of the Khmer Rouge regime in Kampuchea, in which there were massive deportations of urban populations into the countryside without food or shelter, caused over 1,000,000 deaths from starvation.

Cultural influences were responsible for the famines of medieval Europe, as well as those of Asia. The feudal social system combined with enormous overpopulation resulted in extended food shortages, which begat malnutrition, widespread disease such as the Black Death, and famine. From the birth of Christ to 1800, there are records of famine occurring in Europe in 350 different years, while in England during the same period there was a food shortage in one year out of 10. According to historian A. Porter in his *Diseases of the Madras Famine of 1877–79*, it was estimated that famine occurred somewhere in France every six years between A.D. 1000 and the 19th century. Throughout history, the food supply of humankind has been, at best, highly precarious.

The effects of overpopulation worldwide continue to compound the problem. Add to this the rape of the environment, and atmospheric pollution by industrial and nuclear waste, and, short of a grim, Malthusian housecleaning, famine can only grow in this world in which we live.

There is hope. In recent years, relief agencies have come to the forefront, combatting both the causes and the effect of famines. UNRRA (The United Nations Relief and Rehabilitation Administration), WFP (The World Food Program) and FAO (The Food and Agriculture Organization) all represent the United Nations's war upon famine. Voluntary agencies joining in the anti-famine fight include CARE (Co-operation for American Relief Everywhere), Catholic Relief Societies, Save the Children Fund, War on Want, Christian Aid and the League of Red Cross Societies.

Their enemy is as formidable as nature, the universe, human cruelty and stupidity. But they have been successful against such famines as the one in the Bihar section of India in 1967. Their cause is correct, and the only hope of reducing, even fractionally, the growing Fourth World of starvation on this planet.

• • • • • • • • • • • • • •

CHINA

1876–1878

• • • • • • • • • • • • • •

The worst recorded famine in the history of the world was the China famine of 1876–1878. Thirteen million people (according to some missionary sources) or 9.5 million people (according to Chinese government sources) died as a result of this famine, caused by a drought in northern and central China.

The great and terrible famine of 1876–1878, which killed between 9.5 and 13 million people and affected another 70 million, began simply, as the majority of famines do, with a drought.

For three endless years, from 1876 to 1878, not a drop of rain fell upon northern and central China, in the area bordered by the Yangtze River on the south and west, Pe-

king on the north and the Korean border on the east. Normally, this region is beset by yearly monsoons, thus insuring a plentitude of rice and other staple crops of the Chinese diet. But from 1876 through 1878, the monsoons did not come.

The neighboring provinces of Kwangtung and Fuhkien to the south suffered massive crop damage by monsoon-induced floods. The British crown colony of Hong Kong, in the southernmost section of Kwangtung, was deluged with rain.

But not so the immense agricultural area to the north, which was transformed into an immense hell of starvation, murder, slavery and cannibalism.

A normally benign countryside, it was transformed into a savage jungle in which night travel became suicidal. Roving bands of starving men set upon travelers, killing their mules, oxen, camels or horses out from under them. By the second year of the famine, it became unsafe to even rest by the side of the road.

According to the Chairman of the Foreign Relief Committee set up in the coastal city of Tientsen:

In November, 1877, the aspect of affairs was simply terrible. The autumn crops over the whole of Shanzi and the greater part of Chihli and Honan had failed. . . . During the winter and spring of 1877–78, the most frightful disorder reigned supreme along the route to Shansi. Hwailuhien, the starting point, was filled with officials and traders all intent on getting their convoys over the pass. Fugitives, beggars and thieves swarmed. The officials were powerless to create any sort of order among the mountains. The track was completely worn out and until a new one was made, a dead block ensued. Camels, oxen, mules and donkeys were hurried along in the wildest confusion, and so many perished or were killed by the desperate people in the hills, for the sake of their flesh, that transport could only be carried on by the banded vigilance of the interested owners of the grain, assisted by the trained bands, or militia, which had been hastily got together. . . . Night traveling was out of the question. The way was marked by the carcases or skeletons of men and beasts, and the wolves, dogs and foxes soon put an end to the sufferings of any wretch who lay down to recover from or die of his sickness in these terrible defiles. . . . Broken carts, scattered grain bags, dying men and animals so frequently stopped the way, that it was often necessary to prevent for days together the entry of convoys from the one side, in order to let the convoys from the other come over. . . .

The Manchu dynasty may have contributed to the huge death toll by not revealing the extent of the famine to the outside world. Perhaps fearing that a revelation of any internal weakness might bring about a collapse like the one that had befallen its predecessor, the Ch'ing dynasty, in 1811, the Manchus forbade foreign travel through the afflicted area for two entire years.

Still, fragmentary stories began to leak out, and piecemeal descriptions only heightened the horror to those who were told of the catastrophe. Stories (later verified) of "ten thousand man holes"—enormous pits into which the dead were thrown—leaked beyond China's borders.

A Shanghai resident, Frederick H. Balfour, reported in detail his first-hand findings:

The people's faces, are black with hunger; they are dying by thousands upon thousands. Women and girls and boys are openly offered for sale to any chance wayfarer.

When I left the country, a respectable married woman could be easily bought for six dollars and a little girl for two. In cases, however, where it was found impossible to dispose of their children, parents have been known to kill them sooner than witness their prolonged sufferings, in

many instances throwing themselves afterwards down wells, or committing suicide by arsenic.

Finally, by January 28, 1878, the Manchus could hide the facts no longer, and a British investigating envoy opened the drought and famine area to the remainder of the world by dispatching a telegram to his home office: "Appalling famine raging throughout four provinces North China. Nine million people reported destitute. Children daily sold in markets for food. Foreign Relief Committee appeal to England and America for assistance."

The Great Chinese Famine of 1876–1878 remains, to this day, the worst recorded famine in the history of the world.

CHINA

September–November 1939

• • • • • • • • • • • • • • • •

Destruction by the government of a record abundance of crops in the Hunan, Anhwei and Kiangsi provinces of China and flooded crops in the adjacent province of Hopei caused a famine that killed 200,000 by starvation in three months, from September through November 1939.

The enormity of China produces grim ironies. In the fall of 1939, the provinces of Hunan, Anhwei and Kiangsi had bumper crops of rice—25 million bushels, by local government count. It was too much for either the populace or the economy to accommodate, and, to avert a depression, officials and farmers in the region destroyed hundreds of tons of rice.

But at the same time in an adjacent province, 25 million people were being made destitute and 200,000 were perishing from a famine caused by flooding in the Yellow River basin. Ninety of Hopei's 130 districts remained under 10 feet of water for several months, and this in turn wiped out the entire grain and rice crop in this area. Over 500,000 bushels of grain that could have kept the region's inhabitants alive were destroyed by the flood waters.

To add to the problem of starvation, Japan and China were at war, and Japanese troops consistently cut off food and aid supplies that were sent to the area by the International Red Cross. None of these supplies ever reached the starving people they might have saved.

CHINA

1942–1943

• • • • • • • • • • • • • • • •

A combination of a drought, internal political infighting and World War II combined to cause the famine in Honan province in China during 1942 and 1943. Nearly 3 million people died of starvation.

One of the most profound famines in the history of the world took place in the Honan province of China during World War II. It was a natural disaster compounded by two human factors.

First, there was the war with Japan that had been raging since 1936. By 1943, Japan had occupied much of Honan province.

Second, there was the increasingly uneasy alliance between Chiang Kai-shek, heading the Nationalist government, and Mao Tse-tung, heading the Communist government. United to fight the Japanese in 1937, they fought each other with almost as much vigor as they pursued the war against the Japanese.

Thus, when the great famine of 1942 and 1943 struck this southern province of China, the combination of forces was overwhelming for the people of the province. Of the 30 million people who lived in Honan, close to 3 million died of hunger in one year.

The immediate causes of the famine can be traced to 1940. Until that time, Honan was noted as a fertile province with richer-than-ordinary soil. The cash crop was spring wheat, which the peasants sowed in late autumn and harvested in mid-May. This was followed by the secondary crops of millet and corn, sown after the harvesting of the wheat and gathered in by late autumn. In 1940 and 1941, all crops were poor. In 1942, a full-scale drought hit, destroying all three crops.

No provision had been made by either the government or the populace to deal with the effects of the drought; each assumed that it would not last, and when it did, it was the peasants who suffered.

The central government was slow to react. Crops failed in the summer of 1942. In November, the government sent in observers, and then, instead of sending food to the starving populace, it sent money—$200 million in famine relief funds, most of which disappeared on the way to Honan. By March of 1943, only $80 million of the original $200 million had reached the provincial government. It was put into local banks, collecting interest for the government, while the populace was reduced to eating bark and dying in the streets.

When the money was finally distributed, taxes were deducted up front, and after that, the local banks skimmed off operating costs. Peasants who were subsisting on dried leaves and elm bark had to haul their last sack of seed grain to the tax collector's office. To add to the charade, the government distributed the money in $100 denominations. Wheat could only be bought from the hoarders in small denominations, and the banks charged the peasants for changing the large bills for small ones.

In the midst of this, there was some tiny, almost Machiavellian gesture of food distribution made by the government. Ten thousand sacks of rice and 20,000 sacks of mixed grain were meted out between January and March. This came to slightly less than a pound apiece for 10 million people who had been starving since autumn.

Ironically, just across the border from Honan, in Shensi province, grain was plentiful, as it was in Hupah, on the other side. But ancient provincial distrust and the delicate balance of power and conflict in the central government prevented the shipping of food across the borders of these provinces.

Meanwhile, the extent of the famine was being recorded by Protestant missionaries. Early in the autumn of 1943, mobs of hungry peasants stormed wealthy homes and farms that had, through irrigation, survived the drought, rifling the homes and seizing the standing crops.

Horror stories abounded. The parents of two small children near one mission murdered them rather than hear them beg for food. Some families sold all they could for one last meal and then committed suicide.

Authors and correspondents Theodore H. White and Annalee Jacoby, gathering material for their book *Thunder Out of China,* toured the province in the early spring of 1943. Their written accounts were graphic and terrifying.

A great stink suffused [everything]. Dry sweat, urine, common human filth, scented the morning. The peasants shivered in pulsing reaction to the cold, and their gray and blue rags fluttered and quivered in the wind. . . . When we walked down the street, children followed crying, "K'o lien, k'o lien (mercy, mercy)." If we pulled peanuts or dried dates from our pockets, tiny ragamuffins whipped by to snatch them from our fingers. The tear-stained faces, smudgy and forlorn in the cold, shamed us. Chinese children are beautiful in health; their hair glows then with the gloss of fine natural oil, and their almond eyes sparkle. But these shrunken scarecrows had pusfilled slits where eyes should be; malnutrition had made their hair dry and brittle; hunger had bloated their bellies; weather had chapped their skins. Their voices had withered into a thin whine that called only for food. . . .

There were corpses on the road. A girl no more than seventeen, slim and pretty, lay on the damp earth, her lips blue with death; her eyes were open, and the rain fell on them. People chipped at bark, pounded it by the roadside for food; vendors sold leaves at a dollar a bundle. A dog digging at a mound was exposing a human body. Ghostlike men were skimming the stagnant pools to eat the green slime of the waters . . . .

The city of Chengchow, before the war a thriving center of 120,000 people, contained less than 40,000 by late 1943. In the countryside, it was even worse. White and Jacoby went there, too, and recorded it. "The people were slicing bark from elm trees, grinding it to eat as food," they wrote. "Some were tearing up the roots of the new wheat; in other villages people were living on pounded peanut husks or refuse. Refugees on the road had been seen madly cramming soil into their mouths to fill their bellies, and the missionary hospitals were stuffed with people suffering from terrible intestinal obstructions due to the filth they were eating."

And, as in many famines, cannibalism followed. A missionary doctor told White and Jacoby about a woman who was caught boiling her baby. The authorities let her go when she convinced them that the baby had died before she had begun to cook it. Another woman was caught cutting off the legs of her dead husband. She was also released when it was ascertained that he had died first.

Because of the war, no relief came from the West; because of the Nationalist/Communist face-off, no relief came from within China. Millions died, waiting for nature to right both its wrongs and the ones committed by those in power.

In the winter of 1943, snow did fall, and this irrigated the fields. Passing a field of green wheat, White and Jacoby encountered an emaciated old man. Gesturing toward the field, they told him that there was hope. The man nodded hollowly, and told the writers, "It is fine, yes, but who knows whether we will be alive to eat it?"

By 1944, the Japanese had decided to wipe the province clean of Chinese soldiers and government officials. They did it in three weeks, thanks to armed uprisings by peasants who had been taxed and starved, literally, to death by their own government, and were all too eager to help in rooting that government out, even if it meant aligning themselves with an enemy of their country. They must have thought this enemy might, at least, feed them.

EGYPT

3500 B.C.

• • • • • • • • • • • • • • • •

An inscription on a tomb on the island of Sihel, off the coast of Egypt in the Mediterranean, dating back to the Third Dynasty, leaves a fragmentary but revealing picture of the first recorded famine, in Egypt, 3500 B.C.

The earliest recorded famine, which occurred in Egypt in the third millennium B.C., was preserved visually in a re-

lief that survives on the causeway of the Fifth-Dynasty Pyramid of Unas in Sakkara. The relief shows emaciated famine victims apparently consoling each other. Their faces and posture in which they are frozen reflect, as if in a long distance mirror, the twisted and wasted forms of Biafran children in the 1980s.

The written account was found in an inscription on a tomb on the Mediterranean island of Sihel, created in the reign of Djeser during the Third Dynasty. The inscription was restored and re-written centuries later, during the time of the Ptolemies, and offers a remarkable insight not only into the physical effects of famine—which are, not surprisingly, the same as those experienced by famine victims today—but also into the very attitude of those in power 5,000 years ago:

I am mourning on my high throne for this vast misfortune [says the ancient, anonymous chronicler of this first famine] because the Nile flood in my time has not come for seven years. Light is the grain; there is lack of crops and of all kinds of food. Each man has become a thief to his neighbor. They desire to hasten and cannot walk. The child cries, the youth creeps along, and the heads of the old men are bowed down; their legs are bent together and drag along the ground, and their hands rest in their bosoms. The counsel of the great ones in the Court is but emptiness. Torn open are the chests of provisions, but instead of contents there is air. Everything is exhausted.

EGYPT

1708 B.C.

• • • • • • • • • • • • • • • •

The beginning of the biblical, seven-year famine in Egypt has been set by scholars in 1708 B.C. Located in both Egypt and Palestine, it killed tens of thousands.

The Great Famine of the Book of Genesis ("And the famine was over all the face of the earth . . . and the famine waxed sore in Egypt . . .") took place, by consensus of historians and biblical scholars, in 1708 B.C.

The passage of time and intervening conflict have erased most of the first-hand information concerning the event. What is known is that it was at the time of Egypt's Middle Kingdom, when its pharaohs had been replaced by rulers from Syria and Canaan, and strict control over agriculture and the use of the land was, like much of the country, in disarray.

Thus, crops failed, corruption in the distribution system kept food from the populace, and for seven years, from 1708 to 1701 B.C., famines and plague ranged back and

75

forth across Egypt and Palestine. Tens of thousands died of starvation in both countries.

EGYPT

A.D. 1064

• • • • • • • • • • • • • •

Forty thousand people died in the eight-year famine that gripped Egypt from A.D. 1064 to 1072. Drought caused the famine; crime and cannibalism exacerbated its effects.

An eight-year famine ravaged Egypt from 1064 to 1072. During that time, approximately 40,000 Egyptians died from starvation, and crime and cannibalism were rampant. W. R. Aykrod quotes survivors in his study, *The Conquest of Famine:* "Organized bands kidnapped the unwary passenger in the desolate streets," noted one observer, describing a creatively cruel twist upon this ancient custom: ". . . principally by means of ropes furnished with hooks let down from latticed windows."

The famine was the result of a drought brought on by the unusually low state of the Nile in 1064, which made irrigation impossible. At that time, Egyptian farmers customarily depended upon the regular overflowing of the Nile's banks to irrigate their crops. For eight years, this natural phenomenon did not occur, and the resultant drought caused famine and then pestilence.

EGYPT

1199

• • • • • • • • • • • • • •

One hundred thousand people died in Egypt in the famine of 1199, which was caused by a failure of the Nile River to provide natural irrigation to the crops bordering it. Increased food prices were secondary culprits. Medical science advanced when Islamic law was softened, allowing the first autopsies to be performed.

The cause of medical science was tangentially advanced and crime and cannibalism reached new lows in a record-breaking famine once again caused by a drought that was brought on by the failure of the Nile to overflow its banks (see previous entry). This time, the low state of the river occurred in 1199. Over 100,000 Egyptians lost their lives, either through starvation or at the hands of their fellow human beings. In the city of Maks alone, 20,000 perished.

In no other recorded famine until that time were such extremes of human desperation reached. Murder and cannibalism were rampant. The drought, caused by the drying up of the fields neighboring the Nile, was extraordinarily widespread and continued for three years, through 1202.

Ironically, the human-induced consequence of drought, economic deprivation and starvation because of decreased food supplies and increased prices, produced the only positive outcome of this otherwise grisly period in Egyptian history.

Sometime in the early part of 1200, Abdul Latif, a physician from Baghdad, observed an increased number of people emigrating from Egypt to Arabia, Yemen and Syria. Questioned about their reasons, they answered that they were moving on because of spiraling food prices brought on by the drought-caused famine in the Nile River valley.

More and more refugees poured into the cities of Egypt and its neighboring countries. The cities could not accommodate them, and so, instead of starving at home, they starved in strange surroundings, on city streets, or were murdered by roaming bands of brigands who sometimes lived, according to Latif, on the excrement of animals.

The bodies of the starved, mutilated or murdered were everywhere, and local law enforcement officials gradually began to ignore the Islamic law forbidding the dissection of bodies for medical experimentation. Thus, anatomists like Abdul Latif and his colleagues were able to perform the first crude autopsies on record.

This event, however, was overshadowed by the horror. Perhaps in no other famine on record did cannibalism reach such vast proportions. Children particularly were caught, slaughtered and roasted as if they were lambs or pigs. And, most difficult to believe of all, these children were often eaten by their own mothers and fathers.

Latif recorded this nightmare of nightmares. "I myself saw a small roasted child in a basket," he wrote. "They carried it to the Emir and led in at the same time the mother and father of the child. The Emir sentenced both of them to be burnt alive."

Once these cannibalistic offenders were publicly and municipally roasted, they were considered legal food and distributed to the masses for consumption.

Other examples of cannibalism are part of the public record of the time. Friends were invited for an evening and slaughtered and eaten by the host and hostess. Repairmen were called to homes and butchered as they worked. It was proof beyond contradiction of the theory that hunger is a pervasive motivation for many of mankind's most heinous crimes.

ENGLAND

1069

• • • • • • • • • • • • • • • •

In 1069, following the Norman Conquest (1066), a famine raged over the northern counties of England. Over 50,000 died.

Thousands sold themselves into slavery and more than 50,000 others perished in a deep and pervasive famine that overran the northern counties of England in 1069, shortly after the Norman Conquest of 1066.

Records of the time give no specific reason for the famine. They only describe it, in some detail: ". . . between Durham and Yorke lay waste, without inhabitants or people to till the ground, for the space of nine years . . ." states the *Harleian Miscellany*. ". . . Many were forced to eat horses, dogs, cats, rats and other loathsome and vile vermin," the record continues, "yea, some abstained not from the flesh of men. . . ."

ENGLAND

1976

• • • • • • • • • • • • • • • •

A freak drought in South Wales brought on a summer famine, of sorts, in England in 1976.

By the last quarter of the 20th century, the more primitive and criminal tendencies of famine-stricken human beings had been all but tamed, and in the summer of 1976, the British even managed to treat their plight, in the worst drought in 500 years, with a certain degree of lightness.

Centered in South Wales, which normally is treated to heavy downpours and then misty stretches of unrelieved precipitation, the drought brought on a dry spring in 1976. By the end of May, crops were withering all over the British Isles.

Marion and Arthur Boyars, two London publishers writing to a friend, chronicled the summer:

> *June: . . . tankers hauling water to rural areas, heath fires in Somerset. Greatest shortage of potatoes in memory. They cost more than Mediterranean oranges.*
>
> *July: Passersby cheer lady in Chiswick for walking the street cool and naked. Pleasure boats ordered off the canals. The Thames looks sick, low, muddy. . . .*
>
> *August: Water cut off overnight in South Wales. . . . Authorities with power to fine waterwasters accused of sending spy planes to spot green gardens. . . . Queen decides to let royal gardens die. London's fountains turned*

> *off. . . . Clouds of smoke from burning forests and heaths. Drought grips all western Europe. Shortage of beef, wine, milk saves Common Market huge price subsidies. Rainy London day makes news on the telly. St. James's and Hyde parks are like deserts. . . . Water-diviners do a roaring business.*
>
> *September: Wales . . . worries about cutback in factories of big water users—American industrial chemicals, plastics. . . . Water for homes cut off in parts of southwest England.*
>
> *Mid-September: Finally! Torrential rains! Six months later: Rain still falling. English again living under umbrellas.*

ETHIOPIA AND THE SUDAN

1983–1988

• • • • • • • • • • • • • • • •

Over 1 million people have died so far in a famine that reached its peak between 1984 and 1986, and is partially caused by natural factors and partially the result of civil wars in Ethiopia and the Sudan.

Most of Africa is marginally less prone to drought and famine than Asia, but inter-tribal warfare, generations of poor farming practices and complex civil wars have increased the impact of famine upon its populace. Today, in the 1990s, while most of the world gets wealthier, 150 million Africans are, in the words of the United Nations Food and Agricultural Organization's Director General, Eduard Saoums, ". . . in the most serious economic distress and shortage of food, which may reach proportions of hunger and malnourishment on a massive scale."

Even in the best of times, Africa is, by Western standards, a poor continent. It depends upon farm products for the survival of the 12 billion people who live in its 12 countries, and most of the agricultural methods it uses are ancient and sometimes counter-productive. For instance, the nations of the sub-Saharan region—Chad, Niger, Mauritania, Mali, Upper Volta, Gambia and the Cape Verde Islands—lose valuable agricultural land each year as the Sahara Desert advances southward at an average of five miles per year, while rainfall has decreased 25 percent in the last 20 years.

The lack of rainfall is a natural phenomenon. The encroachment of the Sahara, however, is worsened by unwise overfarming and overgrazing by sheep and cattle. South of the Sahara, where trees once stood and greenery abounded, there is now nothing but barren, eroded land.

In countries like Zimbabwe, rebuilding after an eight-year war, with its northwest portion suffering from year after year of drought, there is little hope for self-sufficiency in the near future. Governmental corruption in Ghana has created food shortages for 10 million people.

So, Africa is a land that has been and will, for the foreseeable future, continue to be a region in which drought and famine hold the upper hand over the populace, at least while that populace is governed by warring tribal and governmental factions.

No two nations in Africa exemplify this situation more dramatically than the neighboring states of Ethiopia and the Sudan. Since 1983, both countries have been wracked by drought, famine and civil war. Their governments have been accused of genocide through starvation. Both countries have, to a certain extent, been used as pawns between the East and the West—the governments of the United States and the USSR—supporting those in power (or guerrilla groups as the case may be) and adding to the general turmoil and privation.

A pivotal year was 1983. As the USSR-supported, Marxist government seemed to have the upper hand in Ethiopia, a truce was requested by the United Nations to end the fighting. But 1983 was also the year that the civil war between the North and South of Sudan began. In this case, the U.S.-supported government of the country advertised itself as a democracy, though its Islamic Fundamentalists were responsible for Islamic law being proclaimed throughout the entire country, thus pitching a battle between Arab Muslims in the North and Christians and others in the South. The battles, drought and famine—both natural and forced by the government—would, between 1983 and 1988, claim 1 million lives in the Sudan, and as of the writing of this, the dying, the fighting and the famine are still continuing, in varying degrees.

To sort out this tangle of troubles, it is necessary to go back nearly 20 years:

In 1973 and 1974, several hundred thousand people in West and East Africa died of famine and attendant malnutrition, while the Western world was absorbed in the economic crisis precipitated by OPEC's dramatic oil price rise. As a consequence, little aid came to the starving of Africa, and, according to some analysts, this made the truly terrible famine which peaked in 1984–1986 even worse than it might have been. In fact, the Marxist government of Ethiopia seized upon this assumption based upon some fact as a smoke screen to cover its heartlessly extravagant expenditure of $200 million on a celebration to mark the 10th anniversary of its coming to power, while millions of poor Ethiopians were threatened with starvation, and hundreds were dying of it every day.

It could be that the problems of famine might once have been successfully addressed, for, beginning in 1984, various International Relief Organizations had begun to make

inroads against famine and disease. But the problem of constant population shifts caused by refugees being driven from one part of the country to the other have made prior planning almost impossible. Supplies may be in abundance in one area and pitifully inadequate in others, with virtually no chance of swapping supplies, since even U.N.-marked supply convoys have been attacked and destroyed by Somali guerrillas.

This sort of activity goes back to 1980. At this time, 1.8 million of the 5 million people in Ethiopia affected by famine were from the Ogaden region of the country, where ethnic Somalis conducted frequent guerrilla raids against governmental outposts and villages. Frequently, these raids occurred in Gamu-Gofa, in the southwest, where the drought had hit the hardest, where virtually no rain fell in 1980 and the U.N. officials visiting Gamu-Gofa, Baje, Harar and Wallo reported that 50 percent of the 600,000 cattle in the land had died of starvation, too.

As the years 1981 and 1982 dragged on, irrigation even became pointless. Rivers dried up, while tides in the Indian Ocean forced themselves upward, leaving the water brackish. Even if the marketing policies of some of the African countries had been perfect, there was little food to market. More and more of the population turned nomadic, wandering from place to place and talking of 1968, the last year of good rains in the subSahara region.

In Ghana, in 1983, the hot wind that usually comes in January lasted twice as long as it normally does, fanning brush fires that destroyed both fields and food storehouses. Along with the drought, the fires cost Ghana a third of its annual food production.

Finally, in mid-1983, most of the world woke up and began massive efforts to stem the tide of starvation in Africa. In September of that year, the U.N. urged a truce between the Ethiopian government and the guerrillas. The U.S. administration under Ronald Reagan, reluctant to send foodstuffs through Ethiopia's Marxist government, finally came down on the side of humanity and upped its expenditures for relief to something over $10 million.

By the end of 1984 the U.N. reported in a *New York Times* story that "up to 7,000,000 Ethiopians [were] said to be 'at risk of starvation.'" Many others were dying of attendant diseases.

U.N. teams discovered horrifying conditions under which the populace had lived for a decade. In the 10 years since the government had taken over in a military coup, virtually no land had been irrigated and little had been done to correct environmentally destructive agricultural practice. Farmers in the north were farming in ways that eroded the land completely. Forests were cut down, overgrazing by livestock grew, and the government did nothing—or worse. It dropped the prices it would pay for grain, through

A terribly malnourished child is cared for by her mother in a relief camp in Bati, Ethiopia. U.N. Photo/John Isaac.

its government-owned Agricultural Marketing Corporation, thus discouraging farmers from producing a surplus, or selling whatever surplus they were able to produce.

"The fact is," one U.N. worker noted, "many farmers hoard their excess grain, not to sell later but because they'd rather have the food than the little money the government would pay them for it."

Meanwhile, as the drought dragged on, hundreds of Ethiopians died daily. Projections put the number that would starve to death between May 1984 and May 1985 at half a million.

"Many others, particularly children, will suffer problems for the rest of their lives, including impaired physical and mental growth," said High Goyder, field representative of the British-based relief organization Oxfam.

The workers who toured the camps which were feeding tens of thousands daily described conditions ranging from grim to hellish. "At Korem, for example, things have improved," noted William Day of Save the Children, another independent relief agency. "[In the feeding center 225 miles north of Addis Ababa,] three weeks ago, 150 were dying . . . every day. Three days ago [November 1984], that figure was down to 40."

It was a comparative improvement; but the deaths from famine continued. At camps in the Ethiopian highlands, severe cold and the resulting hypothermia killed many. Lacking other shelter, thousands of people dug holes in the ground and surrounded the rims with rocks as their only protection against winds and frost. Disease invaded even these camps. Typhus, pneumonia, dysentery, meningitis and measles claimed the lives of hundreds.

Meanwhile, various governments blamed each other for the problem, while the dying went on, and nomads filtered into feeding centers, where they set up their way of life in *tukuls*—low gumdrop-shaped huts fashioned from grass mats and sticks. One such woman, in Harerge, in eastern Ethiopia, said to a *Times* reporter in December 1985, "All the animals died because of the drought. For three years' duration there was nothing. We don't have any sheep or goats, and we can't do anything now even if the rains come."

That sort of hopelessness extended to many of the 1.2 million people in Harerge who were affected by this prolonged dry spell, described by a representative of another relief organization, Interact, as a "green famine. There's sorghum in the fields, but there's no seed on it. The maize is withered," he concluded. Thus, the starving would not, could not be fed in the foreseeable future.

By January 1985, the relief supply to Ethiopia from the U.S. had increased to $40 million. But the Ethiopian government was misusing much of this, utilizing blankets and supplies as bait to supposedly resettle hundreds of thousands of Ethiopians from the poor and overcrowded North to the fertile and underpopulated South. The hidden agenda may have been genocidal. Weakened by starvation and disease, hundreds of thousands of these refugees died by the sides of roads already littered by the corpses of humans and animals.

Finally, in 1986, the rains came, and the drought dissipated. But all of the problems did not miraculously cure themselves with a change of weather. A "normal" situation in Ethiopia means importing 15 percent of food needs and feeding 2.5 million people in residual pockets of famine. (During the peak famine years of 1984–1986, 6.5 million people were being fed.)

In January 1987, Ethiopia's leader, Colonel Mengistu Halle Mariam, began a three-year drive for food and self-sufficiency, saying that "hunger has left its indelible scar on the history of our country, the honor and morale of our people."

Dead cattle and devastation are mute evidence of the gigantic drought that has ravaged Ethiopia and the Sudan since 1984. U.N. photo.

Noble words. But the underpayment for farmers' produce, plus the resettlement horror of January 1985, which was to be resumed, made U.N. agencies look with some trepidation upon the Ethiopian government's ability to handle poverty, drought and famine. Not only that. In late 1987, U.N. convoys bearing food were attacked in the drought stricken provinces of Iritrea and Tigre by The Eritrian People's Liberation Front, an anti-government guerrilla group. Thirty-five trucks were set afire, incinerating food supplies that were on their way to thousands of starving Ethiopians.

And more problems arose: Now, the civil war in Sudan, Ethiopia's neighbor to the west, accelerated to full fury, and hundreds of thousands of refugees from Sudan began to pour over the borders into Ethiopia. Tens of thousands of these refugees walked hundreds of miles, and the roads in Sudan, as they had been in Ethiopia a few years earlier, became littered with the corpses of those who had died of starvation along the way, or from the blows and bullets of Sudanese militiamen.

Because the Sudanese government represented a semblance of democracy, the Reagan Administration sent $1.7

billion in aid to it. Over $1 million a day was to be spent on distributing food. But independent relief agencies were barred from the country, and the army was given the responsibility of distributing the food. As a result, much of it went to the army rather than to the starving populace.

To complicate matters, massive floods paralyzed the country in August 1988. When these subsided, various U.N. representatives and relief agencies that began to filter into the country saw evidence of genocide through neglect. As in Ethiopia, masses of people were herded together by militiamen and moved from place to place. Many of them died along the way. But, whereas in Ethiopia, there was some evidence of positive sense to the moves, there was none in Sudan, except to kill off the populace. Country dwellers were moved to cities, urban dwellers to the country. Neither could live in these strange surroundings, and so they died.

Disease rose like a wraith. Tuberculosis swept the ravaged countryside.

Finally, in May 1989, a truce was declared between the north and the south of Sudan. For the first time, the International Red Cross was allowed in. Food supplies were in the country already, but the government had not distributed them. A crisis atmosphere prevailed. The May rains were imminent, and when they struck, roads would be washed out and transport of these foodstuffs would be severely hampered. A massive international airlift was begun, and, for a moment, at least, these two poor, drought and famine-plagued countries would look forward to some hope of reducing the devastation of death by starvation.

HOLLAND

1944–1945

• • • • • • • • • • • • • • •

The most extreme example yet of human manipulation of natural forces to bring about a natural disaster was the 1944–1945 famine in western Holland. Nazi occupiers brought on a two-year famine that killed 10,000.

Athough the death toll from the famine of 1944–1945 in Western Holland was 10,000—relatively small compared to the millions that have perished in other famines—its circumstances and placement in history make it important. Unlike other famines caused entirely by natural circumstances, this famine was purposefully created by the occupying Germans during World War II and specifically designed to bring about mass starvation. The natural resources that supplied food were intentionally manipulated.

Prior to the beginning of World War II, the Dutch lived on an excellent diet containing an abundance of animal products, with wheat and rye as the staple cereals. However, most of their food was imported, including fodder for livestock. And to add to a precarious internal balance, much of the butter, cheese and eggs produced in Holland was exported.

The war broke out in 1939, and it became immediately apparent to the Dutch that they would have to stockpile imports against a possible blockade. This they did, but their facilities were inadequate, and by the beginning of 1940, rationing of all food, including fodder, was instituted.

It was only an interim measure that soon became outdated. The Germans invaded Holland in May 1940 and not only confiscated the stockpiles but commandeered, for their own armies, 60 percent of everything that was produced agriculturally in Holland.

The Dutch made do with the remaining 40 percent by self-imposed rationing, by cutting down on the production of pigs and poultry, and by increasing the planting of potatoes. The eastern part of the country, where most of the farms are located, naturally fared better than the low-land, industrial west, but overall, the entire populace managed to survive.

Then, in September 1944, the Dutch government in exile ordered a nationwide railroad strike. At the same moment, General Bernand Law Montgomery launched an airborne attack on Arnheim, on the border between eastern Holland and Germany, as a prelude to an advance on the Ruhr. There were huge casualties on both sides, and the attack was judged a failure. The strike went on.

But the worst was to come. Retaliation was the rule in occupied countries, and Seyes-Inquart, the Nazi Reichskommissar, immediately cut off all movement of food from the north and east into western Holland. The Reichskommissar warned that unless the strike was terminated, famine would result.

And it did, rapidly. By October, stocks of food began to be depleted. Ships with cargoes of food that were already in harbor were boarded by German soldiers, and their cargoes were confiscated and destroyed. Factories and warehouses of food were emptied and their contents carried off. Eastern Holland became isolated.

Those who could went out into the country and foraged for food on bicycles with handcarts. After a while, even the few potatoes or sugar beets that were lying untended in abandoned fields had been gathered up.

People began to die. The elderly perished first, then those who lived alone, and then, as the famine deepened, families started to starve.

In certain towns, "starvation hospitals" were set up—waystations, where people could check in for a prescribed period to be fed and then discharged to make room for others. The diet in the hospital, shared alike by doctors, nurses and patients, was anything but grand:

Breakfast: 1 slice of bread; 1 cup of tea.
Lunch: 2 potatoes, a small portion of "vegetables," some watery sauce.
Dinner: 1 or 2 slices of bread, 1 plate of soup, 1 cup of "coffee substitute."

In desperation, Dutch doctors sent an open letter to the Reichskommissar, Seyes-Inquart:

We hold your Administration responsible for the dire shortage of even the most necessary foodstuffs. The want and distress of the Dutch people living in the most densely populated parts of the occupied territory increase day by day. The ration allotted to adults has a nutritive value of only 600 to 800 calories. That is even less than half what is needed for an adult to survive, even when resting; it is less than a third of what is required for work. The small stocks of food which many families had been able to put aside are disappearing or are already exhausted . . . extra rations for the sick and aged have been withdrawn altogether.

As a result of serious malnutrition, insufficient clothing and the great shortage of fuel, endurance has been seriously undermined, so that there is an increase of grave illness. These evil consequences are made even more serious by the shortage of means for carrying on medical work, cleansing and disinfection. Tuberculosis, dysentery, enteric fever and infantile paralysis are rapidly increasing in severity, while epidemics of diphtheria and scarlet fever have already reached proportions formerly unknown in Holland. The danger of typhus must be seriously faced.

The Occupying Authorities are to blame for these conditions. In the first place, because they broke International Law by transporting to Germany the large reserve supplies available in 1940, and in the years following 1940, by carrying off a considerable portion of the livestock and food produced in our country. Secondly because, now, in 1944, they are, by confiscation and abduction of nearly all transport material, preventing the Dutch people from distributing the remaining food satisfactorily over the whole country. . . .

The letter was, needless to say, never answered. But by this time, the tide of war had turned, and British and Americans, aware of the famine, were organizing teams of doctors and trained personnel to fan out over western Holland immediately after the liberation.

As it turned out, the relief teams entered ahead of the Allied armies. Seyes-Inquart, increasingly repentant as he received an avalanche of hysterical memos from Berlin, advising him to break down the sea-dykes and flood western Holland, met secretly with Allied and German officers and arranged for a non-military medical mission, under a flag of truce, to pass through the lines and treat the starving.

The rescue team was greeted by the cheerful faces of the thin people on the street. Their ruddiness was in stark contrast to the emaciated bodies and faces of those in emergency hospitals and in bed at home, suffering from famine edema and lingering on the verge of death.

The official report, issued after the liberation of Holland, noted that the Dutch famine was within days of becoming ". . . a very terrible catastrophe. Had the German occupying forces held out another two or three weeks against the Allied attack, nothing could have saved hundreds of thousands in the towns of the western Netherlands from death from starvation."

INDIA

1769

• • • • • • • • • • • • • •

Eighteen months without rain in the northern part of India from 1769 through 1770 produced a drought which created a monster famine that killed 3 million people.

Three million people perished in the three-year famine that followed an 18-month drought in the Ganges Plain of Northern India, known as Hindustan, from 1769 to 1770.

No rain fell throughout the entire area, from the Himalayas on the north to the Decca Plain on the south, and from Punjab to Assam, for a year and a half. When the monsoons finally returned, and crops began to grow again, the farmers who might have harvested them had already died of starvation. Thus, the crops that might have fed and saved thousands also died, unpicked and unprocessed.

The devastation was widespread and dramatic. Entire villages became devoid of human beings. According to one written record, in many of these villages ". . . the air was so infected by the noxious effluvia of dead bodies, that it was scarcely possible to stir abroad without perceiving it. . . ."

According to others, the air was alive with the cries of those who were in various stages of starvation, a sound and a sight that those who witnessed it were never wholly able to forget.

INDIA

1790

• • • • • • • • • • • • • •

More than 1 million residents of the western province of Baroda in India died in a famine caused by a two-year drought, from 1790 through 1791.

An extensive famine climaxed in cannibalism among families when crop ruination and an absence of monsoons in the western province of Baroda, India dried the countryside to dust from 1790 to 1791.

For almost two solid years, no crops were able to grow or be harvested in this province of India that had heretofore been regarded as a rich agricultural area. When the remnants of the scorched crops were exhausted, desperate residents of the area turned to cannibalism—even among families. Over 1 million perished, either from starvation or murder.

INDIA

1833

• • • • • • • • • • • • • •

Over 200,000 died in the Guntoor Famine, caused by a drought in the Madras Presidency of southeastern India in 1833.

Portions of the Madras Presidency, in the southeast of India, were scenes of widespread human suffering during 1833. Over 200,000 persons died of starvation in what later became known as the Guntoor Famine, since the greatest concentration of drought and consequent famine occurred in this district.

According to some British authorities, the official death figures were actually skewed on the conservative side, to save face for the British colonial government. In actuality, it was the most serious famine to occur in India since the beginning of the British occupation in 1757.

INDIA

1866

• • • • • • • • • • • • • •

Off-schedule monsoons caused a famine in the southern Indian provinces of Bengal, Orissa and Behar in 1866, killing 1.5 million people.

In an odd twist of fate, an abundance of rain was responsible for the immense famine that caused the deaths of more than 1.5 million residents of the southern provinces of Bengal, Orissa and Behar in India in 1866.

The regularity and abundance of monsoons have always been the basis of India's agricultural economy. Irrigation of crops is dependent on the monsoons. Without them, famine results.

The monsoons arrived in 1866, but not on schedule. The first rains arrived two months before the beginning of planting season and ceased before the sowing began. The later rains, upon which farmers depended for sustenance of the crops and which regularly arrived at the end of September and October, did not arrive at all.

Thus, a million and a half people died of starvation and its related diseases of cholera and scurvy.

INDIA
1876–1877
• • • • • • • • • • • • • •

India's largest recorded famine, in which 6 million people died, occurred in the Madras presidency and the Bombay district of Poona from 1876 to 1877. Brought on by an extensive drought, its devastation was deepened by the spread of cholera, which was responsible for half of the recorded deaths.

The most extensive famine in India occurred in the two years of 1876 and 1877. More than 6 million people starved or succumbed to cholera within the Madras Presidency and the Bombay district of Poona.

The onset of the so-called Great Famine began two years earlier when the customary monsoons did not materialize. To make matters considerably worse, no appreciable rainfall occured between monsoon seasons. There were a few short-lived rainstorms during the two years—enough to raise hopes—but these hopes were short-lived, as an unrelieved drought consumed whatever crops managed to break through the dry earth.

By October 1876, nine districts of the Bombay Deccan had been hit by famine, and malnutrition, coupled with polluted drinking water, conspired to produce 3 million deaths by cholera. It was one of the most tragic instances of drought and famine on record.

INDIA
1898
• • • • • • • • • • • • • •

One million residents of a 300,000-square-mile area of southern and western India died in a drought-induced famine in 1898.

Over 61 million people were affected and 1 million died of starvation and related diseases in the immense famine of 1898 which ranged over 300,000 square miles of southern and western India.

Once again (see preceding two entries), a solid two years of insufficient rainfall and the failure of crops came together to produce a famine of major proportions that resulted in enormous loss of life, with its ancillary horrors of scurvy, cholera, leprosy, murder, cannibalism, poverty and mass misery.

As in any drought, the scarcity of even the most basic staples of wheat and rice spawned an alarming rise in prices. Women and men, paid two and a half cents a day for hard physical labor, could not afford a minimal amount of grain to sustain their families. As a result, families were decimated. Fathers and mothers died, and children joined the vast, destitute armies of people who wandered the countryside in search of work.

These starving nomads were in turn exploited by entrepreneurs who sometimes gave them three cents a day in salary for several days labor. A precious few survived the trek and the first few days of hard labor. Others, less fortunate and more desperate, were forced to survive by eating berries, roots, thorny cactus and grass seed. Some resorted to cannibalism.

An ancillary result of this particular famine was the proliferation of so-called "poorhouses." These were nothing more than exploitation centers which traded marginal amounts of food in exchange for near-slave labor, prostitution and crime.

There were good people including missionaries and government officials who offered aid during the famine. Reverand J. Sinclair Stevenson was one of these who recorded some of his efforts to stem the tide of mortality in Parantij, Giujarat: "My chief work was to take care of orphans . . ." he wrote, "but often you get them . . . just in time to fill your cemetery. . . . To go out every morning and whenever we see a child lying beside its dead mother, we, of course, take it back with us. Yesterday morning, within two hundred yards of our house, I saw sixteen corpses; today, within the same distance, ten. Must people really see ribs and skeletons to make them give?"

INDIA
1943
• • • • • • • • • • • • • •

The immense Bengal famine of 1943, in which 1.5 million died, was caused by a confluence of factors, natural and man-made. World War II, wrong decisions by the Indian government and human greed were the man-made factors. Heavy rains, a typhoon and river flooding were the natural ones.

For 40 years before the Bengal famine of 1943, there had been no famines in India. In fact, the British pointed with pride to the apparent fact that one of the triumphs of the Raj was the elimination of famine in India.

But in 1943, a combination of natural and man-made factors converged and changed the records forever.

The man-made causes, so pervasive in this scenario, began on January 15, 1942, when the Japanese captured Singapore, in one of their first major victories of World War II. Following this, Burma was overrun and captured within two months. Thousands of refugees from Burma poured into Bengal through Assam and Chittagong, carrying with them not only horrible stories of atrocities but a virulent form of malaria.

The invasion of Bengal by the Japanese was expected at any moment. That it never occurred, and that the Japanese remained merely a menacing presence on the borders of Northeast India from then until the end of the war in August 1945 did nothing to decrease the tension of expectation or the preparations for it.

Two of these preparations, in early 1942, paved the way for famine. First, stocks of paddy and rice in excess of local requirements were removed from coastal areas in the delta that were perceived to be vulnerable to invasion. Instead of being earmarked for the future needs of the populace of Bengal, this rice was distributed in Calcutta.

Secondly, in order to further frustrate the awaited Japanese, all boats capable of carrying 10 passengers or more were removed from the province. This not only cut the transport lines for the populace, it also removed the only means local fishermen had of getting their catch and distributing it to the area.

These were devastating decisions on the part of the Indian government, and they were not helped by natural conditions in Bengal. In 1941, there was a poor harvest of rice. During 1942, a combination of heavy rains and increased exports weakened the supply of rice still further. On October 11, 1942, a typhoon, accompanied by three tidal waves, struck the western districts in the delta, inundating 3,200 square miles of it, causing a sizable loss of life and the destruction of all of the standing crops and stocks of rice. Even in the areas away from the coast, the level of rivers was raised, which caused the flooding of approximately another 400 square miles.

All of these influences, plus the factor of human greed, conspired to raise the minimum price of rice, which is the staple of the Indian diet and accounts for 80 percent of the caloric intake of the average inhabitant of Bengal.

From a price of approximately six rupees per maund (82 pounds) in January 1942, the price of rice skyrocketed to 40 rupees per maund in June of that year. By the end of 1943, it was reckoned that the unprecedented profits made in the buying and selling of rice had reached Rs 150 crores, which translates into approximately $24 million.

The toll on humanity was far more grim. By June 1943, the price of rice was fantastically out of reach for the poor. Landless laborers, small tradesmen, weavers and potters who had managed marginal livings were forced, in order to buy food, to sell at cut-throat prices their domestic utensils, ornaments, tools, clothes, even the doors and windows of their dwellings to more fortunate neighbors. Eventually, their short rations began to dwindle, while the residents on the other side of the economic fence, those who could buy and store rice, began to reap monumental profits.

By May, the death rate from starvation began to rise in six districts in the Delta, particularly in Chittagong. In June, it was double the quinquennial average and three to four times the normal July average.

The government in Calcutta remained unaffected by this situation until August, when thousands of people began to drift into the city, propelled there by rumors that food was to be had. They were a placid army, begging for food, often dying in the street just outside locked storehouses that were filled with the very rice that could have prevented their deaths. The dying were the poor, used to accepting their misfortune, and by the time they reached Calcutta, most of them had sunk into the apathy that precedes death by starvation.

Author W. R. Aykroyd, who was a member of the National Inquiry Commission appointed in July 1944 by the government of India to investigate the causes of the famine, recalled, in his book *The Conquest of Famine*, the scene in the outlying districts:

In August I was traveling by rail from Madras to Calcutta. . . . It was customary for the Madras-Calcutta mail to pick up a dining car at Khargpur Junction, some thirty miles outside Calcutta, to provide first and second-class passengers with breakfast. I stepped cheerfully down from my compartment en route for a hearty meal. The whole platform was thronged with emaciated and ragged people, of all ages and sexes, many half-dead, hoping to board a train for Calcutta. What I remember is a loud, bleating, wailing noise which the starving crowd made, a combination of begging and misery. . . . I could not eat breakfast in the dining car and went back to my compartment.

The death rate from the famine reached a peak in December 1943. In its early days, most deaths were caused by starvation, but later, hundreds of thousands of deaths were attributed to smallpox, cholera and malaria.

The government of Bengal tried to stem the tide of deaths. But their methods were too little, too late—distracted, at that, by the war and the perceived necessity of keeping the factory workers adequately fed and thus capable of turning out material for the army to defend India against a Japanese invasion which never occurred. Thus, out of 260,000 tons of rice that the government bought at exhorbitant prices from profiteering dealers, 140,000 tons were used to feed Calcutta, while only 65,000 tons were sent to rural Bengal, where the famine began and was raging most furiously.

It would take the end of the war to end the famine, and the Commission would estimate that one and a half million victims would be officially counted. But this figure was, at best, conservative, according to Aykroyd, who noted, ". . . whenever I come across [the historical figure of 1.5 million dead] I remember the process by which it was reached. I now think it was an underestimate, especially in that it took too little account of roadside deaths, but not as gross an underestimate as some critics of the Commission's report, who preferred 3 to 4 million, declared it to be. The lower figure is tragic enough."

INDIA

1972

• • • • • • • • • • • • • • •

Drought in the Ganges basin caused the 1972 famine which affected most of India and killed 800 people.

Over 800 persons died of heat exposure or starvation, 50 million residents of India were affected, and the Indian economy was $400 million poorer as a result of a combined heat wave and drought that struck 14 Indian states in May 1972.

May is generally a benign month in India in terms of hot weather. In this particular year, however, the annual monsoons that enter the Bay of Bengal and soar up the Ganges basin, generally watering the crops and lowering the temperature, failed to arrive. As a result, thousands upon thousands of acres of sugar cane and jute broiled on the vines or failed to mature, while the sun baked the land and kept the thermometer at an even 110 degrees for nearly a month.

When the rains finally came, the soil had been so devastated, it washed away in gigantic mud flows, making the resowing of crops extraordinarily difficult.

IRELAND

1845–1850

• • • • • • • • • • • • • • • •

One fourth of the entire population of Ireland—2,209,961 people—either died of starvation or emigrated as a result of the Great Potato Famine of 1845–1850.

If the sources of a national, binding emotion can be traced to one event, the Irish hatred of all things British would have to be traced to the Great Potato Famine that raged across this small and verdant country for five years, from 1845 to 1850. During that time, fully one quarter of the country's population was eliminated, either from death or emigration—1,029,552 died of starvation, typhoid, typhus or scurvy and 1,180,409 emigrated, mostly to America—and the seeds would be sown for a deepseated enmity that would erupt in a bloody revolt whose echoes and actuality continue to reverberate into the present.

A short 45 years before the famine, Ireland was, if not rolling in wealth, at least touched by it. But with the departure of Wellington's forces in 1815, its Irish contingent was abruptly thrown upon the Irish labor market, glutting it.

That might have been absorbed, since Ireland has an abundance of rich soil and the crops to prove it. But the British withdrew more than Wellington. They were, the Irish soon found, experts in extraction through tariff and taxation. The Corn Laws imposed impossible tariffs on small landowners and funneled herds of cattle, boatloads of oats, rye and corn away from Ireland's increasing population and into England. "Immense herds of cattle, sheep and hogs," reported Irish writer John Mitchel, "floating off on every tide, out of every one of our thirteen seaports . . ."

And so, while the populace of Ireland continued to multiply (in 1800 it reached 5 million—a population exceeding that of America at the time), its breadbasket continued to empty, until the Irish, along with the Belgians, earned the name of "potato-eaters," after the new staple of their diet.

And so Ireland was not a pretty sight in the early 1800s. Poverty was everywhere, and, with most of its agricultural output being exported to the ruling British, hunger soon followed. Thomas Carlyle, touring the land, wrote, "Never saw such begging in the world. . . . Often get in a rage at it . . . [beggars] storming round you, like ravenous dogs round carrion . . . human pity dies away into stony misery and disgust at the excess of such scenes."

Worse was to come when British landlords evicted tens of thousands of starving peasants when they were unable to pay their rent. The Earl of Lucan in County Mayo, euologized by Alfred, Lord Tennyson in his "Charge of the Light Brigade," evicted 40,000 peasants from the hovels upon which he was collecting rent.

And then the potato blight hit. It was a chance for the British to save both their honor and millions of lives. Instead, the Earl of Lucan stepped up his evictions and his rents. The *London Times* Irish correspondent, the Reverend Sidney Godolphin Osborne, called these actions "philanthropic," claiming that they helped stabilize populations. Gentle Tennyson added his voice, noting that "Kelts are all made furious fools. They live in a horrible island and have no history of their own worth the least notice. . . . Could not anyone blow up that horrible island with dynamite and carry it off in pieces—a long way off?"

So much for disaster relief in the 19th century.

In Ireland itself, misery spread like the black plague. Large parts of the population, swelled to 8.2 million in 1845, were existing on "lumpers," a gray tuber used for pig fodder in all other parts of the world, and water.

When even this was reduced by blight, starvation began to increase. Tens of thousands died in the privacy of their homes; others perished along the sides of public roads. Along with cholera and scurvy, there was death by exposure as a result of mass evictions when peasants could no longer harvest wheat crops with which to pay their rent. There were incidents of cannibalism. Shallow graves were dug along the sides of roads, but the graves were frequently raided by hungry dogs, who dismembered the corpses and scattered them about the countryside.

In *The Black Prophet*, William Carleton wrote, "The roads were literally black with funerals, and as you passed from parish to parish, the deathbells were pealing forth in slow but gloomy tones, the triumph which pestilence was achieving over the face of our devoted country—a country that was every day filled with darker desolation and deeper mourning."

Still, the ships loaded with grain and produce continued to set out from Ireland's 13 ports, while other ships loaded with emigrants began to fill with the nearly 2 million who would flee Ireland and give rise to its continuing reputation as a country whose greatest export was its young men. But in the 1840s, these emigrants found life scarcely better elsewhere. In England, they were treated as pariahs and forced into hovels and cellars. In America, they met similar resistance, the infamous "No Irish Need Apply" signs everywhere, forcing them to gather in Irish ghettos in Boston, New York and Baltimore, where a half million of them would perish, miles away from home.

England did make some halfhearted attempts to establish work projects in Ireland—hard labor at low wages, building roads to nowhere. The large public projects that might have turned the death rate around were lost in Parliamentary squabbles. Benjamin Disraeli remarked, "One day the Pope, the next day potatoes." Lord Salisbury, as prime minister, compared the Irish to "Hottentots," incapable of both self-rule and self-survival.

Only Lord John Russell, speaking in the House of Lords on March 23, 1846, voiced some concern and responsibility. "We have made Ireland, I speak deliberately—we have made it the most degraded and most miserable country in the world. . . . All the world is crying shame upon us; but we are equally callous to our ignominy and the results of our misgovernment."

But his remarks would be buried beneath indifference and other matters, like the beginning of the Anglo-Sikh War in India. Time would be the curer of Ireland's famine and the sustainer of its rage.

JAMAICA
1788
• • • • • • • • • • • • •

A series of major hurricanes left much of Jamaica unfarmable in 1777. By 1788, a resultant famine killed 15,000 of the island's 25,000 slaves.

Both the rulers and the ruled, the privileged and the underprivileged were affected by a huge famine that swept through the island of Jamaica in 1788. Landowners and slave masters lost money. Fifteen thousand of the 25,000 slaves on the island lost their lives.

The famine had its roots in a series of violent hurricanes that swept through the island in the fall of 1777. The devastation from these hurricanes was particularly felt by the 775 sugar plantations, owned by whites, worked by slaves. Over 200 of these estates lay in utter ruin after the hurricane left, unfarmable until more financing could be brought from England.

In the ensuing six months, before rebuilding funds could arrive and the moderately damaged plantations could be replanted, work disappeared for the island's slaves. And their masters refused to feed them if they did not work. Riots erupted throughout the colony and dozens of whites were killed. But the riots proved ultimately ineffectual, and by the end of the six months, over two-thirds of Jamaica's slave population had perished from starvation.

NIGERIA
1968
• • • • • • • • • • • • •

One hundred thousand died—most from ancillary reasons—in the drought-caused famine in Nigeria from 1968 through 1973.

Nigeria, in the Sahel region of Africa, is one of the most drought-prone areas of the world. Over and over, thousands die when rain refuses to fall, rivers dry up and crops wither.

The six-year drought that began in 1968 and ended in 1973 claimed 100,000 Nigerians. The causes of their deaths were recorded in a startling report by medical missionary Dr. John A. Dreisbach, a 30-year resident of the area who noted, in the National Geographic Society's 1978 survey of natural disasters, *Powers of Nature:* "I saw thousands of cattle carcasses. . . . Nomads who once owned them were in relief camps eating gift food sent by the rest of the world. We saw much malnutrition and sickness. In their weakened condition, many people died of pneumonia, measles, and whooping cough. I saw little starvation as such."

It was there. But it only accounted for a fraction of the overall death rate. More than three-quarters of the deaths were from disease—typhus, pneumonia, measles and whooping cough.

RUSSIA

1921–1923

• • • • • • • • • • • • • • • •

The Russian famine of 1921–1923, in which over 3 million people died, was caused by a combination of drought, the depletion of granaries from World War I, a civil war and an international blockade.

Although the Volga River basin in Russia is one of the richest sources of agriculture in the world, it is also one of the most vulnerable to drought. Since A.D. 900, Russia has suffered over 100 famines, and one of the worst of these occurred in 1921. More than 30 million people were affected by it; over 3 million died from it.

The causes of the famine were twofold. First, was a lack of rain in 1920, followed by a complete drought in 1921 that left one of Europe's most productive cornlands a blackened waste.

That in itself would not have been enough of a natural setback to cause a famine that covered an area of a million square miles and affected so many millions of people. It was the economic effect combined with this that produced the cataclysm of 1921–1923.

During World War I, granaries in Russia were depleted, and most of the able-bodied farmers were conscripted into the army.

Immediately following World War I, Russia became embroiled in civil war, which did not conclude until 1920.

During that time, fully half of the arable land lay fallow. And if this were not enough, Russia was blockaded by other nations until 1921, thus preventing any slack in domestic supplies from being made up through imports.

The new Bolshevik government found itself in great trouble. Seven provinces on the Volga were in drought and in need. In the province of Samara alone, 70 percent of the cornfields had failed completely, and without help, most of the peasants would not survive the winter. By September 1921, 1.2 million people were already starving.

Several international relief organizations were formed, and the most prominent of them was the English and American Society of Friends, which faithfully recorded the event. Michael Asquith, a member of the first Quaker unit to be headquartered in the town of Buzuluk, in Samara, documented the famine in his book *Quaker Work in Russia 1921–23.* By September, when Asquith's party arrived, the populace was already subsisting on grass and acorns, a diet that was rapidly killing most of the young children, who could not digest it. Asquith wrote:

I saw in practically every home benches covered with birch or lime leaves. These are dried, pounded, mixed with acorns, some dirt and water, and then baked into a substance which they call bread, but which looks and smells like baked manure. . . . There are practically no babies and those that survive look ghastly. The mothers have no milk and pray that death may come quickly. . . . All the children have distended stomachs, many are rachitic and have enlarged heads. . . . According to Government figures, ninety percent of the children between the ages of one and three have already died from the famine. . . .

The first snowfall took an enormous toll; one Quaker reported seeing 40 people die in one morning at the beginning of November.

The Government attempted to stop the death of children by setting up receiving homes, distributing homes and permanent homes. These became graphic exercises in futility, shelters where the young went to die. One receiving home in Buzuluk was described in detail by a Quaker worker:

As a home it was intended for 50 children, but yesterday 654 children were crammed within its walls. On such days as many as 80 are brought in. The stench inside was indescribable . . . as we entered we became aware of the continual wailing sound that goes on day and night. In each room . . . there were at least a hundred children packed like sardines in canvas beds—six on a bed intended for one, and underneath the beds as well. The typhus cases, some of them completely naked, lay on straw in a separate room. They had neither bedding, medicines nor disinfectants, though we had been able to give them a little soap and clothing. They had no doctor.

Each morning the attendants picked out the dead from the living and put them in a shed to await the dead cart which every day makes its round of the Children's Homes.

One home's record summarizes the situation: "Admitted, 1,300; Died 731."

As the famine increased, cannibalism occurred, but it was not as widespread as in other famines of this extent. Still, the Friends Relief Committee met and decided to give up buying cheap sausages when some were found to contain human flesh.

It was not until the middle of 1922 that the International Russian Relief Commission was able to surmount various bureaucracies and begin to set up soup kitchens— a process that had succeeded in the waning days of the Great Irish Potato Famine (see p. 85)—to feed up to 2 million people.

Finally, in the autumn of 1923, a sizable Russian harvest was reaped, and the International Relief Commission turned its attention to clothing the poor, replacing farm equipment and harnesses that had been boiled and eaten, importing farm horses from Siberia and tending to some 13,000 abandoned children. It was a baptism by fire and famine for the new Soviet Government.

USSR

April–December 1975

• • • • • • • • • • • • • • •

Few died in the Soviet famine of 1975, but the economic impact of the loss of a wheat crop caused the starvation of tens of thousands in Third World countries.

Although there was little or no loss of life from the extreme drought that swept across the USSR from early spring through the end of 1975, the worldwide economic impact was immense. Deprived of most of its wheat crop, the Soviet Union bought millions of tons of wheat from the United States, Canada and Argentina. As a result, American farmers reaped a bonanza, and the price of bread doubled worldwide—a situation that caused starvation and deprivation in Third World countries thousands of miles from the drought itself.

Statistics of the 1975 drought in the USSR were characteristically withheld from the rest of the world, but what is known is that the absence of rain in a small spot near Kybyshev, between the Volga River and the Ural Mountains in April of that year was the harbinger of far worse conditions to come.

Ninety percent of the USSR's wheat is grown in a fertile triangle formed by the Baltic, Black and Caspian Seas. Ordinarily, this is an ideal spot for wheat: rolling plains, rich soil, a steady but not overly abundant supply of rain which irrigates the soil without leaching it out. In 1975, Russian farmers relied exclusively upon natural irrigation to keep their huge wheat crop healthy, despite the fact that the Soviet Union's farmlands are the most drought-plagued in the world.

In 1975, the rains did not come. The great plains east of the Urals baked under unrelieved skies all summer. By autumn, the rich topsoil blew off farms in enormous, dun-colored clouds.

Autumn passed; winter set in with no appreciable precipitation but with widespread drought and poverty. It finally took the onset of the deepest part of the Russian winter, in January 1976, for snow to reirrigate and enrich the soil enough to prepare it for a successful early spring planting.

UNITED STATES
MIDWEST

1909–1914

• • • • • • • • • • • • • • •

Several thousand died in the Great Plains drought of 1909– 1914, in which unique and ineffectual methods of inducing rain were employed.

Although mild in comparison to the Great Dust Bowl of the 1930s (see following entry), the Great Plains drought of 1909–1914 caused widespread deprivation. For five years, the winter winds brought nothing but cold and the spring breezes only isolated showers. Summers were unconscionably hot, and crops either did not germinate or withered on the vine.

This was the age of rainmaking folktales. In the 1870s, settlers had been lured to the Southwest desert by folklore that stated that "rain follows the plow." In the 1890s, perhaps taking their cues from Indian rain dances, farmers paid as much as $500 to itinerant and ineffectual rainmakers.

In the drought of 1909–1914, famous cereal magnate C. W. Post, hearing from Civil War veterans that rain always followed heavy bombardments, employed armies of men to set off scores of dynamite explosions. The hope was that the first explosions would cause clouds and the later ones rattle rain loose from these clouds. It didn't work. Only time and the cycle of nature returned rain to the parched land.

The effects of the great drought and famine of the 1930s in the American Midwest are etched into the faces of a mother and her child, two of thousands made homeless and forced to wander from shelter to shelter, temporary job to temporary job. Library of Congress.

UNITED STATES
MIDWEST

1934–1941
· · · · · · · · · · · · · ·

Thousands of farmers-turned-migrants died when a combination of drought, unwise use of land, and bank foreclosures converged to cause the Great Dust Bowl of 1934–1941.

A combination of natural and man-made circumstances brought on the famous "Dust Bowl" drought of the 1930s, in which 25,000 square miles of the midwestern United States became one vast wasteland of dried soil and unproductive land. More than 300,000 farmers and their families, driven off their ancestral land by a combination of a hostile nature, the economics of the Great Depression and their own folly, became a vast, exploited army of nomads, chronicled vividly in John Steinbeck's powerful novel, *The Grapes of Wrath*.

The troubles of this area began during World War I, when the high price of wheat and the needs of the Allied troops encouraged farmers to expand their wheat fields into pasture land. By cramming their livestock into abbreviated grazing pastures and plowing under every square foot of available land and planting it with wheat, these farmers made small fortunes in a short period of time.

But when the war ended, demand shrank to its prewar levels, and these same farmers returned the plowed fields to their livestock without first properly seeding and preparing them. Within a few years, the cattle's hooves pulverized the unprotected soil, and when strong winter winds blew in from the northwest, this topsoil was borne eastward on the wind.

Now, a combination of forces gathered to produce drought and famine. The topsoil that was blown away was gone forever. Spring and summer rains became more infrequent. Beginning in 1934, the northwest winds blew relentlessly from December to May, picking up not only the soil but seeds that had lain in it for six months without sprouting. Tumbleweeds whirled across the landscape, fetching up against fences and houses. Stock tanks were emptied of water and filled up with dust. The dry soil lifted itself in thousand foot clouds that obscured the sun, engulfing farmhouses and forcing itself inside, into cook pots and beds. Traces of dust and wisps of winter wheat were driven by these winds as far east as New York and Washington.

In July and August, the bitter northwest winds were replaced by furnace blasts from the deserts of the Southwest. The bare land baked under horrendous heat which often reached and sustained, for days on end, temperatures of 110 degrees—enough to kill rattlesnakes.

The wind-driven dustclouds resembled horizontal tornadoes, according to Kansas farmer and author of the memoir *Empire of Dust*, Lawrence Svobida, who described conditions in his state to the National Geographic. When a duststorm came, he said,

> *You got inside the house quick, watched the cloud coming, and felt it envelop you. I've known storms to last 12 hours. Dirt clicked like sleet against the window glass.*
>
> *You'd hear almost continuous thunder, and the crackle of lightning—the friction of dust particles throws off a lot of static electricity. Streaks of it ran back and forth around metal structures—gasoline pumps, for instance. Radio aerials lit up like fiery crosses. That was scary. Static electricity made the ignition systems on cars fail. That could be fatal if you got caught on the road in a storm.*

Lives were claimed by these storms. Thirty-mph winds with gusts up to 60 mph blew enough dirt into the nostrils of cattle to suffocate them.

"Dust did kill some people I knew," Svobida remembered. "One young fellow about my age spent his last day alive plowing in a dust storm, trying to roughen the topsoil to keep the wind from blowing it away. He stumbled into the doctor's office that night to be told he was dying on his feet, filled up with dust."

These assaults of man upon nature and nature upon man were fatal, but not altogether insurmountable. A drought cannot last forever.

But this occurred during the time of the Great Depression, and it formed the final third of the equation. The Depression brought on an overload of poverty, starvation and hopelessness, which, piled upon the other misfortunes, collapsed the strongest will. Farms that contained some planting room could count on small subsidies—usually under $1,000 a year—for, ironically, *not* raising wheat they could not raise anyway.

Even with the Dust Bowl tragedy, there was a surplus of wheat in the U.S. in the 1930s. But those farmers who had only grazing land which would grow nothing starved, and were eventually run off their land by the banks holding mortgages the farm families could no longer pay.

And so that great, nomadic migration began. The disparagingly named "Oakies" (even though most of them came from Kansas), set out for California with all of their possessions strapped to broken-down cars and trucks, lured by promises of jobs and prosperity. Once there, they were turned away, or, if they were employed, were paid not in money but in company scrip, worthless anyplace but at the exorbitantly priced company store.

Finally, in 1940, the rains came, and a decade of normal-to-wet weather combined with regrassing and erosion-preventing procedures revitalized the Central Plains of the United States and restored its reputation as the "Breadbasket of the Nation."

But that was too late for many of the migrant workers who had lost both their land and their belongings in the 1930s. Thousands of them perished miles from their roots.

UNITED STATES
VIRGINIA
JAMESTOWN

1607

• • • • • • • • • • • • • • •

A consuming fire caused the death by starvation of 62 of the original 100 settlers of the Jamestown Colony in 1607.

One hundred settlers established the first English settlement in Jamestown, Virginia in 1607. By the end of that year, 38 of the original 100 remained alive. The other 62 died of starvation following, not a drought, but a fire.

On January 7, 1607, a devastating fire of unknown origin swept through the colony, consuming lodgings, clothing—and what was most important—provisions. Most appalling was the fact that the fire occurred in the midst of a particularly bleak and bitter winter. With neither shelter nor the means to grow food, homeless and threadbare colonists froze to death in various stages of starvation.

FLOODS

. . . .

•   •   •   •   •

THE WORST RECORDED FLOODS

•   •   •   •   •

* Detailed in text

Bangladesh
* (1970) (see CYCLONES)
(1972)
* (1974)
(1987)
* (1988)

Brazil
* Tubarao (1974)

China
(1851–1866)
* (1887)
* (1911)
(1931)
* (1939) (see FAMINES AND
DROUGHTS)
(1949)
* (1950)
* (1954)
Canton (1915)
Eastern Shensi Province (1942)
Foochow (1948)
* Fukien Province (1948)
* Kwangtung (1982)
Hankow (1908)
* Hankow (1935)
Hong Kong (1906)
Hupeh(1926)
Kaifong (1642)
Kweichow (1938)
Senchow (1933)
Shantung Province (1957)
* Sichuan Province
(1981)

Colombia
(1970)

Denmark
Zealand (1717)

England
(48)
(1099)
Cheshire (353)
* Lynmouth (1952)

France
(1208)
* Frejus (1959)

Germany
* North Sea Coast (1962)

Greece
Attica (1760 B.C.) (The "Second
Deluge")
Deucalion (1504 B.C.) (The "Third
Deluge")

Guatemala
(1949)

El Salvador
(1982)

Haiti
* (1935)

Holland
* (1530)
* (1570)
(1916)
* (1953)
* Dort (1421)
Friesland (1228)
Friesland (1646)
* Leyden (1574)

India
(1864)
(1955)
Bengal (1876)
* Bengal (West) (1978)
Bihar (1961)
* Gujaret (1968)
Gujaret (1970)
Lahore (1947)
* Morvi (1979)
Punjab (1787–1788)
Rajputana (1943)
Surat (1959)

Indonesia
Lomblem Islands (1979)

Iran
* Farahzad (1954)

Italy
* Belluno, Pirago, Villanova,
and Rivatta (1963) (see
AVALANCHES AND
LANDSLIDES)
* Florence (1966)

* Po Valley (1951)
* Stava (1985)

Japan
* (1896)
* (1964)
* (1972)
Kyushu (1953)
Tokyo (1947)

Java (and Sumatra)
(1883) (see VOLCANIC ERUPTIONS,
Krakatoa)

Manchuria
Harbin (1932)

Mozambique
Quelimane (1971)

North Vietnam
(1971)

Norway
(1219)

Pakistan
Punjab, Sind (1972)

Peru
Huaraz (1941)

Poland
(1813)

Portugal
Lisbon (1967)

Russia
* St. Petersburg
(1824)

Salandria
(1287)

Scotland
Glasgow (758)
* Inverness (1829)

Sicily
(1161)

South Korea
* (1972)

Spain
(1617)
* Barcelona, Sabadell, Tarrasa
(1962)
Consuegra (1891)

Sudan
* Khartoum (1988)

Thailand
  ˙ (1988)
Tibet
  Himalayas (1970)
  ˙ Shigatse (1954)
Tunisia
  ˙ (1969)
Turkey
  (1946)
United States
  ˙ California (1928)
  ˙ Colorado (and Montana,
    Kansas, Wyoming and New
    Mexico) (1965)
  ˙ Colorado (1976)
  Connecticut

  ˙ Putnam (1955)
  Florida (1928) (see HURRICANES)
  ˙ Kansas (1951)
  ˙ Mississippi River (1874)
  ˙ Mississippi River (1890)
  ˙ Mississippi River (1912)
  ˙ Mississippi River (1927)
  ˙ Mississippi River (1973)
  ˙ Ohio (and Indiana and Illinois)
    (1913)
  ˙ Ohio (1937)
  ˙ Oregon (1903)
  ˙ Oregon (and Washington,
    California, Idaho and Nevada)
    (1964)
  Pennsylvania

  ˙ Johnstown (1889)
  South Atlantic Coast (1893)
  South Dakota
  ˙ Rapid City (1972)
  Texas
  ˙ Galveston (1900) (see
    HURRICANES)
The World
  ˙ (2400 B.C.) (The Great
    Deluge of the Book of
    Genesis)
Yugoslavia (and Romania)
  (1970)

CHRONOLOGY

˙ ˙ ˙ ˙ ˙ ˙ ˙ ˙

˙ Detailed in text
2400 B.C.
  ˙ The World (The Great Deluge
    of the Book of Genesis)
1760 B.C.
  Attica, Greece (The "Second
    Deluge")
1504 B.C.
  Deucalion, Greece (The "Third
    Deluge")
A.D. 48
  England
353
  Cheshire, England
758
  Glasgow, Scotland
1099
  England
1161
  Sicily
1208
  France
1219
  Norway
1228
  Friesland, Holland
1287
  Salandria
1421
  April 17
  ˙ Dort, Holland
1530
  November 1

  ˙ Holland
1570
  November 1
  ˙ Holland
1574
  October 1–2
  ˙ Leyden, Holland
1617
  Catalonia, Spain
1642
  Kaifong, China
1646
  Friesland, Holland
1717
  Zealand, Denmark
1787
  Punjab, India
1813
  Poland
1824
  November 19
  ˙ St. Petersburg,
    Russia
1829
  July
  ˙ Inverness, Scotland
1851
  China
1864
  October 5
  India
1874
  April

  ˙ Mississippi River
1876
  Bengal, India
1883
  August 26
  Java (and Sumatra) (see
    VOLCANIC ERUPTIONS,
    Krakatoa)
1887
  ˙ China
1889
  May 31
  ˙ Johnstown, Pennsylvania
1890
  January–April
  ˙ Mississippi River
1891
  June 20
  Consuegra, Spain
1893
  August
  United States, South Atlantic
    Coast
1896
  ˙ Japan
1900
  August
  ˙ Galveston, Texas (see
    HURRICANES)
1903
  June 14
  ˙ Oregon
1906

Hong Kong,
China
1908
April 14
Hankow, China
1911
September
* China
1912
April
* Mississippi River
1913
March 25
Ohio (and Indiana and Illinois)
1915
June 12
Canton, China
1916
January 14
Holland
1926
August 4
Hupeh, China
1927
April
* Mississippi River
1928
March 13
* California
September 10
Florida (see HURRICANES)
1931
August
China
1932
August 3
Harbin, Manchuria
1933
September 1
Senchow, China
1935
July 4
* Hankow, China
October 22
* Haiti
1937
January
* Ohio
1938
June 11
Kweichow, China
1939
China (see FAMINES AND
DROUGHTS)
1941
December 14

Huaraz, Peru
1942
September 28
Eastern Shensi Province,
China
1943
August 4
Rajputana, India
1946
May 12
Turkey
1947
September 17
Tokyo, Japan
September 29
Lahore, India
1948
July 6
Foochow, China
August 7
* Fukien Province, China
1949
July 17
China
October 14
Guatemala
1950
August
* China
1951
July 12–31
* Kansas
November
* Po Valley, Italy
1952
August 15
* Lynmouth, England
1953
February 1
* Holland
June 27
Kyushi, Japan
1954
August
* China
August 10
* Shigatse, Tibet
September 17
* Farahzad, Iran
1955
August 19
* Putnam, Connecticut
1957
July 21
Shantung Province, China
1959

September 18
Surat, India
December 3
* Frejus, France
1961
October 9
Bihar, India
1962
February 17
* North Sea Coast, Germany
September 26
* Barcelona, Sabadell, Tarrasa,
Spain
1963
October 9
* Belluno, Pirago, Villanova, and
Rivalta Italy (see AVALANCHES
AND LANDSLIDES)
1964
July 18–19
* Japan
December
* Oregon
1965
June 16–26
* Colorado (and Montana,
Kansas, Wyoming and New
Mexico)
1966
November 4–6
* Florence, Italy
1967
November 26
Lisbon, Portugal
1968
August 7–14
* Gujaret, India
1969
September–October
* Tunisia
1970
June 1
Yugoslavia (and Romania)
July 22
Himalayas, Tibet
September
Gujaret, India
November 12
* Bangladesh (see CYCLONES)
November 12
Colombia
1971
January 31
Quelimane, Mozambique
August 30
North Vietnam

1972
  March 13
      Bangladesh
  June 9
    · Rapid City, South Dakota
  July 17
    · Japan
  August 12
      Punjab, Pakistan
  August 19
    · South Korea
1973
  April–May
    · Mississippi River
1974
  March 24
    · Tubarao, Brazil

  July–August
    · Bangladesh
1976
  July 31
    · Colorado
1978
  September
    · Bengal, India
1979
  July 17
      Lomblem Islands,
      Indonesia
  August 9
    · Morvi, India
1981
  July
    · Sichuan Province, China

1982
  May
    · Kwangtung, China
  September 17
      El Salvador
1985
  July
      Bangladesh
  July 19
    · Stava, Italy
1988
  August 4–5
    · Khartoum, Sudan
  September–November
    · Bangladesh
  November
    · Thailand

· · · · ·

FLOODS

· · · · ·

At first glance, the causes of floods seem easy to discover and simple to define: melting snow, frequent storms, heavy rainfall.

But these obvious factors form only a small part of the story. This single most catastrophic natural disaster known to humankind—one study found that between the years 1947 and 1967, 173,170 persons died as a direct result of riverine floods, whereas the grand total of 18 other categories of catastrophe, including hurricanes, tornadoes, earthquakes and volcanoes, came to just 269,635— springs from a multiplicity of subtle, complex factors.

One of these is inevitability, manifested in time, tides, and the hydrologic cycle—an endless, natural circle of stabilization, in which water passes from the oceans into the atmosphere, onto the lands, through and under the lands, and back to the oceans. As certainly as the moon will rise and set, rivers will rise and fall. And as certainly as the seasons change, the hydrologic cycle will continue. For 3 billion years, the total amount of water on the Earth and in its atmosphere has been almost exactly the same. And if it has remained this way for 3 billion years, it is fairly safe to say that it will probably stay that way for the next 3 billion years—unless, in our reckless disregard for the world's ecosystems, we upset that balance as we have in other natural phenomena.

This water balance and its cycle is achieved by a combination of the sun's heat and the pull of gravity, both of which constantly recycle moisture, which evaporates and enters the air as vapor, then condenses and falls back to Earth as rain or snow. Thus, though it may boggle the mind, it is entirely possible that the glass of water you drink today could very well have been Cleopatra's bathwater. Or, if that image is a little distasteful, consider that the water in your swimming pool could very well have fallen as snow on Hannibal's troops.

There is also an interesting and perhaps controversial side to the scientific theory of the hydro-logic cycle, and that is that if all of the water in the atmosphere at any given time were suddenly to be loosed upon the Earth, it would cover the planet to a depth of only a fraction of an inch. Believe this—as most scientists do—and the great deluge of biblical times, which must have been thousands of feet deep, and for which there is much archaeological and historical evidence (see p. 135) could not have occurred.

Naturally, the hydrologic cycle does not manifest itself regularly in one place. If it did, there would be neither deluge nor drought. It constantly shifts, from time to time and place to place, taking from here and overfeeding elsewhere.

Thus a logical inference to draw from this is the constant warning that if you live near a river or a sea, sooner or later, you're liable to experience a flood.

Why, then, do humans build some of their finest cities near rivers? The answer is twofold: commerce and food. Since Mesopotamia, rivers have been arteries of commerce. Even Barotseland tribesmen in the northwestern floodplains of Zambia float goods on the Zambesi, and when the flood season arrives, they simply move to higher ground and wait it out.

As far as food is concerned, humankind learned early that alluvial soils (soils deposited by moving water) were the richest for growing crops. According to one estimate, as many as 1.5 billion people, or one-third of the world's population, still depend upon alluvial soils for food. Small wonder, then, that cities, towns, villages and farms are commonly located on the floodplains of rivers, or on the seashore. In the U.S. alone, nearly 3,800 settlements, each one of them containing 2,500 people or more, are located in spots that are prone to flooding.

What is worse, the farming and construction methods employed in these locations often contribute to flooding. Vegetation captures precipitation, often before it hits the ground, and returns it to the atmosphere. Denuding the landscape by grazing, tilling, building, or the feckless felling of trees removes that process.

Certain soil characteristics also contribute to flood potential. If the ground is coarse and composed of sand or gravel, rain water is absorbed quickly. But if the ground is fine, composed of clay, for instance, less water gets through, and runoff is inevitable. Sooner or later, of course, no matter what the character of the soil, the water level above subterranean, less permeable rock—known as the water table—will be reached, and will back up to the surface, also causing runoff.

Not surprisingly, the most resistant surface is caused by human construction. The present, wholesale concretizing of the landscape allows for no absorption, and so cities create their own threats of flood through runoff.

This man-made flood potential has forced humankind to invent methods to divert and/or contain waters swollen by precipitation, tidal waves, tsunami or melting snow. These include dikes, diversions and dams. But none of these have been effective against a major catastrophe. In fact, flash floods and bursting dams are the most calamitous of all flood disasters, because they are unpredictable, and because those who live in the path of potential danger frequently develop a tragically false sense of limitless security.

But there is simply no defense against unleashed water. A gallon of it weighs about 8.5 pounds; a cubic foot of it weighs approximately 62 pounds; and a bathtub-full—one cubic yard—weighs approximately three-quarters of a ton.

Now, try to contain an astronomically large amount of this heavy substance behind concrete or earthern walls, and you get a rough idea of the pressures that dams and dikes must withstand. The reservoirs of dams impound colossal amounts of water. Lake Mead, behind Hoover Dam on the Colorado River, is 115 miles long, and has a capacity of 1.4 trillion cubic feet of water, or 10.5 trillion gallons, or, as scientists measure it in acre feet (one acre foot is the equivalent of one acre of land covered by water to a depth of one foot), 32 million acre feet.

All well and good if the dam holds. But consider the other characteristic of water besides its volume and its weight: its force. An inch of rainfall descending 1,000 feet and draining one square mile has the energy potential of 60,000 tons of TNT, or three times the force of the Hiroshima nuclear bomb. Once this energy enters a stream or a conduit, it concentrates itself into a battering ram that can destroy stone buildings and bridges and lift tons of debris and fling them around like discarded toys.

The velocity of a river is largely determined by gravity. The greater the volume of water and the steeper the grade, the faster it goes—within certain limits. The friction caused by the combination of the Earth's surface beneath, the air above and even within the water itself usually keeps it at a maximum of around 20 mph. Still, given all of those factors, the potential for disaster is staggering.

So, compound this with the natural forces of extreme rainfall, seasonal storms, the natural inclination of the hydrologic cycle to concentrate itself in selective areas, and other human factors, and you have the makings of a cataclysmic flood. And why, if all of this is known, is the casualty rate from floods so sorrowfully high?

Perhaps it is because human beings make compromises, with life, and with nature. Like our perception of death, we feel that maybe it might not happen to us. And the price of these compromises and illusions is often measured in the casualties caused by floods.

• • • • • • • • • • • • • •

BANGLADESH

1970

• • • • • • • • • • • • •

(See CYCLONES)

BANGLADESH

July–August 1974

• • • • • • • • • • • • •

Over 2,000 died, more than a million were injured and millions were made homeless by a monsoon-created flood that covered Bangladesh throughout July and August of 1974.

Bangladesh, the world's most densely populated country and one of the world's 10 most heavily populated countries, is, in terms of natural disasters, an accident waiting to happen. And, sadly enough, that accident occurs practically every year. Every year, the monsoon rains come, and every year, the land, which is, at its highest point, a mere 300 feet above sea level, is flooded, killing anywhere from scores to thousands, rendering millions homeless, causing crop loss and disease and starvation.

Both the Ganges and the Brahmaputra Rivers empty into Bangladesh, and even in normal times, the country is composed almost entirely of tiny islands surrounded by rivers, canals and other waterways. This allows for easy irrigation, and the alluvial soil is rich enough to support abundant harvests of rice, cashews and spices, upon which—along with textiles and paper products—the country's economy is based.

In the past, this natural state of affairs was controllable. But in recent years, the snows have increased in the Himalayas, where the two rivers originate, and the deforestation of Nepal continues. And so, as the inevitable monsoons return, the richness of the soil is depleted, as, year after year, the crops are washed away by floodwaters, composed of melting snow, mudslides and monsoon rains.

The monsoons were unusually severe in July 1974—more so, residents noted, than in 20 years. Seven of the 20 states of India were affected by serious flooding. By the beginning of August, the floodwaters had reached Bangladesh, and the delta region of that country, already soaked by monsoon rains, disappeared under water. By the middle of August, two-thirds of the country was flooded, and 80 percent of the annual summer crop was destroyed, along with the seedlings planted for the main winter crop. Officials estimated that at least 40 percent of the annual food output of 12 million tons was lost in the floods.

But these statistics pale in contrast to the human suffering, borne stoically by the inhabitants of hundreds of villages that were completely inundated with such regularity that the more farsighted families had built bamboo living platforms in nearby trees.

Cut off from the rest of the world, their food supply under water, those who did not drown in August 1974 frequently succumbed to starvation or disease. In total, more than 2,000 died, more than a million were injured and millions were made homeless.

In the village of Sunamganj, 160 miles northeast of the capital city of Dacca, a 45-year-old farmer, Mohammed Ahmadullah, spoke in despair to a reporter for the *New York Times*. His village of 4,000 remained under water for over a month, while its inhabitants huddled either on their tree perches or in the local school building. The cattle they owned were left standing in four feet of water, where they died, one by one.

"We can eat their flesh but we cannot cook," Mr. Ahmadullah told the Western reporter. "We have no fuel. Our stock of rice is exhausted. We have eaten the seeds meant for the next crop."

Their resistance to infection lowered by starvation, the people of Bangladesh then became victims of typhoid and cholera, spread by the stagnation and pollution of the sewage systems. In the 2,000 relief camps established by the government and the U.N. relief organizations, the death toll from these two diseases reached 100 a day in the month of August. By October, 15 million starving citizens of this stricken country were without homes, food and jobs. Thirty-five million had been affected by the disaster.

The World Health Organization established a headquarters in Dacca to combat the cholera epidemic that established itself in September, and the government of Bangladesh appealed to the rest of the world to help them through a period of starvation. Help came over the next few months, but it came slowly, and people continued to starve to death through the winter of 1974–1975.

BANGLADESH

September–November 1988

● ● ● ● ● ● ● ● ● ● ● ● ● ● ●

Indiscriminate deforestation in the Himalayas was the major cause of the devastating flood in Bangladesh at the end of 1988. Independent estimates reported 5,000 dead; official figures placed the death toll at 2,100. Three-quarters of Bangladesh disappeared under water, and half of its people were rendered homeless.

Deemed "man-made" by Tom Elhaut, director for projects in Bangladesh for the International Fund for Agricultural Development, the horrendous floods that engulfed three-quarters of that country from September through November of 1988 were also called by U.N. relief agency officials, "one of the worst natural disasters of the century."

Casualty figures varied according to the source. John Hammock, director of Oxfam America estimated that 5,000 died; Bangladesh's foreign minister, Hamayun Rasheed Choudhury, set the figure at 2,100. Both reported that three-quarters of the country had disappeared under water, and half of its people were rendered homeless by overflowing rivers caused by heavy rains in June that were compounded by unusually severe monsoons in August, September and October.

Yearly monsoons are both a bane and a blessing to Bangladesh (see STORMS). They provide the natural flooding that sustains the rice crop which forms the staple of the diet of Bangladesh. But the man-made destruction of the Earth's ecosystem in the 20th century, accounted for the severity of this disaster, and caused Elhaut to look at the floods of 1987 (see STORMS: MONSOONS) and 1988 and admit, sadly, that "This phenomenon is bound to recur. These are the first two years of a sustained series of catastrophic floods."

The man-made causes of the 1988 flood took place in the Himalayas, upriver from Bangladesh. Indescriminate deforestation and soil erosion in the Himalayas removed natural barriers to the monsoon rains, and dikes built to shield development projects only exacerbated the problem. The Nepalese forests were subjected to the same wanton and wholesale destruction as the rain forests of the Amazon. A population increase in Nepal heightened the demand for wood faster than the trees could be replaced and growing herds eroded the remaining grasslands. Thus, the flood-swollen rivers, carrying tons of silt, rushed annually into Bangladesh's rivers and streams, which in turn became clogged with silt and overflowed onto dry land. Downriver, the water finally drained into the Bay of Bengal in India, which created barrages to slow the rivers long enough for the silt to drop to the bottom before it flowed into Calcutta Harbor. But this construction also caused the rivers to back up into Bangladesh, thus exacerbating the floods.

Added to this was the difficulty of achieving regional cooperation among Bangladesh, India, Nepal, Bhuttan, Tibet and China, because of India's reluctance to share power with China in the region. It was an international recipe for disaster.

This fear was voiced by Thomas Drahman, the Asia regional manager for CARE, after surveying the area by helicopter: "I hate to sound hyperbolic, but this could be one of the largest natural disasters of the century."

To those villagers huddled on tin rooftops or in trees, fighting off poisonous snakes who climbed into the same trees for shelter, it must have been that, and more. In the village of Nichkasia, in the Bhola district, 550 drowned, and the rest went without food for days. An 11-year-old girl named Fajilatunnesa told *New York Times* reporters that she had survived for four days on a small package of biscuits.

No deaths were attributed to starvation because of the country's extensive stores of food, collected for just such purposes, but thousands were made homeless and thousands more died of disease. In Bhola alone, 70,000 people were rendered homeless. An estimated 3 million people in the entire country contracted diarrhea or dysentery.

More than 85 percent of the population of the country was thrown out of work as a result of the floods, and its economic activity was brought to a virtual standstill because of destroyed factories and equipment. Most of the livestock and crops were totally destroyed.

Ironically, the contemporaneous Hurricane Gilbert in Jamaica occupied the attention of many of the relief agencies of the world, thus reducing aid and attention to Bangladesh. The U.S. sent $125 million to Jamaica for hurricane relief and only $3.6 million to Bangladesh. It fell to Japan to be the greatest donor, sending $13 million and rescue workers to the stricken region, where they joined private and U.N. relief agencies in the nearly hopeless task of rebuilding and rehabilitation.

BRAZIL
TUBARAO
March 24, 1974

• • • • • • • • • • • • • • •

Two hundred people drowned and over 100,000 were made homeless when the rain-swollen Tubarao River overflowed its banks and spilled into the city of Tubarao, Brazil on March 24, 1974.

Tubarao is a city of 65,000 nestled in one of the final curves of Brazil's Tubarao River before it snakes into the Atlantic Ocean. Under ordinary circumstances, the river flows peacefully past Tubarao towards the river's nearby outlet.

In March 1974, torrential downpours swelled the river and accelerated its flow. Days and nights of rain caused streams and rivers to begin to overflow all over Brazil, and on March 24, at high tide, the swollen Tubarao River, flowed over its banks. Once freed of its customary path, the river's water became a juggernaut, smashing houses flat in the suburb of Sao Joao—50 people were crushed to death in one house near the flooded river bank. Within moments, every street in Tubarao was flooded, and buildings disappeared up to their first stories. Two hundred people drowned, and more than 100,000 fled to higher ground.

The surrounding countryside was wrecked. Over 8,000 head of cattle drowned, and growing crops of rice, potatoes, corn and cassava were washed from the earth. The final damage to property would total $250 million.

CHINA
1887

• • • • • • • • • • • • • • •

Depending upon the record-keeping source, between 1.5 million and 7 million people perished, and over 2,000 towns, villages and cities were inundated and destroyed when the Yellow River overflowed its banks in China's northern provinces in late spring of 1887.

The worst flood disaster in modern recorded history, which claimed somewhere between 1.5 million and 7 million lives, occurred in the spring of 1887 in the northern provinces bordering upon China's Yellow River.

Beginning in 2297 B.C., when the first flood was recorded by Chinese historians, the Yellow River (or Huang Ho), a 3,000-mile-long carrier of the silt which gives it its proper name, has consistently, in the rainy summer season, raged over its banks, causing floods and famines and earning it its second name, "China's Sorrow."

On the other hand, China's agricultural plain gained its richness from the Yellow River. In fact, the great North China Plain, which extends over much of Honen, Hopeh and Shan-tung provinces, was formed alluvially over many millenia from the waters of the Yellow River. This is China's agricultural heartland, producing the corn, kaolin, winter wheat, vegetables and cotton that form the basis of its economy.

The river has its origins in the Kunlun mountains of Northwest Tsinghai Province. From here, it flows generally east through a series of gorges to the fertile Lan-chou valley. Here, it develops into a slow-moving stream as it flows around the "great northern bend" that skirts the huge Ordos desert. The west end of this bend passes through the heavily populated oasis of the Ningshia agricultural district, a source of cereals and fruits. At the northwest corner of the bend, it divides into small fingers of tributaries which were helped by ancient constructions to form natural irrigation sources. At the northeast corner, more fertile fields, farmed without irrigation until 1929, receive the Yellow River's largess of moisture.

From here, the Yellow River plunges south, through the loess region, where it picks up most of the yellow silt that has earned it its name. As the river picks up speed and power and bridges the Great Wall, it turns east, through the San-men gorge and onto the Great Delta it has formed at its mouth and which is constantly meandering towards the Po Hai, a portion of the Yellow Sea.

During the winter, the Yellow River shrinks to a trickle, barely visible from the banks it nurtures; in the spring it overflows its banks and has caused major floods more than 1,500 times since 2297 B.C. The spring of 1887 was the worst instance.

Heavy rains throughout the entire province of Honan had swollen the river that spring, and the first incursion occurred at a sharp bend near the town of Cheng Chou. Generations ago, the town had erected a protective wall, and the population attempted to shore it up against the torrent that battered it. The wall failed, and within seconds, both populace and town were engulfed by 20 feet of swirling water.

Day after day, the surging river waters slammed into towns, inundating or washing them away—a total of 600 located near its banks, including the walled city of Chungmow. It continued to consume crops, animals, towns and people in a 40-mile-wide swath, with floodwaters that reached 50 feet in depth.

By late November, eyewitness reports had started to filter through to the English-language *North China Herald.* "Every night," a correspondent in Anhwei Province related, "the sound of the winds and waters, and the weeping and crying, and cries for help, make a scene of unspeakable and cruel distress. It is slow work going from terrace to terrace against often both wind and tide; on these terraces from a dozen to 100 families were often congregated. Of houses, not more than one or two in 10 are left with walls in ruins and half under water. Men rest on tops of these houses, and those of the old who do not die of hunger, do of cold."

Straw ricks became rafts that refugees clung to, ". . . which," the correspondent continued, "in a high wind are driven along the water, each with its weeping load of men and women. The tops of poplars which lined the roads now float like weeds on the water, but here and there an old tree with thick strong branches has strong men clinging to it crying for help. In one place a dead child floated to shore on the top of a chest where it had been placed for safety by its parents, with food and name attached. In another place a family, all dead, were found with the child placed on the highest spot . . . well covered with cloths."

A missionary later told *Goldthwaite's Geographical Magazine:*

In Cho-chia-kow itself fifty streets are swept away, leaving only three business streets, on the north side, which are all flooded. The west and south parts of the city are on opposite sides of the stream. The whole area is one raging sea, ten to thirty feet deep, where there was, only a month ago, a densely populated, rich plain. The newly gathered crops, houses and trees, are all swept away, involving a fearful loss of life and complete destruction of next year's harvest. The river is all coming this way now, and a racing, mad river it is. The mass of the people is still being increased by continual arrivals, even more wretched than the last. There they sit, stunned, hungry, stupid and dejected, without a rag to wear or a morsel of food.

The devastation left behind when the flood waters eventually receded was awful to behold, and the final statistics would never be accurately computed. By 1889, when the Yellow River was at last back to normal, pestilence added its afflictions to flood and famine, and an estimated half a million people died of cholera.

CHINA

September 1911

• • • • • • • • • • • • • • •

Over 200,000 died and a half million were made homeless when the Yangtze River flooded the Chinese provinces of Nganhwei, Ichang, Hupei and Hunan in September 1911.

Over 100,000 people died of drowning, another 100,000 perished from starvation and hundreds more were murdered by roving bands of starving marauders when China's Yangtze River burst its banks in September 1911.

The so called "water basin" of the 700-square-mile area that includes the provinces of Nganhwei, Ichang, Hupei and Hunan and the city of Shanghai is a rich and lush area, housing 2 million people and feeding much of the surrounding area. It was turned into an inland sea by the floodwaters of the Yangtze in 1911. Nothing survived—no crops, no cattle and very few human beings.

Typical of the devastation was the condition of the city of Suchow, situated on the Grand Canal near Tai Lake. This proud population center of over 1,000,000 was noted for the exquisite silks its artisans and mills produced for royalty and wealthy Westerners. In September, the floodwaters of the Yangtze, swollen by repeated rains, funneled through the canal, completely submerged the town within the first hour of the flood. Thousands were drowned instantly; others fled to the drier countryside. As days passed and the floodwaters failed to recede, robber bands formed, and one of these bands from Suchow sacked the American Baptist Chapel near Quisan, murdering the missionaries and leaving the chapel a scarred wreck.

Other Western missionaries wrote home of the macabre sight of thousands of wooden coffins floating down the Yangtze, as one of the largest cemeteries in the district was flooded.

Ultimately, over a half million refugees from countryside and city alike fled to Manchuria and Mongolia, never to return.

CHINA

1939

• • • • • • • • • • • • • •

(See FAMINES AND DROUGHTS.)

CHINA

August 1950

• • • • • • • • • • • • • •

Official figures record that 489 persons drowned and 10 million were made homeless by flooding from the Hwai and Yangtze rivers in eastern China in August 1950.

The Communist government of China refused to release final statistics on the flood caused when the Hwai and Yangtze rivers overflowed their banks in August 1950, inundating much of the provinces of Anhwei, Kiangow, Honan, Hopei, Hupei, Hunan, Kiangsi and Kwangtung.

What is known is that the hardest hit province was Anhwei, a low-lying section of eastern China that has traditionally suffered enormous losses of life and property from flooding. The government admitted to the death by drowning of 489 persons, but Western observers concluded that this was a gross underestimate.

Official figures were a little more accurate regarding property damage. More than 890,000 dwellings were destroyed, leaving 10 million people homeless; 5 million acres of cultivated land were left under flood waters for a long period of time, rendering 3.5 million acres of it untillable and unworkable for the entire planting season.

In terms of effect upon the food supply and material devastation, the flood of 1950 must emerge as a major catastrophe.

CHINA

August 1954

• • • • • • • • • • • • • •

Over 40,000 drowned and over 1 million were made homeless by floods caused by the overflowing of the Yangtze and Hwai rivers in China in August 1954.

Old records as well as ancient structures were swept away by the monumental flood of August 1954, caused by torrential rains and the overflow from the swollen Yangtze and Hwai rivers. Over 40,000 people drowned, hundreds of villages and towns disappeared, and the flood waters rose to a level of 96.06 feet.

According to Peking Radio, the "heaviest rainfall in a hundred years" preceded the flood. It was enough to swell the Yangtze, the sixth largest river in the world, into a raging torrent that ultimately burst its embankments, exploding into the rich rice fields of the Peking-Shanghai-Hankow triangle.

For millenia, this sunken valley had been ideal for rice growing but dangerous for settlers. Prior to the Communist takeover of China in 1948, the U.S. had attempted to reverse the flow of the river by proposing a TVA dam—it would have been the largest in the world—and a reservoir system.

Instead of the American plan, the leading Chinese Communist architect, a woman named Chien Chen-ying, designed, in the Soviet mold, a dam that was constructed completely on the surface of the soil. Three million workers completed this monumental but ultimately flawed structure. Like similarly constructed dams before it, the large dam crumbled like a sand castle against the advancing floodwaters.

At one break point in the dam, 200 soldiers and 10,000 peasants with mats strapped to their backs linked arms to form a human wall. For three hours, they remained shoulder to shoulder, while the floodwaters battered at this concrete and human barrier. Finally, the waters won, crumbling the wall and sweeping several thousand soldiers and peasants to their deaths. More than the dam crumbled that day; Mao Tse-tung's first Five Year Plan was also turned to ruin.

CHINA
FUKIEN PROVINCE

August 7, 1948

• • • • • • • • • • • • • • • •

More than 80 percent of the Chinese province of Fukien was destroyed, 1,000 drowned and 1 million were made homeless by a flood caused by the overflowing of the rain-swollen Min River on August 7, 1948.

Two solid months of torrential rains preceded the flood of August 7, 1948, which drowned 1,000 people, sent 1 million refugees onto the higher ground of the surrounding hills and destroyed more than 80 percent of the Chinese province of Fukien.

The Min River, Fukien's principal source of irrigation for its plentiful rice crop, is ordinarily a benign resource. But the cloudbursts of June and July of 1948 filled the river to overflowing, and on the night of August 7, squads of gong beaters shouting "Chiu ming! Chiu ming!" ("Save life!") preceded the floodwaters. Practically every shelter within a few miles of the river bank was destroyed, and for weeks, floating debris and bodies drifted with the currents in the Min.

A curious sidelight of this flood involved a political duel of words between the Communists and the Nationalists, both of whom were vying for the power that the Communists would claim within a year. The Communists, via Peking Radio blamed the Nationalists for the tragedy: "It is impossible to complete dike repair work because of constant Nationalist raids . . . . We request Nationalist troops and air forces to cease their obstruction."

Almost simultaneously, the Nationalists, through Nanking Radio were firing their salvos of accusation: "Since their occupation of this area, Communists have methodically destroyed dikes. With floods coming they are wildly firing accusations against the Central Government . . . . We hope they will show a sense of humanity and withdraw . . . ."

CHINA
KWANGTUNG

May 1982

• • • • • • • • • • • • • • •

Four hundred thirty people drowned and over 450,000 were rendered homeless when the North River flooded the Chinese province of Kwangtung in May 1982.

The populous province of Kwangtung, in the southeast of China was pelted with nearly 24 inches of rain in 13 hours early on May 12, 1982. As a direct result, the North River rose to its highest level since 1949, burying roads under six feet of water, inundating 286,000 acres of farmland and collapsing 46,000 homes. Forty bridges spanning the river collapsed under the rising floodwaters; dikes meant to contain the river were leveled. Before two days passed, Guingyuan and Yingde counties were entirely under water.

The floodwaters spread with alarming speed and force for several days, sweeping away more than 20 miles of the main rail line between Canton and Peking (or Beijing). Some travelers arriving in Hong Kong reported being stranded in trains for 30 hours as the waters rose and landslides blocked the tracks.

After the first five days, Chinese television began to show army units rescuing stranded peasants, some huddled on rooftops. Military aircraft dropped tons of biscuits, clothing and candles. Sailors, piloting landing craft and rubber dinghies, rescued others.

In all, over 100,000 troops were pressed into service to rescue the more than 450,000 marooned and displaced people. Less fortunate were the 430 who died in this tragic and unexpected disaster.

CHINA
HANKOW

July 4, 1935

• • • • • • • • • • • • • •

The Yellow River flood of July 4, 1935 killed 30,000 and rendered 5 million homeless in the North China Plain.

When the Yellow River burst its banks on July 4, 1935, it inundated 6,000 square miles of the North China Plain. Thirty thousand died, 5 million were left homeless and the damage was estimated at $300 million.

The flood was caused by torrential downpours that swelled the Yellow River until it broke through the levee in western Shantung province. In an alarmingly short amount of time, the breach extended until it measured 1.5 miles in length. River water poured through this breach at the rate of 3.79 million gallons per second, and all buildings and life, both animal and human, were swept before it.

While rescue attempts—most of them futile—were launched, an army of 35,000 peasants was organized to repair the levee. First, 15,000 of the workers constructed four dikes into the river a short distance above the break to deflect the tumultuous flow of the water.

Simultaneously, on the far bank, 20,000 more workers excavated a canal around the levee, the break and the main channel of the Yellow River. For two solid months, while the dead and the dying were collected, and medical facilities were readied for a possible plague, this work continued.

It took another month to rebuild the broken levee and reduce the gap to 130 feet. At this point, the canal on the opposite shore was opened, and the river, still swollen, was diverted to it. With pressure off the levee, workers dumped bales of kaolin stalks into the breach, added bags of earth and sand, and waited several days for the silting to close in minor leaks. At this point, the river returned to its normal flow, and the breached levees held. It was a method that worked well after the fact. But it did little to save lives.

In July 1981, a combination of natural overabundance and human foolishness combined to provide the Sichuan Province, China's most populous (100 million people) province, with one of the worst flood disasters of this century.

For three decades preceding the disaster, the province's watershed area, in the upper reaches of the Yangtze River, had been virtually swept clean of trees. This wholesale and wanton deforestation had allowed the water from normally heavy summer rains to fill the river's tributaries, building up force and sweeping tons of valuable topsoil downriver. This not only reduced the amount of land available for crops; it created a potential hazard, since the force of flooding water is increased many times by the addition of silt and soil.

Ironically, the reason for this denuding of the landscape was agricultural reform. Under the edicts of Mao Tse-tung, farmers were authorized to strip the land of trees in order to plant wheat and corn, and to plow up grasslands in the north that had held back the deserts.

The resultant ecological chaos came to a head in early July 1981, when the Yangtze River, swollen from a three-day rain, overflowed its banks. Within hours, bridges, roads and over 400,000 structures were leveled or swept before the raging floodwaters. The highest tide of the century swept unchecked through the Yangtze gorges and then, in an 18-foot-high wave, smashed against the pride of China, the $2.2 million Gezhou Dam.

The dam held, but this did little for the land upstream of it, which contained Sichuan's two largest cities, Chengdu and Chongquing. Backwaters swept the record-breaking tide even higher, and more and more land disappeared under water.

Two hundred thousand workers were formed into an army that shored up dikes along the riverfront, hauling huge rocks with their bare hands or on shoulder poles.

The effort tamed the torrents and saved millions of lives particularly in Hubei Province. But when the waters finally receded, the death toll would still be appalling: 753 were dead, 558 were missing, 28,140 were injured and 1.5 million were made homeless.

CHINA
SICHUAN PROVINCE

July 1981

• • • • • • • • • • • • • •

Ecologically unsound practices produced the flood in China's Sichuan Province in July 1981. Seven hundred fifty-three drowned, 28,140 were missing and 1.5 million were made homeless.

ENGLAND
LYNMOUTH

August 15, 1952

• • • • • • • • • • • • • •

A flash flood totally destroyed the town of Lynmouth, England on August 15, 1952. Thirty-four people died; the remaining 1,200 residents were made homeless.

The quaint seaside town of Lynmouth derives its name from an old Anglo-Saxon term meaning "the town on the torrent." For centuries it contradicted its name, and with its cobbled streets and thatched houses and benign climate served as a haven for such 19th-century poets as Percy Bysshe Shelley, and, later, as a seaside resort for vacationing Londoners.

The flood that destroyed the village in August 1952 was of the flash variety, caused by torrentially intense and sustained rains, which swelled the West and East Lyn rivers in north Devon. Lynmouth itself sits in a narrow Y-shaped valley at the confluence of the two rivers. Originating in 39 square miles of the Chains of Exmoor, which is a heather-coated plain, the two normally placid and stream-like rivers funnel through gorges punctuated by oak forests and plunge some 1,500 feet in four miles before joining together for a short, final fall to the sea.

For the entire first two weeks of August 1952, rain fell intermittently and heavily over the entire area. August 15, a Friday, was a particularly dismal day. Three inches of rain had fallen, and by evening, the East and West Lyns were swollen and roiling.

At dinner time, the rain stopped, but only momentarily. From 6:30 until 11:30 P.M., over six inches of rain fell on Lynmouth.

At 7:30 P.M., a canal carrying water to Lynmouth's hydroelectric station roared over its banks, crashing into the generators, and the plant went dead. A backup emergency diesel system was brought on line, but by 9 P.M. this too shut down, leaving Lynmouth in darkness, which made the invasion of the debris-laden flood all that more terrifying.

By 9:30, the flood waters had roared down the gorges above Lynmouth and had begun to take down trees and brick walls of homes that had heretofore rested a comfortable 30 feet above the ordinary flow of the twin rivers. Thomas Floyd noticed the garden wall of his property starting to crumble. Before he could get back to his home to warn his family, the floodwaters roared into his yard. He managed to seize a piece of brickwork that withstood the flood; the eight other members of his family, trapped in the house, drowned.

The next morning, as is often the case after a natural disaster, was brilliant and calm. Lynmouth had been demolished; 93 houses were either swept away or irreparably damaged, 132 vehicles were swept out to sea, and at least 34 people were dead. Those who survived did so through luck or fate. The 60 guests in the Lyndale Hotel, for instance, managed to scramble to safety on the upper floor of the hotel. The next morning, they were able to step out of their upperstory sanctuary directly onto a rocky flooring composed completely of huge boulders. Beyond the village, on the beach, the detritus of the flood was strewn for miles. Splintered lumber, broken telegraph poles, pretzelized steel girders, ruined automobiles and thousands of saplings that had been uprooted and peeled of their bark by the grinding action of the flood, lay everywhere. They would continue, in some fraction, to remain as reminders of the terrible dark night of August 15, 1952.

FRANCE
FREJUS
December 3, 1959

• • • • • • • • • • • • • • •

The collapse of the Malpasset Dam above the small town of Frejus, France caused the destruction of most of the village and the death of 419 residents on December 3, 1959.

Four hundred nineteen residents of the small town of Frejus, located near Cannes on the French Riviera, were swept to their deaths in a few terrible moments on the night of December 3, 1959.

For two years, the Malpasset Dam, a supposed miracle of modern engineering designed by world famous engineer Andre Coyne, had doled out water from a five-mile-long by two-and-a-half-mile Alpine lake, supplying water for a number of Riviera towns and irrigation for the Reyran valley, the major source of Europe's peaches. The dam, begun in 1952 and completed to much fanfare in 1957, had been accepted as a monumental example—much like the local Roman ruins of a gladiator's arena—of humankind's ability to build to last.

Not so. Without warning and with a thunderous roar, the dam gave way, splitting in half and unleashing a 15-foot-high juggernaut of water that roared downhill and into the sleeping village. Trees, bridges and buildings were ripped apart; livestock and human beings were tossed, doll-like, downstream. In a few moments it was all over. Most of the village was destroyed, except for one landmark, which remained unscathed: the Roman ruins.

GERMANY
NORTH SEA COAST
February 17, 1962

• • • • • • • • • • • • • • •

Germany's most serious flood of the 20th century occurred on February 17, 1962, when a storm-agitated North Sea breached seawalls and flooded most of the coastline. Three hundred forty-three people drowned; 500,000 were made homeless.

Three hundred forty-three residents of the North Sea Coast of Germany were drowned on February 17, 1962, when the waters of the sea, churned by a hurricane, breached seawalls and roared inland, swelling rivers and streams in an echo effect that exceeded the first inundations along the seacoast. Thousands of homes and buildings were swept from their foundations or collapsed by the flood waters, thus rendering 500,000 homeless. More than $6 million in damage was caused by this, the most serious flood along Germany's coast in modern times.

In the first few hours of the flood, the Elbe River rose to particularly extended heights, engulfing the city of Hamburg and killing 281, inundating a large part of the city of Bremen and isolating the island of Krautsand for days.

A distinctive quality of this flood was its suddenness and its longevity. Though the storm that was its origin blew itself out in hours, the flood continued for days, as its floodwaters pushed inland, decimating ancient breakwaters and buildings. In Schleswig-Holstein and Lower Saxony, rich agricultural land was rendered temporarily useless, as crops washed away and livestock drowned. With little opportunity for runoff, the fields were turned into marshes for weeks, and did not return to their true character for a multitude of months.

HAITI

October 22, 1935

• • • • • • • • • • • • • • • • •

Over 2,000 drowned in the floods caused on the island of Haiti by the so-called "hairpin hurricane" of October 22, 1935.

More than 2,000 people lost their lives to floodwaters spawned by a hurricane that swept across Haiti on October 22, 1935. (See HURRICANES, p. 181.) The "hairpin hurricane," so called because of the pattern of its path, hit Jamaica head on, pouring huge amounts of rain on the island in a very short time, swelling rivers and streams, and catching farmers unaware in their fields.

These workers formed the bulk of the casualties from floodwaters, and the plantations in which they worked suffered $2 million in economic damage. For days, livestock and human bodies floated on the increasingly stagnant waters that covered plantations like some murky inland sea.

HOLLAND

November 1, 1530

• • • • • • • • • • • • • • • • •

The North Sea, powered by gales, breached Holland's dikes on November 1, 1530, causing the most catastrophic flood in Holland's history. Four hundred thousand people drowned; entire villages disappeared.

Forty percent of the land area of Holland lies beneath sea level, and most of the country is actually land reclaimed from the sea. Bounded by the North Sea on the north and west, by Belgium on the south and by West Germany on the east, it is crossed by drainage canals, and the main rivers, the Scheldt, the Maas, Ijssel, Waal and lower Rhine are canalized and interconnected by artificial waterways that are linked with the river and canal systems of Belgium and West Germany.

The country has always been thickly populated, and, from its earliest recorded history, has served as a battleground for many of Europe's fiercest wars. In the 1500s, the so-called "low countries" were under the rule of the House of Hapsburg, represented on the throne by Charles V—who would, in the 1550s, give them to his son Philip II of Spain.

In 1530, Holland was a prosperous country, protected from the rest of Europe by the Hapsburgs and from the sea by a system of dikes. On November 1, 1530, after a furious gale which whipped the North Sea into a frenzy, the dikes gave way. With no high ground available for escape, 400,000 hapless people drowned. Hundreds of homes and entire villages were inundated and collapsed, and the property damage, in today's figures, amounted to the billions.

HOLLAND

November 1, 1570

• • • • • • • • • • • • • • • • •

Gale-driven waves from the North Sea breached Holland's northwestern dikes on November 1, 1570, drowning 50,000 people and destroying the northern provincial capital of Friesland.

Forty years to the day following the most destructive flood in Holland's history (see previous entry), its rebuilt dikes gave way once more under the assault of gale-driven waves from the North Sea.

For days before, these newer, stronger dikes were battered by heavy seas. Finally, at high tide on November 1, the dikes in the northwestern part of the country crumbled, once more cutting wide swaths of destruction throughout the countryside, wiping out dozens of villages and drowning more than 50,000 people. Friesland, the capital city of this northern province, was totally destroyed. Twenty thousand residents of the city perished in the first assault of the floodwaters.

At the time of the flood, Holland was at war with Spain, and the Spanish blamed the flood, which occurred on All Saints' Day, on the Calvinism of the Dutch, ". . . the vengeance of God upon the heresy of the land . . ." according to one account of the period.

HOLLAND

February 1, 1953

• • • • • • • • • • • • • • • •

Fifty of Holland's primary dikes melted away under the assault of the North Sea on February 1, 1953. One thousand eight hundred thirty-five people drowned; 72,000 were evacuated; 43,000 homes were either damaged or demolished.

A horrendous death toll of 1,835 followed the breaching of 50 of Holland's primary dikes in the pre-dawn hours of February 1, 1953. It was one of the worst floods in modern history and in all of Holland's history. Over 72,000 people were evacuated, 3,000 homes were totally destroyed and 40,000 were damaged in a tragedy that was intensified by a false sense of security.

Until then, the 10-foot dikes of Holland had held for nearly 400 years against enormous assaults. Thus, when hurricane winds of over 100 mph moved 15 billion cubic feet of water from the Atlantic Ocean into the North Sea and continued to drive high tides and waves at the dikes from January 29 through January 31, the Dutch felt no particular sense of alarm. But a few minutes before dawn on the next day, February 1, the combination of battering wind and increased water volume finally combined to crush 50 dikes simultaneously. Within minutes, 133 towns and villages were buried beneath the onrushing water. It took virtually no time at all for the flood waters to rise to the tops of town towers.

The populace, caught unaware, improvised survival procedures. Residents of Burghsluis, Stellendam, Ouddorp and Kortgene escaped the waters by climbing through upper windows and floating or swimming to the roofs of houses. Many of those who hesitated to pack bags or rescue valuables were drowned instantly. One man chose to stretch out on his dining room table. Water gushed into his home and turned the table into a raft. The next day, rescuers found him alive, floating just beneath the ceiling beams of his dining room.

In one of these villages, a couple who were to be married the next day used their bodies to hold an embankment together for 36 hours at the height of the punishing assault of rain and wind and water. The embankment held; the human beings who had morticed it did not. When rescuers reached them, she was dead, and he had gone mad.

In Kortgene, in a move that would be duplicated almost exactly a year later in China by Chinese soldiers and peasants (see FLOODS, China, August, 1954, p. 102), a hundred fishermen linked arms and pressed their backs against one crumbling dike. The town constable, strolled by, looked at them curiously, refusing to heed their cries to him to ring the alarm bell. His reasoning: the water at his feet was merely the overflow from a few high waves and the dike was impregnable. In the next few minutes he was proved wrong. The dike gave way and soldiers and constable barely escaped with their lives.

Elsewhere, terror rippled through villages awash with the floating carcasses of drowned people and livestock. When the waters receded, as they would in a few days, the stench was enormous and overwhelming. Over half a million acres were under salt water, 625 square miles of agricultural lands would be rendered temporarily useless. By the end of the first day, 12,000 soldiers of the Dutch Army and helicopters of the Royal Netherlands Air Force joined vessels of the Royal Netherlands Navy in rescuing clumps of survivors clinging to chimneys and bell towers.

Within a week, 25 of the world's nations had rallied to the support of a reeling Holland. Food, medical supplies and personnel, including battalions of engineers, super amphibious ships, helicopters and planes from the United States. Even England and Belgium, ravaged by the same storm sent rescue teams and money. The cleanup was swift and efficient; the price tag would run into the hundreds of millions.

HOLLAND
DORT

April 17, 1421

• • • • • • • • • • • • • • • •

The second worst flood in Holland's history, on April 17, 1421, was caused by heavy winds and prolonged rain. One hundred thousand people drowned and the city of Dort was leveled.

The second worst flood disaster in Holland's history (the worst was in 1530) [p. 106]; the third worst [see previous entry] was in 1953) took place in and around the city of Dort, in the southern part of Holland. A deluge that had lasted for days, whipped by strong winds, swelled both the North Sea and the Waal River that flowed from it and past Dort and the nearby city of Dordrecht.

On April 17, 1421, the dikes surrounding the city burst, and battering rams of water rushed onto the thickly populated countryside. Even in 1421, Holland contained an average of 500 people per square mile, and within a day, more than 100,000 drowned. The city of Dort was not merely inundated; it was totally destroyed. Seventy-two villages surrounding it were also obliterated, never to rise again. The city of Dordrecht, prior to this April flood a solid portion of the mainland of Holland, was permanently detached by the gushing waters of the Waal River. To this day, Dordrecht remains surrounded by water.

HOLLAND
LEYDEN

October 1–2, 1574

• • • • • • • • • • • • • •

The tide of war was turned, literally, when a storm-driven flood drowned 20,000 occupying Spanish troops near Leyden, Holland on October 1, 1574.

Holland was at war with Spain in October 1574, and things were going badly for William the Silent and the Dutch populace. The Spanish Duke of Alba, engaged in subjecting the Godless, Calvinist Netherlanders in the name of the Inquisition, had successfully surrounded the walled city of Leyden. While they were unable to storm the city because of the fierce determination of the inhabitants, who had chosen to fight to the last grain of powder, the Spanish were having some success in cutting off all supply lines, thus starving the city's defenders and inhabitants alike.

Starvation was and still remains a weapon of war (see FAMINES AND DROUGHTS), and, according to historian A. H. Godbey, the dwellers of the besieged city ". . . were digging up every green thing, devouring roots of grass, old leather, offal, anything that could in the least aid to sustain life . . . so long as a dog barked in the city the Spaniards might know they held out."

The situation was desperate indeed, and a miracle was clearly needed to save the absentee William the Silent and the defenders of Leyden. The miracle arrived, ironically, in the person of a natural disaster. A fierce storm struck the coast on the night of October 1, 1574, and North Sea waves crumbled dikes miles away from the encamped Spaniards. By October 2, the roaring floodwaters reached the Lowlands surrounding Leyden, and an estimated 20,000 Spanish troops drowned.

The tide literally turned that day, and, with the reinforcements of floodwaters firmly in place, the defenders of Leyden joyously declared the siege at an end.

INDIA
BENGAL (WEST)

September 1978

• • • • • • • • • • • • • •

Monsoon rains caused extensive river flooding in India's Bengal state during September, 1978. Thirteen hundred drowned and 15 million were made homeless.

In four months of torrential monsoon rains and repeated flooding, 1,300 people lost their lives, 15 million of Bengal's 44 million people were displaced, 26,687 head of cattle drowned, and 1.3 million dwellings were destroyed. The economic loss was put at $11.3 million. Unofficial estimates were two and sometimes three times that amount.

The cataclysmic flooding that took place in the summer and fall of 1978 in northern India and profoundly affected one in 18 Indians, began with the expected, annual monsoon rains. By September 5, rivers were regularly overflowing their banks in seven northern states, forcing hundreds of thousands to flee their inundated villages. Reports began to filter into New Delhi of survivors in West Bengal perched in housetops and in trees. In the Midapore district, west of Calcutta, the United News of India reported that the first patients of the inevitable cholera outbreak were being treated on the roof of the area hospital because the ground floor was under water.

By the next day, which was the Day of Id, the Muslim festival marking the end of a month of fasting, the monsoon-fed Yamuna River overflowed its sandbag dikes and flooded the low-lying suburbs of New Delhi. More than 200,000 residents were evacuated, but not all of them were saved. According to Lt. Governor D. R. Kholi, speaking to the Associated Press, at least 20 persons, including some women and children, drowned when an army boat rescuing flood victims capsized in the river.

Water overflowed New Delhi's main crematorium and flooded the nearby cremation site of the late Prime Minister Jawaharlal Nehru, which had become a national monument. Two thousand flood victims taken to a stadium north of New Delhi were forced to flee when water surrounded the building. Road and rail traffic to and from New Delhi was in chaos. Four main bridges across the Yamuna were closed, and the trunk road to the northwest was submerged in knee-deep water for 12 miles.

The flood waters traveled southward, rising to record levels and overrunning low-lying areas of Agra, the site of the Taj Mahal, the 17th-century tombs of Itimaduddaula, and the holy cities of Benares and Mathura. Workers toiled feverishly to protect the Taj Mahal by piling sandbags around it.

Southeast of the Taj Mahal, the Mathura region was swamped. The famed Dwaradhesh Temple, a landmark in what is considered to be one of the seven sacred Hindu cities, disappeared under the rising flood waters. Two-story houses in nearby Sudamapauri and Mathura's Masai railway station also vanished under the rising, silt-stained and disease-carrying floodwaters.

By mid-September, the waters peaked. The Taj Mahal was not damaged, and the Krishna Janma Bhoomi temple complex at Mathura, said to be the birthplace of Lord Krishna, the Hindu diety, was also spared, but thousands of pilgrims, housed in hostels nearby, were trapped in their quarters.

Slowly, the waters receded, as army units ranged over the countryside, delivering food and medical supplies. But toward the end of September, heavy rains again began to

fall near Calcutta, forcing the Ganges River to overflow its banks, trapping army troops and residents alike in seven districts in West Bengal. The city of Calcutta was under five feet of water, and in Durgapur, west of Calcutta, the power plant was flooded, plunging the city into a 48-hour period of absolute darkness.

Within a day, more than 20,000 persons were rescued from flood-lit districts. Nearly 300 villages in the already flood-ravaged district of Midnapore were again inundated.

By September 29, Calcutta was entirely cut off from the rest of India. Low-lying districts of the city were under 10 feet of water, and some 500 houses collapsed, while tens of thousands of Calcutta's pavement dwellers were forced to seek shelter in school buildings. Railway tracks leading out of Calcutta were entirely washed away and all of the major roads were under at least a foot of water.

But the worst was yet to come. For days, the 7 million residents of Calcutta would be without fresh food supplies. Gougers who had food raised their prices by 100 percent,

Improvised transportation is the only alternative for residents of a village in India's Bengal state during the monsoon flood of September 1978. CARE photo.

making the acquisition of life-sustaining staples by the poor absolutely impossible.

And then, in October, more rain fell, and more flooding hit western Bengal. Some areas received 21 inches of rain in three days, inundating some recently dried out villages for as much as three weeks. Fewer than 10 percent of the 30,000 mud-walled dwellings were left standing in the Midnapore district 30 miles west of Calcutta. "The disaster is so total that books on relief management never envisaged any natural disaster of this magnitude," said state spokesman Dr. Nitish Sangupta to the Associated Press.

With this new onslaught of floodwaters, food shortages increased dramatically. In some districts bands of refugees raided relief trucks, including some bearing CARE supplies. Armed police were pressed into service to accompany the relief caravan. Karen Kandeth, a relief worker, lamented, "It is the worst flood I've seen in this country and I've been with CARE for 17 years and I've seen a lot of floods."

It would be weeks before order and disease would be brought under control by Indian and World Relief Agencies, and months before the devastation would be cleared.

INDIA
GUJARET

August 7–14, 1968

• • • • • • • • • • • • • • •

Monsoon rains caused the Tapti River to flood Gujaret state in India on August 7, 1968. Over 2,000 people died, either from drowning or cholera.

Over 1,000 people were drowned when the Tapti River in the Indian state of Gujaret overflowed its banks on August 7, 1968. For a solid week, the monsoon-swollen river waters swirled across the countryside, inundating and uprooting crops, smashing farm structures, sweeping other, smaller ones ahead of it like so many bobbing corks.

The city of Surat was one of the first major population centers to feel the floodwaters. Within hours it was submerged under 10 feet of water, and remained that way for a full seven days.

But the aftereffects of this flood were, in many ways, far worse. In Gujaret and the neighboring state of Rajasthan, over 80,000 head of cattle drowned. The corpses of these cattle were considered sacred, and so rotted, untouched in the streets, and this, coupled with the widespread contamination of the drinking water throughout the state, ignited

a cholera epidemic which killed at least a thousand people.

INDIA
MORVI

August 9, 1979

• • • • • • • • • • • • • • •

The Machu Dam 2 near the city of Morvi, India burst on August 9, 1979, allowing the Machu River to flood the city. The official death toll was 1,000; the unofficial, 5,000. Seventeen thousand people were evacuated from the area.

A spectacular flash flood was unleashed on August 9, 1979, when a rain-weakened dam burst in Gujarat state, four miles above the city of Morvi, which is 300 miles northwest of Bombay.

Prior to the collapse of the Machu Dam 2, 25 inches of rain fell on the region in a 24-hour period, which is the usual amount for a whole year in this arid region of Saurashtra, bordering the Rann of Cutch. The Machu River, which the dam had heretofore comfortably contained, was turned into a raging monster. Even the dam's 52-foot height and its ability to withstand pressures of 200,000 cubic feet per second was not enough, and it burst with a gigantic roar, sending tons of water in a 20-foot-high wave crashing forward, sweeping dozens of villages into obliteration and smashing into the city of Morvi with its population of 60,000 unprepared citizens.

Fully 60 percent of the dwellings in the city were leveled in minutes. Mud, debris and water engulfed streets and buildings, suffocating and drowning thousands. (The official death toll would be placed at slightly more than 1,000. Unofficial sources claimed that it was nearer 5,000.)

Within minutes, the flood waters receded, leaving silt covered chaos behind. A blanket of mud, which was 19 feet high in some outlying areas of Morvi, reached well up into the second stories of buildings within the city. Roadways were littered with strewn bodies.

The city's central telephone exchange was crushed by the floodwaters; thus, word of the tragedy was slow in reaching the outside world, and relief teams were not dispatched until the following morning. High winds and a steady rain made these efforts even more difficult. Still, the army was able to evacuate 17,000 people within the first week following the disaster.

Local officials, faced with this sudden disaster, seemed unable to cope, and by the end of the week, a state investigation into the reasons for the fumbling first relief efforts was ordered. The findings would be inconclusive.

International relief agencies would soon appear; the army would recede as quickly as the flood waters had; and the state would grant relatives of each victim cash compensation equivalent to $125.

IRAN
FARAHZAD

September 17, 1954

• • • • • • • • • • • • • • •

A sudden storm washed a mountain shrine in Farahzad, Iran into a gorge on September 17, 1954. Two thousand pilgrims worshipping in the shrine were swept to their deaths.

In the middle of September 1954, several thousand Iranian pilgrims arrived in Farahzad, the location of a mountain shrine called Imam Zadeh David. The shrine clung to the side of a slope giving onto a gorge that plummeted thousands of feet to a valley floor. Next to it were dozens of cottages designed to house pilgrims to the shrine.

On the night of September 17, 1954, a torrential rainstorm hit the area, uprooting trees, unleashing mountain streams, sending torrents of water cascading down the mountainside. Three thousand pilgrims were worshipping in the shrine when it suddenly let go of the side of the mountain and plunged downward, taking the cottages with it. It fell to the bottom of the gorge, where it was rapidly blanketed by rain water, rivers and streams, which combined to flood the gorge. Over 2,000 pilgrims drowned within minutes; most of the bodies were carried miles downstream, where they remained, unrecovered, for days.

ITALY
BELLUNO, PIRAGO, VILLANOVA, AND RIVALTA

October 9, 1963

• • • • • • • • • • • • • • •

(See AVALANCHES AND LANDSLIDES, Italy, Belluno)

ITALY
FLORENCE

November 4–6, 1966

• • • • • • • • • • • • • • •

One hundred forty-nine people drowned, over 100,000 were trapped in their homes for days and millions of dollars worth of priceless art works were either destroyed or damaged when the River Arno overflowed its banks and flooded Florence, *Italy on November 4, 1966. A combination of heavy rains and human neglect—some of it centuries old—caused the flooding.*

In the 19th century, poet Elizabeth Barrett Browning called the River Arno where it flowed into Florence, "This crystal arrow in the gentle sunset."

On the rain-soaked morning of November 5, 1966, novelist Katherine Taylor, observing the Arno from the fortunate safety of her upper-story apartment, described it as ". . . a snarling brown torrent of terrific velocity, spiraling in whirlpools and countercurrents that send waves running backward."

For centuries, the Arno had been both of these and more, but on the night of November 4, 1966, it would once again prove that Florence is a city built in the wrong place. In a few hours, it would be transformed into a dung and mud heap. Thousands of priceless art treasures would be destroyed forever and thousands more damaged. One hundred fourteen people would drown in the surrounding countryside; 35 would perish in the city, and 500,000 tons of mud would be deposited within its environs—one ton for each man, woman and child living in Florence. Over 100,000 citizens of this Tuscan paradise would be trapped in their upper-story dwellings.

For over 900 years the Arno had overflowed its banks regularly and relentlessly. In the years between 1177 (the year of its first recorded flood) and 1761, the Arno crested its banks 54 times, with a major flood on the average of every 26 years and a severe, catastrophic flood every hundred years.

In 1545, Leonardo da Vinci drew up plans for an intricate set of dams, lakes and locks that would prevent further flooding. They were never utilized. In August 1547, Bernardo Segni recorded a huge flooding of the Arno, writing, ". . . because very great numbers of trees had been cut down for timber . . . the soil was more easily loosened by water and carried down to silt up the bottoms of the rivers. In these ways, man had contributed to the disaster. . . ." Late on the third of November, 1966, modern men compounded the unwise farming habits of their ancestors.

They had help from nature. The entire month of October 1966 was unrelievedly wet and gloomy. But the first two days of November were crisp and clear, and November 4th, the anniversary of the end of World War I in Italy and a national holiday was anticipated to be an auspicious and fair one. But a blinding downpour occurred on November 3. In fact, during the 48 hours of November 3 and 4, Florence and the Arno would receive 19 inches of precipitation, which was more than one-third of the area's average annual rainfall.

It seems, however, that the operators of the Penna hydroelectric dam some 29 miles above Florence were not paying attention during the deluge of the previous weeks, and did not release water from the dam in gradual, small doses. Rather, they let it go all at once, in a huge mass, which put an impossible strain the Levane hydroelectric dam four miles downstream. In turn, the operators here were faced with a disturbing decision: whether to open the gates and flood the valley. Signora Ida Raffaelli, who lived below the Levane dam, remembered for the world press later, "I was appalled to see the gates slowly opening, and immediately an enormous wall of water started coming down the Arno toward us. I screamed to my sister and we ran for our lives."

Well that they did, for the Arno roared on, straight for Florence. Between 9 P.M. and 11 P.M. on November 4, the river rose 18 feet in the city. Romildo Cesaroni, an elderly watchman was patroling the famed Ponte Vecchio to warn shopkeepers of any danger. By 11 P.M., the water was roaring by at 40 mph, a mere three feet below the bridge. Huge tree trunks were slamming into the bridge. Cesaroni began to telephone shopkeepers, who came running to reclaim their valuables.

By 3 A.M., the waters had engulfed the bridge, and floating automobiles were smashing into it, causing it to shudder and tug at its moorings, which had been dynamited by the Germans in World War II. But miraculously, the bridge held.

Now, the lower parts of the city began to disappear under water. Underground transformers started to short out. Furnaces exploded. The antiquated sewer system, built 300 years before, gave way under the tremendous force of the water backing into it, and human waste shot like a geyser out of manholes, blanketing the city with a horrendous stench. Fuel oil from the furnace rooms floated out on the water, coating walls and buildings.

The old part of the city, on the river bank, also housed the city's poorest residents, and many of them drowned that night in their apartments. In the Santa Teresa prison, the floodwaters climbed to 13 feet, and the prisoners were herded to the top floor, where they summarily overpowered their guards. Eighty of them then clambered to the roof, where, to the cheers of other stranded Florentines in their apartments, some of them tried to escape by leaping onto tree trunks and other debris that sped by. Not many were successful.

In another part of the city, at the Cascine Park race track, handlers frantically struggled to load 270 horses into vans to evacuate them ahead of the flood waters. They only managed 200; 70 horses drowned, and two days later, when the waters receded, their corpses were incinerated by rescuers with flame throwers to prevent the spread of disease.

At exactly 7:26 A.M., every electric clock in Florence stopped, and power was not restored for 24 hours. Outer bridges leading from the city were washed out, roads were blocked, railroad tracks were covered. Florentines were isolated from the world.

The worst destruction took place while the guardians of the richest collection in the world of Renaissance art were busy elsewhere. Slowly, this universal treasure was dissolved, torn apart or forever stained with the oil-laden waters. Before dawn, this destruction spread into the low-lying Piazza Santa Croce. In the ancient church of Santa Croce, the water climbed to a height of 20 feet, covering the tombs of Galileo, Michelangelo, Niccolo Machiavelli and Antonio Rossini. Donatello's relief of the Annunciation was smeared with the oil and sledge-stained water. Next door, in the church museum, the famous 15-foot painted Crucifix by Giovanni Cimabue, the father of western art, was completely destroyed as the waters continued to climb and consume it. At the baptistry in the Piazza del Duomo, five of Lorenzo Ghiberti's 10 monumental bronze panels of Old Testament scenes were ripped from the portals that Michelangelo had named the "Gates of Paradise." At the Institute and Museum of the History of Science, the director, Maria Luisa Righini-Bonelli, edged along an inches-wide third floor ledge 28 times, saving priceless precious objects, including several of Galileo's telescopes from the Uffizi Gallery. In the basement of the Biblioteca Nazionale Centrale, a million books and manuscripts were turned to pulp by the flood waters.

Meanwhile, elsewhere in the city, rescue efforts began. Newspaper editor Franco Nencini witnessed helicopters lifting stranded people from housetops. One old woman, clinging to a rescue rope from the helicopter, tired midway to safety, and dropped to her death in the roaring floodwaters.

At the hospital of San Giovanni di Dio, patients were carried to upper floors when the generators flooded and the elevators failed. The food supply was rapidly covered with oily water, and all that workers were able to salvage were 10 chickens and 20 bottles of mineral water, which provided sustenance for the entire hospital until emergency food could be brought.

All day, the rain continued, without a sign of letting up. Finally, at 6 P.M., a delegation from the national government in Rome arrived. *Nazione* editor Enrico Mattei, accompanying the group, described the scene:

Behind a curtain of driving rain, pierced here and there by dim, mysterious lights, the Piazza San Marco was a storm-tossed lake. This lake was fed by a violent torrent which poured down from the Piazza dell'Annunciata, lapped at the church and went swirling off down the Via Cavour in the direction of the Cathedral. Beneath the grim rumbling of the water, we could hear a subdued murmur of human voices.

The voices belonged to the survivors. Five thousand families would be left without a place to live; 6,000 of the 10,000 shops in the city would be destroyed.

Still, Florence belonged to the world, and the world responded almost immediately. The skies had scarcely cleared when the first contingents of rescue workers from 10 European countries, America and Brazil arrived. Sustaining gifts from England, Germany, Austria and the Soviet Union began to arrive. Scotland sent blankets, water pumps and vaccines. The U.S. dispatched food, clothing, generators and prefabricated houses. The Dutch sent engineers who brought water-decontamination equipment, and Israel provided a Christmas vacation on kibbutzim for more than 100 homeless children.

But the worst task, the cleanup, lay ahead. Students from the Florence branches of Stanford, Syracuse and Florida State universities plunged in immediately. Because they wore blue jeans, they were lovingly referred to by Florentines as "Blue Angels." For two weeks, the students formed human chains from the basements of the Biblioteca Nazionale, passing up water-logged manuscripts and books to upper floors, where they were carefully blotted with a special paper to absorb the moisture. From here, the books were loaded into U.S. Army trucks and sent to tobacco-drying kilns in central Italy, overseen by some of the planeloads of scholars and restoration experts who had arrived upon the scene from all over the world.

Ghiberti's priceless panels were discovered, buried in the muck. They were returned to their places on the Gates of Paradise. Michelangelo's statues, coated thickly with talcum, then scrubbed with powerful detergents, seemed hardly the worse for wear. Donatello's 500-year-old wooden sculpture of Mary Magdalene, restored with solvents and surgical lancers, seemed in better condition than it had been before the flood. But Cimabue's Crucifix was irreparable, as were invaluable frescoes.

More than half of the million books damaged in the flood have, as of this writing, been restored and rebound. More are continuing to be worked on, as are the frescoes, the paintings, the statuary. But, millions of lire later, projects designed to build more dams upriver on the Arno to put into practice some of Leonardo's plans have been shelved for lack of funds. And so, at any time, Florence may be—as it has for much of its history—flooded again.

ITALY
PO VALLEY

November 1951

• • • • • • • • • • • • • • • •

Over 100 drowned when dikes and canals were inundated in the Po Valley in November 1951. Crop loss was placed in the millions of lire.

From ancient times, the Po Valley has undergone constant and regular inundation, thus making it a rich source of agriculture. Grain, sugar beets, livestock and fruits feed not only the principal cities of Turin, Asti, Milan, Bresica and Verona, but much of the rest of Italy and parts of Europe. But it was not until the 1930s that attempts were made to control the floodwaters of the River Po and its tributaries, the Dora Baltea, Tanaro, Ticino, Adda and Oglio. An elaborate system of hydraulically controlled dikes and canals were installed, designed to drain off excess waters, refocus the tidal flow and protect the populace, livestock and crops of the valley.

And for 20 years and a World War, it held. But then, in November 1951, torrential rains fell on the valley for weeks. The force of the river, swollen by the unceasing downpours, fed into the tributaries faster and more vigorously than the hydraulic controls could handle. Dikes began to crumble, then dissolve completely. Levees were swept clean as floodwaters crested, then crashed through them.

Tens of thousands of people were trapped by the sudden and unexpected flooding. Over 100 people were drowned, 30,000 head of cattle were destroyed, and the damage to the valley's crops climbed into the millions of lire.

ITALY
STAVA

July 19, 1985

• • • • • • • • • • • • • • • •

The collapse of an earthen dam caused a flash flood in the resort of Stava, Italy on July 19, 1985 that killed 250 and injured nearly 1,000.

Stava is a small resort community in the Dolomite Alps, about 40 miles south of the Austrian border. Its unusual countryside, made up of pine forest and broad, green meadows, its Alpine houses overlooking winding, cobblestone streets that rise and fall along the hillsides and its spotless villages make it a favorite tourist attraction and vacation spot for Italians and Austrians.

July 1985 was the height of a particularly busy tourist season. The area's four hotels, the Erika, the Stava, the

Miramonti and the Dolomiti were filled; several civic groups had organized excursions, and children's camps were thickly populated in this particularly placid and sylvan part of the Flemme Valley.

About a half mile above Stava was an earthen dam, built to hold back two artificial lakes which were used to purify minerals from a nearby fluorite mine. Fluorite is used in glass-making, and the Prealpi Mining Company, which owned the dam, was one of Italy's most successful producers of this mineral.

Over the years, the earthen dam had built itself up, and large amounts of chemical sediment had accumulated on the bottom of the lakes, thus increasing the weight and pressure on the dam. Over the months preceding July 1985 trees had been cut in preparation for the expansion of the pools.

In the days before July 19, heavy rains fell.

At 12:20 P.M. on Friday, July 19, with a roar that sounded to one local resident like an earthquake, the dam gave way, and an immense white wall of water thundered toward the crowded resort. "I saw the end of the world," a survivor told reporters. "I saw a white wall coming toward me. I couldn't tell if it was fire or what."

The enormous wave, made more lethal by mud and debris, smashed into Stava, collapsing three of its four hotels, the Stava, the Erika and the Miramonti, and partially collapsing the fourth, the Dolomiti. Following the Stava River, the floodwaters roared into the nearby town of Tesero, damaging bungalows and a bridge over the Avisio River, which ultimately absorbed the rest of the wave of mud, houses, trees and bodies.

The floodwaters had ripped a brownish-gray swath two to three miles long through pastures and forests of the Flemme Valley. Trees were stripped and uprooted, houses were cut in two, and cars were upended and buried, their wheels sticking out of the mud.

Almost immediately, rescue workers began to dig through the overwhelming effulgence of mud and slime. Alma Bernard, a hotel owner in Tesero, said to reporters, "Many families were wiped out with their houses. Earth and mud covered [everything.]" Another survivor, identified only as Pietro, said he had seen his 48-year-old brother, Lucio, climb a tree to escape the mud-laden tidal wave. "But then a second wave carried him away," he added.

It was a grisly sight for rescuers manning bulldozers, rescue trucks and ambulances, or merely digging with anything that was at hand. One young soldier, doing his compulsory military service nearby and pressed into rescue duties, spoke of his horror at digging through the mud with a shovel and finding a child, its head crushed. Guiseppe Zamberletti, the Minister of Civil Protection, said, in a news conference to reporters, that in the case of 15 bodies, disfigurement was so severe that it was impossible even to determine the victims' sexes.

A rescue worker from Bolzano wept when asked for a description of his work. "I felt helpless," he said. "I knew that under that moving sand, there were so many people who were suffocating. And I could not do anything to save them."

However, there were hopeful stories, as well. Maria Assunta Cara, a Sardinian, was pulled alive from the wreckage of a hotel around dawn. She had been buried up to her mouth in mud for 18 hours.

For days, traffic jams of rescue vehicles clogged the mountain roads around Stava. Bodies were taken to a hospital in Cavalese, three miles southwest of Stava, and to a school in Tesero, which was converted into a morgue.

The countryside looked as if some indescriminate war had been waged back and forth across it. Commenting on the view from a helicopter, Zamberletti related, "The sites of the hotels and houses had to be pointed out to me. It's as if they never existed."

All in all, 250 people died and nearly a thousand were injured. It would be the worst tragedy from a collapsed dam since 1963, when a dam burst at Longarone, 35 miles away, and killed 1,800 (see AVALANCHES AND LANDSLIDES).

The Italian Parliament, acting upon multiple complaints and petitions, investigated criminal culpability and negligence on the part of the Prealpi Mining Company and local officials responsible for supervision of the dam. Because of a complex history and multiple responsibilities, coupled with inadequate proof of any single act of negligence, the charges were ultimately dropped.

JAPAN
1896

• • • • • • • • • • • • • • •

Twenty-seven thousand people drowned when a giant tsunami inundated the Japanese coastline on the Sea of Japan in 1896. No specific date is recorded.

Tsunamis (see EARTHQUAKES, Introduction) have worked particularly destructive havoc in the Sea of Japan. Entire villages have been obliterated or displaced by these gigantic, seismically-caused waves that appear without warning, create their havoc in minutes or seconds, and then disappear as suddenly and unceremoniously as they have appeared.

The second most catastrophic tsunami-caused flood in Japan occurred in 1896, 13 years after the horrendous explosion of Krakatoa, which created 100-foot waves that drowned more than 36,000 people. (See VOLCANIC ERUPTIONS AND NATURAL EXPLOSIONS, Krakatoa.)

This particular tsunami was the product of a gigantic undersea earthquake 700 miles from Japan's coastline. A series of tsunamis were set in motion by this earthquake; they rolled over the coast of Japan in rapid-fire progression, wiping out villages, changing the coastline and drowning 27,000 people. (See EARTHQUAKES, Japan, 1896.)

JAPAN

July 18–19, 1964

• • • • • • • • • • • • • •

A combination of an earthquake and heavy rains conspired to flood the coast of Japan bordering on the Sea of Japan on July 18, 1964. One hundred eight people died; 233 were injured; 44,000 were made homeless.

A series of multiple natural disasters set the stage for a fatal flood along the Sea of Japan on July 18 and 19, 1964.

First, a minor earthquake rumbled through Niigata, laying waste to much property along the seacoast, but causing very few deaths. Immediately after the earthquake, torrential rains followed, ceaselessly.

Swollen rivers began to crumble structures that had been loosened and weakened by the earthquake. The sides of hills began to break away and slide towards the villages nestled at the bottom of these hills.

Before the end of the day on July 18, 150 bridges had collapsed, and nearby dikes which had also been weakened by the repeated shocks of the earthquake, cracked and fell in more than 200 separate places.

The onslaught of water, rain and landslides collected together to destroy several villages and 295 homes in the small cities of Ishakawa, Toyamma, Niigata, Tottori and Shimane.

One hundred eight people either drowned or were crushed by mudslides and collapsing buildings, 233 were injured and an astonishing 44,000 were made homeless.

JAPAN

July 17, 1972

• • • • • • • • • • • • • •

Extremely heavy rains caused river flooding throughout Japan on July 17, 1972. Three hundred seventy people drowned; 70 were reported missing.

A week of heavy rains swelled rivers and streams and caused a series of floods throughout an area that covered almost the entirety of Japan in the middle of July 1972. Landslides added to the destructive force of rain and flood, particularly in the farming districts, which were flooded beyond recognition.

By the time the waters receded, and the rain ceased, 370 people had drowned, 70 were missing and the crop loss was estimated at $472 million.

RUSSIA
ST. PETERSBURG

November 19, 1824

• • • • • • • • • • • • • •

The River Neva overflowed its banks in and near St. Petersburg, Russia on November 19, 1824. Over 10,000 people drowned.

More than 10,000 people drowned in the swirling floodwaters of the River Neva on November 19, 1824, near St. Petersburg, Russia. It would remain the worst flood in the history of the Neva, which is now called the Svir.

In 1824, St. Petersburg was the winter home of the Czar, and his troops and consorts were everywhere that November. All were threatened by the roaring floodwaters. According to one report, ". . . a regiment of Carabineers, who had climbed to the roof of their barracks, were drowned."

Carriages and horses were swept away; the homes of the privileged as well as peasant shacks were inundated and sometimes swept from their foundations. Practically every dwelling in the city, including the Winter Palace, was flooded to the top of its first story.

Nearby, the coastal city of Kronstadt was also inundated. Refuse swept into dwellings and open places not only from the river banks but from the sea. A 100-gun navy ship was floated from its berth and ended up in the middle of Kronstadt's marketplace.

By the time the waters had receded, 10,000 people were dead, the property damage amounted to millions of rubles, and there were too many homeless to count.

SCOTLAND
INVERNESS

July 1829

• • • • • • • • • • • • • •

Hundreds drowned when floods caused by giant storms inundated Inverness, Scotland in July 1829.

Enormous thunderstorms raged over the Inverness area of Scotland throughout the month of July 1829. Drops of rain powerful enough to kill small animals and birds pounded. All of the streams and rivers running northward from the mountains to the sea were filled to overflowing. By the middle of the month, tremendous torrents of water began to roar down mountainsides into the hapless valleys below. The Findhorn Gorge filled to overflowing so that only the tops of great trees were visible above the water.

Cottages in these gorges were picked up and flung ahead of the raging waters. Farms, bridges, mills and factories were sucked into the flood and disappeared. One huge wave lifted a 65-foot stone arch from a bridge into the air and carried it, floating like a raft on the raging waters, for miles before it finally sank.

The entire plain of Forres was flooded to the Moray Firth. Findhorn Village became an island, its people marooned on the upper stories of their homes. For weeks, broken furniture and vehicles dammed the streams. Fertile soil was replaced by gravel in the fields. In the rivers, hundreds of salmon were dashed to pieces or choked by the sand. Nearly all the bridges in the area were swept away, and four sawmills were completely destroyed. The dead numbered in the hundreds.

SOUTH KOREA

August 19, 1972

• • • • • • • • • • • • • •

Six hundred thirty-eight people died and 144,000 were made homeless in river and stream flooding caused by heavy rains in South Korea on August 19, 1972.

The rain that fell relentlessly in Seoul, South Korea on August 19, 1972 measured 17.8 inches, which was a record.

No terrain can withstand this sort of attack from the heavens for long, and within hours, swollen rivers and streams, some of them redirected by massive landslides brought on by the downpours, flooded Kyonggi, Kangwon and North Chungchong provinces. Overnight, 463 would drown or be crushed by collapsing houses inundated by falling mud or pounding floodwaters.

Thirteen separate landslides occurred within the city of Seoul itself, accounting for 175 deaths. Here, 127,000 inhabitants were made instantly homeless, 158 were injured and 34 were reported missing.

Areas outside Seoul were similarly affected but because of smaller concentrations of population, the casualty figures were smaller. The city of Yongwol, 90 miles southeast

of Seoul, was completely submerged, forcing its entire population of 17,000 to flee in panic. In Suwon, an ancient city wall collapsed under the assault of floodwaters, demolishing hundreds of homes. The agricultural losses were staggering; the loss of buildings was likewise enormous. But what was most appalling was the small amount of time it took to wreak such widespread havoc.

SPAIN
BARCELONA, SABADELL, TARRASA

September 26, 1962

• • • • • • • • • • • • • •

Floods following catastrophic amounts of rain killed 445 and rendered 10,000 homeless in Barcelona, Sabadell and Tarrasa, Spain on September 26, 1962.

Famed painters Salvador Dali and Pablo Picasso auctioned off some of their paintings to aid the 10,000 homeless residents of Barcelona following the enormous floods of September 26, 1962. When the worst flood disaster of modern times hit this premiere city of the Costa Brava, 445 were killed.

Torrential rains followed by heavy floods totally submerged the nearby villages of Sabadell and Tarrasa, and damage to agriculture and the closely packed dwellings of not only Barcelona but the stuccoed towns that border it resulted in a high economic toll.

SUDAN
KHARTOUM

August 4–5, 1988

• • • • • • • • • • • • • •

The city of Khartoum, in Sudan, was flooded when the Nile overflowed its banks on August 4, 1988. Over 100 drowned, hundreds were injured, and over 1 million were made homeless.

Khartoum, located where the Blue and White Niles join to make the Nile River that flows into Egypt, is the capital of Sudan, Africa's largest country. Ordinarily, Khartoum's population totals 334,000, but in August 1988, that figure had been swollen by an additional 1.5 million refugees, fleeing the civil war in Sudan's south. Most of these refugees lived in makeshift shelters of mud thatch and cardboard in shantytowns on the fringes of Khartoum, and it was this ancillary city of displaced persons that was most catastrophically hit when the floods of August 1988 poured through Sudan's capital.

Torrential rains soaked the city and its surrounding countryside on August 4 and 5, 1988. In the space of 48 hours, over eight inches of rain fell, compared with a total of less than two inches of rain in the previous year.

The Nile boiled furiously, overflowing its banks, rising higher, according to the Sudanese Irrigation Ministry, than at any other time in this century. Within a very short time, all of the roads leading in and out of the city were washed away, including the one paved road between the city and Port Sudan on the Red Sea. This would make later rescue and relief attempts hazardous to the point of impossibility.

Electricity was cut off early on when two thermal electricity plants were damaged by flood waters and five of the six turbines serving the national electrical supply were knocked out.

Streets of Khartoum were turned into high-speed streams; houses were flooded to the upper stories; automobiles and buses were overturned and smashed into stores and buildings; livestock drowned on the outlying farms. Without

electricity—it would not return for four days—the life of the city virtually ground to a stop.

But the true carnage took place in the shantytowns. According to Sudanese Ambassador to Kenya, Omar el-Sheik, "The shantytowns were completely washed away, leaving 1.5 million completely homeless. The rains made a bad situation worse. Houses of unbaked clay just washed away."

Water supplies were rapidly contaminated, and outbreaks of malaria, cholera and typhoid began to erupt shortly after the flood waters eased. Access to the city was restricted to helicopters, which flew in food, tents, medical help, mobile generators, water tanks and water purification tablets. The treatment of the injured was hampered by the loss of electricity, and when power was finally restored four days later, scores of people, including a worker for the International Committee of the Red Cross, were electrocuted as eroded pylons fell, bringing power lines down with them.

A residential section of Khartoum is totally inundated during the Sudan flood of August 4, 1988. CARE photo.

117

Final casualty figures were hard to come by. Over a hundred were known dead, hundreds were injured, and more than 1.5 million were totally without shelter. It would be months before relief efforts by Egypt, Britain, the United States, Italy, Saudi Arabia and the United Nations Disaster Relief Organization would restore some semblance of normalcy to the city and its displaced hordes.

THAILAND

November 1988

• • • • • • • • • • • • • •

Torrential rains caused a huge flood in Thailand in November 1988. Over 1,000 drowned; over 100,000 were rendered homeless.

A combination of natural and man-made conditions joined to produce one of Thailand's greatest natural calamities. Over 1,000 drowned, hundreds were reported missing and at least 100,000 people were made homeless by enormous floods that raged through Thailand's southern regions and throughout northeastern Malaysia.

Five days of heavy rainfall beginning on November 19, 1988, swelled streams and rivers throughout this largely agricultural region. The situation was compounded by illegal logging activity. In addition to the indiscriminate elimination of forests that had hitherto contained flooded land, logs were left piled along river banks and in areas that, because of the absence of trees, turned instantly into moving quagmires.

When the rain reached torrential proportions, land that had been bound tightly by the roots of trees and protected by enormous umbrellas of leaves became malleable, and huge mudslides developed. Uncollected logs, left where they had fallen and often hidden in the mass of mud and water and other detritus, were swept up in the mudslides.

In the province of Nakhon Sri Thammarat, about 360 miles south of Bangkok, entire villages were mowed down by this murderous combination, and entire settlements were leveled within minutes, leaving nothing alive or standing.

Roads were blocked by flood waters, rail lines and telephone service were disrupted. Gangs of looters navigated the flooded streets of deserted villages in large trucks, scooping up whatever they could carry.

In the countryside, 700,000 acres of orchards and rice paddies were inundated, 1,000 shrimp farms were destroyed, and nearly 300 bridges were either damaged or swept away. The total cost of the carnage exceeded $400 million.

TIBET
SHIGATSE

August 10, 1954

• • • • • • • • • • • • • •

The overflow of Lake Takri Tsoma, above Shigatse, Tibet on August 10, 1954 caused a flood that killed between 500 and 1,000 people.

A flash flood drowned between 500 and 1,000 people in Shigatse, the second largest city in Tibet, on August 10, 1954.

For months, the Nyang Chu River, which snakes through the high Himalayas (Shigatse itself is located at an elevation of 12,800 feet) had been swollen by pounding, daily rainfall. Its overflow normally ran into Lake Takri Tsoma, where it was safely absorbed. The lake, which hovers near and slightly above Shigatse, had been a natural safety valve for as long as anyone alive could remember—enough so that the Palace of the Western Paradise, housing the Panchern Lama, the religious leader of three million Tibetans who regarded him as the reincarnation of Buddha, had been built below it.

But on August 10, 1954, Lake Takri Tsoma failed in its function, and with a thunderous roar overflowed its banks, sending driving cataracts of water roaring downhill and into the palace. Towers and wings that had stood for centuries crumbled under the onslaught of the water, filling the palace's courtyards and drowning scores of Buddhist monks at prayer.

The Lama escaped unscathed. The Communist household troops who simultaneously served him and held him prisoner in his palace were all killed when their barracks collapsed on them, and the Providential differentiation was not lost upon devout Tibetans.

TUNISIA

September–October 1969

• • • • • • • • • • • • • •

An extended period of rain resulted in widespread flooding in Tunisia in September and October of 1969. Five hundred forty-two people drowned; hundreds of thousands were made homeless.

For 38 days in September and October of 1969—just two days short of the Biblical record—it rained over the entirety of Tunisia. Every river, stream, pond and lake first filled, then overflowed its basin. The Zeroud and Margeu-lil rivers became roaring torrents, carving out the alluvial

Citizens join in the monumental cleanup after the Tunisian flood of September 1969. CARE.

banks that formerly bordered them, inundating fields and villages. Eighty percent of Tunisia was under water by mid-October, and by the end of the month, the death toll would reach 542.

The rivers crested at an astonishing 36 feet above normal, and the force of their overflow actually moved 100-ton concrete anchoring slabs on the scores of bridges that spanned their normally tranquil waters. Thirty-five major spans were washed away completely; near one, a $7 million irrigation project was obliterated.

The rich soil that supported Tunisia's agriculture was shoveled up by the floodwaters and washed into the Mediterranean. Farmers lost everything—buildings, crops, animals and in many cases their own lives. One hundred thousand head of livestock were drowned, their bloated and rotting carcasses causing health hazards for months. This, plus the total destruction of crops in the country, caused widespread sickness and death from disease and starvation.

Help came swiftly from the rest of the world: The U.S. offered $4 million in loans; West Germany provided $2.5 million in loans. France, Belgium, the Netherlands and Spain sent contingents of engineers to help in the recon-

struction of the destroyed bridges. Russia sent blankets and food. All in all, 80 nations responded with aid, and when it arrived, it was consumed hysterically by wild-eyed, starving refugees.

The door of the helicopter carrying food and piloted by U.S. Air Force Major Robert McDougal was ripped completely off by starving villagers. Once they had pulled the food parcels from the helicopter, these same villagers clawed at each other, in feeble fights over food they had not seen in weeks.

UNITED STATES
CALIFORNIA

March 13, 1928

• • • • • • • • • • • • • •

The collapse of the St. Francis dam caused heavy flooding in Southern California on March 13, 1928. Four hundred twenty people drowned.

Four hundred twenty people drowned in the early morning hours of March 13, 1928, when the St. Francis dam burst and sent a 120-foot-high wall of water roaring past Los Angeles and into the Pacific Ocean, 44 miles from the dam site.

The dam was a mere two years old when it was totally destroyed by the water it was to have contained, but it was probably doomed from its inception.

The creation of William Mulholland, the man who conceived and built the 233-mile-long aqueduct through the Sierra Nevada Mountains that carried water and provided hydroelectric power to the city of Los Angeles, this monumental system included 52 miles of tunnels blasted through the rock faces of the eastern slope of the Sierra Nevadas.

Forty-five miles north of Los Angeles, the mouth of one five-mile-long tunnel emptied over a precipitous cliff that plunged 1,000 feet into the San Fransicquito Canyon. Here, Mulholland constructed two concrete power stations that harnassed the plunging water into electricity for the city.

Shortly after this, Mulholland made the most unwise decision of his life, mapping out a huge dam that would be built across the canyon midway between the two power stations. Its reservoir, supplied by the aqueduct's surpluses, would store enough water to supply Los Angeles for one entire year, in case of an emergency.

Mulholland refused to heed the warnings of geologists who knew that the ground upon which he was building the dam was composed of a combination of conglomerate (which ultimately dissolves into mud in water) and mica schist (which has a habit of breaking into thin, flat, slate-like pieces). To add to the dilemma, the dam was built along a geologic fault.

But the grand dam went up, 205 feet high, 700 feet wide and 175 feet thick at its base. Impounded in the reservoir behind it were 38,000 acre-feet of water.

The dam began to show cracks almost from the very beginning. Water dribbled continuously from its base. On the morning of March 12, 1928, a large crack appeared on the conglomerate side, and inspections were made, but the leak was judged by Mulholland himself to be insignificant.

At 11:58 P.M. on March 12, the dam gave way. Lights in Los Angeles flickered, a house above power station Number 2 began to shudder and the lights went out. With a tremendous roar, several 3,000-ton sections of the dam were swept ahead of a roaring, thundering wave comprised of 12 billion gallons of water, cascading down toward the Santa Clara Valley, nine miles away.

In a construction camp, 150 men slept in their tents. Miraculously, 66 of them rode the wave to safety; the others were drowned. On California Highway 126 in the Santa Clara Valley, 50 automobiles, carrying 125 people, were swept off the road by the raging floodwaters. Later, some of these cars were found buried in mud more than 20 miles from the highway.

Broadening out, the waters slowed into a two-mile-wide collection of sludge, pieces of houses and fencing and other detritous which ultimately crept into the Pacific Ocean.

The final inquest and investigation laid the blame on the one man who had acquired not only fame but the ability to make unilateral decisions about dam sites. The 73-year-old William Mulholland accepted the blame and the responsibility for 420 deaths.

UNITED STATES
COLORADO (AND MONTANA, KANSAS, WYOMING AND NEW MEXICO)

June 16–26, 1965

• • • • • • • • • • • • •

Twenty-three people drowned in Colorado, Montana, Kansas, Wyoming and New Mexico when the Arkansas River flooded the territory through which it ran from June 16 to 26, 1965.

The Arkansas River spilled over its banks in the middle of June 1965, bringing woe to the citizens of Colorado, Montana, Kansas, Wyoming and New Mexico. Of all of the states, Colorado was the hardest hit. Fourteen of the

23 dead were drowned in Colorado; the property damage in the state exceeded $120 million.

Entire villages disappeared under the flood waters in the northeastern part of the state, among them, Fort Morgan, Brush and Sterling. In the normally placid city of Denver, murky floodwaters covered a mile-wide part of it, immobilizing transit and rendering commercial establishments uninviting, to say the least. It would be the end of the summer before the villages and cities would return to normal, and longer than that for the agricultural sections of the state to begin to produce again.

UNITED STATES
COLORADO

July 31, 1976

• • • • • • • • • • • • •

One of the most tragic flash floods in U.S. history, caused by astonishing rains, turned Colorado's Big Thompson River into a hellespont on July 31, 1976. One hundred thirty-nine people drowned; 600 were missing.

Looking at Colorado's Big Thompson River in normal times would make the average person scratch his or her head in disbelief at its name. More a stream than a river, it measures roughly 18 inches in depth and several feet across from the time it leaves its headwaters in the Rocky Mountains until it finds its junction with the South Platte River, 78 miles downstream. On the night of July 31, 1976, it measured 32 feet in depth, demolished motels and automobiles, washed out bridges, floated concrete slabs and rocks weighing hundreds of tons for miles, and drowned 139 people. Six hundred more would remain missing in one of the most tragic flash floods in history.

Through the first 21 miles of its run, the Big Thompson descends 5,000 feet to the town of Estes Park; two miles east of there, it sluices into the 25-mile-long gorge of Big Thompson Canyon, a narrow alleyway in which it drops another 2,500 feet before wandering for 30 miles along flat land to the South Platte.

Big Thompson Canyon is a wilderness area that usually contains around 600 people. But Saturday, July 31, 1976, was the beginning of a three-day celebration weekend of the centennial of Colorado. The motels and campgrounds of the canyon were filled to overflowing, and the estimate of its population that day was around 3,500.

Late in the afternoon of the 31st, a line of thunderstorms formed from central Kansas to eastern Colorado, eventually deteriorating into a 12-mile band of intense activity that spread from Estes Park to the town of Drake. At approximately 6:30 P.M., an intense rainstorm hit. It

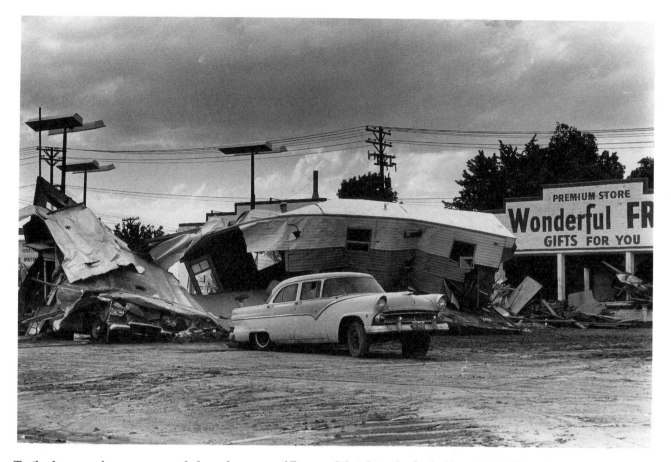

Trailer homes and cars were tossed about the streets of Denver, Colorado in the flood of June 16, 1965. American Red Cross.

would continue for four and a half hours without letting up and would dump more than 12 inches of water into the upper one-third of Big Thompson Canyon—exceeding the average yearly rainfall in the region.

Despite advanced meteorological technology used to track the storm, the occupants of the canyon received no warning of the potential danger. Two satellite specialists in Kansas City were preoccupied with two larger storm systems developing in the Southern Mississippi River Basin over Missouri and Arkansas. Backup video equipment used to flash radar findings to Denver was down for repairs. Thus, from the time of the 7:35 P.M. weather forecast that mentioned "the possibility of flooding in low-lying areas," until the first frantic reports of a river gone instantly wild by state troopers at 8 o'clock, the occupants had no way of knowing the seriousness of the situation.

Tragically enough, many of those who were told to evacuate by the state police did not believe that they were in mortal danger, and by then, events had speeded up enough so that the troopers could not spend time trying to convince the unconvinced.

"Raindrops a half-inch in diameter were coming straight down," reported one trooper. "My slicker pockets filled with water almost instantly." Shortly after 8 P.M., the Colorado Highway Patrol Office at Greeley, 43 miles east of Estes Park, received a report that part of U.S. Highway 34, a scenic route that passes through Big Thompson Canyon and parallels the river, had a washout. Two troopers were dispatched—William Miller and Hugh Purdy. Miller sent a frantic message before he abandoned his floating car and swam to safety: "We've got to start taking people out. . . . My car's gonna be washed away. . . . I've got a real emergency here!" And then, seconds later: "The whole mountainside is gone. There is no way. I'm trying to get out of here before I drown."

Purdy was less fortunate. His message, "I'm stuck. I'm right in the middle of it. I can't get out," turned into his epitaph. His battered body was recovered later eight miles downstream.

By now, the incredibly engorged river was racing forward at a velocity of more than 20 feet per second. Bursting out of the canyon's mouth, the floodwaters roared on at a rate of 233,000 gallons per second. "Campers were being washed away and big propane tanks were coming downstream, spinning like crazy, starting to explode," recalled one survivor. Another saw Highway 34 ripping apart, "sending 10 to 12 foot chunks of asphalt high into the air."

"You could hear the people inside . . . cars screaming for help," said Mrs. Dorothy Venrick, who lived about 250 feet from the river in the town of Drake. "Above the roar of the river and the sound of homes smashing into each other, you could hear [them]. . . . It made your heart sick to stand there and know that there was nothing you could do."

"While I was outside on the porch," recalled Mrs. Barbara Nicholson, of Loveland, "I heard this sound echoing in the canyon. It sounded like three freight trains off in the distance . . . then I saw the water rising on our property."

Mrs. Nicholson's daughter, Christine, and her husband, Howard, attempted to rescue the Baileys, two neighbors. "The water knocked all of us down," related Christine Nicholson. "Suddenly we were in the flood—drifting past houses and getting struck by a lot of debris."

"You've got to realize that by the time the flood hit us, it wasn't just water," continued Mr. Nicholson. "There was a lot of solid material—dirt, rocks, buildings, cars and concrete—that was carried along with us."

Further downstream, emergency medical technicians John McMaster and George Woodson, of Loveland, set out on an emergency call in their ambulance on Highway 34 on the night of the 31st, and were calmed by the sight of the river downstream. "The river was nice and low and moving along slowly," said McMaster afterward. "It was so peaceful you could have gone out fishing on it."

But a few miles upstream, they found the swollen river, debris and roadblocks. Since they were driving an ambulance, they were waved through. A few miles of growing debris, and they realized they were in the wrong place. As they were turning the ambulance around, they heard the roar of the main floodwaters approaching them. "There was a huge, choking dust cloud ahead of the water," remember McMaster. "Then the water hit us like a big freight train. It picked up our ambulance about fifteen feet into the air and slammed it into a V-shaped wedge on one of the canyon walls."

The two jumped clear as the water picked up the ambulance a second time and flung it against the opposite canyon wall, smashing it to pieces. The two men climbed the canyon wall until they found a perch 50 feet above the highway. The perch was insecure. McMaster lost his footing and plunged downward toward the water. "I fell

about twenty-five feet straight down, but as I fell I put out my arm and caught a rock," he recalled.

The water climbed up to his waist, but fortunately receded before it could rise higher. The two remained in the canyon until daylight, when they were lifted out by one of the many helicopters that plucked hundreds of survivors from the horrendously scarred and debris-scattered canyon.

The toll was tremendous. A motel log was found, with 28 registered names. Neither the motel nor any of the registered guests was ever found.

It would take months to clear the wreckage. Clarence Johnson, of Drake, remembered, for the national press, the Army Corps of Engineers coming into his yard to clean it of rocks. "They used the biggest tractors I ever saw," he said. "One rock they moved from in front of our house weighed 10 tons, they said. There were three huge rocks a little way from our house that couldn't be moved. An engineer estimated that each weighed a hundred tons."

UNITED STATES
CONNECTICUT
PUTNAM
August 19, 1955

• • • • • • • • • • • • •

Swollen by Hurricane Diane, the Quinebaug River destroyed its dams and flooded Putnam, Connecticut, causing no deaths but spectacular property damage.

On the night of August 18, 1955, Hurricane Diane, the second of two back-to-back hurricanes—the other was named Connie—(see HURRICANES, U.S., East) pelted Putnam, Connecticut with eight inches of rain. Prior to that, Connie had dumped four inches on this small (pop. 8,200) riverfront, colonial town.

On the morning of August 19, the Quinebaug River, customarily contained by a series of old stone and earth dams 20 to 50 miles north of Putnam, erupted. One by one, the dams crumbled under the onslaught of the swollen river, and within moments, waves five feet high sent plumes of spray cascading over river banks, wiped away roads and took out bridges, carved up railroad embankments and crashed headlong into the town.

Fortunately, the rising of the river and the falling of huge amounts of rain were duly recorded by weather bureaus throughout the East, and state police and civil defense personnel preceded the flood by a safe margin, evacuating as many people as they possibly could. The residents of Connecticut cooperated fully and by the time the roaring floodwaters, clocked at 25 mph, roared into the town, it was vacant. Not one person was lost in this flood.

There was, however, considerable and spectacular property damage. Just above the town, water poured into a warehouse stocked with 20 tons of magnesium. Magnesium is noted for, among other things, its volatility when placed in contact with water. The warehouse went up in a gigantic eruption of flame and water, and hundreds of barrels of burning magnesium were launched into the raging floodwaters. They, too, exploded along the way, sending plumes of water and flame 250 feet in the air.

Some holdouts were plucked from rooftops by National Guard helicopters after the first passage of the river. Others returned a week later to assess the $13 million worth of property damage caused by the flood.

UNITED STATES
KANSAS

July 12–31, 1951

• • • • • • • • • • • • • •

Fifty-three days of rainfall preceded the flood of the Kansas River on July 12, 1951. Fifty were killed; hundreds of thousands were evacuated.

The costliest flood in U.S. history up to that point (over $1 billion dollars) and the worst ever in the Central Plains claimed 50 lives and came after a solid 53 days of rainfall that totaled 16 inches by the middle of July.

Most of this relentless deluge fell in the basin of the Kansas River; the rest found its way into the Arkansas and Neosho rivers.

There was warning of the impending flood. By late May most of the smaller rivers in Kansas and northern Oklahoma had burst their banks. On May 22, the small city of Hays, Kansas was inundated by water from nearby Big Creek.

As June wore on, low-lying farmlands and cities throughout the state were on constant alert for floods. By the end of the month, all of the area drained by the Kansas River had absorbed all of the water it could. Scientists estimated that the soil in the area could safely hold only two more inches of rain. Much more than that would fall.

By the afternoon of July 11, all of the larger rivers in Kansas were over their banks, and the highest flood crest ever seen in the state moved down the length of the Kansas River.

Manhattan, Kansas, located on the Kansas River at the point at which it joins the Big Blue River, was hit by flood waters on the night of July 12, 1951. In minutes, more than half the town was under five feet of water, and thousands of people had been made instantly homeless.

At dawn of the 13th, the flood waters reached Topeka, cresting three and a half feet higher than the previous record height, set in 1903. The city was cut in two as water topped levees and flood walls. Twenty-five thousand people were evacuated; railyards, factories and businesses were gutted or destroyed, and a large section of the city became an unpopulated lake.

Many miles downstream, the floodwaters poured across the Sante Fe railroad tracks for 55 hours, trapping 337 people aboard the passenger train *El Captain*. From here, they sped on to the thickly populated twin cities of Kansas City, Kansas and Kansas City, Missouri where 35-foot-high dirt-and-rock dikes had been built 40 years ago to shield the stockyards, packing plants, railyards, flour mills and grain elevators from flooding. On the Missouri side of the river, an eight-foot-high by three-foot-thick concrete wall had been added as reinforcement.

But by Friday, July 13, the Army Corps of Engineers estimated that the debris-laiden river would broach these dikes easily. Workers toiled into the night, adding sandbags to the dikes. Their efforts were fruitless, and in the middle of the night, the dikes gave way. Roaring floodwaters rammed through the railyards, blanketing $50 million worth of locomotives, freight cars and buildings. Factory whistles and police sirens set up a wail, warning people to evacuate the path ahead of the flood. Twelve thousand people scurried for the bluffs beyond the town.

In moments, most of the buildings in Kansas City, Kansas were covered up to their second stories. Outside of town, six square miles of homes, grain elevators and manufacturing plants were under as much as 30 feet of water.

On the Missouri side of the river, the reinforced dike held, but by midday on the 13th, it, too, began to waver under the assault of 500,000 cubic feet of water per second. Refugees from Kansas were threatened for the second time. Within two hours, the Kansas City stockyards were under 10 feet of water. Six thousand hogs and sheep that were not moved to higher overhead shoots drowned.

Dead animals, smashed homes, uprooted trees, splintered telephone poles plummeted through the city. An enormous steel tank loaded with diesel oil floated into an area where two other, building-size tanks loaded with gasoline floated. The diesel tank became entangled with a live electric wire, exploded, and as the flame spread across the water to the other two tanks, a chain reaction of multiple explosions flung fire in all directions, igniting a naptha tank which went up like a volcano. Within minutes a quarter mile square sea of fire ignited, and despite efforts of firemen in boats to put it out, it burned for five days.

The wreckage of a home and boathouse following the Kansas flood of July 1951. American Red Cross.

The wreckage was enormous. Twenty-five hundred homes were totally destroyed. Streets of the two Kansas City were filled with 16 million tons of silt and sand. Only one of the 13 rail lines servicing the area was operable. Only two out of the 17 highways running into it were open. Seventeen major bridges had been washed away. Two million acres lay under polluted water. And only 10 percent of the area's sewers, water and power systems were left in working order.

The floodwaters crashed on into the Missouri River, but workers in Jefferson City, downstream, saved its main bridge by piling nearly 100 tons of scrap metal on it.

Within days, President Harry Truman, a native of nearby Independence, Missouri, made $25 million of Federal Emergency Aid available, and sent in the Red Cross and other relief agencies. It would be nearly a year before a semblance of normalcy would return to the area.

UNITED STATES
MISSISSIPPI RIVER

April 1874

• • • • • • • • • • • • • • •

Two hundred to 300 people drowned in Mississippi and Louisiana in the first recorded flooding of the Mississippi River, during April 1874.

The first reported flooding of the Mississippi River was sketchily told, largely because the areas hit were rural ones, where, in 1874, communication ranged from nonexistent to feeble.

What is known is that an estimated 200 to 300 people were drowned in the floodwaters of the Mississippi that had been swollen from melting snow and heavy rains in the early spring of 1874. Tens of thousands of acres of

124

OVERFLOW OF THE MISSISSIPPI.—SCENE NEAR HICKEY'S CREVASSE, LA.—SKETCHED BY C. E. TINGUE.

A graphic depiction of the first recorded Mississippi flood, in April 1874, caused by melting snow and heavy spring rains. Frank Leslie's Illustrated Newspaper.

farmland and grazing land in Louisiana and Mississippi were inundated, and over a thousand head of livestock were killed in hundreds of locations at which early levees had been erected.

UNITED STATES
MISSISSIPPI RIVER

January–April 1890

• • • • • • • • • • • • •

At least 100 drowned and 50,000 were made homeless by the seemingly endless flooding by the Mississippi River of its entire valley between January and April of 1890.

The spectacular Mississippi River flood of 1890 was a long time coming. Beginning soon after New Year's, with melting snows swelling its headwaters at Cairo, Illinois, the Mississippi kept on rolling over its banks and its levees, right up until the end of April, when it inundated three thousand square miles of Louisiana, rendered 50,000 persons homeless and drowned at least 100.

A former steamboat pilot sadly concluded: "I have lived on the river for thirty years, and I have studied it, for it was my business to do so. I have been steamboating all that time. I am now certain that I don't know anything about it, or about what ought to be done to it."

What had been done since the flood of 1874 (see previous entry) and the flash floods of 1882, was a strength-

ening and lengthening of the levee system. Perhaps anything would have been too little and too late. The river washed away the dikes, the levees, the extra sandbags, and, in some cases, the men and women who were frantically piling on the sandbags in one last effort to stem the roaring tide.

First warnings of the impending flood were issued by the United States Signal Service in December. Massive snowfalls in Ohio would, they said, cause flooding. And certainly enough, on January 1, 1890, the Mississippi rose to 18 feet in Cairo, Illinois and continued to rise after that, at a rate of one and three-eighths feet a day.

By the end of February, Memphis, Shreveport, Vicksburg and New Orleans were threatened, and by the end of March, the river was breaching its banks at Arkansas City and Memphis, drowning dozens and covering thousands of acres.

By April 3, Greenville, Mississippi was inundated and most of its 10,000 residents had removed themselves to nearby high ground.

The Morganza Bend, south of this, suffered greatly in the middle of April when 400 feet of dikes and levees collapsed simultaneously, drenching the countryside and collapsing many nearby homes.

Finally, by April 24, the entire Mississippi Valley was all or partially under water, from Illinois to Baton Rouge, Louisiana. Three thousand square miles of land in Louisiana alone were under water, and it would be months before the destruction would be cleared.

UNITED STATES
MISSISSIPPI RIVER

April 1912

• • • • • • • • • • • • • •

Two hundred fifty people drowned and 30,000 were rendered homeless by a Mississippi River flood, caused by melting snows, in April 1912.

April has always, it seems, been the cruelest month for those who live along the banks of the Mississippi River, particularly in those years when the winters to the north have been severe and full of snow. In 1912, 250 drowned, 30,000 were made homeless, and at least $10 million in damages were caused by floodwaters that were first fed by melting snows in tributaries of the Mississippi and then swollen by falling rains.

On April 2, troops that had been brought into Cairo, Illinois to build up and hold the dikes, ran for their lives as the river shot up like a geyser over the barriers and roared into the Mobile & Ohio train yards.

During the next week, river towns in Kentucky began to fill up with water, turning them into muddied lakes.

As usual, the worst flooding occurred in Mississippi, in Bolivar County, where great loss of life occurred and thousands of acres were inundated. The cities of Beulah and Benoit were turned into Southern Venices, and it would be weeks before they would return to some semblance of normality.

UNITED STATES
MISSISSIPPI RIVER

April–July 1927

• • • • • • • • • • • • • •

A long rainy period culminated in a long flood in the Mississippi River Valley, from April to July 1927. Local and federal statistics conflict; from 246 to 500 were killed and 650,000 were rendered homeless in the flood.

Between 246 and 500 people drowned, 650,000 were made homeless, 2.3 million acres of land were inundated and a staggering $230 million in damages were caused by a series of monumental Mississippi River floods from Tennessee to New Orleans between April and July of 1927.

The floods originated in August 1926, almost a year before the recession of floodwaters. Heavy, nearly ceaseless rains began to fall throughout much of the Mississippi's drainage basin. The deluge continued into the winter. On New Year's Day, 1927, the Cumberland River, a tributary of the Mississippi, stood at a depth of 56.2 feet, which

was 41 feet above its level before the rains began in August. In Cairo, the Ohio River stood at 44.9 feet. In August, it had measured 18.1.

The rains let up in February and resumed in March, and on April 19, the Mississippi broke loose, riddling the levees at Mound Landing, above Greenville, Tennessee with small drill holes of rushing water that erupted into boiling bubbles on the outside wall of the levees. All through the night of April 20, small farmers and townspeople worked in a downpour, attempting to shore up the levee. But, according to flood historian William Percy, ". . . about daylight, while the distraught engineers and labor bosses hurried and consulted and bawled commands, while the 5,000 Negroes with 100-pound sandbags on their shoulders trotted in long converging lines to the threatened [weak] point, the river pushed, and the great dike dissolved under their feet."

Scores were swept to their deaths there and in Greenville, where General Alexander G. Paxton of the Engineers recalled ". . . three words that I shall remember as long as I live—'There she goes!' "

One planter remembered the crest of the river as a "tan-colored wall seven feet high, and with a roar as of a mighty wind." Over two million acres of farmland were submerged, under water which swirled around eastern hills and flowed into the basin of the Yazoo River, and then back to the main stream of the Mississippi near Vicksburg.

Across from Mound Landing, on April 21, the levee at Pendleton, Arkansas burst. "You could hear it roaring a long ways off," noted Robert Murphy, who lived below Pendleton. "Kind of like, they say, a tornado. Near about that loud." In Arkansas City, 32 miles downstream, streets that had been dry at noon were flooded enough to drown people, and did, by 2 P.M.

A secondary danger, backwater flows from main streams into tributaries, threatened those living along the Arkansas River all the way upstream to Little Rock, 100 miles from the Mississippi. Near Pine Bluff, which was 60 miles from the mouth of the Arkansas, 500 people crowded together on Free Bridge, a mile-long steel span across the Arkansas.

They didn't realize the danger of being stranded when access roads flooded. For three days and nights, in a cold rain, they remained on the span, isolated by waters that were too turbulent to allow rescuers to reach them from the river. When the survivors were finally taken off by boat, two babies had been born on the bridge.

By the middle of May, the floodcrest had traveled southward to Louisiana. On May 17, the supposedly impregnable Atchafalaya levee at Melville crumbled. "The water leaped through the crevasse with such fury that it

Small towns like this in Illinois were totally inundated, and stayed that way for weeks during January 1927, when 25 days of steady rain melted snow and swelled the Mississippi above flood stage. Library of Congress.

spread into three distinct currents," reported Turner Catledge in the Memphis *Commercial Appeal,* "One force shot straight west. . . . A second current raced north, quickly eating out 50-foot sections of the Texas & Pacific Railroad embankment . . . a third current struck out from the south . . . washtubs, work benches, household furniture, chickens and domestic animals were floating away."

One more city would be jeopardized by the rushing floodwaters, New Orleans. A difficult solution was decided upon: the dynamiting of the Caernarvon levee just below the city. This would drain the water off to the southeast, but it would mean that the thinly populated parishes of St. Bernard and Plaquemines would be inundated.

The advantages of saving New Orleans and draining off the upstream floodwaters won out over the protests of the inhabitants of the two parishes. State authorities trucked out the refugees, and the National Guard moved in to oversee the demolition.

The first attempt was a spectacular failure. Fifteen hundred pounds of dynamite, buried in the top of the dike, lifted tons of earth into the air and dropped them back in exactly the spot from which they had been loosened. Finally, diver Ted Herbert volunteered to place the charges at the levee's base. Twice, he nearly drowned in the strong current which twisted his diving helmet askew, nearly strangling him. The third attempt succeeded, and New Orleans was saved.

Seven states had been inundated by the flood, and now 33,000 rescue and relief workers poured in under the joint direction of Secretary of Commerce Herbert Hoover and the American Red Cross's James Fieser. Hoover's success in the effort was widely credited with helping him in his later, successful campaign for the presidency.

His influence and a radio appeal immediately brought in $15 million for rescue efforts. The railroads provided trains and 6,000 riverboats of all sizes, from 700-ton river

Workers sandbagging levees on the Mississippi River during the enormous floods of April through July 1927. More than 650,000 were made homeless by this natural catastrophe. Library of Congress.

steamers to tiny skiffs. Sawmills on the river went to work and made 1,000 boats in 10 days. Navy planes circled the area, as the Coast Guard manned the larger boats, and engineers studied possible future courses of flood waters.

Interestingly enough, some of the most effective and personal rescue work was achieved by bootleggers from the swamps. Their high-speed escape boats proved particularly valuable. Historian Percy reported, "No one had sent for them, no one was paying them, no one had a good word for them—but they came. They scoured the back areas, the forgotten places, across fences, over railroad embankments, through woods and brush, and never rested."

UNITED STATES
MISSISSIPPI RIVER

April–May 1973

• • • • • • • • • • • • • • • •

Twenty-five drowned and 35,000 were made homeless by the April–May 1973, Mississippi River floods, caused by melting snow.

The work of Herbert Hoover and his commission in 1927 (see previous entry) prevented the enormous floods of 1973

from reaching the catastrophic proportions of the 1927 event. Still, this region suffered the inundation of 13 million acres of land, the displacing from their homes of 35,000 people and 25 deaths.

The winter of 1973 was a severe one, with heavy snowstorms that killed hundreds of head of livestock in the northern portion of the Mississippi drainage system. And spring was scarcely any better; heavy rains began in March and continued into early April, preventing the sowing of spring crops in Wisconsin. Rain melted the snow quickly, and pressure began to build in the 340 storage basins built at a cost of 10 billion dollars as a result of the 1927 catastrophe.

But the basins held. By early April, more than 7 million acres in the upper floodplain of the Mississippi were under water, and the storage capacity had been reached. Floodgates were opened, and the excess drained into Lake Pontchartrain, away from New Orleans. The dikes held, and the floodwaters dropped.

But the rain continued, and by early May, the drained water had been replaced and much more added to it. At Keithburg, Illinois, a levee broke and three feet of water gushed into the main street of the town. Fifteen city blocks disappeared underwater and downstream, Hannibal, Missouri was flooded under six feet of water. In Quincy,

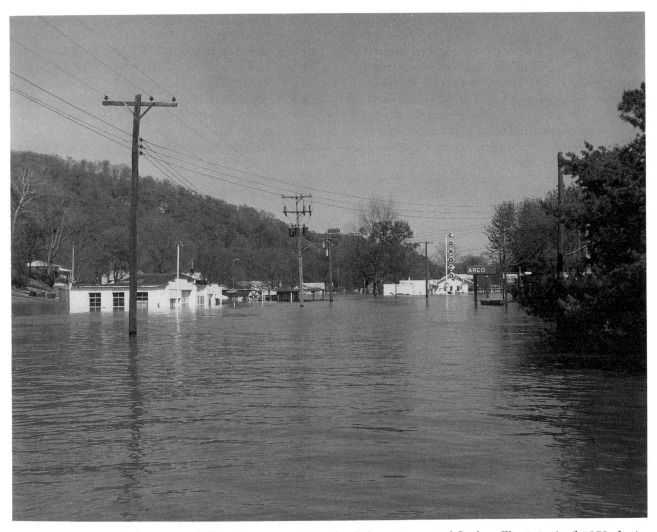

Flood waters from the Mississippi and Illinois rivers totally inundated the main street of Grafton, Illinois in April 1973, forcing the evacuation of 900 of the town's 1,100 residents. American Red Cross.

Illinois, 4,000 people had to be evacuated from their riverside homes, and now, more and more levees toppled and more and more campsites and resort communities disappeared under the Mississippi's muddy torrents. In Missouri, as dike after dike disintegrated, 30,000 acres of farmland were drowned in water, mud and silt.

Finally, at the beginning of June, the rains ceased, and the waters receded. Despite the damage, most of the levees had held, and it was generally estimated that without the constructions that had resulted from the 1927 floods, property damage would have risen another 7 billion dollars, and human casualties would have soared into the hundreds.

UNITED STATES
OHIO (AND INDIANA AND ILLINOIS)
March 25, 1913

• • • • • • • • • • • • • • • • •

Five hundred people drowned and over 175,000 were rendered homeless in a flood in lands adjacent to the Scioto, Mad, Miami and Muskingum rivers in Ohio, Indiana and Illinois on March 25, 1913.

The second worst flood of the 20th century in America (see FLOODS, United States, Pennsylvania, p. 132 and FLOODS, United States, Mississippi River, 1927, p. 126) took place on March 25, 1913. Five hundred people drowned, most

129

of them in Dayton, Ohio; over 175,000 people were made homeless; and over $147 million in damage was recorded from the several days that the Scioto, Mad, Miami and Muskingum rivers ran amok, inundating cities and farmland alike.

For decades, the population of Ohio, Indiana and Illinois rested secure in the assumption that the levees they had constructed would contain the swelling of these rivers. But by the middle of March, levees in southern Indiana, Illinois and Ohio had already been breached by river waters swollen from weeks of steady rain. In three days, according to a reporter in the *Cleveland Leader,* 18 billion tons, or 575 million cubic feet of water fell on Ohio. It was enough to make the Miami River smash through its dikes above Dayton, Ohio. Almost simultaneously, the Mad River broached its banks and roared toward Dayton.

Within minutes, the city was under seven to 12 feet of water, and its 125,000 residents climbed to the upper stories of buildings, some of which collapsed under them. Seven thousand refugees sought shelter in landmark office towers such as the Bretheren Publishing Company, the Conover Building, the Calahan Bank, and the National Cash Register Building, whose 70-year-old president, John H. Patterson, immediately set out by rowboat to rescue drowning swimmers in the city's streets.

In those first few moments of the flood, all communication in and out of Dayton was severed as the city's sole telephone line snapped under the pressure of falling poles.

An 18-year-old Ben Hecht, then a cub reporter for the *Chicago Journal,* was one of the first newspapermen to arrive and report on the scene. He was nothing if not persevering, taking the train as far as he could from Chicago, walking through heavy snows, fast talking two trainmen into loaning him their handcar, which he pumped into town, while ducking the shots of militiamen and deputies ordered to shoot potential looters and strangers on sight.

In his book of recollections, *Child of the Century,* Hecht recalled spending the day in a canoe, ". . . paddling through flooded Dayton, interviewing other boatmen and gathering data on the catastrophe. . . ."

He had plenty to report, from the grotesque to the grim. In downtown Dayton, a dead horse floated through the broken doors of the First National Bank and was later found standing behind the bars of a teller's cage. A sow managed to make it to the second floor lingerie department of a large clothing store before drowning.

Martin Ellis and his wife found themselves marooned on top of the Algonquin Hotel in Dayton, when the hotel's front doors became blocked by a team of horses. "The

water traveled like a sheet to the east," recalled Ellis, "passing over the city. A panic followed. People ran to the tops of buildings and were brushed off like flies. My four children were home. We lived on North Main Street. We saw the top of our house burn. . . . My wife couldn't stand it. . . ." Mrs. Ellis leaped into the raging waters and drowned.

The age of the horse-drawn vehicle saved some, who clambered atop swimming animals and thus saved themselves.

Meanwhile, the rest of Ohio was also disappearing under torrents of wild water. Train passengers, passing Toledo, witnessed wholesale destruction in that city as it filled with water and refugees stopped the train and clambered aboard. According to passenger Perry Hillister, "The wind was raw, too, and some of them were nearly frozen when we took them aboard. . . . Toledo was struck badly. The lower part of the city was under water."

Individual acts of heroism abounded. Ben Hecht described the telegraph operators in Miami Junction, who manned their posts for 30 hours: "Some have dropped from exhaustion," he reported. "The Western Union men, who were the first to break into the city, haven't slept since Tuesday. 'Safe.' 'Safe.' the monotonous words of rescue and death have jammed the wires since the first one was opened. . . ."

Students at Wesleyan University in Delaware, Ohio were responsible for saving scores of lives. One unnamed student saved 30 people by swimming back and forth in the raging current. A boatload of other students saved a woman and her three children who were dangling from a railroad bridge by maneuvering under them and catching them as they dropped, one by one, into the boat.

In Columbus, Ohio, Midwestern ingenuity accounted for the survival of the George Roller family. As the flood approached their home, they somehow managed to maneuver the family cow through the kitchen door, and upstairs, where it was accorded its own private bedroom in return for providing themselves and their neighbors with milk for five days, until the waters receded.

As the Scioto River also rose, the towns of Troy and Tadmore were submerged entirely under water. Portsmouth, Columbus, Circleville and Chillicothe were flooded. In Indiana, the Wabash River rampaged through Terre Haute and Lafayette, and the White River slammed into the western suburbs of Indianapolis. But it was in Ohio that the greatest destruction and loss of life took place.

There was a huge outpouring of relief supplies and Red Cross help from across the country, but it would be well into 1914 before the damage to dikes, buildings and farmland would be remedied.

UNITED STATES
OHIO

January 1937

• • • • • • • • • • • • • •

Twenty-five days of steady rain caused the Ohio and Mississippi rivers to bridge their levees in Ohio in January 1937. One hundred thirty-seven people died primarily from fires and explosions; 13,000 were made homeless.

A flood of fearsome proportions was generated by 25 straight days of torrential downpours which dumped an estimated 15 trillion gallons of water on the Ohio River Basin during the month of January 1937. This in turn swelled the Ohio all the way from West Virginia to its mouth in Cairo, where it emptied an unprecedented tide of water into the Mississippi.

From Pittsburgh, Pennsylvania to Cairo, levees crumbled and cities were inundated. The waters rose to a depth of 10 feet in the streets of Cincinnati, and Louisville, Kentucky was likewise inundated. Over 204,000 square miles—more than 8 million acres—of floodplain and farmland, town and city were affected by the Ohio's raging floodwaters, and 13,000 homes were swept away.

Ironically, practically all of the 137 deaths that occurred were not from drowning, but from fires and explosions. On January 16, the Louisville Varnish Company went up in flames. Gas explosions caused by the displacing of mains in the flood erupted in Louisville for two weeks, as they did in Ironton, Ohio.

At Cairo, the Army Corps of Engineers was forced to dynamite the left-bank levee when the Ohio crested at 63 feet. Downstream on the Mississippi, thousands of workers manned the levees, and each of them held, thus, preventing the overflow that might have recreated the 1927 flood disaster (see p. 126).

The Red Cross commandeered 5,400 boats to conduct rescue work on the Ohio. Hundreds of people were scooped from the roofs of crumbling houses, 300 emergency hospitals were set up and 3,600 nurses arrived to staff them. It would take more than $25 million in relief funds to administer to the injured and displaced alone.

UNITED STATES
OREGON

June 14, 1903

• • • • • • • • • • • • • •

Three hundred twenty-five drowned and one third of the town of Heppner, Oregon was destroyed when a flash flood, the product of a hail and rainstorm, transformed Willow Creek into a killer torrent on June 14, 1903.

A lightning-fast hail and rainstorm that lasted a mere half hour triggered a flash flood at 4 P.M. on June 14, 1903, in the foothills of the Blue Mountains of Oregon, near Willow Creek. An enormous amount of rain fell in those 30 minutes, enough to turn Willow Creek into a raging, churning dynamo that generated 25-foot-high waves and sent them crashing into nearby Heppner.

For almost an hour, the floodwaters raged through the town, sweeping away 200 buildings—one third of the town—and drowning 325 people. In the short space of an hour and a half, nature changed the face of an entire community, caused $250 million in damage, and dramatically altered the population of this formerly peaceful place.

UNITED STATES
OREGON (AND WASHINGTON, CALIFORNIA, IDAHO AND NEVADA)

December 1964

• • • • • • • • • • • • • •

Fifty were killed and over 12,000 homes were destroyed in the "Christmas Week" floods that roared through Oregon in December 1964, and, to a lesser degree, affected Washington, California, Idaho and Nevada.

The Christmas Week floods of 1964 affected five states—Oregon, Washington, California, Idaho and Nevada, destroying over 12,000 homes and killing 50 people. But by far the greatest damage and loss of life occurred in Oregon, where the cause of the flood originated.

A cold front from Alaska brought plummeting temperatures and a record snowfall in the Cascade Mountains and the surrounding countryside during the middle of December. Shortly before Christmas, meteorological conditions reversed, and sharply rising temperatures produced a sudden thaw. More than a foot of mountain snow melted each day for three straight days, and this, compounded by steady rains, swelled the Willamette, John Day and Deschutes rivers considerably beyond their floodstages.

During Christmas week, paper mills were wiped away, and tides 75 feet above normal overflowed dams, crumbled roads and uprooted bridges. The newly constructed 160-foot bridge across the John Day River near Estacada was hit while holiday travelers were crossing it. With one horrendous roar, it split in the middle, hurtling one car and its driver into the floodwaters below and thoroughly terrifying other motorists and their passengers who narrowly escaped the same fate.

Civil Defense crews and Red Cross personnel were flown into the stricken areas of the state by helicopters on Christmas Day. It would be after New Year's before major cities like Portland and Corvallis would dry out.

UNITED STATES
PENNSYLVANIA
JOHNSTOWN

May 31, 1889

• • • • • • • • • • • • • • •

Over 2,500 died and thousands were made homeless when the South Fork Dam collapsed, and the Conemaugh River roared into Johnstown, Pennsylvania on May 31, 1889.

"Run for your lives! The dam has burst!" was a line in a joke in Johnstown, Pennsylvania before May 31, 1889. After that date, it became a grim reminder of a monumentally cataclysmic day in which, in the space of one hour, over 2,500 people lost their lives as 4.5 billion gallons of water weighing 20 million tons burst through a sorrowfully neglected and obsolete earthen dam above that Pennsylvania steel city. The water laid waste to everything and everybody in its thundering descent.

Johnstown is located in the flat land where the Little Conemaugh River and Stony Creek come together to form the Conemaugh River. In 1824, 14 miles upstream of Johnstown, engineers hired by the state of Pennsylvania began a 12-year project that would create a system of canals, between Pittsburgh and Johnstown. The system would allow barges to move between the cities and be the last link in a chain of canal and rail conduits between the coal mines, iron deposits and limestone quarries near Jamestown and the commerce hub of Pittsburgh.

Thus, work began on the South Fork Dam, in its time, the largest earthen dam in the world, holding back the largest man-made lake in the world. Looming 100 feet above the old creek bed, its dirt atop an arched stone culvert rose a mere 72 feet in height. However, it measured 272 feet thick at its base, 10 feet at its top, and stretched 931 feet from rock wall to rock wall. The culvert housed five cast-iron pipes, each two feet in diameter, which would, through the regulation of valves in a nearby wooden tower, discharge water from a two-mile-long, mile-wide 70-feet-deep reservoir that contained approximately 5 billion gallons of water. In addition, a spillway 72 feet wide was cut nine feet deep into the rock abutting the eastern end of the dam.

From the time the dam was finished, it was obsolete. By this time, canal-rail links had been replaced by purely rail links through the Allegheny mountains, and so, in 1879, Pennsylvania sold the dam and its reservoir for $2,000

to promoter Benjamin F. Ruff. Ruff then incorporated the South Fork Fishing and Hunting Club, and sold $2,000 memberships to, among others, Andrew Carnegie, Andrew Mellon, Henry Clay Frick and Philander C. Knox. Cottages and a clubhouse were built, and makeshift repairs were made to the deteriorating dam. Hemlock branches, tree stumps and straw were used to patch up holes. The discharge pipes were removed, and the outlet was filled in, thus leaving only the spillway to prevent floods from topping the dam, whose crest was lowered to accommodate a 20-foot roadway. The spillway itself was blocked by debris when a fish-catching, iron mesh net was strung across it.

The residents of Johnstown were not altogether unaware of the dangers from flooding that these modifications posed. Every year there was flooding of some sort, including the famous "pumpkin flood" of 1820, when thousands of pumpkins floated into the city from farms upstream.

Thus, in 1880, Daniel J. Morrell, the president of the Cambria Iron Company, retained an engineer to inspect the dam. His findings were disquieting, but nevertheless Ruff stated publicly, "You and your people are in no danger from our enterprise."

Nine years later, at the end of May 1889, an unusually heavy storm struck the mountain region of western Pennsylvania, saturating 12,000 square miles of earth that was already soaked by the sudden melting of 14 inches of snow the month before. Rivers were full to their banks, and the lake above Johnstown had filled to the point at which tons of water were already hurtling through the partially blocked overflow channel. (It was later calculated that up to 75,000 gallons of water per second were entering the lake by way of swollen feeder streams and the rainfall. The spill was only equipped to handle 45,000 gallons per second. And that was when it was entirely clear of debris.)

On the morning of May 31, 1889, a crew of 30 men, overseen by South Fork Fishing and Hunting Club president Colonel E. J. Unger and accompanied by engineer John G. Parke, attempted to shore up the dam. "Rip-rap"—the small stone wedges that had supported the dam—were beginning to fall away from the top, and no amount of shoveling of more earth onto the dam or attempts to clear away the obstructions in the fish gratings was going to forestall the inevitable.

At 11 A.M., the 23-year-old engineer mounted a horse and began a solitary ride through the valley to warn residents to evacuate.

At 3:10 P.M., the dam gave way. According to one witness, "When the dam broke, the water seemed to leap, scarcely touching the ground. It bounded down the valley, crashing and roaring, carrying everything before it." A wall of water 150 feet high rushed toward the village of South

The wreckage left behind after the South Fork dam burst above Johnstown, Pennsylvania on May 31, 1889. Library of Congress.

Fork at an estimated 50 mph. The village was wisely built on high ground, and only 24 houses were swept away.

But now, as the waters plunged forward, they picked up flotsam—houses, trees, the stones of a railroad bridge—a few miles downstream from South Fork. A freight train waiting to cross the bridge was abruptly shifted into reverse by its engineer, John Hess, when he received a telegraphed warning of the water's arrival. He backed the train six miles downstream to East Conemaugh, just ahead of the flood.

While the train had been backing up, the floodwaters had smashed into the village of Mineral Point, wiping it out, killing 16 persons and sending its Methodist Church spinning and hurtling downstream.

In the Pennsylvania Railroad yard and roundhouse at East Conemaugh, 33 Consolidation model locomotives, weighing, with their tenders, 170,625 pounds apiece, were suddenly picked up—along with 315 freight and 18 passenger cars—and flung about as if they were toys. One

engine was later found buried in rock and sand nearly a mile from its original location.

After gutting East Conemaugh, the now lethal debris-carrying wave careened through the town of Woodvale, uprooting 800 buildings, killing close to 1,000 of its residents and smashing 255 houses to tinder. Hundreds of people were seen hanging from pilings and rooftops as their improvised rafts were driven furiously downstream.

Moments later, the water hit the steel mills of the Gautier Wireworks, bursting its boilers and sending a towering plume of steam hundreds of feet into the air.

At a little after 4 P.M., the enormous wave, containing the remains of houses and factories, railroad cars and engines, trees, telegraph poles, steel rails, rocks and the bodies of hundreds of people and animals, reached the outskirts of Johnstown. It would take 10 minutes to span the city and in those 10 minutes more than 1,000 people would die. "In an instant," according to one reporter, "the deserted streets became black with people running for their lives. The flood came and licked them up with one eager and ferocious lap."

Within seconds, enormous stone buildings collapsed under the assault of the wave, trapping hundreds who doubtless thought these buildings would offer them safe haven. The German Luthern Church and YMCA, both stone monoliths, crumbled and fell in on themselves. All of the municipal buildings were flattened. The Hulbert House, an elegant brick hotel, fell, drowning all 60 of its guests, who were trapped on a third floor staircase leading to the roof and supposed safety.

Families were decimated. Parents saw their children slip, one by one, from roofs into the water. Others were miraculously saved when they transferred themselves—or were transferred by the swirling currents and the persistance of fate—from one floating cluster of wreckage to another.

Finally, just below Johnstown, the flood waters encountered a stone railroad bridge standing 32 feet above the normal river level. It remained standing, and the mountain of debris and river piled up against it. One huge, heaving mass of ruined homes, parts of the landscape and human beings, both alive and dead, rose to a height of 30 feet and extended back into Johnstown for 30 blocks.

Coal stoves containing live coals had been picked up by the flood; a railroad car loaded with lime caught fire when its contents reacted chemically with the water. By 6 P.M., the mountain piled against the bridge had become a massive pyre of flame. People caught in the mass struggled to free themselves.

"It reminded me of a lot of flies on flypaper, struggling to get away, with no hope," said one observer. Another witness reported, "As the fire licked up house after house and pile after pile, I could see men and women kiss each other goodbye and fathers and mothers kiss their children. The flames swallowed them up and hid them from my view, but I could hear their shrieks as they roasted alive."

Two hundred people were pulled from the debris; countless others perished. The next day, more survivors were dug from under the rubble; others were found in the wreckage of their homes. One five-month-old baby was discovered nearly a hundred miles downstream in Pittsburgh, floating on the floor of a ravaged house. For weeks, bodies floated downstream and surfaced, threatening a spread of disease.

Help came quickly, and lasted through a long, horrible summer. Among the hundreds who arrived was Clara Barton, one of the founders of the American Red Cross. "The Angel of the Civil War Battlefields," then 68 years old, worked tirelessly for five months, distributing $500,000 worth of money and materials and supervising the building of three large structures to provide shelter to the thousands of homeless refugees.

All summer long, the city rehabilitated itself. Over $3 million in aid and workers filtered in, and Johnstown gradually took shape again.

UNITED STATES
SOUTH DAKOTA
RAPID CITY

June 9, 1972

• • • • • • • • • • • • • • • •

Torrential rain and the collapse of two dams brought about the flooding of Rapid City, South Dakota on June 9, 1972. Two hundred sixty-three people died; hundreds were injured; 1,200 homes were destroyed.

A flash flood that devastated Rapid City, South Dakota and collapsed two nearby dams began with an unexpected 10-inch rainfall on the night of June 9, 1972. By 9 P.M., Rapid Creek, which ran directly through the heart of the city, had swollen from a creek into something resembling a large river. Twenty feet wide in the afternoon, it was 400 feet wide after 9 P.M.

Within minutes, undermined buildings began to crumble and wave-driven waters started to smack against telephone poles and wooden dwellings, which collapsed like piles of matchsticks. Most residents of the city were either in bed or lounging before their television sets, which had reported no warnings.

Harold Higgins, a local reporter, later told the *New York Times*, "I was standing in the middle of [a] road when a four-foot bank of water came down the creek." Trailers shot by him like racing speedboats. "It [was] like a war zone," he went on. ". . . fires all over the place, and nothing [could] be done about it because the city [was] cut in half by the flooding of Rapid Creek."

Meanwhile, the dams at Canyon Lake and Deerfield burst, and the nearby village of Keystone was swept entirely away by the rushing waters. Not one building remained standing, and the death toll was high.

While residents were still huddled on rooftops or clung to trees and high promentories of land, 1,800 South Dakota National Guardsmen, quartered in Camp Rapid on the western edge of the city, moved in with rescue vehicles.

For days afterward, bodies floated through the streets and were unearthed when debris was sifted. Refrigerator trucks were used to pick up and store the bodies to prevent the spread of disease.

Shortly thereafter, President Richard Nixon declared Rapid City and its surroundings a national disaster area, which brought federal funds into the stunned area. When the casualties were counted, 236 people were reported dead, 1,200 homes were destroyed, another 2,500 were damaged and 5,000 automobiles were wrecked beyond use. Hundreds of people were injured and the damage was reckoned at $100 million.

UNITED STATES
TEXAS
GALVESTON

August 1990

• • • • • • • • • • • • • •

(See HURRICANES.)

THE WORLD

2400 B.C.

• • • • • • • • • • • • • •

Scientific evidence indicates that the Great Deluge of the Old Testament probably occurred in approximately 2400 B.C., and covered the known world at that time.

Of course, the date of the Great Deluge and Flood of the Book of Genesis must be approximate. There are no written records of the precise day and hour, nor is there universal agreement about the year or the location. But scientific evidence gathered within the past 50 years has confirmed that such a flood actually did take place.

Consider the synchronicity of myths from various civilizations. The Chinese have a story of a universal deluge that, according to some historians, must have occurred at the time of the Biblical deluge. Although there is no evidence of widespread disaster in this account, there is evidence that there was flooding on an enormous scale.

Peruvian records speak of a huge inundation occurring before the time of the Incas. The story parallels that of Noah, except that in it, six people were saved from the flood, and they owed their lives to a float. Geological evidence likewise proves that there have been many cataclysmic inroads of the sea into this region.

The coastal area of Chile, near Concepcion, has a long history of flood disaster, and the native Araucanian Indians have a flood legend. Earthquakes and sea waves permeate this story, and, in recorded history, earthquakes and sea waves repeatedly struck the area, including the devastating one of 1751. What is particularly fascinating is that the tribal legend parallels the Mosaic Deluge in that only a few people were saved by taking refuge on a mountaintop, although no ark is mentioned. Even today, when earthquakes occur in Chile, people of Indian descent flee to the mountains in fear that the sea will again cover the world.

There is also archeological evidence. In 1872, George Smith, a young official in the British Museum, discovered a portion of the story of the Great Deluge and Flood on a broken tablet taken from the library at Ninevah. It spoke of a ship docking on the mountain, and a dove being set forth.

Other excavations at Nippur in the lower Euphrates valley yielded a library of over 20,000 tablets, made before 2000 B.C., and in one of the Sumerian texts, an Assyrian version of the Flood was discovered. In it, there is a hero who is a priest and king, a godly man very much like Noah. In it, God warns the hero, and a ship is mentioned.

The most dramatic archeological find, however, was uncovered in 1929 near the pre-2000 B.C. dead city of Ur on the Euphrates River in what is now Iraq. A 62-foot section was cut at Ur that showed some evidence of having been occupied by humans. In one part of the section, there is a 10-foot stratum of clay or sand in which there is no evidence of human life. Below this, there are remains of a human civilization that are consistent with remains found above the clay or sand interruption. Normally, it would take a very long time to accumulate 10 feet of silt, but the comparative thicknesses and the evidence below the belt of sand and clay show that this took place in a very short time.

Add to this the evidence from the Summerian civilization, which occupied Mesopotamia from 5000 B.C., forward, in which records indicate that the period around 2400 B.C. was one of abnormally heavy rainfall in West and Central Asia.

PLAGUES AND EPIDEMICS

· · · · · · · · · · · · · · · · · ·

THE WORST RECORDED PLAGUES AND EPIDEMICS

• • • • •

CHRONOLOGY

• • • • • • • •

1340
Italy (plague)
1348–1666
• Europe ("Black Death"—"second pandemic")
1386
Smolensk, Russia (plague)
1493
• Europe (syphilis epidemic)
1505–1530
• Italy (typhus epidemic)
1507
West Indies (smallpox epidemic)
1518
• France (St. Vitus's dance epidemic)
1544
Budapest, Hungary (typhus epidemic)
1560
Brazil (smallpox epidemic)
1625
Great Britain (plague)
1632
France (plague)
1656
Italy (plague)
1665
• Great Britain (plague)

1672
Naples, Italy (plague)
1721
Massachusetts (smallpox epidemic)
1760
Syria (plague)
1792
Egypt (plague)
1793
• Pennsylvania (yellow fever epidemic)
1799
Africa (plague)
1812
India (plague)
• Russia (typhus epidemic)
1826–1837
Europe (cholera epidemic)
1832
• London, Great Britain (cholera epidemic)
1846–1860
• The World (cholera epidemic)
1855–Present
• The World (plague)

1876
India (see FAMINES AND DROUGHTS)
1889
The World (influenza epidemic)
1896–1907
• India (plague)
1899
• California (plague—"third pandemic")
1903
Panama (yellow fever epidemic)
1910–1913
China (and India) (plague)
1917–1921
Russia (typhus epidemic)
1918–1919
• The World (influenza epidemic)
1921–1923
India (plague)
1926–1930
India (smallpox epidemic)
1958
India (smallpox, cholera epidemic)
1974
India (smallpox epidemic)
1980–Present
• The World (AIDS epidemic)

PLAGUES AND EPIDEMICS

• • • • •

Of all natural calamities, plagues and epidemics affect the human population of the Earth most directly and most devastatingly. And although other natural disasters may be more spectacular and abusive to buildings and landscapes, plagues and epidemics bear a disquieting resemblance to the neutron bombs that scientists dangled tantalizingly before the public in the early days of the atomic age, bombs which destroyed people but left cities standing. Plagues and epidemics also destroy people. Only people.

And they have a disturbing longevity about them. Tornadoes are over in an instant; volcanic eruptions in minutes; floods, earthquakes and hurricanes in hours. Only famine and droughts, in some circumstances, challenge plagues and epidemics in longevity.

Strictly speaking, there is only one transmitted disease to which the term plague can be rightly applied: bubonic plague, the *Rattus rattus* of antiquity. This disease spread by rodents is graphically chronicled in the cuneiform writings of Babylonia.

The plague bacillus, *Pasteurella pestis*, is spread among rodents by *Xenopsylla cheopis*, a flea that inhabits the fur of these rodents. These fleas also like to feed on the blood of humans, and thus, most plagues involve mass movements of rats, which invade the environs of man. When the host rat dies, its fleas, in search of food, attack humans.

When this vector bites, and infection occurs, there is a swelling of human lymph nodes, causing buboes (which is derived from the Greek word *boubon*, meaning groin or swelling in the groin). Often if the victim does not succumb to the primary infection, the organism often invades the lungs causing pneumonic plague, a secondary infection. Each results in a high fever, which is followed by delirium, vomiting, bleeding and eventually death.

For centuries, bubonic plague roared through the inhabited world with mysterious velocity. In fact, the connection between fleas, rats and plague was not made until the end of the 19th century.

Even though Babylonian writing reported large quantities of rats, it did not link them to the pestilence that occurred at the same time. Nor did medieval historians writing of the Black Death make this connection.

It is only through informed hindsight, through connecting large migrations of rats and fleas, that medical historians have been able, in the 20th century, to put together the pattern, history and magnitude of plagues.

Epidemics can arise from a number of sources and are transmitted in a variety of ways. Again, before modern medicine it was universally accepted that plagues and epidemics alike were transmitted either through the intervention of the gods or through miasmas, or vapors. Thus, medieval families would often seal their homes from the inside, while the infection raged unchecked within their tightly packaged dwellings, killing them all.

One of the most persistent epidemics is cholera. A water-borne disease that is spread through sewage-contaminated rivers or urban water supplies, it is characterized by profuse diarrhea, vomiting, muscular cramps, dehydration and ultimate collapse. Rampant in the 19th century, it is still with us today.

Other epidemics such as yellow fever, syphilis, poliomyelitis, influenza, encephalitis and puerperal fever (a hospital-related epidemic disease) have been largely brought under control through the efforts of modern medicine. Still, wherever starvation, privation or unsanitary conditions prevail, epidemics can occur.

A word, however, about what we term "epidemic." Each year, local television and radio stations broadcast illustrated maps and lectures about certain epidemics—of influenza, for instance. These localized epidemics are certainly worth recording, and will, alas, be worthy of note for the foreseeable future. The influenza virus, to cite one, has a vicious habit of adapting itself to new vaccines. As soon as a vaccine is developed to stem the tide of one strain, another develops. The only bright note in this frustrating picture is that in modern times, at least, these epidemics tend to limit and localize themselves.

Two current epidemics, however, do not limit and localize themselves, and they have sinister possiblities. The first, Lyme disease, often evades detection in its early stages by disguising itself behind symptoms of lesser afflictions—flu, allergies, etc. It is also a young epidemic, whose impact has yet to be felt in a wide geographical sense. AIDS, the second pervasive epidemic of today, which has entered its adolescence, has the potential, unless a cure is soon found, of escalating into one of the most devastating pandemics in all of recorded history.

And that final term, "pandemic" is worth a close examination, for it has given rise to a certain amount of confusion and conflict among medical historians and scientists. A pandemic is generally defined as an epidemic or plague that affects an enormous number of people across a wide geographic area.

The first of the three great plague pandemics, is generally thought to have begun in the 15th year of the Roman emperor Justinian I (thus its sobri-

quet, "The Plague of Justinian"). It raged from A.D. 531 until roughly A.D. 650, approximately 100 years.

The second pandemic, also agreed upon by most historians, is that of the Black Death. It began in 1348 and lasted over 300 years, until 1666 and the Great Fire of London—although some few historians seem to think that its pandemic stage lasted only four years.

The third pandemic began in China in 1892, and, according to some historians, ended 15 years later. To others, however, it continued until 1959. And to others, notably Charles T. Gregg in his compelling case study, *Plague!*, published in 1978, it is still with us. "Plague is now neighbor to us all," he states unequivocally, "for many, only a few hours away, at most a day's journey distant. Plague is a willing handmaiden to famine and war; these threaten us still—perhaps more so than ever. The plague bacillus and its hosts show increasing signs of resistance to antibiotics and pesticides. This raises the specter of our most potent weapons against the pestilence splintering in our hands at that moment when they are most needed."

· · · · · · · · · · · · · · ·

EUROPE

1348–1666

· · · · · · · · · · · · · · ·

In the 300 years of its existence in Europe, from 1348 to 1666, the bubonic plague known as the Black Death killed 25 million people. Its demise was due to three possible causes: the fire of London, the change of seasons and an improvement in sanitation.

The immense, horrific bubonic plague that roamed and ravaged Europe for 300 years killed 25 million people, or one-third of the population of Europe at that time. The Black Death, as it was known, is considered to be the most deadly natural catastrophe in recorded time.

Worse than a war, since it recognized no national boundaries, more cruel and painful in its attack upon its victims than an earthquake, and more terrifying, because of its hidden nature, than the eruption of a volcano or the coming of a hurricane, the Black Death—so called because it was first carried by black rats—held all of western civilization in its thrall for generations.

The first evidence of *Pasteurella pestis*, the parasite responsible for the disease, as nearly as historians and scientists can ascertain, was in 1334, in the vicinity of Lake Issyk-Kul in the province of Semiryeschensk, in what is now the Kirgiz Soviet Socialist Republic, and called by Charles T. Gregg in his study, *Plague!*, ". . . part of the primordial plague reservoir of central Asia."

Carried by black rats transporting fleas which were infested with *Pasteurella pestis*, the plague spread south and east to China, India and then west to Turkistan.

In 1347, in the Crimean trading port of Kaffa (which is now the southern Russian city of Feodoiya) a group of enterprising Genoese traders became trapped in a years-long seige by the Janibeg Kipchak Khan. Kaffa was the major port for goods from Genoa, but that made little difference to the Khan, who held Kaffa hostage, fighting off any and all invaders, except one: the Black Death. The disease arrived early in 1348 and mowed down his long limbed Tartar troops as surely as if they had been defeated by overwhelming military forces.

According to the contemporary account of Gabriel de Mussis, a Piacenza notary who is thought to be an eyewitness: "Infinite numbers of Tartars and Saracens suddenly fell dead of an inexplicable disease . . . and behold the disease invaded all the army of the Tartars . . . every day . . . thousands were killed . . . the humors coagulated in the groins, they developed a subsequent putrid fever and died, all council and aid of the doctors failing. . . ."

The Khan, ever resourceful and barbaric, decided to use the corpses of his fallen army as ammunition and thus launched the first known biological warfare attack. "The Tartars," de Mussis continued, "fatigued by such a plague and pestiferous disease, stupefied and amazed, observing themselves dying without hope of health ordered cadavers placed on their hurling machines and thrown into the city of Caffa [sic], so that by means of these intolerable passengers the defenders died widely. Thus there were projected mountains of dead, nor could the Christians hide or flee, or be freed from such disaster . . . they allowed the dead to be consigned to the waves. And soon all the air was infected and the water poisoned, corrupt and putrefied, and such a great odor increased. . . ."

The contaminated Genoan sailors now boarded their boats and sailed back to Italy, infested with the fleas themselves, and unleashing, down the anchor ropes and into the Italian port, hordes of black rats that were similarly contaminated. The Genoans, however, were not the only ones spreading the Black Death into Europe. Sixteen galleys brought plague to Italy, and only four of them came from Kaffa. Twelve others, bearing returning Crusaders from Constantinople, docked in Messina, Sicily at roughly the same time. The Crusaders were already infected.

By the end of 1348, all of Italy was blanketed by plague, and most of France was beginning to feel its grim affects. Switzerland was infected by August, as was England, via a ship from Calais that put into the Dorsetshire port of Melcombe. By the end of 1349, Scotland, Ireland, Denmark and most of Germany were under its influence. Norwegian ships carried the plague as far as Iceland, where the entire population would be wiped out, and to Poland and Russia, both of which would be contaminated by 1351.

The number of fatalities was astronomical. Half of the population of Italy died. Nine out of every 10 residents of London succumbed. In the year 1348, 1,244,434 inhabitants of what is now Germany were killed by the plague. In the Russian city of Smolensk, only five persons remained alive by 1386.

It was not a pretty death. According to Michael Plateinsis of Piaza, quoted in Johannes Nohl's study, *The Black Death*: "Those infected felt themselves penetrated by a pain throughout their whole bodies and, so to say, undermined. Then there developed in their thighs or on their upper arms a boil. . . . This infected the whole body and penetrated it so far that the patient violently vomited blood.

This . . . continued without intermission for three days, there being no means of healing it, and then the patient expired."

Thoroughly terrified and helpless, the potential victims of the plague began to act in decidedly inhuman ways. "Not only those who had intercourse with them died, but also those who had touched or used any of their things . . ." continued Platiensis. "Soon men hated each other so much that, if a son was attacked by the disease, his father would not tend him. If, in spite of all, he dared to approach him, he was immediately infected and . . . was bound to expire within three days. . . ."

In Florence, the plague was at its worst, so much so that the Black Death was sometimes referred to as the Plague of Florence. Here, according to Giovanni Boccaccio in *The Decameron*, "[some] went about, carrying in their hands, some flowers, some odoriferous herbs and other some divers kind of spiceries, which they set often to their noses, accounting it an excellent thing to fortify the brain with such odours, more by token that the air seemed all heavy and attainted with the stench of the dead bodies and that of the sick and of the remedies used."

In Parma, Francesco Petrarch echoed this: "Alas, my loving brother, what shall I say? How can I begin? Where shall I turn? Everything is woe, terror everywhere. You may see in me what you have read in Virgil of the great city, with 'everywhere tearing pain, everywhere fear and the manifold images of death.' Oh, brother, would that I had never been born or that I had already met my death!"

In France, the papal city of Avignon, the residence of Pope Clement VI, was horrendously invaded by the plague. An unidentified canon, writing to his family in Belgium and quoted in George Deaux's book, *The Black Death 1347*, chronicled the sad scene: ". . . one-half, or more than a half of the people at Avignon are already dead. Within the walls of the city there are now more than 7,000 houses shut up; in these no one is living, and all who have inhabited them are departed; the suburbs hardly contain any people at all. A field near 'Our Lady of Miracles' has been bought by the Pope and consecreated as a cemetery. In this, from the 13th of March, 11,000 corpses have been buried. . . ."

Later, Pope Clement would consecrate the Rhone River so that surplus corpses might be dumped into it. The Pope himself would survive, protected by two huge fires kept burning night and day on either side of him.

In England, William Dene, a monk of Rochester, recorded the scene: "To our great grief, the plague carried off so vast a multitude of people of both sexes that nobody could be found who would bear the corpses to the grave. Men and women carried their own children on their shoulders to the church and threw them into a common pit. From these pits such an appalling stench was given off that scarcely anyone dared even to walk beside the cemeteries."

And so it went throughout all of Europe. Frantic to escape the pain and horror and inevitable death of the plague, victims turned to physicians who knew no more than they how to cure or prevent the scourging sickness, but who continued to experiment with all sorts of palliatives.

Some doctors prescribed human fecees to be worn around the neck in a bag. Others prescribed bathing in and drinking urine. Leeches and dried toads and lizards were applied to boils to suck out the poison. Butter and lard were lathered into open wounds. Testicles were run though with needles. The blood of freshly slain pigeons and puppies was smeared on feverish foreheads. A French physician, Guy de Chauliac, sliced open the boils and inserted red hot pokers into the open wounds. This primitive purification method did meet with some success with those who didn't die from a heart attack, go into irreversible shock, or become insane from the pain.

There was, too, the problem of the "poisoned rooms" of those who died from the plague. Fresh milk was placed on a platter in the middle of a sick room to absorb the poisoned air. An anonymous London physician offered the following prescription for decontaminating a home in which a plague victim died: ". . . take large Oynions pale them and lay three or foure of them upon the ground, let hem l ie ten daies, those picled Oynions will gather all the infection into them that is in one of those Roomes, but burie those Oynions afterwards deep in the ground."

Bewildered that neither physicians nor priests could stop the Black Death, many poor souls turned either to extreme piousness, or, despairing of a God whom they felt had turned from them, turned to hunting down scapegoats, to unregenerate licentiousness and voluptuousness, to amulets and charms, or even to devil worship. In many respects, the Black Death set civilization back centuries.

There were isolated pockets of positiveness; some of the very pious set in place some traditions that have endured. The villagers of Oberammergau, for instance, vowed to present a religious performance at intervals forever if the dread hand of the pestilence was lifted from them. Their vow was given toward the end of the plague, in 1634, and the plague left them. They still present their Passion Play.

But these shafts of sunlight in a dark time were perhaps brighter for their rarity. The zealous and feverish in their religious fervor, did monumental ill. The flagellants, the so-called "Brethren of the Cross" roamed the countryside, arriving in village squares, where they performed their rituals of self-flagellation in atonement for the sins that had

supposedly brought on the plague, while at the same time probably spreading the plague itself by their travels.

The search for scapegoats fueled anti-Semitism. In May 1348, the Jewish communities in three cities of southern France were exterminated. Aged and newborn, healthy and firm, men, women and children were all savagely murdered. In September of that same year, a Jewish physician in Chillon, Switzerland confessed, after having been brutally tortured, that he and other members of the Jewish community had poisoned the wells. The news spread fast, and all over Europe, some 60 large and 150 small Jewish communities were wiped out in 350 separate massacres.

A nursery rhyme and a fairy tale found their roots in the plague.

> *Ring around the Rosies,*
> *Pocket full of posies,*
> *Achoo, Achoo,*
> *All fall down.*

This was a description, supposedly, of the habit of wearing garlands of flowers in plague time to ward off miasma. However, the failure of the remedy is evidenced by the last two lines, in which the wearers gasp and fall dead on the spot.

The more cheerful fairy tale involves the Pied Piper of Hamelin, the German town afflicted by the plague and a rising rat population in 1348 and again in 1361. Historically, the facts pretty much parallel the story and Robert Browning's poem: An army of rats invaded Hamelin. The town corporation hired an itinerant ratcatcher. When the rats were cleaned out, and the ratcatcher demanded his fee, the corporation offered him a pittance. The ratcatcher stormed out of town, swearing revenge. Meanwhile, the children of Hamelin gathered up the rat corpses that were littering the streets and tossed them into the swift-flowing River Wescr. But, having been exposed to the plague, the children died, and they were buried in a new cemetery dug on the side of Koppelberg Hill, the place in the tale in which the earth opened up and the Pied Piper and the children disappeared forever.

Unaffected by the measures of God or man, the plague persisted, as did its manifestations in the consequent habits of the populace. All sorts of remedies and penances continued to be tried—some effective, some not. Dancing was one of the more macabre ones that did not. In this fanatical act of penance, thousands of victims would dance wildly on platforms erected for them in public squares, in a goulish, aptly named Dance of Death, until they dropped from fatigue or the effects of the plague. Others trampled on them, thus assuring their deaths.

In a more effective method of containing the plague, the tradition of quarantine was put into practice for ships in port. Forty days (probably because of its religious significance) was the time assigned to ships kept at anchor in various ports, and, although this probably prevented the spread of the plague into these ports from ships at sea, it also set some ships adrift, as every man aboard succumbed to the Black Death.

All in all, it was a dolorous time of the world, a Veblenian way of trimming down a population that had strained the natural resources of Europe. The one weapon that could have conquered the plague—sanitation—would be implemented in 1666, when the plague would suddenly disappear. Some credited its end to the London fire; others to the change of seasons. Few realized at the time that it was probably soap and water that were responsible.

For details concerning the end of the Black Death, see PLAGUES AND EPIDEMICS, Great Britain, London, 1665, p. 146.

EUROPE
1493

• • • • • • • • • • • • • •

Millions not afflicted by the Black Death died in a 50-year epidemic of syphilis that ravaged Europe from 1493 to 1543.

In the midst of the Black Death, parts of both Europe and the New World were riven by a 50-year epidemic of syphilis. Its origins are contradictory. According to one school, the so-called "Columbian School" quoted by J. F. D. Shrewbury in an article, "The Saints and Epidemic Disease" in the *Birmingham Medical Review*, the disease was endemic among the natives of the West Indies, and was transmitted sexually by the Carib women to the sailors of Columbus, who then imported it into Europe.

A much more persuasive case than the Columbian one can be made for the *Morbus Gallicus* or "French Disease" theory, in which the disease originated in France in 1493, and then spread from there to Spain, the islands of the Mediterranean and Italy via the French army of King Charles VIII. Giovanni di Vigo, surgeon to pope Julius II, blamed its entrance into Italy on the seige of Naples, in 1494, and Rodrigo Ruiz de Isla, in his *Treatise on the Serpentine Malady*, reaffirmed this: "In . . . 1494 the most Christian King Charles of France who was then reigning having gathered a great army passed into Italy. And at the time he entered the country with his host many Spaniards infected with this disease were in it and at once the camp began to be infected with the aforesaid malady and the French, as they did not know what it was, thought it came from the atmosphere of the region. The French called it the disease of Naples."

Whatever the source, it was a new disease, which the poet, physician and philosopher Girolamo Fracastoro named syphilis in his essay, "Syphilis or the French Disease," Sipylus, the son of Niobe, who claimed that she should be worshipped equally with Leto the mother of Apollo because she had borne seven times as many children as Leto. In retaliation for this effrontery, Apollo destroyed all her sons.

It apparently took little time for physicians to discover that the disease was transmitted sexually. Armies left the then fatal disease behind as they invaded, and subsequent armies contracted it from female citizens with whom they had sexual intercourse. Fracastoro described the progress of the disease on an "illustrious YOUTH [sic] of Verona":

. . . The wretched man, too confident to fear such dire mischance, was attacked by this disease. . . . By slow degrees that shining springtide, that flower of young manhood, fell to ruin as his vital force declined; then, dreadful to relate, foul corruption fastened on his wretched limbs, and deep within, the larger bones began to swell with loathsome abscesses. Foul ulcers (shame on the mercy of heaven!) began to devour the fair eyes which the light of day loved to look upon; to feed, too, on nostrils gnawed away by bitter wounds. And then, doomed too soon by unkind fate, the luckless youth left behind him the now hateful air of heaven and the light of day. . . .

Treatment evolved swiftly; mercury was used to dissolve the scabs, and this treatment was continued into the mid-19th century. Still, millions would die in this epidemic of the end of the 15th and beginning of the 16th century, but according to British Researcher R. S. Morton, "With the spread of the Renaissance influences of education, sophistication in dress, and improved personal hygiene, the complex known so widely as *Morbus Gallicus* faded from central Europe. Residuals were found in the most backward areas, causing sporadic outbreaks."

In the 20th century, first arsenic-bismuth and then penicillin were introduced to treat syphilis and thus prevent further epidemics. Still, the disease is reported to be on the increase.

FRANCE
1518

• • • • • • • • • • • • • •

Hundreds danced themselves to death in an outbreak of an unexplained affliction termed "St. Vitus's dance" in France in 1518.

The curious outbreak of St. Vitus's dance in Strasbourg, France in 1518 was, conceivably, a side effect of the religious and fanatic dancing that accompanied the Black Death (see p. 142). According to medical historian George Rosen of Yale University, this epidemic of continued dancing occurred

> . . . *eight days before the feast of Mary Magdalene [when] a woman began to dance, and after this went on for some four to six days she was sent to the chapel of St. Vitus at Hohlenstein, near Zabern. Soon thereafter, more dancers appeared and the number grew until more than a hundred danced at a time. Eventually, the municipal council forbade all public gatherings and music, restricted the dancers to two guild halls, and then sent them off to the chapel of St. Vitus. According to one account, more than four hundred people were affected within four weeks. . . .*

Hundreds literally danced themselves to death in this, one of the strangest epidemics ever.

GREAT BRITAIN
LONDON
1665

• • • • • • • • • • • • • • •

The end of the Black Death occurred in England in 1666. Some historians and writers of the time, among them Samuel Pepys, insisted that it was a self-contained "English Plague" that lasted for a mere two years.

Although most historians consider the Great Plague of London actually to mark the end of the Black Death, which began in 1348 (see pp. 142–145), others consider it to be a separate event, confined solely to London and the surrounding countryside.

It was Samuel Pepys, in his diaries, who graphically chronicled the Plague of London:

> *20th [June] . . . Walked to Redriffe, where I hear the sickness is, and indeed it is scattered almost every where, there dying 1,089 of the plague this week. . . . Lord! to see how the plague spreads! it now being all over King's Streete, at the Ace, and next door to it, and in other places. . . . 12th [August] . . . The people die so, that now it seems they are fain to carry the dead to be buried by daylight, the nights not sufficing to do it in. . . . 31st . . . the plague having a great encrease this week, beyond all expectation, or almost 2,000, making the general [Mortality] Bill 7,000, odd 100; and the plague above 6,000. Thus the month ends with great sadness upon the*

publick, through the greatness of the plague everywhere throughout the kingdom almost. Every day sadder and sadder news of its encrease. In the City died this week 7,496, and of them 6,102 of the plague. But it is feared that the true number of the dead this week is near 10,000. . . . 16th October . . . I walked to the Tower; but, Lord! how empty the streets are, and melancholoy, so many poor, sick people in the streets full of sores; and so many sad stories overheard as I walk, everybody talking of this dead, and that man sick, and so many in this place, and so many in that. And they tell me that, in Westminster, there is never a physician and but one apothecary left, all being dead. . . .

The disease was spread to the surrounding countryside. A village tailor in the tiny village of Eyam in Derbyshire, received a box of patterns and some articles of discarded clothing from London. He would be the first of 85 members of the tiny village to die of the plague.

Finally, November and its frosts seemed to stop the growth of the plague. The Great Fire of September 2–6, 1666, is also thought to have ended it.

GREAT BRITAIN
LONDON
1832

• • • • • • • • • • • • • •

Sixty-eight hundred Londoners died from a cholera epidemic, introduced from Germany in 1831. The epidemic would last for one year.

Cholera came to the British Isles via a ship from Hamburg which docked at Sunderland in the north of England in October 1831. It would be February 1832 before the first case would be reported in London, but the terrified populace would soon realize its full impact.

According to Francis Sheppard, in his book, *London 1808–1870: the Infernal Wen,* "[the disease] with its usual unpredictability [leaped] to outlying districts such as St. Marylebone and Hoxton. By the autumn, when few new cases were occurring, some 5,300 Londoners had died, and during the second short attack in 1833 there were another 1,500 victims."

London hospitals were ill equipped to handle the victims of the disease. Sanitary conditions were being improved in St. Bartholomew's Hospital as a result of new discoveries regarding the spreading of germs. However, modifications were not completed when the epidemic struck. Thus, hastily improvised houses were utilized, often over the extreme objections of neighbors. They were actually dying houses. Fully half or more of the patients admitted never left.

As devastating as this first exposure to cholera was for Londoners, it would pale before the arrival of the next invasion, termed the "third pandemic," which would dock in England within a short 16 years (see p. 152).

GREECE

431 B.C.

• • • • • • • • • • • • • • •

Hundreds of thousands of citizens of Athens died from the so-called "Plague of Thucydides," a combination of typhus and measles, from 431–427 B.C.

The so-called Plague of Thucydides took place in 431 B.C., one year into the Peloponnesian War. It lasted for two years, then reoccurred for a year at the end of 427 B.C. Actually an epidemic of several mysterious diseases (post analysis by medical historians identify it as a combination of typhus and measles), it affected hundreds of thousands of soldiers and citizens of Athens alike. Ironically, the largest fatality rate at first took place among the physicians themselves, since the epidemic proved to be wildly contagious.

According to Thucydides, in his chronicle of the Peloponnesian War, ". . . the disease is said to have begun south of Egypt in Aethiopia; thence it descended into Egypt and Libya, and after spreading over the greater part of the Persian empire, suddenly fell upon Athens."

The first incidents of the epidemic came after the Peloponnesian army, under the command of the Lacedaemonian king Archidamus, had invaded and established itself in Attica, where it set about ravaging the country and presumably spreading the disease. "It first attacked the inhabitants of the Piraeus," continues Thucydides, "and it was supposed that the Peleponnesians had poisoned the cisterns, no conduits having as yet been made there. It afterwards reached the upper city, and then the mortality became far greater."

During the summer of 431 B.C., Thucydides reported that his army and the population of Athens was in remarkably good health. And then, ". . . all in a moment, and without apparent reason, were seized with violent heats in the head and with redness and inflammation of the eyes. Internally the throat and the tongue were quickly suffused with blood, and the breath became unnatural and fetid. There followed sneezing and a hoarseness; in a short time the disorder, accompanied by a violent cough, reached the chest; then fastening lower down, it would move the

stomach and bring on all the vomits of bile to which physicians have ever given names. . . ."

Convulsions followed, then

> *. . . the body externally was not so very hot to the touch, nor yet pale; it was of a livid colour inclining to red, and breaking out in pustules and ulcers. But the internal fever was intense; the sufferers could not bear to have on them even the finest linen garment; they insisted on being naked, and there was nothing which they longed for more eagerly than to throw themselves into cold water. And many of those who had no one to look after them actually plunged into the cisterns, for they were tormented by unceasing thirst, which was not in the least assuaged whether they drank little or much. They could not sleep; a restlessness which was intolerable never left them. While the disease was at its height the body, instead of wasting away, held out amid these sufferings in a marvellous manner, and either they died on the seventh or ninth day, not of weakness, for their strength was not exhausted, but of internal fever, which was the end of most; or, if they survived, then the disease descended into the bowels and there produced violent ulceration; severe diarrhea at the same time set in, and at a later stage caused exhaustion, which finally with few exceptions carried them off. For the disorder which had originally settled in the head passed gradually through the whole body, and, if a person got over the worst, would often seize the extremeties and leave its mark, attacking the genitals and the fingers and the toes; and some escaped with the loss of these, some with the loss of their eyes. Some again had no sooner recovered than they were seized with a forgetfulness of all things and knew neither themselves nor their friends.*

When neither physicians nor priests could offer cures or even some relief from the suffering, the populace lapsed into lawlessness and anti-religious fever. With the end of the scourge, Athens once again pulled itself together into an orderly and dedicated city-state.

INDIA

1896–1907

• • • • • • • • • • • • • • •

The third pandemic had its origins in China in 1892, but its first devastation occurred in India from 1896 to 1907. During that time, nearly 5 million Indians died of plague.

The third pandemic of bubonic plague affected a broad geographic area. It is, however, generally agreed that it had its beginnings in the Yunnan province of China in

147

1892, but did not acquire world attention until it reached Canton in the spring of 1894. From here it was a short distance to Hong Kong, with its trade connections to the ports of the Pacific in India, Australia, Japan and America.

India, at least in the first stages of this pandemic, seems to have been most mortally affected, despite the fact that the plague bacillus had been discovered in 1894 and vaccine inoculation was introduced into India in 1897. Perhaps because of faulty communication, the immensity of the population or ancient religious beliefs and practices, the average annual death toll was 548,427 in India. For the period from 1889 to 1908, plague deaths in India would account for 47.88 percent of these deaths.

As in the Black Death, the second pandemic, (see pp. 142–145), this plague was exported by ship, to ports in Asia, South America, Australia, Africa, Europe and even San Francisco, on the west coast of the U.S. (see p. 150 for the development of this pandemic).

ITALY

1505–1530

• • • • • • • • • • • • • • •

A typhoid epidemic raged through Italy from 1505 to 1530, killing hundreds of thousands.

Typhus (a rickettsial disease transmitted by human body lice) and typhoid (a Salmonella bacillus found in human waste which is transmitted by contaminated food and water) have long been known as the basis for epidemics. Even in the second century B.C., a 56-mile aqueduct was built to supply Rome with fresh water, since the Romans recognized the importance of clean household water and sanitation in the combatting of waterborne disease.

Still, in the 16th century A.D., epidemics of typhus and typhoid were common throughout Italy, particularly between 1505 and 1530, when hundreds of thousands succumbed to them. Girolamo Fracastoro chronicled the disease and its fevers, which he said were ". . . vulgarly called 'lenticulae' (small lentils) or 'puncticulae' (small pricks) because they produce spots which look like lentils or flea-bites. . . ."

Fracastoro described the onset of this form of typhus as gentle, in fact so mild that most victims waited until too late to call a physician. A general kind of lassitude was reported until the seventh day, when ". . . the mind would wander; the eyes became red, and the patient was garrulous; the urine was usually observed to be at first pale, but consistent, but presently red and clouded, or like pome-granate wine; the pulse was small and slow . . . about the fourth or seventh day, red, or often purplish red spots broke out on the arms, back and chest, looking like flea-bites . . .though they were often larger and in the shape of lentils, whence arose the name of the fever. . . ."

ROME

452 B.C.

• • • • • • • • • • • • • • •

Epidemic pestilence swept through Rome in 452 B.C. killing thousands, among them, many members of the Roman Senate.

An epidemic hit Rome in 452 B.C. that not only killed thousands of citizens, but reached into the high councils, killing Sextus Quintilius, one of the consuls, Spurius Furius (who had been appointed to succeed him), four of the tribunes and an untold number of senators.

Despite the planning engineers who already realized the importance of uncontaminated water (see previous entry), the general populace seemed to ignore such good advice, and thus this epidemic (most likely typhoid) spread quickly and viciously. Entire households perished and then, because of the disposal methods of the bodies of rich and poor alike, the infection was spread through both the air and the water supply.

According to Greek scholar and historian Dionysius of Halicarnassus:

. . . they burned the bodies and committed them to the earth, at the last, either through a disregard of decency or from a lack of the necessary equipment, they threw many of the dead into the sewers under the streets and cast far more of them into the river; and from these they received the most harm. For when the bodies were cast up by the waves upon the banks and beaches, a grievous and terrible stench, carried by the wind, smote those who were still in health and produced a quick change in their bodies; and the water brought from the river was no longer fit to drink, partly because of its vile odour and partly by causing indigestion. . . .

As in the case of most early epidemics and plagues, the populace called upon physicians and priests, and when neither could help them, gave up all pretense of morality. As German classical historian Barthold G. Niebuhr pointed out in his *History of Rome*, "Pestilences, like inhuman military devastations, corrupt whom they ruin. . . ."

However, in the case of this particular pestilence, reform in some Roman laws resulted. As Niebuhr also pointed out, "Very calamitous times however serve to awaken a sense of the defects of existing institutions; many cheer themselves with the belief that the correction of these would restore their past prosperity; and this motive unquestionably seconded the proposals made at Rome, after the pestilence and the military reverses, for the reformation of the laws."

ROME

A.D. 541–590

• • • • • • • • • • • • •

Millions died during the first pandemic, called the "Plague of Justinian" which spread over the Roman Empire from A.D. 541 to 590.

The first of the three great pandemics (the second was the Black Death, the third began in China, spread to San Francisco at the end of the 19th century and continues today—see introduction to this section for details) occurred in the year 541, during the 15th reign of the Roman emperor Justinian I. Thus, its title, the "Plague of Justinian."

The coming of the plague was reportedly heralded by a 20-day, spectacular nighttime display by Halley's comet in 531. Its departure was marked by Pope Gregory the Great crossing the Tiber on the Bridge of Hadrian, heading a procession to Saint Peter's to pray for relief from the pestilence. There, the pope saw the Archangel Michael standing on Hadrian's mausoleum, sheathing a bloody sword. At that moment, the plague ceased, and thereafter a chapel was erected atop Hadrian's tomb, called Saint Michael's in the Clouds.

Procopius of Caesarea chronicled the first appearance of the plague in Constantinople (then Byzantium), where it was brought, apparently by Egyptians living in Pelusium. From there, it proceeded to Alexandria, then to Palestine, and from there, it spread over the entire Roman Empire.

Procopius goes on to write what has become to be known as the first detailed description of bubonic plague: ". . . a bubonic swelling developed," he wrote, "and this took place not only in the particular part of the body which is called 'boubon' [groin], that is below the abdomen, but also inside the armpit, and in some cases also behind the ears, and at different points on the thighs. . . ."

He then proceeds to describe the classic spreading of bubonic plague, from the victims to the attendants of the victims, of the enormous anguish of the patients, who rushed from their houses, attempting to immerse themselves in the sea or to throw themselves from great heights.

"Death came in some cases immediately, in others after many days, and with some the body broke out with black pustules about as large as a lentil and those did not survive even one day, but all succumbed immediately. With many also a vomiting of blood ensued without visible cause and straightway brought death. . . ."

However, the vigilant Procopius did notice that:

. . . in those cases where the swelling rose to an unusual size and a discharge of pus had set in, it came about that they escaped from the disease and survived, for clearly the acute condition of the carbuncle had found relief in this direction, and this proved to be in general an indication of returning health; but in cases where the swelling preserved its former appearance there ensued those troubles which I have just mentioned . . . those who were without friends or servants lay unburied in the streets or in their desolate houses. . . . Corpses were placed aboard ships and these abandoned to the seas . . . Physicians could not tell which cases were light and which severe, and no remedies availed.

Despite the detailed study of the effects of the bubonic plague upon its victims, none of these learned men, nor even the historian Edward Gibbon, writing in his *History of the Decline and Fall of the Roman Empire* in the late 18th century had discovered that it was spread through rats, fleas and bacilli. To Gibbon,

. . . during three months, five and at length ten, thousand persons died each day at Constantinople. . . . No restraints were imposed on the free and frequent intercourse of the Roman provinces: from Persia to France, the nations were mingled and infected by wars and emigrations; and the pestilential odour which lurks for years in a bale of cotton, was imported, by the abuse of trade, into the most distant regions.

RUSSIA

1812

• • • • • • • • • • • • •

Nearly 100,000 Russian and French soldiers died from typhus in 1812 in Russia. Napoleon's retreating soldiers then spread the epidemic over parts of Germany, Austria, Switzerland and France.

Typhus, the persistent microorganism that is halfway between being a louse-born virus and a louse-born bacteria, (see PLAGUES AND EPIDEMICS, Rome, 541–590, above) has been described by Columbia University professor Hans Zinsser as ". . . the inevitable and expected companion of war."

This was the case when Napoleon invaded Russia in 1812. The Russians employed a scorched earth policy, and thus, deprived of even basic sanitation, French troops suffered severely from dysentery and diarrhea on the way to Moscow. It might have weakened them. At any rate, by the time they reached Smolensk, on August 14, 1812, they were no match for the typhus infection that beset them in that city. By mid-September, when they reached Moscow, the French army was riddled with the disease, and, according to Friedrich Prinzing, in his book, *Epidemics Resulting from Wars*, ". . . when Napoleon's army withdrew from the city it left behind several thousand typhus-fever patients, almost all of whom died—only the stronger patients were taken along on wagons." But, predictably, the epidemic did not respect boundaries of nationality. Sixty-two thousand Russian soldiers, who pursued the French army, were also felled by typhus.

On December 8, the remaining bits and pieces of the French Army crossed Lithuania (then Vilna), and 30,000 soldiers died there, most of them of typhus. These soldiers spread the disease to civilians, who in turn spread it through much of what was formerly the USSR west of an imaginary line running north and south through Moscow.

It did not stop there. Pressing on in their retreat, the French troops fanned out over a large part of Germany, France, Switzerland and Austria, leaving typhus behind wherever they went.

UNITED STATES
CALIFORNIA

1899

• • • • • • • • • • • • • •

The third pandemic, bubonic plague, which began in China and India (see pp. 147–148) was brought to the West via San Francisco, in 1899.

The third pandemic, which began in China in 1892 (see p. 147) traveled to San Francisco in 1899, where it flourished and spread. There is evidence that the third pandemic is still with us (see PLAGUES AND EPIDEMICS, the world, 1855–Present, p. 152).

On June 27, 1899, the S.S. *Nippon Haru* arrived in San Francisco harbor from Hong Kong via Honolulu. Two cases of plague had occurred on the ship and she carried plague-infected rats, much like the Genoese ships that spread the Black Death to Europe in the 1300s (see pp. 142–145). There were two Japanese stowaways aboard the *Nippon Haru*, who apparently jumped overboard before the ship reached quarantine on Angel Island. When the stow-

aways' corpses were fished from the bay two days later, they were found to be riddled with plague bacilli.

All was quiet until nine months later, when the body of a Chinese man, Wing Chut King, was discovered in the basement of the Globe Hotel in the heart of Chinatown. An autopsy revealed that he had died of bubonic plague.

The Board of Health of San Francisco immediately cordoned off the 12 square blocks of Chinatown, and a search was launched among the 25,000 inhabitants for more corpses. However, San Francisco at the time was controlled by conservative business interests and railroad and lumber magnates, who saw the plague scare as a threat to their profits.

Working through sympathetic newspapers—which included every newspaper except William Randolph Hearst's *Examiner*, they launched a campaign to minimize the danger. The *San Francisco Bulletin* skewered Board of Health head Dr. J. M. Williamson in verse:

Have you heard of the deadly bacillus,
Scourge of a populous land,
Bacillus that threatens to kill us,
When found in a Chinaman's gland?

Under fire from all sides, health officials lifted the quarantine of Chinatown two days later. Now, the fight between the Board of Health and the business interests escalated, while the plague, unattended, grew. Extremism blunted the arguments of both sides. Governor Henry T. Gage insisted that there was no plague in his state, and dismantled the Board of Health, but not before the board had announced a plan to remove all Chinese in the city to detention camps on Angel Island and to demolish Chinatown.

Finally, U.S. Surgeon General Edward Wyman and President William McKinley took a hand, and, beginning on April 8, 1901, saw to it that Chinatown was scrubbed clean. The new governor of California, George C. Pardee, was a practicing physician, and he soon cleaned out the corrupt health practices of his predecessor.

But the damage had been done. The plague was spreading. On February 29, 1904, a 33-year-old woman died of the plague in the town of Concord, California, northeast of San Francisco. Until that time, there had been 121 reported cases in San Francisco and only five outside the city. The mortality rate was 97 percent.

For years, the books were then closed on the so-called San Francisco epidemic. But, according to some scientists, this was merely the beginning of the third pandemic, one that would claim millions and that still rages through most of the world.

UNITED STATES
PENNSYLVANIA
1793

• • • • • • • • • • • • • • •

Four thousand residents of Philadelphia died in a yellow fever epidemic in 1793.

Yellow fever arrived in Cuba from Veracruz in 1761. The following year, British forces besieged Havana, contracted the disease in large numbers, and brought it back to Philadelphia. There was a moderate outbreak in the city that year, but then, for 30 years—from 1763 to 1793—no cases of yellow fever were reported.

Then, in August 1793, it reappeared in Philadelphia and from that month until the October frost, when it abated, 4,000 people would die of the disease.

According to publisher Mathew Carey, an eyewitness,

The consternation of the people . . . was carried beyond all bounds. Dismay and affright were visible on the countenance of almost every person. Most people who could . . . fled the city. Of those who remained, many shut themselves in their houses and were afraid to walk the streets. . . . Many were almost incessantly purifying, scowering, and whitewashing their rooms. Those who ventured abroad, had handkerchiefs or sponges impregnated with vinegar or camphor at their noses. . . . The corpses of the most respectable citizens, even if they did not die of the epidemic, were carried to the grave, on the shafts of a chair, the horse driven by a negro, unattended by a friend or relation, and without any sort of ceremony. People shifted their course at the sight of a hearse. . . . The old custom of shaking hands fell into such general disuse, that many were affronted at even the offer of a hand.

Two theories raged in Philadelphia almost as furiously as the epidemic. The contagionists, led by Oliver Wilcott Jr., the comptroller of the U.S. Treasury, argued that it was transmitted overland as easily as by ship, and that quarantining would do little to avoid outbreaks of yellow fever.

The anti-contagionists, led by James Hutchinson (himself a victim of the epidemic) and Noah Webster, also argued against quarantining, and cited instead filthy conditions on the wharves—a recent outbreak, they argued, had begun in damaged coffee that had putrefied on one of the wharves, and in a proclamation, declared that the only cure could be "extensive sanitary measures, including sewer construction, waste removal, broad streets planted with trees, numerous open squares, large house lots, and an end to overcrowding—in short, comprehensive city planning, sanitation and housing reform."

It was good advice that went unheeded. Quarantine still remained Philadelphia's chief weapon against yellow fever. And so, the epidemic inched northward to New York City and killed 2,000 there in 1798.

THE WORLD
1200 B.C.

• • • • • • • • • • • • • • •

The first recorded plague struck the Philistines in 1200 B.C., and they, bearing the Ark of the Covenant, spread it throughout the known world.

The first recorded plague is the one which beset the Philistines in 1200 B.C., and which is recorded in the Bible in the Book of Samuel. The Philistines in this year defeated an army of nomadic Hebrews at Eben-ezer, captured the sacred Ark of the Covenant, and carried it in triumph to Ashdod, a city near the Mediterranean Sea.

But their triumph was immediately tainted, according to 1 Samuel 5:9: "the hand of the Lord was against the city with a very great destruction: and he smote the men of the city, both small and great, and they had emerods [swellings] in their secret parts."

The description makes it clear that bubonic plague had invaded the army of Philistines, probably from a stricken ship. If it had originated in the Ark of the Covenant, as the Bible notes, it would have been mentioned in the Old Testament.

Wherever they took the Ark, the Philistines took plague, too. They moved from Ashdod inland to Gath, then to Ekron. The plague followed them. Terrified, they trundled the Ark of the Covenant into a cart pulled by two milk cows. If the cows took the Ark to the Hebrew border town of Beth-shemesh, they reasoned that the Lord of Israel was responsible for the plague, and had indeed smitten them.

The cows took the Ark into the field of the Beth-shemite Joshua, stopping alongside a huge stone. Israel rejoiced, but not for long. In 1 Samuel 6:19, the Bible chronicles the inexorable progress of the plague: "And he smote the men of Beth-shemesh, because they had looked into the ark of the Lord, even He smote of the people fifty thousand and three score and ten men: and the people lamented because the Lord had smitten many of the people with a great slaughter."

THE WORLD
1846–1860

• • • • • • • • • • • • •

The 15-year cholera epidemic that roamed the world from 1846 to 1860 killed millions.

For 15 years, cholera swept the world. When it began in India, in roughly 1840–1841, it was generally conceded that great plagues and epidemics were either forms of supernatural punishment or the result of "miasmic vapors." However, by 1849, John Snow, a pioneer in inhalation anesthesia, proved, in a highly conclusive paper that won him a 30,000-franc prize from the Institute of France, that cholera was waterborne and taken into the system by mouth.

The epidemic spread throughout India in the early 1840s, completely covering the country by 1846. From there, it spread to the Philippines and China in one direction and to Persia in the other. By 1848–1849, it had consumed Europe. From there, it leaped to Canada and the U.S. via immigrant ships from Europe. New York, New Orleans and ports along the Mississippi, Arkansas and Tennessee rivers were infested. By early 1849, all of the United States east of the Rockies was infected, and tens of thousands died monthly.

By the 1850s, Snow's theories had become widespread, and efforts were made to decontaminate water supplies. But by that time, the cholera had spread from Texas south to Mexico, to the West Indies, Cuba and Jamaica, the Bahamas, Puerto Rico, Venezuela and Brazil. There would be no corner of the world that would escape this scourge, which John Snow, according to Norbert Hirshhorn and William Greenough's account in *Scientific American* in 1971, carefully mapped London and ". . . determined that most of the people who had died had drunk water from the Broad Street pump. The water, drawn from the Thames River, had the taste and odor of sewage. Snow advised the guardians of the parish to remove the pump handle, and the epidemic quickly waned. . . ."

Snow's contaminated water theory was soon dramatically confirmed. In 1854, London was struck by another severe cholera outbreak. In the intervening years, one of the two private water companies serving the city had changed its water source, drawing from a clean area of the Thames instead of the sewage-laden area. Among the users supplied by this company, relatively few persons succumbed to cholera. There were 461 deaths in a 14-week period, or 2.6 per 1,000. In the population served by the other company, which was still drawing from the sewage-laden waters, there were more than 4,000 deaths from cholera, or 15.3 per 1,000.

THE WORLD
1855–Present

• • • • • • • • • • • • •

A modern theory proposes that the third pandemic of bubonic plague, which began in 1855, is still with us today. According to these theorists, it has been confined to Africa since 1959, but this is only a temporary confinement.

According to a convincing case made by Charles T. Gregg in his book *Plague!*, the horror of bubonic plague, which accounted for the Black Death that once decimated one-third of the known world (see pp. 142–145) is still with us.

According to Gregg, the so-called third pandemic wound down in 1959 when the total of world deaths dropped from nearly 5,000 in 1953 to a little more than 200 in 1959.

But more recent incidents of plague have been found to occur in areas characterized by poor sanitation practices, famine or starvation. The carriers of the disease, rats and fleas, seem to thrive in these conditions. Outbursts of plague have occurred in Madagascar, where 132 cases were reported from 1953 to 1958 with a 72 percent mortality rate, and between 1960 and 1970, when another 143 cases were reported with a fatality rate of 52 percent. In the Zaire outbreak in 1960, the fatality rate was 80 percent, and in Nepal in February 1966, 12 out of 13 cases were fatal.

THE WORLD
1918–1919

• • • • • • • • • • • • •

Over 22 million people died in the mammoth influenza epidemic of 1918–1919. Its true source has never been accurately traced, but it has been established that returning servicemen from World War I helped to spread it.

The monumentally devastating influenza epidemic of 1918–1919 killed more than 22 million people in practically every corner of the globe. This was more than twice the total killed in World War I, which was at least partially responsible for the rapid progression of the pandemic.

One theory has it that the virus began in Fort Riley, Kansas and was spread through Europe by American soldiers. But throughout history, epidemics have generally followed an east to west pattern, and this theory has generally been discounted.

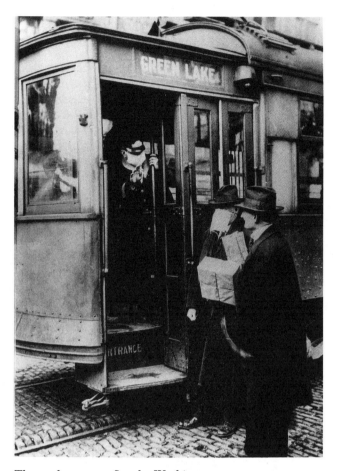

The conductor on a Seattle, Washington streetcar wears a surgical face mask distributed by the Red Cross during the worldwide influenza epidemic of 1918. American Red Cross.

Other historians have claimed that it was introduced into Europe by Chinese labor battalions that landed on the coast of France. Still others blamed it on Russian soldiers arriving from Vladivostok, others said it developed from an earlier bronchitis noted in Spain (it was generally called the "Spanish Influenza"), others blamed it on a confluence—and presumably an inter-infection—of American with European and African troops in the north of France.

Thus, the true source of the great influenza epidemic will probably never be accurately known. But whatever the sequence of events and the source, the pandemic made its first dramatic appearance in America on August 28, 1918, in Boston via a sailor on a transport tied up in the port. According to medical historian Henry A. Davidson, "It infected New England like a forest fire. In Massachusetts alone it killed 15,000 civilians in four months, plus an unknown number of others whose deaths were erro-

neously classed as 'pneumonia,' 'encephalitis,' 'meningitis' or masked under other rubrics."

Within days, the epidemic had traveled the length of the East Coast, but that was only the beginning. Some of the sailors on the same boat were transferred to Michigan and Illinois, and in September and October of 1918, one out of every five soldiers stationed in the United States was felled by influenza. Twenty-four thousand died. (Thirty-four thousand were killed in World War I from other causes.)

Makeshift emergency hospitals were set up in major cities and at major military encampments, but they were short-staffed because of the war. Fortunately, the outbreaks of the disease were short-lived. There would be one or two weeks of rapid dissemination of the disease, followed by two or three weeks of deaths, and then the epidemic would rapidly subside. The third week of October was the peak of the epidemic in the nation's major cities, particularly New York, New Orleans and San Francisco. In all three cities, the mortality rate was roughly 28 percent.

The rest of the world did not fare quite so well. A staggering 12 million died in India alone. In Argentina, the mortality rate was a low 120 per 100,000 people, in England and Wales it climbed to 680 per 100,000, in South Africa it was 2,280 per 100,000.

What was astonishing about this pandemic was its ability to reach into remote sections of the world. In cloistered islands of the South Pacific, where respiratory diseases were all but unknown, whole populations were wiped out. The *Sydney Daily Telegraph* described the situation in Samoa: "As at one time 80 or 90 percent of the people were lying helpless, many died from starvation who might probably have recovered, for even when rice milk and other items were sent out and delivered, the survivors were too weak to prepare and apportion the food."

New Zealand recorded 6 million influenza deaths, and some settlements in Alaska were completely eliminated.

THE WORLD

1980–Present

• • • • • • • • • • • • • • • •

From the first reported case in the U.S., in 1980, AIDS has spread worldwide. Current projections estimate there will be 40 million AIDS sufferers by the end of the 1990s.

AIDS (Acquired Immune Deficiency Syndrome) is the possible pandemic of the 21st century. "Anyone who has the least ability to look into the future," noted Dr. Ward Cates of the U.S. Centers for Disease Control in 1989, "can already see the potential for this disease being much worse than anything mankind has seen before."

Epidemiologists are fairly certain that the AIDS virus originated in Central Africa, where it was originally harbored by green monkeys. The generally accepted theory states that the virus was mutated in a way that made it able to attack humans. According to Dr. Myron Essex, of the Harvard School of Public Health, a mechanism may have evolved in these monkeys to control the virus that infects them, so that they remained healthy, while those that they bit became infected with the virus.

Generally speaking, the level of health in Africa has deteriorated in the 20th century while the health of the more affluent nations of the world has grown better. The transfer of the virus from human to human was unwittingly accomplished in the late 1970s and early 1980s through health workers using a single needle to inject a number of patients with penicillin and other drugs. In 1986, *Newsweek* reported that 10 percent of the blood stocks in Zambia were contaminated with AIDS; it was easy to contract it during transfusions.

But the largest early transmission of the disease in Africa is thought to have been sexual. Since multiple heterosexual partners (some Africans infected with AIDS were reported to have had an average of 32 sexual partners) and visits to prostitutes constituted a way of life in Central Africa, the disease spread quickly and alarmingly.

From Africa, some theorists state that the disease was spread to the Caribbean by natives, and was then picked up by American homosexuals, many of whom had made Haiti a vacation spot of choice in the 1970s. Haiti hotly contests this, although medical investigators from the Centers for Disease Control and the University of Miami Medical School, as well as doctors from Cornell University traced the first cases of AIDS-related diseases to Port-au-Prince in 1979, two years before the first well documented cases of what was later called AIDS were found in San Francisco and New York.

In 1981, a young male homosexual in San Francisco was found to be suffering from a severe fungal infection to which he had little immune reaction. Shortly afterward, he developed *pneumocystis carinii* pneumonia (PCP). At roughly the same time, a dermatologist in New York encountered two cases of Kaposi's sarcoma (KS) in one week, both in young male homosexuals.

It would be 1982 before the virus was given the name HIV, and there are no records of who named it, but in 1980–81, Dr. Michael S. Gottlieb of the University of California at Los Angeles noted that several men he had examined had contracted *pneumocystis carinii* pneumonia, or PCP—a rare type of pneumonia that is caused by a small protozoan organism of a mere two to four nanometers in size (a nanometer is one billionth of a meter). Discovered in 1955, it first appeared in malnourished infants housed in displaced person camps after World War II, and then only in cancer patients, or in organ transplant recipients, whose immune systems had become weakened.

At roughly the same time, Dr. Alvin Friedman-Kien of New York University Medical Center diagnosed a young, gay man with Kaposi's sarcoma, a particularly uncommon, slow-growing cancer customarily seen among elderly men of Mediterranean extraction. The cancer, rare in the U.S. but prevalent in equatorial Africa, is a tumor of the blood vessels. In this disease, the lining of the body's small vessels becomes stippled with irregular tumor cells which cling to the inner walls. When the lymph nodes and internal organs are affected, the tumor can clog narrow blood vessels; thus, limbs that are affected may become swollen and internal organs congested and enlarged.

In older patients, this process takes anywhere from eight to 30 years to develop. In young AIDS patients (the vast majority are in their thirties) it becomes fatal in three.

At first, AIDS was thought to be a strictly homosexual disease, transmitted sexually. Then, it was discovered that the transmission was through the blood, and intravenous drug users and hemophiliacs, who must receive constant blood transfusions, were added to the list of people at risk. By early 1983, heterosexual recipients of blood transfusions were also thought to be potentially at risk. Then, in Africa, heterosexual transmission of the disease was discovered to be a common occurrence.

It would be 1984 before the AIDS virus would be isolated by two researchers, Dr. Robert C. Gallo of the U.S. National Cancer Institute, and Dr. Luc Montagnier at the Pasteur Institute in Paris. (In 1990, Dr. Gallo admitted that he had used some of Dr. Montagnier's early findings to reach his breakthrough, and acknowledged that the French research team actually isolated the virus.)

The findings revealed that the virus reproduces itself, killing, in an accelerating fashion, T-4 lymphocytes, a subgroup of white blood cells that play a major role in defending the body against infections like PCP and some cancers.

Unfortunately, the discovery of AIDS coincided with a resurgence of conservative political and religious philosophy in the U.S. The fact that the disease first seemed confined to homosexuals caused the government to do little about it. "The poor homosexuals," Nixon speechwriter and Reagan staff member Patrick Buchanan said in 1983. "They have declared war on nature, and now nature is exacting an awful retribution." The Reverend Jerry Falwell and his moral majority preached like sermons, and other conservative spokespersons advocated everything from 20th century leper colonies to summary executions for victims of the nascent pandemic. Historical perspective will undoubtedly compare the behavior of modern-day American politicians with the panic that surrounded the Black Death in medieval Europe (see pp. 142–145).

By the time Surgeon General Dr. C. Everett Koop had shaken the U.S. administration into a grudging acknowledgment that an epidemic cannot be controlled by moral pronouncements, the epidemic had burst full force upon the world. In the U.S. the victim count grew from one in 1980, to 12,000 in 1985, and 38,312 in 1987, and of that figure, 22,057 died. By 1989, the estimate of infected individuals in New York State alone—the state with the largest number of AIDS cases—would rise to 400,000, and of those 400,000, scientists further estimated that 88 percent to 90 percent of them were still untested, and therefore probably freely spreading the disease. The National Institute of Health in 1989 estimated that up to 1.5 million people throughout the United States were already infected with AIDS, and that by 1992, the number of deaths would total 263,000.

Europe's statistics are scarcely less alarming, with constantly escalating figures in every country, ranging, in 1987, from 1,980 in France to 1,298 in Germany. Researchers estimate that there will be 40 million people infected with AIDS worldwide by the end of the 1990s.

The search for a cure still continues. But there is still a lack of federal support for research. Prevention and education measures are still fought by conservative groups in the U.S., and the FDA has blocked the testing of new drugs, including those designed to alleviate the symptoms of AIDS. Some desperate patients and their families travel to clinics in Mexico and Europe in search of miracle cures.

Social programs fail to help alleviate the financial burdens of AIDS patients and their families—it costs $125,000 to treat the average, terminal AIDS patient—and some drug companies practice price gouging with newly developed treatments.

The only hope in preventing what will certainly be one of the grimmest, cruelest and most cataclysmic of all pandemics from developing fullblown in the 21st century will be the discovery of a vaccine. Researchers are cautiously optimistic.

CYCLONES

. . . .

THE WORST RECORDED CYCLONES

CHRONOLOGY

CYCLONES

Cyclone is the generic name given to storms that rotate around a core of low pressure in a counterclockwise direction in the northern hemisphere and in a clockwise direction in the southern hemisphere. This circular movement is caused by a combination of two forces: (1) the contrast between the low core, or axis of atmospheric pressure and the relatively higher pressure surrounding it, and (2) the Coriolis Effect, which, simply stated, is the tendency for any moving body on or above the Earth's surface to drift sideways from its course because of the rotation of the Earth. In the northern hemisphere, this deflection is to the right of the motion; in the southern hemisphere, the deflection is to the left. The combination of these two forces sets up what is termed a "cyclonic pattern."

This establishes the pattern of the storm; further characteristics of low pressure systems contribute to the destructive forces within the heart of the cyclone. The force of air moving over the Earth's surface is affected by objects in its path or variations in the Earth's surface. For instance, on or near the surface of the Earth, there is a frictional drag on air currents, which causes them to spiral inward toward areas of low pressure, and this in turn builds up cyclonic forms. This is compensated for by currents that rise upward from the center of this bowl of low pressure, forming a chimney of rising air. These currents, in turn, eventually cool at high altitudes, which then increases the humidity of the air. Thus, in any region of low pressure, clouds and high humidity come into being, and are characteristic of not only cyclones but storms in general.

As cyclones intensify, they often spread outward, sometimes reaching a radius of 500 miles or more—although this is a relatively unusual size.

Finally, cyclones generally fall into two major categories: middle latitude and tropical.

Middle latitude cyclones, which can form over either land or water, are sometimes associated with waves or ripples along polar fronts and generally move from west to east along with the prevailing winds.

Tropical cyclones, which occur over warm, tropical oceans, in their formative stages usually move toward the west with the flow of the trade winds, and when mature, curve towards the poles.

A tropical cyclone that has matured to severe intensity is called a hurricane when it occurs in the Atlantic Ocean or its adjacent seas, a typhoon when it occurs in the Pacific Ocean (or adjacent seas) and a cyclone when it occurs in the Indian Ocean region.

BANGLADESH (EAST PAKISTAN)

November 12, 1970

The cyclone of November 12, 1970 in Bangladesh is widely considered to be the worst natural disaster of the 20th century. Between 300,000 and 500,000 were killed by a combination of wind and water.

On November 12, 1970, five months before it became Bangladesh, East Pakistan experienced the worst disaster of the 20th century. The combination of a killer cyclone and a tidal wave said to be 50 feet high caused a death toll of between 300,000 and 500,000. Winds of up to 150 mph lashed the East Pakistan Coast, the Ganges Delta and the offshore islands of Bhola, Hatia, Kukri Mukri, Manpura and Rangabali.

Bangladesh is roughly the size of Wisconsin with an enormous population of over 95 million people. It borders on India and Burma and consists mainly of a low plain cut by the Ganges and Brahmaputra rivers and their delta. A Hindu portion of India until 1947, the area became part of East Pakistan and remained so until its declaration of independence from Pakistan in March 1971. Alluvial and marshy along the coast, with hills only breaking this monotony in the extreme Southeast, it has one of the rainiest climates in the world, and is thus a breeding ground for tropical monsoons.

Ironically enough, this, the worst disaster of the century was first dismissed as a false alarm. Barely a month earlier, on October 23, 1970, a small cyclone had frightened the inhabitants of the Ganges Delta into evacuating the environs, and only minimal damage resulted. But this false alarm brought with it a false sense of confidence, and when, on November 11, 1970, an American weather satellite warned of a giant cyclone heading toward the same region, Radio Pakistan ignored it. Uninformed, the huge population slept blissfully as this meteorological monster pounded inexorably toward it.

The storm hit in the middle of the night of November 12. Cyclonic winds pushed a tidal wave of at least 20 feet—some said—50 feet—in height towards islands whose highest ground level rested a maximum of 20 feet above the sea's surface. Thus, when the wave curled over and crashed upon the thatched roof houses and paddies of these islands, it absolutely consumed them, and only the second stories of the manor houses of a few well-to-do farmers were saved.

Most houses were smashed into piles of soaked straw, and the sleeping inhabitants were swept out to sea by the roaring current. Moments later, the storm made landfall with winds of 150 mph. Houses, hospitals, power lines were instantly collapsed, cutting off all communication with the outside world. It would be two days before the rest of Pakistan would know of the calamity, and by then the tragedy would have climbed to monumental proportions.

More than 20,000 inhabitants of one island alone disappeared into the sea without a trace; corpses covered the land like grim cobblestones. They were scooped up from the islands and thrown into the sea, where they floated toward the land. There, inhabitants lined the beaches, shoving the beached corpses back out to sea with bamboo poles.

Disease spread rapidly. Cholera ravaged the island of Rangabali. Rice paddies turned the color of blood. Vultures circled constantly, and the smell of death and decaying corpses hung like a sickly sweet mist over the entire area. Water was unobtainable; food supplies were spoiled or tainted by disease.

Within two days, medical supplies, personnel and food began to be airlifted into the region from the rest of the world. America and Great Britain ferried in the largest amount of supplies and engineers to reconstruct the transportation and health-support systems. But, air drops of food supplies caused further misery in the form of food riots.

It would be months before the dead would be collected from the streets of the demolished city of Patuakhali and its surrounding fields and paddies, and months more before the International Red Cross would be able to stem the rampant spread of cholera and typhoid in the region.

BANGLADESH

May 25, 1985

• • • • • • • • • • • • • •

Ten thousand people perished in the cyclone that hit Bangladesh on May 25, 1985, and destroyed 80 percent of the dwellings of the seven islands at the mouth of the Meghna River.

Bangladesh is no stranger to cyclones and tidal waves, nor to monumental loss of life because of both. In 1942, when it was still part of India, 40,000 people lost their lives in a cyclone; in 1963, when it had become Pakistan, 22,000 perished in a windstorm; in 1965, 30,000 and 10,000 died respectively in two more windstorms; in 1970, a staggering 300,000 died in the worst cyclone of the century (see p. 161).

On May 25, 1985, a cyclone struck, preceded by a 15- to 20-foot wall of water that ravaged seven islands at the mouth of the Meghna River, part of the delta system in the Bengal basin. The disaster killed 10,000 people, 500,000 head of cattle and flattened 80 percent of the area's dwellings.

The 400-square-mile area affected embraces approximately one-eighth of Bangladesh's 95 million people, contains nearly 1,000 islands (some of which disappeared entirely in this storm) and is located southeast of Dhaka, the capital. The most severely battered islands were Sandurip, Hatia, Mahash Khali, Bhola, Ulir Char, Char Clerk and Dhal Char.

This part of Bangladesh is beset by monsoon rains twice a year, from the east in the fall, and from the west in the spring. Half of these monsoon rains coincide with the annual May rice harvest, and, in May 1985, the population of 10 million was swelled by 300,000 migrant workers brought in to assist in the harvest.

Although the cyclone was detected three days earlier in the Indian Ocean by satellite, there is no record of a warn-

Survivors of the Bangladesh cyclone of May 25, 1985 huddle together, waiting for shelter and food. Rudolph von Bernuth, CARE.

ing being sent to Bangladesh. Thus, workers and dwellers on the islands were swept into the sea by the sudden, monumental waves that roared across the islands. Only a few survivors made it to the concrete cyclone shelters.

Winds of over 100 mph ripped the roofs from thatched-roof houses and submerged the main town on the island of Hatia under three feet of water. Miraculously, only seven people in the city of 40,000 were killed.

The next day, relief aid began to arrive from Europe and the U.S. But most of these supplies did not arrive before much of the populace had been forced to survive on rancid food and salt water.

INDIA
BACKERGUNGE

October 31, 1876

• • • • • • • • • • • • • •

Two hundred thousand residents of the Indian city of Backergunge died from wind, water and cholera caused by the

wreckage and pollution of a cyclone that struck the city on October 31, 1876.

One hundred thousand people were killed when a gigantic cyclone roared into the Indian city of Backergunge on October 31, 1876. Sitting at the mouth of the Megna River, Backergunge is also serviced by the Bay of Bengal, which is a well known sluiceway for cyclones.

The warning signs of this tragedy formed a classic pattern. For several days prior to the arrival of the storm, above average tides had flooded the shores of the Megna River. Thus, when a huge tidal wave, pushed by the storm, broke over these shores and the outlying islands, they were instantly inundated under water that reached 40 feet in depth at certain points.

The death toll from drowning in Backergunge was swollen within weeks by another 100,000, who succumbed to disease—probably cholera—caused by the pollution of the water supply by the storm.

163

Families were separated and decimated by the 1985 Bangladesh cyclone. Rudolph von Bernuth, CARE.

INDIA
BAY OF BENGAL

October 7, 1737

• • • • • • • • • • • • • •

A cyclone which struck the Bay of Bengal on October 7, 1737, killed 300,000 residents of that thickly populated part of India.

The tidal wave caused by the cyclone of October 7, 1737 wrecked 20,000 ships that were anchored in the harbors of the Bay of Bengal, and, crashing over the shorelines, particularly at the mouth of the Hooghly River, went on to claim 300,000 lives.

Densely populated in the 18th century because of the huge amount of shipping that originated within the Bay of Bengal's fairly sheltered environs, this area was easy prey to a storm that claimed the greatest death toll up to that time in that region.

INDIA
CALCUTTA

October 5, 1864

• • • • • • • • • • • • • • •

Striking at high tide, a cyclone devastated Calcutta on October 5, 1864, killing over 50,000 people. Nearby cities were untouched.

The great killer cyclone of 1864, which instantly drowned more than 50,000 inhabitants of the bustling city of Calcutta on the morning of October 5, was a selective storm. Sinking more than 200 ships, sending a 40-foot tidal wave over the docks and into the streets of the city, it seemed to localize itself solely in and around Calcutta. Nearby coastal sites such as Contai remained blissfully dry and happily unaffected.

The high water level of the northern part of the Bay of Bengal makes cities like Calcutta particularly vulnerable to storms at times of high tide. (The 1833 cyclone claimed 50,000 lives, and 300 of the surrounding villages were destroyed.) October 4, 1864, was a time of extremely high tide, thus aiding the 40-foot storm wave, when it slammed into the city.

In moments, the city was almost entirely submerged, which accounted for the great number of drownings. Disease, brought on by the polluted water supply, killed another 30,000 during the following weeks.

INDIA
CORINGA

December 1789

• • • • • • • • • • • • • •

Three tidal waves and a cyclone battered Coringa, India in December 1789, killing 20,000.

Located at the mouth of the Ganges River, the city of Coringa was completely destroyed and 20,000 of its inhabitants were drowned by three tidal waves spawned by a cyclone that hit the city at the end of 1789.

Although detailed information is sparse, it was apparently the first of the three waves that did the major damage, sinking most of the ships moored in the harbor, flooding every alley and small street, crushing businesses, government buildings and the thatched roof dwellings that housed much of the city's population.

The second wave, less intense than the ones before and after it, hit the area a glancing blow, saving most of its fury for the countryside surrounding the city.

Over 50,000 were killed when this cyclone tore through Calcutta, India on October 5, 1864. Illustrated London News.

The third wave followed the path of the first, adding measurably to the depth of the water in the city and the surrounding countryside. It went on to hit Yanaon, a town nearby.

Enormous quantities of mud and silt choked the entrance to the mouth of the river, hampering the search for bodies and cloaking the ruins of a once bustling city now reduced to one building and the shattered remains of its smashed docks.

It took the rebuilders of Coringa many years to reconstruct their ancient city after the triple waves of the cyclone of 1789 (see preceding entry). And then, 40 years later, a gigantic 40-foot tidal wave, spawned by an enormous cyclone, once again wiped out the city, destroying 20,000 vessels in its harbor and killing 300,000 people.

It was one of the worst cataclysms ever to hit this cyclone-ravaged area, and the ancient city of Coringa was never wholly rebuilt after it.

INDIA
CORINGA

November 1839

• • • • • • • • • • • • • • • •

Three hundred thousand people lost their lives in a cyclone and tidal wave that assaulted Coringa, India in November 1839. The city was never entirely rebuilt.

INDIA
ORISSA DISTRICT

October 12, 1967

• • • • • • • • • • • • • • • •

Hardly anyone survived the cyclone that struck the Orissa district of India on October 12, 1967.

Orissa, a primitive state consisting of small villages and located some 200 miles south of Calcutta, keeps no records, and so the precise number of fatalities from the killer cyclone of October 12, 1967 remains unknown. Suffice it to say that only a small percentage of humans survived.

All but a handful of the buildings—most of them thatched palm roofed huts held together by mud—were flattened as if a giant fist had driven them into the earth. Mingled with the wreckage of the huts were banana, palm and banyan trees, all of them uprooted and crushed.

On the one-lane roads, steel I-beams that had been used to hold electric lines were bent into U-shapes. The rice crops that ordinarily rimmed the roads were destroyed without a trace.

One unique circumstance makes this particular tragedy outstanding and strange. Ordinarily, a mass destruction of livestock is taken care of by nature, for vultures strip the carcasses clean. In the Orissa cyclone, every bird, as well as every animal was killed. There were no vultures to clean the thousands of decaying animal carcasses, which permeated the disaster site with their fearsome stench for months.

HURRICANES

. . . .

THE WORST RECORDED HURRICANES

• • • • •

* Detailed in text

Barbados
(1694)
* (and Martinique, St. Lucia and St. Eustatius) (1780)
(1782)
* (1831)

British Honduras
* Belize (1931)

Cape Santa Cruz
(1481)

Caribbean
* Hurricane Janet (1955)
* Hurricane Inez (1966)
* (and Mexico and Texas) Hurricane Gilbert (1988)
* Hurricane Joan (1988)

Cuba
* (1926)
(1933)
* Hurricane Flora (1963)
Havana (1768)
* (and Florida) Havana/Florida (1944)
* Santa Cruz del Sur (1932)

Curacao
(1877)

El Salvador
(1934)

England
* (1703)

Grenada
* (1956)

Guadeloupe
* (1666)
* (1928)

Haiti
* (1909)
* Hurricane Jeramie (1935)
* Hurricane Cleo (1964)
* Hurricane Flora (1963)
* Hurricane Hazel (1954)

Holland
* Leyden (1574)

Honduras
(1941)

* (1955)
* Hurricane Hattie (1961)

Jamaica
* (1784)
* Hurricane Charlie (1951)

Leeward Islands
Twin hurricanes (1747)

Lesser Antilles
Besseterre (1650)

Martinique
(1680)
* (1695)
* (1881)
(1891)

Mexico
* (1909)
Manzanillo (1959)
* Tampico (1933)
* Tampico (Hurricane Hilda) (1955)
* Yucatan (Hurricane Gilbert) (1988) (see HURRICANES, Caribbean, Hurricane Gilbert)

Montego Bay
* (1780)

Newfoundland
* (1775)

Nova Scotia
* (1873)

Puerto Rico
* (1533)
* (1825)
* (1899)
* (1932)
* Hurricane Donna (see HURRICANES, U.S., Florida)

Santo Domingo
* (1780) (see HURRICANES, Montego Bay)
* (1834)
* (1930)

St. Croix
* (1772)

United States
Alabama

* Mobile (1819)
* Mobile (Hurricane Frederic) (1979)
East
(1849)
(1944)
* Hurricane Hazel (1954)
* Hurricanes Connie and Diane (1955)
* Hurricane Donna (1960)
* Hurricane Eloise (1975)
* Hurricane David (1979)
Florida
(1758)
* Keys (1906)
* Keys (1935)
Key West (Hurricane Donna) (1960)
Miami
* (1926)
* Hurricane Cleo (1964)
* Okeechobee (1928)
* St. Jo (1841)
* Straits (1919)
Georgia
* (1893)
Louisiana
* (1812)
* (1893)
* (and Mississippi) (1909)
(1918)
* Last Island (1856)
Mississippi
* Hurricane Elena (1985)
New England
* (1773)
* (1815)
* (1841)
* (1938) (see HURRICANES, New York [Long Island] and New England)
* (1944)
* Hurricane Carol (1954)
New York (Long Island) and New England

North Carolina
  * (1713)
Southern U.S.
  * Hurricane Audrey (1957)
  * Hurricane Camille (1969)

  * Hurricane Juan (1985)
Texas
  * Galveston (1900)
  * Galveston (1915)
  * Indianola (1886)
West Indies

(and Florida) (1928)
  * Hispaniola (1495) (first reported
      hurricane, by Columbus)
Hispaniola (1509)
  * Trois-Islets (1766)

CHRONOLOGY

• • • • • • • •

* Detailed in text
1495
  June
    * Hispaniola, West Indies (first
        reported hurricane, by
        Columbus)
1509
  July 10
    Hispaniola, West Indies
1533
  July 26–August 31
    * Puerto Rico
1574
  October 1
    * Leyden, Holland
1650
    Besseterre, Lesser
      Antilles
1666
  August 4
    * Guadeloupe
1680
  August 3
    Martinique
1694
  September 27
    Barbados
1695
  October 20
    * Martinique
1703
  November 27
    * England
1713
  September 16–17
    * North Carolina
1747
  October 24
    Leeward Islands (twin
      hurricanes)
1758
    Florida

1766
  August 12
    * Trois-Islets, West Indies
1768
  October 25
    Havana, Cuba
1772
  August 31
    * St. Croix
1773
  August 14
    * New England
1775
  September 9
    * Newfoundland
1780
  October 3
    * Montego Bay
  October 10
    * Barbados
1782
    Barbados
1784
  July 30
    * Jamaica
1812
  August 19
    * Louisiana
1815
  September
    * New England
1819
  July 27–28
    * Mobile, Alabama
1825
  July 26
    * Puerto Rico
1831
  August 10
    * Barbados
1834
  September 23

  * Santo Domingo
1841
  September
    * St. Jo, Florida
  October 3
    * New England
1849
  October 6
    Eastern United States
1856
  August 13
    * Last Island,
      Louisiana
1873
  August 24
    * Nova Scotia
1877
  September 21
    Curacao
1881
  August 18
    * Martinique
1886
  August 19
    * Indianola, Texas
1891
  August 18
    Martinique
1893
  August 27
    * Georgia
  October 1
    * Louisiana
1899
  August 8
    * Puerto Rico
1900
  September 8
    * Galveston, Texas
1906
  October 18
    * Florida Keys

1909
August 23
* Haiti
August 27
* Mexico
September 10–20
* Louisiana and Mississippi
1915
August 16
* Galveston, Texas
1919
September 9–10
* Florida Straits
1926
September 17
* Miami, Florida
October 20
* Cuba
1928
September 10
West Indies (and Florida)
September 12
* Guadeloupe
September 16
* Okeechobee, Florida
1930
September 3
* Santo Domingo
1931
September 10
* Belize, British Honduras
1932
September 26
* Puerto Rico
November 9
* Santa Cruz Del Sur, Cuba
1933
September 1
Cuba
September 24
* Tampico, Mexico
1934
June 8
El Salvador
1935
September 2

* Florida Keys
October 22
* Haiti (Hurricane Jeramie)
1938
September 21
New York (Long Island) and
New England
1944
September 8–16
* New England
September 14
Eastern United States
October 13
* Havana, Cuba (and Florida)
1951
August 17
* Jamaica (Hurricane Charlie)
1954
August 26–31
* New England (Hurricane Carol)
October 12
* Haiti, Eastern and Southern
U.S. (Hurricane Hazel)
1955
August 4–18
* Eastern United States
(Hurricanes Connie and
Diane)
September 19
* Tampico, Mexico (Hurricane
Hilda)
September 22
* Caribbean (Hurricane Janet)
September 27
* Honduras (Hurricane Janet)
October 12
* Haiti (Hurricane Hazel)
1956
September 22
* Grenada
1957
June 27–30
* Southern United States
(Hurricane Audrey)
1959
October 27

Manzanillo, Mexico
1960
September 4–12
* Eastern United States (Hurricane
Donna)
1961
October 31
* Honduras (Hurricane Hattie)
1963
September 30–October 9
* Cuba (Hurricane Flora)
1964
August 22–27
* Florida and Haiti (Hurricane
Cleo)
1966
September 24–29
* Caribbean (Hurricane Inez)
1969
August 17
* Southern United States
(Hurricane Camille)
1975
September 22–27
* Eastern United States (Hurricane
Eloise)
1979
August 31–September 8
* Eastern United States (Hurricane
David)
September 11
* Mobile, Alabama (Hurricane
Frederic)
1985
August 30–September 2
Mississippi (Hurricane Elena)
October 27–November 5
* Southern United States
(Hurricane Juan)
1988
September 12–19
* Caribbean (Hurricane Gilbert)
October 17–23
* Caribbean (and Mexico and
Texas) (Hurricane Joan)

HURRICANES

A hurricane is a tropical cyclone which takes place over the North Atlantic Ocean and is characterized by windspeeds greater than 75 mph.

There are four stages in the development of a full blown hurricane: 1) tropical cyclone, 2) tropical depression, 3) tropical storm, 4) full hurricane. These storms generally form over the tropical North Atlantic, often off the west coast of Africa, and mature as they move westward. But, although a great many incipient cyclones on the way to becoming hurricanes may form in this way, only an average of 3.5 per year reach tropical storm stage. Usually occurring over the Caribbean Sea or the Gulf of Mexico, only one to three of these tropical storms approach the eastern coast of the United States each year.

Occasionally, hurricanes develop off the west coast of Mexico and move northeast, thus threatening the coastal areas of Texas.

Hurricanes generally have a lifespan of from one to 30 days. They thrive over tropically heated water and are transformed into extratropical cyclones after prolonged passage over the cooler waters of the North Atlantic. Once they make landfall, they decay rapidly.

This dispassionate description may convey a benign picture of hurricanes. But just the opposite is true. In fact, in an average hurricane, the release of latent heat from the condensation of water vapor provides as much energy as the detonation of 400 20-megaton hydrogen bombs. Fortunately for those in a hurricane's path, only 2 percent to 4 percent of this heat energy is translated into the kinetic force of the winds' motion—still enough of a percentage to cause immense damage from hurricane winds, and secondary damage from the flooding that results from the coastal storm surge and tropical rains that generally accompany the storm.

The precise conditions necessary to spawn a hurricane are not entirely known, although Project Stormfury, a U.S. Government program designed to develop ways of defusing hurricanes at their source is currently studying this in depth. What is known is this: A mature hurricane is nearly symmetrically circular in form, sometimes extending to a diameter of 500 miles. Within a chimney of superheated, tropical air, is a so-called "eye"—a space of calm and often blue sky that is usually 20 miles in circumference. Surrounding this is the "eye-wall," the place of greatest danger and turbulence. This is where the inward-spiraling, moisture-laden air is shot aloft, causing condensation and the release of dangerous, latent heat—the source of the energy of the storm. After reaching tens of thousands of feet of altitude, this energy is expelled toward the storm's periphery. But at the location of the wall, the upward velocity of the air, mixed with condensation, forms a combination of maximum high winds and furious precipitation.

Clouds spread outward from this wall in spiral bands parallel to the wind direction, thus forming the hurricane's characteristic shape, and giving way from persistent rain at the storm's core to tropical showers along its outer rim.

Hurricanes generally move at speeds of about 10 mph on their westward track, often picking up speed as they curve toward the north pole, usually at 20 to 30 degrees north latitude, but often in a more complex and unpredictable pattern. Predicted or unpredicted, hurricanes are capable of causing enormous destruction and staggering loss of life.

BARBADOS (AND MARTINIQUE, ST. LUCIA AND ST. EUSTATIUS)

October 10, 1780

• • • • • • • • • • • • • •

In an 8-day trip through Barbados, Martinique, St. Lucia, St. Vincent and St. Eustatius, the hurricane that entered the area on October 10, 1780 killed 20,000.

The great hurricane of 1780 roared through Barbados on the 10th of October, 1780, totally leveling the entire island, killing 6,000 on the island itself and a total of nearly 20,000 on its 8-day rampage through Barbados, Martinique, St. Lucia, St. Vincent, St. Eustatius and Puerto Rico.

The intense destruction of Barbados resulted from the full fury of the storm passing directly across it. An entire day of increasing rains and rising winds preceded the final destruction of every tree and every building on the island, including its Government House, which, with its three-foot-thick walls was heretofore thought to be hurricane-proof. (Major General Cunningham, governor of Barbados, and his family escaped unharmed by hiding in a storm cellar.) The terror was increased by the fact that the eye of the storm passed over the island at night, and thus whole families were buried in the rubble of their dwellings as they slept.

Once the storm crossed Barbados, it smashed an entire British fleet anchored off St. Lucia, then barreled on to Martinique, which it also flattened, destroying a French fleet of an estimated 40 ships and drowning 4,000 French soldiers and sailors. On St. Lucia, 9,000 persons lost their lives to the storm.

After the devastation of Barbados, Martinique and St. Lucia, the storm reeled over open water, sinking a score of other ships and eventually blowing itself out someplace past Puerto Rico.

BARBADOS

August 10, 1831

• • • • • • • • • • • • • •

Fifteen thousand people died in the hurricane of August 10, 1831 in Barbados.

A huge hurricane, pushing a series of tidal waves before it, was first sighted as it roared into the island of Barbados on August 10, 1831. Compounding the human toll of 1,500 was the incredible loss of property: $7.5 million worth, which in current value totals hundreds of millions.

As in the 1780 event (see preceding entry), trees were uprooted, and scarcely a dwelling was left standing. In addition, millions of dollars worth of crops were laid to waste, inundated by water and stripped clean by wind.

A day later, the same storm slammed into Haiti, raced on to Cuba, totally submerged several small islands, careened through the Gulf of Mexico and eventually made landfall at New Orleans, after which it blew itself out over the mainland of Louisiana.

BRITISH HONDURAS
BELIZE

September 10, 1931

• • • • • • • • • • • • • •

A small but powerful hurricane slammed into Belize, British Honduras on September 10, 1931, killing more than 1,500 people.

With winds exceeding 132 mph, a compact but deadly hurricane ran through the Caribbean from Barbados on September 6, 1931, to British Honduras on September 10. Its full force slammed into the small city of Belize, where it picked up a score of ships and flung them through the streets of this normally busy port.

A coastal surge pushed inland from the storm filled the streets of Belize, drowning over 1,500 inhabitants and causing over $7 million in damage.

CARIBBEAN
HURRICANE JANET

September 22, 1955

• • • • • • • • • • • • • •

Five hundred people died and 60,000 were rendered homeless by Hurricane Janet as it carved its destructive path through the Caribbean on September 22, 1955.

The Caribbean season of 1955, with 11 hurricanes, was the most extraordinary and disastrous to date, and Hurricane Janet was one of the worst of them.

Packing winds of 114 mph, Janet, an immense storm that originated off the coast of Venezuela, claimed over 200 lives in Honduras and 300 in Mexico, made over 60,000 homeless and caused millions of dollars in damage to the coastal areas of Mexico, Honduras, Veracruz, Tampico and the U.S. Navy Hurricane Observation State at Swan Island, located off Cape Gracias a Dios.

Janet claimed its first lives in the first recorded wreck of a hurricane hunter plane. The Navy Neptune flew out of

Jacksonville on September 26, 1955, with nine crewmen and two Canadian news photographers. Early in the morning of September 27, Lieutenant Commander G. B. Windham reported penetrating the eyewall at an altitude of 700 feet and announced that winds in the eyewall were clocked at 150 mph. That was the last message received from the plane, which was never found.

The second victims were also personnel, stationed, along with U.S. Weather Bureau personnel, on Swan Island. The center of the storm passed over the tiny island, destroying all of its buildings with the exception of its mess hall, whose refrigerator exploded. When the winds reached 150 mph, the roof of this one remaining building was ripped off, soaking seven men with 500 gallons of diesel fuel from a roof tank.

All of the foliage on the island was destroyed, including 10,000 coconut palms which were snapped off at a uniform height of 15 feet. The beaches were carpeted with dead fish, almost all with their eyes popped out. Fortunately, there was no loss of human life.

From here, the storm proceeded to Honduras, where it killed an estimated 200 inhabitants of Corozal, a small Honduran city. Exiting Honduras, it menaced the coast of Mexico, ricocheting off the beaches, demolishing huts and buildings in the ancient city of Chetumal in the state of Quintana Roo, as well as other sites in the Yucatan.

But its most horrendous fury was saved for last. Refueled by the tropical waters of the Caribbean, it crashed into Tampico with unabated, monstrous force, ripping countless homes asunder and rendering over 60,000 people homeless.

A grim aftermath occurred when the Panuco and Tamesi rivers, swollen by the coastal surge and tropical downpours, overflowed their banks, disgorging countless poisonous rattlesnakes into the nearby villages, and increasing the total number of dead from the storm.

CARIBBEAN
HURRICANE INEZ

September 24–29, 1966

• • • • • • • • • • • • •

More than 2,500 people were killed, 3,000 were injured and 250,000 were made homeless by Hurricane Inez's five-day stay in the Caribbean, from September 24 to 29, 1966.

Over 2,500 residents of Haiti, Cuba and the Dominican Republic died in the onslaught of Inez, the Caribbean-spawned hurricane that raged for five days (September 24–29, 1966) laying waste to over a hundred million dollars worth of crops, flattening villages and injuring an esti-

mated 3,000 people. Over 250,000 were forced to evacuate their homes—150,000 in Cuba alone.

A particularly furious storm, with winds clocked at 160 mph, Inez hit Haiti the hardest, turning some of its countryside into a valley of death, with corpses piled high enough to dominate the devastated landscape. The town of Jacmel, a hitherto peaceful enclave on the southwest coast of Haiti, reported a death toll of 1,000. Accurate figures were hard to come by from the dictator, Francois Duvalier, but huge crop damage was reported.

The Dominican Republic suffered complete destruction of all crops on the island. Homes were completely flattened (in the town of Oviedo the only building that remained standing was the town hall). More than 1,000 people were reported injured, and 200 were known dead.

The coastal areas and river banks of Cuba were overrun by the coastal surge of Inez, sending 150,000 persons fleeing from their inundated homes and farms. Hundreds more, caught in the path of waves and wind, drowned or were felled by falling trees and houses.

CARIBBEAN (AND MEXICO AND TEXAS)
HURRICANE GILBERT

September 12–19, 1988

• • • • • • • • • • • • •

The gigantic Hurricane Gilbert killed over 350 people in the Caribbean, Mexico and Texas between September 12 and 19, 1988. The National Hurricane Center established it as the most violent storm in its annals, and the worst hurricane ever to occur in the Western Hemisphere.

The worst hurricane ever to hit the Western Hemisphere cut a 2,500-mile-wide path of stupendous destruction as it crossed the Caribbean westward from September 12 to 19, 1988. It wreaked nearly $10 billion worth of havoc and killed more than 350 people, as it roared across the Caribbean with winds of up to 200 mph.

In the Caribbean, Haiti, the U.S. Virgin Islands, the British Virgin Islands, St. Lucia, Puerto Rico, the Dominican Republic, the Cayman Islands and, particularly, Jamaica suffered everything from mild to extreme damage. Mexico's Yucatan Peninsula, which is normally spared hurricanes, suffered huge damage. Brownsville, Texas, where the storm eventually ran ashore, suffered minor damage, but the storm continued to move upward from Texas, spinning off 41 tornadoes that killed three people in Texas and Oklahoma, flooding land near rivers in both states, and spreading moisture as far north as Chicago. The last casualty of the storm was a 50-year-old pilot from Santa

Fe, New Mexico who was killed on September 17, when his plane broke apart while flying near Muskogee, northeast of Oklahoma City, in heavy rain produced by the storm.

Gilbert began its short but destructive life off the coast of Africa in late August and traveled the trade winds, arriving in the eastern Caribbean at the beginning of September, 1988.

On Sunday, September 11, it grazed the southern tip of Haiti, drowning 10 people and engulfing hundreds of head of livestock. Roads were completely cut off to this peninsula and the banana crop was destroyed. Simultaneously, its winds struck the Dominican Republic and the U.S. and British Virgin Islands. Damage was slight to the Virgin Islands; utility poles were toppled, there was some livestock and crop loss on the British Virgin Islands, and there were numerous power outages. In the Dominican Republic, however, the flooding and crop damage were far more widespread. Five died on the island, 100 families were rendered homeless, and the main electricity relay station was blown down, blacking out much of the capital city of Santo Domingo.

Squarely in the path of Gilbert lay the island of Jamaica. It had not had a visit from a hurricane in 37 years, but this one would hit it head on, at 9 A.M. on the morning of September 12. By this time, Gilbert's winds had climbed to 145 mph. It slammed into Kingston, swept across the banana plantations and livestock farms, and lifted the roofs from 80 percent of the homes on the island. Trees were leveled as if a cosmic buzzsaw had rushed through the countryside. Four out of every five homes were rendered uninhabitable; once the storm had passed, more than a million people would be affected, and 500,000 made homeless.

In Kingston, all 82 patients from the National Chest Hospital were moved hastily after the hurricane chewed through 50 feet of roof, spewing the remnants of solid wooden beams like toothpicks across the hospital garden.

At another public hospital, the storm crushed its kitchen and flooded the maternity ward. Two days later, doctors and nurses there were still standing in rubber boots in water an inch deep delivering babies in a hallway.

Seventy percent of the dwellings in Kingston, home to a fourth of Jamaica's 3.4 million population, were either damaged or destroyed.

Twenty-five people died on Jamaica; the banana and poultry crops of the entire island were completely wiped out. Communication with the island would be impossible for days. All in all, Jamaica suffered $8 billion in damages, making it the greatest natural disaster in that island's history.

But the storm had not finished its destruction. Back over the tropical waters of the Caribbean, it intensified still further, and both American and Soviet hurricane watchers (the Soviets were based in Cuba) flying into it were astonished by the pressure in its eye: 26.13 inches—the lowest ever recorded for a hurricane in the western hemisphere. (The only lower pressure in a hurricane, 25.69 inches, was recorded on October 12, 1979, in the eye of Hurricane Tip as it rocketed across the Pacific Ocean between Luzon in the Philippines and Iwo Jima in the western Pacific.)

Something else was odd about Hurricane Gilbert. Ordinarily, the eyes of hurricanes measure from 20 to 25 miles across. Gilbert's eye measured a mere eight miles in diameter. Thus, it resembled a tornado more than a hurricane, and this, according to Frederick J. Gadomski, a climate analyst at Pennsylvania State University, probably accounted for the extremely violent winds—now clocked at 200 mph—within its eyewall.

By Tuesday night, September 13, the storm was upgraded to a force 5 storm—the highest force rating possible. Accorded the title of the century's fiercest storm, it headed due west, passed 20 miles south of the Cayman Islands, where it leveled trees and disrupted electricity and telephone service and headed straight for Mexico's Yucatan Peninsula. With wind gusts of 218 mph and a storm surge that sent 23-foot-high waves curling over beachfronts, Gilbert slammed into the Yucatan at daybreak on Wednesday, the 14th.

The night before, 20,000 residents of the coastal areas of Yucatan state, including 6,000 tourists—90 percent of them American—were evacuated from the beachfront resort areas of Quintana Roo State and housed in schools, hospitals and government buildings inland.

Well that they had been, for, as it had in Jamaica, the storm began systematically to peel the roofs from homes and other buildings, uproot trees, smash docks and topple communications towers. The storm cut a 90-mile-long swath across the Yucatan, wrecking the banana crops, flattening thatched roof houses and rendering small villages on the edge of the fabled Yucatan jungle, where Mayan ruins vie with the undergrowth, ghost towns. The devastation in the city of Cancun was extreme; businesses were wrecked, debris was everywhere. Seventeen people were dead; 300,000 people were made homeless. Ninety percent of the corn and fruit crops were destroyed. In Cancun and Cozumel, posh resort hotels were severely battered. The Club Med lost half of its installations.

Meanwhile, the storm roared on. Honduras, Nicaragua and Guatemala all reported deaths, mostly by drowning, and extensive damage to crops and animal herds. Sheets of rain pelted Brownsville and Galveston, Texas. Over

175,000 people were evacuated from northern Mexico. City officials on Galveston Island asked the city's 70,000 residents to leave. In Houston, space agency officials delayed the first space shuttle launching since the *Challenger* disaster in January 1986 because the hurricane threat in Houston was interferring with the work of engineers on the project. Prisoners from four Houston area prisons were moved to facilities further north for the duration of the storm. A hurricane warning was posted from Tampico in northern Mexico to Port O'Connor near the middle of the Texas coast, and a hurricane watch extended as far north as Louisiana.

Dozens of tornadoes, spawned by the storm, whirled through the Lower Rio Grande Valley of Texas and brought wind gusts of up to 82 mph on the Texas Coast at South Padre Island, ripping tin roofs off stores and homes, overturning mobile homes and automobiles. Tornadoes ripped the roof off an apartment building in Brownsville.

Off the Texas coast, the Coast Guard received rescue calls from three shrimp boats that tried to outrun the storm but wound up caught in rough waters. Helicopters quickly found one boat, the *Ki II* of Venice, Louisiana and picked up her crew of five. A sisters boat, the *Ki I*, ran aground, and its three-man crew survived, as did the third shrimper and its men.

An estimated 20,000 people stayed at shelters in the Brownsville area, and roughly that number were housed in shelters in Matamoros, across the border, including 3,000 who stayed in railroad cars.

The storm, whose winds had weakened over the Yucatan Peninsula, and whose eye had widened from eight miles to 50, made its final landfall at 5:30 P.M. Friday, September 16th (Mexico's Independence Day) just south of the border city of Matamoros, Mexico. Its sustained winds were still 120 mph, enough to topple trees, devastate houses and cause the most tragic occurrence of its 2,500 mile trek.

Four buses, loaded with a reported 200 passengers stalled near the overflowing Santa Catarina River near Monterey. Trying to avoid the flooding, the buses detoured unwisely and soon found themselves mired on a two-lane highway, engulfed by the raging rain-swollen waters of the Santa Catarina.

Panicked passengers soon clambered to the roofs of the buses. For six hours they remained there, buffetted by winds and rain, while the waters slowly rose around them and rescuers tried to reach them—to no avail. Four police officers drowned when the tractor they were using as a rescue vehicle overturned in the water and they were swept away. Two civilian rescue workers in a boat fell into the floodwaters.

Finally, all four buses toppled over, spilling their passengers into the raging waters, and sweeping them downstream, past their rescuers. Only 13 of the 200 passengers were saved; some of the drowned were fished from the water as far away as Cadereyta, 35 miles from the site of the tragedy. Some of the bodies were never found.

All in all, more than 350 people lost their lives to Hurricane Gilbert, 750,000 were made homeless and at least $10 billion in damage was caused by this, the most ferocious storm of the century.

If anything positive can be gleaned from this, it is this: Modern, up-to-date forecasting techniques and the willingness of populaces to follow the warnings undoubtedly kept the statistics from matching the size and tragic intensity of the storm. Had it occurred 75 years earlier, the casualty figures would have been a hundred times worse.

CARIBBEAN
HURRICANE JOAN
October 17–23, 1988
• • • • • • • • • • • • • •
The first Atlantic hurricane to cross over land and continue as a Pacific tropical storm, Hurricane Joan killed 500, made over 60,000 homeless and destroyed scores of villages and towns in the Caribbean from October 17 to 23, 1988.

The second deadly Atlantic hurricane in six weeks (see HURRICANES, Caribbean, Hurricane Gilbert, p. 175) in the Caribbean, Joan was also the first recorded Atlantic hurricane to cross over and continue as a tropical storm in the Pacific. After devastating parts of Nicaragua on October 22, it headed over the Pacific, assuming a new name and a new identity. Weakened by its crossland passage, it became Pacific tropical storm Miriam and threatened San Salvadore, Guatemala and Mexico.

Nearly 500 people lost their lives to Joan in Nicaragua, Costa Rica, Panama, Colombia and Venezuela as the hurricane wandered for six days across the Caribbean and finally, with winds of 155 mph, slammed into the coast of Nicaragua at Bluefields. This city of 60,000 was 90 percent destroyed, "practically disappear[ing] from the map," according to the Managua daily *El Nuevo Diario*.

Off the coast of Bluefields, a deep water port that Bulgarian engineers had been building was 60 percent destroyed. The winds uprooted the breakwater, pulling 10-ton concrete sections from their moorings.

Houses were splintered into kindling; dikes and dams burst; mudslides buried entire villages. Shrimp packing plants in El Bluff, near Bluefields, were flattened. Every house was smashed on Little Corn and Great Corn Islands, 45 miles east of Bluefields, and the Great Corn's only clinic was destroyed.

Many refugees from the Contras, who lived in tin and wood shacks along the riverbeds near Managua were forced to flee from their homes, which were washed away by roaring, overflowing riverwaters.

In Nicaragua alone, 360 people died, 178 were seriously injured, 110 were reported missing and 29,000 were made homeless. Seventy-six bridges were wiped out by flood waters. "This could be the worst natural disaster in Central American history, but people don't realize it because we didn't have 50,000 victims," commented Nicaraguan Social Security Minister Reynaldo Antonio Tefel.

In neighboring Costa Rica, eight people were killed when a dike burst in the town of Neily, 10 miles from the Panama border. In Costa Rica's mountains, the Terraba River rose almost five feet in an hour of pounding rain, then burst its banks and flooded the village of Cortes, forcing its 2,000 inhabitants to flee. Throughout Costa Rica, 1,500 homes were destroyed, six hospitals and health centers were severely damaged and 55,000 people were forced to evacuate their homes.

But the greatest casualties in both human life and ecological loss were centered in Nicaragua, which, because of the presence of its Communist Sandinista government found nearby disaster aid hard to come by. Flying in the face of its normally humane attitude towards the victims of natural disasters, the Reagan Administration failed to respond to Nicaragua's pleas for relief aid and sent nothing. Cuba and the Soviet Union sent 25,000 tons of food, medicine and other necessities and 300 construction workers to rebuild 1,000 homes in Bluefields.

In terms of longterm destruction, the gutting of 70 percent of the fishing fleet, the entire crop in the south of Nicaragua and more than 600,000 acres of its rain forest was incalculable. "To rebuild a town of 25,000 is possible with the right amount of aid," commented Interior Minister Tomas Borge, "but the ecological damage to our rivers and forests is apocalyptic."

A similar conclusion was expressed by Sandinista commentator Sofia Montenegro, who dubbed her country "The nation of Sisyphus. Damned country!" Montenegro went on, in an article in the official newspaper *Barricada*:

Once more in ruins! How many times will we have to rebuild what has been destroyed?

This new catastrophe, devastating but above all unfair for a country already worn down by war and enemy siege, gives one a sense that the effort to raise Nicaragua up is futile and hopeless. Against the background of aggression, the hurricane seems not a caprice of nature, but rather a joke, a hideous conspiracy by who knows what Indian

gods against our absurd mortal efforts. It produces a strange and atavistic rebellion against our apparent destiny to plant again and again, without ever harvesting anything.

CUBA

October 20, 1926

• • • • • • • • • • • • • • •

Every window in Havana, Cuba exploded from the force of the hurricane that raced through Cuba on October 20, 1926, killing 650 and rendering 10,000 homeless.

The monumental hurricane that battered Cuba for six hours, from early morning until the late afternoon of October 20, 1926, packed winds that climbed to 130 mph, strong enough to explode every window in downtown Havana, kill 650 people, render 10,000 homeless, sink dozens of boats in Havana Harbor, and cause $100 million in damage.

Roaring into the harbor of Havana in the early morning of October 20, the storm pushed a 25-foot-high coastal swell that swamped huge steamers like the *Puerto Tarafa*, which went instantly to the bottom with all hands. The *Maximo Gomez* was turned into a juggernaut, ramming a score of other ships and sending them under the roiling waters of the bay before an enormous swell sent it careening ashore.

Matanzas and Pinar del Rio provinces were devastated; the small town of Batapano, located at the extreme southern end of Havana Province suffered a death toll of 300, which was 15 percent of its total population of 2,000. Inhabitants of Santa Maria del Rosario, Fajardo, Guanabocoa, Jaruco and Minas were trapped and crushed within their collapsing dwellings. The next day, these villages had virtually disappeared from the horizon.

A distraught officer at the Cuban army headquarters and Camp Columbia walked out to the middle of the parade field and committed suicide at the height of the storm. Other members of the army reacted with more equanimity by assisting what was left of the Havana police force in digging through wreckage for survivors.

When the coastal surge broke over Havana's sea wall, it drove trolleys, automobiles and people ahead of it, snapping off trees as if they were twigs, crushing one four-year-old boy against a hospital wall and drowning or maiming rescue workers under collapsed walls or automobiles.

The famous American monument to the dead of the U.S. battleship *Maine*, which was blown up in Havana harbor in 1898, was toppled, its marble columns sheared

Injured survivors of Hurricane Flora are loaded aboard helicopters in Haiti in September 1963. CARE photo.

off at centerpoint, its stone eagles liberated and sent flying, never to be reclaimed.

By the time the storm, which had now centered itself inland where it destroyed crops and farmhouses, had veered out to sea and headed toward Key West, there was hardly any means left to broadcast the news of the wholesale and horrible destruction to the outside world.

CUBA
HURRICANE FLORA

September 30–October 9, 1963

• • • • • • • • • • • • • • •

Hurricane Flora, which remained in Cuba for 10 days, from September 30 through October 9, 1963, killed over 1,000 and made 175,000 homeless. Proceeding to Haiti, it killed 5,000 and rendered 100,000 homeless on that island.

The paths of hurricanes can be by the book, moving westward along the trade winds and then curving northward toward the poles. Or, they can behave erratically, and this was the reason that Hurricane Flora caused such unbridled havoc on Haiti and Cuba during 10 horrendous days and nights—September 30 through October 9, 1963.

Fidel Castro accused the United States of deliberately withholding information from Cuba about the imminent danger posed by the threatening storm, which wiped out one-fourth of that island country's sugar crop, 90 percent of its coffee crop, killed over 1,000 persons and rendered more than 175,000 homeless. (Later, apparently reconsidering his hasty accusation, the Cuban leader filed for United States disaster aid.)

What increased the cataclysm in Cuba was the longevity of the storm. It spent five days crossing and recrossing Cuba, particularly over its easternmost quadrant. Here, it claimed 1,000 lives and accounted for the crushing of the homes destroyed, and erased the once abundant and rich crops of sugar and coffee that formed the basis of Cuba's economy in 1963.

Francois Duvalier's subjects on Haiti also fared badly, as the hurricane whipped through that island, felling forests, unceremoniously tilling fields, and swelling streams into roaring rivers. Duvalier, noted for undercounting victims, nevertheless admitted that scores of villages had simply disappeared, 5,000 persons had died, and 100,000 had been rendered homeless.

CUBA (AND FLORIDA)
HAVANA/FLORIDA

October 13, 1944

• • • • • • • • • • • • • • •

Possessing an eye that was 70 miles in diameter and 167 mph winds, a deadly hurricane struck Cuba, killing hundreds.

The great freak Havana-Florida hurricane, born in the Gulf of Colombia, packed incredible force. For 12 long hours, it clocked 167-mph winds, which threw huge schooners used for sponging two and a half miles inland near Batabano, where hundreds died. From here, the storm headed directly for Florida, through the Gulf of Mexico, passing, with an eye that was 70 miles in diameter, through the space between Ocala and Jacksonville.

From this point, the storm skirted the coast, making no landfall as it rocketed up between Nantucket and Cape Cod and on to the colder waters of Nova Scotia, where it would ultimately die at sea.

CUBA
SANTA CRUZ DEL SUR

November 9, 1932

• • • • • • • • • • • • • • •

A hurricane with 210-mph winds killed half the population of Cruz del Sur, Cuba—2,500 people—on November 9, 1932.

A ship's captain off the coast of Cuba on November 9, 1932 recorded in his log that the winds that roiled the seas around him into a furious froth and bounced his vessel like a youngster on a pogo stick were "infinite."

That may have been an exaggeration, but to the 4,000 inhabitants of Santa Cruz del Sur in Cuba that same day, the winds recorded at 210 mph might just as well have been beyond measurement. The mighty forward motion, the incredibly high winds of this monster hurricane churned up a gigantic tidal wave which curled forward and smashed into the Cuban city full force.

Within minutes, Santa Cruz del Sur was flattened beyond recognition, and 2,500 people—more than half of the city's population—had lost their lives, mostly from drowning. There were simply no shelters for the inhabitants to escape the violent fury of this storm, even if they had had adequate warning.

ENGLAND
November 27, 1703

• • • • • • • • • • • • • • • •

The hurricane of November 27, 1703 drowned 30,000 sailors off the coast of England, countless others on land, and crushed 5,000 houses in Gloucestershire, Sussex, Kent, Oxfordshire, Somersetshire, Northampton, Suffolk and Worcestershire.

Daniel Defoe, the creator of *Robinson Crusoe,* must have drawn some inspiration from the raging sea caused by the enormously destructive hurricane of November 27, 1703. Slamming into the southern coast of England, it sank 300 ships, killed an estimated 30,000 sailors at sea, caused the deaths of an incredible—though unrecorded—number of cattle and people, and tumbled or crushed 5,000 houses in Gloucestershire, Sussex, Kent, Oxfordshire, Somersetshire, Northampton, Suffolk and Worcestershire.

It was, in fact, Defoe, then a pampleteer, who is responsible for whatever records survive of this 18th-century catastrophe.

For 14 days prior to making landfall, the storm lashed at the English coast with pelting rain and high wind squalls, softening it up for the final blow, which, when it came, virtually scoured the harbors of Grimsby, Falmouth, Bristol, Gravesend, Plymouth and Cowes clean of the ships and seamen of the French, Russian and English fleets which happened to be unlucky enough to be riding at anchor in these ports when the storm struck. Even ships inland, on the River Thames, were demolished as they were driven either into each other or onshore.

The wind turned tiles into flying missiles, flinging them through the air at enormous speed and driving them, according to Defoe, ". . . from five to eight inches into the solid earth." Other solid pieces of dwellings—bricks, timber, sheets of lead and iron—were lifted from buildings and sent soaring murderously above the earth.

Even after the storm careened inland, its devastation continued. The next day, a prodigious tide that was said to be six to eight feet higher than normal roared over seawalls and river banks, killing still more people and cattle.

GRENADA
September 22, 1956

• • • • • • • • • • • • • • • •

Two hundred people died and practically every building on the island of Grenada was destroyed in the 127-mph hurricane of September 22, 1956.

In one five-hour nightmare of destruction, a hurricane packing winds of up to 127 mph barreled into Grenada on September 22, 1956, killing 200 persons and destroying almost every building on the 120-square-mile island.

The Crown Colony of England (it would become an associated state of Britain 12 years later, in 1967, and gain full independence in 1974), primarily a resort, had been amply warned of the impending storm. A day earlier, the hurricane had roared in from the Atlantic and ripped across Barbados, 98 miles northeast of Grenada, killing 30 persons and flattening over 40,000 homes.

But even radioed warnings, the firing of cannons in the harbor of Saint George's and frantically pedaling policemen on official bicycles failed to prevent the catastrophic loss of life.

Saint George's was particularly hard hit, losing not only its buildings but its warehouses and piers, the heart of its commercial and tourist area. It would take almost a year, with copious American and British aid, before Grenada would return to any semblance of stability and serenity.

GUADELOUPE
August 4, 1666

• • • • • • • • • • • • • • • •

More than 2,000 French sailors were drowned when a violent hurricane struck Guadeloupe on August 4, 1666.

After surviving a minor sidehand sweep from a hurricane in 1665, Guadeloupe received the full force of what has been recorded as one of the most violent storms of the 1600s in the western hemisphere, on August 4, 1666. Over 2,000 French sailors alone were drowned when a troop fleet was sent to the bottom of the Caribbean by the monster storm surge that roared ahead of the hurricane.

First coursing through St. Christopher and Martinique, the storm was not abated a bit by this brief landfall and went on to slam into Guadeloupe with full force, sinking every sailing vessel either at anchor or at sea near the island. A six-foot-thick defense wall surmounted by huge cannons was crumpled like paper by the pounding of the same waves that demolished the ships it was supposed to shelter.

The sugar crop that the French had been nurturing with imported slaves was wiped out in a matter of hours. It would take years before it would be reinstated and the colony transformed into one of the world's richest growers and exporters of sugar.

GUADELOUPE
September 12, 1928

• • • • • • • • • • • • • • •

Six hundred people died without warning when a surprise hurricane hit Guadeloupe on September 12, 1928.

The same storm that meandered into Puerto Rico on September 13, killing 300 persons and causing $50 million in damage, laid waste to Guadeloupe the day before, causing the deaths of 600 people.

The mammoth storm was a slow mover, and this, in the computer-controlled forecasting atmosphere of today would have assured a much smaller fatality figure. But the fact that most of the dead were caught in their fields or on village streets indicates that warning failures were the primary cause of the magnitude of this disaster.

HAITI
August 23, 1909

• • • • • • • • • • • • • • •

(See HURRICANES, Mexico, 1909, p. 184.)

HAITI
HURRICANE JERAMIE
October 22, 1935

• • • • • • • • • • • • • • •

Over 2,000 died when one of the first named hurricanes, Hurricane Jeramie, the aptly named "hairpin hurricane," hit Haiti on October 22, 1935.

More than 2,000 farmers, most of them caught at work, were killed when Hurricane Jeramie, one of the first named hurricanes, slammed into Haiti on October 22, 1935.

Jeramie was nicknamed "The Hairpin Hurricane" because of the abnormal path it followed. Ordinarily, hurricanes travel predictably along the trade winds and then turn toward the polar north. This hurricane originated in the western Caribbean, traveled eastward, and slammed into Jamaica, where it wiped out over $2 million in sugar plantations, and then veered, not north, but south.

Thus, neither weather forecasters nor the population of Haiti were at all prepared for the fatal onslaught of the storm which hit most devastatingly in the agricultural regions of the southwest, killing farmers, crops and livestock.

HAITI
HURRICANE CLEO
August 22, 1964

• • • • • • • • • • • • • • •

(See HURRICANES, United States, Florida, Hurricane Cleo, p. 199.)

HAITI
HURRICANE FLORA
October 9, 1963

• • • • • • • • • • • • • • •

(See HURRICANES, Cuba, Hurricane Flora, p. 179.)

HAITI
HURRICANE HAZEL
October 12, 1954

• • • • • • • • • • • • • • •

(See also HURRICANES, United States, East, Hurricane Hazel, p. 190.)
Villages were buried and cities devastated, 1,000 were killed and over 40,000 were made homeless when Hurricane Hazel visited Haiti on October 12, 1954.

Sometime before dawn on October 12, 1954, Hurricane Hazel smashed into Haiti's southern coast with 125-mph winds. Before it left the island, it would kill nearly 1,000 people and render over 40,000 homeless. Soil and crops of coffee, sugarcane, beans, rice and corn were washed out to sea.

Near the capital, Port-au-Prince, torrential rains at the heart of the storm washed tons of mud over the village of Berly, burying alive all but two of the town's 260 inhabitants. In Jacmel, a city of over 8,000 people, the wind sheared off the faces of buildings, exposing the interiors to the soaking storm. Monumental tides caused by the storm surge of the hurricane pummeled the coast, washing over the seashore villages of Les Cayes on the tip of the southern peninsula.

Heading northeast, the storm seemed to blow itself out against Haiti's mountains, after leaving its destructive aftermath of tuberculosis, typhoid and typhus. U.S. Navy observation planes and Weather Bureau experts pronounced it tamed. But Hazel, heading for the Carolinas, was about to be reborn.

HOLLAND
LEYDEN

October 1, 1574

• • • • • • • • • • • • • •

Twenty thousand occupying Spanish soldiers were drowned when a hurricane destroyed dikes near Leyden, Holland on October 1, 1574.

The siege of Leyden had gone on for many days before a gigantic wind and rain storm of hurricane force hit this lowland city, located on the old Rhine River in Holland. Spanish troops, warring against William the Silent, were in the process of starving out the populace of this ancient, walled city.

They were having little luck. The plucky Netherlanders were, according to historian A. H. Godbey, ". . . devouring roots of grass, old leather, offal, anything that could in the least aid to sustain life. . . ." But the Spanish soldiers, who ringed this city that dated back to Roman times, held fast.

On the night of October 1, 1574, a hurricane arrived, lashing against the coast some distance beyond the encamped Spanish soldiers. The dikes gave way before the storm surge, flooding the lowlands and drowning an estimated 20,000 Spanish troops. The siege of Leyden was over. (See also FLOODS, Holland, Leyden, p. 108.)

There is an equally persuasive version of this same incident that states that there was no storm, and that William the Silent was the one who smashed the dikes, thus allowing the fleet of the Beggers of the Sea (crews of patriotic privateers chartered in 1569 by William to harass Spanish shipping) to sail across dry land and subdue the Spanish. Belief in either depends upon a choice of historian.

HONDURAS

September 27, 1955

• • • • • • • • • • • • • •

(See HURRICANES, Caribbean, Hurricane Janet, p. 174.)

HONDURAS
HURRICANE HATTIE

October 31, 1961

• • • • • • • • • • • • • • •

Carrying winds clocked at 200 mph, Hurricane Hattie struck Honduras on October 31, 1961, killing 400.

Hurricane Hattie, the eighth hurricane of an ordinary season in 1961, proved to be a distinctly out of the ordinary storm when it slammed into Belize, the capital of Honduras, with winds that were gauged from 160 to 200 mph. Two hundred seventy-five people died in this city, most from drowning when a series of 10-foot tidal waves crumbled seawalls and piers, and rose to the third stories of buildings near the waterfront. Days later, debris and mud still clung to the third-story floors and walls.

After wreaking its havoc on Belize, the storm plummeted on toward smaller villages, leaving only three buildings standing the town of Stann Creek. The waves continued to roll in, inundating such islands as Caulker and Turneffe Cays, and burying many inhabitants under mud and collapsed homes. The final tally of dead reached 400, with countless others missing and presumed swept out to sea.

JAMAICA

July 30, 1784

• • • • • • • • • • • • • • •

The only known record of the Great Cape Verde Hurricane of July 30, 1784 was kept by American poet Philip Freneau, who favored imagery over statistics.

The Great Cape Verde Hurricane of 1784 was given an odd sort of immortality when it was recorded in verse by American poet Philip Freneau, a witness and near victim of this catastrophic, meteorological monster.

On July 30, Freneau, sailing as supercargo on the brig *Dromelly*, heading for Jamaica, found himself suddenly surrounded by darkness, roaring winds and mountain-high waves. The ship nearly went to the bottom, which would have eclipsed the early career of this journalist turned seaman.

Shaken, he later set down the following—the only known—account of the storm, which he titled "Verses, made at Sea, In a Heavy Gale." Short on statistics, it is abundant in imagery and terror:

> *Happy the man who, safe on shore,*
> *Now trims, at home, his evening fire;*
> *Unmoved, he hears the tempest roar,*
> *That on the tufted groves expire.*
> *Alas! on us they doubly fall,*
> *Our feeble barque must bear them all.*
> . . . .
>
> *While death and darkness both surround,*
> *And tempests rage with lawless power,*
> *Of friendships's voice I hear no sound,*
> *No comfort in this dreadful hour—*
> *What friendship can in tempests be,*
> *What comforts on this raging sea?*
>
> *The barque, accustomed to obey,*
> *No more the trembling pilots guide.*
> *Alone she gropes her trackless way,*
> *While mountains burst on either side—*
> *Thus, skill and science both must fall;*
> *And ruin is the lot of all.*

JAMAICA
HURRICANE CHARLIE

August 17, 1951

• • • • • • • • • • • • • • •

Fifty-four people were killed, 2,000 injured and 50,000 made homeless on the island of Jamaica by Hurricane Charlie on August 17, 1951.

Hurricanes were first given women's names in 1953. Two years before that, in 1951, they were noted alphabetically by the Navy as Able, Baker, Charlie, etc. Thus, Charlie was the third of the 12 hurricanes of that season. It began life gently enough in the Atlantic, and then in the Lesser Antilles. But, by the time it finally blew itself out, 54 people died, 2,000 were injured, and 50,000 were rendered homeless.

On August 16, Jamaica forecasters warned that the storm was on a course running east and north, which would allow it to miss Jamaica. But by 8:30 P.M. it took an unexpected shift, crashing into the old town of Morant Bay, located on the coast of St. Thomas Parish. Every coco

palm that had hitherto lined that town's streets was flattened in a matter of minutes. Every house was smashed, and the Yallahs Valley was stripped of topsoil and crops, which were washed out to sea.

Winding up now, with winds of 125 mph, the storm spun on towards Port Royal, the former pirate hangout, where it demolished the waterfront, sweeping wharves, warehouses and rum shops out to sea.

Heading inland, the storm lay waste to 12 parishes, wiping out 90 percent of the banana export trade and a large percentage of the coconut industry. Thousands of coco palms fell, cocoa crops were inundated and washed away by torrential downpours, and 154 people either drowned, were buried under fallen houses and debris, or were crushed by crazily blown timbers.

The storm wore itself out at sea near Tampico, but the devastation it left behind would number in the millions of dollars.

MARTINIQUE
October 20, 1695

• • • • • • • • • • • • • • •

An incomplete but colorful account of the great hurricane of October 20, 1695, on Martinique was left by Father Jean-Baptiste Labat.

The monstrous hurricane of October 20, 1695 was recorded in sketchy form by Father Jean-Baptiste Labat, a scourge and a legend to the native population of Martinique.

Father Labat, a torturer of natives who, when he caught them practicing their black magic whipped them and then rubbed the raw wounds with lime juice and red pepper, still survives in legend as a figure galloping through hurricanes, living on as an evil spirit responsible for the ills of the people he both hated and oppressed.

Certain that hurricanes were caused by divine intervention he wrote, ". . . this compression and rarefaction of the air [brought on by either the movement of Earth around the sun or the sun around Earth] is the cause of the winds. They are not here by accident."

Caught in the rising winds of October 20, Father Labat galloped on horseback to his church and snatched the Holy Sacrament from the altar. Tucking it under his arm, he remounted his horse, and, through winds so strong he had to clutch at the neck of his horse, galloped across meadows that resembled a sea of waves. Thus, the legend and the longevity of Father Labat.

MARTINIQUE

August 18, 1881

• • • • • • • • • • • • • • •

Seven hundred people were killed in a deceptively small hurricane that hit Martinique on August 18, 1881.

Hurricanes that seem small by comparison to others can often outdo the damage wrought by their bigger brothers. Through a combination of bad reporting and complacency, a compact, self-contained hurricane hit Martinique a crippling blow in the early evening of August 18, 1881. The huge storm surge sent waves crashing into this volcanic, windward island, flooding the streets of Fort de-France and inundating the vast sugar fields that, since 1654, had governed the economy of this island and covered 80 percent of its land area.

The storm continued to batter the island for four hours, and when it finally smashed up against Pelée, the island's volcano, it split and veered out to sea. It left behind 700 dead and over $10 million in damage to livestock, buildings and flooded sugar crops.

MEXICO

August 27, 1909

• • • • • • • • • • • • • • •

Over 1,500 people died in the assault upon Tampico, Mexico by 1909's worst hurricane, on August 27 of that year.

In 1909, multiple hurricanes hit the Caribbean. The worst hurricane of the year began its life to the east of the Windward islands on August 20. For two days it roiled the waters of the Caribbean, first hitting Puerto Rico a glancing blow, then completely leveling the city of St. Nicholas, in Haiti.

On August 24, with winds clocked at 60 mph, Cuba received a moderate brushing from the storm.

But that was a mere respite. Drawing more energy from the superheated waters of the Yucatan Channel, the hurricane's winds cranked themselves up to speeds exceeding 100 mph in the next two days, sideswiped the coast of Texas and barreled full force into the northeastern provinces of Mexico. A combination of high winds and torrential rains swelled this region's rivers, and by the time the hurricane had passed on August 28, over 1,500 people had been killed.

MEXICO
TAMPICO

September 24, 1933

• • • • • • • • • • • • • • •

There is no official record of the human loss from the hurricane that hit Tampico, Mexico on September 24, 1933, causing $5 million in property damage.

In September 1933, at the depth of the Depression and the height of the hurricane season, two major storms ravaged the city of Tampico within the space of 10 days.

No estimate of fatalities was kept from this killer storm, largely because thousands of unemployed persons from outside of Tampico had gravitated to the city, swelling its population and muddling the statistics.

What is known is that the hurricane approached from the southwestern Gulf of Mexico, pushing a strong storm surge of sea water ahead of it. By the time the waters had receded and the winds had ceased, over $5 million in property and agricultural damage had been caused.

MEXICO
TAMPICO
HURRICANE HILDA

September 19, 1955

• • • • • • • • • • • • • • •

Three hundred people died when Hurricane Hilda hit Tampico, Mexico on September 19, 1955.

Three hurricanes battered Tampico in the season of 1955: Gladys, Hilda and Janet (see HURRICANES, Caribbean, Hurricane Janet, p. 174). However, it was Hilda that did the most damage and which, with its awesome power, was described by Mexico's then-president Adolfo Ruiz Cortines as ". . . the worst disaster in the city's history."

The bustling city of 110,000, located on the Panuco River a few miles inland from the Gulf of Mexico, was wearily cleaning up the debris from Gladys when Hilda roared into its docks, smashing its oyster and shrimp fleet and the piers that contained loads of cattle, hides and other agricultural products saved from Gladys's fury.

The strong storm surge swelled the Panuco River to its greatest height in 30 years, funneling it into the streets of the city. Before it left, Hilda had flooded half the city and drowned 200 people.

A month later, Janet would deliver the third strike, drowning another 100 people and bringing the total of property destruction for the three storms to $42 million.

MONTEGO BAY

October 3, 1780

• • • • • • • • • • • • • •

The first hurricane to be assiduously tracked, the great Atlantic hurricane of October 3, 1780, killed over 25,000 people on Montego Bay, Martinique and St. Eustatius, and was felt as far north as New England.

The greatest Atlantic hurricane of the 18th century is also the first hurricane in history to be tracked. The day-to-day logbooks of a British fleet of 27 ships that, had it not been decimated by the storm, might have carried out a plan to capture Puerto Rico, collected more minutae on this storm than hundreds that came after in supposedly more meticulous and scientific times.

The storm first struck the Jamaican town of Savanna-la-Mar at 1:00 P.M. on October 3. The flimsily constructed English houses, crowded below their tide marks, were easy targets for the storm surge, and by evening, the undertow had sucked the supporting sand away and many of these houses were swung, with people in them, out to sea, never to be found again.

By morning, there were no homes left below the high water mark, and the only visible survivors were on ships that were hurled up on the marshes far inland.

Meanwhile, the storm coursed northward toward Montego Bay, where four ships of the British Navy were anchored. When the full fury of the hurricane hit, crashing across the island, it either smashed the ships to bits in the harbor or foundered them at sea. Only a handful of men survived, as their ships were thrown against the rocks of Cabo de la Cruz on the coast of Cuba.

The storm, spawning ancillary cyclones, continued to whirl through the Indies, sending its effect as far north as Newport and Rhode Island, pushing tides up into bays and toppling windmills, loose shutters and washlines, thus earning it the title in New England of the "line storm."

Meanwhile, the main storm whirled over Barbados, reducing it to mud, debris, dead cattle and corpses. The few survivors were given the unprecedented sum of 80,000 pounds in relief aid by Lord Rodney, the British Protectorate.

The center continued, passing over St. Lucia, which was flattened. The only cheerful news out of that battered place was that the storm drowned a plague of ants that had been eating the sugar cane. Three British ships—the *Vengeance*, the *Deal Castle*, and the *Thunderer*—were either smashed on the rocks or sent spinning out to sea, never to be heard from again. As far away as Grenada, 15 Dutch ships were slammed against the rock-strewn shore.

The storm crashed into Martinique, demolishing ships, towns, churches, houses and a hospital, and killing 9,000 people. On the Dutch island of St. Eustatius, every building was smashed and washed out to sea and 5,000 people were drowned.

On the morning of October 15, the storm moved up the Mona Passage, its rain squalls extending to Puerto Rico and Santo Domingo. It swallowed the island of Mona whole and disabled two British ships, the *Ulysses* and the *Pomona*, which had survived the first battering a few days earlier.

From here, this monster storm curved eastward, soaking the East Coast of the United States and tormenting ships at sea to the extent of shearing off their topsails. Finally, spending itself out over open water, it reached the latitude of Great Britain, after at one point covering, in its gigantic width, the distance from Newfoundland to St. George's Channel.

NEWFOUNDLAND

September 9, 1775

• • • • • • • • • • • • • •

Four thousand people died in the hurricane that struck Newfoundland on September 9, 1775. Accounts of the storm's passage and effect conflict.

On September 2, 1775, while British redcoats and American militiamen fought in North Carolina, an Atlantic hurricane swept ashore, killing 150 people and wiping out the corn crop in Pasquotank County. Some reports say the storm continued on through Virginia and blew itself out over Pennsylvania. Others say that it curved out to sea again, hitting Newfoundland on September 9, and wiping out, in one awful afternoon, its entire fishing fleet.

Whether the September 9 hurricane was a new storm or the North Carolina one, it was devastating for Newfoundland. Unwarned, hundreds of fishing boats were caught offshore when the storm struck, and every one of them was lost. Four thousand sailors and fishermen lost their lives that day.

On shore, roofs tore away, chimneys disintegrated and entire houses were lifted from their foundations and transported by the winds until they eventually either exploded or collapsed. In all, the loss of ships, land, buildings and produce was estimated to total a staggering 140,000 pounds, or $350,000 in today's dollars.

NOVA SCOTIA

August 24, 1873

• • • • • • • • • • • • • • • •

At least 600 died and 1,032 ships foundered in the hurricane that devastated Nova Scotia on August 24, 1873.

While it may be true that the death toll of pre-20th century hurricanes is abnormally tilted towards perished sailors, it is also true that the military kept far better records in those days than civil authorities. Thus, the fact that the roll of an estimated 600 lost lives in the great Nova Scotia hurricane of 1873 is composed mostly of ships' crews tells as much about record keeping as it does about the location and the impact of the storm.

Roaring in from the sea lanes, where it left in its wake 190 ships or boats either foundering or ripped from stem to stern by its enormously high winds, this hurricane shot up the Gulf of St. Lawrence on August 24, 1873. Its winds and storm surge engulfed no less than 1,032 ships, anchored in the supposedly protected ports of Nova Scotia, Newfoundland and Cape Breton. The ships were either driven ashore, split asunder or sent to the bottom. Property damage from the storm, which eventually blew itself out in the Canadian Provinces, was estimated at a staggering $5 million.

PUERTO RICO

July 26–August 31, 1533

• • • • • • • • • • • • • • • •

Nearly 2,000 people—almost all of them slaves—died as a result of three successive hurricanes that assaulted Puerto Rico from July 26 to August 31, 1533.

Puerto Rico had only been settled for 25 years (Ponce de Leon had named it Puerto Rico in 1508, although Columbus had actually discovered it in 1493) when the triple hammer blows of three major hurricanes battered this rich paradise on July 26, August 23 and August 31, 1533.

The Spanish had all but swept the island clean of gold in the early 1530s and had executed most of the native Arawak Indians. Boatload after boatload of slaves from Africa were brought in to plant and work the sugar plantations that would replace the gold deposits.

Thus, when the first of the three major storms hit, it claimed its greatest loss of life among these slaves, many of whom had not been provided with adequate shelter.

When the second storm struck, even the poor shacks being erected to replace those demolished by the first storm were not yet in place, and still more slaves were drowned.

By the morning of September 1, 1533, nearly 2,000 people, almost all of them slaves, had been killed by the three storms, and the sugar cane fields lay flooded and useless. Overlooking the casualties, the Spanish conquerors sent envoys back to Spain to request more slaves to rebuild and work the gutted plantations and repopulate the island.

PUERTO RICO

July 26, 1825

• • • • • • • • • • • • • • • •

Three hundred seventy-four people died and nearly 1,200 were made homeless on Puerto Rico as a result of the hurricane of July 26, 1825.

Residents of Puerto Rico have become accustomed, if not inured to storms. But Santa Ana, the monster hurricane of July 26, 1825 was a particularly memorable one.

The storm first laid waste to Guadaloupe, then bore down on Puerto Rico with winds strong enough to collapse 7,000 buildings over the entire length of the island. Three hundred seventy-four people, most of them trapped and crushed in buildings or buried under falling walls or flying debris, lost their lives to the storm, and nearly 1,200 were rendered homeless.

PUERTO RICO

August 8, 1899

• • • • • • • • • • • • • • • •

The entire island of Puerto Rico was laid to waste by the hurricane of August 8, 1899, called the worst Caribbean storm of the 19th century. Over 3,000 died.

More than 3,000 people were killed by the most ferocious Caribbean storm of the 19th century, which literally laid waste to the entire length of the island of Puerto Rico from early in the morning until late at night on August 8, 1899.

The only city that escaped the wrath of this particular monster was San Juan. Winds were a mere 90 mph by the time San Ciriaco, as the storm was called, reached there. When it roared into the port of Humacao, its first landfall, its winds were clocked at 125 mph—enough to send multiple tidal waves crashing over wharves and through streets. Further inland, Aguadilla received winds of over 100 mph, which peeled the tiles from roofs and turned metal stripping into flying knives which decapitated some of those fleeing from the storm. Twenty million dollars in property damage seems slight compared to the monumental loss of life in this killer storm.

PUERTO RICO
September 26, 1932

• • • • • • • • • • • • • • •

Two hundred twenty-five died, 3,000 were injured and 75,000 were made homeless by the killer hurricane that struck Puerto Rico on September 26, 1932.

Winds measuring 120 to 150 mph toppled the weather tower in San Juan during the night of September 26, 1932. San Ciprian, as this storm was called, made landfall at Ceiba, then tore swiftly through the island of Puerto Rico, killing 225 people, injuring 3,000, rendering 75,000 homeless and causing $30 million in property damage. Its tenure was short but devastating; within a day it had blown itself out over Mexico.

PUERTO RICO
HURRICANE DONNA

• • • • • • • • • • • • • •

(See HURRICANES, United States, East, Hurricane Donna, p. 193.)

ST. CROIX
August 31, 1772

• • • • • • • • • • • • • • •

Hundreds were killed and the course of history was changed by the hurricane that struck St. Croix on August 31, 1772.

If a few—a very few—hurricanes can be categorized as ill winds blowing some mite of good, the hurricane of August 31, 1772, would certainly qualify as one of those select storms.

Alexander Hamilton, confidential aid to George Washington and later America's first Secretary of the Treasury, was born illegitimately in 1757 on Nevis, one of the small British Islands of the West Indies, to a 20-year-old mother divorced from an older husband. In 1772, at the age of 15, he was employed in Nicholas Crueger's counting house

on the nearby Danish island of St. Croix. He was hardworking, a financial wiz, a sometime manager of Mr. Crueger's entire operation, and therefore headed for wealth and comfort as a business manager on St. Croix.

But the hurricane of August 31—a giant that wrecked all of the ships anchored in Dominica, killed hundreds and destroyed 2.5 million pounds of prime muscovado sugar in unroofed warehouses—slammed into St. Croix, Hamilton's life and American history, all at once. The following day, still shaken by the fury of the storm, Hamilton wrote, in part, to his father the following summation of it:

I take up my pen just to give you an imperfect account of one of the most dreadful hurricanes that memory, or any records whatever, can trace, which happened here on the 31st ultimo at night.

It began about dusk, at north, and raged very violently till ten o'clock, then ensued a sudden and unexpected interval, which lasted about an hour. Meanwhile the wind was shifting round to the southwest point, from whence it returned with redoubled fury and continued so till near three o'clock in the morning. Good God! What horror and destruction—it is impossible for me to describe—or you to form any idea of it. It seemed as if a total dissolution of nature was taking place. The roaring of the sea and wind—fiery meteors flying about in the air—the prodigious glare of almost perpetual lightning—the crash of the falling houses—and the ear-piercing shrieks of the distressed were sufficient to strike astonishment into Angels. A great part of the buildings throughout the island are levelled to the ground—almost all the rest very much shattered—several persons killed and numbers utterly ruined—while families running about the streets unknowing where to find a place of shelter—the sick exposed to the keeness [sic] of water and air—without a bed to lie on—or a dry covering to their bodies—our harbor is entirely bare. In a word, misery in all its most hideous shapes spread over the whole face of the country—a strong smell of gun powder added somewhat to the terrors of the night, and it was observed that the rain was surprisingly salt. Indeed, the water is so brackish and full of sulphur that there is hardly any drinking it . . .

Hamilton's father, no doubt feeling a tingle of paternal pride, submitted the letter to the editor of the *Royal Danish-American Gazette*, which printed it in its October 3, 1772 issue. A group of wealthy planters read it and decided that the boy had promise. Together, they raised enough money to send young Alexander Hamilton away from the limited future of the islands to the promise of King's College (now Columbia University) and a college education.

SANTO DOMINGO

October 3, 1780

• • • • • • • • • • • • • •

(See HURRICANES, Montego Bay, p. 185.)

SANTO DOMINGO

September 23, 1834

• • • • • • • • • • • • • •

Thousands were killed by the so-called Padre Ruiz Hurricane that struck Santo Domingo on September 23, 1834.

The hurricane of September 23, 1834—known as the "Padre Ruiz Hurricane" because it occurred simultaneously with the burial of a highly respected and popular priest—flattened a large portion of Santo Domingo during its ravaging stay there.

Thousands were killed in the entire country; Dominica, the small, lush, volcanic island to the west of Santo Domingo had been mangled by the storm three days earlier, and 200 of its inhabitants lay dead as a result.

In addition to the enormous loss of life brought about by the storm, huge tracts of forest and crops ready for harvest along the Ozama River were crushed and flooded. Fishing and transportation boats on the river sank, and their crews, trapped by the force and suddenness of the storm, went to the bottom with their boats.

SANTO DOMINGO

September 3, 1930

• • • • • • • • • • • • • •

Four thousand people died, 5,000 were injured and every wooden building was destroyed in Santo Domingo during the 200-mph hurricane of September 3, 1930.

The numbing effects of the hurricane of September 3, 1930 upon Santo Domingo, the capital of the Dominican Republic, were swift but telling. In a mere four hours, 4,000 people died, 5,000 were injured and 9,600 buildings—every one of the wooden structures in the city—were demolished. When the skies cleared that night, a mere 400 stone buildings remained, stark sentinels in the midst of $40 million worth of damage.

The eye of the storm passed directly over the city, giving its inhabitants a 30-minute respite before the storm

surge that would be whipped up by the sudden wind flow from the opposite direction.

The hurricane struck Santo Domingo at almost exactly noon, when the city was most crowded. Tourists and natives alike sought shelter in the hotels, which were thought to be the most solid structures. And they did stand—minus their shutters, windows, doors and skylights.

The dictator Rafael Trujillo narrowly missed being one of the storm's victims when his executive offices began to come apart around him. Accompanied by his plenipotentiary, he scampered swiftly through the chaotic streets, finally taking refuge in Fort Ozama.

When the sun broke through the next morning, prisoners were turned loose from the jails to assist in the grim cleanup, which included burning bodies in huge funeral pyres. Martial law was declared to protect the remaining food supplies. The water supply was totally destroyed by the storm, and the casualty figures were swollen by hundreds who died of typhoid fever, the result of drinking contaminated water.

UNITED STATES
ALABAMA
MOBILE

July 27–28, 1819

• • • • • • • • • • • • • •

More than 200 people were killed by winds and life-threatening debris—including snapping turtles and alligators—washed up by a hurricane that hit Mobile, Alabama on July 27, 1819.

Possibly one of the oddest hurricanes of the 19th century struck Alabama Bay on the night of July 27, 1819. The storm was odd not because of its size, which was described by one observer as "the most severe and strongest that ever blew on this coast since I came to it," and not because of the number of ships it sent to the bottom of the Gulf, nor its death toll of over 200. It was unique in the fact that many of its casualties were caused not by the storm itself but by some of the debris washing up into the streets of Mobile at the height of the storm: hordes of snapping turtles and alligators.

The hurricane roared up Mobile Bay on the evening of July 27, 1819, taking four hours to wind up and hit the city of Mobile its most devastating blow, when the eye passed over the city around midnight. The sudden shift of wind caught residents by surprise. As is often the case, they were lulled into false security by the momentary calm

An entire residential area of Santo Domingo is flattened in the hurricane of September 13, 1930. American Red Cross.

of the storm's eye. The sudden rush of wind from the opposite direction carried high tides into the city, pummeling buildings and collapsing them, and carrying a lethal load of snapping turtles and alligators through the city streets. Fully half of the 200 casualties were blamed on alligator and turtle bites. Huge ships were floated onto dry land. Dauphin and Water streets became the docking point for an immense brig; other smaller vessels moored at other locations.

A few captains had the good sense to weigh anchor and escape up the Pearl River, where it was possible to ride out the storm. Others, like the *Favorite,* were thrown against reefs at Henderson Point, which splintered the ship's hull but did not effect casualties in her crew. The man of war *Firebrand* was not so lucky. Her captain and seven crewmen were in New Orleans when the storm struck. The first in charge, left to protect the ship and crew, appar-

ently either made the wrong decision or no decision at all, and when the Captain and his group returned on the morning of July 28, they found the ship with its capsized hull jutting up from a sandy shoal known as "The Square Handkerchief." The crew, confined to its quarters, apparently drowned.

Along the banks of Mobile Bay, whole herds of cattle were swept from the shore. A mere three buildings were left standing at Pass Christian, and water six feet deep churned through the streets of Bay St. Louis (both Mississippi cities), undermining and collapsing scores of buildings, some with inhabitants inside.

Although the storm reached its fingers out as far as Biloxi, Mississippi and New Orleans, damage was slight there, and, though it must have made itself felt in Pensacola, that Florida city was still under the control of Spain, and no reports were released from it.

UNITED STATES
ALABAMA
MOBILE
HURRICANE FREDERIC

September 11, 1979

• • • • • • • • • • • • • •

Hurricane Frederic, the worst storm ever to strike the Mobile, Alabama area, caused mass evacuations—nearly 450,000 people were moved out before it struck—and this kept the casualties low. One hundred ten people died.

Hurricane Frederic plowed ashore at beleaguered Dauphine Island (see HURRICANES, United States, Mississippi, p. 202) 25 miles south of Mobile, Alabama, on the night of September 11, 1979 with winds of 100 mph. It was the worst storm ever to hit the Mobile area, one that, it was predicted, would carve up and destroy Dauphine Island, a small, 16-mile-long spit of populated sand that rose only 10- to 15-feet above sea level. Since the tides were expected to climb at least that high, experts figured that the end was in sight for this Alabama resort haven.

But Dauphine Island would survive, and so would Hurricane Frederic, but not before turning Mobile and Dauphine Island into twin war zones.

The storm, with an eye 50 miles in diameter, had been closely tracked by the U.S. Weather Bureau. As a result, 400,000 people were evacuated from coastal areas along a 400-mile strip from Pensacola, Florida to Biloxi, Mississippi. The air force evacuated 9,000 service personnel and dependents stationed at the Tyndall Air Force Base near Panama City and 1,000 Florida National Guardsmen assisted in that state's evacuation plan. As a result, the loss of life—110—was low, considering the fury of the storm, which, when it hit Mobile shortly after midnight, had narrowed its eye to 20 miles in diameter, thus increasing its power and wind velocity to 130 mph.

The wind pummeled the city like a giant fist. The south wall and part of the roof of the City Hall collapsed. Other buildings were flattened as if a bomb had gone off inside. Broken power lines snaked across streets, setting fires before the power went off. Three stores in a major shopping area went up in flames during a downpour, and the sky was lit by blue flashes as power transformers blew up.

In the surrounding towns, some evacuation centers had their roofs ripped away, forcing refugees to flee. Inshore, along the Alabama-Mississippi state line, the low-lying towns of Bayou LaBatre, Theodore and Grand Bay received the full force of the storm. At Theodore, a house containing 15 people was demolished, leaving them stranded in an open field at the height of the storm.

At Bayou LaBatre, the Herbert McKinney family spent the night in a gravel pit 30 miles inland because they could not afford a motel. When they finally returned, by sawing their way through roads barricaded with fallen pines and monster oak limbs, they found only battered remnants of their mobile home. Around them, groves of pecan trees were flattened in rows as militarily correct as those of a cornfield.

At sea, the 230-foot freighter *Mary's Ketch*, out of Grand Cayman Island, went dead in the water during the height of the storm. It survived waves ". . . as high as the mast . . ." according to a radio message the Coast Guard received from its captain.

Seventy-five foot shrimp boats were driven ashore as if they were rowboats. A stacking effect of rising water occurred when the storm surge rushed into Mobile Bay, which was already swollen by the storm's heavy rains.

And what of Dauphine Island? The causeway to it from the mainland was wiped away like a toy construction. Twenty-seven stubborn residents rode out the storm on the island and survived by huddling together in an Army radar bunker. The island was a sea of crushed homes. Deputy Sheriff Bud Wilson, a resident of the island, gathered other homeowners around him on the roadside leading to the causeway and said to his neighbors, "Why don't we all gather around and cry?"

Fortunately, few people lost their lives during Frederic, although the damage in Alabama was $493.3 million and in Mississippi $175.5 million. Between David (see p. 194) and Frederic, the two brotherly storms that hit roughly the same area within a period of two weeks in September 1979, 1,567 died, 600,000 were made homeless and $3 billion in damages were caused.

UNITED STATES
EAST
HURRICANE HAZEL

October 12, 1954

• • • • • • • • • • • • • •

Hurricane Hazel killed over 1,300 in its passage from Haiti up the East Coast of the United States on October 14, 1954.

Hurricane Hazel gave plenty of warning before it slammed into the coast of the Carolinas. Two days earlier, it had blasted Haiti with 125-mph winds, ripping off the fronts of buildings in Jacmel, washing tons of mud over the village of Berley and burying all but two of the village's 260 inhabitants. Sweeping over the southern end of the peninsula, it killed another 1,000 people and rendered 40,000 homeless, toppling banana trees and washing away fields of beans, rice, coffee, sugar and corn.

That was devastation enough for one storm, and, to the relief of the local residents, Hazel, after crossing the island, headed out to sea. However, a huge high pressure area—an anticyclone—settled down during the night of October 12, blocking Hazel's retreat. She re-formed, and, armed with an extremely small eye (Naval weather planes had great difficulty remaining within it and were constantly threatened by the 150-mph winds of the eyewall), headed straight for the outer banks near Cape Fear.

All night on October 1, warnings were broadcast to the remaining inhabitants of this area to evacuate, and most did. On the morning of the 15th, the storm hit with full force, packing a 20-foot storm surge (added to a 10-foot tide). Miles and miles of houses literally exploded as the waves and wind struck. The ground was pushed into the inland waterway. Of Long Beach's 377 buildings, 352 were absolutely destroyed. At Holden Beach, 200 were erased. Ocean Isle was swept bare; Myrtle Beach, Windy Hill, Crescent Beach, Cherry Grove, Robinson Beach, Colonial Beach and Wrightsville were horribly damaged. One-half of the taxable wealth of Carolina Beach was swept away. Shrimp boats were washed onto the verandas of some of the remaining dwellings. Nineteen people lost their lives, and over $136 million of damage was done to property, chiefly by sea water.

But Hazel wasn't through yet; on she careened, up through Virginia, the District of Columbia, Maryland, Delaware, Pennsylvania, New Jersey and New York State,

High tides and storm surges, whipped to a froth by Hurricane Hazel, demolished waterfront homes in Swansboro, North Carolina on October 15, 1954. American Red Cross.

mowing down power lines, trees, crops, poultry houses and tobacco barns. The losses due to power failure and the flooding of dams, rivers and lakes were astronomical.

By the time the storm had reached upstate New York, Hazel had diminished to an extratropical cyclone with heavy rains and wind gusts of 90 mph. It was on the cusp between hurricane and cyclone, and should have blown itself out in the Alleghenies. But again, a blocking system, this time a cold front over Chicago, redirected it towards Toronto, a city unaccustomed to hurricanes.

Hazel cranked itself up again. Its rains increased and its winds rose in gusts to 120 mph. Above Toronto, north of Lake Ontario, four rivers carried more than six billion gallons of water to the city and the land surrounding it. Over this area, Hazel collided with the cold front from Chicago. The resulting water vapor condensed into an explosion of rain.

In Toronto, hurricane warnings were lifted after 7 P.M. on the night of October 15. What weather bureau experts failed to anticipate was the effect of the torrential rains of Hazel. Upriver of Toronto and its environs, 113 tons of water per inch of rainfall fell for six hours. The Humber River suddenly overflowed its banks in a black wall of water. The Little Don River soon followed, washing out roads, uprooting houses and sending them spinning downstream. Forty concrete bridges were wiped out. The sewage plant in the town of Kitchener was gutted. Every house was surrounded by water and many washed away in Woodbridge.

The next morning, an army of rescue workers was marshaled to rescue families trapped on the roofs of floating houses throughout a silt-covered countryside that had once been green and populated.

Hazel had by now blown northeastward, out of North America, beyond Greenland. Her effects would eventually be felt off the coast of Norway. In Toronto alone, she would leave over $100 million in property damage.

Altogether, the three hurricanes of 1954—Carol, Edna and Hazel—would cause $1 billion in property damage and claim over 150 lives in the United States, and thousands more in the Caribbean.

UNITED STATES
EAST
HURRICANES CONNIE AND DIANE

August 4–18, 1955

• • • • • • • • • • • • •

Occurring back to back, hurricanes Connie and Diane killed 310 people and caused $1.5 billion in property damage from August 4 to 18, 1955 in large areas along the East Coast of the United States.

Considered to have created the worst storm impact upon the eastern seaboard of the United States in this century, the back-to-back fury of hurricanes Connie and Diane killed 310 people and caused $1.5 billion in property damage to coastal areas in the Carolinas, Virginia, Delaware, Maryland, Pennsylvania, New Jersey, New York, Connecticut and Massachusetts.

Connie, the first of the fatal sisters, was first sighted by a Navy Neptune weather plane in the southeastern Atlantic. The plane invaded the storm's eye and measured winds of 125 mph, which caused the Weather Bureau and the Red Cross to call for an evacuation of the Carolina beaches. On the 11th of August, ten-foot-high rollers thundered into Myrtle Beach, North Carolina, crushing it, and then roared on to Wilmington and Pimlico Sound.

Thousands warned by the weather bureau evacuated the area, but in New Bern, North Carolina, 41 residents met their deaths through drowning, auto accidents or electrocution from live wires that fell into the swirling flood waters.

By the 12th of August, Connie had sideswiped New York with gale winds and had blown itself out over Pennsylvania. But Diane was right behind her, following the same path until she got to the vicinity of New Jersey. There, instead of veering inland, Diane curved northeastward, smashing into coastal areas from New Jersey to Boston, where the storm finally took a right turn into the North Atlantic.

Monumentally high tides, brought on by the storm surge overflowed the banks of Connecticut's Naugatuck, Still and Mad rivers. Winsted, Connecticut was inundated with 12 feet of brackish water. In Putnam, a magnesium plant was broken apart and hundreds of barrels of burning magnesium floated through that town's streets, exploding sporadically and sending cascades of white hot metal 250 feet in the air.

Diane blundered on tearing up Revolutionary War–era coffins in the cemeteries of Woonsocket, Rhode Island and grimly floating them down the swollen rivers. In Massachusetts, the roaring, swollen waters of the Concord River ripped apart the historic Revolutionary bridge where the "shot heard round the world" was fired.

Six eastern states were declared disaster areas by the federal government immediately after Diane departed, and local, state, federal and private relief supplies and money began to flow into the area.

UNITED STATES
EAST
HURRICANE DONNA
September 4–12, 1960

● ● ● ● ● ● ● ● ● ● ● ● ●

One hundred forty-three people died as a result of Hurricane Donna, which originated in the mid-Atlantic, traveled through the Leeward Islands to Puerto Rico, on to Florida, and up the East Coast of the United States to the Gulf of St. Lawrence, from September 4 to 12, 1960.

Hurricane Donna was a long-distance traveler. From the time it originated in the mid-Atlantic until it blew itself out in the Gulf of St. Lawrence, ultimately claiming 143 lives, it had covered more than 5,000 miles.

Its path took it across the Leeward Islands and through Puerto Rico, which suffered a death toll of 106 from the 150-mph winds.

From here, Donna directed its roaring fury on the Florida Keys, slamming into Key Largo with winds that had climbed to 180 mph. Roofs flew through the air, boats were ripped from their moorings and sent surfing out to sea. Trees were felled by the hundreds, and scores of residents barricaded themselves within the cement walls of the Florida Keys Electric Cooperative Association, where they were bombarded by sparks from the generator before it finally went dark, too.

Leaving the Florida Keys, the storm skirted the East Coast. But by now, enough sophisticated weather data had been gathered from U.S. Weather Bureau airplanes to warn coast dwellers to leave their homes. Thus, only 22 persons were killed by the storm in the U.S.

UNITED STATES
EAST
HURRICANE ELOISE
September 22–27, 1975

● ● ● ● ● ● ● ● ● ● ● ● ●

Hurricane Eloise killed 45 and made hundreds of thousands homeless as it ripped up the East Coast of the United States between September 22 and 27, 1975, spawning destructive tornadoes, which caused additional damage.

Eloise was a double-barreled storm that caused as much damage after it had supposedly died than it did at the peak of its youth. First sighted in the Caribbean as a tropical storm that claimed 42 lives on two Caribbean islands, it was upgraded on September 22 to a full hurricane when its winds climbed to 115 mph. It proceeded to bear down on a 150-mile-long, crescent-shaped stretch of Gulf of Mexico coastal lands in Louisiana, Mississippi, Alabama and Florida.

Landfall finally occurred on the morning of September 23, 1975, on a 40-mile stretch of beach between Fort Walton Beach and Panama City, Florida. The hurricane's winds were now 130 mph, making it the worst storm to hit the area in almost half a century. What was worse, Eloise, like a great many hurricanes, had spawned along its rim a group of killer tornadoes which raced over other parts of Florida, Alabama and Georgia, causing floods and extensive wind damage.

Three early morning twisters struck Fort Walton Beach, Hartford, Alabama, and an area near Jacksonville, Florida, collapsing homes and businesses, knocking out 90 percent of Fort Walton's electricity and causing $20 million in property damage. In nearby Panama City, which suffered $50 million in damages, motels were flattened and the roof of a shoe store was picked up and blown away, as winds scattered shoes like confetti.

That there was only one death attributed to Eloise along the gulf was not a result of the wise judgment of its residents. Many waited until the very last minute before evacuating their beachfront homes. When 15-foot-high waves driven by the 130-mph winds began to cut through the dunes and the wind to peel roof after roof from houses, the inhabitants finally crowded the causeways to the mainland. J. D. Hembree, a construction supervisor for a new condominium project at Destin, said later, "I decided to ride this thing out, but when that first break crested those dunes, I thought, 'J. D., ole boy, you've made a mistake.' "

Although only one person in this area died, hundreds were injured, 17,000 were rendered homeless, and a total of more than $150 million in damages was left behind by Eloise, which headed northward, where it was soon to fire its second barrel.

A quirk of the atmosphere sent the storm due north, through the Washington D.C. area, Pennsylvania and New York state and city. A blocking system of high pressure kept it in place for five days, during which time it dumped 7.89 inches of tropical precipitation on that area. Streams, rivers and sluiceways were turned into raging, roaring tides, and in Pennsylvania, 20,000 people were driven from their homes as the Susquehanna and Juniata rivers overflowed their banks.

In the Washington, D.C. metropolitan area, thousands were affected, as the worst rainstorm in 41 years—actually the backlash of Eloise—flooded every major commuter route in and out of the city. Approximately 600 persons were evacuated from Laurel, Maryland, midway between Washington and Baltimore, when flood gates on a reservoir were opened to keep it from collapsing.

In the area of Alexandria, Virginia, boats evacuated many of the 400 who had to move out. Refugees were taken from the tops of cars, from trees and from partially submerged homes and businesses in Maryland.

Industries, homes and schools around Elmira, New York were evacuated. In New York City, all of the major access routes were flooded, as were basements and first stories of homes in Queens, Brooklyn and Staten Island. A state of emergency was declared by Mayor Abraham Beame.

The fall crops in rural New York were ruined and the property damage was estimated to be in the "tens of millions." Ironically, there were only two deaths reported from Eloise's second coming: one 83-year-old motorist was swept to his death when he ventured from his car on the Hutchinson River Parkway in White Plains, New York, and an 11-year-old boy drowned in an overflowing brook near Mt. Pleasant, New York, thus bringing the fatality count to a total of three.

UNITED STATES
EAST
HURRICANE DAVID

August 31–September 8, 1979

• • • • • • • • • • • • • •

Fourteen hundred fifty-seven people died and hundreds of thousands were made homeless by Hurricane David, on its path, from the Caribbean island of Dominica, through Puerto Rico, the Dominican Republic and the Eastern Coast of the United States from Florida to New England, from August 31 to September 8, 1979.

Hurricane David first hit the tiny eastern Caribbean island of Dominica on August 31, 1979, killing 22. It then lunged toward Puerto Rico, where it claimed 16 lives and made 1,500 homeless. From here, it blundered directly into the Dominican Republic, where it killed over 1,000 people and rendered 150,000 homeless, 90,000 of them in Santo Domingo alone.

Its 150-mph winds and huge storm surge ripped chunks of concrete loose from sidewalks and crushed cars waiting on a dock. Hotels were smashed. Power poles were broken off at their bases and palm trees were uprooted. A long concrete walkway along George Washington Avenue in Santo Domingo was shredded and its remains hurled across the street. Waves broke directly into the lobbies of oceanfront hotels.

In the tiny town of Padre las Casas in the Ocoa Mountains 75 miles southwest of Santo Domingo, 400 Domini-

The remains of a luxury Florida condominium after Hurricane David's assault on the eastern United States, August 31, 1979. CARE.

cans who had sought refuge in a church and school drowned when flood waters from the Yaque River swept through both buildings. The few who escaped death in that village were forced to climb to the top of the church steeple. Fifteen people were killed when winds collapsed a concrete block church in San Cristobal, 12 miles west of Santo Domingo.

Ninety percent of the nation's crops were destroyed—although the nation's precious sugar crop, which had already been harvested and bagged, escaped unharmed—and damage estimates exceeded $1 billion, including $350 million damage to agriculture, $130 million to business and industry, $30 million to housing and $30 million to the electrical system. A week after the storm's passing, 150,000 people were still homeless and uncounted thousands were in need of food, medicine, clothing and water.

While aid was being organized to help the Dominican Republic, which was already under the threat of the visitation of a second storm, Hurricane Frederic, David headed toward Florida. It had weakened somewhat when it made landfall near Palm Beach; its winds were clocked at between 75 and 90 mph. Still, the storm spanned a 220-

mile stretch of coastline, stretching as far north as the Carolinas.

The hardest hit area appeared to be South Melbourne Beach in Brevard County, Florida, where a tornado associated with the storm ripped the roof and rear wall from the Opus 21 condominium, sucking furniture and appliances from the building.

Fortunately, most of the area's 220,000 residents either left themselves or were evacuated, although some refused to leave. (A police dispatcher in Daytona Beach admitted in frustration, "they're just laughing at us," and 27 diehard drinkers remained in the Sand Spur Bar, on the beach at Cocoa Beach, Florida. Fortunately, their hurricane party had a happy, if hungover, ending.)

Ultimately, only four people lost their lives in Florida in the storm, including two who suffered heart attacks while shuttering their homes, one killed when his car overturned on rain-swept Interstate 95, and another electrocuted when his sailboat mast hit a power line as he towed his boat out of the Keys. The property damage was in the millions.

After smashing through Florida, David once more headed out to sea, gathered energy, and then, on the afternoon of September 4, slammed into the Georgia–South Carolina Coast. Its first landfall whipped the barrier islands near the border of Georgia and South Carolina with 70- to 90-mph winds, then hit Savannah, Georgia a slashing blow.

The downtown streets of this colonial city, population 120,000, were quickly rendered impassable, choked with the remains of stately trees and other debris. One large oak was split in two by a lamp post and traffic signal hurled by the storm.

In the lush resort of Hilton Head, South Carolina, 30 miles north of Savannah, vacationers gleefully ignored evacuation orders and became isolated when the James F. Byrne Causeway, linking the resort to the mainland disappeared beneath David.

In Charleston, South Carolina, immense waves broke over the High Battery wall at 7:15 P.M., flooding East Bay Street and sending rolling water onto the lawns and over the porches of century-old homes. Undeterred, a crowd of about 50 people cavorted in the spray, yelling and drinking beer, apparently oblivious to the danger.

Outside of Savannah, farms and yards were covered with sea water. On the 17 small islands lying off Savannah, which housed 18,000 people, wind damage was devastating. The 70-year-old lighthouse on Tybee Island was abandoned early by the Coast Guard, but five men and a woman holed up in it with beer and sandwiches, determined to tough out the storm. They fled when the pounding of waves threatened to crush in the lighthouse's seaward door.

And David had still not ended his destruction. Downgraded to a tropical storm, it was nevertheless capable of claiming eight lives and leaving more than 2.5 million residents of the Northeastern United States without power.

A combination of abnormally high tides brought on by a rare total eclipse of the moon, residual winds of 55 mph and accompanying tornadoes caused huge breakers to slam into the coastal Northeast, uprooting trees, inundating highways, toppling power lines, and forcing yet another mass evacuation. Sixteen more people died, among them, policeman Alvin Williams who dove into a raging torrent in Woodbridge, New Jersey in an attempt to save two 10-year-old boys from drowning. Instead, all three were sucked into a storm sewer, never to be found again.

The storm wove northward, knocking out power for more than 300,000 people in Connecticut, bowling over trees and more power lines in New York's Mohawk Valley. Ultimately, it would blow itself out over Newfoundland.

The death toll from the storm in the United States would be set at 19. But the lives that were disrupted by David would number in the millions.

UNITED STATES
FLORIDA
KEYS

October 18, 1906

• • • • • • • • • • • • • • •

One hundred twenty-nine people died during the hurricane that struck the Florida Keys on October 18, 1906.

The Overseas Highway and the Florida East Coast Railroad were under construction when the first important hurricane of the 20th century barreled into the little group of islands called the Florida Keys.

A day before, the hurricane had hit Cuba with minimal winds of 50 mph—an indication to local weather forecasters that Florida had nothing about which to be concerned.

But on the night of the 17th, the storm picked up power from the moisture of the Caribbean, and by the morning of the 18th, when it slammed into Sand Key, its winds had increased to minimum speeds of 75 mph. The storm surge washed across the Key, demolishing the houseboats that sheltered the workmen, smashing at the rock embankments, and drowning 124 workmen and five others.

The partially constructed road and railway held firm. But 30 years later, they would be destroyed by another hurricane.

UNITED STATES
FLORIDA
KEYS

September 2, 1935

• • • • • • • • • • • • • •

Gusts of wind clocked at 250 mph drove a monster hurricane into the Florida Keys on September 2, 1935. Four hundred people, many of them veterans of the 1932 Washington Bonus March, were killed.

The great Labor Day hurricane of September 2, 1935 was a true monster, packing winds of from 150 to 200 mph and gusts of an unbelievable 250 mph. It left behind 400 dead and injured hundreds more. The villages of Mate-cumbe, Tavernier, Rock Harbor and Islamorada were totally destroyed.

But it was the death of 121 of the 716 inhabitants of Camp Number 5, located near Snake Creek on lower Matecumbe Key that drew world attention to this storm and its victims. Camp Number 5 housed World War I veterans, survivors of the famous 1932 Bonus March on Washington, during which members of the Third U.S. Cavalry, under General Douglas MacArthur, rode full herd onto their fellow veterans, whose only crime was protesting Congress's failure to pass a bill for the payment of their bonus certificates.

Two marchers in this so-called Bonus Army lost their lives that August day. Three years later, what remained of the Bonus Army was spread out over the country in work camps, such as Camp Number 5, tucked away from public

The relief train that was overtaken by the September 1935 hurricane and its storm surge in Key West, Florida. Better planning and less bureaucracy might have saved hundreds of lives. Mattock Photo from the American Red Cross.

view. Their task: to build a government road, for which they received 30 dollars a month and all the food they could eat.

Most of them, by this time, had become outcasts. Some were drunks, and some suffered from shell shock. Some were hardened misfits. All were an embarrassment and a shame to the country that had conscripted them to fight and then had abandoned them.

Most of the natives of the Keys distrusted and disliked this ragtag army. Only Ernest Hemingway, it seemed, who knew some of them, pleaded their cause in *The New Masses:* ". . . they were all that you get after a war," he wrote, "but who sent them there to die?"

And die they would, most of them from a hurricane that was first recorded on August 31 northeast of Turks Island. It was a small hurricane, as hurricanes go—merely 10 miles across. But when it reached Andros Island on September 1, it was already a giant in force, if not in size. Northeast storm warnings were posted from Fort Pierce to Fort Myers, and caution was advised for the Florida Keys.

The next day, September 2, was Labor Day. Three hundred fifty veterans from the Keys camp were in Miami, attending a ball game. The wind was high in Miami, but not nearly so high as it was in the Keys by 12:15 that afternoon, when Captain Edney Parker telephoned the Florida East Coast Railroad. An evacuation train that was supposed to be ready and waiting at Homestead in case of just such a storm wasn't there, nor had it been prepared. It was finally made up in Miami and departed at 4:25, arriving in Homestead after 5 P.M. From there, it slowly backed down the track to evacuate the veterans, who by now had abandoned Camp Number 5 and were huddling along the railway embankment.

Storm waves began to crash over the banks. Windborn sand drew blood as it knifed into their faces. As night began to fall and the train still didn't arrive, some of the men went back to the camp.

Sometime after 8 P.M., J. A. Duncan, the keeper of the Alligator Reef Light went out onto the observation platform to check the light. A black mass of water suddenly loomed over the lighthouse. He jumped for the ladder and held fast as tons of sea water crashed over him, shattering the glass and the lenses. Duncan reported that the wave seemed to be 90 feet high. In reality, it was 20 feet high and powered by 250-mph gusts of wind.

On over the Keys the wave rushed, slicing roofs off houses, floating homes and beds and their inhabitants out to sea. At 8:30, it hit the 10 cars of the rescue train, which had finally arrived, uprooted the track, smashed the trestles, and knocked over every car but the engine. It roared on into Camp Number 5, leveling every building, sending timbers and roofs and bodies swirling out to sea.

The eye, with its brief calm center, passed over Lower Matecumbe Key, plummeting the barometer to 26.35 inches, the lowest reading yet recorded for a western hemisphere hurricane.

By morning, in the 10-mile-wide swath cut by the storm, hardly anyone was left alive. Everything was destroyed—buildings, docks, roads, viaducts, trees, the railroad and its bridges. Many of the dead had been washed out to sea and would never be seen again. Bodies were found hanging among overturned and stripped mangroves, buried in sand and debris, or in sunken wrecks of boats. Hardly any survivors were without injury.

All communication with the Keys was cut off. Some of the injured, hanging in trees, died of thirst, without help. Cisterns were choked with debris and fouling salt water. Finally boats reached the mainland at Homestead, and help arrived in the form of Coast Guard amphibians and cutters bearing supplies, administered by the National Guard and boys from the Miami CCC (Civilian Conservation Corps) camp.

The National Guard command ordered all of the bodies to be cremated. The Red Cross set up headquarters, telling people who had been left with nothing that to get help they had to submit "plans for rehabilitation." A storm of bitterness broke, the WPA (Works Projects Administration) ordered an investigation to settle blame for the tragedy, particularly the reason that the train did not arrive until it was too late for it to have any role in rescuing the veterans. Eventually, tempers cooled, orders were rescinded, and the investigation abandoned. The veterans group was fragmented and those who had survived the storm were quietly sent elsewhere.

UNITED STATES
FLORIDA
MIAMI
September 17, 1926

• • • • • • • • • • • • •

The hurricane of September 17, 1926 struck Florida at the height of the great land boom. Five hundred people died, 25,000 were made homeless, and over $760 million of property damage resulted.

The great Florida land boom had just passed its fevered peak when the Miami hurricane of September 17, 1926, struck. When the final toll was counted, the property damages in Miami alone totaled a staggering $760 million. One hundred fifteen people lost their lives in Miami; 300 were killed in Moore Haven and dozens in Fort Lauderdale; 25,000 people were rendered homeless.

A devastated beachfront in Miami, Florida following the hurricane of September 17, 1926. Striking at the height of the Florida land boom, the hurricane killed 500, made 25,000 homeless and set the boom back considerably. Library of Congress.

The storm originated in the Cape Verde Islands on September 15th, brushed Puerto Rico, and roared into Miami at approximately 7:30 P.M. on September 17. There was no warning. The Weather Bureau reported a tropical storm nearby, but issued no warnings for the steadily increasing northeast winds.

By midnight, waves were crashing over the breakfronts and the wind had climbed to 120 mph, blowing away house roofs and the instrument shed at the top of the Weather Bureau. People trying to crawl to safety were crushed by trees or bricks, and water was foaming everywhere.

The devastation was horrendous. Concrete office floors weighing five tons were broken up and carried for 50 feet by the flood waters. Trees, automobiles and entire families were buried under the drifting sand.

Salon Maritime, a palatial real estate office in Coral Gables, lost its roof and filled first with sand, then with five hundred thousand gallons of fresh water when the Roman Pool next door split in two. By dawn, a policeman and a real estate agent still clung to its chandelier, as sea water mixed with fresh water and rose beneath them. Finally, they floated through the door on a piano.

At 6:47 A.M., the eye of the storm passed overhead. Unwarned, people poured out of shelters, and when the gale suddenly leaped anew out of the south at 128 mph (which made this storm one of the fiercest in Florida history) many were instantly killed by blown timbers or falling, weakened walls. The tide crashed in from the opposite direction, sucking the two men on a piano back inside the wreckage of the real estate office. They would climb from here onto the oversize mantel and remain there until they were rescued, 10 hours later.

On the storm raged, obliterating the boom town of Moore Haven on Lake Okeechobee, hitting Fort Lauderdale, falling on Pensacola. Shacks, flimsy buildings and billboards were blown entirely away.

The cleanup would take weeks. More than 2,000 workmen were hired for the job, cutting up fallen trees, burning wreckage and collecting rotting fish. The wholesale carnage brought about by the collapse of flimsy, expensive buildings built during the boom led Miami to revise its

Building Code, which would later become a model for all hurricane endangered cities in Florida.

UNITED STATES
FLORIDA
MIAMI
HURRICANE CLEO
August 22–27, 1964

• • • • • • • • • • • • • •

One hundred thirty-three people died when Hurricane Cleo traveled from Guadaloupe to Miami from August 22 to August 27, 1964.

Spawned in the Caribbean, where it located itself for four days, August 22–26, 1964, Hurricane Cleo killed 120 people in Guadaloupe and Haiti with 100-mph winds and enormous storm surges.

On August 27, its fury was turned on Miami. By this time, its maximum winds had climbed to 135 mph, and the waves it sent roaring over breakwaters of the famous resort's oceanfront sank, smashed or overturned hundreds of boats, from dinghies to six-figure yachts.

The so-called "Gold Coast," that strip of beachfront property that housed the poshest hotels and vacation homes, was particularly hard hit. More than 1,200 homes and offices suffered wind and/or water damage. For weeks, streets were buried under debris and mud. The final damage accounting totalled $200 million in property loss. Fortunately, thanks to modern forecasting methods, only 13 people lost their lives in Miami. If the storm had struck 20 years earlier, the loss might have been catastrophic.

UNITED STATES
FLORIDA
OKEECHOBEE
September 16, 1928

• • • • • • • • • • • • • •

Six hundred people died in Guadaloupe, 300 in Puerto Rico when a major hurricane ripped across these islands in early September 1928. But its most tragic visit was to the Florida

Shacks are turned into lean-tos after Hurricane Cleo rampaged through Haiti on August 22, 1964. CARE photo.

Everglades, where 2,500 people drowned from the storm surge of Lake Okeechobee.

In 1928, there was no flood control along Lake Okeechobee's shores, protecting the lake towns of the Everglades and their surrounding farms from being destroyed by an overflow from this, the second largest fresh-water lake wholly within the United States. It took the hurricane of September 16, 1928, in which a staggering 2,500 people—some said more—drowned to convince both the state and federal governments that drastic flood control measures were necessary, if the Everglades were ever to be a safe, habitable and agriculturally profitable area.

The hurricane was a monster, a vicious killer right from its start, somewhere off the African coast. It crashed across Guadaloupe on September 12, leaving over 600 dead. On the next day, which was the feast of San Felipe, its 235-mile-wide presence made itself fatally felt in Puerto Rico, where it caused $50 million in damage, killed another 300 people and rendered 200,000 homeless.

On the night of September 16, moving with a kind of terrible grandeur, it hovered over and smashed its way through West Palm Beach, where the barometer plunged to 27.43, a new low up to that time. Word spread that the Everglades, particularly the area around the 730 square miles of Lake Okeechobee was directly in the path of the storm. Moore Haven would not have to be warned; it had been flattened two years earlier by another killer storm. But border places like Bare Beach, Lake Harbor, Belle Glade, Pelican Bay, Pahokee and Canal Point were active resort areas on the afternoon of Sunday, September 17.

By 6 o'clock, the winds were strong enough to overturn automobiles and strip roofs from shacks and houses. In Belle Glade, 500 people crowded into the Glades Hotel and 150 crammed themselves into the Belle Glade Hotel. On Lake Okeechobee itself, a group of women and children huddled on a barge.

When the full fury of the storm hit, the lake was completely emptied of water, which in turn was hurled towards an inadequate mud dike and the towns below it. Needless to say, the dike melted under the force of the water, and the land south of the lake was completely inundated. No trees, telephone poles, canals or houses were visible above the surface of the water from there to the sea, 30 miles away.

In Belle Glade, the Belle Glade Hotel was torn from its foundations, but it held together and continued to shield its refugees from the projectile-riddled winds. The Glades Hotel took in water up to its second floor, but the inhabitants there just moved above the high water mark and survived. The remainder of the town was demolished. Fifty houses were swept away.

In Pelican Bay, everyone drowned, either in their homes, or trying to escape on the roads. On Ritta Island, many who had climbed to the roofs of their houses to escape the flood waters were crushed by falling trees. Others, climbing trees, were killed by the fatal bites of water moccasins swarming up the trunks or along the tops of ridges that jutted up above the roaring waters.

The women and children on the barge miraculously survived.

The next day, the water receded only slightly. Militia men and boy scouts, pressed into rescue service, fished for bodies, both human and animal, from the brackish waters that covered everything. Later, they tied the dead together and towed them behind launches to railroad platforms. Seven hundred were buried in a long trench in West Palm Beach. Finally, after four days of hot sun, the only solution was to burn the dead in huge funeral pyres.

It would take two years of lobbying to convince the Hoover Administration in Washington to approve a bond issue of up to $5 million to support a plan for state flood control over the 12,000-square-mile Okeechobee-Everglades area.

UNITED STATES
FLORIDA
ST. JO

September, 1841

• • • • • • • • • • • • • • •

Nearly 4,000 people—the entire population of St. Jo, Florida was killed when the town was totally destroyed by a hurricane in September, 1841.

A few miles from Apalochiola, on the banks of the Apalochiola River, the high-living boomtown of St. Jo reveled night and day. A collection of saloons, shops and small businesses, it was a thriving town of 4,000 in 1841. The only unhappy citizens were its local preachers, who rode around the countryside denouncing St. Jo as a hellhole of wickedness, destined to be destroyed by fire or flood.

Half of that destiny came dramatically true in September 1841, when a colossus of a hurricane slammed into the boomtown on its way eastward across the state from the Gulf of Mexico. Within hours, every single building in St. Jo was demolished. Almost every person in town was either drowned or crushed under the falling buildings or flying debris. Today, the only evidence that St. Jo ever existed at all is a cluster of deteriorating gravestones.

UNITED STATES
FLORIDA
STRAITS

September 9–10, 1919

• • • • • • • • • • • • • •

Seven hundred seventy-two people died in a hurricane that whipped up the Florida Straits from September 9 through 10, 1919.

What was reputed to be the largest, most destructive hurricane of the 20th century began as a minor disturbance near Santo Domingo on September 2, 1919. Before it finally subsided near Corpus Christi, Texas 12 days later, 772 people would lose their lives to the storm.

After Santo Domingo, the hurricane made landfall at Key West, Florida, where its 80-mph winds stripped the weather service of some of its recording instruments. The full fury of the storm slammed into this city, collapsing buildings, flooding streets, uprooting trees, overflowing mud dams and ultimately causing $2 million in property damage.

Settling into the Florida Straits, the storm laid to waste the sea lanes, capsizing 10 vessels. There were survivors from most of these ships, but the *Valbanera*, a Spanish cruise ship, was unceremoniously and tragically swamped before safety precautions could be taken, and it went rapidly to the bottom of the Gulf of Mexico near the Dry Tortugas, drowning 400 vacationing passengers and 88 crew members.

The killer storm maintained its size and power when it blundered ashore at Corpus Christi. Its outer winds, holding at an even 60 mph, lashed at Galveston and Miami. But the fury of its center was saved for Corpus Christi, where it sent storm surges up to 16 feet high through the city streets, toppling tall buildings and pulverizing houses, farms and businesses. When a watery, calm dawn finally broke over the city on September 15, $20 million in damage had been caused, and 284 people lay dead from the horrendous destructive force of the storm.

UNITED STATES
GEORGIA

August 27, 1893

• • • • • • • • • • • • • • •

Over 1,000 were killed by the hurricane that struck Georgia and North Carolina on August 27, 1893.

By the time they reach the southeastern coast of the United States, most hurricanes curve northeastward toward the pole. The hurricane of August 27, 1893, however, behaved differently. Packing huge winds, it produced a roaring, consuming tidal wave that totally inundated islands off the Georgia and North Carolina coast.

Property damage was estimated to approach $10 million, and more than 1,000 people were reported killed by the storm.

UNITED STATES
LOUISIANA

August 19, 1812

• • • • • • • • • • • • • •

Fatality figures were not kept, but hundreds were known to have died in one of the first hurricanes to be recorded in Louisiana, on August 19, 1812.

One of the first hurricanes to be recorded in Louisiana slammed into the shore area west of the Mississippi River and followed its entire length on August 19, 1812.

Its first impact flattened buildings in New Orleans, turned streets into streams and collapsed the historic Market House with its supposedly indestructible 24-inch diameter columns.

Settlers along the river were routed from their homes and fields or drowned in them. Fifty-three ships either anchored in or sailing upon the Mississippi were, as one writer of the time put it, "crushed to atoms." Others sank with their crews aboard.

Further up the river, at Fort St. Philip, a contingent of American volunteers was billeted in anticipation of a British attack. Flood waters roared through the fort, and the wind shattered its buildings, all except the barracks, which were fashioned from thick logs. Some survived here, but 45 others perished, adding to the unrecorded fatalities that occurred from New Orleans to Fort St. Philip.

UNITED STATES
LOUISIANA

October 1, 1893

• • • • • • • • • • • • • • •

Two thousand people were killed by a small, forceful hurricane that struck Louisiana on October 1, 1893.

Small hurricanes, if wound up tight, can cause as much damage and loss of life as more grandiose and far reaching ones. Such was the compact hurricane that caromed into the coast of Louisiana between Port Eads and New Orleans on October 1, 1893.

The storm, unannounced by the primitive weather forecasting methods of the time, pushed a 12-foot-high storm surge ahead of it, and it was this that drowned, according to one report, 2,000 people working the fields and the fishing boats of that rich area of Louisiana.

Boats that had not been made fast were swept out to sea with their crews aboard; the fishing shacks and curing sheds that lined the docks were swept away in minutes, or crushed in seconds.

The storm swept inward, than outward again toward the coast, laying waste to millions of dollars worth of property throughout the South Atlantic States before it finally headed out to sea and self-extinction.

UNITED STATES
LOUISIANA (AND MISSISSIPPI)

September 10–20, 1909

• • • • • • • • • • • • • • •

Three hundred fifty people died in the hurricane that hit Louisiana and Mississippi in September, 1909.

A giant hurricane that developed off the Leeward Islands, traversed the Caribbean and sideswiped Cuba. Ten days later it slammed into the Louisiana coast 50 miles west of New Orleans, crumbling carefully constructed dikes at the mouth of the Mississippi River with a moderate storm surge.

The winds of the storm were not enormously strong in comparison to other, later storms that had already hit the region (see two previous entries). But combined with high tides in the Gulf, the storm swelled the Mississippi a full three feet above the high water mark.

Lake Borgne, located outside of New Orleans, overflowed its banks and united with the onrushing waves from the Gulf of Mexico. All the wire supplying electricity to the city and carrying communication both in and out of it was swept away.

The large storm continued on, devastating coastal Mississippi and parts of Florida. At Pensacola, ships safely moored in the harbor were overturned by the storm surge and scores of people, trapped in such supposedly, secure vessels as the steamer *Romanoff* perished. Scores of small towns simply disappeared along with their populations as the storm swept over them.

In Louisiana and Mississippi, 350 people were killed and over $5 million in property damage was sustained by this long-lasting and extensive hurricane.

UNITED STATES
LOUISIANA
LAST ISLAND

August 13, 1856

• • • • • • • • • • • • • • •

The entire population of Last Island, Louisiana—several hundred people—drowned when a huge hurricane submerged the island on August 13, 1856.

Last Island, off the Louisiana Coast, was pelted with nearly 14 inches of rain during the week preceding the arrival of the colossal hurricane that would eventually destroy it.

These meteorologically correct conditions set up a classic scenario for disaster on August 13, 1856. At approximately 2 P.M. on that day, huge waves, produced by the storm surge began to pound the island. Residents were blinded by both the rain and wind-driven sand. Those who chose to row out to the steamer *Star*, which was anchored in the bay, would survive, although by the end of the storm the ship would be stripped back until only her hull and boilers remained.

Those who decided to climb to the highest point on the island were less lucky, for within hours, the entire island would be submerged, the waters of the Gulf of Mexico closing over it like a green and murky blanket. Only the nearly destroyed ship with its survivors could attest to the island's existence.

UNITED STATES
MISSISSIPPI
HURRICANE ELENA

August 30–September 2, 1985

• • • • • • • • • • • • • • •

Although there were no fatalities, over 1 million people were either evacuated or affected by Hurricane Elena, which wandered through Louisiana, Alabama, Mississippi, and Central and Northern Florida from August 30 to September 2, 1985.

Like a drunken sailor, Hurricane Elena wove and dipped around the Gulf of Mexico from August 30 to September 2, 1985, threatening New Orleans, Alabama, Mississippi and Central and Northern Florida.

On August 30, it appeared that the 300-mile-wide hurricane would come ashore somewhere near Pensacola, Florida, and some 125,000 people were evacuated from Louisiana and Florida coastal areas, while oil companies airlifted 20,000 people from their offshore oil rigs. Governor Edwin Edwards of Louisiana declared a state of emergency for 14 parishes in Louisiana, and 15,000 people in Alabama evacuated their homes, condominiums and mobile homes. The National Guard moved into the Florida panhandle.

But instead of hitting the coast where it logically should have, Elena stalled and churned over the warm gulf waters about 50 miles west-southwest of Cedar Key in Central Florida. Rains and tidal surges 8 to 12 feet high battered the coast on August 30 and 31, and high tides closed the three main bridges crossing Tampa Bay. The storm was behaving like 1950's Hurricane Easy, which had lingered off Florida's Gulf coast, dumping 38 inches of rain in 24 hours—a national record.

At midday on August 31, two tornadoes spun off the main storm. One hit the Kennedy Space Center at Cape Canaveral, causing no damage. The second injured seven people when it slammed into a mobile home community near Leesburg, destroying 54 trailers and damaging 83 others.

On August 31, Elena intensified, doubled back and once again threatened the Gulf Coast east of New Orleans with winds of up to 125 mph. By changing its course, the hurricane, which had been snaking and bobbing across the Gulf of Mexico since the previous Thursday, now menaced many of the same people who had been given an all clear late on Friday. Hundreds of thousands of people were again ordered to flee inland.

Still remaining offshore, the storm rolled up the coast of Northwest Florida, battering seaside towns from Apalachiola to Fort Walton Beach. As the eye passed near Panama City, winds on the fringe of the storm caused power failures as far away as Pensacola. At Port St. Joe, Bill Eagle, a police dispatcher said he had just heard from a neighbor. "Bill, your roof just blew right by my house," the neighbor reported. There was a short pause. "Bill," the neighbor continued, "your pump house just whipped by, too."

Now, its upper-air currents apparently diminishing, the storm wobbled towards New Orleans, simultaneously climbing on the Saffir-Simpson scale to a grade 3 hurricane.

But again, the predictors were wrong. On September 1, instead of making landfall in Louisiana, the storm came ashore further north, near Biloxi, Mississippi. The storm's winds, which exceeded 110 mph, peeled roofs off homes, toppled trees and power lines and demolished structures in Biloxi and Gulfport.

Dauphine Island, a resort community southwest of Mobile, Alabama was particularly hard hit. A 12-foot tidal surge crashed over the west end of the island, sweeping away 50 homes, uprooting trees and floating debris at lethal speeds inland.

In Gulfport, a tornado ripped into a storm shelter, injuring one person and forcing another 380 to flee into the night. A fire in the same city destroyed an apartment complex, leaving 130 people homeless. The roof of a center for the elderly in Biloxi was collapsed by a tornado, forcing paramedics to crawl through the rubble to rescue an estimated 200 people.

All in all, over a million residents of the wide area either hit or threatened by Elena had their lives and often their living spaces disrupted by the storm. The ultimate loss in homes and agriculture would rise to $543.3 million, making it the costliest storm on record until that time.

UNITED STATES
NEW ENGLAND

August 14, 1773

• • • • • • • • • • • • • •

There are no casualty statistics for the hurricane that cut a wide path through New England on August 14, 1773. Widespread damage is known to have resulted from the storm.

Cows grazed on the Boston Common in 1773, but they were sent home early on the night of August 14, as a slashing rain began to whip across the salt marshes and the 2,000-foot length of Long Wharf. All up and down the New England coast, the wind had been rising, and by nightfall, waves were breaking over the docks and smashing into warehouses and ropewalks.

In Charleston, waves cracked the wharves as they smashed down upon them. Bunker and Breed's Hills were eroded and Cambridge was flooded. Houses were shuttered and safe in Boston itself, but the farmhouses along the Merrimack River were ripped from their foundations as the river overflowed its banks. Houses, barns and windmills collapsed, and apple orchards were stripped and broken, cornfields turned into vistas of mud, and cattle drowned or felled by flying planks.

Salisbury Point, Amesbury and Haverhill were ripped by tornadoes that grew along the edge of the storm, and ships in Boston and a score of other harbors along the coast were torn from their moorings and thrown up against the rocks of the shore, where they burst apart, or simply capsized, often with all hands aboard.

The hardy colonists started rebuilding as soon as the sun rose on August 15. No casualty statistics survive. There are only accounts of wagons rumbling in from Roxbury and Dorchester to the maritime settlements, laden with supplies and men to repair homes, raise sunken ships, and get the thriving trade with the Indies and Africa back in business. These efforts, however, were shortlived; a year later, King George would shut down the port of Boston, with even greater effect than the hurricane of 1773.

UNITED STATES
NEW ENGLAND

September 1815

• • • • • • • • • • • • • • •

Eighty-five vessels were sunk in the "September equinoctial gale of 1815," which was obviously a hurricane. No casualty records were kept, but it is safe to assume that many drowned aboard the sunken ships.

Originating near the Island of St. Bart's, the "September equinoctial gale of 1815," as it was called, slammed into Providence, Rhode Island in September, pushing a storm surge ahead of it that raised the tides in Narragansett Bay 12 feet above normal, and swept away the bridge that connected the two parts of Providence. Thirty-five vessels, anchored at the head of the Bay, were completely demolished. Water rose to the tops of second-story windows in some houses; men from a wrecked brig on the river crawled over floating debris until people taking refuge on the roofs of nearby houses tossed them lines and pulled them to improvised safety.

Sixty vessels went to the bottom of Boston Harbor. Roofs were ripped from houses in Cambridgeport, Salem, Gloucester, Reading, Newburyport, Danvers, Saugus, even as far north as Wells, in Maine.

Point Judith light was destroyed. In Connecticut, New London, Groton, Norwich and Stonington suffered wind and water damage; sea water was picked up by the roaring winds and flung more than 40 miles inland, scalding the sides of buildings and trees with salt.

No casualty figures were kept, but the lesson of the storm prodded the residents of much of New England, and especially Providence, to burn and replace the wrecks of dilapidated wooden warehouses with brick ones. In fact, as a result of the storm, the entire architecture of the city underwent a generous, noticeable facelift.

There was no warning of the storm that whistled and screeched all night on the third of October 1841, felling trees, smashing windows, collapsing walls and buildings. In the harbors, boats simply disappeared. The next morning, it was as if winter had come early. Trees were stripped or felled in meadows white with salt. Every village and farm was piled high with debris and dead livestock.

But the worst and most tragic damage was done to the Cape Cod fishing fleet, which had headed out on October 1 for the George Bank, where the cod were running. Between 40 and 50 vessels foundered and split apart in the roiling sea whipped by the storm. They washed up on the beaches from Chatham to the Highlands the next morning. Gloucester, Dennis and Hyannis Port all lost some of their finest schooners and their proudest men. At Cape Ann, 14 of the fishing fleet were washed ashore at Pigeon Cove, where fish houses, fish flakes, 60 barrels of mackerel, 200 barrels of salt, 300 empty barrels and a catch that would have brought $50,000 to its fishermen and their families were completely wiped out by the storm.

These were the bald and horrible facts. Probably from the safety of an inner city shelter, Oliver Wendell Holmes immortalized the storm in verse that hardly plumbed its terrible depths:

> *Lord how the ponds and rivers boiled*
> *And how the shingles rattled*
> *And oaks were scattered on the ground*
> *As if the Titans battled*
> *And all above was in a howl,*
> *And all below a clatter,—*
> *The earth was like a frying pan*
> *Or some such hissing matter.*
> *I lost—oh, bitterly I wept*
> *I lost my Sunday britches.*

Tragedy, as well as beauty, sometimes seems to rest in the eye of the beholder.

UNITED STATES
NEW ENGLAND

October 3, 1841

• • • • • • • • • • • • • • •

Hundreds of fishermen drowned in the hurricane that struck New England on October 3, 1841.

UNITED STATES
NEW ENGLAND

September 21, 1938

• • • • • • • • • • • • • • •

(See HURRICANES, United States, New York (Long Island) and New England.)

UNITED STATES
NEW ENGLAND

September 8–16, 1944

• • • • • • • • • • • • • •

Three hundred eighty-nine people were killed in the New England hurricane of September 8–16, 1944, which followed a unique inland path from North Carolina northward.

Largely following the path of the September 21, 1938 hurricane (see HURRICANES, New York (Long Island) and New England), a monster storm, born off the West Indies, would ultimately claim 389 lives and cause $50 million in damage along a 500-mile front.

After bringing slight damage to Puerto Rico, the Bahamas and the Florida Keys, the storm swerved inland at North Carolina. At this point, Colonel Lloyd B. Wood, deputy chief of the Army Air Corps' Weather Division, took off from Washington, D.C., piloting an A-20 Havoc light bomber. Colonel Wood flew straight through the incredible 140-mph winds of the storm to its eye. His reports made the killer hurricane one of the best charted storms in history up to that time, thus keeping the death toll down.

Despite the fact that it had made landfall, the hurricane maintained powerful winds and barreled northward across the Carolinas, Maryland, Delaware and then into New Jersey. At Sea Isle, New Jersey only 300 of the resort's 700 dwellings escaped without severe damage. In Asbury Park, 200 feet of that city's municipal fishing pier was torn up and washed away. In Atlantic City, the famous boardwalk was ripped apart.

By September 14, the storm, now packing winds of 95 mph, slammed into New York City, skipping the villages of eastern Long Island that had been so severely devastated by the 1938 storm. Skyscrapers swayed and pedestrians were whipped by stinging rain and flying debris, but the metropolis remained fairly undamaged.

Not so New England, which felt the storm's final fury. Tens of thousands of ancient, towering trees were toppled, bringing down electrical lines—which in some cases caused fires—and wiping out telephone service for more than 300,000 residents. Bridges crumbled, waterfront houses were washed away in a moment, salt spray whitened the land along the coast, but few people lost their lives. Most of the fatalities in New England took place at sea, where scores of vessels, both military and civilian, foundered with their crews aboard.

After covering a total area of close to 1,000 square miles, the storm finally blew itself out off the coast of Newfoundland.

UNITED STATES
NEW ENGLAND
HURRICANE CAROL

August 26–31, 1954

• • • • • • • • • • • • • •

Five thousand tourists and fishermen were stranded on the tip of Long Island by Hurricane Carol, in late August 1954. Forty-five people died as the storm continued on to ravage New England.

Born in the so-called horse lattitudes well east of Jacksonville, Florida, Hurricane Carol made an inauspicious entrance into the world on August 26, 1954. If a convergence of forces—a Bermuda high and a western high pressure area that arrived from the Rockies—hadn't created a sluiceway up the Atlantic cost, Carol might have remained an inconsequential storm.

But such was not the case. Unlike the 1944 hurricane (see previous entry), the Weather Bureau failed to issue hurricane warnings to the crowds enjoying Labor Day weekend on the Long Island beaches. Fortunately, Carol struck Long Island at low, rather than high tide. No huge tidal wave hit, but the storm surge was strong enough to strand 5,000 tourists and fishermen at Montauk, at Long Island's tip, where the surge scoured out roads and railroad tracks, isolating that community.

By the time the storm hit the coast of Connecticut, the Weather Bureau had still not issued hurricane warnings. The storm crest hit Narragansett Bay at high tide, smashing into Misquamicutt Beach and sweeping away 200 homes.

Pushed by 120-mph winds, the surf exploded against the beaches of Block Island, Rhode Island and Martha's Vineyard, Massachusetts, filling fresh water ponds with salt water. On the island of Martha's Vineyard, Vineyard Haven, West Chop, Edgartown and particularly Menemsha were flattened by the winds and buried under piles of wreckage.

In Newport, Rhode Island, the venerable casino collapsed. Travelers in cars were swept off coastal highways by sudden waves. In South Kingston, eight carloads of people who had fled from their summer cottages were stranded, and many drowned. A 35-foot wave overwhelmed Westerly and Watch Hill, Rhode Island. The center of Providence was flooded up to the 1938 high water mark.

In Massachusetts, New Bedford harbor was inundated by waves, broken boats, docks, yachts, draggers, sailboats, trawlers, tugs and houses. Fishermen were washed off boats and drowned. A fire in Wareham was fought by firemen struggling through chin-high water.

A normally tree-lined country road in Westhampton Beach, Long Island was turned into a lumber yard after the hurricane of September 21, 1938. The wreckage consisted of the remains of once palatial beach houses smashed to splinters by a 20-foot storm surge. Quogue Historical Society/Pat Shuttleworth.

Finally, hurricane warnings filtered through from the Weather Bureau, just as the wooden spire of Boston's Old North Church cracked, shuddered and fell. It had fallen once before, exactly 150 years ago in the New England hurricane of 1804.

Worcester County suffered severe crop damage, and in the city of Worcester, one Harry R. Davis was blown to his death from the 10th story of a downtown office building when he opened a door on a fire escape.

Maine suffered tree, boat and dock damage, as, unannounced to its inhabitants, Carol swept northward into Canada, where it would blow itself out. Behind her, she would leave 45 dead and millions of dollars in property damages.

UNITED STATES
NEW YORK (LONG ISLAND) AND NEW ENGLAND

September 21, 1938

• • • • • • • • • • • • •

Four hundred ninety-four people died, over 100 were missing, and 1,754 were injured in the September 21, 1938 hurricane that hit Long Island, New York and ultimately blew itself out over New England.

The Long Island hurricane of September 21, 1938, was born some 600 miles northeast of Puerto Rico (called Porto Rico in 1938) four days before, on September 17, traveling rapidly along the prevailing trade winds, west-northwest. Two days later, it was headed on a collision course

The storm surge of the Long Island/New England hurricane inundated roads a mile and a half inland on the south shore of Long Island. Quogue Historical Society/Pat Shuttleworth.

with Miami, and hurricane warnings were posted for the Florida coast.

The storm then veered northward, and by the night of September 20, was 400 miles due east of Jacksonville and picking up speed.

The conditions for this hurricane to make landfall over Long Island and New England were just right. A long tongue of warm, moist air hung in a line from the Carolinas to Long Island, where it had been raining heavily for two days. But no such storm had hit Long Island since October 6, 1849—nearly a hundred years before.

That morning, fishing boats went out, as usual. The weather forecast was for showers. But the situation deteriorated rapidly during the day, and when the National Weather Bureau finally issued gale warnings, radio stations were giving priority to a speech by Adolf Hitler being shortwaved from Europe.

When the storm inched its way into Long Island, around noon, few people believed it was more than an autumn gale. But by mid-afternoon, when it slammed full force into Westhampton Beach, where the eye would pass, tide

levels had risen 18 feet above normal, and waves measured another 12 feet. Telephone poles were picked up like match sticks and became flying trajectories. A tidal wave, estimated to be 20 feet in height, broke over the dunes and swept away hundreds of beachfront homes. Water rushed over the mainland, as survivors floated miles inland on pieces of houses, parts of boats and even oil and water tanks. Steeples were stripped from the tops of churches; the 100-year-old cupola from the top of the Presbyterian Church in Sag Harbor was lopped off as if a sword had sliced through the tower.

By evening, the storm had blown itself out over the mountains of Vermont, where, a week later, records from the town hall in Southampton were found strewn across the New England countryside. State troopers were brought in to restore order in the devastated vacation land of the south shore of Long Island. Bridges that connected the mainland to the barrier beach no longer existed. Looters had already appeared and by midnight, patrols of local citizens, armed with clubs, walked the battered beaches and darkened towns. Country clubs were turned into tempo-

The Main Street of Westhampton Beach, Long Island during the 1938 Long Island/New England hurricane. Quogue Historical Society/
Pat Shuttleworth.

rary morgues; school buildings became combination hospitals and shelters.

It would be months before the silt-covered villages and towns would recover and years before the multi-million dollar reconstruction would approach completion.

UNITED STATES
NORTH CAROLINA

September 16–17, 1713

• • • • • • • • • • • • • • •

Seventy people died in the onslaught of a furious hurricane that hit North Carolina on September 16, 1713.

In the sparsely colonized area of the North Carolina coast at the beginning of the 18th century, a fatality figure of 70 was impressive and calamitous. That it was brought about by a hurricane whose winds reached 100 mph makes this early storm notable for its viciousness and toll.

Charleston, Cape Fear and Port Royal were the hardest hit areas, although the storm did slice over three miles inland, across the salt marshes surrounding these settlements.

One of the first casualties of the storm was the 80-foot-high lighthouse on Sullivan's Island. Able to withstand the screaming winds during the earlier parts of the storm, it was no match for its final, accumulated fury, and after swaying precipitously, it finally snapped in two like a dried branch.

Seaside cottages were undermined and swept out to sea with their inhabitants, who thought—as most did in those times—that home was the safest haven. Most drownings, in fact, took place in this way. Farmers in their fields, pedestrians on the streets of Charleston, and crews aboard the schooners and sloops that were driven inland or capsized in the harbors also drowned.

UNITED STATES
SOUTH
HURRICANE AUDREY

June 27–30, 1957

• • • • • • • • • • • • • • •

Hurricane Audrey, the out-of-season hurricane that struck the southern United States on June 27, 1957 killed 534, injured thousands and destroyed 40,000 homes.

Ordinarily, the hurricane season begins in August. Thus, when, on June 27, 1957, a tropical depression in the Gulf of Mexico, 350 miles southeast of Brownsville, Texas unexpectedly developed into Audrey, the first hurricane of the season, residents of the Texas and Louisiana Bayou country refused to believe early Weather Bureau warnings.

Such was not the case with residents of Galveston and Port Arthur, Texas. Hearing radio reports that the 105-mph winds of Audrey had already claimed their first casualties—nine men killed when a 78-ton fishing boat was hurled into an oil rig—the inhabitants of these two cities evacuated their gulfside homes, and casualties there were relatively minimal.

After brushing these two Texas cities, Audrey flung itself toward the Louisiana coastal villages of Grand Chenier, Creole and Cameron. The storm slammed into these thickly populated villages at 97 mph, shoving a storm wave ahead of it that inundated streets, uprooted trees and houses, and sent automobiles whirling through streets.

Cameron, Louisiana was the worst hit. Homes were demolished and strewn across the countryside. The entire village virtually disappeared beneath the roiling waters of the Gulf. A tidal wave consumed the entire countryside as if it had been swallowed whole. One doctor remained in the local medical center, tending to the injured, while his own family was swept away. His children were never found; his wife was discovered clinging to a piece of driftwood 20 miles from Cameron.

When the storm finally blew itself out over Ohio and Pennsylvania, it had left behind 534 dead—mostly from Cameron—and 40,000 destroyed homes.

UNITED STATES
SOUTH
HURRICANE CAMILLE

August 17, 1969

• • • • • • • • • • • • • • • • •

The largest recorded storm ever to hit a heavily populated area of the United States, Hurricane Camille, with winds of close to 200 mph killed at least 360, injured thousands and left tens of thousands homeless.

Hurricane Camille, described by Dr. Robert H. Simpson, then head of the National Hurricane Center at Miami, Florida as ". . . the greatest recorded storm ever to hit a heavily populated area of the Western Hemisphere," began its life off the coast of Africa and was first sighted by hurricane watch planes on August 14, 1969 in the Caribbean, 480 miles south of Miami. From then until its demise over Newfoundland four days later, the storm wreaked

incredible havoc—causing more fatalities in fact, in an aftershock than it had in its initial assault upon Louisiana and Mississippi.

That more people weren't killed by this killer storm can largely be credited to the advanced methods of hurricane reporting. From the time it was first sighted, Camille was closely tracked. It brushed by the western tip of Cuba with no effect except accelerated winds. By Friday, August 15, it had entered the Gulf of Mexico, with gale-force winds spreading 150 miles ahead of it.

On August 16, as pressure dropped within the storm and its winds rose, weather forecasters predicted landfall in southern Florida. But that night, the storm changed direction and headed towards New Orleans. An Air Force plane, entering the eye, clocked winds of nearly 200 mph and a barometric reading of 26.61—the second lowest barometric pressure ever recorded. The lowest—26.35—was recorded in the eye of the great Labor Day hurricane of 1935 over Key West. (See HURRICANES, United States, Florida, Keys, 1935, p. 196.)

By noon the next day, Camille had aimed her fury directly at the bayou country of Mississippi and Louisiana. Two hundred thousand people boarded up their houses and headed for higher ground. The area just west of Gulfport, Mississippi received the full force of Camille—winds of 190 mph and a storm surge that sent awesome 25-foot waves roaring through the tiny resort city of Pass Christian. That city's Trinity Church literally exploded in a gust of 200-mph wind, burying 11 people who had taken shelter there.

Beach houses were swept out to sea. In one luxury condominium, the steel and concrete Richelieu Apartments, 12 people gathered for a hurricane party, ignoring the pleas of local police to evacuate the area. All 12 perished when the building collapsed on them. Slightly up the beach from the Richelieu, a motel was flattened when several ocean-going ships riding the crest of the 25-foot waves plowed into it.

By 2 A.M., the wind had subsided, and local police, accompanied by a fleet of Navy amphibious DUCKS manned by Seabees plied the waist-deep waters, looking for survivors. Every house in town, they discovered, had been either destroyed or badly damaged. Bodies floated on the water; natural gas lines were smashed; electricity was gone; the water was contaminated. When the sun rose, hundreds of deadly cottonmouth snakes swarmed out of the swamps and into town, trying to escape the flooding.

In all, 137 people died and 500 were injured in the area in and around Pass Christian, which was soon put under martial law while nearly a million pounds of food, fresh water and medical supplies poured in from as far away as Arizona.

But meanwhile, Camille was far from dead. For reasons not quite clear to meteorologists, the storm had either conserved some of her original cargo of rain or had in some manner acquired fresh quantities. Instead of blowing out over the land mass of Tennessee and Kentucky, she seemed to gather new power, and by the time she had unexplainably turned east and crossed the Blue Ridge Mountains into Nelson County, Virginia, she was still a menace. Thirty-one inches of rain fell during the night of August 19—more than 400 million gallons of water within a period of four hours. Scientists afterward noted that rain of this magnitude occurs on an average of only once in a thousand years.

Now, mudslides were added to the devastation caused by Camille. At Holcomb Rock the James River rose from eight feet on August 18 to 47.5 feet on August 19. Families, sleeping through what they thought was just another rainstorm, were buried under tons of mud. Nearly 200 people lost their lives in Nelson County, and $100 million worth of property was simply washed away. The Tye and Rockfish Rivers overflowed; trees were uprooted; bridges washed away and highways and railroad right of ways were undercut and disappeared.

After Virginia, Camille went out to sea and eventually blew herself out over the open waters of the Atlantic near Newfoundland.

UNITED STATES
SOUTH
HURRICANE JUAN

October 27–November 5, 1985

• • • • • • • • • • • • • • •

More than 60 people were killed, hundreds were injured and thousands were made homeless by Hurricane Juan, when it struck the southern coast of the United States on October 27, 1985.

Hurricane Juan was a wanderer, causing as much damage after it was downgraded to a tropical storm as it did when it qualified as a full-fledged hurricane.

As a hurricane, with winds of up to 85 mph, Juan first roared into the Gulf of Mexico on October 27, 1985, swamping boats and oil rigs and stranding some 1,400 people in Grand Isle, Louisiana when they failed to evacuate over the causeway. By nightfall, the only power in town was in City Hall and the high school gymnasium, which, lit by a portable generator, was turned into a storm shelter for the 70 percent of the villagers who chose to stay on the island.

In the Gulf, waves that often reached heights of 18 feet, driven by 75- to 80-mph winds, pummeled oil rigs. Ten people were stranded on a semi-submersible offshore rig whose supporting legs partly collapsed after catching fire. *Miss Agnes*, a boat used to ferry workers to the offshore oil rigs, capsized, drowning two crewmen. Other crewboats ran aground.

Juan made landfall shortly before dawn on October 28 along the south-central Louisiana coast, then bounced out into the Gulf again, where it knocked down two more oil rigs. At 3 P.M. on October 29, it again made landfall near Lafayette, Louisiana, about 100 miles west-northwest of New Orleans. Waves over 20 feet high and tides 10 feet above normal rushed inland, flooding areas in New Orleans and on the west bank of the Mississippi River and forcing over 2,000 people from their homes in Louisiana and from 5,000 to 6,000 in Mississippi.

Tornadoes spun off the edges of the hurricane, causing isolated damage in Mississippi, Alabama and Florida, and dumping 7.25 inches of rain on southeastern Texas.

By October 30, damage from Juan was estimated at $1 billion. Seven deaths had been recorded, 50,000 homes were flooded in Louisiana and $110 million in damage had been done to the Louisiana sugarcane crop. Several multimillion dollar oil rigs were either capsized or badly damaged and three bodies were recovered from a 52-foot-long drilling barge that capsized in a marshy ship channel 20 miles east of New Orleans. Six people were rescued from a foundering shrimp boat 150 miles off the coast of Galveston, Texas.

Now packing winds of 65 mph and downgraded to a tropical storm, Juan continued to hit the coast, dumping 10 inches of rain on New Orleans and eight inches at Pensacola, Florida; Baumont-Port Arthur, Texas; and Alexandria and Boothville, Louisiana. By the night of the 30th, approximately 2,500 people who had been evacuated from their homes were still waiting in 23 Red Cross shelters for flood waters to drop in 10 southern Louisiana parishes.

Moving back into the Gulf of Mexico, Juan briefly cranked itself up to near hurricane status, then weakened as it came ashore near Gulf Shores, Alabama, alongside the Florida state line, and headed towards Georgia. In some frustration, M. K. Renfroe, the Escambia (Florida) Country Civil Defense Coordinator commented: "It was predicted there would be more than the usual number of storms this year, but they didn't say they would be weird."

In Louisiana, flood waters kept 50,000 homeless, and by now, coffins were floating out of mausoleums.

Juan continued northward, spreading devastation everywhere. Twenty-six people lost their lives in Virginia and Maryland, and thousands more fled their homes when swollen rivers, fed by the rains from the last, tattered rem-

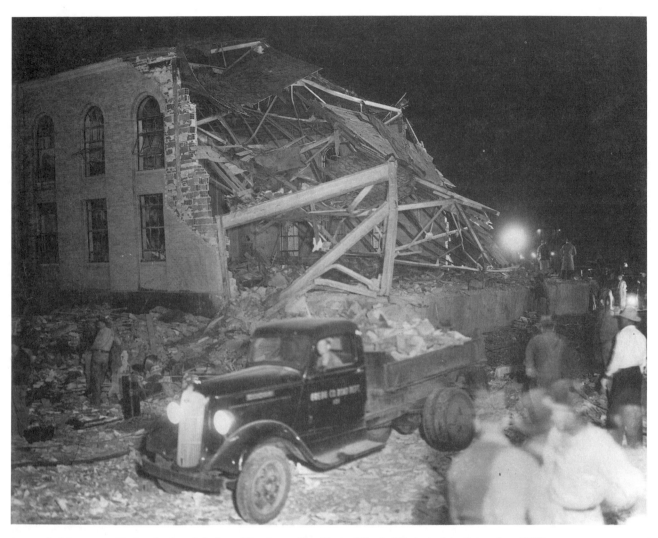

A wrecked house amid the detritus left from Hurricane Camille in Biloxi, Mississippi in September 1969. American Red Cross/Ted Garland.

nants of Juan pummeled the mid-Atlantic states. Six one-ton cannisters of poisonous chlorine gas were washed into the James River from a plant near Lynchburg, Virginia and they roared like torpedoes past concrete bridges that, had they been hit by the cannisters, would have been demolished in fiery, explosive splendor.

Governor Arch Moore of West Virginia mobilized the National Guard; up to 60 barges ripped loose from moorings on the Monongahela River and evening rush hour traffic was tied up in Pittsburgh as the police closed bridges while some of the barges swept past.

Towns in Pennsylvania were inundated by flood waters that had not reached such levels in the past 100 years. Twenty people were listed missing, 10 more reported dead, more than 2,000 more were rendered homeless in Virginia, West Virginia and Pennsylvania. The James River

flooded approximately 40 square blocks of warehouses and small businesses in low-lying areas of Richmond, Virginia, and historic sites around Washington D.C. were sand-bagged against the expected rise of the Potomac River.

By the time Juan had blown itself out, over 60 people would be dead, thousands homeless, and the total damage would reach nearly $2 billion.

UNITED STATES
TEXAS
GALVESTON

September 8, 1900

• • • • • • • • • • • • • •

Six thousand people died, 6,000 were injured and tens of thousands were rendered homeless by the huge hurricane that hit Galveston, Texas on September 8, 1900. It was one of the last untracked storms in the history of the United States.

Six thousand people—one-seventh of the population of Galveston—were killed and an equal number were injured by the monster hurricane that struck the city on September 8, 1900. This event is an example not merely of the deadly force of tropical hurricanes, but of the dramatic contrast in weather reporting methods between 1900 and today.

In 1900, the U.S. Weather Bureau was unable to detect storms while they were still at sea; in fact, it was not until five years later, in 1905, that ships began to send weather reports directly to the Washington Weather Bureau. Of course, whether or not the Washington Weather Bureau would evaluate this data correctly is another story. In 1900, Isaac and Joseph Cline, two brothers who manned the Galveston branch of the Weather Bureau, had reason to doubt that.

In hindsight, it seems that the storm was born somewhere off Venezuela in late August. It blew down telegraph lines on Antigua on August 30, raked Haiti on September 2, and dumped 12.5 inches of rain on Santiago, Cuba on September 3.

But once the storm left Cuba, Washington lost track of it. Meteorologists assumed that it would curve north and hit Florida. But the storm defied the pattern and instead headed due west, toward Galveston. The Weather Bureau still predicted that it would make landfall east of Galveston.

By the afternoon of Friday, September 7, the booming waves hitting the beach could be heard all over town. Dr. Isaac Cline and his brother Joseph determined that the wind was coming not from the northwest, as it would if the storm were to hit east of them, but from the northeast.

By 5 A.M. on Saturday, September 8, the tide had risen high enough to flood four blocks of the city—and at a time when the wind was blowing against the tide. People

Six thousand people—one-seventh of the population of Galveston, Texas—drowned or were buried under falling debris in the great hurricane of September 8, 1900. Six thousand more were injured and tens of thousands were left homeless. Library of Congress.

began to wade through ankle deep water to work (in 1900 almost everyone worked on Saturday), and by 8 A.M., the rains began.

By 10 A.M., the waves had increased in force and size. Groups of curiosity seekers, huddled under umbrellas, went down to the beach to watch the surf as it smashed into beach cottages and other obstructions, sending plumes of spray 20 feet into the air. By this time Dr. Cline had mounted a horse-drawn cart to ride up and down the beach, warning sightseers and residents to move to higher ground. The tide was already five feet above the high water mark and rising at a rate of nearly a foot an hour.

At 11:15, Joseph Cline received word from Washington to change the wind warnings from northwest to northeast. The storm would stay out at sea, the U.S. Weather Service confidently predicted. Against regulations, Dr. Cline wired hurricane warnings up and down the coast. He wrote later, ". . . neither emergency nor hurricane warnings for the disaster were received from the forecaster in the Washington office."

By the afternoon, half the city of Galveston was under water, and all the telegraph lines were down but one. Joseph Cline sent one last message to the National Weather Bureau, stating that the storm was upon them. Two bridges to the mainland had fallen, and a causeway was inundated. The city was completely cut off.

By early evening, the wind had risen enough to shear off roofs and hurl timbers through the air at enough velocity to kill hundreds of people trying to wade to safety through the flooded streets. The anemometer on the roof of the Weather Bureau blew off after first registering 120 mph.

The wooden barracks at Fort Crockett, in the southwestern part of the city, washed away, carrying with it seven soldiers who had remained behind to guard it. Huge rafts of debris—battered and crushed remains of houses and people—planed through the streets, carried by the current out toward the Gulf. A thousand people crowded into the Tremont Hotel lobby, climbing the stairs just ahead of the rising water.

Dr. Cline found 50 people besides his family huddled in his house that evening. A moment later, water roared into the first story of the house, reaching Dr. Cline's armpits. Moments after all 50 had climbed to the second story, a railroad trestle collapsed on the house, splitting it asunder and spilling its inhabitants out into the raging floodwaters. Joseph Cline grabbed two of Dr. Cline's children and escaped through a window; Dr. Cline grabbed his baby and clambered aboard some floating wreckage. His wife and 31 of their friends were trapped in the wreckage that sank beneath the water.

Over 700 people sought shelter in the city hall. It collapsed, killing 50 and injuring hundreds more. The Rosenberg school caved in on a score of people huddled inside it. St. Mary's Infirmary collapsed on hundreds, leaving only eight survivors.

The cemeteries were scooped clean of coffins. One metal one weighing 200 pounds floated as far as Virginia Point. An ocean liner was torn from its moorings. It rocketed down the channel, ramming all three bridges to the mainland and ripping them apart, thus cutting off three major avenues of escape.

At dawn, the sun rose on a scene of incredible carnage. Limbs of trees, pieces of buildings, piles and piles of rubble stretched as far as the eye could see. Nothing but the larger buildings of Galveston were left standing, and one of them, fortunately, was the Levy Building, which contained the record of the storm.

In addition to the flooding, two billion tons of rain had fallen on this hapless city during a 24-hour period. Six thousand people died in the city; another 2,000 more bodies were scattered for miles along the coast on either side of it. Many bodies had been swept out into the Gulf. Others were piled into funeral pyres and burned, for health reasons.

Chaos reigned. Some survivors went insane. Several shot themselves when they discovered the bodies of loved ones. But the worst was yet to come. Hundreds of looters scurried into the city, many arriving by boat from the mainland. The militia was called in, and over the next two days hundreds of looters were executed on the spot.

The tally from the storm was ruinous. Once the fourth wealthiest city in the nation, Galveston had lost half of its taxable property in the storm—a loss of over $20 million.

Still, two lessons were learned and put to immediate use: First, a seawall, a foot higher than the highest waves of the 1900 storm was built between the city and the Gulf. It still stands, with one major modification (see following entry).

Second, the Weather Bureau of the United States appointed Dr. Isaac Cline to direct the nation's first scientific study of hurricanes, so that no hurricane would ever again surprise a city quite the way this one did.

UNITED STATES
TEXAS
GALVESTON

August 16, 1915

• • • • • • • • • • • •

Two hundred seventy-five people were killed when the Galveston Seawall, built after the 1900 hurricane, collapsed under the force of the storm surge set in motion by the hurricane of August 16, 1915.

Human beings still try, in spite of experience, to erect structures designed to thwart nature's furies. This futile effort resulted in the construction of the giant seawall at Galveston, Texas after that city was devastated by the great storm of 1900 (see previous entry). The 11-mile-long structure was built of granite, timbers and concrete, 16 feet thick at its base and between 17 and 19 feet high and designed in a concave curve to give it added strength. It was thought to be impermeable to anything natural forces could fling against it.

But like all seawalls, it proved to be no match for nature.

The hurricane of 1915 was first sighted off Cape Verde on August 10, 1915. Barely more than a gale, with winds of 60 mph, it continued on a track that took it past Guadaloupe and Dominica. Fifteen years earlier, the U.S. Weather Bureau would have lost track of it at this point. But, thanks to the efforts of Galvestonian Dr. Isaac Cline, the bureau since 1905 was pinpointing hurricanes with increasing accuracy.

This one cranked its forces up, turned into the Gulf of Mexico, and now, brandishing winds of 120 mph, headed straight for Galveston. Both local and national Weather Bureaus warned of its coming. But the residents of Galveston, for the second time in 15 years, went about their normal business, confident that their new seawall would hold.

When the storm hit, during an abnormally high tide, the waves it pushed ahead of it rose to 21 feet, easily broaching the wall and in some places penetrating it. Water roared into the business district, funneling furiously through its streets and covering them to the second stories of most buildings. Two hundred seventy-five people were drowned or crushed by the force of the water and falling debris, and a record $50 million in damages was caused before the storm roared inland, where it quickly dissipated.

The game survivors of the second Galveston disaster in a decade set about elevating the seawall to a uniform 19.2 feet. No other hurricane for more than 75 years has conquered this man-made structure. Not yet, at least.

UNITED STATES
TEXAS
INDIANOLA

August 19, 1886

• • • • • • • • • • • • •

One hundred seventy-six people lost their lives when a hurricane hit Indianola, Texas on August 19, 1886, absolutely destroying it.

On August 18, 1886, Indianola, Texas was a thriving town. On August 20, 1886, it was totally demolished and later deserted. The cause was a hurricane that slammed into it on August 19, flattening every house and killing 176 people, including its weather observer, I. A. Reed, who, while fleeing from the storm was struck from behind and decapitated by flying timber.

The giant hurricane moved in from the Gulf, first making landfall between Lavaca and Matagorda bays. Its wind velocity was only 72 mph, but its concentrated force, colliding with Indianola in the form of both winds and a storm surge of building-crushing force, flattened, crumbled or gutted every structure in town. What it didn't destroy it washed away, scattering the remains of these structures on the plains beyond.

The following day, the small number of survivors picked through the wreckage of homes, personal possessions and dead animals, which were strewn everywhere. Nothing was salvagable. The town would have to be rebuilt from the bottom up, and rather than do that, its inhabitants decided to leave and settle elsewhere. To this day, only the rubble left from the passage of the storm remains.

WEST INDIES AND FLORIDA
September 16, 1928

• • • • • • • • • • • • •

(See HURRICANES, United States, Florida, Okeechobee, p. 199.)

WEST INDIES
HISPANIOLA

June 1495

• • • • • • • • • • • • •

Christopher Columbus recorded the hurricane that slammed into Hispaniola in June, 1495 and sank the Pinta *and the* Santa Maria. *He did not record human casualties.*

The first hurricane to be documented was recorded by none other than Christopher Columbus. In Hispaniola to rout out and enslave the Indians and establish a colony, Columbus was preparing to leave for home when the hurricane surged out of the Atlantic, crossed the lesser Antilles and slammed into Hispaniola, the second largest island of the West Indies, located between Cuba and Puerto Rico. Discovered and claimed for Spain by Columbus in 1492, the island was a rich trove of subtropical forests and fields, ideal for growing coffee, cocoa and sugarcane.

The native Indians were used to the frequent hurricanes, and Columbus and his crew had encountered one at sea in September of the famous first voyage. Still, he was as helpless as the horrified settlers when this giant storm roared into the island, uprooting trees from the rain-softened ground, toppling them in windrows. Huts were flattened and buried under the whirling mud; some settlers were buried in their crushed dwellings.

In the harbor, ships strained at their anchors, broke loose, turned over and sank. The *Pinta* and *Santa Maria* both went to watery graves, with some hands aboard. Only the *Nina* remained afloat.

It would take 10 months for Columbus to salvage enough from the wreckage of the two sunken caravels to build another, which he called the *Santa Cruz.* During that time he also built more forts on the island, exacted tributes of gold from the Indians under threat of slavery or death, and, besting the record of the hurricane, killed or hunted down with dogs thousands of native Indians.

WEST INDIES
TROIS-ISLETS

August 12, 1766

• • • • • • • • • • • • •

The ruination caused by the hurricane of August 12, 1766, on Trois-Islets, a small village on Martinique, set in motion a succession of events that would eventually unite Napoleon Bonaparte and his future empress, Josephine.

In the French West Indies, 1765 and 1766 were bad years for hurricanes. And the small village of Trois-Islets, which clings to the rocky southern coast of Martinique and is composed of a few narrow houses, a cobbled square and a church, was hit particularly hard in the middle of the second season.

History would probably have passed by Trois-Islets had it not been for the fact that in 1763, in this tiny town, the wife of Lieutenant Joseph-Gaspard Tascher gave birth to her second girl, Marie Josephine Rose, who would later, as the wife of Napoleon Bonaparte, be known as Empress Josephine of France.

On the night of August 12, 1766, a storm slammed into Trois-Islets, collapsing many of the town's houses, uprooting trees, flooding the sugarcane fields, and collapsing the slave quarters on "La Pagerie," the sugar plantation owned by Lieutenant Tascher.

As the fury of the storm mounted past midnight, slaves escaped from their smashed huts and huddled in the mansion with the Tascher family.

But the mansion proved no match for the storm. Tiles blew off the roof, then the entire roof was lifted off and the screaming wind and torrential rain rushed in, forcing both family and slaves to flee to the shelter of an old stone sugar house whose walls were two feet thick.

The following day, the plantation lay in ruins. Tascher was forced to sell his slaves, and for the next 10 years, Josephine would grow up in the stone sugar house. She was eventually bundled off to France, where she married a nobleman who was decapitated during the Revolution. She returned to Martinique and the old sugar mill, and finally, as a merry widow, returned to France with a ticket to immortality.

ICESTORMS AND SNOWSTORMS

. . . .

THE WORST RECORDED ICESTORMS AND SNOWSTORMS

• • • • •

* Detailed in text

ICESTORMS

France
* Chartres (1359)

India
Moradabad (1853)
* Moradabad (1888)

United States
Central (1951)
South (1948)

SNOWSTORMS

Bulgaria
(1936)

Europe
* (1956)

Himalayans
* (1950)

Iran
(1972)

Japan
(1931)

Sweden
(1719)

Turkistan (Djetisusisk)

(1928)

United States
Atlantic Coast (1922)
California
(1952)
* Truckee Pass (Donner Party) (1846–1847)
* East (1947)
* (1958)
New England (1898)
* Northeast (1888)
* Northeast (1958—March)
Northwest (1891)
Southwest (1886)

CHRONOLOGY

• • • • • • • • •

ICESTORMS

1359
* Chartres, France
1853
Moradabad, India
1888
April 30
* Moradabad, India
1948
January 24
Southern United States
1951
November 2
Central United States

SNOWSTORMS

1719
Sweden
1846–1847
October 28, 1846–April 21, 1847
* Truckee Pass, California
(Donner Party)

1886
January 6–13
Southwestern United States
1888
March 11–14
* Northeast United States
1891
February 8
Northwest United States
1898
January 31
New England, United States
1922
January 27–28
Atlantic Coast, United States
1928
January 12
Turkistan (Djetisusisk)
1931
January 12
Japan
1936
February 11

Bulgaria
1947
December 26
* Eastern United States
1950
November–December
* Himalayas
1952
January 13
California
1956
January–February
* Europe
1958
February 7–10
* Eastern United States
February 15–16
* Northeastern United States
March 19–22
Northeastern United States
1972
February 10
Iran

. . . . .

ICESTORMS

. . . . .

Icestorms may precede or follow snowstorms and are usually composed of a combination of sleet and hail.

Sleet is precipitation of small, partially melted grains of ice. These grains of ice are formed in two ways, either by drops of rain falling through a layer of air with a temperature below freezing, or from snowflakes that have fallen through a layer of air with a temperature above freezing. Unlike hail, which can fall at any time of the year, sleet only falls in winter.

Although sleet is an annoyance, it rarely causes the wholesale disruption that hail does, and thus, the casualties and damage figures in the following section will be entirely attributable to the effects of hailstones.

Hail is precipitation in the form of pellets of ice or a combination of ice and snow. Usually, hailstorms occur during the passage of a cold front, or during a thunderstorm.

Small hailstones are simple structures formed when the surfaces of snow clumps melt and re-freeze, or become coated with water droplets which subsequently freeze. Thus, they have a soft center and a hard outer coating.

Large hailstones, which have diameters of from one-half inch to—in rare cases—five inches, are more complex, and the theories on their formation vary. Generally, they are composed of alternating layers of hard and soft ice. One theory has it that they are formed in clouds, when supercooled raindrops freeze on dust particles or snowflakes. These tiny hailstones are then blown upward and downward, repeatedly, by winds within the cloud. Each time they descend and pass through a region whose temperature is above freezing, they collect moisture, and each time they are blown upward into a region in which the temperature is below freezing, they either freeze or accumulate a layer of snow. The stones continue to grow until they reach a weight that the winds will no longer support, after which they fall to the ground.

Another theory suggests that hailstones fall through varying pockets of air, gaining layers by passing through air containing varying amounts of water.

Whatever the method of formation, falling hailstones have caused astonishing damage and loss of life.

. . . .

FRANCE
CHARTRES

1359
. . . .

One thousand men and 6,000 horses in the army of Edward III were killed by a destructive hailstorm in 1359 near Chartres, France.

In 1359, if old chronicles are to be believed, one of the most prodigious and devastating hailstorms of all time struck the army of Edward III, just outside of Chartres.

It occurred during the 22nd year of the Hundred Years' War. Edward, claiming the French crown, had already captured Calais and Crecy and approached Chartres heading an elite corps of horsemen and soldiers.

Suddenly, a fierce rain and lightning storm struck the army. Within moments, raindrops had turned to hailstones the size of goose eggs, which, in a matter of moments, pounded some 1,000 men and 6,000 horses to death.

Reversing his trek towards Chartres, Edward escaped unharmed and went on to sign the treaty of Calais with Philip of Burgundy.

INDIA
MORADABAD

April 30, 1888

• • • • • • • • • • • • • • •

Two hundred fifty people died in India's worst hailstorm on April 30, 1888.

In the same year that the famous blizzard of '88 pounded the Northeastern United States with high winds and snow (see p. 227), the worst hailstorm in the history of India killed 250 people, caused widespread havoc among livestock, and atomized windows, glass doors and unreinforced roofs.

Older residents of India were no strangers to damaging icestorms. In 1853, a hailstorm pounded 84 people and 3,000 head of cattle to death, and in 1855, another storm killed dozens of farmers in the fields of Naini Tal.

But for sheer fury and damage, the 1888 storm was considered to be the worst, since it was accompanied by a giant windstorm that lifted roofs, uprooted porches, shook walls and drove hailstones said to be the size of eggs and oranges into buildings, animals and people.

When it was over, ridges of ice one- to two-feet deep remained on the ground, and buildings looked as if they had been pummeled with giant lances. The bodies of farmers and livestock beaten to death by the hail laid partially buried in the white carpet of ice that would soon melt in the spring heat.

SNOWSTORMS

Snow in its most benign form is what children and romantics wait for from the first turn of the calendar towards November and the first drop of the thermometer below freezing. Snow has a way of softening the sharp edges of urban environments and providing the tools of play for imaginative youngsters.

But in its less benign form, when it roars into our lives in the form of a blizzard, it can be a killer.

Snow itself is precipitation formed by the sublimation of water vapor into solid crystals at temperatures below freezing. This sublimation generally takes place around a dust particle, in the same way that rain drops are formed, except that snowflakes emerge as symmetrical, hexagonal crystals, no two of which are alike. The difference in size and shape is the result of the matting together of several crystals, caused by the descent of these snowflakes through air warmer than that of the cloud in which they originated.

On an average, 10 inches of snow is equivalent to 1 inch of rain, and the factors determining rainfall are roughly those affecting snowfall.

Blizzards, then, are winter storms that are characterized by low temperatures, high winds and driving snow, as a hurricane is characterized by tropical temperatures, high wind and driving rain. According to the U.S. Weather Bureau, which evolved the parameters of blizzards in a 1958 definition, a snowstorm becomes a blizzard when the winds reach 35 mph, and the temperature dips below 20°F. In the U.S., blizzards are most common in the Northern Great Plains States, but they also occur as far south as Texas and as far east as Maine.

EUROPE

January–February 1956

Nearly 1,000 died in a record series of snowstorms that blanketed Europe in January and February 1956.

One of the fiercest winters on record gripped the entire European continent in January and February 1956. Close to 1,000 people died as a result of prolonged cold and a repeated series of blizzards that roared out of Siberia and blanketed Europe from Norway to the Mediterranean with repeated, paralyzing snowstorms. The French Riviera received its first snow in years, and the first snow in memory blanketed parts of North Africa.

Adding to the danger of frostbite and exposure, roving bands of wolves and wild boar, forced from their lairs to forage for food, wandered into villages. Near Kalambaka in central Greece, a pack of wolves attacked children returning home from school. In Italy, Germany and Belgium, similar attacks occurred.

The capital cities of Paris, London, Madrid and Athens were brought to a standstill by the numbing cold and ferocious blizzard conditions.

While the northern countries such as Norway, Denmark, Sweden, West Germany and Czechoslovakia merely suffered the effects of a particularly severe winter, the Mediterranean area experienced extreme economic damage because of the annihilation of its crops.

In Italy, fruit and vegetable crops were severely damaged. Spain suffered close to $100 million in agricultural damage. Citrus crops, hit with the cold before they could be picked, were totally destroyed. Fifty thousand people employed in the citrus groves of the southeast Mediterranean seaboard were thrown out of work.

Olive groves in both Spain and Greece were ravaged. In Greece alone, frost and flood damage to crops, trees, livestock and installations such as bridges, dams and culverts was estimated at millions of dollars.

In Turkey, the effects of the cold produced huge floods, particularly in Thrace and along the Ceyhan River in southern Turkey.

In mid-February 1956, President Dwight Eisenhower sent millions of dollars in supplies and seed for replanting crops to stricken countries who requested aid.

HIMALAYAS

November–December 1950

• • • • • • • • • • • • • • • •

Over 500 perished in the horrific trek of several thousand refugees from Communist China through the high passes of the Himalayas in November and December 1950.

The background of the story begins in 1948, when Chinese Communists conquered most of Northern China. By 1949, all of the Chinese Nationalists were driven off the Chinese Mainland, and the People's Republic of China was established, with Mao Tse-tung as Chairman and Chou En-lai as Premier and Foreign Minister.

By 1950, the Chinese Communists were in firm control, joining North Korea in pushing U.N. forces under General Douglas MacArthur back from the Manchurian border to the 38th parallel.

These are the neat lines of history. Contained within them are the human stories of refugees and loyalists to the Nationalist regime who were forced to flee from their destroyed homes.

In early November 1950, several thousand Muslim Chinese set out with food, provisions and what they could salvage of their possessions to emigrate over the Himalayan passes into India. Like the Donner Party (see following entry), they were not seasoned travelers, and numbered among them wealthy dignitaries. In this case, the dignitaries—Isa Yusuf, Secretary General of the former Nationalist Government of Sinkiang, and Colonel J. A. Sabri, formerly of the Nationalist Army garrison in Sinkiang's capital, Urumchi—may have unwittingly contributed to the tragedy, for when 50 caravans reached the China-India border in mid-November, Communist soldiers detained them for weeks, forcing them to surrender arms, extra clothing and valuables.

Yusuf and Mohammed Amin, Deputy Governor of the province, were imprisoned, and Yusuf was hanged by his wrists from a rafter in the makeshift prison for an entire night. The remainder of the refugee party was forced to remain nearby, and in so doing, consumed half of their food supply.

The party finally set forth toward the Himalayan passes in early December—far too late in the year for safe passage through trails that often climbed to 18,000 feet. Yusuf and Amin finally bribed their guards and escaped, joining the remainder of the refugees as they set out to climb into swirling snowstorms which coated ice-plated trails.

All of the travelers began the passage on horseback. But as they reached higher elevations the snow accumulated to a depth of six feet and the horses died. The thin air made the blood gush from the nostrils of humans and horses alike, and headaches were constant and debilitating.

As the horses began to perish, some of the refugees were forced to wait behind. The first of the band began to die from the exposure and cold.

At night, the caravans attempted to make camp on the glassy ice, but many had no tents and lay exposed to the elements. Mothers with nursing children found their bones frozen into hunched positions as they tried to shelter the infants in their arms. Extremities—both hands and feet—began to freeze.

As the bands of refugees plodded through the treacherous ice and snow in a desperate race against dwindling supplies, they were forced to abandon relatives and friends. Those who stayed behind to help died by the side of the trail.

One man left his wife in the snow to push on with their three small children. Half an hour later, he was able to obtain a horse. He mounted it and went back for his wife, and found her frozen to death in the snow. By the time he had returned to his children, they were suffering from frostbite.

Finally, near Christmas, the survivors of the trek reached Leh, the 12,000-foot-high capital of Ladakh Province in Kashmir. Two hundred remained there, some 700 miles from their starting point. The remainder went on to Srinagar, where winter deepened, darkening the plight of those who were still suffering from frozen extremities. Secretary General Yusuf brought his family of five through safely only to see his 7-year-old daughter die in Srinagar on Christmas Day of tetanus resulting from frozen feet. Days later, his 8-year-old son's frostbitten foot had to be amputated.

Altogether, nearly one-quarter of the several thousand who began the trip through the Himalayas perished, and those who survived would be forever scarred by the experience.

UNITED STATES
CALIFORNIA
TRUCKEE PASS

October 28, 1846–April 21, 1847

• • • • • • • • • • • • • • • •

Approximately 100 members of the Donner Party, a group of pioneers ill-suited for pioneering, perished in the snows of Truckee Pass, California in the winter of 1846–1847.

The Donner Party, about which volumes have been written, was a group of slightly more than a hundred businessmen and their families who had decided to quit the relatively humdrum existence of Springfield, Illinois for the untested promise of California.

Led by Jacob Donner and James F. Reed, they began their westward journey on April 14, 1846, but through a series of mishaps and misfortunes, did not reach the most treacherous terrain of their trip until October. Some accounts state that they were warned not to attempt to cross the Sierras until spring; others that they were promised safe passage by guides who later abandoned them. At any rate, around 90 of the party reached Truckee Lake (now known as Donner Lake) high in the Sierras, on October 28, 1846. And there, the snow began to fall, in great, blustering abundance.

The group hastily began to erect shelters, which, from their very concept, were inadequate. There was no time to build cabins; tents and lean-tos were all they could manage. An account by one of the survivors states, "The snow came on so suddenly that we had barely time to pitch our tent, and put up a brush shed . . . one side of which was open. This brush shed was covered with pine boughs, and then covered with rubber coats, quilts, etc. . . ."

The storm continued, day and night. All of the passes through the Sierras were blocked by the steadily accumulating snow. Hunting parties that went out for food supplies came back empty-handed. From October to mid-December, several unsuccessful attempts were made to drive men and cattle through the waste-high snow to the summit. All failed.

Food supplies continued to dwindle. First cattle, then horses, and finally dogs were killed, dried and eaten. Finally, on December 16, a party of 17 men and women, led by poet-woodsman C. T. Stanton, set off in desperation to scale the summit and bring help to the slowly starving inhabitants at the Donner camp. They were apparently the first to revert to cannibalism when their meager supplies of six days' worth of dried beef gave out, and their fellow explorers died around them. Stanton, their leader, was one of the first to perish. Three days after the

beginning of the trek, he went snowblind, and two days after that, he built a tiny fire, wrote a poem to his dead mother, and died.

On the survivors battled, through sudden blizzards and waist-high drifts. Two Indian guides were killed and eaten by the dwindling band of semi-delirious travelers.

Thirty-two days later, on January 17, 1847, seven survivors reached an Indian camp on the western slopes of the Sierras. Gaunt, ravaged, sometimes unintelligible, they pleaded with whomever would listen to them to send rescue parties to bring back the remaining men, women and children who might still survive at the camp on Truckee Lake.

One of the men who immediately set out with a rescue party was James Reed, one of the original organizers of the party, who had been exiled from it at the beginning of October when he had killed another man in a fight. Ironically, Reed had reached California safely, while his wife and children remained at the top of the pass.

Back at Truckee Lake, Jacob Donner, the party's other organizer, was dead. The only food available was green rawhide, which was boiled down to a barely edible, glue-like substance. But even that gave out, and, when the children began to die, these survivors also turned to cannibalism, stripping the flesh from those who were dying around them each day.

The misery mounted; the snows continued. Finally, the first of three rescue parties sponsored by the philanthropic California pioneer Captain J. A. Sutter broke through the summit snow and reached the horror of the Donner campsite on February 19, 1847. What they saw was indescribable. Skeletons, their flesh half ripped away, and the remnants of shelters littered the snow. In the midst of this, looking scarcely different from the corpses, was a gaunt band of 48 survivors, some of them already insane.

James Reed arrived in the second party. His wife and two daughters had survived, and would write about their experience later. Trials were held, murder charges were brought against those who had reverted to cannibalism, and then dropped. There was simply no precedent for the horrors experienced by the Donner Party.

UNITED STATES
EAST

December 26, 1947

• • • • • • • • • • • • • • • •

Fifty-five died in a colossal snowstorm that paralyzed New York City and its suburbs, Connecticut and New Jersey on December 26, 1947. The storm established a new record for snowfall in the area.

An extraordinarily vicious snowstorm swept in from the Atlantic at 5:25 A.M. on December 26, 1947, descending upon the eastern U.S., and eclipsing the previous snowfall record of the fabled Blizzard of '88 (see p. 227) in 12 hours. It took 30 hours for the 1888 storm to accumulate 20.9 inches; during the 1947 storm, from 5:30 A.M. until midnight of the 26th, 25.8 inches of snow paralyzed New York City. At times, the snowfall exceeded three inches an hour.

The only benign aspect of this storm was the fact that it was not, as in 1888, accompanied by hurricane force winds. Thus, it did not qualify as a full-fledged blizzard. Still, 99 million tons of snow fell on New York City alone and brought the huge city and other parts of the eastern seaboard as far north as northern Connecticut and as far south as Washington, D.C. to an absolute, silent standstill.

Fifty-five people died, some of exposure, some of heart attacks from shoveling snow, some in fires ignited by makeshift heating devices invented when power lines weighted with ice were severed. One hundred eighty fires were reported in the first 24 hours after the snowfall ended in New York City, further straining the 25,000 police and firemen already battling the snow. In Philadelphia, five brick buildings in the downtown warehouse and wholesale district burned out of control, causing an estimated $1 million in damage. Four hundred firemen, hampered by icy streets and residual snow, battled the blaze for nearly five hours before bringing it under control. Two of them received leg fractures when a brick wall collapsed on a fire engine; eight others were less seriously hurt. Only the fact that the buildings were commercial properties, unoccupied during the weekend, accounted for the relatively low number of casualties.

Public transportation on the eastern seaboard ground to a muted stop for two days. Mayor William O'Dwyer, in California for the Christmas holidays, could not return to New York until Sunday, three days after the storm struck. He immediately went on radio, assuring the public that his deputy mayor, Vincent Impelliteri, had kept the wheels of the city moving, and that food and fuel supplies would soon be getting through to the snow-locked city.

Seventy-three freighters, loading or unloading on the then-busy docks of New York City and Hoboken, New Jersey were forced to suspend activities. Because of low visibility, decks banked high with snow and the absence of docking crews, five passenger liners either did not leave on time or docked late. The *Queen Mary* postponed a scheduled sailing for 12 hours, awaiting most of her 860 passengers, who could not get to the dock. Snow prevented the Coast Guard from maintaining its watch at Breezy Point for three days. Some commuter trains were stalled for up to 14 hours on runs that normally took under an hour to accomplish. Abandoned cars tied up main thoroughfares for a week.

Some price gouging was reported, with some New York City cabdrivers charging the equivalent of weekly salaries for rides. In one part of the Washington Heights section of Manhattan a grocer was cited for charging 35 cents for a quart of milk and 24 cents for a loaf of bread.

Still, tales of heroism abounded. Volunteers from the wartime Civilian Defense Corps, the army, navy and Red Cross put themselves at New York City's disposal. State troopers of the Hawthorne Barracks in Westchester County, north of New York City, wearing snow shoes, hauled toboggans loaded with milk, bread and other foods to marooned residents.

An unidentified young sailor rescued a 50-year-old bridge operator who had been trapped in a snow-covered automobile for 21 hours a half mile away from his job at the Mill Basin Bridge in Brooklyn.

A policeman delivered a baby in Maspeth, Queens when the family doctor could not make it through the drifts in time.

Police cars were used for ambulances when ambulances could not get through snow clogged streets. The Morro Limousine Service in Brooklyn could not free its 18 limousines for ambulance service, and began to receive an average of 25 calls an hour to transport sick persons to hospitals. Radio station WNEW broadcast an appeal for horse-drawn sleds to transport the sick, and the need was met.

In one bizarre case, policemen who pursued a larceny suspect in Harlem had to carry him to a hospital after they had shot him in the legs. No ambulance was available.

Metropolitan Opera star James Melton, who lived on a farm six miles from Westport, Connecticut, shoveled snow from his backyard on the Saturday afternoon after the storm so that a chartered helicopter could land and take him to LaGuardia Field. From here, a limousine scooped him up and got him to his engagement on the Metropolitan's Opera Quiz of the Air. Still wearing his raccoon coat, Melton dashed to the broadcasting room. Boris Goldovsky, who had been pinch-hitting, shifted over and the panting singer expressed his opinion about American opera and volunteered an answer about off-stage music in *Don Giovanni*.

Also admirable was the performance of the post office, which, demonstrated its slogan, "Neither sleet, nor snow, nor dark of night shall stay these couriers. . . ." Mail deliveries took place on time, even at the height of the storm.

UNITED STATES
EAST

February 7–10, 1958

• • • • • • • • • • • • • • •

A monumental blizzard swept through the entire United States, from the Rocky Mountains to the eastern seaboard from February 7 through 10, 1958. Sixty died and cities were immobilized from upstate New York to Jackson, Mississippi.

One of the most severe blizzards on record swept through the United States from the Rocky Mountains to the eastern seaboard for three days in February, 1958, killing 60 people, stranding tens of thousands, and causing economic damage in the hundreds of thousands of dollars.

Upstate New York was hit the hardest, when a series of new storms swirled in on February 9, blowing 40 inches of snow into drifts up to 15 feet high, snarling transportation, marooning hundreds, immobilizing industries and closing schools and businesses. Twenty-six inches of snow fell overnight between February 9 and 10, stranding 50,000 workers in the Syracuse-Utica area. The General Electric Company shut down all four of its plants in Utica. By early afternoon on Monday, all of the airports in the region had suspended activity.

The entire New York Thruway was closed off, and stalled vehicles dotted the roads in most of New York State. In Baldwinsville, on the outskirts of Syracuse, the faint sound of an automobile horn led rescuers to a car buried beneath a huge drift. It had been there for two days. Inside the car was a woman with both of her legs frozen. Her husband lay dead beside her.

At Augusta, in central New York, state police abandoned a stalled patrol car and trudged 15 miles on snowshoes to aid a marooned farm wife and her eight children. The family was taken to shelter on toboggans.

Milk farmers in Ontario and Tompkins counties were forced to dump their milk because they could not deliver it. One dairy that normally shipped 84,000 quarts a day was only able to deliver 9,000 at the height of the storm.

The effects of the blizzard and cold extended offshore and into the South. The Cunard liner *Saxonia* battled fierce headwinds and ferocious seas for 36 hours before finally limping into port in New York City. Up to two inches of snow fell as far south as Vicksburg and Jackson, Mississippi. In that state, bus service was suspended, schools were closed and motorists were warned to stay off highways.

UNITED STATES
NORTHEAST

March 11–14, 1888

• • • • • • • • • • • • • • •

Four hundred people died in the Blizzard of '88, which raged in the northeastern United States from March 11 through 14, 1888.

The famous "Blizzard of '88" was a four-day, raging snow-and-wind storm that claimed 400 lives and $7 million in property damage in an area that extended from Maryland to Maine. Its fury was particularly felt in New York City, where wind gusts climbed to nearly 100 mph, the snowfall exceeded 20 inches and drifts climbed to heights of nearly 20 feet.

Occurring at a time when weather forecasting was decidedly unsophisticated, the storm was at first greeted with the innocent joy most snowstorms receive. But by midnight, most East Coast cities had lost not only power, fire alarm systems and transportation facilities but hope that the snow would ever end.

By the second day of this roaring blizzard, sustained by hurricane force winds, the frozen bodies of homeward bound office workers began to dot the drifts. Those foolhardy enough to venture out into the raging storm sank up to their armpits in snow. By the end of the second day, Boston, New York and most large cities had been brought to a virtual standstill. Hotels were packed to capacity, their lobbies carpeted with sleeping refugees from the storm, which continued to howl into its third day.

Telephone and telegraph lines were downed and communication, even within major cities, was impossible. The major stock exchanges were closed for three days. Without power, without light, families built fires to survive, often igniting their homes in the process. Fire companies could not be contacted, or, if reached, could not get through the towering drifts.

Equally destructive were the winds. Fishing boats off the coast and even in harbors were swamped and sunk. Walls and roofs of houses were torn away, and the families within the homes froze to death, or, after finally being rescued and given shelter, died from the effects of prolonged exposure to the cold and the elements.

By the second day of the storm, all manner of improvised shelters were full to overflowing.

On March 13, a bridge of ice appeared, spanning the East River between Manhattan and Queens. Some foolhardy adventurers tried to cross it and were pitched into the icy waters when a change of tide shattered the bridge.

The winds calmed and the snow diminished to flurries on March 14, and a combination of bonfires and an

A bustling New York City was brought to a standstill by the famed blizzard of 1888. The corner of Pierpoint and Fulton streets, normally awash in activity, is a quiet snowscape on the day following the storm. Library of Congress.

emerging, warm March sun melted the mountains of snow quickly, but the cleaning up, restoration of power, and the counting of the dead would go on for months.

UNITED STATES
NORTHEAST

February 15–16, 1958

• • • • • • • • • • • • • •

Only five days after a monster blizzard struck the eastern United States, an even more severe snowstorm blanketed the Northeast on February 15 and 16, 1958. Over 500 died and the entire Northeast, from Washington D.C. to Maine was immobilized.

The worst snowstorm in U.S. history from the viewpoint of human casualties struck the Northeast on February 15, 1958. More than 500 persons were killed, and millions of dollars in crop and property damage resulted from this two-day blizzard that brought the nation's capital to a complete standstill, and left only the janitor to answer the telephone at the U.S. Weather Bureau.

Various cities and their populations experienced various depths of snow and cold. It was 48 degrees below zero in Wisconsin and 26 degrees below zero in Bismarck, North Dakota. Lebanon, New Hampshire recorded a record snow depth of 60 inches, and Michigan City, Indiana was buried beneath 54 inches of closely packed snow. For the first time in history, the locks at Lake Michigan were frozen shut by ice blocks eight feet thick.

New York City was virtually closed down, as its new snow-fighting equipment, purchased after the 25.8-inch snowfall of 1947 (see p. 225), failed to open public thoroughfares.

The Beltway outside of Baltimore was completely shut down when two tractor trailers jackknifed across its entire width. Some of the passengers and drivers in the thousands of cars halted by the accident died of frostbite.

At nearby Bowie racetrack, over 4,000 fans were stranded by the onset of the fast-moving storm. As quickly as state troopers in half-tracks and jeeps opened the access road to the track, gale winds closed it behind them. Eventually, they too were stranded with the 4,000 sports enthusiasts at the track. It would be another day before all would be rescued by emergency Pennsylvania Railroad trains.

On February 16, Washington D.C. resembled a ghost town. Over 80 percent of government employees did not report for work. No transportation—public or otherwise—operated in the paralyzed seat of national government until late on the second day of the storm.

TORNADOES

. . . .

THE WORST RECORDED TORNADOES

CHRONOLOGY

1896
  May 27
    • St. Louis, Missouri
1903
  June 1
    • Gainesville, Georgia
1913
  March 23
    • Omaha, Nebraska
  December 11
    Freetown, Sierra Leone
1917
  May 26–27
    • Midwest and South United
      States
1920
  March 28
    • Chicago, Illinois
  April 20
    Southern United States
1924
  April 29–30
    • Southern United States
1925
  March 18
    • Illinois, Indiana and Missouri
1927
  May 9
    • Poplar Bluff, Missouri
  September 29
    • St. Louis, Missouri
1932
  March 21–22

  Southern United States
1936
  April 2–6
    • Southern United States
  October 30
    India
1938
  September 29
    • Charleston, South Carolina
1942
  June 12
    • Oklahoma City, Oklahoma
1945
  April 12
    • Oklahoma, Arkansas and
      Missouri
1947
  April 9
    • Southwestern United States
1951
  January 4
    Madagascar
  June 8–10
    Southern United States
1953
  May 11
    • Waco, Texas
  June 8
    • Flint, Michigan
  June 9
    • Worcester, Massachusetts
1955
  May 25

    • Udall, Kansas
1965
  April 11
    • Midwestern United States
1967
  September 20
    Texas
1970
  April 30
    • Oklahoma City, Oklahoma
1971
  February 21
    Natchez, Mississippi
1972
  April 2
    Bangladesh
1973
  April 13
    Bangladesh
1974
  April 3
    Xenia, Ohio
1984
  March 29
    • North and South Carolina
1985
  May 31
    • Northeast United States
1987
  May 22
    Saragosa, Texas

234

• • • • •

TORNADOES

• • • • •

In contrast to a cyclone, a tornado covers a relatively small area of ground. But it is also much more violent and destructive. In fact, for sheer, concentrated energy, there is very little else in nature that compares to this kind of storm.

There is no doubting a tornado by those who see it coming, or hear its explicit, roaring freight-train sound. Surrounded by rain, thunder and lightning, a dark, funnel-shaped cloud extends from the cumulonimbus cloud from which it was formed to the ground. Within this funnel, air rotates violently. The tornado rises and falls, twists about, and wherever it touches earth, it causes instant and enormous destruction.

The diameter of a tornado ranges in size from a few feet to a mile. Within it, there are two types of violent wind: the winds rotating in its walls can achieve speeds of 200 to 300 mph; the winds in its updraft at the center may reach 200 mph.

The atmospheric conditions necessary for the formation of a tornado include high humidity, great thermal instability and the convergence of warm, moist air at low levels with cooler, drier air aloft—a condition that explains the frequent presence of tornadoes within or accompanying hurricanes.

Tornadoes can travel distances from a few feet to a hundred miles, usually in a northeasterly direction at a speed of between 20 and 40 mph. In the U.S., the greatest concentration of tornadoes is usually over the central and southern plains and the Gulf states.

• • • • • • • • • • • • • • • •

ENGLAND
WIDECOMBE-IN-THE-MOOR

October 21, 1638

• • • • • • • • • • • • • •

Fifty members of a congregation were killed and 12 were injured when a tornado entered a church in Widecombe-in-the-Moor, England, on October 21, 1638, during a Sunday service.

The tiny hamlet of Widecombe-in-the-Moor earned itself the sub-title of "The Evil One's Residency" when a tornado struck it on Sunday morning, October 21, 1638. Local authorities blamed the devil for timing the arrival of the storm to coincide with the commencement of the morning worship service, when the entire population of the town was gathered within the hamlet's only church.

Lightning often accompanies tornadoes, and in this case, a fireball was unleashed as lightning struck the church just as the storm's winds arrived. According to records left by parishoners, ". . . most part of [the congregation] fell downe into their seates, and some upon their knees, some on their faces, and some one upon another, with a great cry of burning and scalding, they all giving themselves up for dead . . ." and one Mistress Ditford reported that she had ". . . her gowne, two wastcoates, and linnen next to her body burned cleane off."

Far worse, however, seemed to be the effect of the twister itself, which apparently entered the church, flinging the congregation against the stone walls of the structure, killing 50 people and injuring 12 more.

UNITED STATES
GEORGIA
GAINESVILLE

June 1, 1903

• • • • • • • • • • • • • •

Two hundred three people were killed and thousands were injured when a tornado struck Gainesville, Georgia at the beginning of the shift in the local cotton mill on June 1, 1903.

The worst storm disaster in the southern United States to that date occurred on the morning of June 1, 1903, when a twister slammed into Gainesville, Georgia. The characteristic, dark and funnel-shaped cloud appeared suddenly, with little warning, and most of the fatalities occurred in the downtown area, where people were instantly buried under collapsing and exploding buildings.

The storm arrived at precisely the hour that 750 employees of the city's largest cotton mill punched in for the day. The twister hit the mill broadside, crushing parts of it, and flinging other sections scores of feet into the air. In the mill and in the city 203 persons died, and nearly a thousand were seriously injured. (See also TORNADOES, United States, South, 1936, p. 247.)

UNITED STATES
ILLINOIS
CHICAGO

March 28, 1920

• • • • • • • • • • • • • • •

The worst tornado to strike Chicago killed 28, injured 325 and destroyed 113 buildings on March 28, 1920.

Twenty-eight people lost their lives when the great tornado of March 28, 1920, slashed through Chicago. Three hundred twenty-five people were injured, 113 buildings, were demolished and over $3 million in property damage made this the most destructive of the six major tornadoes to strike this city. (Others hit on May 25, 1896; April 6, 1912; May 18, 1926; April 1, 1929 and May 1, 1933.)

The storm remained chiefly in the northwestern portion of Chicago, centering on Melrose Park, in which 10 people died. It was an unusual storm that included huge hailstones, along with the thunder, lightning and rain that accompanied its path. Power lines were snapped like toothpicks. Animals were flung crazily about. Streetcars and automobiles were overturned. A freight car, packed with 1,500 pounds of unidentified cargo, was lifted 40 feet in the air and deposited on the roof of a train station.

The storm lasted only an hour, from 12:15 to 1:15 P.M. But to those caught in it, it seemed to last for decades.

UNITED STATES
ILLINOIS, INDIANA AND MISSOURI

March 18, 1925

• • • • • • • • • • • • • •

Six hundred eighty-nine people died, 2,000 were injured and over 15,000 were made homeless by the tornado that rolled through Illinois, Indiana and Missouri on March 18, 1925.

Ordinarily, tornadoes give warning of their coming by their characteristic funnel-shaped clouds. Ordinarily, tornadoes move at approximately 45 mph for roughly 13 miles in a path that is usually less than a quarter of a mile wide. But the famous tri-state tornado, a storm that has been called ". . . perhaps the worst tornado that has ever occurred anywhere in the world . . . ," defied all of these rules. Its path was three-quarters of a mile wide. It traveled for 219 miles. And worst of all, its covering cloud was so close to the ground that hardly anyone saw the hidden funnel within it. Thus, the 689 who were killed, the 2,000 who were injured and the more than 15,000 who were rendered homeless in the three hours and 18 minutes of the storm's fury probably never knew what hit them.

Formed by the collective massing of a cold low pressure system from Canada and a warm and wet low pressure system from the Gulf of Mexico, the tri-state tornado was one of eight that formed on the morning of March 18, 1925.

It first touched the ground at about 1 P.M. in Reynolds County, Missouri and then began its 60-mph race toward the northeast. Eleven people died, buildings were collapsed and trees uprooted as it roared towards the Mississippi River.

Across the river, Gorham, Illinois was totally obliterated by the storm. Ninety people were killed and 200 were injured.

The same fate awaited the larger city of Murphysboro, which was also left in ruins seconds after the storm struck. Over 150 of the 200 blocks that comprised the city were totally destroyed; 234 people were crushed by falling buildings; 800 were injured; 11 steam engines lay on their sides in the railroad yard. The fires, some of which accounted for the fact that more than 8,000 people would be homeless by nightfall, raged without control. The town's water supply had also been destroyed by the storm.

DeSoto, Illinois felt a particular fury from the tornado, which was described by resident F. M. Hewitt as a ". . . seething, boiling mass of clouds whose color constantly changed. From the upper portion came a roaring noise as of many trains. Below this cloud was a tapering dark cloud mass reaching earthward."

Wooden houses were blown apart as if dynamited. A mother and her two-week-old baby miraculously survived when falling roof timbers formed a protective tent over their bed. The 100 who died in DeSoto died violently, many of them through dismemberment or from splinters of wood that were driven into them by the wind with the force of bullets.

The storm seemed to feed on destruction, gathering power and speed. Near Zeigler, Illinois it lifted the Illinois Central Railroad Bridge from its concrete base. Sixty-four houses were destroyed within two minutes, and 127 people were killed. A two-by-four plank was driven through the side of a metal railroad car. Nearby, a large plank was driven so far into a tree that a man could later stand on the end of the plank without budging it.

As the storm continued on, it picked up a huge grain binder and carried it for a quarter of a mile; further on, it gathered up a touring car and blew it 225 feet through the air before dropping it to the ground. A barber chair was discovered later in a field, miles from the nearest barber shop. A school building was destroyed, but its 16 pupils were picked up and deposited, unhurt, 150 yards away.

Griffin, Indiana was totally destroyed. Thirty-four people were killed, and every house was so badly damaged that there was no shelter left in the town for the survivors.

Finally, at 4:18 P.M., the tornado blew itself out near Princeton, Indiana, but not before cutting a grim path of destruction through that town. It demolished buildings, flung furniture and belongings over the countryside, and in one case, popped open the doors of a car containing four miners, pulled the passengers and driver from the car, dropped them, unhurt by the side of the road and tore the car into little pieces, scattering its remains along several miles of road.

UNITED STATES
KANSAS
IRVING

May 30, 1879

• • • • • • • • • • • • • •

Fifty people were killed and the entire town of Irving, Kansas was leveled by a multiple-barreled tornado on May 30, 1879.

One normal size tornado hit the tiny town of Irving, Kansas on the late afternoon of May 30, 1879. It caused minimal damage and no loss of life, and the inhabitants were just picking themselves up and brushing themselves off when the sky turned an unearthly black, shot through with red and purple flashes that seemed to give off smoky, sulfurous fumes. It was a mass of whirling, superheated air that contained in its two-mile-wide swath not one, but a dozen tornadoes.

Within minutes, the bundle of storms had slammed into the little town, leveling or blowing apart every building, leaving behind them the sort of scene that only a cosmic steamroller could have created. Records on the frontier were casual in 1879; around 50 people were killed, according to reports, but no estimate was made regarding either the injured or property damage.

UNITED STATES
KANSAS
UDALL

May 25, 1955

• • • • • • • • • • • • • •

One hundred one people died and at least 500 were injured when a tornado struck Udall, Kansas on May 25, 1955.

Throughout the United States, 1955 was a particularly bad year for tornadoes. Normally, about 150 of them occur in any 12-month period. In 1955, nearly 900 were recorded. Without touching the ground, one of these killed the 15-man crew of a B-36 bomber flying over Sterling, Texas.

One of the most destructive of them to come to Earth entirely destroyed the farming town of Udall, Kansas, 22 miles south of Wichita, killing or injuring half its population and scarring the rest with the horrible memory of the black night of May 25, 1955.

At 9:30 P.M., the twister smashed through Blackwell, Oklahoma near the Kansas border. Five hundred homes were destroyed there; 19 people were killed and 493 were injured. A refrigerator was flung with so much force into a tree that refrigerator and tree fused into one inseparable mass. The pavement on the streets of Blackwell was peeled up like an apple skin. Automobiles were flung to the top of two-story buildings.

At 10:30, hail began to fall on Udall, lit by flashes of brilliant lightning, intermixed with rain driven almost parallel to the ground by a roaring, teeming wind. The twister struck with such force and rapidity, most local residents had no time to get to their storm cellars.

Eighty-two people died; more were buried under the rubble, or struck by pieces of windows, walls and roofs that were turned into flying missiles when the sudden drop in outside pressure exploded houses. Every home was damaged. The Community Center was destroyed, although those who were attending a meeting there that night escaped injury by crowding against the west wall. As the pressure outside the building dropped, the roof exploded upward and the wind carried away the walls on the north, east and south sides of the building. Only the west wall held, protecting the 12 women and children who huddled against it.

The town's huge cement and metal grain elevator was demolished. Every car in town was damaged so badly that none could be started. A visiting policeman filled his car with injured and drove them to the hospital in Belle Plain, nine miles away.

Word spread quickly about the destruction of Udall, and within hours, dozens, then thousands of rescuers descended upon the scene. The Kansas National Guard and the Air Force sent detachments, beds, bedding, a crane, a wrecker and food. A dairy in Wichita sent in a gasoline-powered generator and searchlights. The Red Cross and Salvation Army brought in food. A car dealer from Mulvane sent all of his station wagons to serve as ambulances. The rebuilding began quickly.

UNITED STATES
MASSACHUSETTS
WORCESTER

June 9, 1953

• • • • • • • • • • • • • • •

The worst tornado in New England's history killed 62, injured more than 1,200 and destroyed 4,000 buildings in Worcester, Massachusetts on June 9, 1953.

The tornado that struck Worcester, Massachusetts at 5 P.M. on June 9, 1953, remains the worst tornado ever to strike New England. Moving at 36 mph, the twister traveled through 46 miles of Massachusetts, roaring through Holden and Shrewbury and claiming 28 lives in these two towns before fusing with another tornado and slamming into Worcester.

Sixty-two people perished in this cataclysmic collision of forces which twisted several steel towers that had been built to withstand winds of 375 mph. More than 4,000 buildings were destroyed; over 1,200 people were injured.

One man, in a newspaper report, related that his wife went out to rescue the dog as the storm struck.

"She opened the door and that is the last we saw of her," he said. "She just went up into the air and out of sight."

The property damage estimate of $52 million was the highest ever recorded in the United States for tornado destruction.

UNITED STATES
MICHIGAN
FLINT

June 8, 1953

• • • • • • • • • • • • • • •

One hundred sixteen people were killed and 386 homes were totally destroyed when a twister hit Flint, Michigan on June 8, 1953.

In terms of grim tornado statistics, 1953 challenged even 1955. From January to June of that year, 250 twisters rampaged through Michigan and Ohio, killing 28 and injuring over 350. But it was the 251st tornado that was by far the worst.

It began around 8:30 P.M. on June 8, 1953, in Flushing, Michigan, a suburb of Flint. In the manner of most twisters, its path was contained but viciously ravaging. Within minutes, it had flattened buildings, exploded others and ripped the roofs from the suburban settlements along the Coldwater Road and the Flint River. Three hundred eighty-six homes were totally obliterated, 525 others were severely damaged. But the worst of it was the human toll:

The worst tornado in New England's history was captured as it slammed through Holden, Massachusetts on June 9, 1953. Sixty-two people died, 1,200 were injured and over 4,000 buildings exploded. Library of Congress.

Forty-five drive-in moviegoers were killed and scores were injured when a tornado tore through Flint, Michigan in June 1953.
American Red Cross.

116 victims were trapped indoors and crushed to death by this killer tornado.

UNITED STATES
MIDWEST

April 11, 1965

• • • • • • • • • • • • • •

On April 11, 1965, 37 tornadoes tore through the Midwest, killing 271 and injuring over 5,000.

Palm Sunday, April 11, 1965, will be long remembered by survivors of what has been called the "worst tornado epidemic in history." On that day, an amazing total of 37 tornadoes formed from the warm, humid thunderstorm conditions that prevailed over a wide area of the Midwest, including Kansas, Missouri, Illinois and Iowa. Before the day ended, 271 people were dead, more than 5,000 had been injured, and the property damage totaled $300 million.

UNITED STATES
MIDWEST AND SOUTH

May 26–27, 1917

• • • • • • • • • • • • • •

Three hundred ninety-seven people died in a series of tornadoes that traversed Illinois, Louisiana, Mississippi, Missouri, Kansas, Tennessee, Indiana, Kentucky, Alabama and Arkansas on May 26 and 27, 1917.

An unusual, perhaps freakish series of tornadoes invaded seven states in two days, from May 26 to 27, 1917, killing 249 and causing more than $5.5 million in property damage. Illinois, Louisiana, Mississippi, Missouri, Kansas, Tennessee, Indiana, Kentucky, Alabama and Arkansas fell victim to a collection of killer storms that—in the usual behavior pattern of tornadoes—demolished some buildings while sparing others nearby, killed some people and spared others only feet away.

In Konts, Indiana one of the largest, most opulent estates in town was transported more than a city block, without so much as unseating the curtains hung in its many windows. A Catholic church in Andale, Kansas standing directly in the path of another twister, remained intact when the storm took an abrupt turn.

Other locations were less lucky. A tornado that, in its 293-mile journey from Missouri to Indiana established the record as the tornado that traveled the longest continuous distance ever, left a wide swath of smashed farms, toppled grain elevators and mangled automobiles. The northern section of Mattoon, Illinois was virtually eliminated from the map, and 110 persons lost their lives there. Charleston, Illinois suffered a similar fate when a different tornado slammed into it, demolishing 221 homes and killing 38 residents of that medium-sized town.

UNITED STATES
MISSISSIPPI
NATCHEZ

May 7, 1840

• • • • • • • • • • • • • • • •

Three hundred seventeen people died and 109 were injured when a tornado struck Natchez, Mississippi on May 7, 1840.

Nine inches of rain punctuated by huge hailstones preceded a tornado that followed the Mississippi River northward and slammed into Natchez, Mississippi at 2 P.M. on May 7, 1840. In the five minutes the tornado took to traverse the city, it chewed up the riverfront, demolished two residential areas, killed 317 people, injured 109 and caused a staggering—for 1840—$1.26 million in property damage.

Pieces of houses were later found 30 miles away from the city. Sheets of tin from roofs were scaled through the air like scimitars with a similar, murderous effect. Houses, their windows shut, exploded when the pressure around them suddenly plummeted.

The most tragic occurrences, however, took place on the river, near the docks. Two large steamers crowded with passengers and 60 flatboats were simultaneously capsized by the storm, drowning a large percentage of their passengers and crews.

UNITED STATES
MISSOURI
MARSHFIELD

April 18, 1880

• • • • • • • • • • • • • • • •

The collision and consequent fusion of two tornadoes killed 101 and injured 600 in Marshfield, Missouri on April 18, 1880.

Two tornadoes collided in Marshfield, Missouri on April 18, 1880, and that cataclysmic meeting of forces combined to erase the town from the face of the Earth. Not one structure was left unaffected. All were splintered, pounded into the earth or exploded sky high. One hundred one people died; 600 were injured seriously. Over $2 million in damages was recorded—an incredible amount in 1880, in a thinly populated corner of the United States.

UNITED STATES
MISSOURI
POPLAR BLUFF

May 9, 1927

• • • • • • • • • • • • • • • •

One hundred forty-two people were killed by a tornado that struck Poplar Bluff, Missouri and parts of Oklahoma, Texas and Kansas on May 9, 1927.

Ninety-two residents of Poplar Bluff, Missouri were killed by one of a series of tornados that left another 50 dead in Oklahoma, Texas, Kansas and other parts of Missouri on May 9, 1927.

The storm, which caused over $1 million in damage to the small city, slammed into the middle of its business district at 3:15 P.M., while children in the East Side School were finishing their afternoon classes. Several children were killed; many more were trapped and injured in the collapsed school.

Most of the fatalities in the downtown part of Poplar Bluff took place in its three largest hotels. Its newest structure, The Melbourne Hotel, was hammered into the ground, trapping and killing those inside it. The four-story Drucker Hotel suffered a similar fate, but some of its inhabitants were saved by brick walls. They had to wait a number of hours before being rescued. The Harris Hotel—a wooden structure—did not collapse entirely, but was swept by a huge fire that roared out of control, threatening the rest of the business district. Even before the fire department could reach the Harris, an enormous rain squall generated by the storm doused the flames.

Relief arrived soon after the storm in the form of troops to prevent looting and a trainload of doctors, nurses and medical supplies.

UNITED STATES
MISSOURI
ST. LOUIS

May 27, 1896

• • • • • • • • • • • • • • • •

A tornado containing 560-mph winds killed 306 residents of St. Louis, Missouri and injured 2,500 on May 27, 1896.

If the estimate of weather expert Frank H. Bigelow is to be believed, the winds within the vortex of the immense killer tornado that ravaged St. Louis, Missouri on May 27, 1896, were traveling at an amazing speed of 560 mph.

The evidence of horrendous ruination, superphenomenal in its scope, gives credence to Bigelow's estimate:

Spikes of trees and shards of houses in Russiaville, Indiana are all that remain after the passage of one of 37 tornadoes that tore through six states on Palm Sunday, 1965. American Red Cross/Jack Shere.

306 killed, 2,500 injured and more than $12 million in property damage, and all of it accomplished in 20 minutes. Straws were driven with the force of a rifle bullet six inches into a tree trunk. A six-by-eight wooden plank was pounded four feet straight into the ground. A farmer's spade burrowed six inches into another solid tree trunk.

This, the most violent storm ever to visit St. Louis, was preceded by spectacular thunder and lightning, first observed, according to an official of the United States Weather Bureau, ". . . at 5:00 P.M., an hour before the tornado occurred. This continued with short intermissions until 5:45 P.M., when it became almost continuous. . . . At 6:00 P.M., when the tornado occurred, the whole west and northwest sky was in a continuous blaze of light. Intensely

vivid flashes of forked lightning were frequent, being outlined in green, blue, purple and bright yellow colors against the dull yellow background of the never ceasing sheet lightning."

Somewhere within this web of color and light was the tornado, which, uncharacteristically, was not formed in a funnel, but rather as a mass of black clouds. At 6:10 P.M., it roared into the city limits, rocketed across six miles of densely populated parts of the city, exploding homes, driving trees like medieval pikes through thick walls, crushing, with its awful velocity, entire city blocks.

And then it was gone, across the Missouri River, leaving behind it raging fires, the cries of the wounded and the dying and thousands of bewildered, sometimes crazed survivors.

UNITED STATES
MISSOURI
ST. LOUIS

September 29, 1927

• • • • • • • • • • • • • • •

Eighty-five people died and over 1,300 were injured when a tornado struck St. Louis, Missouri on September 29, 1927.

One of the most horrendous happenings in the five-minute passage of the tornado that killed 85, injured over 1,300, caused $100 million in property damage and virtually wiped out a large part of St. Louis's southwest section, was the presence of mysterious sheets of flame that scores of inhabitants swore they saw, whipping like grim, fluttering curtains down streets and abruptly disappearing against walls of buildings.

In contrast, one of the most *inspiring* happenings was the conduct of the two radio stations, KMOX and KFVE—KFWF had suffered a demolished antenna as a result of the storm and so was rendered silent—in directing rescue efforts and appealing for outside aid. Stationing himself on the roof of the Chase Hotel, KFVE broadcaster Patrick Convey, following a game plan that had been evolved two years earlier by the local Disaster Committee, was able to direct units of the Red Cross, Fire Departments, National Guard, American Legion and Boy Scouts to specific disaster sites. At ground level, KMOX's George Junkin kept in further contact with rescuers and, working around the clock, appealed for relief supplies and money. Because of this, it only took hours for medical attention, food, clothing and money to arrive in the city, thus preventing the spread of fires and the seemingly inevitable aftermath of looting.

The twister announced its approach shortly before 1 P.M. on September 29, 1927. The noontime air suddenly thickened, thunder growled in the distance and lightning flashes illuminated the fast approaching black and orange clouds.

The full impact of the twister struck at 1:05 P.M., exploding homes, shearing off chimneys, hurling building blocks and automobiles through the air, collapsing streetcars, felling trees and telephone poles, ripping live wires from their protective moorings.

Survivors on the ridges of the city reported that the twister churned up the earth as if some sort of cosmic plow had touched down. In East St. Louis, Granite City, Madison, and Venice, Illinois, and throughout St. Louis itself, over 1,800 dwellings were either exploded or slammed into the ground.

A period stereoview captures the havoc wrought by the 560-mile-per-hour winds of the tornado that struck St. Louis, Missouri on May 27, 1896. The view is of the corner of Rutger and Seventh streets, where seven of the 306 residents who were killed by the storm lost their lives. Library of Congress.

A devastated landscape reflects the passage of the worst tornado to ever hit Omaha, Nebraska. The 1913 twister killed 115, destroyed 600 homes and seriously damaged 1,100 others. Library of Congress.

UNITED STATES
NEBRASKA
OMAHA

March 23, 1913

• • • • • • • • • • • • • •

A giant tornado hit Omaha, Nebraska on March 23, 1913, killing 115, destroying 600 homes and seriously damaging 1,100 others.

The worst tornado ever to smash into Omaha, Nebraska was documented on its way toward its grim mission of destruction by *Topeka Daily Capital* reporter Milton Tabor, who was picnicking at the time: "The tornado," he wrote, "whirled furiously over our heads. We looked up into what appeared to be an enormous hollow cylinder, bright inside with lightning flashes, but black as blackest night all around. The noise was like ten million bees, plus a roar that beggars description."

Tabor must have witnessed this sometime between 5:30 and 6:00 P.M. on the late afternoon of March 23, 1913. At approximately 6:00 P.M., the tornado touched down at Forty-fourth and Frances streets, then tumbled on northeastward to Center Street, near millionaires' row in West Farnum. Before it would leave, 12 minutes later, it would claim 115 lives, destroy 600 homes, seriously damage 1,100 others and rob the economy of this midwestern city of $3.5 million in property damage.

The path of the tornado was limited to a small area—one-quarter of a mile in width and five miles in length—but within that path, horror reigned.

Barn roofs were lifted and sent flapping through the air. On Mayberry Street, a family was crushed at the dinner table when their home folded in upon them. At Forty-eighth and Leavenworth streets, a streetcar was lifted off its tracks and capsized, with all of its passengers inside. A baby was killed in its father's arms by flying glass.

The huge stone palaces built by millionaires in the Bemis Park District were no match for the combined forces of wind, hail, sleet and rain generated by the storm. Roofs were peeled away, windows were exploded outward, and monumental stones were flung like baseballs from yard to yard.

Not only the wealthy were affected. At Twenty-fourth and Grant streets, the Idlewild Poolhall collapsed upon 20 pool-playing patrons, crushing them to death.

And even the dead were not left undisturbed. In West Lawn cemetery, cadavers were ripped from their graves, spun skyward within the tornado's eyewall and flung yards from the graveyard.

The continuing rain extinguished fires set by the tornado, but that was only the beginning of a massive cleanup effort that would take months to complete.

UNITED STATES
NORTH AND SOUTH CAROLINA

March 29, 1984

• • • • • • • • • • • • • •

A freak series of 24 tornadoes ripped through North and South Carolina on March 29, 1984. Sixty-one people were

243

killed, 1,000 were injured and nearly 3,000 were made homeless. New York and New England were also affected.

An unusual set of atmospheric events on March 29, 1984, produced an immense storm system that would send 24 tornadoes through North Carolina, scatter thunderstorms accompanied by hurricane force winds and blinding snow into New York, topple a 103-year-old lighthouse in Nantucket and raise wind levels to over 115 mph on Mount Washington, New Hampshire.

The gigantic storm system was born when a vast body of warm, moist air from the Atlantic was driven over cold, dry air descending from Canada. At the same time, an unusually active jet stream blew across the top of the storm system, sweeping the topmost clouds downward into an anvil shape and setting up huge updrafts of air. These factors converged to form, according to Joe Friday, deputy director of the National Weather Service, ". . . one of the most severe general cyclonic storms in recent history."

The worst damage came in North and South Carolina, where 61 people were killed, 1,000 were injured, nearly 3,000 were rendered homeless, and damage estimates climbed to $200 million. The tornadoes, racing along a 260-mile path across both of these states, missed most thickly populated urban areas, but wreaked havoc in rural spots, tossing mobile homes about like pieces of cardboard and shearing the roofs off homes and businesses alike.

Red Springs, North Carolina was one of the few towns struck dead center by a tornado, which touched down in the town's main street, blowing apart businesses, flattening a school and knocking down hundreds of 200-year-old oak and pecan trees that had lined the elegant, residential area of the city. A 3-year-old boy was killed when the roof of a church collapsed upon him and other refugees from the approaching tornado, and more than 300 houses and 100 mobile homes were severely damaged.

In the northern part of South Carolina, the storm hit the towns of Anderson, Winnsboro (where one person was killed), Newberry and Bennettsville (where seven people perished when a twister slammed into an apartment building and shopping center).

The group of twisters then entered North Carolina's sandhills and tore through the coastal plain, including the towns of Maxton, Shannon, Red Springs, Parkton and Mount Olive. People and homes were blown ". . . all over the fields . . ." according to Mark Tartis of the Emergency Division of Scotland County, North Carolina.

Before the giant storm system would blow itself out over New England, hundreds of thousands of homes would be robbed of power and some of their roofs. But the greatest siege of terror occurred in North and South Carolina, which

one North Carolina survivor described to a reporter as ". . . the hand of God reaching down to crush us."

UNITED STATES
NORTHEAST
May 31, 1985

• • • • • • • • • • • • • •

Ninety-three people were killed and over 2,000 were injured when more than 24 tornadoes traversed the northeastern United States on May 31, 1985.

Ninety-three people lost their lives and over 2,000 were injured when more than two dozen tornadoes slashed through Central Ontario to parts of Ohio, Pennsylvania and New York on the evening of May 31, 1985. A combination of warm, humid air from the Gulf of Mexico, cooler air from the north and a cold front appearing from the west sent giant hailstones hurtling through the air in Ohio and Pennsylvania and spawned the tornadoes—which churned along at 200 mph with a deafening noise that witnesses compared to freight trains or jets.

In Ontario, where the tornadoes first touched down, the heaviest damage occurred north of Toronto, were 12 died and 150 were injured. Eight people died in Barrie, the site of the Barrie Racetrack, where cars and trucks were strewn crazily around the track and terrified horses, freed from their partially demolished stalls, ran wild over the countryside.

In Ohio, over $4 million damage was caused as the twisters virtually destroyed the village of Newton Falls, crushing or exploding 300 homes, turning much of the downtown area into rubble and setting off numerous fires. Nine people were killed in Youngstown, when a tornado cut a 200-foot swath across three and a half miles of the town.

New York State suffered only property damage, but neighboring Pennsylvania was hit extremely hard. The state suffered hundreds of millions of dollars of damage—more than in any other area visited by the storm. In Atlantic, Pennsylvania five people were killed, dozens of homes, a grain mill and a 312-foot microwave tower were pulverized. In Wheatland, a steel plant that employed 500 people simply disappeared. Mayor Helen M. Duby and her family escaped to their cellar, and when they emerged, the town of 1,122 was gone. "It was like a nightmare," she said.

In Butler County, eight women at a tupperware party tried to make it to a storm cellar outside the house. Seven

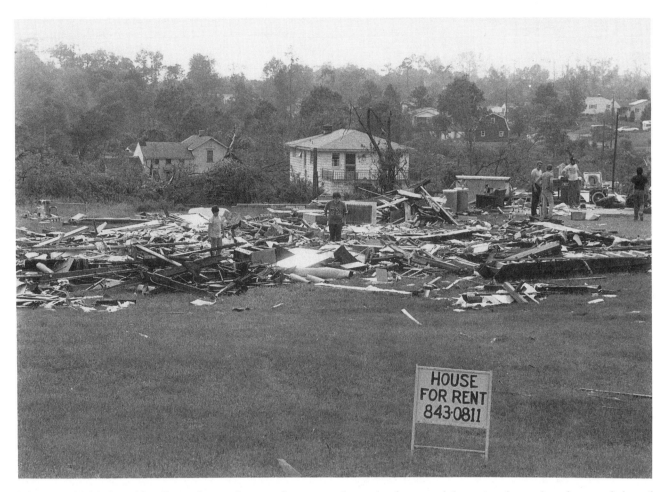

A house in North Sewickley, Pennsylvania that was for rent, no longer is after one of the series of tornadoes that raged through western Pennsylvania, southwestern New York and eastern Ohio on May 31, 1985. American Red Cross/Joseph Matthews.

succeeded. The eighth was found in a creek two miles away, dead.

Albion, in northeastern Pennsylvania was struck shortly after 5 P.M. Martha Sherman, the Red Cross disaster co-ordinator, noted that a warning appeared on her television screen only seconds before the tornado struck her block. The storm roared through, turning tall maples trees into missiles, sending them through the air and dropping them half a mile from where they had been rooted. Automobiles were flung about like plastic toys. When the storm passed, there was little left of the town, and what remained was unrecognizable.

In the wake of the tornado, roads were sealed off to the stricken towns to prevent looting, and the National Guard hauled 500-gallon water tanks to many areas, since many private wells were now inoperable.

UNITED STATES
OKLAHOMA
OKLAHOMA CITY

June 12, 1942

• • • • • • • • • • • • •

Thirty-five people died and 30 were injured on June 12, 1942, in still another Oklahoma City tornado.

Sometime during the night of June 12, 1942, a tornado touched down in a residential section of Oklahoma City, Oklahoma killing 35 sleeping citizens in their collapsing and exploding dwellings. Thirty more were taken to hospitals the following morning. More than 100 homes were blown apart by the nocturnal twister, and more than $300,000 in damage was caused to both the residential and neighboring business district of this city that—more than any other city in the United States—is the victim of constant assaults by tornadoes.

245

UNITED STATES
OKLAHOMA
OKLAHOMA CITY

April 30, 1970

• • • • • • • • • • • • • • • •

Because of the population's response to early warnings, there was no human loss when a tornado hit Oklahoma City on April 30, 1970.

The area of frequent tornado activity that runs from Texas northward through Oklahoma, Kansas and Iowa is known to its residents as "Tornado Alley." Perhaps because the people in this area pride themselves in "sensing" tornadoes before television and radio reports warn of them, perhaps because they know, through experience, to heed forecasters' warnings, the twin twister that hit Oklahoma City at around 2 A.M. on April 30, 1970, caused monumental damage but killed no one.

A torrential thundering deluge had hit at 11:30 P.M. the night before, filling storm drains and flooding parts of the city. Up until 2:20 A.M., when the first house collapsed, cleanup crews were busy clearing flooded drains and streets. But during that time, radio and television reports constantly warned of approaching tornadoes. Shortly after 2 A.M., the radar at the Emergency Operating Center noted a funnel 12 miles from the city moving toward it at nearly 50 mph.

At 2:20, the two funnels smashed into the northwestern section of the city, while warning sirens wailed. The tornadoes hit the earth, bounced, and hit again. And again. Telephone lines snapped, showering glistening displays of sparks skyward and earthward. Houses and other buildings exploded. A semi-trailer was flung onto its side at Interstate 40 and Council Road.

In 20 minutes, the storms were gone. Emergency crews fanned out over the affected area, a thickly populated Oklahoma City suburb. Twenty miles of it had been scoured clean by the storm, and millions of dollars of property damage was recorded. But, again, because of training and reporting, there were no serious injuries and no deaths.

UNITED STATES
OKLAHOMA, ARKANSAS AND MISSOURI

April 12, 1945

• • • • • • • • • • • • • • • •

One hundred twelve people were killed when a series of tornadoes traveled through Oklahoma, Arkansas and Missouri on April 12, 1945.

A series of tornadoes raged through Oklahoma, Arkansas and Missouri on April 12, 1945, and, although damage was extensive in Arkansas and Missouri, Oklahoma suffered the majority of the 112 deaths and hundreds of thousands of dollars in damage.

In Oklahoma, Oklahoma City was sideswiped by the storms and four other nearby towns received great damage: Rowland, Boggy, Red Oak and Greenwood Junction. But the worst damage and the greatest loss of life occurred in Antler, Oklahoma, the town first hit by the storms. A small hamlet of 3,000, it lost all of its power and its residential area was torn asunder, with scores of houses flung wildly apart by explosions and the flattening force of the twister. Sixty-three people were killed—including the owners of the town's only funeral parlor—and hundreds were injured.

UNITED STATES
SOUTH

February 19, 1884

• • • • • • • • • • • • • • • •

Over 800 people died and over 10,000 were made homeless when 60 tornadoes traversed the southern United States on February 19, 1884.

More than 60 tornadoes tore through the southern states on February 19, 1884, flattening dwellings, killing more than 890 people and rendering over 10,000 homeless. The entire town of Davisboro, Georgia was destroyed, as well as several other small farming villages in six southern states. The twisters, of unusual ferocity, arrived in split seconds, with almost no warning in certain cases. Reports, mostly contained in Frank Leslie's *Illustrated Newspaper* were rife with accounts of entire families being crushed within houses when one of the 60 twisters struck.

UNITED STATES
SOUTH

April 29–30, 1924

• • • • • • • • • • • • • • • •

One hundred fifteen people died and more than 1,500 were made homeless when 22 tornadoes raised havoc in the southern United States on April 29 and 30, 1924.

Twenty-six towns in South Carolina, Georgia, Alabama, Arkansas, Louisiana and Mississippi were obliterated by 22 tornadoes that touched down in the southern United States during the two-day period of April 29 and 30, 1924. Riv-

Stripped trees, bodies and a war-torn landscape were all that remained of multiple areas of the southern United States after a series of 60 tornadoes ripped back and forth across the area on February 19, 1884. Frank Leslie's Illustrated Newspaper.

erside Mill, South Carolina was particularly hard hit, losing its entire business district, half of its residences and a $500,000 mill. Over 1,500 became homeless in that town alone.

A total of 115 people lost their lives and a conservative estimate of the storm's damage reached $10 million.

203 people died and nearly a thousand were injured did inhabitants remember such devastation.

Ironically, Gainesville was also hit the hardest in this series of storms; its entire downtown section was demolished by the tornado that roared into this town 55 miles outside Atlanta at 8:45 A.M. on the morning of April 6. Without warning the tornado slammed into the Cooper Pants Manufacturing Company, destroying it and killing 125 people instantly.

In the middle of town, the hotel, the First Baptist Church and virtually every one of the downtown area's 630 buildings was either flattened or damaged, and 33 businesses were whisked off their foundations. Only the new post office and federal courthouse remained unscathed.

Five days before, at the same hour of 8:45, the first of the tornadoes had sideswiped Gordo, Georgia and roared through Cordele, Georgia and Greensboro, North Carolina. In Cordele, a 12-mile-long, 400-foot-wide swath was cut through the town's center, 23 people were killed, 600 were injured and 289 buildings were lost.

Between the 2nd and 6th of April, Coffeyville, Booneville and Auburn, Mississippi; Columbia, Fayetteville and LaCrosse, Arkansas; Elkwood and Red Bay, Alabama; and Acworth, Woodstock and Lavonia, Georgia felt the storms' furies.

On the last day of the storms' multiple crisscrossings of the six states, Tupelo, Mississippi was hit a devastating blow. The small town with a population of 10,000 suffered a loss of 195 lives in the space of a few tumultuous moments. Office buildings were turned into hospitals as the town's only hospital was filled beyond capacity. Fires threatened to add to the damage, but fortunately, rains appeared shortly after the storm passed and extinguished what the local fire department could not.

UNITED STATES
SOUTH

April 2–6, 1936

• • • • • • • • • • • • • •

Multiple tornadoes killed 421 and injured 2,000 in the southern United States from April 2 through 6, 1936.

On the five days of April 2,3,4,5 and 6, 1936, a veritible firestorm of tornadoes touched down in six southern states— Alabama, Arkansas, Georgia, Mississippi, North Carolina and Tennessee. Four hundred twenty-one people lost their lives, 2,000 were injured and property damage was estimated in excess of $25 million. Not since the notorious twister of June 1, 1903, in Gainesville, Georgia in which

UNITED STATES
SOUTH CAROLINA
CHARLESTON

September 10, 1811

• • • • • • • • • • • • • •

Over 500 people were killed by the noon-hour tornado that struck Charleston, South Carolina on September 10, 1811.

A southerly gale blew through Charleston, South Carolina through most of the morning of September 10, 1811. But by noon, the winds had calmed. Citizens went about their ordinary tasks, only mindful of an odd pinkness that seemed to paint the underside of the clouds that remained clustered over the city.

Deathly calms are notoriously the harbingers of storms to come, and this was precisely the case in Charleston that day. At approximately 12:30 P.M., the air began to thicken, and a telltale, dark, funnel-shaped cloud bore down directly upon the city. Within moments, it had cut a swath of devastation through the crowded noontime streets, uprooting and twisting trees into odd shapes, blowing up buildings and killing more than 500 people.

UNITED STATES
SOUTH CAROLINA
CHARLESTON

September 29, 1938

• • • • • • • • • • • •

Five tornadoes struck Charleston, South Carolina simultaneously on September 29, 1938, killing 32 and injuring 150.

Five twisters at once slammed into Charleston, South Carolina on the morning of September 29, 1938. In less than 2 hours more than $2 million in property damage was sustained, 32 people were killed and 150 more were hospitalized.

The first tornado was a relatively mild one, setting up a feeling of complacency in the public—a blueprint for disaster. The second and third, touching down a mere two miles apart, caused the most damage and loss of life. While the second twister hit the city directly, the third, more powerful one first hit land on James Island, and then ran

into the city for another 1,600 feet, destroying everything in its path. The fourth and fifth merely splintered what had already been demolished.

UNITED STATES
SOUTHWEST (TEXAS, OKLAHOMA AND KANSAS)

April 9, 1947

• • • • • • • • • • • • •

The most destructive and widest tornado ever to hit the Texas panhandle killed 169 and caused millions of dollars in property damage throughout the southwestern United States on April 9, 1947.

The tornado of April 9, 1947 was a record breaker. It traveled in the widest path ever recorded—one and a half miles (the width of a tornado's path is usually measured in feet)—and was the most destructive tornado in the entire history of the Texas panhandle.

Its first recorded touchdown was in the small (population 500) town of White Deer, Texas. Normally, tornadoes only sound like freight trains. This one struck a freight train just outside of White Deer, lifting it from the tracks as if it had been made by Lionel. Fortunately, only three people were injured in this small town, but a goodly portion of its few buildings were demolished.

The still smaller hamlet of Glazier, Texas (population 125) was the next stop for the tornado. It flattened every building in town except the schoolhouse, killed 16 people,

Tornado cones sweep across the southwestern United States on April 9, 1947. American Red Cross.

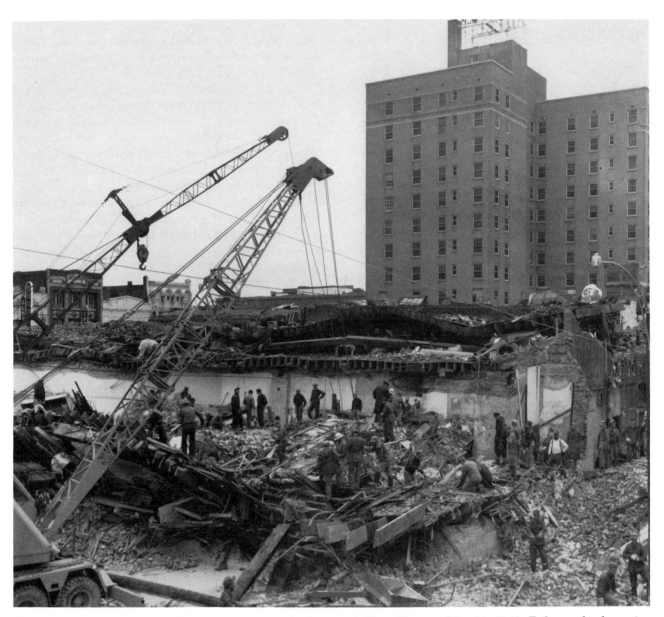

Rescuers probe through the wreckage left by the tornado that struck Waco, Texas on May 11, 1953. Failure to heed warnings resulted in the deaths of 114 people. Smithsonian Institution.

and transported two 200-pound men—C. S. Wright and Art Beebe—30 feet in the air for nearly 300 yards before dropping them, unhurt, into the debris.

On the twister proceeded, demolishing Higgens, Texas, where it killed 45 people, and set fires that even rain and golf-ball-sized hailstones failed to extinguish.

After destroying the town of Shattuck, Texas, the tornado crossed the border into Oklahoma, and wreaked its greatest havoc in the town of Woodward which was also the largest town on its itinerary. One hundred blocks of

Woodward were blown off the face of the Earth, 95 people were killed and for the few minutes the tornado took to rage through the town, the air was filled with flying pieces of houses, roofs, roadsigns and automobiles.

It was the last location to suffer a human toll. White Horse, Oklahoma received a sideswipe, and Kansas, while suffering $200,000 in property damage, reported no deaths.

In all, 169 persons died and more than $15 million in damage was caused in the 221-mile path of destruction left by the April 9, 1947, Southwest Tornado.

UNITED STATES
TEXAS
WACO

May 11, 1953

• • • • • • • • • • • • • •

One hundred fourteen people were killed and 500 injured when a fierce tornado hit Waco, Texas on May 11, 1953.

In 1953, weather scientists were just beginning to realize the value of radar in tracking tornadoes and other violent storms. The Air Force Weather Service had developed a radar network that ran from Omaha, Nebraska to Oklahoma City's Tinker Field, and a week before May 11, it had tested it to the point of satisfaction. It could, evaluators felt, become a useful tool to supplement the tornado watch alerts issued by the U.S. Weather Bureau.

Late in the afternoon of May 10, 1953, a tornado watch alert was issued by the U.S. Weather Bureau for central Texas, warning that a mass of warm, moist air was moving northward from the Gulf of Mexico and was expected to meet a large mass of cold, dry air that had moved in from the north somewhere between Waco and San Angelo.

The population of San Angelo heard and heeded the warning. The population of Waco did not. The resultant tragedy was a primer in preparedness.

Patrolmen of the Texas Department of Public Safety spotted the storm three hours before it hit San Angelo. The twister was a slow mover. Its forward speed was judged to be 15 mph, and it stuck closely to the Concho River valley.

By 2:15 P.M., when the elephant trunk of the tornado's cone touched down in San Angelo, schoolchildren in the Lake View residential section had moved into inside hallways or under desks away from the windows, which had been opened on the side of the building away from the storm. Although the roof of the school lifted off and the windows blew out, no one was injured.

Police began rescue work even before the wind had begun to lessen. Local ambulances arrived upon the scene within 10 minutes. By 3:15 P.M., National Guard and Goodfellow Air Force Base personnel had set up a command post. Still, 11 people died and another 66 suffered serious injury, but the toll could have been far higher. There was hardly anything left of San Angelo's business section.

Now, the storm gathered speed and headed toward Waco. Here, in contrast to San Angelo, there was a minimum of preparation. Hardly any of the 90,000 residents of the city had heard the news about San Angelo. Perhaps because many believed the Indian legend that the "dancing devil" could never dance between the hills that circled the town—a legend accepted so unquestioningly that few Waco residents carried wind damage insurance on their homes and automobiles—the city was caught absolutely unaware.

The tornado touched down on the city's southwest side at approximately 4:45 P.M. It cut a grim swath into the business district, demolishing 83 buildings in a matter of minutes. At the Joy Theater, late afternoon patrons were buried when the arched roof collapsed, and the front of the building exploded into the street.

Steel mailboxes were turned into deadly flying objects; bricks and chunks of cement shot through the air. Automobiles tumbled end over end down city streets. Apparently descending directly on top of the Dennis Furniture Building, the tornado wrenched the top four floors off the ground floor, exploding them into dust and scattering them over a five-block area.

Twenty-five high school boys and older men were playing pool in the Torrance Recreation Hall behind the Joy Theater. Tons of debris from the Dennis Building arched through the air and landed on the Recreation Hall, collapsing its roof and burying all of the men and boys within. None survived.

A steady rain fell after the storm passed on. By 5 o'clock, police, fire department, National Guard and army rescue teams were at work. Human chains were formed to unearth people from beneath mountains of debris.

In the few moments that it took the tornado to traverse Waco, it destroyed two square miles of the city's business district, killing 114 people, injuring 500 and causing $50 million in damage.

Ironically, a month later, on June 8, another tornado struck the same area, bypassing Waco, but killing 11 people in the nearby town of Flint.

TYPHOONS

· · · · · · · · · · · · · · · · · · ·

THE WORST RECORDED TYPHOONS

* Detailed in text

China
    (1926)
    Canton (1862)
    Fukien (Typhoon Iris) (1959)
    Haifung (1881)
    * Hong Kong (1841)
    * Hong Kong (1906)
    Hong Kong (1947)
    Hong Kong (1964)
    Swatlow (1922)
    * Typhoon Wanda (1956)

Formosa
    * Taito (1912)

India
    Barisol (Ganges Delta)
      (1941)

Japan

    * Hakodate (1954)
    Ichinoseki (1948)
    Kiashuni (1281)
    Kyushu (1927)
    Kyushu (1951)
    Loochow Island (1930)
    * Osaka (1934)
    * Tokyo (1918)
    * Typhoon Ida (1958)
    * Typhoon Vera (1959)

Korea
    (1936)
    (1949)
    Typhoon Billie (1967)

Philippines
    (1937)
    (1952)
    (1964)

    * (1970)
    Leyte (1929)
    * Luzon Islands (1944)
    Manila (1928)
    Manila (1929)
    Manila (1936)
    Mauban (1934)
    Mayon (1776)
    Mayon (1875)
    Quezon Province
      (1970)
    * Typhoon Ike (1984)
    * Typhoon Ruby (1988)
    Visayas (1946)

Thailand
    (1962)

Vietnam
    * (1953)

CHRONOLOGY

* Detailed in text

1281
  July 17
    Kiashuni Island,
    Japan
1776
    Mayon, Philippines
1841
  July 21–22
    * Hong Kong, China
1862
  July 27
    Canton, China
1881
    Haifung, China
1875
    Mayon, Philippines
1906
  September 18

    * Hong Kong, China
1912
  September 16
    * Taito, Formosa
1918
  September 30
    * Tokyo, Japan
1922
  August 2–3
    Swatlow, China
1926
  September 30
    China
1927
  September 13
    Kyushu Island, Japan
1928
  November 17
    Manila, Philippines
1929

  May 27
    Leyte, Philippines
  September 3
    Manila, Philippines
1930
  November 14
    Loochow Island, Japan
1934
  September 21
    * Osaka, Japan
  November 14
    Mauban, Philippines
1936
  August 28
    Korea
  October 11
    Manila, Philippines
1937
  August 5
    Philippines

1941
　May 25
　　Barisol (Ganges Delta), India
1944
　December 17–18
　* Luzon Islands, Philippines
1946
　November 13
　　Visayas, Philippines
1947
　October 7
　　Hong Kong, China
1948
　September 17
　　Ichinoseki, Japan
1949
　December 8
　　Korea
1951
　October 14
　　Kyushu, Japan

1952
　October 22
　　Philippines
1953
　September 25
　* Vietnam
1954
　September 26
　* Hakodate, Japan
1956
　August 2
　* China (Typhoon Wanda)
1958
　September 27–28
　* Japan (Typhoon Ida)
1959
　　Fukien, China (Typhoon Iris)
　September 26–27
　* Japan (Typhoon Vera)
1962
　October 28

　　Thailand
1964
　June 30
　　Philippines
　September 5
　　Hong Kong, China
1967
　July 9
　　Korea (Typhoon Billie)
1970
　September 11
　　Quezon Province, Philippines
　October 14–15
　* Philippines
1984
　September 2
　* Philippines (Typhoon Ike)
1988
　October 24
　* Philippines (Typhoon Ruby)

TYPHOONS

For a detailed description of typhoons, consult the section on hurricanes, page 167. In the North Atlantic, this meteorological phenomenon is considered a hurricane, in the Indian Ocean, a tropical cyclone, and in the Western Pacific Ocean, a typhoon. Thus, all of the storms described in this section have taken place in that land area bordering upon the Western Pacific Ocean.

· · · · · · · · · · · · · · · · ·

CHINA
HONG KONG

July 21–22, 1841

· · · · · · · · · · · · · · · ·

One thousand people were killed in the typhoon that struck Hong Kong harbor on July 21–22, 1841. Practically all of the casualties were Chinese; British naval personnel knew of the approaching storm, but neglected to inform the Chinese residents.

The typhoon that roared into Hong Kong Harbor on the night of July 21, 1841, wrecking or sinking every boat except the British frigates anchored there, claimed an estimated 1,000 lives, most of them Chinese fishermen and inhabitants of the junks that dotted the harbor. According to British Navy reports, some waterfront dwellings were also swept into the harbor under the incessant battering of winds, rain and sea.

There was ample warning of the approaching storm. For hours, the telltale purple clouds that signal the onset of a typhoon wandered and brooded over the hills that ring the harbor, and there was continuous lightning and thunder. By 10:30 on the night of July 21, the British Navy's barometers registered 28.50.

However, there seems to be no record of the British Navy efforts either to rescue or warn the Chinese inhabitants. According to the diary of a British officer: "The Chinese were all distracted, imploring their gods in vain for help; such an awful scene of destruction and ruin is rarely witnessed, and almost every one was so busy in thinking of his own safety as to be unable to render assistance to anyone else. . . ."

CHINA
HONG KONG

September 18, 1906

· · · · · · · · · · · · · · ·

An absence of warning again caused a huge death toll among the Chinese of Hong Kong from a typhoon that struck on September 18, 1906. Of the 10,000 dead, only 20 were Europeans.

In the harbor of Hong Kong is a "Typhoon Gun"—a cannon that is fired to signal the impending approach of a typhoon. The fact that the gun was not discharged until 8:40 P.M. on the night of September 18, 1906, a mere 20 minutes before a typhoon roared into Hong Kong Harbor, may account for the ghastly death total of 10,000.

It was a horrendous storm, with winds of 100 mph or more, and a storm surge that was powerful enough to sink 22 medium-sized steamers, 11 heavy ships and more than 2,000 junks and sampans.

Within a half hour after the gun exploded, the 2,000-ton American steamer S.P. *Hitchcock* was blown ashore, and the 1,698-ton German steamer *Petrarch* was catapulted by wind and waves onto the steamers *Emma Luyken* and *Montreagle*. The hulls of both of these smaller steamers were crushed by the *Petrarch*, which then careened into the Kowloon wharf, demolishing a large chunk of it.

The *San Cheung*, a heavy steamer, did tremendous damage when it snapped its mooring cable and was flung around the harbor like a menacing toy ship, ramming and sinking dozens of other ships. Its captain, trying to grab and steady the ship's wildly spinning wheel, broke his fingers in the attempt.

In the Kowloon District, hundreds of houses were turned into fragmentary, lethal weapons, as their roofs were torn off, and the bamboo walls splintered and knifed through the air, killing or injuring hundreds of people. Rickshaws, some with passengers inside, were flung crazily through the air.

The worst toll of human life and property fell on the native Chinese. Of the 10,000 dead, only 20 were Europeans whose brick homes withstood the storm, and afterwards, there was justifiable criticism for their refusal to take in Chinese victims of the storm.

Still, there were acts of heroism. A large wooden drawbridge spanned the waterway leading to the boat club lagoon, a logical shelter for the wildly pitching junks and sampans and other small boats. Thousands of coolies raised this bridge by hand at the height of the storm, and hundreds of small boats scurried for shelter. Unfortunately, the fury of the storm drove into the lagoon, too, wrecking every boat in it. The next morning, it was possible to walk across the lagoon on the wreckage of sunken boats.

At the height of the storm, dozens of Chinese men braved the collapsing piers to thrust bamboo poles into the raging waters, allowing hundreds of drowning boatmen and their families, dumped from sampans and junks, to climb to safety.

H. R. Bevan, a legendary soldier of fortune, spotting a coolie who was picked up by the wind, rammed into a lamppost and then flung into the water, joined forces with an Indian constable. The constable removed his turban, unravelled it and held onto one end while Bevan looped the other around his waist and leaped into the water, rescuing the coolie as he was about to go underwater for the last time. The coolie survived, as did Bevan, who, in true soldier of fortune fashion, disappeared before he could be either rewarded or thanked.

CHINA
TYPHOON WANDA

August 2, 1956

• • • • • • • • • • • • • •

Typhoon Wanda killed 2,000, injured 1,200 and made 38,000 homeless when it hit the Chinese coastal provinces of Anhwei, Chakiang and Kiangsu on August 2, 1956.

Nearly 2,000 people lost their lives, 1,200 were injured and 38,000 homes were demolished in the gigantic typhoon that ravaged Anhwei, Chakiang and Kiangsu provinces on August 2, 1956.

The provinces, located on the China coast, are widely separated, but this made no difference. The typhoon struck on a wider front than any other typhoon in recent history, tearing up crops, wiping out villages and farms and drowning livestock and people alike.

Warned of the imminent approach of the storm, peasants near Shanghai attempted to harvest the rice crops, already battered by the worst heat wave in a century. Their efforts proved futile; one-third of the rice crop of the three provinces was destroyed, as well as 40 percent of the cotton crop.

FORMOSA
TAITO

September 16, 1912

• • • • • • • • • • • • • •

A typhoon with winds of over 200 mph killed 107 and injured 293 in the city of Taito, Formosa on September 16, 1912.

Over 200,000 houses in Taito, on the island of Formosa, were flattened or blown apart by the winds of an immense typhoon that struck the island on September 16, 1912. According to sketchy records, winds of over 200 mph roared into this tiny Portugese island separated from the mainland of China by the Strait of Formosa. These monstrous winds pulverized the fishing fleet, and the consequent storm surges inundated the rice and sugar fields, wiping out that island's two major agricultural industries.

One hundred seven people were killed, either by debris unleashed by the furious wind, or from drowning. Another 293 were severely injured.

JAPAN
HAKODATE

September 26, 1954

• • • • • • • • • • • • • •

Sixteen hundred people died in the typhoon that hit Hakodate, Japan on September 26, 1954, 1,000 of them in a ferryboat capsized by the storm.

Statistics never tell the entire human story, but in the case of the killer typhoon of September 26, 1954, the casualty figures completely obscure the bizarre balance struck by this storm. Sixteen hundred people died. But over 1,000 of these 1,600 drowned in one place in a matter of minutes.

The September 26 typhoon was one of 15 which raged over Japan in 1954. Some were slight; others immense. None took the toll of human life that this storm did.

Other storms glanced off Japan's outward islands. This storm hit the mainland squarely, roaring in with extremely high winds and extraordinarily high tides.

The 4,300-ton ferry *Toyu Maru*, which used to transport people between Hokkaido and Honshu, made its customary trips that day. Unwisely, perhaps, it left Hokkaido as the storm approached. Midway there, the storm struck, its eye passing directly across the ferry's path. Buffeted by the winds within the eyewall of the storm and swamped by the heavy seas, the ferry's engines gave way in the Tsugau Straits.

Through some herculean effort, the captain and crew of the ferry managed to keep her afloat. Powerless against the currents, the ferry was swept against a reef at the entrance to Hakodate harbor. The boat overturned, spilling its 1,000 passengers, including 50 Americans, into the sea, where they all drowned.

JAPAN
OSAKA

September 21, 1934

• • • • • • • • • • • • • •

Four thousand people died when a monster typhoon struck Osaka, Japan on September 21, 1934.

Despite the devastation caused by countless typhoons throughout Japan's history, the builders of Osaka, because they had not felt the fury of these ravaging storms for more than a generation, constructed buildings not meant to withstand storms—including schools, hospitals and even an insane asylum. These vulnerable structures stood directly in the midst of a classic storm path, one which the furious typhoon took that bore down directly upon the city on September 21, 1934.

The outer fringes of the monster storm containing winds of 50 mph struck Kyoto, Kobe and Tokyo glancing blows. The typhoon hit Osaka dead center, with winds exceeding 125 mph. Osaka's major industry was textiles. In one afternoon, 3,082 factories were destroyed, literally blown to pieces, as hundreds of workers were killed in the disintegrating buildings.

The Sorojima Leper Hospital was ripped apart, killing 200 of its 560 inmates. The insane asylum was flattened, and 50 more died under its wreckage.

Eighty-seven schools were wrenched from their foundations during the middle of the school day; 420 children were killed in their classrooms and another 1,000 were seriously injured when pieces of the buildings shattered and became decimatingly airborne.

All in all, 4,000 people died in the storm, most of them residents of Osaka.

JAPAN
TOKYO

September 30, 1918

• • • • • • • • • • • • • •

One of the worst typhoons in Japan's history slammed into Tokyo on September 30, 1918, killing 1,619 and making 139,000 homeless.

In Japan, as in the rest of the world, weather forecasting methods and warning systems were in a relatively primitive state in 1918. Thus, when the residents of Tokyo went to bed on the night of September 30, they settled in with a fair amount of serenity, thinking they were only receiving another rainstorm.

By 3 A.M., however, the wind velocity had reached 100 mph, and the fragile structures in the poorer sections of Tokyo had begun to blow away, tumbling against each other and crushing inhabitants both inside and outside the dwellings.

The Kasai and Sunamura neighborhoods, near the waterfront, were turned into raging sluiceways with nine-foot-high waves roaring over the waterfront and rushing through the streets. Hundreds drowned.

Even such sturdy structures as the Seiyoken Hotel and the Ebisu Brewery collapsed against the assault of wind and waves. Ancient pine trees that had withstood centuries of lesser typhoons were uprooted. Most astonishingly, the windows of some houses seemed to explode outward, suggesting an abrupt drop in air pressure that usually only occurs in tornadoes.

The devastation was immense. Six hundred twenty-nine people died within the city. Another 990 deaths occurred in its outskirts. When 200,000 houses both in and outside Tokyo were demolished by this severe typhoon, 139,000 were rendered homeless.

JAPAN
TYPHOON IDA

September 27–28, 1958

• • • • • • • • • • • • •

Over 600 were killed, thousands were injured and 1,200 were made homeless by Typhoon Ida, which hit the Izu Peninsula near Tokyo, Japan on September 27 and 28, 1958.

More than 600 people lost their lives, thousands were injured and 1,200 were reported missing in the onslaught of Typhoon Ida, which slammed into the Izu Peninsula, 70 miles south of Tokyo on September 27, 1958. This plot of land is rich in rice paddies, supplying Japan with a goodly portion of the staple of its diet. The storm destroyed most of the Izu Peninsula's crop that year, flooding 120,000 acres of rice paddies.

The Eguro, Kano and Arakawa Rivers, swollen by torrential rains and wind-driven storm surges, overflowed their banks, taking down 244 bridges, washing away 1,000 homes and creating 1,875 muddy landslides. More than 10,000 residents of the area were rendered homeless by the combination of winds and floodwaters.

JAPAN
TYPHOON VERA

September 26–27, 1959

• • • • • • • • • • • • •

Japan's worst typhoon, Typhoon Vera, hit central Honshu Province on September 26, 1959. Five thousand people died, 15,000 were injured and 400,000 were made homeless.

The worst typhoon in Japan's history struck central Honshu Province on September 26, 1959, killing 5,000 people, injuring more than 15,000, rendering 400,000 homeless and causing $750 million in damages.

Powered by 135-mph winds, the storm slammed into the coastline from Nagoya to Tokyo on the night of September 26, flinging the 7,412-ton British-owned freighter *Changsha* onto the beach at Nagoya.

Yokohama and Tokyo were hit first; 92-mph winds roared down the canyons of their urban streets, forcing floodwaters ahead of them. From here, the storm flung itself inland across central Honshu Province, then turned north and traversed the island, wrecking the provinces of Toyama, Yamagata, Akita and Niigata.

The city receiving the worst of the storm was Nagoya, which was celebrating its 70th anniversary. An early casualty of the storm was a series of Golden Dolphins affixed to its 350-year-old castle in commemoration of the anniversary.

The Nagoya lumber yards, heavily stocked with logs waiting to be cut into planks were turned into ammunition dumps by the storm. Floated loose by the floodwaters, and propelled by the winds, the logs shot down streets in Nagoya, ramming in doors and walls.

As the floodwaters rose, hundreds of people were swept out of their homes before the homes themselves collapsed. Over 5,800 houses in Nagoya alone were destroyed by the winds or the flood waters. Even modern apartment buildings fell, often burying their inhabitants under the rubble.

On the day following the storm, 25,000 people wandered or swam over their devastated homes. Thieves were so plentiful and persistent they often robbed homes that were still occupied. A police force of 1,100 men was finally formed to control the looting.

Further tragedy occurred when dysentery and typhus, spread by polluted water, claimed more lives.

PHILIPPINES

October 14–15, 1970

• • • • • • • • • • • • •

Three successive typhoons killed 1,500 and rendered 500,000 homeless when they struck the Philippines on October 14 and 15, 1970.

Three typhoons in a row ravaged southern Luzon, Mindanao and smaller islands in the Philippines during two terror-filled days, on October 14 and 15, 1970.

There was no discernible pattern to the destruction; the storms crisscrossed the islands, striking with an average velocity of 100 mph and completely destroying an astonishing 90,000 homes in 24 provinces. In all, 1,500 died and over 500,000 were made homeless by these rampaging typhoons. The islands' crops were destroyed, cities were rendered powerless and the damage was reckoned in the millions.

The Philippine government was overwhelmed by the cleanup job. Red Cross disaster relief supplies and other aid quickly arrived from China, Canada and the Soviet Union.

PHILIPPINES
LUZON ISLANDS

December 17–18, 1944

• • • • • • • • • • • • •

The worst storm disaster to strike the United States Navy hit Admiral "Bull" Halsey's fleet off Luzon in the Philippines on

December 17 and 18, 1944. Seven hundred ninety people drowned, three ships and 156 airplanes were destroyed, and 28 ships were crippled.

During World War II, the weather warning apparatus for the U.S. Navy in the Pacific was located in Honolulu. It was efficient and up to date for the time, but when, on December 16, 1944, a 300-mile-wide, monster typhoon bore down on Admiral Halsey's Third Fleet, which was cruising off the Luzon Islands of the Philippines, the Honolulu weather station was unable to chart the typhoon's course.

Thus, the worst storm disaster to strike the United States Navy approached without warning. Seven hundred ninety seamen would drown, three ships and 156 airplanes would be lost, and 28 ships would be crippled.

The Third Fleet had just come from assisting General Douglas MacArthur and his troops, who had landed on the main island of Luzon. It was resting and refueling just east of the Philippines when the storm struck, on December 17, with 150-mph winds and waves that rose 100 feet above equally menacing troughs in the sea.

The fleet had already been battered by war. Most of its ships had been in continuous service since Pearl Harbor, three years before. Thus, the 24 hours of repeated pounding by immense waves, pelting rain and enormously powerful wind sent some to the bottom and ripped rivets, rigging and armor plate from others. One hundred fifty-six airplanes were torn from their moorings on the decks of the fleet's aircraft carriers.

The Flagship Command attempted, in the early hours of the storm, to maintain order. But the power of the storm was such that this soon became impossible, and the fleet scattered, each ship seeking its own means of survival.

The 1,500-ton Destroyer *Monohan*, a veteran of 12 battles, keeled over early, pounded repeatedly by gigantic waves. She was driven to the bottom with 256 officers and crew aboard; only six survived.

The *Hull*, a sister ship to the *Monohan*, was likewise thrown over on its side, whipped from quadrant to quadrant by waves and wind, pummeled by huge rollers and eventually sent to the bottom.

The 2,000-ton *Spence* tipped over as a 100-foot-high wave slammed it down into a seemingly bottomless valley of churning water. One officer and seventy enlisted men were flung into the water, and, although the wind and waves ripped lifejackets from some of them, all 71 managed to survive.

The magnitude of the disaster drove the Naval Command to establish another Weather Control Station on the island of Guam to oversee storm conditions in that part of the Pacific.

PHILIPPINES
TYPHOON IKE

September 2, 1984

• • • • • • • • • • • • • • • • •

Typhoon Ike, packing winds of 137 mph, struck the Philippines on September 2, 1984, killing 1,363, injuring over 300 and making 1.12 million people homeless.

Typhoon Ike, the worst recorded storm of this century to hit the Philippines, slammed into the southern part of these Pacific islands on September 2, 1984, with winds of 137 mph. Ike killed an estimated 1,363 people, injured more than 300 and rendered 1.12 million homeless.

The storm uprooted trees, darkened the provincial capital of Mindanao, 450 miles south of Manila, and flattened homes and businesses across six southern provinces. In Mainit, a lake overflowed, drowning 200 people, and on Negros Island, near Cebu, 59 people died when the storm surge completely engulfed the island. Surigao del Norte and del Sur provinces were the worst hit by the storm. Ninety percent of the crops in the Surigao region were destroyed, and the day after the storm struck, Constantino Navarro, the Mayor of Surigao City appealed for immediate food assistance, stating that rice stocks in his area would only last for 10 days.

At first, President Ferdinand Marcos refused aid from outside of the Philippines, declaring that ". . . everything is under control . . ." and "The policy has been to rely on our own resources."

But the $4.4 million in government aid released by Marcos soon proved inadequate, and the Philippine president requested aid, which was immediately forthcoming from the United States and Japan.

Meanwhile, Ike roared on to the China Seas, whipping the southern China coast. Thirteen people were reported missing at sea off the city of Bethai after enormous winds swept the coast of the Guangxi-Zhuang Autonomous Region on September 6, 1984. Factories and houses collapsed in Bethai, Qinzhou, Fangcheng and the area around the regional capital of Nanning.

PHILIPPINES
TYPHOON RUBY

October 24, 1988

• • • • • • • • • • • • • • • • •

Three hundred fifty-six people died—240 of them aboard a capsized ferry—and 110,000 were made homeless when Typhoon Ruby hit the Philippines on October 24, 1988.

Typhoon Ruby, the strongest typhoon to hit the main island of Luzon in the Philippines since Typhoon Patsy in 1970, slammed into the coast 50 miles east of Manila on October 24, 1988. Three hundred fifty-six people died in the storm—240 of them aboard the ferry *Dona Marilyn*, that sank in 140-mph winds with 500 passengers and crew aboard at the height of the typhoon. This monster storm made 110,000 Philippine residents homeless and caused $45 million in damage. The islands were saturated with nine inches of rain in a 24-hour period, causing massive flooding, mudslides and washed out bridges.

Twenty-six people died in central Antique province when a bus went off a bridge and into the Sibalom River during the storm.

The dramatic *Dona Marilyn* disaster was the second such sinking within a year in the Philippines, following the horrendous *Dona Paz* collision with an oil tanker on December 20 off the central part of the islands.

The 2,846-ton *Dona Marilyn* was carrying fewer than half its capacity of 1,279 passengers when it left Manila at 10 A.M. Sunday, October 23. It was scheduled to arrive about 24 hours later in Tacloban, the provincial capital of Leyte.

But at 11:30 A.M. on Monday the 24th, the vessel's crew radioed Manila to say they were changing course because of choppy water. At 1:10 P.M., they radioed Manila again. This time it was a distress signal stating that they had encountered large waves and were taking on water. It was the last message received from the sinking ferryboat, which went down in the Visayas Sea just short of its destination of Leyte Island.

Later that day, two survivors were rescued from the water, eight were rescued from a nearby island and five from another. The next day, 135 more were discovered alive on a third island. Seventy-six other people lost their lives on the Philippine mainland from drowning or injuries received from falling debris.

VIETNAM
September 25, 1953

• • • • • • • • • • • • • • • •

Over 1,300 were killed, over 100,000 were made homeless, and the U.S. Air Force Base in Otsu, Japan was almost destroyed by a typhoon that struck Vietnam on September 25, 1953.

A typhoon that killed 21 persons and caused $1.9 million in damage to the United States Air Force Base in Otsu, Japan slammed into the central coast of Vietnam on September 25, 1953. Its 90-mile-wide swath cut through the central part of the country, wiping out the entire rice crop of the two provinces traversed by the storm.

In the countryside, 1,300 people either drowned or were crushed by collapsing huts or flying debris. In the capital city of Hue, 325 miles north of Saigon, massive numbers of people died, and a large percentage of the city's structures were flattened.

At the storm's end, over 100,000 would be left without homes or shelter.

STORMS

. . . .

THE WORST RECORDED STORMS

CHRONOLOGY

STORMS

The following storm disasters are collected together because they occur too infrequently to
justify a section of their own.

All are self-explanatory, with the exception of
monsoons which possess distinct and individual
characteristics.

Simply stated, monsoons are winds that change
direction with the change of seasons in India and
Southeast Asia. In the winter, they bring no moisture; in the summer they carry with them torrential
rains, which, when unleashed, cause large amounts
of human and crop damage.

The change in wind direction results from changes
in air temperature over land masses and oceans.
In winter, the wind change that causes monsoons
results from an area of high pressure that develops
over southern Siberia, out of which dry winds cross

India from northeast to southwest, and Southeast
Asia directly from north to south. The wet, or
summer monsoon formation is a little more complex: Its source is an area of low pressure which
develops over Southeast Asia as the land mass
slowly warms. As the low pressure area deepens,
moisture-heavy air from the oceans is drawn toward
it. Then, this air cools as it ascends the slopes of
mountain barriers in Asia and India, and, losing
its ability to retain moisture, releases it in torrential
rainfall.

Since the destruction from monsoons almost
always manifests itself in floods, consult the separate section on floods (p. 91) for additional information on the effects of monsoons in India and
Southeast Asia. Only two monsoons are included
in this section.

· · · · · · · · · · · · · · ·

ENGLAND
LONDON FOG

December 1952

· · · · · · · · · · · · · ·

*London's deadliest fog occurred in December 1952. Twelve
thousand people died from ingesting soft-coal smoke, sulphur
dioxide, chemical fumes and gasoline fumes contained in the
fog.*

London's fogs are both legendary and picturesque—to all
but those who have experienced them. Formed by a combination of stalled warm air masses and the smoke given
off by thousands of soft-coal stoves and factory chimneys,
they have, for centuries, literally strangled a large part of

the populace of this city, bringing its commerce to a stop,
hospitalizing many and killing more.

Even the interiors of theaters, restaurants and other public
places whose doors to the street opened and closed frequently were not exempt from the notorious fog. The dense,
pungent, opaque air would roll into movie theaters, ob-
scuring the screen and making the auditorium uninhabitable.

The deadliest fog ever settled over London in December
1952. Soft-coal smoke, sulpher dioxide, chemical fumes
and gasoline fumes collected in the atmosphere, intensifying as the warm mass lingered. Four thousand people
died from ingesting the fumes, and another 8,000 eventually died from its aftereffects.

It was this catastrophic fog that brought about the four-
year study that would produce England's Clean Air Act.

ENGLAND
LONDON
FOG

December 3–7, 1962

· · · · · · · · · · · · · ·

One hundred thirty-six people died and 1,000 were hospitalized in the last lethal London fog, from December 3 through 7, 1962.

Great Britain's Clean Air Act of 1956 had scoured the London air of most pollutants. But certain industries were still sending great quantities of sulphur dioxide into the air in and around England's capital city.

Thus, when another air inversion brought on a heavy fog on December 3, 1962, 136 elderly persons succumbed to the fumes and another 1,000 were hospitalized.

The *New Yorker's* London correspondent gave the following colorful description: "The fog floated visibly, like ectoplasm, into theaters, cinemas, and shops, where sales assistants stood around gossiping among the sparsely populated wastes of Christmas presents. In the evenings, the West End was as empty as on a night in the blitz. . . . If you had felt the urge to do so, you could have danced in the eerie middle of Piccadilly in safety, if not in comfort."

That, apparently, was after the first casualties of the fog conditions, and after London's 5,000 red double-decker buses were pulled from the streets after two of them collided, injuring 13 passengers. A train motorman was drowned when he stepped from his cab and, not realizing he had stopped on a bridge, plummeted into 40 feet of water. Scores of pedestrians were run down by motorists, driving blind.

Perhaps the only positive advantage of this fog was the use it was put to by the British Ministry of Aviation. It successfully tested a new blind flying system at London Airport.

ENGLISH CHANNEL
WINDSTORM

January 16, 1974

· · · · · · · · · · · · · ·

A freak windstorm with 100-mph gales killed 36 people and sent numerous ships to the bottom of the English Channel on January 16, 1974.

Completely outside the hurricane season and without the snow that would qualify it as a blizzard, a freak windstorm with 100-mph gales whipped up 55-foot-high waves in the English Channel on January 16, 1974.

The 2,088-ton Cypriot freighter *Prosperity* swirled out of control in the middle of the channel in the midst of the storm, which finally drove it aground on a reef off the island of Guernsey. Eighteen of its crew members drowned.

The *Merc Enterprises,* a 781-ton Danish freighter also went down in the storm, taking with it eight crew members.

The storm then struck the coast of Brittany and battered the 2,447-ton freighter *Marta,* 10 miles off the coast of Ostend, Belgium, causing the craft to catch fire. Hours afterward, the *Marta,* missing one of her seamen who had leaped with his clothes aflame into the water, limped into Ostend harbor, which by now was calm.

Other fatalities occurred in different locations. Six fishermen in Brest and Brittany were lost when their boats disappeared. At Dawlins, in Devon, two boys were swept off a seawall and into the Channel. Almost instantly, a wave scooped up one of the boys and swept him safely ashore. A 16-year-old girl was lost from a Brest ferry when wind-powered waves washed across the ferry's decks.

INDIA
MONSOON

October 7–12, 1955

· · · · · · · · · · · · · ·

One of India's worst natural disasters occurred as a result of floods generated by the monsoons of October 7–12, 1955. Seventeen hundred people were killed and 28,000 villages were totally destroyed.

When monsoon rains struck Orissa province from October 7 through 12, 1955, the population was caught unprepared.

The results were horrendous. According to the estimate of Dr. Francois Daubenton of the International Red Cross, 1,700 persons lost their lives and 28,000 villages were wiped off the face of the Earth, obliterated by the roaring flood waters from eight rivers; 3,500 square miles of cropland were flooded and rendered useless.

In India and Pakistan, thousands of people clung to trees, their only refuge above the roaring waters fed by downpours and whipped by the monsoon winds. Over 300,000 persons were evacuated by Indian paratroopers. The International Red Cross and other International Relief agencies were quick to converge upon the disaster site. The United States alone sent 10,000 tons of wheat to the devastated area.

(See also FLOODS, p. 91.)

THAILAND
MONSOON

September–December 1983

• • • • • • • • • • • • •

Ten thousand people died, 100,000 contracted water-borne diseases and 15,000 were evacuated as a result of the monsoons that raged throughout Thailand from September through December 1983.

The three months of monsoon rains that engulfed Thailand from September through the middle of December, 1983, caused more than $400 million in damage and 100,000 people to contract water-borne diseases. Ten thousand died in floods, and 15,000 were evacuated. Many of those who stayed cut their feet on submerged glass and other obstacles, and one hospital reported 20 cases and two deaths from leptospirosis, a disease once common in the trenches of World War I.

The storms caused the worst flooding in 40 years in the capital city of Bangkok, and brought to the attention of city planners the uncomfortable fact that, like Venice, Bangkok was sinking.

For two centuries, the city, built on low ground, had been drained by a network of canals. As urban sprawl took over, the canals were blocked or simply paved over, thus causing the massive flooding following the monsoon.

Thus, after floods, some city streets resembled riverbeds, with gravel and boulders littering them; others like the aftermath of some recent battle.

Finally, after an exchange in which Admiral Tiam Makarandanda, the Governor of Bangkok, accused the Interior Minister and his Irrigation Department of relieving flooded farmlands east of the city by pumping water into the suburbs, the Interior Minister replied—with what he believed to be supreme logic—that both men, after all, had the people's best interest at heart. An impatient and truly logical King Phumiphol Adulet asserted, in a national address, that unplanned construction had blocked Bangkok's drainage.

Cowed by the king's knowledge of hydraulics and stung by his criticism, the Cabinet of Thailand approved a $40 million series of drainage schemes designed to build flood-gates, dredge canals and install permanent pumps. It had taken the carnage of a monsoon to bring this about. (See FLOODS, Thailand, 1988, p. 118.)

TUNISIA
RAIN

September–October 1969

• • • • • • • • • • • • •

Thirty-eight consecutive days of rain produced flooding over 80 percent of Tunisia in September and October of 1969. Five hundred forty-two people were drowned, 100,000 were made homeless and 250,000 became refugees in other countries.

An unprecedented 38 consecutive days of rain fell over Tunisia in late September and early October, 1969. Every river in the country was swollen beyond its banks, and over 80 percent of the country was flooded, from the Gulf of Bou Grara to the Gulf of Tunis.

Many of the rivers crested without warning in the middle of the night. Once unleashed, the floodwaters rampaged over the countryside, rising 36 feet above their normal levels, ripping apart 35 major bridges and washing away a $7 million irrigation project.

One hundred-ton concrete blocks were shoved out of the way like children's toys and millions of tons of valuable loam were washed into the Mediterranean. One hundred thousand head of cattle and other livestock drowned.

The human toll was staggering: 542 people drowned; more than 100,000 were rendered homeless and a quarter of a million people became temporary or permanent refugees from the storm and the floodwaters.

Starvation was the immediate effect of the catastrophe. Villagers, wild with hunger, ripped the door off one U.S. Air Force helicopter that landed, some weeks later, in the remains of one gutted town. All told, 84 nations sent relief funds and supplies to alleviate the human toll and the $200 million in damage brought on by a deluge that was just two days short of the Biblical one, and, to the human beings caught in it, nearly as devastating.

VOLCANIC ERUPTIONS AND NATURAL EXPLOSIONS

. . . .

THE WORST RECORDED VOLCANIC ERUPTIONS AND NATURAL EXPLOSIONS

. . . . .

CHRONOLOGY

. . . .

• Nicaragua (Coseguina)

1883

August 26–27

• Java (Krakatoa)

1897

June 23–30

• Philippines (Mayon)

1902

May 8

• Martinique (Pelee)

May 7 and 8

• West Indies (La Soufriere)

October 24

• Guatemala (Santa Maria)

1906

April 4

• Italy (Vesuvius)

1909

Indonesia (Kelut)

1911

January 30

• Philippines (Taal)

1919

• Java (Keluit)

1931

December 13–28

• Java (Merapi)

1944

March 18

• Italy (Vesuvius)

June

• Mexico (Paricutin)

1951

January 21

• New Guinea (Lamington)

1956

March 30

• Kamchatka, USSR (Bezymianny)

1960

May 21–30

Chile

1980

May 18

• United States (Mt. St. Helens)

1985

November 13

Colombia

1991

June 10–15

• Philippines (Mt. Pinatubo)

VOLCANIC ERUPTIONS AND NATURAL EXPLOSIONS

• • • • •

If drama and spectacle were the stuff of natural disasters, then volcanic eruptions would be their benchmark, for there is probably nothing more terrifying or splendid than the eruption of a volcano. It is cataclysmic, often climactic, and frequently instantaneously horrible in its consequences. Cities, civilizations and cultures have been either wiped out or forever changed—and in one case, that of Vesuvius's hermetic sealing off of Pompeii—revived.

There is also something primeval and mysterious about this spurting forth of the interior contents of the Earth upon which we live. For the moments of the eruption of a volcano, we are plunged backward in time to that sort of prehistory of which legends are made, that time when the solid ground upon which we walk and base our assumptions of reality was a shifting, amorphous mass of matter, and the Earth as we know it was establishing itself in a very theatrical way.

Volcanic eruptions are still, to this day, somewhat of a mystery. Volcanologists can only study the aftereffects of a volcanic explosion. The cause and sources of such an event are buried too deeply within the Earth—perhaps down to its very core—to explore scientifically. And they are likely to remain that way for the remainder of human existence on this planet.

Still, we do know more about the 516 active volcanoes on the Earth at this moment than, say, Pliny did when he described the eruption of Vesuvius in A.D. 79.

First of all, the true, real volcano is merely a vent, or a series of vents in the Earth's crust, through which the forces of the Earth's interior are released into the atmosphere, often violently. The mouth of the vent is referred to as the crater. The large, more or less circular depression—if it is more than a mile in diameter—formed either by collapse or by explosion of the volcano, is the caldera. Crater lakes sometimes form in these calderas.

The vent is like a chimney, connecting the atmosphere with a reservoir of molten matter known as magma. The smoke that seems to come from these vents is actually condensed steam, frequently mixed with dust particles until it is dark in color. The so-called fire of a volcano is the reflection of the red-hot material on the vapor clouds above the volcano. And the lighting observed playing around and through this vapor cloud is actually St. Elmo's fire, caused by a characteristic abundance of static electricity in the atmosphere around a volcanic explosion.

Volcanic mountains—which we often mistake for volcanoes—are formed after a series of explosions have deposited cooled matter blasted forth from beneath the Earth's crust around the vent. In fact, the highest mountains in the world were formed, over millions of years, through the accumulation of volcanic detritus.

There are three varieties of material expelled from volcanoes: liquid (lava), fragmental (pyroclastics, such as ash, mud and rocks) and gaseous—usually sulphur dioxide if it comes from beneath the Earth, but sometimes a hybrid formed from contamination of the atmosphere.

And lastly, the explosions from a volcano do not always shoot straight up from its cone, as 19th-century romantic artists have depicted them. On the contrary, the most lethal and cataclysmic of volcanic explosions occur in the sides of volcanic mountains.

Volcanologists have been able to plot the major belts of volcanoes on the Earth: The Mid-Atlantic range, going through the West Indies; the Cascade Range in the Pacific Northwest; the Hawaiian Range; the unnamed string of mountains that occurs along the north shore of the Mediterranean and extends eastward through Asia Minor into the Himalayas and beyond.

The theory of plate tectonics (see EARTHQUAKES, Introduction, p. 17) established some of the causes of the eruption of volcanoes. In one theory, volcanoes appear where two plates are pulling apart, thus releasing a surge of magma from beneath the plates. The Mid-Atlantic Ridge, for instance, exists along the seam at which the Eurasian and American plates begin to move in opposite directions. Here, volcanic islands such as Iceland, the Azores and Tristan de Cunha have been formed.

The second cause for the formation of volcanoes, according to this theory, comes where plates collide, or slide over or under each other. When one plate slides beneath the other, it melts and churns as it descends into the bowels of the Earth. Molten material simultaneously rises to the surface and erupts there, forming new land. These collisions or grindings created the Caribbean Islands, the volcanic peaks of Central America and the Cascade Range.

The third type of volcanic formation occurs in the middle of a plate. According to Earth scientist Dr. Robert Decker, "Somehow, a hot spot in the Earth's mantle melts a hole through the middle of a plate, allowing molten material to spill out on the surface. The Hawaiian Islands are a perfect example of this process—they are right in the middle of the huge Pacific plate."

Volcanologists have classified volcanoes into four categories, ranging from the least to the most destructive, and those of the Hawaiian type are considered the least destructive—in fact, Mauna Loa, the fabled mountain of Hawaii does not appear in this section, nor does Fujiyama in Japan because neither have had catastrophic explosions, at least in recorded history.

In the Hawaiian category of volcano, there is a relatively quiet effusion of basaltic lava unaccompanied by explosions or the ejection of fragments.

The Strombolian type of volcano (named for Stromboli, in the Lipari or Aeolian Islands north of Sicily) is characterized by continuous but mild discharges, in which viscous lava is emitted in recurring explosions. The ejection of incandescent material produces luminous clouds.

The Vulcanian category of volcano, typified by Paricutin (see p. 296), is more explosive. Here, the magma accumulates in the upper level of the vent but is blocked by a plug or hardened lava that forms at the orifice between consecutive explosions. When the explosive gases have reached a critical pressure within the volcano, masses of solid and liquid rock erupt into the air, and clouds of vapor form over the crater, but they are not incandescent, as in the Strombolian type.

The most violent and destructive type of volcano is the Pelean type, named after its prototype, Pelee (see p. 292). Here there is an emission of fine ash, hot gas-charged fragments of magma and superheated steam in an incandescent cloud that moves downhill with the speed of a major hurricane. Thus, thousands of people are often caught absolutely unaware and are simply ground under by superheated mud, steam and molten, falling ash and rocks.

Volcanoes rarely erupt without warning. The problem in the past has been the disregard of warning signs, namely earthquakes. Even in modern times, people situated near volcanoes ignore common sense and the warnings of experts.

• • • • • • • • • • • • •

GREECE
SANTORINI

1470 B.C.

• • • • • • • • • • • • •

Santorini, in the Aegean Sea, erupted cataclysmically in the summer of 1470 B.C. Experts theorize that it was the cause of four major prehistoric events recorded by Plato and documented in the Bible.

The overnight disappearance of Atlantis. The parting of the Red Sea. The plague of darkness that allowed the Children of Israel to leave Egypt. The disappearance of the Minoan Civilization. If the theories of Professor George A. Galanopoulos, the director of the Seismological Laboratory of the University of Athens, are to be believed, all of these legendary happenings are inextricably linked by a single, cataclysmic cause: the monumental eruption of the volcano Santorini, located in the Aegean Sea, 131 miles southeast of Athens and 68 miles north of the island of Crete.

Santorini (a medieval Italian corruption of Sant' Irene, the patron saint of the volcanic island of Thera) is one of a series of volcanoes that form an island arc bordering the former Aegean land mass. According to Dr. Galanopoulos, Santorini's first subterranean explosions took place in the Pleistocene Age, after which the cone of Santorini, along with a number of accompanying cones, grew to a height of 5,300 feet above sea level.

This growth was apparently uneventful. Then, in the summer of 1470 B.C., Santorini erupted with incredible force, enough to atomize its summit, collapse the cones of several nearby volcanic mountains and send an enormous geyser of molten rock skyward, over the islands of the Mediterranean, Crete and part of Egypt. An area of 77,200 square miles was completely covered with the ash from this gigantic explosion which sent a cloud of poisonous vapors and sun-blotting darkness over Egypt and the eastern Mediterranean that lasted for days and possibly weeks.

The caldera (the depression formed by the volcano's explosion) of Santorini was enormous, more than three times the area of the caldera of Krakatoa. If Plato and Dr. Galanopoulos are to be believed, it was, until the moment of the eruption, the lost colony of Atlantis.

When the top of Santorini blew off in 1470 B.C., it took with it all of the structures and all of the people of this fabled empire, and deposited them on the floor of the Mediterranean Sea.

The legend and reality blend convincingly. First, although Santorini initially erupted in the Pleistocne Age and was active enough to build itself to a height of 5,250 feet, it probably was inactive enough for a civilization to have been built on its summit. Second, this summit measured 32.05 square miles—not enough space for a huge civilization, but certainly large enough for one of the size of either Athens or Sparta, comparable civilizations of the time.

The story of Atlantis—the advanced, island empire that sank beneath the sea in a single day and night—is told by Plato near the opening of *Timaeus* and in more detail in *Critias*. The tale is credited to Critias, an Athenian political figure in the Socratic circle, who in turn heard it when he was 10 years old from his 90-year-old grandfather, who had heard it from his father, a friend of Solon, the founder of Athenian democracy.

The Irazu Volcano, located in Turrialba, Costa Rica is typical of the Central American chain of volcanos that have erupted periodically from earliest recorded history to today. U.N. photo.

An engraving depicting the 1866 eruption of Nea Kameni, Santorini, Greece. National Geophysical Data Center.

Solon, it seems, was a progressive and a free thinker, who believed in outlawing contracts where personal freedom was involved. This brought about his 10-year exile in Egypt, where he learned from the priests of Sais, one of the ancient cities of the Nile delta, the story of an island empire larger than Libya and western Asia combined, located outside the Pillars of Hercules (now the Straits of Gibraltar), which, 9,000 years earlier, had disappeared in a single day and night beneath the water.

Two problems arose for some historians. One was the small size of the caldera that supposedly contained the civilization; the other was the 9,000 year figure recorded by Solon. However, in 1956, Dr. Galanopoulos, examining the refuse from a severe earthquake on Thera, concluded that, among other misinterpretations of history, a misplaced decimal would make the 9,000 figure 900, and thus locate the disappearance of Atlantis at 570, approximately the time of the explosion and decimation of the summit of Santorini. Dividing the land area of Libya and Western Asia by 10 also diminishes the area to that of the caldera of Santorini.

Fascinating. But the possibility that the eruption of Santorini was also the destruction of Atlantis is only one-fourth of this intriguing theory. The disappearance of the first true civilization in the Mediterranean area, the Minoan civilization, which developed in Crete and the adjacent islands, also happened around 1400 B.C. At the same time, the Mycenaean civilization, which contained a multitude of Minoan traditions, suddenly appeared in southern Greece.

It seems reasonable to assume, then, as the Irish scholar K. Y. Frost did in a 1939 newspaper article titled "The Critias and Minoan Crete" and as did the Greek archeologist S. Marinatos, who carried out excavations at the Minoan palaces of Crete, that the Minoan civilization was not destroyed by foreign invaders, but was, instead, buried under the pumice falling from a gigantic, cataclysmic natural catastrophe of an unparalleled violence. The cataclysm? The eruption of Santorini, 75 miles to the north of Crete.

The conclusions of both Dr. Marinatos and Dr. Galanopoulos—who, while investigating a mine shaft after the earthquake of 1956, discovered the ruins of a stone house in which he found two small pieces of wood and some human teeth, which radiocarbon dating proved to have come from approximately 1400 B.C.—were that a giant tsunami, caused by the eruption of Santorini, destroyed most of the Minoan civilization, and its survivors went to Greece, where they founded the Mycenaean civilization. This, too, was a responsible conclusion: Tsunamis were not uncommon in the region around Crete (recorded ones from earthquakes submerged parts of Alexandria, Egypt in A.D. 365, and the southeast coast of the island of Amorgas, about 40 miles southeast of Santorini, was inundated in 1956), so the theory could be true.

And if that was not enough, the conclusions of these two gentlemen had been prepared for in the 19th century by French engineers who built the Suez canal and mined the thick volcanic ash layer on Thera for the manufacture of cement used in the construction of the canal. Under the ash layer, they found remains of a civilization which was clearly pre-Greek, but whose age was then unknown.

So much for Atlantis and Minoa. Now, Galanopoulos, fired by his first discoveries, went on to speculate upon other effects of this monster eruption.

Continuing with his tsunami tracing, he used it to explain the Biblical parting of the waters of the Red Sea, which allowed the Children of Israel to escape the pursuing forces of the Pharaoh. The parting, according to Professor Galanopoulos, was brought about by the withdrawing of the sea a half hour or so before the tsunami struck, thus exposing a large area of the sea bottom near the shore.

All of this gains credibility when one considers that the date of approximately 1450 B.C. is usually assigned by Biblical scholars as the time of the exodus of the Children of Israel from Egypt. Noticing this, Professor Galanopoulos also concluded that the great plague of darkness brought by the Lord to compel the Pharaoh to let these children go was the same volcanic cloud that darkened all of the region after the explosion. "And the Lord said unto Moses," it says in Exodus 10:21–22, "stretch out thine hand toward heaven, that there may be darkness over the land of Egypt, even darkness which may be felt. And Moses stretched forth his hand towards heaven; and there was a thick darkness in all the land of Egypt for three days."

Considering the fact that there was total darkness for 22 hours at a distance of 130 miles and for 57 hours at a distance of 50 miles from the collapse of the caldera of Krakatoa in 1883 (see p. 289), it is not only possible but probable that darkness continued for at least 3 days over Egypt in 1470 B.C.

Thus, four legends from four sources might very well have had their basis in the fact of one calamitous natural explosion—one that, if the theories that link these legends to it are even nearly true, is extraordinary, perhaps monumental—not only in its persuasive actuality but in its effect upon the history of the world, its legends, its civilizations, and its beliefs.

GUATEMALA
SANTA MARIA

October 24, 1902

• • • • • • • • • • • • • •

Six thousand people were killed when Santa Maria, a 12,361-foot volcano in western Guatemala erupted on October 24, 1902. An area of 125,000 square miles was covered by volcanic ash and stone.

Santa Maria, a volcano rising 12,361 feet above the flat coffee plantations of western Guatemala, erupted with a roar that was heard 500 miles away in Costa Rica on October 24, 1902.

It was an explosion of enormous proportions. An entire side of the mountain blew away, sending farmhouses into the air and crushing those which remained with horrendous showers of gigantic boulders. In fact, most of the 6,000 people who perished were crushed to death in their homes when this lethal rainfall of rocks, some of them weighing a ton or more, descended upon them.

The rest were killed by the lava flow whose pumice stone and ashes eventually covered an area of 125,000 square miles to a depth of eight inches.

The eruption cloud lingered for weeks and climbed to a height of 18 miles before dissipating. The eruption would rank as one of the worst in the entire history of volcanic explosions.

ICELAND
LAKI

January–June 1783

• • • • • • • • • • • • • •

Twenty thousand people—one-third of the population of Iceland—were killed by the monumental, multiple eruptions of Laki, a 15-mile-long series of 100 craters and vents near Lakagigar, from January to June, 1783.

A small, thinly populated country abutting the Arctic Circle, Iceland seems like anything but a volatile place. And yet Iceland is one of the most volcanically active places in the world. Straddling the mid-Atlantic Ridge, it has, during its 1,100 years of recorded history, experienced an eruption on the average of once every five years.

In 1783, it was the site of a monumental volcanic explosion that produced the world record for casualties. It took place over a span of six months and consumed nearly 20,000 lives, or one-third of the population of the country.

"Basically," Dr. Sigurdur Thorarinsson, the dean of Icelandic geologists, told National Geographic writer William R. Gray in 1978, "Iceland is part of the ocean floor. We simply happen to be sitting over a plume where more magma [hot rock] has been released and therefore more terrain built."

The residents of Iceland had ample warning of this cataclysmic disaster. First, there was the long-term knowledge that Iceland is situated on the northern rim of one of the major concentrations of volcanoes in the world. In a more immediate sense, they experienced, prior to the eruption, a long series of seismic upheavals over several weeks of escalating ground movements and a roiling sea that erupted periodically in enormous geysers, whirlpools and water spouts which intensified the tides enormously.

The seas literally steamed in the few days before Laki's eruption, and the 50,000 inhabitants of Iceland, most of them farmers and families of farmers, had become so thoroughly terrified from the weeks of upheavels that they had retreated within their homes, where they locked the doors and windows.

Laki, near Thingvellir, is a 15-mile-long slash in the Earth, with over 100 craters and vents pockmarking it. The center of activity was near Lakagigar, one of its largest craters, in a practically deserted part of Iceland. On June 11, 1783, the mountain called Skaptar Jokul, near Lakagigar, erupted with a cataclysmic roar, splitting open the entire 15-mile-long fissure. The gas pressure and rock-melting heat spewed forth a powerful and prodigious lava flow. Within hours, the normally placid and huge River Skapta was dried up and replaced by a lava flow 200 feet wide and from 400 to 600 feet deep. The moving lava, fueled by repeated eruptions that continued like grim, deafening echoes, moved relentlessly and purposefully to the sea, where it turned the water into steam, killing the fish for miles.

Ashes filled the air and blotted out the daylight. The grasslands for 50 miles around the mountain were poisoned, and grazing cattle and sheep died by the thousands. According to one report, "The hills were dotted with decaying carcasses. The air was filled with horrible stench." Seventy percent of Iceland's livestock would die within the next two years.

Once put in motion, the volcanic forces did not ease. The enormous lava flow, the largest in history, poured forth from this 15-mile-long fissure, in various places, alternately creeping and racing across a staggering 23,400 acres of land, laying waste to it, and creating cloud upon cloud of noxious fumes from the decaying vegetation.

It was the largest lava flow ever recorded, covering an estimated 20 cubic miles. To early volcanologist Professor E. Bischoff, it was ". . . the greatest eruption of the world—the lava, piled, having been estimated as of greater volume than is Mont Blanc."

The lava streams crossed and recrossed the landscape, swallowing up entire villages, bypassing some and then returning to consume them on a second or third pass. Two major streams of running lava, one 40 and the other 50 miles long, roared along at an average depth of 100 feet. Eventually, they would reach widths of 15 and seven miles, thus totalling an amount of molten lava that was sufficient to cover 1,000 square miles to a depth of 150 feet. More than 9,000 villages perished of asphyxiation from the poisonous fumes or were buried and incinerated by the lava flow.

Those who reached the sea were in no less danger. The lava flow reached the beaches and inched into the sea. But before that, the heavy cloud of ashes descended upon it. According to Professor Bischoff, "The ashes fell in such volumes into the ocean that the fish deserted the coast. The flying clouds of dust spread to Europe. The appalling horror of the scene can hardly be imagined. Death stalked abroad in his most repulsive form."

While the eruptions continued, those who had escaped the lava flow and its immediate lethal effects died of starvation when both crops and fish were eliminated by the volcanic fallout.

Some sense of the enormity of this disaster can be imagined when it is compared to that of Vesuvius in its most angry times. At its worst, Vesuvius's lava flow covered only a square mile to a depth of 25 feet. Thus, its most extensive lava field was only .006 as extensive as that from this eruption of Skaptar Jokul, in the volcanic ridge of Laki.

ITALY
SICILY
ETNA

1226, 1170, 1149, 525 B.C.

• • • • • • • • • • • • • • •

The written records of the earliest eruptions of Etna, while vivid in imagery, are lacking in statistics. Nevertheless, they provide a picture of a constantly erupting volcano that repeatedly destroyed the city of Catania.

Myth has surrounded Mt. Etna as certainly as the volcanic clouds that have frequently obscured its 10,870-foot peak. Overlooking the Mediterranean from the eastern coast of

Sicily, Etna is Europe's highest, grandest volcano, and one of its only active ones today.

Scientists, and particularly volcanologists, have never ceased to be interested in Etna, since, in its dormant moments, it provides a moment of frozen time, a relic from the prehistory of the earth.

Etna may also represent the height of man's foolishness. Its base, which spans some 87 miles in circumference, is also the location of dozens of villages and a major city, Catania. Catania has been buried and dug out, destroyed and rebuilt, over and over. And yet, human beings still choose to live there, knowing full well that Etna could at any time explode and bury buildings, people and landscape.

The early eruptions of Etna were explained in religious terms by the Greeks who witnessed them. The first three recorded ones, those of 1226, 1170 and 1149, were attributed to the expulsion of Hercules from Sicily and the wrath of Zeus. Another theory postulated that Etna was the workshop of Haphaestus and Cyclops—a direct parallel to the Icelandic myth that blamed the eruptions of Heclas on the workshop activity of the fire god Thor.

No less a figure than Pythagoras recorded an explosion that took place in 525 B.C., and Thucydides set to tablet another major eruption in 477 B.C.: "In the first days of this spring the stream of fire issued from Etna as on former occasions, and destroyed some land of the Catanians who live upon Mount Etna which is the largest mountain in Sicily. Fifty years, it is said, had elapsed since the last eruption, there having been three in all since the Hellenes have inhabited Sicily."

The most detailed and literary reportage of the volcanic activity of Etna during Greek times was by the poet Pindar. In 474 B.C., he brought to center stage Typhon, whom he claimed was manacled and imprisoned in the mountain by Zeus. "He is fast bound by a pillar of the sky," wrote Pindar, "even by snowy Etna, nursing the whole year through her dazzling snow. Whereat pure springs of unapproachable fire are vomited from the inmost depths; in the daytime lava streams forth a lurid rush of smoke; but in the darkness a red roiling flame sweepeth rocks with uproar to the wide, deep sea. . . . That dragon-thing [Typhon] is what maketh issue from beneath the terrible, fiery flood."

Virgil waxed eloquent over Etna, too:

But Etna, with her voice of fear,
In weltering chaos thunders near.
Now pitchy clouds she belches forth
Of cinders red, and vapor swarth;
And from her caverns lifts on high
Live balls of flame that lick the sky;

Now with more dire convulsion flings
Disploded rocks, her heart's rent strings.
And lava torrents hurls today
A burning gulf of fiery spray . . .

Lucretius, on the other hand, chose a more scientific approach.

"I will explain in what ways yon flame, roused to fury in a moment, blazes forth from the huge furnace of Etna," wrote Lucretius.

First the nature of the whole mountain is hollow underneath, underpropped throughout with caverns of basalt rocks. Furthermore in all caves are wind and air, for wind is produced when the air has been stirred and put in motion. When the air has been thoroughly heated, and raging about, has imparted its heat to all the rocks around, whenever it comes in contact with them, and to the Earth, and has struck out from them fire burning with swift flames, it rises up and then forces itself out on high, straight through the gorges; and so carries its heat far, and scatters far its ashes, and rolls on smoke of a thick, pitchy blackness, and flings out at the same time stones of prodigious weight—leaving no doubt that this is the stormy force of air.

Again the sea to a great extent breaks its waves and sucks back its surf at the roots of the mountain. Caverns reach from this sea as far back as the deep gorges of the mountain below. Through these you must admit that air mixed up with water passes; and the nature of the case compels this air to enter in from that open sea, and pass within, and go out in blasts and so lift up flame, and throw out stones, and raise clouds of sand; for on the summit are craters, as they name them in their own language, what we call gorges and mouths.

An inaccurate report, it nevertheless attempts an explanation of one of the most splendid and terrifying of all natural disasters.

When Rome absorbed Sicily, the mythology of the mountain was turned over to the likes of Seneca, who turned the attention of his readers and listeners to the apocryphal tale of two brothers involved in the very real eruption of Etna in 477 B.C., an eruption that almost totally destroyed the city of Catania. According to Seneca, these two brothers carried their aged parents on their backs and fled from the city and the lava. But they could not outrun natural forces, and the lava overtook them. And then, like the Red Sea, the ocean of lava parted on either side of the family: "The flames blushed to touch the filial youths, and retired before their footsteps," writes Seneca. "On their right hand fierce dangers prevailed; on their left were burning fires. Athwart the flames, they passed in triumph. . . . The devouring flames fled backward and checked themselves around the twin pair. At length they issued forth unharmed, and bore with them their deities in safety."

After the eruption of 477 B.C. Catania was rebuilt and would withstand the eruption of 396 B.C., which obliterated the town of Naxos and killed all but a handful of its 500 inhabitants.

But when Etna again erupted in 122 B.C., huge, tumbling clouds of ash caved in the roofs of hundreds of houses, and prompted Rome to grant its Sicilian colonies a stay of taxation for 10 years—thus establishing the first recorded example of disaster aid from a government.

ITALY
VESUVIUS

August 24, A.D. 79

• • • • • • • • • • • • • • •

Practically all of the inhabitants of Pompeii and those unable to evacuate Herculaneum perished as a result of the horrific eruption of Mt. Vesuvius on the afternoon of August 24, A.D. 79.

One of many volcanoes in the Naples area, Vesuvius first began life as a submarine volcano in the Bay of Naples, then emerged as an island and finally was joined to the land by the filling and upbuilding of its eruptive products. Its first eruptions are believed to have occurred after the retreat of the last Ice Age, which would make it roughly 10,000 years old.

However, since the ancients made no record of Vesuvius' volcanic activity, the mountain was most likely dormant for hundreds or perhaps thousands of years before the cataclysmic explosions of A.D. 79, which destroyed the cities of Pompeii and Herculaneum.

The district's earliest known inhabitants called themselves Oscans, and they were primitive cattle herders. Around 800 B.C., the Greeks arrived and settled in eagerly. There were forests full of game. The soil around the mountain, loaded with ancient deposits of mineral-rich ash, was amazingly fertile. Apples, pears, figs, cherries, melons, almonds and pomegranates prospered. It was possible to grow two or three crops of wheat, barley and millet annually, and vegetables and grapes flourished everywhere.

Small wonder then that the twin cities of Pompeii, on the slope of Vesuvius, and Herculaneum, at the foot of the mountain and on the rim of the Bay, grew and flourished, and when Rome conquered Greece in 88 B.C., Pompeii became a jewel in the imperial crown, with its own council, Temple of Jupiter and a forum. Gauius Quinctius Balbus, a Roman speculator, erected an amphi-

An artist's depiction of Pompeii during the cataclysmic eruption of Vesuvius in A.D. *79.* Library of Congress.

theatre capable of accommodating 16,000 spectators, the entire population of the city, while they watched gladitorial games. Ironically, these games would be in progress on the afternoon of August 24, A.D. 79.

In 62 A.D., nature offered a warning to the residents of the slopes of Vesuvius. A gigantic earthquake shook the area, tumbling public buildings, wiping out villages and reducing a large part of Pompeii and Herculaneum to rubble. Despite this event, for the next 17 years, new temples, better, more grandiose baths, houses, taverns and theaters rose in both cities.

And there they remained until the afternoon of August 24, A.D. 79, when, with a stupendous roar, Vesuvius woke from a long sleep and erupted, sending incandescent ash skyward in a huge, seething cloud. Lightning flashed through this geyser of ash that blew outward and upward at unbelievable speed, bombarding the countryside and the two cities with showers of stones and fragments of pumice. Ultimately, the western wall of the volcano blew away and fell into its widening crater.

At the bottom of the mountain at Miseneum on the westernmost point of the Bay of Naples, Pliny the Elder, who, as Gaius Plinius Secundus, commanded the oar-powered war galleys in the bay, was roused by the spectacle. His nephew, Pliny the Younger, then a lad of 17, wrote two letters to the Roman historian Tacitus, one of his uncle's experiences and one of his own, and they constitute the first recorded eye-witness accounts of a volcanic explosion:

About one in the afternoon, my mother deserted him [Pliny the Elder] to observe a cloud which had appeared of a very unusual size and shape . . . a cloud, from which mountain was uncertain at this distance, was ascending, the form of which I cannot give you a more exact description of than by likening it to that of a pine tree, for it shot up to a great height in the form of a very tall trunk, which spread itself out at the top into a sort of branches . . . it appeared sometimes bright and sometimes dark and spotted, according as it was either more or less impregnated with earth and cinders. . . .

Pliny the Elder ordered his ship to proceed toward the cloud. As they drew closer, hot cinders fell onto the ships. Pliny also describes a "sudden retreat of the sea," which indicates that a tsunami might also have occurred that afternoon.

Pliny the Elder disembarked. Climbing the side of the mountain, he made contact with his friend Popomponianus.

They consulted together whether it would be most prudent to trust to the houses, which now rocked from side to side with frequent and violent concussions as though shaken from their very foundations; or to fly to the open fields, where the calcined stones and cinders, though light indeed yet fell in large showers and threatened destruction. In this choice of dangers they resolved for the fields. They went out then, having pillows tied upon their heads with napkins; and this was their whole defense against the storm of stones that fell round them.

Pliny the Elder now reached the shore, with the idea of putting out to sea, but the sea was roiling with waves and steam, and he laid down to sleep. Then, "He raised himself up with the assistance of two of his servants, and instantly fell down dead; suffocated, as I conjecture, by some gross and noxious vapor. . . ."

Pliny the Younger's conjecture has been challenged by historians. His uncle, they conclude, must have died of a heart attack, not asphyxiation from volcanic gases; otherwise, his companions would have all died, too.

Meanwhile, Pliny the Younger, left with his mother at Miseneum, recorded his own observations for Tacitus. Setting out from his tottering home, he noticed that:

A panic-stricken crowd followed us, and (as to a mind distracted with terror every suggestion seems more prudent than its own) pressed on us in dense array to drive us forward as we came out . . . we stood still in the midst of a most dangerous and dreadful scene. The chariots, which we had dared to be drawn out, were so agitated backwards, and forwards, though upon the most level ground, that we could not keep them steady, even by supporting them with large stones. The sea seemed to roll back upon itself and to be driven from its banks by the convulsive motion of the earth; it is certain . . . the shore was considerably enlarged, and several sea animals left upon it.

It now grew rather lighter, which we imagined to be rather the forerunner of an approaching burst of flames (as in truth it was) than the return of day; however, the fire fell at a distance from us; then again we were immersed in thick darkness, and a heavy shower of ashes rained upon us, which we were obliged every now and then to stand up to shake off, otherwise we should have been crushed and buried in the heap. . . . At last this dreadful darkness was dissipated by degrees, like a cloud or smoke; the real day returned, and even the sun shone out, though with a lurid light, like when an eclipse is coming on. Every object that presented itself to our eyes (which were extremely weakened) seemed changed, being covered with deep ashes as if with snow.

It was thus the morning of the third day since the first eruption of Vesuvius.

Pliny did not describe the fate of Pompeii and Herculaneum. For years, the two cities would remain buried and silent—Pompeii under 25 feet of pumice and ash, and Herculaneum under a mud flow 65 feet deep.

The world ignored the two metropolises. A new city, Resina, rose above the site of Herculaneum, and grape vines grew where Pompeii once was. Ironically, it would take almost 1,600 years and another cataclysmic eruption of Vesuvius before the twin towns would be unearthed, and the story of that fateful day would be reconstructed.

But there would be no shortage of descriptions of the last hours of Pompeii once excavators and archaeologists began to dig through the hardened ash and pumice which killed at least 2,000 of its inhabitants.

Vesuvius's first major eruption following the A.D. 79 cataclysm occurred in 1631 (see p. 283). Shortly after that eruption, workers excavating civic water systems and irrigation reservoirs came upon a few Roman coins, which they pocketed. Shortly after this, the site was looted by scavengers until the beginning of the 18th century, when a well digger unearthed a cache of alabaster and marble.

From then until 1860, various high-level looters arrived, unearthing statues, artifacts and pieces of buildings. Among them was Sir William Hamilton, the British envoy to Naples from 1764 to 1800, and an amateur archeologist, who sold artifacts to the British Museum for a small fortune.

It would remain for the 37-year-old archeologist Guiseppi Fiorelli to bring responsibility to the search for the lost city and the events of that August afternoon in A.D. 79. What he—and some before him—discovered was that the particular combination of pumice and ash had in fact hermetically sealed the city against the destruction of time. He unearthed an amphitheatre along with the skeletons of gladiators, discovered in positions they must have been assuming when the first fall of molton ash occurred. A sealed bakery oven contained blackened loaves of 1,800-year-old bread. Wall murals were preserved with their colors intact.

The bodies of those killed by the eruption had of course decomposed soon after they were buried by the falling ash, but their imprints in the ash were absolutely intact. Fiorelli gave the last hours of Pompeii a tragic immediacy by pumping liquid plaster of paris into these perfect molds. thus reproducing the people they had contained as they had looked at the very moment of death.

Two Roman soldiers who were evidently being punished at the time of the eruption were found intact, locked in stocks. The temple of Isis was unearthed, and in it, on a pedestal, was a statue of the goddess draped in purple and gold. In the next room was the body of a priest holding an axe in his hand, and in another room was a priest sitting at dinner, apparently confident that the temple would protect him from the deadly ash falling in the streets of the city. In another area, a man was discovered in an upright position, a sword in his hand and his foot resting on a pile of silver and gold. Around him lay the bodies of five would-be looters he had apparently killed in defense of his possessions.

Outside of the city proper, in the suburban villa of Diomed, 18 adults, a boy and an infant were discovered in a vault. "To the skulls of the children cling their long, blonde hair," stated one historian, who went on to detail a scene in which the family sought shelter in the cellar of the villa, while the servants tried to make off with the family's valuables. Near the gate of the villa, two skeletons were uncovered, one holding a bunch of keys and a large sum of money, and the other clutching two silver vases.

"In the house of Faun," reconstructed another anonymous excavator/historian, "stood the skeleton of a woman, her hands raised over her head. Her scattered jewels lay about the floor. Endeavoring at length to leave the house, she found the doorway blocked with ashes. The flooring of the upper rooms began to fall, and she lifted her arms in a vain attempt to stay the crumbling roof. Thus she was found."

A large number of residents of both Pompeii and Herculaneum were discovered with their hands or cloths to their mouths, apparently trying to keep out the lethal gases. Numerous bodies were found near the sea, often with their possessions clutched in their hands. They were obviously struck down while trying to escape.

Excavators decided that Pompeii maintained a high standard of living before the cataclysm that snuffed out its life. There were 118 bars and taverns offering food, drink and diversion to traders and merchants from all over the Roman Empire. Some had gaming rooms and others showed evidence of having provided prostitutes. A thermopolium (a tavern specializing in hot wine) had walls inscribed with the names of women—possibly the sort of Andalusian dancing girls who, in the words of Martial, ". . . with endless prurience swing lascivious loins." "Lucilla sells her body," trumpeted one piece of graffiti, while another, left by one Livia about someone named Alexander chided, more ironically and prophetically than she could have dreamed, "Do you think I would mind if you dropped dead tomorrow?"

Into the 20th century, excavations unearthed new, preserved remains of Pompeii's doomed populace. On August 29, 1991, workmen clearing space for a service hut discovered the mummified bodies of eight people, one a teenage girl wearing a ring, indicating that she was a slave. Their faces, wrapped in tunics to protect them from the gases that may have killed them, were turned toward the town wall and the sea, a mere 200 yards away.

Herculaneum, excavated from under its gigantic mausoleum of mud, would yield very few bodies, leading to the assumption that the muddy mass of fine ash, lava fragments and pumice which invaded every nook and cranny of the city had not reached there in the first cataclysmic moments of the eruption, but probably crept in sometime during the three days of darkness. Thus, most of the populace had a chance to escape the lethal wrath of Vesuvius.

ITALY
ETNA
1169

• • • • • • • • • • • • • •

Catania was again destroyed by the eruption of Mt. Etna in 1169, and over 15,000 of its inhabitants died. In Messina, hundreds of refugees were drowned in an ancillary tsunami set in motion by the eruption.

Catania was again (see p. 000) the object of Etna's falling ash and charging lava in 1169. According to legend, when Etna erupted and sent huge rivers of lava tumbling toward the town in 251, terrified residents went to the tomb of St. Agatha, removed the veil that covered the remains of the saint, held it up against the lava flow and thus stemmed this furious fulmination of nature just before it would have consumed them.

And so, when Etna exploded with a gigantic, earth-rocking roar in 1169, thousands of peasants crowded into the great cathedral of Catania, while the bishop and 44 Benedictine monks again employed St. Agatha's veil to protect them. But this time, the immense combination of an earthquake and the blowing out of one side of Etna's cone in a huge blast of molten ash and fire overwhelmed the city built on the slopes of a natural time bomb.

Almost instantaneously, more than 15,000 citizens of Catania, including everyone in the cathedral, were either crushed to death by falling buildings or burned by falling ash and advancing lava.

All over Sicily, and particularly in Syracuse and Ajo, fountains first turned brackish and then bloody. The earth pitched and rocked all over the island, as hundreds of citizens of Messina, running to the beach to escape both the earthquake and the eruption, were met by an enormous tsunami, which roared across the beaches, flooded half the city and drowned scores of refugees and residents.

ITALY
VESUVIUS

December 16, 1631

• • • • • • • • • • • • • •

Estimates of between 4,000 and 18,000 dead resulted from a monumental eruption of Vesuvius on December 16, 1631.

Vesuvius erupted from time to time after the cataclysmic explosions of A.D. 79 that buried Pompeii and Herculaneum (see pp. 280–282), but, from all accounts, these were minor outpourings, causing little damage or loss of life. Eruptions were recorded in 203, 472, 512, 685, 993 and 1036. The eruption of 472 is noteworthy, since it is reported to have spread ashes over all of Europe and caused alarm as far away as Constantinople. The 1036 explosion marked the first time that lava flowed out of Vesuvius. Even the great catastrophe of A.D. 79 consisted entirely of fire and ash.

But the cataclysm of 1631 ranked in fury and effect alongside that of A.D. 79, with the added dimension of death and destruction by lava.

There was also an added similarity to the A.D. 79 eruption in that the volcano had been quiescent for nearly 500 years—long enough for the sides of the crater to be covered with brushwood and for a plain upon which cattle grazed to exist at its bottom. It was, in other words, the same soft scene that preceded the earlier holocaust, and which in part accounted for the monstrous loss of 18,000 human lives (more conservative estimates have put it at 4,000) and 6,000 animal lives in 1631.

The mountain began to erupt on December 16, 1631, with echoing explosions and the rising of a huge pink cloud which brought instant darkness and a rain of lethal cinder and ash. Some inhabitants of the villages that had sprung up along the mountain's slopes were burned to death by falling flames and red hot cinders; the survivors fled down the mountainside to Naples.

On the morning of the 17th, two fissures opened on the southwest side of the cone and floods of molten lava erupted from them, breaking into seven streams and rushing down the slope at enormous speed, invading the towns of San Giorgio a Cremano, Portici, Pugliano, La Scala and the western portion of Torre del Greco. Tongues of lava slipped into the sea, causing it to boil and send gouts of steam skyward.

On the evening of the 17th, mud began to rain down on Naples. Huge mudflows invaded not only the villages on the slopes of Vesuvius and the north slope of Mt. Somma, but San Giorgio a Cremano, Portici and Resina—the town built upon the site of Herculaneum. A long peninsula of land was formed and extended nearly a mile into the sea. More lava spit from the fissures on the side of the mountain, accompanied by strong explosions, adding to the stygian darkness that covered the area.

More villages were destroyed by lava and mud flows. Six and a half feet of ash and cinders fell in Naples, and then, to add to the destruction, tremendous deluges of rain descended during the last week of December, particularly on the north slope of Vesuvius, where the ash fall was the heaviest.

The cone of the mountain was reduced in height by 51 feet, and the crater was enlarged to more than twice its diameter before the eruption. From that year forward, Vesuvius's periods of repose would never extend beyond seven years.

ITALY
ETNA

March 11, 1669

• • • • • • • • • • • • • •

The worst eruption in the long and explosive history of Mt. Etna occurred on March 11, 1669. There were at least

20,000 dead, although other estimates have run from 60,000 to 100,000.

The worst explosion in Mt. Etna's long history (see pp. 278–280) was preceded by three days of monstrous earthquakes, in which the entire town of Nicolosi was swallowed up. On March 8, 1669, a whirlwind swept across the summit of the mountain, blotting out the sun, and the earth shook with increasing ferocity. The climatic explosion occurred at dawn on March 11, resulting in a giant fissure 12 miles long and six feet wide in the side of the mountain.

An astonishing red-white light emitted from the crevice as six craters erupted great gouts of flame and smoke. By the end of the day, a seventh crater had appeared, shooting white-hot stones, sand and ashes over 90 square miles of the Sicilian countryside.

The seventh crater was also the source of an immense lava flow, and it was this, combined with the poisonous vapors and rain of ashes, the blasts of fire and showers of boulders caused by repeated earthquakes and the splitting of the great central crater from the mountain that caused over 20,000 deaths (some reports set the figure at anywhere from 60,000 to 100,000).

Fifty towns were buried under the rivers of molten lava, including Pietro, Camporotondo, Mascalia and Misterbianco. As the lava flow inched toward Catania, scooping up cornfields and vineyards which boiled eerily on it surface, prayers were offered up by priests clutching the veil of St. Agatha. One man, Diego de Pappalardo, attempted a single-handed salvation of his doomed city.

Gathering 50 cohorts, clad in wet cowskins to protect themselves from the lava's intense heat and wielding long iron bars, de Pappalardo set out to divert the lava stream away from Catania by breaking down the lava-made levees of cooling substance at the sides of the flow. The game group smashed a hole in one levee, high above their city, and a tributary of molten lava worked its way through the breach, slowing the main stream.

However, this tributary was pointed directly at the village of Paterno, 11 miles northwest of Catania. Its citizens were justifiably horrified. Some 500 set out, armed with any weapon they could find, to undo the work of Diego de Pappalardo and his workers. This they did in short order, and the levee breach soon clogged and the lava stream, restored to full and formidable volume, resumed its descent directly towards Catania.

There, it came upon a 60-foot-high stone wall, erected by Catania to withhold future lava flows. The wall held for three days, as tons of lava built up against it. On the third day, a weak spot gave way and with a horrendous roar, the river of lava poured through the streets of Catania.

An English ambassador, in Sicily to report on the destruction, wrote, "I could discern the river of fire to descend the mountain, of a terrible fiery or red color, and stones of a paler red to swim thereon, and to be as big as an ordinary table . . . of twenty thousand persons which inhabited Catania, three thousand did only remain; all their goods are carried away, the cannon of brass are removed out of the castle, some great bells taken down, the city gates walled up next the fire, and preparations made by all to abandon the city."

Once more, Etna destroyed Catania, and once more, its residents stubbornly rebuilt it.

ITALY
VESUVIUS

May–August 1779

• • • • • • • • • • • • • • •

Close to 1,000 people died in the eruptions of Mt. Vesuvius from May through August 1779.

Various cyclic eruptions marked the continuation of Vesuvius as an active volcano, particularly in the latter part of the 18th century. In May 1779, a fissure opened on the northeast side, and lava poured from it throughout the month of June, covering the countryside and destroying several villages.

On August 8, huge explosions rocked the mountainside and a liquid fountain of fire rose from the crater to a height of two miles. This blazing, undulating column of fire directed itself toward the town of Ottaiano. As it fell, it covered the side of the cone with a band of red-hot scoria (a basaltic type of volcanic ejecta) more than a mile in width. Because they could not see the crater which was hidden by the rim of Mt. Somma, the inhabitants of Ottaiano were caught unawares, and were unable to escape the bombardment of red-hot scoria and cinders.

Sir William Hamilton, who had recorded earlier eruptions of Vesuvius, was an eyewitness to this:

The sight of the place [Ottaiano] was dismal, half buried under black scoria and dust, all windows towards the mountain broken, some of the houses burnt, the street choked with ashes—in some narrow streets to a depth of four feet, so that roads had to be cut by people to reach their own doors. During the tempestuous fall of ashes, scoria and stones, so large as to weigh a hundred pounds, the inhabitants dared not stir out—even with vain protec-

tion of pillows, tables, wine casks, etc. on their heads. Driven back wounded or terrified, they retreated to cellars and arches, half stifled with heat and dust and sulphur, and blinded by volcanic lightning—through 25 minutes this horror lasted; then suddenly ceased, and the people took the opportunity of quitting the country, after leaving the sick and bedridden in the churches. One more hour of this frightful visitation and Ottaiano would have been a buried city like Pompeii.

Nearly a thousand people died.

ITALY
VESUVIUS

February 1793–July 1974

• • • • • • • • • • • • • • •

Nearly 1,000 residents of Torre del Greco, at the base of Mt. Vesuvius, were killed in a series of explosions between February 1793 and July 1794.

Earthquakes shook the earth near Vesuvius beginning in February of 1793, and finally, on June 15, strong explosions opened a fissure between Resina and Torre del Greco low on the southwest side of the old Somma cone. Along this fracture, which was a half mile in length, lava poured in a single stream. In a matter of six hours, from 10:00 P.M. until 4:00 A.M., this molten river invaded Torre del Greco, flowing down its main street in a path 1,200 to 1,500 feet wide.

Again, Sir William Hamilton recorded the scene:

Huge masses of white smoke were vomited forth by the disturbed mountain and formed themselves at a height of many thousands of feet above the crater into a huge, ever-moving canopy, through which, from time to time, were hurled pitch-black jets of volcanic dust, and dense vapors, mixed with cascades of red-hot rocks and scoriae. The rain from the cloud canopy was scalding hot.

As the lava rushed forth from its imprisonment, it streamed a liquid, white and brilliantly pure river, which burned for itself a smooth channel through a great arched chasm in the side of the mountain. It flowed with the clearness of honey in regular channels, cut finer than art can imitate and glowing with the splendor of the sun.

Nearly 1,000 people, mostly residents of Torre del Greco, were killed.

ITALY
VESUVIUS

April 4, 1906 and March 18, 1944

• • • • • • • • • • • • • • •

Nearly 2,000 were killed in Vesuvius's two final eruptions, on April 4, 1906 and March 18, 1944.

Close to 2,000 people lost their lives in the last two paroxysmal explosions of Vesuvius, in 1906 and 1944.

The 1906 eruption began early in the morning of April 4, when a fissure opened on the southwestern side of the cone—which had added to its height until it had reached 4,338 feet above sea level. Lava began to flow from this fissure, and toward midnight, another flow, some 1,200 feet lower, began.

Meanwhile, roaring activity began to build in the crater, and suddenly, with a violent report, the top of the cone blew off, sending enormous blocks of old lava soaring into the sky. Dubbed "lava bombs" by observers, these boulders of ash and stone weighed up to two tons and collapsed homes and churches with their occupants inside. In the village of San Giuseppe, 105 parishioners were crushed to death as they sought shelter from the fiery eruption in the local cathedral.

On the morning of April 6, a third fissure tore open a slash in the side of the mountain, spouting molten lava which descended toward and eventually covered the town of Torre Annunziata. For the next two days, fresh lava flows and enormous quantities of fresh scoria and rocks covered the countryside and parts of the towns of Terzigno, Ottaiano and San Giuseppe.

The culmination of the eruption came with a great "gas blow-off" which began at 3:30 A.M. on April 8, and continued for 12 to 15 hours. The tremendous outrush of gas, which by its force enlarged the crater and carried away the upper part of the mountain's cone, was a fearsome spectacle.

There was so much ash left by the explosions of Vesuvius this time that "hot avalanches" occurred for days afterwards, and when heavy rains fell toward the end of April, mudslides caused extensive damage in and near Ottaiano.

The eruption of March 12–21, 1944, occurring at the height of World War II, did extensive damage too, but accounted for little loss of life. The heaviest destruction was from the lava flow which began on March 18. Somma, Atrio de Cavallo, Massa and San Sabastiano were inundated by the molten mass, which was 100 yards wide and 30 feet deep. As it passed through the towns, it left only a smoking lava field and the ruins of some of the houses. Other lava streams poured from the west side of the cone,

The April 4, 1906 explosion of Mt. Vesuvius was the next to last major eruption of that dramatic volcano. Three new fissures opened on the volcano's slopes in this thunderous eruption, which climaxed in a giant, 15-hour gas blow-off on April 8. Illustrated London News.

cutting and blocking the railway and the Funicolare Vesuviana. At the same time, explosive activity in the crater increased in violence, throwing out huge quantities of ash and scoria.

Milton Bracker, there to report the war for the *New York Times*, was aghast:

> Those who watched Vesuvius in action this morning will never forget it. The crater, from which alternately oozed or spurted the fiery volcanic matter, was forgotten in the presence of a prong of lava . . . [which] was like the monstrous paw of an even more monstrous lion, slowly inching forward toward his prey.
>
> The lava was white-hot; it was orange-gold, with occasional black patches, undulating like waves. As the stream advanced, great boulders cracked off and tumbled down, setting fire to small fruit trees . . . the general sound was like that of an infinite number of clinkers rolling out of a furnace, but sometimes a great chunk of rock bent rather than broke. Its effect was like that of the devil's own taffy being pulled and twisted to suit his taste. . . .

JAPAN
UNSEN

April 1, 1793

• • • • • • • • • • • • • •

Unsen, the volcano which gave the island of Unsen its name, blew itself apart on April 1, 1793, sinking the island and drowning all 53,000 of its inhabitants.

The 20-year period between 1780 and 1800 was one of extreme volcanic and earthquake activity. Dozens of islands were formed. The Satsuma Sea was rife with ripples of volcanic ridges asserting themselves, rising and forming islands.

At the same time, established volcanoes exploded with extraordinary force. Sakurajima, according to records of the time, ". . . blew out so much pumice material that it was possible to walk a distance of twenty-three miles upon the floating debris in the sea." Asama, according to these same records, ". . . ejected many blocks of stone—one of which is said to have been 42 feet in diameter—and a lava stream 425 miles in length."

But the most cataclysmic explosion occurred on the island of Unsen on April 1, 1793. Huge earthquakes and violent, summit-smashing eruptions from Unsen, the volcano, erupted with an ear- and earth-shattering roar on that day, sending ripples through the side of the mountain and great lava-spitting fissures all the way to the sea.

The entire island, mountain and all, disappeared into the sea, taking an estimated 53,000 people to their deaths. (See EARTHQUAKES, pp. 47–48.)

JAVA
PAPANDAYAN

1772

• • • • • • • • • • • • •

Three thousand people were killed in the eruption of Papandayan, on Java, in 1772. The explosion destroyed the mountain and turned its slopes, formerly dotted with 40 villages, into a lake of lava.

A cataclysm of enormous impact occurred in Java in 1772, when the 8,750-foot-high volcano Papandayan literally blew itself to pieces and then sank into a huge, sulphurous and boiling lake of lava.

Before this horrendous event, 40 villages and several towns with prosperous outlying plantations had existed placidly on Papandayan's slopes, while the steam and smoke from its green sulfur deposits wafted benignly into the sky.

But in 1772, without a rumble of warning, the entire mountain exploded, sucking 3,000 people, herds of cattle and the 40 villages that had previously existed on it into its lethal lake.

"The area that was sunk down was fifteen miles long and six broad," recounted one historian. "No day of judgment painted by Angelo or Dore could ever match that actual horror of the solid mountain sinking into the earth with human beings on its slopes—its huge bulk going down as a ship goes down into the deep."

JAVA
MIYI-YAMA

1793

• • • • • • • • • • • • •

Fifty-three thousand people were reported to have died in the explosion of Miyi-Yama, on Java, in the Indonesian archipelago.

The Indonesian archipelago that contains the densely populated island of Java includes 130 volcanoes—a fifth of the world's total.

One of the worst tragedies ever resulting from a volcanic eruption occurred on the island of Kiousiou, off Java, in 1793. Miyi-Yama, that island's governing volcano erupted in a huge explosion of mud and water that year, and although specific details are unavailable, the historian Engelbert Kampfer recorded an absolute inundation of all of the neighboring plains around the volcano, and a staggering death toll of 53,000 people.

JAVA
TAMBORO (TAMBORA)

April 5–12, 1815

• • • • • • • • • • • • •

An estimated 1.7 million tons of debris were flung into the air during the eruption of Tamboro, also known as Tambora, on the island of Sumbawa in Java, from April 5–12, 1815, thus causing the famous "year without a summer." Nearly 49,000 natives were killed in this monumental explosion, which blew the top off the volcano.

The most spectacular volcanic explosion in the history of the world caused the famous "year without a summer" in 1815. Quoits pitchers on the village green of Plymouth, Connecticut wore overcoats on the Fourth of July, and laundry that was hung out to dry on June 10 in the same village froze on the line. In France crops were so scanty that grain cars on the way to market had to be guarded against bands of starving citizens and wry New Englanders referred to the year as "Eighteen hundred and froze to death."

On April 12, 1815, the 13,000-foot-high volcano called Tamboro (or Tambora) blew itself asunder, sinking the island of Sumbawa, on which it is located, and killing all but 26 of the 12,000 natives instantly. Another 37,000 on neighboring islands died as a result of starvation and disease. It blew an estimated 1.7 million tons of debris into the sky. Most of this fell to earth in the vicinity of Sumbawa within a few hours, thus accounting for the staggering death toll. But the remainder was pulverized into a talc-like dust, light enough to remain suspended in the atmosphere. This dust was carried into the stratosphere, where it began to circle the Earth, reflecting incoming sunlight back into space, robbing the Earth of some of its heat and causing the spectacular orange sunsets that English painter J. M. W. Turner would record for posterity.

That was the effect upon the world. The immediate impact upon the human beings directly affected by the cataclysmic action of this giant among titans was more monstrous and considerably more awesome.

It began on the evening of April 5, 1815, with preliminary explosions deep within Tamboro's crater. Sir Stamford Raffles, the Lieutenant Governor of Java, thinking there might be either a vessel in distress or rebels attacking one of the nearby British outposts, dispatched both troops and two boats from Batavia (now Jakarta) to search the Java Sea for survivors. He found none. The captain of the East India Company's armed cruiser *Benares*, 900 miles to the east at Macassar on the island of Celebes, was also unsuccessful in locating the pirates he thought had unleashed a volley of artillery fire.

But later in the month Raffles did find a local surviving raja from Sumbawa who offered an eyewitness account, which Raffles recorded. According to the account, on April 6, the day after the first explosions, a light dusting of ash began to fall over a 400-mile radius. On Sumbawa, the first eruptions of Tomboro, the huge mountain covered with vines and pastures, sent enormous rocks and quantities of red hot ash into the sky, dropping both upon hundreds of homes on Sumbawa and nearby Bima, and crushing these homes from the sheer weight of the ash.

Between April 6 and April 10, the explosions increased in violence and the ash turned to red hot, glowing boulders. And then, according to the raja, "About seven P.M. on the 10th of April, three distinct columns of flame burst forth, near the top of Tamboro mountain, all of them apparently within the verge of the crater; and after ascending separately to a very great height, their tops united in the air in a troubled, confused manner. In a short time, the whole mountain appeared like a body of liquid fire extending itself in every direction.

"Stones at this time fell very thick . . . some of them were as large as two fists, but generally not larger than walnuts."

Now, a unique phenomenon occurred. A giant whirlwind struck, ". . . which blew down nearly every house in the village of Saugar [a town 25 miles from the center of the eruption]. In the part of Saugar adjoining Tamboro, the whirlwind's effects were much more violent, tearing up by the roots the largest trees, and carrying them into the air, together with men, houses, cattle and whatever else came within its influence."

Simultaneously, a huge tsunami formed, and reaching between 12 and 30 feet in height, moved outward from the island, crashing into neighboring ones and drowning hundreds.

On and on the explosions went, tearing the mountain to bits, blowing away its top and ripping away its sides.

An enormous cloud rose from this holocaust, blotting out the sun for 400 miles around, and causing a three-day night that was, according to one of Raffle's correspondents, "blacker than the deepest darkness imaginable."

The mountain would continue to rumble and belch fire for three months, but by April 18, Raffles felt that it was quiescent enough to send a shipload of rice to feed the starving survivors of Sumbawa and the surrounding islands. Lieutenant Owen Phillips, the ship's commander, found a scene of heartrending desolation and disaster. The once majestic mountain was now flattened down to a plateau. Most of the island was coated with a two-foot-thick mantle of ash and mud. The sea around the island was thickly jammed with thousands of uprooted trees and immense, floating islands of pumice, which had trapped enough gas in its vesicles to keep it afloat.

Many of the 127,000 survivors of Sumbawa and the other islands were already racked by a virulent cholera, which had broken out immediately after the eruption. The rest waded despondently in the knee-deep ash, ready to trade their most valued possessions for a mere few ounces of rice. Along the roads, corpses were strewn like mileposts, and the handful of survivors in the villages foraged in the interior for the few remaining heads of edible palm and stalks of plantain.

Raffles later speculated that if all the ash given off by Tamboro had been gathered, it would have made ". . . three mountains the size of Mont Blanc, the highest of the Alps, and if spread over the surface of Germany, would have covered the whole of it two feet deep."

The ash and mud fill was not confined to Sumbawa alone, nor were the casualties. More than three feet of ash covered the entire island of Tombock, 100 miles from Tamboro. As a result, everything growing on the island died, and an estimated 37,000 people perished by starvation on Tombock. Add up the casualties and the primary and secondary destruction, and Tamboro's eruption becomes the most deadly volcanic explosion in recorded history.

There is an ironic footnote to the "year without a summer" effect of the explosion. For years, no one made a connection between the volcanic catastrophe and the weather that produced snowfall over all of New England in June and killer frosts everywhere. Some scientists suggested sunspots; others blamed it on a large collection of icebergs in the North Atlantic.

But if Benjamin Franklin had still been alive, he might very well have made the connection instantly. In 1784, he had attributed the unusually cold winter to "a dry fog" that was caused by eruptions in 1783 of Mounts Asama in Japan and Laki in Iceland. But no one remembered this, and, in fact, one theorist in 1815 actually blamed the widespread use of Franklin's lightning rods for upsetting a

A drawing of the ash cloud from the 1883 eruption of Krakatoa, Indonesia. One of the largest volcanic eruptions in history, the explosions were heard more than 4,000 kilometers (2,500 miles) away, and atmospheric effects were recognized around the world. National Geophysical Data Center.

natural flow of warming electricity from the Earth's core, thus bringing on the worldwide frost.

JAVA
KRAKATOA

August 26–27, 1883

• • • • • • • • • • • • • • • •

Krakatoa, on Java, exploded with the loudest sound yet known to man on August 26, 1883, in the most ruinous and lethal of all volcanic eruptions. Two hundred thousand died from fire, molten lava, descending ash and rocks or the 120-foot-high tsunami caused by the deafening detonation.

What may have been the greatest cataclysm in the history of the world took place on August 27, 1883, when Krakatoa, the volcanic island located in the Sunda Strait be-

tween Sumatra and Java, blew itself to pieces in a massive eruption. Five cubic miles of rocks and ash and a seven-mile-high gout of steam were shot into the atmosphere, exploding with the loudest sound known since man evolved. The ensuing shock waves circled the Earth seven times, and created a 120-foot-high tsunami, or tidal wave, that drowned 36,000 people.

The ultimate death toll would reach an estimated 200,000, and it would probably have been greater, had Krakatoa been an inhabited island. It was, instead, the uninviting stump of an ancient volcano that might well have erupted in the same way in some prehistoric time. The string of islands that formed the Kandanga range along the southeast coast of Java may have been part of one vast volcano. Certainly, the linked volcanic upthrusts of Perboewatan, Danan and Rakata were all part of the prehistoric caldera, or summit rim of an ancient, immense volcano, encompassing Krakatoa.

The mountain had been somnolent from 1680 to 1883, and the 1680 explosion had been merely a flow of andesitic obsidian, or volcanic glass, from the vent of Perboewatan. Still, it was from this same vent that the initial explosions occurred on May 20, 1883. They were small ones, so unimpressive, in fact, that a group of inquisitive Europeans chartered a steamer on May 27 to visit the island and observe what one adventurous member of the party described as a "vast column of steam issuing with a terrific noise from an opening about 30 yards in width," near the crater of Perboewatan. The group also noticed that Rakata and Verlaten were covered with fine ash and that the vegetation, although unburned, had been killed.

From then until June 19, the area was quiet. Then, the small explosions resumed, and the countryside underwent a metamorphosis of deterioration.

On August 11, 1883 Captain Fercenaar, chief of the topographical survey of the neighboring island port of Bantam, stepped ashore on the island of Krakatoa. It trembled beneath his feet. And worse: it looked like some alien world. Twenty inches of dust covered the entire island. Three vapor columns reached skyward, and 11 new eruptive foci that had not been there before May were spurting steam and ash. The thoroughly terrified captain left after a few hours of record taking.

For 15 days, until August 26, activity quieted, and then the rumbles resumed and became explosions. At 1:00 P.M. on August 26, the first of these detonated from the bowels of Krakatoa, rattling windows on nearby islands, rippling the earth for a hundred miles in each direction. At 2:00 P.M., an immense, black cloud ascended above Krakatoa to a height of 17 miles. It crackled with St. Elmo's fire. On a ship 40 miles distant from the volcano, a Captain Wooldridge noted, "Krakatoa was a terrifying glory . . .

it looked like an immense wall, with bursts of forked lightning darting through it, and lazing serpents playing over it. These bursts of brilliancy were the regular uncoverings of the angry fires. . . ."

Other volcanoes in the Java chain, once part of that one prehistoric mountain, now began to erupt. Krakatoa's explosions increased in violence until 5:00 P.M., when the first tidal wave formed, crashing against nearby islands and inundating fishing villages, drowning their inhabitants and washing away their boats.

All night and into the morning hours of August 27, the rumblings and explosions continued. Concussions collapsed stone walls, shattered lamps and tore gas meters from their sockets in nearby islands. All over Java and in Batavia, 100 miles away, the noise was loud enough to keep everyone awake, as the china in their closets rattled and their houses shook as if heavy artillery were being fired nearby.

Between 4:40 A.M. and 6:40 A.M., several large tidal waves spread outward from Krakatoa, probably because of the further collapse of the northern part of the island.

By 10:00 A.M., the rehearsal was over, and the main event was ready to occur. Two observers watched, and recorded it. A Dutch scientist, sent by his government to make seismic observations, was climbing a mountain near the town of Anjer on the west coast of Java that morning. According to R. Hewitt, in his book, *From Earthquake Fire and Flood:*

. . . looking towards the island of Krakatoa, about thirty miles away in the Sunda Straits, he suddenly saw a movement among the little boats in the bay. It seemed as though a magnet pulled them from their quiet positions of rest, and they all streamed in the same direction, impelled like the Flying Dutchman by an invisible hand. In a moment they disappeared, swallowed up in a mighty boiling chasm of fire and water. Right across the Straits it appeared that a line of flame stretched towards the island. The crust of the Earth beneath the bay had split, and it seemed as though all the fires of hell burst through the surface waters. The sea poured into the chasm, carrying all the little boats to their doom. Hissing steam added to the inferno. . . .

"It grew darker and darker," wrote R. J. Dalby, a seaman on a Liverpool clipper. He continued:

The already loud rumblings grew louder, and now they seemed all around us. The gusts of wind increased to such a hurricane as no man aboard had ever experienced before. The wind seemed a solid mass thrusting everything before it, and roaring like an enormous engine and shrieking through the rigging like a demon in torment. The darkness became intense, but the vivid lightning, which

almost blinded us, seemed everywhere. The thunder was deafening. . . .

. . . When we could get a glimpse of the heavens we could see there a terrible commotion: the clouds whirled round at terrific speed, and I think most of us thought that we were in the vortex of a cyclone. But as the noise grew louder and louder, I at any rate reckoned it was something volcanic, especially when, at about noon, it rained a continuous downpour of dust. This seemed a sulphurous, gritty substance, and as we wore only two cotton garments, we were soon completely smothered; burned, choked and almost blinded.

Visibility at this time was about a yard. I seemed isolated, and felt my way about the deck, never loosing my hold of anything handy. You cannot imagine the force of that wind. Occasionally I met others on the same lay as myself, but quite unrecognizable, just moving grey objects in the darkness. Ropes and lines were lashing across the decks like whips. Once I saw two terrified eyes, the eyes of a poor old coolie, peeping from under the boat.

None of us will ever be able to describe the noise, especially one great bang about noon, which is supposed to have been the loudest sound ever heard on earth. . . . It was the very top of Krakatoa going up into the skies. . . . The whole heavens seemed a blaze of fire and the clouds formed such fantastic shapes as to look startlingly unnatural; at times they hung down like ringlets of hair, some jet black, others dirty white. . . .

The seaman was almost right. Powered by the buildup of steam beneath the surface of the Earth, the cone of Krakatoa had been blown to bits, shooting approximately five cubic miles of material into a cloud that extended 50 miles into the atmosphere. Meanwhile, rock fragments from the former cones of Danan, Perboewatan and Rakata collapsed, sinking beneath the sea and turning it into a boiling cauldron.

The sound of this detonation was so immense, it was heard nearly 3,000 miles away, and the shock waves would circle the Earth seven times. On the island of Rodriguez, in the Indian Ocean, 2,968 miles from Krakatoa, an alert Coast Guard observer recorded the sound exactly four hours after the explosion occurred. In central Australia, 2,250 miles southeast of Krakatoa, the noise was also recorded. Flocks of sheep stampeded at the sound of the eruption on the Victoria plains in West Australia, 1,700 miles away. It was as if Pikes Peak had erupted, and the sound was heard all over the United States.

Now, a stygean darkness settled over the area, plunging places 275 miles away into an early night. One hundred thirty miles from the explosion, the darkness lasted for 22 hours; 50 miles away it lasted for 57 hours. Ships 1,600 miles distant reported that dust began to fall on the decks three days after the eruption.

As if they were being conducted, all of the volcanoes in Java began to erupt. Papandayan ripped apart, and seven fissures hurled steaming lava down its slope. Sixty-five miles of the Kandanga range in the Malay Archipelago exploded, disappearing into the sea. Fifty square miles of Java from Point Capucine to Negery Passoerang also sank beneath the ocean.

And now, one of the worst, most lethal effects of the explosion was born. Half an hour after the cataclysmic eruption, a seismic tidal wave was formed and roared into the coasts of Java and Sumatra, wholly or partially destroying 295 towns and killing 36,000 people (some authorities said 80,000), mostly by drowning.

According to N. van Sandick, the engineer of the ship *Loudon*, the scene was horrifying. "Like a high mountain," he wrote:

the monstrous wave precipitated its journey towards the land. Immediately afterwards another three waves of colossal size appeared. And before our eyes this terrifying upheaval of the sea, in a sweeping transit, consumed in one instant the ruin of the town; the lighthouse fell in one piece, and all the houses of the town were swept away in one blow like a castle of cards. All was finished. There, where a few moments ago lived the town of Telok Betong, was nothing but the open sea. . . . We cannot find the words to describe the terrifying events which left us with the sight of such a cataclysm. The thunder-striking suddenness of the changing light, the unexpected devastation which was accomplished in an instant before our eyes, all this left us stupefied. . . .

New volcanic mountains rose from the sea; islands disappeared with all of their inhabitants. At Anjer and Batavia, 2,800 were washed out to sea by the tsunami; 1,500 drowned at Bantam. The captain of the *Loudon*, surviving the tsunami, made for Anjer to warn the Dutch fort. He found the entire garrison dead, except for one sailor who was wandering around through the thickly strewn corpses. The islands of Steers, Midah, Calmeyer, Verlaten, Siuku and Silesi sank beneath the sea, drowning all of their inhabitants. Of the 2,500 workers in the stone quarry on Merak Island, which had previously been 150 feet above sea level, only two natives and a government bookkeeper escaped drowning when the island was suddenly completely inundated by the sea. The German man-of-war *Berouw*, lying off Sumatra, was swept up in the tsunami and tossed inland a mile and three-quarters, where it came to rest in a forest 30 feet above sea level.

Those residents of islands who escaped the water were rained on by white hot stones and lava. At Warlonge, 900

were killed. At Talatoa, 300 were buried beneath lava. Tamarang was consumed by flaming rocks and lava that set every building on fire; 1,800 perished.

Three more lesser explosions rocked the area during the night of the 27th, and the early morning of the next day, and then the mountain finally rested. The destruction was reported by seaman R. J. Dalby. "In place of luxuriant vegetation nothing but a brown sterile barrenness remained," he wrote. "The shores both of Java and Sumatra seemed to have been battered to pieces and burnt up. All manner of wreckage was flying past us. Huge masses of vegetation floated by, and on it we could see enormous frogs, snakes and other strange reptiles. And the sharks!— it was sickening to see them. As for our ship, we had been painting it and tarring the rigging, and now it looked as if we had been through a shower of mustard."

The reverberations of the explosion traveled the globe. According to Robert Ballin in his book, *Earth's Beginnings*, ". . . every part of our atmosphere had been set into a tingle by the great eruption. In Great Britain the waves passed over our heads; the air in our streets, the air in our houses, trembled from the volcanic impulse. The oxygen supplying our lungs was responding also the supreme convulsion that took place 10,000 miles away."

For months, the sky all over the world glowed, prompting Alfred, Lord Tennyson to record the event in verse, in "St. Telemachus":

Had the fierce ashes of some fiery Peak
Been hurled so high they ranged round the globe?
For day by day through many a blood-red eve

. . . .

This wrathful sunset glared . . .

Two-thirds of the main island of Krakatoa had disappeared, and where the land before the explosion had stood anywhere from 400 to 1,400 feet above sea level, there was nothing but a great cavity 900 feet below sea level.

Bizarre lighting and visual effects persisted for months after the explosions. In some parts of the East the sun appeared blue and the moon a vivid green. And because of the movement of dust particles left by the volcanic eruption scientists were able to identify the presence of the jet stream.

JAVA
KELUIT
1919

• • • • • • • • • • • • • •

In a freak result of the eruption of Keluit, on Java, in 1919, its crater lake first shot skyward in a spectacular fountain, and then drowned 5,500 residents of the villages on its slopes.

Keluit, in the chain of volcanic islands in and near Java, is unique in that its active volcano contains a lake within its crater, formed after the eruption of 1901. It has never been noted for stupendous blowouts, but the explosion of 1919 produced a singular and devastating situation.

The volcano, dormant for 18 years, erupted without warning, spewing ash and fire—and water. The entire contents of the lake shot skyward in a spectacular geyser, and then roared down the slopes of Keluit at tremendous speed, drowning 5,500 residents of the valleys at the bottom of the mountain.

Javanese engineers, realizing that a recurrence would undoubtedly produce exactly the same effect, immediately dug a tunnel into the crater, which constantly drained off the water from the lake. This tunnel still exists, and to date, no such catastrophe has recurred in or near Keluit.

JAVA
MERAPI

December 13–28, 1931

• • • • • • • • • • • • • • • •

One of the worst volcanic eruptions of the 20th century, that of Merapi on Java, from December 13–28, 1931, killed more than 1,300.

For nearly three weeks in December 1931, Merapi, one of the largest volcanoes in the Java chain, belched forth a river of lava four miles in length, 200 yards wide and over 80 feet in depth. The white hot flow scorched the earth, set trees afire, and crushed villages in its path.

In addition, both flanks of the volcano blew out, spreading ashes over half of the island to which the mountain gives its name. Over 1,300 people lost their lives in this, one of the most severe volcanic eruptions of the 20th century.

MARTINIQUE
PELEE

May 8, 1902

• • • • • • • • • • • • • • • •

On May 8, 1902 Pelee, on Martinique, exploded, not at its peak, but at its sides. Thirty-six thousand people were killed instantly; hundreds more perished from numerous ancillary effects, including snakebite.

A new classification of volcanic explosions, a new name and respect for a branch of scientific study called volcan-ism, which had hitherto been considered a mere cavern in the greater mountain of geology, and a new record of death and devastation was set by the absolutely cataclysmic convulsion that killed 36,000 persons in a matter of moments, when Mt. Pelee blew itself to bits on the morning of May 8, 1902, and wiped out the city and population of St. Pierre, one of Martinique's primary ports.

Because not the top, but the sides of Pelee blew out in the enormous explosion of that horrendous morning, all volcanic eruptions of this type would henceforth be dubbed Pelean. As for the new respect accorded volcanism, that occurred because President Theodore Roosevelt chose to dispatch, on May 14, the cruiser *Dixie* filled with not only relief supplies, but scientists, and one journalist—George M. Kennan—to distribute the $250,000 worth of relief the U.S. supplied to Martinique after this nearly indefinable natural disaster.

The story begins, as most volcanic ones do, in prehistory, with the formation of the Lesser Antilles, a group of islands which stretch like the piers of a roadless bridge across the entrance to the Caribbean Sea in the shape of a 450-mile arc bowed out toward the Atlantic Ocean, and stretching from the Anegada Passage east of the Virgin Islands almost to the coast of South America.

All are volcanic islands, but only two of them, Mt. Pelee on Martinique and La Soufriere on St. Vincent (see p. 308) have had violent eruptions, and these occurred only 18 hours apart, in 1902.

Pelee is located at the northern end of the island of Martinique of the Lesser Antilles, 4,430 feet above the city of St. Pierre, the largest (population 32,000) settlement on the island.

According to the author Lafcadio Hearn, who visited the city before the eruption of Pelee, it was ". . . the quaintest, queerest, and the prettiest, withal, among West Indian cities; all stone-built and stone-flagged, with very narrow streets, wooden or zinc awnings, and peaked roofs of red tile, pierced by gable dormers. . . . The architecture is that of the seventeenth century, and reminds one of the antiquated quarter of New Orleans. . . ."

That this stone architecture would, in the space of a mere minute, be pulverized into pebbles was probably beyond the most vivid imaginations of St. Pierre's builders, and no eruption of Pelee prior to 1902 gave any indication that it was a dangerous volcano. The explosions of 1767 had killed 16,000, but most of them had lived on its slopes. Since then, its eruptions had been of lesser and lesser degree.

But the holocaust of May had its warnings, which hardly anyone in the local government or local media chose to heed. On April 2, some steaming fumaroles, or vents in the side of the mountain, began to issue sizable quantities

St. Pierre, Martinique lies in pulverized ruins following the eruption of Pelee on May 8, 1902. The monstrous blast wiped out St. Pierre's populace in minutes. Library of Congress.

of steam. On April 23, ash began to fall in the streets of St. Pierre, accompanied by an undeniable odor of sulphur, and some mild earthquake shocks caused dishes to fall from shelves.

From April 25 on, more vigorous, though not truly alarming explosions began to occur, and a boiling sound was heard by those venturing near the crater on Pelee of L'Etang Sec. This had become filled with a 650-foot-wide, steaming lake, alongside of which a 30-foot cone emitted boiling water.

On April 27, the ash fall began to increase, blocking some roads and giving the landscape a wintry look. In addition, many birds and some animals were reported to have been asphyxiated by the poisonous gas rising from the ash.

The local newspaper, *Les Colonies*, described late April in St. Pierre: "The rain of ashes never ceases. At about half-past nine the sun shone forth timidly. The passing of carriages in the streets is no longer heard. The wheels are muffled [in the ashes]. Puffs of wind sweep the ashes from the roofs and awnings, and blow them into rooms of which the windows have imprudently been left open."

Now, the populace became uneasy. Large numbers of St. Pierre's residents left the city, but they were immediately replaced by even greater numbers of refugees from the mountain's slopes. The U.S. consul's wife, Mrs. Thomas T. Prentis, wrote to her sister in Boston, "My husband assures me that there is no immediate danger, and when there is the least particle of danger, we will leave the place. There is an American schooner in the harbor, the *R. J. Morse*, and she will remain here for at least two weeks. If the volcano becomes very bad, we shall embark at once and go out to sea."

After the holocaust of May 8, rescuers would find the charred corpses of both the consul and his wife, sitting in chairs in front of a window that faced Pelee. The bodies of their children would never be found.

But before that, the local cathedral became crowded day and night with praying citizens of St. Pierre. Another resident wrote on May 4, to relatives in France, "I am awaiting the event tranquilly. . . . If death awaits us there will be a numerous company to leave the world. Will it be by fire or asphyxia? It will be what God wills."

Animals were not so contained. *Les Colonies* reported, "In the meadows, the animals are restless, bleating, neighing and bellowing despairingly." At the Usine Guerin, a large sugar mill at the mouth of the Blanche River, just north of the city, an incredible invasion of ants and centipedes overran the premises. Horses in the yard of the mill bucked and bellowed as the ants and centipedes ascended their legs and bit them, while workers doused the horses with buckets of water, in a sidelong attempt to dislodge the creatures. Inside the mill, workers whacked at the centipedes with stalks of sugarcane, while in the nearby villa of the mill owner, housemaids killed them with flat-irons and boiling water.

Meanwhile, in one quarter of St. Pierre itself, snakes, displaced by the rain of ashes, slithered into streets and backyards, killing chickens, pigs, horses, dogs and people who failed to get out of their way. Fifty humans and 200 animals died of snakebite that afternoon.

On May 5, heavy rains falling on the mountain unleashed floods of chocolate-colored water into all of the valleys on the southwest side of Pelee. Shortly after noon on that same day, the same sugar mill that had been invaded by ants and centipedes was destroyed and buried by an enormous avalanche of mud containing huge boulders, rocks and immense trees. Plummeting down the mountain, it consumed the mill in boiling mud in moments, burying 150 men and leaving only one chimney visible. After inundating the mill, the avalanche continued on into the sea, creating an enormous wave that overturned two boats tied at anchor and flooding the lower portion of St. Pierre.

"A flood of humanity poured up from the low point of the Mouliage [the flooded part of St. Pierre]," according to *Les Colonies*. "It was a flight for safety, not knowing where to turn. The entire city was afoot. The shops and private houses are closing. Everyone is preparing to seek refuge on the heights."

And then, one of the more cynical acts of history occurred. Attempting to keep the population in St. Pierre for an upcoming election on Sunday, May 10, the French governor appointed a commission to investigate the danger from the volcano. *Les Colonies* reported, "[Professor Landes of the Lycee concludes that] Mt. Pelee presents no more danger to the inhabitants of Saint Pierre than does Vesuvius to those of Naples." *Les Colonies* went on, editorially, "We confess that we cannot understand this panic. Where could one be better off than at Saint Pierre? Do those who invade Fort-de-France believe that they will be better off there than here should the earth begin to quake?"

In order to emphasize his commission's findings, the governor ordered troops to turn back refugees at the city's outer limits, and to further reassure potential voters, the governor and his wife rode from Fort-de-France to St. Pierre, where, within a day, they would both meet fiery deaths.

Thomas Prentis, the U.S. consul, dispatched what would be his last communication to President Theodore Roosevelt. Recognizing the political manipulations of the governor, the local government and the local newspaper, he bitterly observed, "To abandon the elections would be unthinkable. The situation is a nightmare where no one seems able or willing to face the truth."

All through May 7, Pelee continued to erupt, but the residents of St. Pierre took some cheer in the news that La Soufriere on St. Vincent, 90 miles to the south, had exploded. That, they thought, as they went to bed on the last night of their lives, would relieve the pressure on Pelee.

May 8 dawned serene and sunny. A column of steam rose from Pelee to an extraordinary height, but otherwise there was nothing exceptional or different about its demeanor. At about 6:30 A.M. the ship *Roraima*, its decks coated with ash, steamed into the port at St. Pierre and tied up alongside the 17 other vessels docked at the city's simple roadstead.

And then, at 7:50 A.M. Pelee blew itself to pieces in four, deafening, gunlike reports, discharging upward from the main crater a black cloud pierced with lightning flashes. But this was not the most lethal explosion. It was the lateral ones—the ones that would forever afterward be regarded as "Pelean"—that launched fire and brimstone at hurricane speed down the mountain slope, straight for St. Pierre. In two minutes, all but four people, almost the entire population of St. Pierre—over 30,000 people—would be incinerated, suffocated or blasted to death in an instant.

Every house, every structure in St. Pierre was blown apart or partially destroyed. Trees were stripped of leaves and branches down to the bare trunks. Cement and stone walls, three feet thick, were torn apart as if they were cardboard. The six-inch cannons on the Norne d'Orange were sheared from their moorings and a statue of the Virgin Mary, weighing at least three tons, was carried 50 feet from its base. On the quays and in the warehouses at the port, thousands of barrels of rum exploded, the flaming liquid running through the streets and out into the water of the roadstead.

Small wonder that there were no survivors. The super-heated volcanic gas, kept close to the ground because of its immense density and speed, permeated every corner of the city, allowing almost no one to escape. Even at 11:30 A.M., three and one-half hours after the blast, the heat from the burning city was so intense that a ship from Fort-de-France could not approach the shore.

Most of the ships in the port were overturned by the blast, and their crews and passengers perished in the boiling waters. A day before, perhaps the wisest captain in St. Pierre, a Neopolitan named Marino Leboff, captaining the Italian bark *Orsolina*, brushed past port authorities who refused him permission to sail. "I know nothing about Mount Pelee," he said, ignoring their orders, "but if Vesuvius were looking the way your volcano looks this morning, I'd get out of Naples."

Sixteen of the 18 ships in the harbor at the moment of the explosion capsized. The Quebec-line steamship *Roraima* was engulfed in the onrushing black cloud. Its assistant purser Thompson, recalled the moments before the explosion, when the crew and the captain, who was later killed, gathered to see the sight: "The spectacle was magnificent," he recalled.

> . . . we could distinguish the rolling and leaping red flames that belched from the mountain in huge volume and gushed high in the sky. Enormous clouds of black smoke hung over the volcano. The flames were then spurting straight up in the air, now and then waving to one side or the other a moment, and again leaping suddenly higher up. There was a constant muffled roar. It was like the biggest oil refinery in the world burning up on the mountain top. There was a tremendous explosion. . . . The mountain was blown to pieces. There was no warning. The side of the volcano was ripped out, and there hurled straight towards us a solid wall of flame. It sounded like a thousand cannon. The wave of fire was on us and over us like a lightning flash. It was like a hurricane of fire, which rolled in mass straight down on St. Pierre and the shipping. The town vanished before our eyes, and then the air grew stifling hot and we were in the thick of it. Wherever the mass of fire struck the sea, the water boiled and sent up great clouds of steam. . . . Before the volcano burst, the landings at St. Pierre were crowded with people. After the explosion, not one living being was seen on land. . . .

The chief officer of the *Roraima*, Ellery Scott, recorded the moment it hit. "Then came darkness blacker than night," he wrote. "The *Roraima* rolled and careened far to port, then with a sudden jerk she went to starboard, plunging her lee rail far under water. The masts, smokestack, rigging, all were swept clean off and went by the board. The iron smokestack came off short, and the two steel masts broke off two feet above the deck. The ship took fire in several places simultaneously, and men, women and children were dead in a few seconds."

Only two of its passengers, a little girl and her nurse, survived and they were interviewed later by Dr. Thomas Jagger Jr., the brilliant Harvard geologist. The nurse's account was particularly vivid:

> . . . the steward [who was later killed] rushed past [the cabin, where I was assisting the children in dressing for breakfast] and shouted "Close the cabin door—the volcano is coming!" We closed the door and at the same moment came a terrible explosion which nearly burst the eardrums. The vessel was lifted high into the air, and then seemed to be sinking down, down. We were all thrown off our feet by the shock and huddled crouching in one corner of the cabin.
>
> . . . the explosion seemed to have blown in the skylight over our heads, and before we could raise ourselves, hot moist ashes began to pour in on us; they came in boiling splattering splashes like moist mud without any pieces of rock. . . .
>
> A sense of suffocation came next [but] when the door burst open, air rushed in and we revived somewhat. When we could see each other's face, they were all covered with black lava, the baby was dying, Rita, the older girl, was in great agony and every part of my body was paining me. A heap of hot mud had collected near us and as Rita put her hand down to raise herself up it was plunged up to the elbow in the scalding stuff. . . .

The immense volcanic cloud covered a triangle of absolute destruction and a second zone of damage spreading over 24 square miles. This cloud, formed of superheated steam and other gases, made heavy by billions of particles of incandescent ash and traveling with enough force to carry along boulders and blocks of volcanic material, reached temperatures of between 1,300°F and 1,800°F, which is enough to melt glass.

The city would not cool enough for rescuers to enter it for four days. When they did, they would find unbearable sights of horrible destruction. At the rum distillery, the burned-out tanks, which were massive containers of quarter-inch boiler plate riveted together, looked to one observer "as if they had been through a bombardment by artillery, being full of holes which vary in size from mere cracks at the bottom of indentations to great rents, 24, 30 and even 36 inches across."

Two weeks later, geologists sent by America on the rescue ship *Dixie* would witness, according to Angelo Heilprin of the Philadelphia Geographical Society, ". . . twisted bars of iron, great masses of roof sheeting wrapped like cloth around posts against which they had been flung, and girders looped and festooned as if they had been made of rope."

There were incinerated corpses of families sitting at their breakfast tables, which, because of the selective nature of the freakish cloud that had killed them, were still set with undamaged plates, cutlery and glasses.

A charred woman was found with an entirely intact handkerchief pressed to her lips. Many bodies were naked; their clothing was blown away by the blast. In a jewelry shop, the heat had been so intense that it had fused hundreds of watch crystals into one lump, but in a kitchen not far away, there were still-intact corked bottles of water, and packets of starch in which the granules were untouched.

Only four people escaped the cataclysm of May 8, 1902. Two were outside St. Pierre, and one of these, a young girl named Harviva De Ilfrile, told a harrowing tale of being halfway up the mountain on an errand for her grandmother, looking into the "boiling stuff" coming out of the so-called Corkscrew crater. She ran to the wharf and jumped into her brother's boat, and, turning, saw her brother running ahead of the boiling tide of ash. "But he was too late," she related, "and I heard him scream as the stream first touched then swallowed him."

From here, this small girl somehow launched the boat, and got it to a small grotto in which she and her chums had once played. "But before I got there, I looked back—and the whole side of the mountain which was near the town seemed to open and boil down on the screaming people. I was burned a good deal by the stones and ashes that came flying about the boat, but I got to the cave," she concluded. Days later, she was discovered floating in her charred craft two miles at sea by the French cruiser *Suchet*.

The other survivor of St. Pierre, Auguste Ciparis, a 25-year-old stevedore who was a prisoner in an underground dungeon at the time of the blast later told his story to George Kennan, and then went on to become a major attraction in the Barnum and Bailey Circus. Protected by his subterranean quarters, he nevertheless survived immense, horrendous burns over much of his body. Kennan called the burns "almost too horrible to describe."

Looters streamed into St. Pierre from other parts of Martinique. French soldiers from the cruiser *Suchet* shot 27 men, and then turned their attention to the nightmarish sight of incinerated heaps of bodies.

It would take months before the entire population of St. Pierre could be buried, and during that time, on May 20, Pelee exploded once again, with almost as much force as the paroxysm of the 8th, leveling whatever walls remained in St. Pierre and killing 2,000 more people—most of them rescuers, engineers and mariners bringing relief supplies to the island.

The shipment of supplies and scientists from the United States arrived only hours later, and the scientists would stay for months, while Pelee treated them to one last, more benign spectacle. Sometime around the middle of October, a domelike mass of lava, too stiff to flow, formed in

the crater of L'Etang Sec, and from its surface, a spine or obelisk began to grow. Its diameter was from 350 to 500 feet, and within a few months, it had reached a height of 1,020 feet above the crater floor, or 5,200 feet above sea level. It was twice as tall as the Washington Monument and as large as the great pyramid of Giza.

But it was too unstable to endure, and by September, 1903, it had collapsed—though not before it had been photographed and preserved for all time by the *Dixie* scientists. And while it stood, it seemed to scientist Angelo Heilprin ". . . nature's monument dedicated to the 30,000 dead who lay in the silent city below."

MEXICO
PARICUTIN

June 1944

• • • • • • • • • • • • • • •

There are no official fatality figures for the multiple explosions of Paricutin, the unique Mexican volcano "born in a cornfield." Unofficial statistics vary from "few to none" to 3,500.

Paricutin is the volcano that was described in various popular magazines in 1943 as "the volcano born in a cornfield while the owner watched." This was not quite the way it happened, although the actuality was close enough.

Located 515 miles due west of Mexico City, Paricutin is named for a small Tarascan Indian village of 500 people five miles from the vent of the volcano. It did rise from the cornfield of the nine-acre parcel of land owned by Dionisio Pulido, but this was not its first appearance. For years, that spot of land had contained a small hole around which the local children played. In fact, one of the local inhabitants recalled, 50 years before, playing near it and hearing underground noises like falling rocks and feeling from it "a pleasant warmth."

On February 5, 1943, a series of steadily intensifying earthquakes began to rumble and split the ground near this hole. On February 19, no less than 300 were felt.

On the morning of February 20, Pulido left the village of Paricutin to prepare his farm for planting, and here both the popular legend and the volcano were born. All proceeded normally for most of the day, and then, at about 4:00 P.M., Pulido, his wife Paula, his son and a neighbor Demetrio Toral were thunderstruck by what was beginning to occur in the cornfield.

A fissure had begun to open on either side of the hole. Almost immediately, there was a sound like thunder. Nearby, trees trembled, and the ground swelled to a height

The cinder cone of Paricutin in Mexico. National Geophysical Data Center/U.S. Geological Survey.

of about three feet. Smoke and a fine ash-gray dust began to rise from parts of the fissure.

Then, as the fascinated farmer and his family watched, a loud hissing sound accompanied the thunder, and the odor of sulphur wafted from the opening, followed by "sparks" which ignited pine trees 25 yards from the jagged rip in the ground. This was enough activity for the eyewitnesses, who hurriedly left the scene.

The volcano continued to grow through the night. By midnight, huge incandescent bombs were hurled into the air with a roar, and lightning flashes appeared in the heavy ash column. By 8:00 A.M., when Pulido returned to his transformed cornfield, a cone about five feet high was spitting smoke and rocks with regularity and great violence. By midday, this cone was 25 feet high and growing.

On the 21st of February, the first lava began to flow from the growing cone at a speed of roughly three feet an hour, spreading a slaglike mass of black, jagged blocks about three feet in thickness all over Pulido's transformed farm.

On the evening of February 22, Dr. Ezequiel Ordonez, a veteran Mexican geologist, arrived upon the scene and recorded it officially:

> I was witnessing a sight which few other humans had ever seen, the initial stages of the growth of a new volcano. Tremendous explosions were heard, ground tremors were felt frequently, and a thick high column of vapors with a great many incandescent rocks could be seen rising almost continuously from the center of a small conical mound then estimated to be 55 meters (16.764 feet) high. On the same night I noticed a red glow on the slope of the mound and large incandescent rocks rolled down a low rocky incline with a distinctly peculiar tinkling noise. Upon approaching this low scarp as closely as possible, it was found to be the front of a large lava flow moving from the north side of the base of the mound over a flat cornfield.

Scientists now took over and clocked the progress of the growth of the volcano. By the end of the first week, the cone was 50 feet high; by the end of the first year, it had reached a height of a hundred feet. As it erupted and cooled, as lava flows built and waned, it would grow and shrink, but its height would remain fairly constant at 100 feet.

By the beginning of 1944, most of the lava activity had shifted to the southwest side of the cone, and for the next three years lava emerged from closely spaced vents (or *bocas*, as the Mexicans called them) on this side. The area of the lava vents became known as the *Mesa de los Hornitos*, or Tableland of Little Ovens. The lava flow increased, creating more vents.

Finally, in June 1944, there was a vigorous eruption, and a huge lava flow descended upon the village of Paricutin and the larger town of San Juan de Parangaricutiro. Heavy ash partially buried both communities and there were a few isolated fatalities, but the inhabitants of both towns shoveled the ash from the streets and roofs of houses with the hope of resuming their lives.

That was not to be. The lava continued to flow, slowly enough to allow the Mexican army to force an evacuation of residents who often waited until it was at their very back door before reluctantly leaving. San Juan de Parangaricutiro was destroyed by the advancing lava flow in June 1944. By the end of September, Paricutin had disappeared, set afire and buried by the river of molten rock.

One source states that 3,500 people died on June 10, the day that San Juan de Parangaricutiro was evacuated. This seems highly unlikely, since the town only contained 4,000 residents. More accurate might be the "few to none" estimation by the geologists in residence. Still there are, unfortunately, no official fatality figures.

NEW GUINEA
LAMINGTON

January 21, 1951

• • • • • • • • • • • • •

On January 21, 1951 the Pelean explosion of Lamington, on New Guinea, killed 2,942, most of them from nue ardente, hurricane-force winds laden with steam, hot ash, rock fragments and superheated mud.

"Nue ardente" was the name given to the lethal, hurricane-force winds containing enormously hot ash and rock fragments, steam and superheated mud that characterized the Pelean-type explosion of Mt. Pelee in 1902. (See pp. 292–296.) The tremendous speed (from 36 mph to 300 mph) with which these molten masses erupt from a volcano and descend its slopes make escape almost impossible, as the monstrous fatality figures from Pelee attest.

The January 21, 1951 eruption of Mt. Lamington in New Guinea was precisely the same sort of explosion as Pelee's, with nues ardentes crashing down its slopes and instantly killing 2,942 people. In this case, the principle cause of death was believed to be steam-laden hot dust, so those who found protection from the main force of the nuee ardente in sealed rooms survived. These survivors described symptoms such as pains in the mouth, throat and eyes, followed by a burning sensation in the chest and abdomen and finally, a sense of rapid suffocation—exactly those described by the four survivors of Pelee. As in Pompeii (see pp. 280–282) and St. Pierre, there was rigidity in the bodies of the fallen, caused by the coagulation of the albuminous material in the muscles. Many of those who survived had been severely scalded, but the shielding of their clothing had saved them from burning to death.

The paroxysm which caused such widespread death and destruction occurred at 10:40 A.M. on January 21, 1951, and, although it was described in newspapers as having occurred without warning, Fred M. Bullard, in his exhaustive study, *Volcanoes of the Earth,* insists that there had been plenty of warning, but that, as in the case of Pelee, the warnings had gone unheeded. "Some six days prior to the climactic eruption there was activity in the crater, which as not generally observed or if so was not associated with an impending eruption," notes Dr. Bullard.

Acknowledging that Pelee was known as a volcano and Mt. Lamington was not, Dr. Bullard goes on to chronicle numerous landslides from the walls of the crater, and a two-day emission of a thin column of vapor rising from the crater which identified it unmistakably as an active volcano.

By January 18, gas was belching from the cone, loaded with ash and rising many thousands of feet. Earthquakes increased until they were "almost incessant" at Higaturu, six miles north of the crater.

By January 19, according to Dr. Bullard, there were "blue flashes, tongues of flames, sheet and chain lightning." He goes on: "On January 20, the day before the climactic eruption, a continuous ash-filled eruption cloud rose to a height of 25,000 feet or more. . . . The activity of Mount Lamington during the six days preceding the catastrophic eruption is fairly typical of eruptions of the Pelean type, and, for the future, it is imperative that such activity be reported, its significance appreciated, and the warning heeded."

Dr. Bullard does acknowledge that the prevailing winds carried the ash fall away from the populated and settled areas on the northern and western slopes of Mt. Lamington, thus robbing the inhabitants of the sort of admittedly unheeded warning the residents of St. Vincent received from Pelee in 1902.

At any rate, the final fulguration occurred in the mid-morning hours of January 21, 1951, and when it did, there was no doubting the identity of Mt. Lamington. A series of huge explosions tore the top and the sides from the mountain, producing a huge, ash-filled, mushroom-shaped cloud which within two minutes rose to 40,000 feet and 20 minutes later had climbed to 50,000 feet. The detonation was enormous enough to be heard on the coast of New Britain, 200 miles away.

Bursting forth from the side of the mountain, the nues ardentes catapulted, with ferocious speed and destructiveness, down the mountainside, flattening the rain forest so that not even the stumps of the trees were left, sweeping cataclysmically through buildings so that neither floors, walls nor people were ever found again, and only the foundations remained to give evidence that houses had been there at all.

In a radius of two miles from the crater, the ground was scoured and grooved, as if a gigantic rake had roared through. Charred root ends were sometimes left in the area beyond two miles; and the few trees that still stood exhibited charred and abraded trunks.

This hurricane of fire seemed to act like an FM wave—it bounced off hills and ridges. But then again, there were abberrations within the cataclysmic cloud that flattened St. Vincent, also.

At Higaturu, more than five miles from the crater, an automobile was left, hanging crazily from the tops of two truncated trees, in an attitude more akin to that left by a tornado than a volcanic eruption. Later, scientists concluded that the stupendous velocity reached within tornadoes are possible in nues ardentes when tongues of the wind extended ahead of the main front and a vortex developed. Thus, the fact that in the Pelee eruption and the Mt. Lamington one, clothing was stripped from some victims and not from others nearby.

Further tests led the scientists to conclude that temperatures within the lethal, roaring cloud reached 392°F for a period of 1.5 minutes—enough to incinerate the countryside and everything that lived within it. Many of the valleys surrounding the mountain were filled with thick beds of hot ash which retained heat for months. It was not uncommon to see a log which had been buried in the ash for weeks catch fire when it was suddenly exposed to the air. In places where the ash was protected from ground water and rainfall infiltration, vapor columns rising from the ash had a temperature of 194°F two years later.

After one more cataclysmic explosion, at 8:45 P.M. the night of the 21st of January, Mt. Lamington retreated from spectacular activity and became semi-quiescent. Within 15 years, vegetation had returned to normal, but the slopes have not become repopulated to this day.

NICARAGUA
COSEGUINA

January 22, 1835

• • • • • • • • • • • • • • • •

The most violent eruption in the western hemisphere occurred when Coseguina, in Nicaragua, exploded on January 22, 1835. Eight hundred died.

The eruption of Coseguina in 1835 has been regarded as the most violent eruption in the western hemisphere. The mountain is part of a belt of active volcanoes that extends along the Pacific coast from Guatemala to the Panamanian border and is sometimes called the "Fire girdle of the Pacific." Before the 1835 eruption, Coseguina was regarded as extinct.

Consisting of a great decapitated cone with an oval-shaped crater a mile in diameter, 2,000 feet deep and occupied by a clear blue lake, this 2,850-foot giant first announced its reawakened presence by a white cloud, like an immense plume of feathers, rising from its crest at 8:00 A.M. on the morning of January 20, 1835. The plume was easily visible to the residents of La Union, El Salvador, 30 miles across the Bay of Fonseca.

Within a very short time, the cloud turned gray, then yellow and finally crimson. By 4:00 P.M. some earthshocks

were felt. By 11:00 A.M., the morning sky had been turned deep grey by the volcano's ash, and lamps were lit in La Union.

As the afternoon wore on, heavy showers of flourlike pumice began to fall and the darkness deepened. Terror and confusion followed, aided and abetted by escalating sounds and sights from the volcano. By 4:00 P.M., the darkness had spread to San Miguel, 50 miles to the northeast, and by nightfall, the ash fall had reached as far north as Tegucigalpa, 80 miles away, and San Salvadore, 110 miles to the northeast.

By the next morning, strong earthquakes and subterranean noises frightened people at La Union, and on Tigre Island in the Gulf of Fonseca, 20 miles from the volcano, pumice fragments as large as hen eggs fell. The darkness, which continued for three days, convinced many local residents that the end of the world was at hand, and, according to Richard S. Williams, Jr., who recorded the explosion, "The terror of the inhabitants at Alancho, anticipating the approach of Judgment Day, was so great that three hundred of those living out of wedlock were married at once."

And then, on the night of January 22, the mountain exploded with an immense detonation that was heard as far away as British Honduras, 400 miles distant, where the superintendent at Belize mustered his troops, thinking that there was a naval action off the harbor. In Guatemala City, the enormous explosions were so deafening, the local troops, thinking it was the cannon fire of an approaching army, hastily prepared to defend themselves.

For seven hours, the mountain spewed red hot pumice from its side and top. Absolute darkness enveloped everything and everyone within a radius of 50 miles. Most of El Salvador was obscured, and ash fell as far north as Chiapas, Mexico and on places near the Costa Rican border. Guatemala City remained in darkness until the 27th, although the main eruption lasted only four hours, stopping on the 23rd.

The fall of ash and ejecta was enormous. E. G. Squier stated, in his recording of the eruption in 1859, ". . . the sea for 50 leagues was covered with floating masses of pumice, resembling the floe-ice of the Northern Atlantic."

Anywhere from 12 to 35 cubic miles of ash were reported to have fallen, although Squire's estimate tended toward the lower figure.

Close to 800 natives living at the base of the mountain were killed by the brief and world-shaking eruption. Their violent and unexplained deaths resulted in a superstition passed down through generations of their descendants to this day. It states that the only way to pacify the mountain is to sacrifice a three-month-old infant by throwing it into the crater every 25 years.

PHILIPPINES
MAYON

October 23, 1766

• • • • • • • • • • • • • • • •

Over 2,000 were killed in the second most destructive eruption of Mayon, on Luzon in the Philippines, on October 23, 1766.

The volcano of Mayon rises majestically, 8,000 feet high and six miles from the Albay Gulf on southeastern Luzon Island. Some have called it the most perfectly formed volcano in the world. A volcano of the Etna type, which spews lava flows that warn of an eruption, Mayon was for centuries a source of great superstition to the natives of Luzon. These natives believed that an evil spirit dwelled in its depths, and every once in a while, in search of sacrifice, showered them with ash and rocks and flaming lava.

In 1592, a Franciscan priest, Estaban Solis, gathered several thousand people from various villages and marched them to the foot of the volcano. Their task was to watch him scale the mountain and report that there were no evil spirits in its crater. This he did, and the natives, apparently feeling that he had either proved them wrong or exorcised their devils, rejoiced and joined his church. Their conversion was shortlived. Father Solis inhaled enough sulfurous gas from Mayon to bring about his death less than a year from the exorcism, and his church immediately became depopulated.

Twenty-four years later, in 1616, Mayon erupted with great loss of life. But its second most destructive eruption took place on October 23, 1766. Villages by the score were either swept away, incinerated or buried by an enormous 100-foot-wide lava flow that cascaded down the eastern slopes for two days.

Following an initial explosion and lava flow, Mayon continued to explode for four more days, this time flinging huge quantities of steam and liquified mud. The dun-colored rivers, which measured from 80 to 200 feet in width, crashed down the sides of the mountain in a radius of 20 miles, sweeping it clean of roads, people, animals and the towns of Daraga, Camalig and Tobaco. Over 2,000 inhabitants of the island were killed by the eruption, most of them swallowed up in either the first lava flow or the second superheated mudslides. For two months afterward, the mountain continued to spew ash and belch lava over the countryside.

Mayon, a volcano in the central Philippines, has erupted explosively over 40 times since 1616. National Geophysical Data Center/U.S. Geological Survey.

PHILIPPINES
MAYON

February 1, 1814

• • • • • • • • • • • • • • •

Mayon's worst eruption occurred on February 1, 1814. Over 2,200 people were killed.

The most cataclysmic eruption of the Philippines's most lethal volcano, Mayon, on Luzon, occurred on February 1, 1814.

The entirety of northern Luzon was plunged into a stygean darkness by the enormous cloud of belched fire and ashes that roared from the depths of Mayon that day. There had been warnings; from early in the morning, earthquakes had rumbled through the countryside. This explosion did not send a great deal of lava roaring down the mountainsides, as the 1766 disaster had (see previous entry). Instead, an enormous bombardment of burning stones, sand and ashes shot up into the stratosphere and then fell on the surrounding countryside. Cagsauga and Badiao were totally pulvarized by these falling, flaming rocks. Not one building was left standing in either town.

The surrounding countryside was absolutely devastated. Trees were burned beyond redemption, rivers were dammed and in some places palm trees were buried to their tops; in other locations the ash accumulation reached 30 feet in depth.

Over 2,200 persons died in this, Mayon's most lethal and spectacular eruption.

PHILIPPINES
MAYON

June 23–30, 1897

• • • • • • • • • • • • • •

Over 400 died in Mayon's longest eruption from June 23 through 30, 1897.

Mayon erupted in 1825, killing 1,500, and again in 1835, 1886 and 1888. Its longest eruption in history, however, began on June 23, 1897 and lasted for seven days of ceaseless, horrific volcanic bombardment. Professor Samuel Kneeland, an eminent geologist, on a steamer bound for Iloilo, observed and recorded the volcano's activity five month before the eruption: "[It has] a pillar of cloud by day and [a] pillar of fire by night," he wrote. "[It throws off] pieces of lava six feet in diameter . . . thrown from the crater to a distance of five miles."

Spending his nights and days in constant observation, Kneeland was awestruck by Mayon's grim beauty:

At night the scene was truly magnificent and unique. At the date of my visit the volcano had poured out . . . a stream of lava on the Legaspi side from the very summit. The viscid mass bubbled quietly but grandly, and overran the border of the crater, descending several hundred feet in a glowing wave, like red-hot iron. Gradually fading as the upper surface cooled, it changed to a thousand sparkling rills among the crevices, and, as it passed beyond the line of complete vision behind the woods near the base, the fires twinkled like stars, or the scintillions of a dying conflagration. More than half of the mountain height was thus illuminated.

Had he stayed on until June 23, Dr. Kneeland might have been less poetic in his description of Mayon. On that day, it began its seven-day rain of fire and terror, tossing thousands of tons of white hot stones skyward and burying the town of Tobaco once again. These stones continually

thundered to earth, while huge, steaming fissures opened in the sides of the mountain.

Once again, lava roared down the mountain. Seven miles eastward, the village of Bacacay disappeared beneath 50 feet of lava. In Libog, 100 persons were burned to death by superheated steam and falling rocks, and the villages of San Roque, Misericordia and Santo Nino became death-traps.

For more than a week, night and day were indistinguishable as an enormous black cloud of ashes spread for nearly 100 miles from the eruption. More than 400 were killed.

PHILIPPINES
TAAL

January 30, 1911

• • • • • • • • • • • • • •

In the worst eruption of Taal in modern times, a constantly active volcano in the Philippines, 1,335 were killed and 199 were injured on January 30, 1911.

Taal, a Pelean-type volcano which rises from a volcanic island in the middle of Lake Taal, south of Manila, has had a number of cataclysmic eruptions in its extensive history, but the most devastating of modern times occurred on January 30, 1911.

It was a classic, catastrophic example of the Pelean type of explosion which blows out not only the crater, but the sides of the mountain—often with hurricane force winds and tornadoes—and releases practically no lava, but copious quantities of white hot ash and superheated steam.

The 1911 eruption of Taal typically began with a series of earthquakes, from the night of January 27 through the 29, accompanied by a column of heavy black smoke that rose for miles into the atmosphere, and dropped thin but steady quantities of ash throughout the countryside.

There were minor explosions, accompanied by lightning, mixed in with these earthquakes on January 29. All of this was duly noted by a party of United States engineers camped at Bayuyungan, but none of these prepared the party for the major one, a double eruption that ripped away the floor of the volcano, opened huge fissures in the lake bed, and blasted these men from their beds at 2:20 A.M., January 30.

"Loud rumbling noise was again heard," noted one of the engineers, "and before I could get out of bed an explosion of indescribable severity took place." He continued his report:

Smoke came out of the crater in dense clouds. The rumbling noise grew louder and louder and then came a heavy

A 1965 aerial view of Taal, a volcano in the Philippines. National Geophysical Data Center/U.S. Geographical Survey.

report. I then saw the mud issuing from the crater as a cloud. In a few seconds, I saw this cloud drifting across the lake toward our camp. Our camp was then swept by a heavy wind which broke the tent ropes and threw the tent into the air. This atmospheric disturbance threw me a distance of about fifteen feet. A rain of ashes fell about eight inches deep, the air was oppressive, and we gasped for breath for twenty seconds. For half a minute there was light warm rain, then cold rain for fifteen minutes. A tidal wave from the lake reached the camp a quarter mile back from the shore. We took refuge on higher ground, everything was washed away at the camp, one of the party was slightly burned about the arms with hot ashes, but otherwise we did not suffer injuries.

The fortunate fate of the engineers was not shared by the residents of 13 villages and towns which were obliterated by roaring avalanches of scalding hot mud, peppered with boulders and uprooted trees. For 10 miles in a fan-shaped swath, all vegetation was burned down to the bare earth. Trees were sliced off at the roots. No wildlife survived.

The death and destruction in the towns and villages was enormous. For a distance of six miles, a 31-inch-thick layer of mud, accompanied by poisonous volcanic gases, destroyed all human life and buildings. An area of nearly 800 square miles would eventually be inundated by the ash fallout from the explosion.

Between 3:00 and 3:45 P.M., geologist W. E. Pratt and a photographer ventured near the crater to take pictures. They, too, were luckier than the residents of such towns as Guilot, Bugaan and San Jose, which, along with their populations, no longer existed. "No animal life could have lived on that island," Pratt recorded. "Not a blade of grass escaped. Trees eight inches in diameter were broken, leaving stumps one to two feet high with ends shredded in splinters by the sand and small stones driven by the force of the eruption. A 600-pound boulder fell on top of the highest ridge. A breadcrust bomb of augite and esite was found, one meter in diameter."

Fifteen minutes after the two descended from the crater, the mountain blew again, with almost the same force as the first explosion, which was heard 310 miles away. Hurricane winds swept away what the mud, ash and fire had not already destroyed. A black cloud of ash spread up and into the atmosphere, darkening the skies over Manila, 40 miles away, and visible for a distance of 250 miles.

In total, 1,335 people were killed and another 199 were severely injured. Taal remained quiescent until 1965, when it again erupted, killing 200. To this day, it is an active, dangerous volcano.

PHILIPPINES
MT. PINATUBO

June 10–15, 1991

• • • • • • • • • • • • • • • •

Approximately 200 died and 100,000 were made homeless by the multiple eruptions of Mt. Pinatubo, 55 miles northwest of Manila on Luzon Island in the Philippines from June 10 through 15, 1991. The eruption created 150,000 refugees and forced the closing of Clark Air Force Base and the evacuation of all dependents of both it and Subic Naval Base.

Of the 37 volcanoes in the world that are considered currently active, 29 lie on the so-called Pacific "Ring of Fire" (see VOLCANIC ERUPTIONS AND NATURAL EXPLOSIONS, Nicaragua, Coseguina, p. 299.) Each of these volcanoes plunges into the deep earth under the islands, and thence to the Pacific Plate, on the floor of the Pacific Ocean. When the descending plate reaches a depth of about 60 miles, it produces molten rock that rises to the surface and feeds these volcanoes.

Located on Luzon Island in the Philippines, some 55 miles northwest of Manilla, 4,000-feet-high Mt. Pinatubo, remained a quiescent member of the Ring of Fire for 611 years. It erupted in 1380, causing great damage, but in the interim, some 300,000 Filipinos had settled on its slopes, raising rice and animals and building cities and military installations.

And then, in 1991, the silence was broken. In April, the mountain began to show signs of activity. Puffs of smoke emerged from the crater at its crest. At the beginning of June, small amounts of steam and ash were released, and the rumblings within the mountain informed seismologists that something was about to happen. They issued warnings, and over 12,000 residents were ordered to be evacuated.

On June 10, a moderate eruption occurred, and 16,000 U.S. troops, dependents and civilian employees stationed at Clark Air Force Base, 10 miles east of Mt. Pinatubo, were evacuated to Subic Bay Naval Base, 30 miles to the southwest. The following day, 900 servicemen volunteered to return, to prevent looting.

And then, on the morning of June 12, at 8:41 A.M., Mt. Pinatubo erupted in earnest, spewing a 15-mile-high grey-green mushroom cloud of ash and smoke into a formerly clear and cobalt sky. Rivers of searing gas, ash and 1,800°F molten rock gushed down the lush slopes at 60 mph, setting fire to the underbrush and flooding the rice fields with molten material.

Day turned into night as far away as Manila, and the cloud and its ash fall would reach as far away as Singapore, 1,500 miles to the southwest. Two inches of white ash would descend upon fields, animals and houses, burning and burying them. Armor Deloso, the governor of Zambales Province, who tried to approach the slope after the eruption, told a *New York Times* reporter, "I could not breathe because the ashes were getting into my nose. It's raining ashes. The plants were all covered with ashes."

Roads instantly became jammed with military convoys and refugees, guiding wagons piled with belongings. In the city of Angeles, adjoining Clark Air Force Base, church bells pealed to sound the alarm, and some residents stood frozen in fear on city streets. But the city was considered outside of the danger zone, and their fear quickly subsided. Scientists, reasoning that the magma within the volcano was too thick to flow easily, felt no need to evacuate Angeles, and plans went forward with the parade commemorating Philippine Independence Day.

Late at night on June 12, and again early in the morning of June 13, the volcano erupted again with even more violence, throwing ash and fire 80,000 feet into the air. Terrified residents of the area now frantically loaded cars, trucks and handcarts with their belongings, and jammed roads became nearly impassable.

Victor Gomez, a 53-year-old American who owned a restaurant near the gates of Clark Air Base, was just sitting down to a morning cup of coffee when he heard screams outside of his restaurant. "I rushed outside and there it was," he said. "It looked like a nuclear bomb had gone up, a huge mushroom cloud over the volcano." On the base, Sergeant Richard Johnson of Wilmington, Delaware, who had been at Clark for more than two years was only 37 days away from reassignment in the U.S., told a reporter, "We've had earthquakes, coup attempts, terrorist attacks and now a volcano. This place is cursed. Next thing we'll probably get is a tidal wave."

Volcanic mud appropriates a former village on the slopes of Mt. Pinatubo after its multiple eruptions from June 10 to 15, 1991.
CARE photo.

On June 14, eight more explosions sent ash and steam 19 miles high, hurling the volcanic detritis over both Clark and Subic Bay.

A giant mud flow began to slide down the mountain toward nearby rivers. All day, the mountain continued to erupt, sending plumes of ash 12 miles into the atmosphere.

And then, early in the morning of June 15, nature struck with the other fist. A typhoon, with winds of up to 80 mph, slammed into the eastern coast of Luzon Island, drenching the countryside, adding weight to the ashes, and turning them to white mud. A serviceman was killed when his vehicle slid on the rain-soaked ash. The weight of the rain-coated debris from the volcano collapsed the roof of a bus terminal in Angeles, which was now under serious threat from falling ash and mud. Only 12 of the 100 people inside were immediately extricated, and scores were crushed.

Inch-thick rocks mixed with the falling ash and became lethal bombs, and now refugees from Angeles joined the crush on the roads of fleeing, terrified residents of the surrounding countryside.

The volcano continued to erupt over the weekend of the 15th and 16th. Mudslides and floods devoured homes. An old man on the outskirts of Angeles drowned in a torrent of thick volcanic ash and rainwater. Eight inches of ash turned to mud collapsed buildings.

The Red Cross worked feverishly. Shelters were set up in churches, schools, army camps and gymnasiums in Manila to accommodate the tens of thousands of refugees. Sitting in the shaded bleachers of a Manilla stadium, a young man, Angelo Luciano, told a *New York Times* reporter that his house had collapsed on his wife and him. "Our neighbors dug into the rubble and saved us," he marvelled with a shake of his head.

Meanwhile, volcanologists warned of a 1.8-mile crack that had developed between two craters along the volcano's southern side. The buildup of pressure within the mountain could be enough to blow it apart, they reasoned, much the way Mt. St. Helens had exploded in 1980 (see below).

Heeding the warning, the U.S. government evacuated the remaining 900 servicemen from Clark and ordered all of the dependents and civilian employees of the two bases to be sent home. Seven navy ships loaded the civilians and left immediately for the U.S.

Earlier, the Nuclear-Free Philippines Coalition had charged that if volcanic lava hit Clark Air Force Base, there would be a potential for the release of radiation from weapons stored there. The U.S. military would neither confirm nor deny that it had nuclear arms at Clark, but denied that there would be any radiation danger. The military also claimed that the 8,200 tons of munitions at Clark was not at risk from the explosion of the mountain.

Neither of these assurances was tested. Instead of exploding, the mountain caved in on itself and gradually quieted.

But the devastation left behind was monumental. Two hundred died, most of them during the height of the explosions; 100,000 were rendered homeless. The rice crop was completely destroyed, buried beneath a foot of volcanic ash and rock. Farmers wondered if their soil would ever be fertile again.

In Olongapo, a city of 300,000 adjoining Subic Bay, looting occurred, and a vast food and water shortage developed. By June 18, the water supply had almost run out, and what was there was contaminated with ash. Residents began to break pipes to drain off what little pure water remained. Street vendors made a quick killing selling cloth surgical masks for 35 cents each to residents of Manila who were still choking on the volcanic ash in the air.

The once lush slopes of Mt. Pinatubo resembled a moonscape. In Zambales Province, the hardest hit region of all, as much as three feet of ash and volcanic rock covered everything. "There is nothing left," said Leonardo Mercavado, who owned a small farm. "Is is all ash and sand now."

UNITED STATES
MT. ST. HELENS

May 18, 1980

• • • • • • • • • • • • • • • • •

Sixty-two people—many of them scientists studying the eruption—died in the monumental explosion of Mt. St. Helens, in Washington State, on May 18, 1980.

"I think people need to put all this devastation into perspective," observed Bill Ruediger, a wildlife biologist for the Gifford Pinchot National Forest after the immense eruption of Mt. St. Helens in May 1980. "Although it's totally unique as far as our lifetimes are concerned, it's the way nature is: every couple thousand years she cleans the slate again. What we have here right now is almost a genesis situation."

Known for its pristine beauty, Mt. St. Helens is the youngest and one of the smallest of the mountains of the Cascade Range, which stretches 700 miles south from Canada to California, and is part of the Pacific "Ring of Fire." Only 9,677 feet in height, the mountain was named for the British ambassador to Spain, Baron St. Helens, in 1792 by Captain George Vancouver, a British navigator and explorer in search of the Northwest Passage. Viewing the peak for the first time in 1805 from what is now Portland, Oregon, explorer William Clark noted in his log of the Lewis and Clark expedition, "Mount St. Helens is perhaps the greatest pinnacle in America."

By the time it had exploded in the spring of 1980, the mountain would be reduced to something resembling a partially extracted tooth. The top seemed as though a cosmic fist had pummeled it. The once symmetrical and shapely peak was gone, and in its place, 1,313 feet lower, was an amphitheatre with sheer, 2,000-foot walls opening to the barren area beneath it.

No other major volcanic eruption has been so painstakingly recorded. The energy released in its climactic explosion was charted as being equivalent to that of 500 Hiroshima-type atomic bombs, or 10 million tons of TNT. An area of 232 square miles was scorched into a moonscape. Only 62 people were killed by the enormous blast, and some of those were scientists, there to record the very disaster that claimed them. One victim, Harry Truman, an 84-year-old veteran of the mountain and proprietor of the Mt. St. Helens Lodge on Spirit Lake, met his fate because he refused to evacuate the area when ordered out by state police. Even when a force 5 earthquake rattled objects loose from the walls of his lodge, Truman reportedly took another sip of bourbon, gathered some of his 16 cats around him, and refused to leave his lodge. "I am part of that mountain," he explained. "The mountain is part of me." Giving up, the law authorities made him a deputy sheriff, thus legalizing his suicide. His lodge was buried under red hot ash; his body was never found.

Mt. St. Helens's geological history is short by the world's standards. Explorers heard Indian reports of its early explosions, but generally dismissed them as primitive legends. However, there were a series of eruptions between 1800 and 1857 that were recorded in some detail.

But from 1857 until 1980—a period of 123 years—Mt. St. Helens was, for all intents and purposes, a very quiet volcano.

On March 20, 1980, a magnitude 4 earthquake (see EARTHQUAKES, Introduction, pp. 23–24) shook the area. It was the first of a series of escalating seismic shocks. On March 27, 47 earthquakes of magnitude 3 intensity shook the area, and at noon that day, there was a thunderous explosion near the peak. A news team from the Vancouver *Columbian* commandeered a helicopter and explored the summit, discovering the source of the explosion. According to reporter Bill Steward, ". . . there was a hole in the snow on the north side of the peak. It was smudged with black ash, and the top, especially the north side was shattered." Long, jagged fissures underlay the snow, cracking it in concert with the opened earth beneath.

The next day, a team of scientists in another helicopter affirmed that there had been a phreatic, or steam eruption caused by subsurface water that had trickled down until it hit hot rock and was vaporized. There was clearly a superheated furnace cranking up beneath the surface of Mt. St. Helens.

From the beginning of April, a bulge began to appear on the north face of the cone, just below the summit crater and above an outcropping of lava called Goat Rocks. The bulge covered an area nearly two miles in diameter which had grown as much as 30 feet. It was expanding at a rate of a foot per day, with the displacement nearly horizontal to the north-northwest. Scientists attributed the bulge to pressure from magma rising in the throat of the volcano, and postulated that either an eruption or a devastating avalanche was imminent.

Roadblocks were erected by the middle of April; the danger zones near the mountain and under the bulge were evacuated except for a few diehards like Harry Truman, and some remaining loggers, scientists and their families.

And then, at 8:32 A.M., on Sunday, May 18, 1980, another magnitude 5 earthquake shook the mountain, triggering the climactic, lethal eruption.

Two geologists, Dorothy and Keith Stoffel, had boarded a light plane early that morning to take a look at the volcano. At 8:32, they were directly over the summit, looking down into the crater from a height of approximately 1,000 feet. "The whole north side of the summit crater began to move as one gigantic mass," they later recorded. "The entire mass began to ripple and churn without moving laterally. Then the whole north side of the summit began sliding to the north along a deep-seated slide plane."

What was happening was a tripleheaded explosion: The bulge abruptly broke away, triggering massive mudflows pockmarked with lethal debris. At the same time, a lateral blast of hot, ash-filled gases blew out of the sides of the mountain, and a vertical eruption cloud and ash fall spewed out of the mountain's cone. The geologists narrowly es-

The growing lava dome in the explosion crater of Mt. St. Helens in 1983, three years after the main eruption. National Geophysical Data Center/University of Colorado.

caped being caught in the vertical cloud, and only outflew it by turning to the south, out of its path.

Meanwhile, an enormous avalanche—the largest landslide ever recorded—of more than two-thirds of a cubic mile of rock debris and glacial ice, turned into steam and boiling water by exploding steam and entrapped air, roared down the mountainside at a speed of 155 mph. It splashed into Spirit Lake, struck a ridge beyond, and was then deflected into the northern fork of the Toutle River. The lake and the valley were immediately jammed with debris in depths up to 500 feet. The combination of water and entrapped snow and ice, plus the volcanic debris, combined to form a huge mudflow that continued down the north fork of the Toutle into the Cowlitz River, and from there into the Columbia River.

The mudflow was like hot mortar, carrying jumbles of logs, pieces of bridges and houses and other macabre debris. One observer reported seeing a fully loaded logging truck being carried upright on the surface, submerged only to the lower tier of logs. By the time it had reached the Columbia, the mudflow had slowed to 4.8 mph. It would deposit more than 1 billion cubic feet of sediment into the Cowlitz River, and enough mud would flow on through the Cowlitz to block the shipping channel of the Columbia River completely.

At the same time, geysers of hot gas shot from cracks around the bulge at speeds of up to 250 mph and overtook the avalanche as it rolled down the slope, heating it to temperatures up to 572°F. This combination of a steam blast and fluidized volcanic rock fragments both flattened and incinerated major ridges and valleys over an area of 212 square miles. Entire trees, four to seven feet in diameter, were uprooted and swept away in the zone nearest to the explosion. Beyond this, other trees were stripped of their limbs and bark and snapped like matchsticks. In some places, they were lined up militarily with their trunks pointed away from the direction of the blast. In other places, tornado-like eddies in the blast left piles of trees in mangled heaps. The timber blowdown represented 3.7 billion board feet of lumber, enough to build nearly a quarter of a million homes. It was this avalanche and the lateral blast of hot ash-filled gas that caused most of the loss of life and property. And most of it was over by 9:00 A.M., an astonishingly short period of time for this sort of eruption.

Wildlife on the north slope of the mountain was almost totally erased. According to the Washington State Department of Game, 5,000 black-tailed deer, 200 black bear and 1,500 elk died in the disaster along with all the birds and small mammals in the affected area. An eerie silence would settle over this part of the Earth for a long time to come.

Finally, while the avalanche was developing its full force, a huge eruption cloud, filled with ash, roared from the crater. Within 10 minutes, this cloud that pursued the Stoffels in their observation plane rose to a height of 63,000 feet. Day turned to night everywhere in the area. At Spokane, Washington, 250 miles away, visibility was reduced to approximately 10 feet in mid-afternoon, when the cloud reached there. In Yakima, 90 miles away, up to five inches of ash fell, and lesser amounts rained down on Idaho, central Montana and parts of Colorado. The ash cloud circled the globe in 11 days. For weeks, a belt of ash would color sunsets and affect the world's atmosphere.

As in most such eruptions, a lava dome formed, 600 feet high and 2,000 feet in diameter, and lava began to flow from it. Mt. St. Helens experienced lesser eruptions throughout 1982. There is ample scientific evidence to indicate that its life as an active, dangerous volcano is by no means over.

USSR
KAMCHATKA
BEZYMIANNY
March 30, 1956

• • • • • • • • • • • • •

One of the greatest Pelean-type eruptions ever, the explosion of Bezymianny in Kamchatka, USSR on March 30, 1956 resulted in no recorded loss of life.

The enormous explosion of Bezymianny in the Kamchatka Peninsula of the USSR has largely gone unnoticed because there was no loss of life. However, in intensity, it ranks as one of the greatest Pelean-type eruptions and as such, deserves mention.

Considered to be an extinct volcano, with no record of explosions in historic times, the volcano was ignored when a series of earthquakes occurred in September and October of 1955. Even though the epicenters of the quakes were traced to Bezymianny, it was believed that nearby Kliuchevsky volcano, an active mountain, was responsible.

However, on October 22, 1955, a moderate eruption did develop at Bezymianny, and ash fell until March 29, 1956.

And then, at 5:11 P.M., on March 30, 1956, an enormous explosion ripped open the top of the mountain's snow-covered cone, which had heretofore risen over 10,000 feet above sea level. In seconds, 600 feet were lopped off the volcano and the eruption cloud rose to a height of 28 miles.

G. S. Gorschkov, the Russian volcanologist, described the scene from nearby Kliuchi:

The cloud was curling intensely, and quickly changed its outlines. . . . It seemed to be very thick and almost tangibly heavy. Together with the cloud came also and was growing a rumble of local thunder accompanying incessantly flashing lightning. About 5:40 P.M. when the cloud had already passed the zenith, ash began to fall . . . and by 6:20 P.M., it got so impenetrably dark that one could not see his own hand, even if brought up to the very face. People returning from work were wandering about the village in search of their homes. Peals of thunder were crashing with deafening loudness without any interruption. The air was saturated with electricity, telephones were ringing spontaneously, loud speakers of the radionet were burning out. . . . There was a strong smell of sulphurous gas.

The hot ash deposited over an area of about 193 square miles melted the snow cover and torrential mudflows formed in the valley of the Dry Hapsita River and in valleys located on the flanks of adjacent volcanoes. The torrents swept huge boulders, some weighing hundreds of tons, through the valley, wiping out everything in their paths. Trees were swept away, decapitated or scorched. Three weeks after the explosion, Gorschkov discovered thousands of steam fumaroles rising from the surface of a 100-foot-thick layering of ash over an area of 19 square miles, and thus, the area was named the Valley of Ten Thousand Smokes of Kamchatka, after a similar occurrence in 1912 after the eruption of Mt. Katmai.

WEST INDIES
LA SOUFRIERE

May 7 and 8, 1902

• • • • • • • • • • • • • •

On May 7 and 8, 1902, 1,565 died in the spectacular explosion of La Soufriere, on St. Vincent, 90 miles south of Martinique. The explosion occurred less than a day before the cataclysmic eruption of Pelee on Martinique.

Less than 24 hours before the immense, death dealing eruption of Mt. Pelee on Martinique, (see pp. 292–296), La Soufriere, a 4,048-foot volcano that rises at the northern end of the island of St. Vincent, 90 miles south of Martinique, staged its own spectacular and lethal geological fireworks display.

Although the Carib natives whom Columbus subdued on St. Vincent when he landed there in 1498 did tell tales of La Soufriere's eruptions, the mountain stayed relatively calm, erupting only twice, in 1718 and 1812. Both of these were major eruptions, and the 1812 explosion left behind a crystalline blue crater lake, 1,930 feet above sea level and framed by sheer, 800-foot, canyon walls. For half a century, this lake was a major tourist attraction in the West Indies.

But in April 1901, the mountain seemed to grow restless. Earthquakes rumbled through it and around it, severely enough to cause alarm among the people living on La Soufriere's western slope. But with the end of April 1901, came the end of the earthquakes and the people's panic.

A year later, the earthquakes resumed with greater force, and the inhabitants on the leeward side of the volcano north of Chateaubelair began to evacuate their homes. Well that they did; otherwise, the toll of 1,565 deaths from the explosions that would follow would have been even higher.

Steam began to spit from the volcano at 2:40 P.M. on May 6, and by 10:30 A.M. on May 7, the mountain erupted with a roar. The cloud of steam stretched 30,000 feet above the cone, and by that afternoon, huge, superheated stones started to fall from it.

Panic stricken residents of the slopes of La Soufriere now commenced their evacuation in earnest, but those who attempted to cross the Tabaka Dry River, southeast of the cone, would encounter a torrent of boiling mud and water over 50 feet deep, rumbling down the valley toward the sea.

By 2:00 P.M., the raging explosions increased, as did the clouds of steam and the rain of red hot ash. Suddenly, a dense cloud of hot dust and steam was expelled from the mountain and sped down the mountainside with the speed of a hurricane. One observer described it as ". . . a terrific, huge, reddish-and-purplish cloud," which swept everything and everyone in its advancing path. A nue ardente, or steam-powered cloud of gas and red hot ash, of the Pelee-type, it tumbled, at astonishing force and speed, toward the sea, overturning trees, setting fire to the dwellings it did not flatten, incinerating forests and vegetation over one-third of the entire island.

At Georgetown, 5.5 miles from the crater, red hot stones six inches in diameter fell on the populace like fatal hail. The immense cloud of ash spread out for miles, helped by prevailing winds. At 2:30 A.M. on May 8, it began to fall on the *Jupiter*, a ship 830 miles east-southeast of Barbados, indicating to scientists that the cloud was traveling at a speed of 60 mph.

In the valleys of St. Vincent, ashes accumulated in depths up to 200 feet. The drifts of grey ash would remain hot for weeks, and steam columns emitting from them would ascend upwards for a full mile.

On the rim of the ash, steam condensed into scalding water, mixed with the ash and formed a characteristic hot mud which invaded everywhere. Had there been a major city in the path of this flow, as St. Pierre had been in Martinique, the loss of life would have been as staggering as that of Pelee's. Still, a great number of people lost their lives on the Georgetown side of the Tabaka Dry River, perishing from inhalation of the hot dust, burns from steam and dust, and scalding blows from falling rocks.

Interestingly, 132 persons escaped injury by hiding out in an empty rum cellar in Orange Hill, two and a half miles north of Georgetown. The cellar was only partly underground but, providentially enough, the one window and door it possessed gave onto the side away from the volcano.

Following the cataclysmic 2:00 P.M. eruption of May 8, similar eruptions of La Soufriere continued through May 18.

On May 23, the rescue ship *Dixie*, with relief supplies that had not been unloaded at St. Pierre, and with some of its eminent scientists still aboard, arrived to aid the ravaged populace of St. Vincent.

Armstrong, Betsy, and Williams, Knox. *The Avalanche Book*. Golden, Colorado: Fulcrum, Inc., 1986.

Asquith, Michael. *Quaker Work in Russia 1921–23*. London: Oxford University Press, 1943.

Atwater, Montgomery. *The Avalanche Hunters*. Philadelphia: Macrae Smith Company, 1968.

Aykroyd, W. R. *The Conquest of Famine*. New York: E. P. Dutton, 1975.

Barth, Tom F. W. *Volcanic geology, hot springs and geysers of Iceland*. Washington D.C.: Carnegie Institution of Washington Publications 587, 1951.

Bascombe, Edward. *A History of Epidemic Pestilences*. London: John Churchill, 1851.

Bell, W. G. *The Great Plague of London in 1665*. London: John Lane Bodley Head Ltd., 1924.

Boccaccio, Giovanni. *The Decameron*. Trans. by G. H. McWilliam, Middlesex, England: Penguin Books Ltd., 1970.

Brindze, Ruth. *Hurricanes (Planet Earth Series)*, Alexandria, Virginia: Time-Life Books, 1982.

Brooks, C. E. P. *Climate Through the Ages*. New York: McGraw-Hill, 1949.

Bullard, Fred M. *Volcanoes of the Earth*. Austin: University of Texas Press, 1984.

Conrad, Karia, et al. *Volcans et Tremblements de Terre*. Paris: Deux Corps d'Or, 1975.

Cornell, James. *The Great International Disaster Book*. New York: Charles Scribner's Sons, 1976.

Corti, Egon C. *The Destruction and Resurrection of Pompeii and Herculaneum*. London: Routledge & Paul Kegan, 1951.

Crandell, Dwight R. *Potential Hazards from Future Eruptions of Mount St. Helens Volcano*. Washington D.C. United States Government Printing Office, 1978.

Creighton, Charles. *A History of Epidemics in Britian*. New York: Barnes & Noble, 1965.

Cry, George W. "Tropical Cyclones of the North Atlantic Ocean: Tracks and Frequencies of Hurricanes and Tropical Storms, 1871–1963," *Technical Paper* no. 55, U.S. Weather Bureau, Washington, D.C., 1965.

Dana, J. D. *Characteristics of Volcanoes*. New York: Dodd, Mead and Co., 1891.

Daniels, George C. ed. *Planet Earth: Volcano*. Alexandria, Virginia: Time-Life Books, 1982.

Deaux, George. *The Black Death 1347*. New York: Weybright and Talley, 1969.

Decker, Robert, and Decker, Barbara. *Volcanoes*. New York: W. H. Freeman, 1981.

Defoe, Daniel. *A Journal of the Plague Year*. Middlesex, England: Penguin Books Ltd., 1966.

Douglas, Marjorie Stoneman. *Hurricane*. New York: Rinehart & Company, 1958.

Duffy, John. *Epidemics in Colonial America*. Baton Rouge: Louisiana State University Press, 1953.

Fodor, R. V. *Angry Waters*. New York: Dodd, Mead & Co., 1980.

Fouque, Ferdinand Andre. *Santorini et Ses Eruptions*. Paris: G. Masson, 1879.

Foxworthy, Bruce L., and Hill, Mary. *Volcanic Eruptions of 1980 at Mount St. Helens: The First 100 Days*. U.S. Geographical Survey Professional Paper, 1249.

Fradin, Dennis Brindell. *Disaster! Famines*. Chicago: Children's Press, 1986.

———. *Distaster! Floods*. Chicago: Children's Press, 1982.

Francis, Peter. *Volcanoes*. Harmondsworth, Middlesex: Penguin Books Ltd., 1978.

Fraser, Colin. *The Avalanche Enigma*. Great Britain: John Murray Publishers Ltd., 1978.

Furneaux, Rupert. *Krakatoa*. New York: Prentice-Hall, 1964.

Galanopoulos, A. G., and Bacon, Edward. *Atlantis: The Truth Behind the Legend*. New York: Bobbs-Merrill, 1969.

Gallagher, Dale (ed.) *The Snowy Torrents: Avalanche Accidents in the United States 1910–1966*. Washington: Alta Avalanche Study Center, U.S.D.A. Forest Service, 1967.

Garrison, Webb. *Disasters That Made History*. New York: Abingdon Press, 1973.

General State Printing Office, the Hague: *Malnutrition and Starvation in the Western Netherlands, September 1944/ July 1945, Parts I and II*, 1948.

Gibbon, Edward. *The History of the Decline and Fall of the Roman Empire* (12 vols). London: T. Miller, 1820.

Gorshkov, G. S. "Gigantic Eruption of Volcano Bezymianny," *Bulletin Volcanologique*, ser. 2, 1959.

Grant, Michael. *The Art and Life of Pompeii and Herculaneum*. New York: Newsweek Books, 1979.

———. *Cities of Vesuvius: Pompeii and Herculaneum*. Hammondsworth, Middlesex: Penguin Books Ltd., 1979.

Gregg, Charles T. *Plague!* New York: Charles Scribner's Sons, 1978.

Gribbin, John. *This Shaking Earth*. New York: G. P. Putnam's Sons, 1978.

Halacy, D. S. Jr. *Earthquakes: A Natural History*, New York: The Bobbs-Merril Company, 1974.

Harris, D. Lee. "Characteristics of the Hurricane Storm Surge," *Technical Paper* No. 48, U.S. Weather Bureau, Washington D.C., 1963.

Harris, Stephen L. *Fire and Ice: The Cascade Volcanoes*. Seattle: Mountaineers-Pacific Search Books, 1976.

Hearn, Lafcadio. *Two Years in the French West Indies*. New York: Harper & Brothers, 1890.

Hecker, J. F. C. *The Epidemics of the Middle Ages*. London: The Sydenham Society, 1844.

Heidel, Alexander. *The Gilgamesh Epic and Old Testament Parallels*. Chicago: University of Chicago Press, 1949.

Heilprin, Angelo. *The Eruption of Pelee: A Summary and Discussion of the Phenomena and Their Sequels*. New York: J. B. Lippincott, 1908.

———. *Mount Pelee and the Tragedy of Martinique*. New York: J. B. Lippincott, 1903.

Herbert, Don, and Bardossi, Fulcio. *Kilauea: Case History of a Volcano*. New York: Harper & Row, 1968.

Hewitt, R. *From Earthquake, Fire and Flood*. New York: Charles Scribner's Sons, 1957.

Hirst, L. F. *The Conquest of Plague*. Oxford: Clarendon Press, 1953.

Hoehling, A. A. *The Great Epidemic*. Boston: Little, Brown and Co., 1961.

Hoyt, J. B. "The Cold Summer of 1816," *Annals of the Association of American Geographers*, Minneapolis, Number 48, 1958.

Hoyt, William G., and Langbein, Walter B. *Floods*. Princeton: Princeton University Press, 1955.

Huang Wei. *Conquering the Yellow River*. Peking: Foreign Language Press, 1978.

Johnson, Thomas P. *When Nature Runs Wild*. Mankato, Minnesota: Creative Education Press, 1968.

Johnson, Willis Fletcher. *History of the Johnstown Flood*. Edgewood, New Jersey: Edgewood Publishing Co., 1889.

Judkins, Grant, ed. *The Big Thompson Disaster*. New York: Lithographic Press, 1976.

Kirk, Ruth. *Snow*. New York: William Morrow & Co., 1978.

Lacroix, A. *La Montagne Pelee et Ses Eruptions*. Paris: Masson et Cie, 1904.

Lane, Frank W. *The Elements Rage*. New York: Chilton Books, 1965.

Lauber, Patricia. *Earthquakes*. New York: Random House, 1972.

Leet, L. Don. *Causes of Catastrophe*. New York: Whittlesey House, 1948.

Link, V. B. *A History of Plague in the United States of America*. Public Health Monograph No. 26, U.S. Government Printing Office, 1952.

Luce, J. V. *Lost Atlantis*. New York: McGraw-Hill, 1969.

Ludlum, D. D. *Early American Hurricanes, 1492–1870*. Boston: American Meteorological Society, 1963.

Krafft, Katia and Krafft, Maurice. *Volcanoes: The Story Behind the Scenery*. New York: Hammond, 1980.

Macdonald, Gordon A. *Volcanoes*. New York: Prentice-Hall, 1972.

Mallory, W. H. *China, Land of Famine*. New York: American Geographic Society, 1926.

Marks, Geoffrey. *The Medieval Plague*. New York: Doubleday & Co., 1971.

Marks, Geoffrey, and Beatty, William K. *Epidemics*. New York: Charles Scribner's Sons, 1976.

Marx, Wesley. *Acts of God, Acts of Man*. New York: Coward, McCann & Geoghegan, 1977.

Mather, Kirtley F. *The Earth Beneath Us*. New York: Random House, 1964.

Mayer, Ken M. D., and Pizer, Hank. *The AIDS Fact Book*. New York: Bantam Books, 1983.

McCullough, David G. *The Johnstown Flood*. New York: Simon and Schuster, 1968.

McGrew, Roderick E. *Russia and the Cholera, 1823–1832*. Madison: University of Wicsonsin Press, 1965.

McNeill, William H., *Plagues and Peoples*. New York: Anchor Press/Doubleday, 1976.

Nash, Jay Robert. *Darkest Hours*. New York: Nelson-Hall, 1976.

National Geographic Society. *Great Adventures*. Washington D.C.: National Geographic Society, 1963.

———. *Powers of Nature*. Washington D.C.: National Geographic Society, 1978.

Navarra, John Gabriel. *Earthquake*. New York: Doubleday & Co., 1980.

Nencini, Franco. *Florence: The Days of the Flood*. New York: Stein and Day, 1967.

Newby, Eric. *Slowly Down the Ganges*. New York: Charles Scribner's Sons, 1967.

Newson, Malcom D. *Flooding and Flood Hazard in the United Kingdom*. Oxford: Oxford University Press, 1975.

Palmieri, Luigi. *The Eruption of Vesuvius in 1872*. London: Asher & Co., 1873.

Phillips, John. *Vesuvius*. Oxford: Clarendon Press, 1869.

Pollitzer, R. *Plague and Plague Control in the Soviet Union*. New York: Institute of Contemporary Russian Studies, Fordham University, 1966.

Ponte, G. *Stromboli*. Catania: Associozione Internazionale di Vulanologia, 1952.

Prinzing, Friedrich. *Epidemics Resulting from Wars*. Oxford: Clarendon Press, 1916.

Rittman, A. *Volcanoes and Their Activity*. New York: John Wiley & Sons, 1962.

Rodwell, G. F. *Etna: A History of the Mountain and of Its Eruptions*. London: C. Kegan Paul & Co., 1878.

Rosenberg, Charles E. *The Cholera Years—The United States in 1832, 1849, and 1866*. Chicago: The University of Chicago Press, 1962.

Ross, Frank Jr.: *Storms and Man*. New York: Lothrop, Lee & Shepard Co., 1973.

Schuchert, C. *Historical Geology of the Antillian-Caribbean Region*. New York: John Wiley and Sons, 1935.

Seymour, Jacqueline. *The Wonders of Nature*. New York: Crescent Books, 1978.

Shope, Richard E. "Influenza," *Public Health Reports*. Washington D.C.: LXXIII (1958).

Shrewbury, J. F. D. *A History of Bubonic Plague in the British Isles*. Cambridge: Cambridge University Press, 1970.

Sigerist, Henry E. *Civilization and Disease*. Ithaca, New York: Cornell University Press, 1943.

Sutton, Ann and Sutton, Myron. *Nature on the Rampage*. New York: J. B. Lippincott, 1962.

Tannehill, I. R. *Hurricane Hunters*. New York: Dodd-Meade, 1955.

Thomas, Gordon and Witts, Max. *The San Francisco Earthquake*. New York: Stein and Day, 1971.

———. *The Day the World Ended*. New York: Stein and Day, 1976.

Trevelyan, Raleigh. *The Shadow of Vesuvius: Pompeii* A.D. *79*. London: Michael Joseph Ltd., 1976.

U.S. Weather Bureau. "Summary of North Atlantic and North Pacific Tropical Cyclones," *Climatological Data, National Summary*, Annual.

Verbeek, R. D. M. *Krakatau*. Brussels: Institut National de Geographie, no date.

Vicker, Ray. *This Hungry World*. New York: Charles Scribner's Sons, 1975.

Walford, Cornelius. *A Statistical Chronology of Plagues and Pestilences as Affecting Human Life*. London: Harrison and Sons, 1884.

Ward, Barbara and Dubos, Rene. *Only One Earth: The Care and Maintenance of a Small Planet*. London: Andre Deutsch, 1972.

Ward, Roy. *Floods: A Geographical Perspective*. London: The Macmillan Press Ltd., 1978.

Warmington, E. H., ed. *Pliny: Letters and Panegyricus*. Boston: Harvard University Press, 1959.

Webster, Noah. *A Brief History of Epidemic and Pestilential Diseases*. Hartford, Connecticut: Hudson & Goodwin, 1799.

Wexler, Harry. "Volcanoes and world climate," *Scientific American*, 186, 1952.

White, Theodore H., and Jacoby, Annalee. *Thunder Out of China*. New York: William Sloane Associates, 1946.

Whittow, John. *Disasters: The Anatomy of Environmental Hazards*. Athens, Georgia: University of Georgia Press, 1974.

Williams, Chuck. *Mount St. Helens: A Changing Landscape*. New York: Graphic Arts Center Publishing Co., 1980.

Williams, Howell, and McBirney, Alexander R. *Volcanology*. New York: Freeman, Cooper & Co., 1979.

Williams, Knox, and Armstrong, Betsy. *Snowy Torrents: Avalanche Accidents in the United States 1972–1979*. Jackson, Wyoming: Teton Bookshop Publishing Co., 1984.

Winslow, Charles-Edward Armory. *The Conquest of Epidemic Disease*. Princeton, New Jersey: Princeton University Press, 1943.

———. *Man and Epidemics*. Princeton, New Jersey: Princeton University Press, 1952.

Woodham-Smith, Cecil. *The Great Hunger (Ireland 1845–1849)*. New York: Harper and Row, 1962.

Ziegler, P. *The Black Death*. New York: The John Day Co., 1969.

Zinnser, H. *Rats, Lice and History*. Boston: Little Brown and Co., 1941.

INDEX

3/27/96
4/15/96